ISBN: 9781290439343

Published by:
HardPress Publishing
8345 NW 66TH ST #2561
MIAMI FL 33166-2626

Email: info@hardpress.net
Web: http://www.hardpress.net

INTRODUCTION
TO THE NEW TESTAMENT

INTRODUCTION

TO THE

NEW TESTAMENT

BY

THEODOR ZAHN

PROFESSOR OF NEW TESTAMENT EXEGESIS, ERLANGEN UNIVERSITY

TRANSLATED FROM THE THIRD GERMAN EDITION

BY

JOHN MOORE TROUT, WILLIAM ARNOT MATHER, LOUIS
HODOUS, EDWARD STRONG WORCESTER, WILLIAM
HOYT WORRELL, AND ROWLAND BACKUS DODGE

FELLOWS AND SCHOLARS OF HARTFORD THEOLOGICAL SEMINARY

UNDER THE DIRECTION AND SUPERVISION OF

MELANCTHON WILLIAMS JACOBUS

HOSMER PROFESSOR OF NEW TESTAMENT CRITICISM AND EXEGESIS
AND DEAN OF THE FACULTY

ASSISTED BY

CHARLES SNOW THAYER

DIRECTOR OF THE CASE MEMORIAL LIBRARY

IN THREE VOLUMES

VOL. I.

EDINBURGH : T. & T. CLARK, 38 GEORGE STREET

1909

Printed by
MORRISON & GIBB LIMITED

FOR

T. & T. CLARK, EDINBURGH

LONDON: SIMPKIN, MARSHALL, HAMILTON, KENT, AND CO. LIMITED
NEW YORK: CHARLES SCRIBNER'S SONS

CORRIGENDA

Vol. i. page 260, line 14, *for* Stephanus *read* Stephanas.
Vol. ii. page 425, line 8, *for* Wetzele *read* Wetzel.

AUTHOR'S PREFACE TO THE ENGLISH EDITION

———◆———

I HAVE been asked by Professor Jacobus, who first suggested the plan for the translation into English of my Introduction to the New Testament, and to whose praiseworthy energy the carrying out of the plan is due, to prepare an Introduction for the English edition. This affords me a welcome opportunity to express my hearty thanks, first of all to Professor Jacobus himself, and also to Dr. Thayer, his fellow Professor in the Hartford Theological Seminary, who has seen the entire work through the press, and to the younger theologians, by whom the first draft of the translation has been prepared, for the great sacrifice of time and labour required in order to present this work to the English-speaking public in a form as complete as possible, and at the same time convenient for use. What these difficulties are no one is in better position to appreciate than the author himself, who is responsible for the plan and the style which render his work difficult to read—especially for foreigners—and to translate. Of these difficulties I was very early reminded. I still recall, often with very mingled feelings, the words with which E. Renan[1] once described my book on Ignatius of Antioch (1873): " Quiconque aura le courage de lire ces 650 pages, écrites d'un style obscure et embarassé, possédera réelement les elements pour résoudre la ques-

———

[1] *Journal des Savants* (1874), p. 34.

tion ; mais tout le travail du raisonnement et de la critique restera bien à sa charge." For this criticism, certainly not flattering, I have found a twofold consolation. Whoever attempts to answer definitely a question complex in character and long discussed without satisfactory results, and to prove in as thorough a manner as possible that his is the only possible answer, will certainly not succeed in writing an elegant romance such as the brilliant Frenchman's *Vie de Jesus*. If, with a fair degree of completeness and accuracy, he succeeds in supplying the reader with the elements from which a correct judgment can be formed, he may reasonably crave some indulgence for "the obscure and confused style" which reflects the great variety of the material handled, and of the observations to be made. As regards criticism itself, this very Ignatian question is an instructive illustration of the fact that the wide currency of a critical view is no guarantee that this view will be permanently held. Even Renan admitted that my "uncritical monograph" definitely disposed (definitivement écarté) of the hypothesis of W. Cureton, which was a favourite one in Germany also, that the genuine portion of the Ignatian literature consisted of the brief recension of only three Epistles edited by Cureton himself from a Syriac translation. Renan's judgment on this point has proved correct. At the same time, his own new hypothesis, that only Ignatius' Epistle to the Romans and some sentences in the other Epistles are genuine, found scarcely any acceptance ; whereas to-day the genuineness of the seven Epistles, the attempt to prove which in 1875 was regarded by the majority of critics as a youthful venture, and as evidence of a lack of critical judgment, is almost universally accepted. Such experiences are a plea for patience ; they also strengthen the hope that patient work in the realm of early Christian literature will not be done in vain.

Likewise, in the literary criticism of the New Testament the last forty years have witnessed at least the beginnings of a trend toward betterment. Unhealthy eccentricities in criticism have appeared, especially in the criticism of the Pauline Epistles, but at the same time sound tendencies have made themselves felt. One of these sounder tendencies I hold to be the greater appreciation of the tradition, without which it is impossible for any criticism to make an historical presentation. To be noted also is a modest realisation of the gaps in our knowledge which forbids us regarding all that seems strange to us, and especially what is unintelligible, as evidence against the genuineness of the document in question. To be noted further is an increasing distrust of *a priori* constructions of every kind, and more attention to material and personal details, which were inserted quite unconsciously on the part of the New Testament writers, but which are of inestimable value to us, because frequently they afford us a better insight than do leading ideas, into the connection between literary remains and the circumstances and conditions under which they were produced.

This development of the historical sense among theologians has redounded to the benefit of my Introduction. In one of the reviews of the first volume of the first edition (1897), the reviewer made the conjecture that owing to the great bulk of the work the circulation would not be wide. The conjecture has not proved true. The English translation of the third German edition now completed is to me an encouraging confirmation of the hope with which I ventured to dedicate the first edition to the University of Cambridge. I can only hope that the great and self-denying efforts which the translators have made may be rewarded by a corresponding influence of the work in the wide English-speaking world.

THEODOR ZAHN.

ERLANGEN, *March* 1909.

EDITOR'S PREFACE

———◆———

EVER since the appearance of Dr. Zahn's great work on New Testament Introduction, it has been evident that sooner or later its stores of critical investigation would have to be placed at the disposal of the English-reading world. The problems of New Testament study are too important to allow the results which this renowned scholar's years of scientific study have gathered into the two large volumes of his great book to be permanently locked up in a foreign language.

To release this scholarship, however, was no easy undertaking. A thousand pages of closely printed matter, written in a style often most difficult to follow even in the text, and with notes too constantly abbreviated in the spirit of a scholar's abundant knowledge of the facts, and too frequently confused with indistinct allusions to unfamiliar literature, presented a formidable task of translation, which any set of men might hesitate to attempt, and which was practically impossible for any individual. Notwithstanding, in the spring of 1900 a formal request was made of the author that certain Fellows of Hartford Theological Seminary, Mr. John M. Trout, Mr. Louis Hodous, and Mr. William A. Mather, should be allowed to take the work in hand. Permission was cordially granted them, and being then engaged in study abroad they entered upon the beginning of their work in the summer of that year. During the year several conferences were held with Professor Zahn, to whose helpful suggestions the translators are greatly indebted.

It was fully expected that the larger part of the text would be translated before return to this country would necessitate such engagements in the active ministry as to restrict the time possible to be devoted to the task. To a large extent this hope was realised ; but the early departure to Foreign Mission service of Mr. Hodous and Mr. Mather, who had undertaken the preparation of the notes, left the burden of completing what had been begun practically with Mr. Trout. Upon his shoulders it has rested since that time, and to his faithful and patient efforts, carried on in the midst of pressing pulpit and pastoral cares, is due largely the successful accomplishment of the undertaking.

To his aid in the translation of the notes there came at different times Mr. Rowland B. Dodge, Hartranft Prize Scholar of Hartford in 1905, Mr. Edward S. Worcester, William Thompson Fellow of Hartford for 1901–1903, and Mr. William H. Worrell, John S. Welles Fellow of Hartford for 1906–1908, all of whom laboured with willing sacrifice of time in rendering service to the work. Along with them in translating, but particularly in the extra service of assisting the editor in his supervision of the translation and in the especially laborious care of the proofs, the aid of Professor Charles S. Thayer of the Case Memorial Library of the Seminary has been invaluable. If, in spite of the necessarily scattered and interrupted character of the work which has been carried on through these years, the results are marked with accuracy and completeness, it has been due largely to him. From him has come also the General Index, which places the widely extended details of notice and of reference in the book at the immediate service of the reader. Associated with Professor Thayer in this work for one summer was Mr.

Worrell, and with Mr. Mather before his departure to his foreign ·field was Mr. Frederick B. Hartranft of the Instruction Corps of the Seminary ; while at various times the editor has had the help in reading proof of Mr. John J. Moment of the Class of 1906 and Mr. Alvin C. Bacon and Mr. Watson Woodruff of the Class of 1907 of Hartford Seminary.

It has been a long task, delayed by many and unexpected interruptions, not the least among which was the appearance of the third German edition after the first English volume was practically in print. The labour of correcting the whole translation to the details of all the changes and alterations which the tireless scholarship of the author had wrought into his book seemed beyond accomplishment ; but it has been effected, and the work goes out in every detail a reproduction of the last German edition.

The Editor cannot hope to have escaped altogether the faults rendered likely by such a diversified translating, carried on in such a broken way ; but he has appreciated the fidelity and the enthusiasm of those who have worked with him, and he has believed that it would be no small service that could be rendered to the English-reading scholarship of his day if he could place at its command what this book has to offer of the masterly results of scientific research in a field the treasures of which are ever open to those whose work is patient and whose vision is clear.

HARTFORD, CONNECTICUT,
   April 1909.

CONTENTS

———◆———

ABBREVIATIONS FOR REVIEW TITLES

AJSL. . .	American Journal of Semitic Languages and Literatures.
AJTh. . .	American Journal of Theology.
AOF . . .	Altorientalische Forschungen.
BZ. . . .	Byzantische Zeitschrift.
BbZ . . .	Biblische Zeitschrift.
ChW . . .	Christliche Welt.
Expos. . .	Expositor.
ET . . .	Expository Times.
GGA . . .	Göttingische Gelehrte Anzeigen.
GGN . . .	Göttingische Gelehrte Nachrichten.
JBL . . .	Journal of Biblical Literature.
JbBW . .	Jahrbücher der biblischen Wissenschaft.
JbfDTh . .	Jahrbücher für deutsche Theologie.
JbfKPh . .	Jahrbücher für Klassische Philologie.
JbfPTh . .	Jahrbücher für protestantische Theologie.
JbPK . .	Jahrbuch der kgl. Preussischen Kunstsammlungen.
JHSt. . .	Journal of Hellenic Studies.
JPh . . .	Journal of Philology.
JQR . . .	Jewish Quarterly Review.
JRAS . .	Journal of the Royal Asiatic Society.
JThSt . .	Journal of Theological Studies.
LCBl . . .	Literarisches Centralblatt.
LR . . .	Literarische Rundschau.
MBBA . .	Monatschrift der Berliner Akademie.
MDPV . .	Mittheilungen und Nachrichten des Deutschen Palästina-Vereins.
MGWJ . .	Monatschrift für Geschichte und Wissenschaft des Judenthums.
MVG . . .	Mittheilungen der Vorder-asiatischen Gesellschaft.
NGWG . .	Nachrichten der Königlichen Gesellschaft der Wissenschaften zu Göttingen.
NHJb . .	Neue Heidelberger Jahrbücher.
NJbfDTh .	Neue Jahrbücher für deutsche Theologie.
NKZ . . .	Neue Kirchliche Zeitschrift.
OLZ . . .	Orientalische Litteraturzeitung.

PEF . . .   Palestine Exploration Fund.
RB   . . .   Revue Biblique.
REJ . . .   Revue des Études Juives.
RKZ . . .   Reformirte Kirchenzeitung.
SBAW . .   Sitzungsberichte der Berliner Akademie der Wissenschaften.
SWAW . .   Sitzungsberichte der Wiener Akademie der Wissenschaften.
ThJb . . .   Theologische Jahrbücher.
ThLb . . .   Theologisches Litteraturblatt.
ThLz . . .   Theologische Literaturzeitung.
TQ, TThQ, or }
ThQSc   } (Tübingen) Theologische Quartalschrift.
ThR . . .   Theologische Rundschau.
ThStKr . .   Theologische Studien und Kritiken.
ThTij or }
ThTjd   } Theologische Tijdschrift.
TU   . . .   Texte und Untersuchungen.
TZfTh . .   Tübinger Zeitschrift für Theologie.
WZfKM . .   Wiener Zeitschrift für Kunde des Morgenlandes.
ZfÄgSp or }
ZfÄ   } Zeitschrift für Ägyptische Sprache und Altertumskunde.
ZfA . . .   Zeitschrift für Assyriologie und Verwandte Gebiete.
ZfATW . .   Zeitschrift für Alttestamentliche Wissenschaft.
ZDMG . .   Zeitschrift der deutschen Morgenländischen Gesellschaft.
ZDPV . .   Zeitschrift des deutschen Palästina-Vereins.
ZfHTh . .   Zeitschrift für Historische Theologie.
ZfKG . .   Zeitschrift für Kirchengeschichte.
ZfKTh . .   Zeitschrift für Katholische Theologie.
ZfKW or }
ZfKWuKL } Zeitschrift für Kirkliche Wissenschaft und Kirchliches Leben
ZfLTh . .   Zeitschrift für lutherische Theologie.
ZfNTW . .   Zeitschrift für Neutestamentliche Wissenschaft.
ZfThuK . .   Zeitschrift für Theologie und Kirche.
ZfWTh . .   Zeitschrift für Wissenschaftliche Theologie.

ABBREVIATIONS OTHER THAN FOR REVIEW TITLES

————◆————

BRP	Edward Robinson, Biblical Researches in Palestine.
CIG or CIGr .	Corpus Inscriptionum Græcarum.
CIL	Corpus Inscriptionum Latinarum.
CISem . . .	Corpus Inscriptionum Semiticarum.
Dalman Gr² . .	Dalman, Grammatik des jüdisch-palästinischen Aramäisch, 2te Aufl. 1905.
EB	Encyclopædia Biblica.
Forsch. i.–vii. 1 .	Zahn, Forschungen zur Geschichte des neutestamentlichen Kanons und der altkirchlichen Literatur, 1888–1892.
GAP	Buhl, Geographie des alten Palästina.
Grundriss . .	Zahn, Gr. der Geschichte des alt. Kanons, 2te Aufl. 1904.
HDB	Hastings' Dictionary of the Bible.
HK i.–iv. . .	Handkommentar zum N.T. von Holtzmann, Lipsius, etc., 2te resp. 3te Aufl.
Hoffmann . .	Die hl. Schrift des N.T.'s zusammenhangend untersucht i.–ii. 3 (2te Aufl.) ; iii.–xi., 1868–1886.
Kühner-Blass .	Kühner, Ausführliche Grammatik der griechischen Sprache, 1 Teil, Elementar- u. Formenlehre, 3te Aufl. besorgt von Fr. Blass.
Kühner-Gerth .	Preceding, 2 Teil, Satzlehre, 3te Aufl. besorgt von Bernh. Gerth.
MS	Manuscript.
N.T.	New Testament.
O.T.	Old Testament.
PRE³	Real - Encyclopädie für protestantische Theologie und Kirche, 3rd ed.
RE	Real-Encyclopädie.
S¹	Peshito.
S²	Philoxeniana (only for the four shorter Catholic Epistles and Revelation).
S³	Syriac Text of Thomas of Heraclea.
Sc	Syrus Curetonianus.
Sh	Syrus Hierosolymitanus.
Ss	Syrus Sinaiticus.

Schürer . . . Geschichte des jüdischen Volks im Zeitalter Jesu Christi,
              3 Aufl. i.–iii., 1898–1901 [English translation of 2nd ed.,
              "The Jewish People in the Time of Christ"].
Skizzen . . . Zahn, Sk. aus dem Leben der alten Kirche, 2 Aufl. 1898.
SWP . . . . Memoirs of the Survey of Western Palestine.
TU . . . . . Texte und Untersuchungen.
ZKom. . . . Kommentar zum N.T. unter Mitwirkung von Bachman,
              Ewald, Horn, Riggenbach, Seeberg, Wohlenberg, heraus-
              geg. von Th. Zahn, 1903.
              See also the bibliographies on pages 14, 58, vol. i., and
              bibliographies of commentaries given throughout this
              work in connection with the discussions of the separate
              books of the N.T.

The editors have attempted to make all other abbreviations full enough
to be self-explanatory.

CITATIONS.

Passages in the O.T. are cited according to the figures of the Hebrew
Text ; the O.T. Apocrypha, if not otherwise noted, according to the edition
of Fritzsche, 1871 ; the witnesses for the N.T. text, except as noted above
under S, according to Tischendorf-Gregory ; the Church Fathers according
to the Vienna "Corpus scriptorum ecclesiasticorum latinorum," and "Die
griechischen christlichen Schriftsteller der ersten drei Jahrhunderte,"
herausgeg. von der Berliner Akademie.

INTRODUCTION TO THE NEW TESTAMENT.

I.

INTRODUCTORY REMARKS CONCERNING THE LANGUAGE AND ITS HISTORY.

§ 1. THE ORIGINAL LANGUAGE OF THE GOSPEL.

THE gospel is older than the N.T. Between the time when Jesus proclaimed the coming of the rule of God in His kingdom and the emergence from His Church of the earliest document which has come down to us, possibly some two decades elapsed; and some seventy years passed before the appearance of the last of the writings found in the N.T. collection. Even if the investigation of this oldest Christian literature should result in showing that no single part of it originated on the soil of Palestine, or within the Jewish Christianity of the first generation, we should still be unable, without some knowledge of the language in which Jesus taught, and in which His disciples preached the gospel to the Jews in Palestine, to form a correct conception of the beginnings of Christian literature. For, quite independent of the results of all literary criticism, and especially of the answer to the question whether the N.T. writings were composed, as tradition

2 INTRODUCTION TO THE NEW TESTAMENT

says they were, almost without exception by native Jews, and to no small extent by Palestinian Jews, the fact remains, that the Christian preaching began from Palestine, and that Jews who had no idea of giving up their nationality carried it beyond the limits of their land and nation. This statement, in which Paul (Rom. xv. 27), Luke (Acts xi. 19), and Tacitus (*Ann.* xv. 44) agree, does not require further proof. It does, however, need to be explained why a religious movement, which had its roots in the Judaism of Palestine, produced very soon after it began a distinctive literature which has come down to us only in the Greek language.

The first question that suggests itself concerns the language in which Jesus preached to the people and instructed His disciples (n. 1). Fortunately, in answering this question, we are not left wholly to our knowledge of the linguistic condition in Palestine in Jesus' time,—a knowledge which is still very much in need of clarification and confirmation,—nor are we dependent upon inferences from examples of a similar character. For the Gospels themselves, particularly those which pass under the names of Mark and John, preserve for us not only single words used by Jesus and those with whom He mingled, but also a number of short sayings of His in their original form. There can be no doubt that in introducing these foreign words into their Greek writings with Greek translations attached in various ways (n. 2), the evangelists were firmly convinced that they were reproducing what Jesus said in its original form, and that it was their duty to convey the same also to their readers, though most of these were acquainted only with Greek. Nor could they very well have been mistaken in this belief; for, leaving quite out of consideration the facts to be established later, that the second evangelist was a native of Jerusalem, and the fourth evangelist one of the twelve apostles, an error of this kind would have been possible only if these

Greek authors had been removed from Jesus and those who heard Him by a period of history during which, and by a region of country in which, on the one hand, the gospel was no longer preached in its original language, while, on the other hand, it had not yet come to be propagated by the use of the Greek language. Only in these circumstances could Greek Christians, who were entirely uninformed about the previous history of their faith, have taken for original what was in fact only a translation. But there were no such period and region as those suggested intervening between Jesus and our Gospels. A few years after Jesus' death the gospel made its way directly from Jerusalem to the Greek population of Antioch.

We possess, therefore, documentary evidence concerning the language used by Jesus. While no fragments of His preaching are preserved, all the utterances recorded are important, and were spoken at critical moments. Among these utterances are two expressions used by Jesus in prayer (Mark xiv. 36, xv. 34), one of which is a phrase taken from one of the psalms and used by Jesus in supplication during the agony of His death (Matt. xxvii. 46; Mark xv. 34). From these passages we discover in what language Jesus pondered the words of the O.T. and communed with His God in prayer. As we learn from other passages, He used this same language when He healed the sick and called the dead to life among the people of Galilee (Mark v. 41, vii. 34). This must, therefore, have been the language in which Jesus preached to the people and taught His disciples. But all the sayings of Jesus, and of those among whom He moved, which are preserved to us in their original form, exhibit the same linguistic features. These features are not those of the Hebrew language, or of a confused mixture of Hebrew and some other language; but, with the exception of a few foreign words, more or less modified in form, they are those of the Aramaic (n. 3) or Syriac tongue. For the use of the latter name there is as much historical justification as for the use of the former; since, during the centuries when this language was the dominant one in Palestine, it was very commonly called Syriac by the Jews and by those Christians who were so situated as to be familiar with the linguistic conditions of Palestine and the adjoining regions (n. 4). The only advantage in using the term Aramaic, instead of Syriac, to designate the language spoken by Jesus and by His immediate followers in the early Church, is the fact that we have become accustomed to employ the term Syriac exclusively with reference to the language of the Christian literature of the Syrian national Church, which began to be prepared first in Edessa after the close of the second century.

If we are inclined to the false notion that the language of Jesus was an uncultivated vernacular, a Jewish jargon, the terms Aramaic and Syriac may serve to remind us that we are dealing with a language which, during the five hundred years preceding the advent of Christianity, had gradually spread until it had become the dominant language of western Asia. And in spite of the rivalry with Greek that had existed since the time of Alexander, it maintained this position over wide regions until it was replaced by the Arabic of Islam. It was not without some reason that a Syrian of the sixth century A.D. called it the queen of languages (n. 5). Its reign was a long one. As early as 700 B.C. the Jerusalem court officials could propose to an Assyrian general that he carry on his negotiations with them in Aramaic, in order that the people standing by, who knew only Hebrew, might not understand what was said (Isa. xxxvi. 11 ; 2 Kings xviii. 26). Aramaic was the native language of neither party, but was employed as a medium of intercourse between powers speaking different languages, just as French is used now in negotiations between Russians and Italians.

At the time of the Persian world-empire, Aramaic had already become the official language in which the royal government and the satraps of the western provinces maintained communication with their polyglot subordinates, including those as far removed as Egypt (n. 6). From this time on Aramaic came more and more into use as a living vernacular, especially in districts where heretofore other Semitic languages had prevailed. Long before the time of Christ, the old "language of Canaan," as the Israelites once called their own language (Isa. xix. 18),— because of the fact that it did not differ essentially from the languages of their nearest heathen neighbours,—had ceased to be the spoken language of Palestine and the adjoining regions. Phœnician was no longer spoken in Tyre and Sidon. While this old language continued to be spoken in Carthage, and, after the fall of the Carthaginian State, for centuries longer in the Roman provinces of North Africa, in its original home it had given place to Aramaic or Syriac (n. 7). In the old dwelling-places of the Edomites and the Moabites, and in the entire Nabatæan kingdom, which stretched from the Elamitic gulf to the vicinity of Damascus, Aramaic was the dominating language, as is evident from numerous inscriptions (n. 7), in the time of Christ and of king Aretas iv., father-in-law of Herod Antipas (cf. 2 Cor. xi. 32), whose reign lasted from about 9 B.C. to 40 A.D.

In the midst of Palestine dwelt the Samaritans, a mixed race, who spoke an Aramaic dialect, possibly from the beginning of their history. Nor was the little remnant of the Jewish nation that resettled in and about Jerusalem able to resist permanently this general development. Consequently, when the nation freed itself from its oppressors, and secured a larger degree of independence by the Maccabean revolt, the Jews had ceased to speak their own language. Of course, they did possess something that the neighbouring peoples did not have, in the

large body of literature which had come down to them
from the times of their kings and prophets,—a sacred
literature, to which they now clung as the charter of their
national calling, and as the law of worship, of faith, and
of civil life.   This literature was collected, and new pro-
phetical, historical, and poetical writings were added in
the old and sacred language.   The introduction of
Aramaic forms and words was more strenuously avoided
than in the times before and during the Exile, just because
of opposition to the inroads of the Aramaic spoken by all
the tribes, in the midst of which the little Jewish community had to maintain its existence.   The hymns and
set liturgical forms for use in the temple worship were
taken from the Hebrew Bible.   The Hebrew Bible was
read and expounded to the people in the synagogues, and
there soon grew up a distinct class of learned men who
made it the subject of special study.

In the case of a people whose individuality and continued existence depended so much upon their religion, and
whose religious life was so thoroughly conditioned by its
hold upon its classical literature as was that of the Jewish
people at the time of the second temple, the language in
which this literature was written could not fall entirely
into disuse.   It not only survived in the sacred books and
in inscriptions upon coins (n. 8), but strenuous efforts
were also made to keep it in use as a spoken language.
Jesus the son of Sirach, a resident of Jerusalem, wrote
his book of proverbs in biblical Hebrew about 180 B.C.,
and his grandson in Egypt translated it into Greek after
132 B.C.   Because it was the sacred language, the scholars
gave it preference in their disputations, and as a medium
for the presentation of their traditional lore.   In order to
adapt it to these purposes, by the construction of new forms
and the introduction of foreign words (n. 9), they modified
it into a learned language, the Modern Hebrew of the
Mishnah.   Of the uneducated multitude they spoke with

contempt (John vii. 49 ; Acts iv. 13), and called their language the "speech of the vulgar." At a time when they themselves had to acquire the sacred language of the Scriptures artificially, they protested against the use, in their own learned circles at least, of the living language of daily intercourse (n. 10). But the effort, at least when made with authority and determination, was too late to be effective. Long before the time of Christ this language which the scholars despised, the Sursi, as the Jews of the Holy Land were wont to call it (n. 4), had become the vernacular of Palestine and the adjoining regions on the east and north (n. 11). Like every other Semite who grew up in these regions, the Jew learned Aramaic as his native tongue before he could learn to read and write and to study the Hebrew Bible. The rule laid down by an aged interpreter of the law, that fathers should teach their sons the sacred language first, only shows that the reverse was the general case. The daughters are expressly exempted from this requirement ; nor did anyone expect them to learn Hebrew (n. 10). So that even in families which were zealous for the law the wives had no knowledge of Hebrew. At the time of Christ, Hebrew was, in the strict sense of the word, the native tongue of no Jew. The small sections of country where the Jews lived together closely and in large numbers, were interspersed with and surrounded by other Aramaic-speaking peoples, Samaritans, Syrians, Edomites, and Nabatæans. Within these narrow limits, necessarily, the language was practically homogeneous. Without the aid of an interpreter Jesus conversed with the Samaritan woman from Sychar and with other Samaritans (John iv. 7–43 ; Luke xvii. 16), also with the Syriac-speaking Phœnician woman (n. 7). Syrians serving in the Roman army understood every word of the table-talk engaged in by the Jews, who supposed that what they said was not understood by them (Jos. *Bell.* iv. 1. 5).

This community of language, which can be proved, and which makes it permissible to speak of a vernacular, did not exclude very perceptible differences of dialect. These differences were necessarily all the greater since Aramaic had been but very little employed for literary purposes, and particularly since there was no common literature which brought the various Aramaic-speaking tribes and religious communities together. From His dialect, the Samaritan woman at Jacob's Well is able at once to recognise Jesus as a Jew (John iv. 9), and *vice versâ*. Especially when spoken by Jews, Aramaic must have had a peculiar stamp. The Jewish people were so zealous in the practice of their religion, that a large number of Hebrew expressions taken from the language of the Bible, from the cultus, and from the rabbis, must have been adopted into the language of daily life, and in the nature of the case these expressions were only partly Aramaicised. Just as the Modern Hebrew of the learned classes took on its peculiar form not without being strongly influenced by Aramaic, so it was impossible and not to be expected that Jews throughout the Orient, especially in Palestine, and most particularly in Jerusalem, the seat of national worship and the seat of rabbinic learning, should speak Aramaic without using some Hebraisms. The Jews themselves not infrequently called the Aramaic which they spoke Hebrew, at least they did so in their intercourse with Greeks and Romans in contrasting their language with Greek (n. 12). It was not only their mother tongue, but also their national language, and those who retained it were called Hebrews in contrast to the Hellenists (§ 2). Inevitably, also, the various Aramaic dialects spoken by the non-Jewish part of the population in different districts had their influence upon the Aramaic spoken by the Jews living in these regions. As spoken in Babylon, the language sounded different from what it did in Jerusalem ; nor did all the Jews in

Palestine speak it in exactly the same way. The Galilean was easily recognised in Jerusalem by his pronunciation (n. 13). But these differences, which were not greater than those existing among the High German dialects still spoken (n. 14), must not cause us to overlook the common character of the Aramaic spoken by all "Hebrews," *i.e.* by Oriental Jews who were not Hellenists.

Especially to be rejected as wholly wrong is the notion that at the time of Christ, Hebrew was spoken in Judea and Jerusalem, and Aramaic only in Galilee. According to Acts i. 19, the Aramaic name of the "field of blood" belonged to the language of Jerusalem Jews; and there were other places in and near Jerusalem which had Aramaic names, such as Bethesda (n. 15). On the occasion of the processions in connection with the feast of Tabernacles, and at the triumphal entry of Jesus, the Galilean pilgrims and the inhabitants of Jerusalem joined in shouting the Hebrew *Hoschia-na* in its Aramaicised form *Oschanna* (n. 3, p. 21). No difference is to be observed between Judea and Galilee in the use of the numerous Aramaic proper names which appear in use along with the old Hebrew names (n. 16). There were many Aramaic expressions, frequently employed and long current, that were in use by all "Hebrews," among these some associated with religious thought and life, such as the title Messiah and the party name Pharisees (n. 17). When Josephus, a native of Jerusalem, and a scion of a priestly house, wrote his history of the Jewish War in the "language of his fathers," *i.e.* the language spoken in Jerusalem,—a history which was afterwards re-edited in Greek,—he did so in the belief that it would be intelligible to the Jews on the other side of the Tigris and in Arabia. But, as is quite clear from this intention of Josephus, and from the combined impression of all the statements which he makes relative to the matter, the language which he used was not that of the O.T. nor the learned language of

the rabbis, but the vernacular of Palestine, which was
intelligible to all Jews not entirely estranged from the
national life, regularly spoken by the " Hebrews " proper,
and used by them in correspondence. We have three
official documents (n. 18) dealing with certain questions
about the calendar and tithes, which were issued between
the years 80 and 110 by Gamaliel—probably not the
famous teacher of Paul (Acts v. 34, xxii. 3), but his no less
distinguished grandson—in his own name and that of his
colleagues, *i.e.* of the highest court of the Jews in Jabne.
One of these is directed to the brethren in Upper and
Lower Galilee, a second to those in Upper and Lower
Daroma, *i.e.* Judea and South Palestine, and the third to
the brethren of the Babylonian diaspora, to those of the
diaspora in Media, to the Greek diaspora, and all the
other exiles of Israel. The account in which the three
documents are incorporated is in Hebrew ; the documents
themselves are written in good Aramaic. In view of this
fact, there can be no doubt that the document issued by
the Jerusalem Sanhedrin—which was still in existence—
to the man who afterwards became the Apostle Paul,
introducing him, and giving him authority among the
Jews in Damascus (Acts xxii. 5), was also written in
Aramaic. But if the most learned body of the nation
found it advisable to use this language in its official
deliverances, and if they made no distinction among their
countrymen in Judea, in Galilee, and in the diaspora,
then it necessarily follows that Josephus must have
written his history of the Jewish War of 63–70 in the
same language, since it was prepared with a specific object
in view, and was designed for the propagation of certain
views. An account of this war in Hebrew would have
made about the same impression on Josephus' contemporaries, especially the Jews of Mesopotamia and
Arabia, who were included among those whom the book
was intended to reach (n. 12), that a history of the

Franco-Prussian War of 1870–71 in the language of the Nibelungenlied would make upon modern Germans. In his defence before the Sanhedrin, had not the presence of the Roman commander necessitated the use of Greek (Acts xxii. 30–xxiii. 10), Paul might have spoken Hebrew, at least with the expectation of being understood, only he would have created the impression of delivering a learned address, rather than of defending his life, which was in danger. To have spoken to the excited mob, which he addressed from the steps of the Roman barracks (Acts xxi. 40–xxii. 21), in the learned language of the time, or in the language of an Isaiah, would have been largely a waste of energy, if not a direct occasion for ridicule. The ἑβραΐς διάλεκτος (Acts xxi. 40–xxii. 2), of which he made use, could have been no other than the Aramaic of common daily life. The fact that, in a Hebrew work like the Mishnah, the sayings of those introduced as speaking are usually reported in Hebrew, is no more proof that these persons spoke Hebrew than our Gospels are evidence that Jesus spoke Greek. On the contrary, from the fact that this same Mishnah transcribes in Aramaic single sayings of the Hillel who was born some thirty years earlier than Jesus, and of some of his contemporaries, it is natural to conclude that Aramaic was widely employed even in rabbinic circles (n. 19).

By Jesus' time Aramaic had come into use also in the synagogue services (n. 20). The story related of Gamaliel the elder, the teacher of Paul, how he ordered a targum, or Aramaic paraphrase of the Book of Job, to be buried, does not, of course, prove the existence at the time of such written translations of the law and prophets also, and still less does it prove that such translations were read in the synagogues in place of the sacred text, or along with it. This came later. But the existence of a targum of the Book of Job in the year 40 A.D. does certainly prove that at this time the Hebrew Bible was unintelligible even to men who studied other parts of the O.T. besides the biblical pericopes, parashas, and haphtarahs. Long before the preparation of the written targums which in part have come down to us, and which were made in order to explain to the people the biblical text, understood by them only imperfectly, use was made in the synagogues of oral translations into Aramaic. It is clear, further, that if it was to accomplish its purpose, the exposition and application, *i.e.* the sermon which followed, also must have been in Aramaic. This must have been true also of Jesus' preaching in the synagogues, upon the mountains of Galilee, and in the courts of the temple at Jerusalem.

What we learn from extra-biblical sources concerning linguistic conditions in Palestine at the time simply confirms what we gather from the original testimony of the four Gospels. The language in which Jesus prayed and talked to the multitudes, and to His disciples, was used also in the Church gathered in Jerusalem shortly after His resurrection. This fact is so self-evident as hardly to call for direct proof. Still it is to be observed that the surname which, according to Acts iv. 36, was given by the apostles to Joseph of Cyprus very early in the history of the Church was Aramaic. Besides, the name assigned was not an ordinary one, but was chosen for a particular reason (n. 16). Expressions other than Greek, which we find employed from the very first in the worship of the Greek Churches, such as the Hebrew αμην, which was used without modification in prayer by Aramaic-speaking Jews, the Aramaicised form ωσαννα (n. 3, p. 21 f.), to which is to be added also αλληλουϊα (Rev. xix. 1–6, cf. Mark xiv. 26), were not adopted by the Gentile Christians from the Greek O.T., for not all of them are to be found there. Nor were they taken from the Hebrew Bible, which the Gentile Christians did not possess : they came rather with the gospel from Jerusalem. The occurrence of the Aramaic expression $\mu a \rho a \nu a \theta a$ in the Greek eucharistic prayers of the so-called *Didache* (x. 2) in very close connection with an $a\mu\eta\nu$ and an $\omega\sigma a\nu\nu a$, indicates that these liturgical formulæ originated in a congregation which used Aramaic in its worship. This could have been none other than the congregation in Jerusalem, the Church in Palestine. Paul makes use of the same formula in a passage where he expressly excludes from his greeting to the Church certain strangers who were disturbing the peace of the Church in Corinth, and threatening to destroy the cordial relations between the Church and the apostle (1 Cor. xvi. 22). As we shall see later, the persons for whom this threatening hint was meant were Jewish Christians from Palestine (§ 18, n. 12). By using the language employed in the Church from which they came, the apostle meant to make clear to these men themselves and to the Greek-speaking Christians in Corinth whom he had in mind.

The successors and heirs of the Jewish'-Christian Church in Jerusalem, which ceased to exist after the time of Hadrian, were the Ebionites, who lived in the region east of the Jordan, and in some localities lying farther north in Syria, as Aleppo. As late as the fourth century they continued to cling to their national traditions. According to Epiphanius (*Hær.* xxix. 7), they were well trained in the use of Hebrew, and, like the Jews, read the O.T. in the original; they were also familiar with the rabbinic traditions as far back as the time of Hadrian. But the only Gospel which they used, the so-called *Gospel of the Hebrews*, was an Aramaic book, which is known to have been in existence from the middle of the second century (*GK*, ii. 648–672). Aramaic, consequently, was the language employed in their religious worship from the time of their enforced departure from Jerusalem before the middle of the second century.

The bearing of these results upon the beginnings of
Christian literature must be reserved· until the separate
writings are discussed. But before we proceed to that
discussion, it is necessary to consider another language
element of predominating importance in the wide field of
the apostolic missionary labours, and of great importance
also in Palestine.

1. (P. 2.) G. DE ROSSI, *Della lingua propria di Cristo e degli Ebrei nazionali
della Palestina da' tempi de' Maccabei*, Parma, 1772. The lines here laid down
were followed out by PFANNKUCHE in his article on the vernacular of Palestine
in the time of Christ and the apostles in Eichhorn's *Allg. Bibl. der bibl. Literatur*,
viii. 3 (1798), S. 365–480. Cf., further, FR. DELITZSCH, " Über die paläst.
Volkssprache, welche Jesus und seine Jünger geredet haben," in *Saat auf
Hoffnung*, 1874, S. 195–215. With regard to later utterances of this scholar,
in which he declared Hebrew rather than Aramaic to have been the original
language of Matthew at least, see below, § 55. A. NEUBAUER, " On the
dialects spoken in Palestine in the time of Christ," in *Studia Biblica* (vol. i. of
the Oxford *Studia bibl. et ecclesiastica*), 1885, pp. 39–74. MARSHALL, " The
Aramaic Gospel," a long continued article in the *Expositor*, New Series,
vols. ii.–viii. (1890–1893). A. MEYER, *Jesu Muttersprache. Das Galiläische
Aramäisch in seiner Bedeutung für die Erklärung der Reden Jesu und der
Evangelien Überhaupt*, 1896. E. NESTLE, *Philologica Sacra, Bemerkungen
über die Urgestalt der Evangelien und der Apostelgeschichte*, 1896. G. DALMAN,
*Die Worte Jesu mit Berücksichtigung des nachkanonischen jüdischen Schrifttums
und der aramäischen Sprache erörtert*, Bd. i., Einleitung und wichtige Begriffe.
Nebst Anhang : Messianische Texte, 1898 (Eng. trans. 1902). Of funda-
mental importance from a philological standpoint is G. DALMAN, *Grammatik
des jüdisch-palästinischen Aramäisch*, 2te Aufl. 1905. Also by the same author,
Aramäische Dialektproben, Lesestücke zur Grammatik, etc., 1896. Lexica :
J. BUXTORF, *Lex. chaldaicum, talmudicum et rabbinicum*, 1639 ; J. LEVY,
Neuhebr und chald. Wörterbuch, 4 vols. 1876–1889 ; *ibid. Chaldäisches Wörterbuch über die Targumim*, 2 vols. 1876 ; M. JASTROW, *Dictionary of the Targumim, the Talmud babli and yeruschalmi*, 2 vols. 1886–1903. G. DALMAN,
Aramäisch-neuhebräisches Wörterbuch zu Targum, Talmud und Midrasch, 1897–
1901. Though the rapid development of these studies is very gratifying,
it is too soon to draw from them wide-reaching conclusions as to the history
and doctrine of the N.T. It is a bypath, and not a very alluring one at
that, which leads from Wellhausen's remarks upon the concept " Son of
man " (*Israelit. u. jüd. Geschichte*, 1st ed. S. 312), altogether correct as many
of them are, to the development of these by A. Meyer (*op. cit.* 91 ff.), and from
thence to Lietzmann, *Der Menschensohn* (1896), and back to Wellhausen himself (*Skizzen u. Vorarbeiten*, vi. 187–215). Cf. Dalman, *Worte Jesu*, S. 191–219
(Eng. trans. pp. 234–268) ; Fiebig, *Der Menschensohn*, 1901 ; *ZKom. Matt.*
346–356.

2. (P. 2.) Referring to words of Jesus, Mark v. 41, xv. 34, ὅ ἐστιν μεθερμη-

νευόμενον (cf. Matt. i. 23; Mark xv. 22; Acts iv. 36, xiii. 8; Mark iii. 17, vii. 11, 34, ὅ ἐστιν (cf. Matt. xxvii. 46; Acts i. 19); in Mark xiv. 36 there is simply a juxtaposition of the Aramaic and Greek expressions (cf. Rom. viii. 15; Gal. iv. 6). John sometimes uses the same or similar formulæ, i. 38, 41, 42, ix. 7, xi. 16, xx. 24, xxi. 2; sometimes he notes that a name used by him is Hebrew, without, however, adding a translation, v. 2; sometimes, after designating a place by its Greek name, he tells what it is called in Hebrew, xix. 13, 17.

3. (P. 4.) Aramaic words, which Jesus either used to express His own thoughts or quoted from the speech of His fellow-countrymen, are the following :—(1) Mark v. 41, ταλιθα κουμ (BLℵ) or κουμι (AD, the Latins, S¹, Aphraates, p. 65), to be written טְלִיתָא קוּמִי ; cf. Dalman, Gr.² 150, A. 6 ; 321, A. 1. The Greek variants make it doubtful whether the final i, which in the Semitic character is to be written at any rate, was still audible. The statement of an anonymous onomasticon (ed. Lagarde, 199. 78), that κουμ is masc., κουμι fem., is grammatically correct, but is probably mere book-learning without regard to the actual pronunciation. (2) Mark vii. 34, εφφαθα (so most authorities, εφφεθα DℵᶜLat., æffeta Jerome, Onomast., ed. Lagarde, 64. 2), correctly taken by Mark (ὅ ἐστιν διανοίχθητι) and the Syrian translators (Ss Sh S¹ אתהנח) as a call in the singular addressed to the deaf man, not as a call in the plural—the ending being dropped—addressed to the ears, cf. Dalman, Gr.² 278, A. 1. (3) Mark xv. 34 = Matt. xxvii. 46. In both passages the text has been transmitted in many various forms, partly owing to recollection of the parallel passage. The original reading of Mark is perhaps ελωι ελωι λεμα (ℵCL, λαμα BD, λιμα AKM, λεμα EFG) σαβαχθανι (EFKL, Eus. Dem. x. 8. 14, σαβαχθανει CGH, σαβακτανει ℵ, ζαφθανει DLat., ζαβαφθανει B) ; that of Matthew is perhaps ηλει ηλει (instead of this ελωι ℵ, ελωει B, both drawn from Mark) λεμα (ℵBL, λαμα D, λιμα or λημα most authorities) σαβαχθανι (al. -νει, DLat. ζαφθανει). Of the ancient Syrian translators (Sc lacks both passages, Sh Mark xv. 34), Ss has in Mark אלהי אלהי למנא שבקתני, i.e. exactly like the Syriac rendering of Ps. xxii. 1 ; it has the question in just the same form in Matthew also, S¹ likewise has it similarly in both Gospels, while Sh, on the contrary, has in Matt. xxvii. 46, למא שבקת יתי ; Ss and Sh have אלי as the form of the address in Matthew (pp. 204, 211, only in the latter passage along with it being given the translation אילהי), S¹ has איל in both Gospels ; cf. the writer's Das Evang. des Petrus, 1893, S. 33, 78. Epiphanius, Hær. lxix. 68, Dindorf, iii. 221, cf. lxix. 49, p. 196, remarks on Matt. xxvii. 46, that Jesus spoke the words ηλι, ηλι in Hebrew, following the original text of the psalm, but that He said what follows in Syriac. Lagarde, Gött. gel. Anz. 1882, S. 329, pointed to this passage as proof of the systematic correction of even our most ancient MSS. which is only partially correct. As proof of the historical originality of Matthew's אלי, a form which, while certainly Hebrew, was not unheard in the Targum, is the fact that through this form the misunderstanding of the people (Matt. xxvii. 47-49, xv. 35) becomes more intelligible ; cf. ZKom. Matt. 705, A. 86 (contrary to view held in first and second editions of the Einleitung). Mark, a native of Jerusalem, probably substituted אלהי, to which he was more accustomed, and which in style was more suitable in an otherwise Aramaic sentence. The obscure pronunciation ελωι instead of ελαι, which was to have been expected, probably arose from

dependence on the sound of the Hebrew *elohim, elohai* (cf. Dalman, *Gr.*[2] 156, A. 1), customary in the living language of the Aramaic speaking Jews. On the other hand, the Western reading ζαφθανει in both Gospels, which had found its way also into B in a still more corrupt form (see above), quite certainly points to scholarly knowledge and conscious consideration of the Hebrew text of the Psalms ; cf. Westcott-Hort, *Appendix*, 21. For evidently an *u*, which could easily have fallen out after λεμα or λαμα, is to be supplied ; so that αζαφθανει, an entirely regular transliteration of the Hebrew עזבתני, is to be considered the original form of the reading. The fact, moreover, that D has λαμα in both Gospels (B only in Mark), discloses the effort to make the entire sentence Hebrew,—a result upon which Luther also ventured in both Gospels. We cannot therefore be wrong in judging that the mutilated text ζαφθανει was traced back to the Aramaic שבקתני by those acquainted with Syriac, and was translated, as in D (Mark xv. 34), by ὠνείδισάς με (cf. also Dalman, *Worte Jesu*, i. 43, A. 2 [Eng. trans. 54, n. 1]). (4) Mark vii. 11, κορβαν = δῶρον, in Matt. xv. 5 only the translation. In the εἰς τὸν κορβανᾶν (*al.* -βοναν, -βανα, -βαν) of Matt. xxvii. 6, where the high priests are speaking, and in Jos. *Bell.* ii. 9. 4,—where, however, we should certainly read κορβανας, and not, with Niese, κορβωνας,—the Aramaic stat. emphat. appears. In Mark vii. 11, where the word forms the predicate (cf. Jos. *Ant.* iv. 4. 4 ; *c. Apion.* i. 22), this form was at least not necessary ; hence Ss also in Mark vii. 11, Matt. xv. 5, is content with the stat. absol. קורבן (Sc S¹ קורבני) ; on the other hand, in Matt. xxvii. 6, Ss S¹ have בית קורבנא, Sh בקרבנא. (5) Mark xiv. 36, ἀββα = ὁ πατήρ. This is its only occurrence in the Gospels, but it is found also in Rom. viii. 15 ; Gal. iv. 6, cf. § 2, and, with regard to Bar-abba, below, n. 16. Instead of this, Ss has here as in Matt. xxvi. 39 (πάτερ) אבי, a form which S¹ pedantically enough places as a Syriac translation beside the exact transcription אבא in Mark xiv. 36, and uses elsewhere for πάτερ as well as for ὁ πατήρ intended as a vocative, Matt. xi. 25, 26, xxvi. 39; Luke x. 21. The East Syrians considered אבי better Syriac, while Sh has אבא in Matt. xxvi. 39 ; Luke x. 21. Cf. *ZKom. Matt.* 436, A. 40 ; Schlatter, *Heimat u. Sprache des 4 Evang.* 54). (6) Mark iii. 17, Βοανηργες (*al.* -εργης, -εργες, min. 700 [*al.* 604], ed. Hoskier, βανηργεζ, min. 565 [*al.* 473], ed. Belsheim, βανηρεγες) = υἱοὶ βροντῆς. Ss בני רגש, so likewise S¹ with appended translation בני רעמא. Jerome on Dan. ii. 7, Vall. v. 625, and *Onom.*, ed. Lagarde, 66. 9, demanded nothing less than a change of the text, which was alleged to be corrupt, into *bane* (or *bene*) *reem*. According to Kautzsch, *Gr. des bibl. Aram.* 9, the verb is not רגש, but רגז "to be angry" (Ss S¹ Matt. v. 22). The free translation in Mark is perhaps to be explained on the ground that υἱοὶ ὀργῆς would be very liable to misunderstanding ; cf. Eph. ii. 3 ; Dalman, recently, *Gr.*[2] 144, A. 2 ; 199, A. 3, prefers רגז. The transcription, however, is remarkable. A superfluous *a* in 'Ιωαχεββέδη (Jos. *Ant.* ii. 9. 4, cf. iii. 5. 3—moreover, the text here as transmitted is uncertain) will not explain the superfluous *o* in *Boanerges*. Delitzsch and Nöldeke, *Gött. gel. Anz.* 1884, S. 1023, saw in this an attempt to reproduce a particular Galilean pronunciation ; whereas Dalman, *Worte Jesu*, 39, A. 2 (Eng. trans. 49, n. 2), would prefer to have either *o* or *a* stricken out. (7) John i. 43, Κηφᾶς = ὁ Πέτρος ; in the other Gospels only the translation. With regard to Paul's usage, see below, § 38, on 1 Pet. i. 1. Jerome, *Onomast.* 66. 14 ; 77. 15, says : *Syrum est* ; and rightly : for it is not כף, which occurs only twice in the O.T. and then in the plural, but the very common Syriac word כאפא (so Ss S¹ in John i. 42, and the Syrians generally as the regular substitution for Πέτρος, Sh כיפא). Instead of the translation ὁ Πέτρος we should have expected Πέτρος, or at best πέτρα, without the article (cf. Acts iv. 36); but John shows by this definite form that he felt the determinative force of the stat. emphat. It is established by Matt. xvi. 17 that Jesus gave this new name as a contrast to that which had been given Simon at birth, as the son of his earthly father. Matthew has preserved the Aramaic form בַּר יוֹנָה. According to this the father bore the name of the prophet Jonah, cf. Matt. xii. 39-41 ; Luke xi. 29-32, which was common among Palestinian Jews even in later times (Levy, *Neuhebr. Lex.* ii. 229, "name of many Amoraim, especially in the Jerus. Gemara"). According to the correct text of John i. 42, xxi. 15-17, and two fragments of the *Gospel of the Hebrews* (*GK*, ii. 693, 694, 712), his name was rather John. The latter name is written in the O.T. יְהוֹחָנָן, or when contracted יוֹחָנָן, e.g. Neh. xii. 22 = Ezra x. 6 ; the former spelling as late as the coins of John Hyrcanus (a. 135-105 ; Madden, *Coins of the Jews*, 76-80) and the Targum (*e.g.* 2 Chron. xvii. 15), in which occurs also the shorter form (*e.g.* Jer. xl. 13). The ancient Hebrew pronunciation is reproduced most exactly in Greek by Ἰωανᾶν (2 Chron. xvii. 15 ; Ezra x. 6 ; Jer. xl. 13, xli. 11, etc., in LXX ; Luke iii. 27 ; along with which occur also here and there Ιωαννναν, Ιωαννα, Ιωναν, and in 2 Kings xxv. 23 in Cod. B the altogether incorrect Ιωνα); the next transliteration in the order of precision is Ἰωάνης, the form in the N.T. in Cod. B throughout, even where Tischendorf has not noted it, sometimes also in א Matt. xvi. 14, xvii. 1, 13 ; Cod. L John i. 32. In the Acts, D, which has the sharpened pronunciation everywhere in the Gospels, comes over to the side of B : Acts i. 5, 13, 22, iii. 1, 11, x. 37, xiii. 24, 25, xix. 3, 4. Once, in iii. 4, D alone has this form. This spelling must be attributed to the older recension of Acts, and therefore to the author himself. Moreover, the corresponding female name is spelled Ἰωάνα by BD in Luke viii. 3, and by DL in Luke xxiv. 10. The wide diffusion of the form Ἰωάννης (cf. also יוחני among the Syrians) cannot be due to a mere error of the Greek copyists, but implies that along with the old Hebrew form there was also a sharpened pronunciation current in Palestine ; cf. Dalman, *Gr.*² 179, A. 5. An analogous case is the name of the high priest חָנָן (Jos. *Ant.* xviii. 2. 1 ; *Bell.* v. 12. 2 correctly Ανανος), which we find in the N.T. (Luke iii. 2 ; John xviii. 13 ; Acts iv. 6) written Αννας almost without variants ; for this form certainly cannot be explained as arising from a confusion of memory with the name חַנָּה (1 Sam. i. 2 ; Luke ii. 36 ; Virg. *Aen.* iv. 9). (8) Matt. v. 22 ρακα (BE and most authorities, ραχα א*D and the Latins) is classed with the Talmudic opprobrious term רֵיקָא (stat. emph.), and this is explained as an abbreviation of רֵיקָן. This is the view even of Dalman, *Gr.*² 173, A. 2. The Syrians, who, without any hint that they were dealing with a foreign word, wrote רקא (Ss Sc Sh S¹), seem with better right to have taken it for a Syriac word. Corresponding to the Hebrew רַק (thin, lean, Gen. xli. 19) the word has acquired among the Syrians the meaning "insignificant, despicable," and among the Syriac speaking population about Antioch has been used as a derogatory form of addressing the lower classes, which has become almost meaningless. See, further, *ZKom. Matt.* 24. The μωρέ standing near it is Greek, of course. But since this Greek word occurs quite often in the form מוֹרָה, מוֹרוֹס in the Midrash as an expression for "fool" (Neubauer, *Athenæum*, 1881, ii. 779 ; *Stud. Bibl.*, Oxford, 1885, p. 55 ; Krauss, *Lehnwörter*, i. 50, ii. 328), it follows that the Galileans, who otherwise spoke Aramaic, used this, like many another Greek word, in common life. (9) The Hebrew אָמֵן, originally an adjective, but regularly an exclamation for the solemn confirmation of a prayer, a word of God, and the like. Usually in the LXX it is translated by γένοιτο, but sometimes (1 Chron. xvi. 36 ; Neh. v. 13) is transcribed as ἀμήν, and in this form was immediately introduced into the liturgical use of the Greek Churches, 1 Cor. xiv. 16 ; 2 Cor. i. 20. Even in the mouth of Jesus the single or double ἀμήν is an elliptical exclamation, like ναί in Matt. xi. 9 ; Luke xi. 51, and is by no means an adverb modifying λέγω or the statement introduced by λέγω, that verb being on such a view a parenthetical *inquam*. The latter supposition is excluded by the simple fact that in many cases a ὅτι dependent upon λέγω follows. But a usage peculiar to the speech of Jesus is the ἀμήν, λέγω ὑμῖν (30 times in Matthew, 13 times in Mark, 6 times in Luke, 25 times with doubled ἀμήν in John) at the beginning of a saying which is neither in answer to a question nor in any way related to another saying as its solemn confirmation, as in Jer. xxviii. 6 ; 1 Kings i. 36 ; Rev. v. 14. The usage in Rev. vii. 12, xix. 4, xxii. 20 is not essentially different from that of Jesus. With regard to Rev. iii. 14, see § 68, n. 8. Delitzsch (*ZfLTh.* 1856, S. 422 f.) conjectured that the original form was אָמַר אָנֵא, the latter word being a contradiction for אֲנָא אָמַר. According to him, the Synoptists had given an exact translation, but John, in addition to this, and indeed quite after his manner, imitated the sound. The Babylonian Talmud was the only place where Delitzsch could find instances of the elision of the ר in the case of contraction, and on this account Dalman, *Gr.*[2] 243, will not admit that it occurred in the speech of Jesus ; nevertheless, the conjecture remains probable. (10) Matt. vi. 24 ; Luke xvi. 9–13 μαμωνᾶς (μαμμωνᾶς is poorly attested ; in Church literature it is the prevalent form), מָמוֹן Pirke Aboth ii. 12, Aram. מָמוֹנָא, not infrequent, Levy, ii. 138 f., so also Ss Sc S¹, מָמוֹנָא Sh, Luke xvi. 13. Jerome, *Ep.* xxii. 31 (cf. *Ep.* cxxi. 6 ; *ad Matth.* vi. 24 ; Vall. vii. 36): "Nam gentili Syrorum lingua (*Ep.* 121 : 'Non Hebræorum, sed Syrorum lingua') Mammona divitiæ nuncupantur." *Ibid. Anecd. Maredsol.* iii. 2. 86 : "Mamona in lingua hebræa divitiæ nuncupantur, non aurum, ut quidam putant." Adam. *Dial. c. Marc.* (Lat. ed., Caspari, 37, effaced in the Greek text) : "Mammonam . . . pecuniam dicit gentili lingua," which probably is to be traced back to Theophilus of Antioch, and refers to the Syriac spoken in the neighbourhood of that city, cf. *ZKG*, ix. 232 f., 238 f. ; Iren. iii. 8. 1 (probably dependent upon Theophilus or Justin, or both): "Secundum Judaicam loquelam, qua et Samaritæ utuntur," etc. ; August. *de Serm. in Monte*, ii. 14. 47, and *Serm.* 113 on Luke xvi. (cf. *Quæst. ev.* ii. 34 ; *Enarr. in Ps.* liii. 2) distinguishes the "Hebrew" *mammona*, the meaning of which he knew through Jerome, from the Punic *mammon*, which he knew through his own acquaintance with the language, and which he says means *lucrum* ; cf. Schröder, *Phönic. Sprache*, 30. See also *ZKom. Matt.* 291, A. 6 ; concerning the doubtful etymology, cf. Nestle, *EB*, col. 2914 ; Dalman, *PRE*,[3] xii. 153. (11) σατανᾶς, in the Gospel and Acts, the authors of which regularly use διάβολος (made current by the LXX), used simply by Jesus (this is true of Acts xxvi. 18 also), the only exceptions being Mark i. 13 ; Luke xxii. 3 ; John xiii. 27, and one other passage (Acts v. 3), where it is used by Peter. It is used ordinarily by Paul also (2 Cor. xii. 7, Antiochian reading σατᾶν, as in LXX 1 Kings xi. 14, 23). It is only in his later Epistles, from Eph. iv. 27 (?) on, that it is sometimes replaced by διάβολος. The Aramaic form occurs as early as Sir. xxi. 27 (τὸν Σατανά B* al. -ναν) ; it is found in the Targum, even where it has no support in the original text ; it is used also in the Syriac Gospels, sometimes even for διάβολος, Sc Matt. iv. 1 ; Ss Luke iv. 2, 13 ; Ss Sc John vi. 70 ; S¹ more seldom, e.g. Matt. xiii. 39 ; Sh, on the other hand, regularly. (12) γέεννα occurs outside of the Gospels (Matthew 7 times, Mark 3 times, Luke once) only once, Jas. iii. 6. The Hebrew גֵּיהִנֹּם ; the pronunciation ge-hinnâm, from which the Hellenised form of the N.T. arose by dropping the m, is also that of the Targums and Talmuds. (13) τὸ πάσχα is used by Jesus in Matt. xxvi. 2, 17, 18 ; Mark xiv. 14 ; Luke xxii. 8, 11, 15. Still earlier than this, in the LXX (φασεκ in Chron. only), and hence used also by Philo and Josephus (also spelled φασκα repeatedly by the latter author, Ant. v. 1. 4, ix. 13. 3 ; Bell. ii. 1. 3) regularly in this Aramaicised form of the Hebrew פֶּסַח. In Sh it is written פסחא in Matt. xxvi. 2, 17, 18, Luke xxii. 8, and quite often, though the form פסחא also occurs, Luke ii. 41. In Sc Ss S¹ the form is פצחא. Among the Jews the pronunciation pascha must be older than pischa. (14) σάββατα, as regards its form, treated as the plural of σάββατον, and actually used with a plural meaning in Acts xvii. 2, perhaps also in Matt. xii. 5, 10, 12, Luke iv. 31, is, however, originally the sing. emphat. form שַׁבְּתָא, and denotes : (a) a single Sabbath day, Matt. xii. 1, 11 ; Mark i. 21, ii. 23, iii. 2 ; cf. LXX very frequently, and perhaps even clearer instances in Jos. Ant. i. 1. 1, iii. 6. 6 ; Hor. Sat. i. 1. 69 : "Hodie tricesima sabbata" ; hence also the expressions ὀψὲ σαββάτων, Matt. xxviii. 1, and ἡμέρα τῶν σ., Luke iv. 16, xiii. 14, 16, xiv. 5 ; Acts xiii. 14, xvi. 13, the latter phrase being used by Luke alone of the N.T. writers (in Mark vi. 2 it is an erroneous insertion of the Westerns) ; (b) the week, so at least in μία [τῶν] σαββάτων, Matt. xxviii. 1 ; Mark xvi. 2 ; Luke xxiv. 1 ; John xx. 1, 19 ; Acts xx. 7 ; 1 Cor. xvi. 2. In Mark xvi. 9 this is changed into the un-Jewish πρώτη σαββ., a form corresponding to חַד בְּשַׁבָּא the first day of the week, Sunday. Among the Jews also שַׁבְּתָא, שַׁבְּתָא, or contracted שַׁבָּא, together with שַׁבּוּעַ, had received the meaning of שַׁבּוּעַ "week" (Levy, iv. 493, 506). Since even Josephus, in spite of his etymological learning, according to which σάββατα = ἀνάπαυσις (Ant. i. 1. 1 ; c. Ap. ii. 2. 11), uses ἑβδομάς, which properly denotes a group of seven, a week, also for the seventh day of the week, the Sabbath (Bell. i. 2. 4, 7. 3, ii. 19. 2 ; c. Ap. ii. 39 ; cf. 2 Macc. vi. 11), it is clear that the people generally had ceased to feel the distinction in derivation between שַׁבְּתָא, שַׁבְּתָא, or rather the contracted form שַׁבָּא, and the word for "seven" שְׁבַע, שְׁבַע. Upon this supposition alone is explicable the signification given under (b). (15) Here the writer puts Βεελζεβούλ, a word cited by Jesus from the speech of His opponents as a term of reviling for Himself and for the devil as His ally (Matt. x. 25 ; Luke xi. 18), or put by the evangelists in the mouth of these opponents (Matt. xii. 24 ; Mark iii. 22 ; Luke xi. 15), or adopted by Jesus Himself (Matt. xii. 27 ; Luke xi. 19), and even used in a good sense (Matt. x. 25). The Syrian translators (Ss Sc S¹, unfortunately Sh is wanting in all these passages) have everywhere put for it בעל זבוב, i.e. the Ekron god of flies, 2 Kings i. 2 ; and even a writer as early as Jerome was so convinced of the correctness of this interpretation, that, on the strength of it, he declared the reading *Beelzebub*, which is attested in no Greek MS., to be the only correct one (*Onom.* 66. 11–13), and through his Vulgate presented to the Latin Church this form now so general among us. Not a particle of proof has yet been found in the LXX, the remains of the other Greek versions, the Targum, or the Talmudic-rabbinic literature, which would support the view that the later Jews altered the name of this Ekron god so arbitrarily, or that they took any interest in him at all ; such proof must first be forthcoming before we can rest satisfied with such a *quid pro quo*. Yet even recent writers like Kautzsch, 9 ; Dalman, *Gr.*² 137 ; Graf v. Baudissin, *PRE,*³ ii. 514, content themselves with this explanation. To be sure, the thought of זבל to dung, זָבַל dung, זִבּוּל dunging, and the application of these words to idol-worship, which had become customary (Levy, i. 509 f.), may have contributed to give the name Beelzebub an evil sense ; but this name (and the only forms which have come down to us are Βεελ (or Βεε, or Βε) -ζεβουλ) cannot be a transcription of *sebel* or *sibbul*, consequently the name must have been בְּעַל זְבוּל "lord of the dwelling." By the dwelling is meant naturally not that of God, the temple (1 Kings viii. 13), but the abode of the dead (Ps. xlix. 15), the stronghold of Hades, whence all the powers of destruction break forth (Matt. xvi. 18 ; Luke viii. 31 ; Rev. ix. 1–11, xx. 1–3). Jesus adopts the very word which His adversaries have used. When they call the devil a lord of the abode, they should at the same time consider that as such he has charge of an ordered household which he will not himself wantonly destroy, nor suffer to be plundered by others, so long as he can prevent it (Matt. xii. 25, 29). If they apply the name to Jesus Himself, He can appropriate it when reminding the disciples that He is the master of the house in which they form the household (Matt. x. 25). The first word of the compound name has the Aram. form, the second is Hebrew as well. Here belong also words which were spoken by those about Jesus, but as to which it is not expressly recorded that He used them Himself : (1) ῥαββί, רַבִּי, was the customary form with which the pupil addressed the teacher (John i. 38, translated by διδάσκαλε 8 times in John, 4 times in Matt., 3 times in Mark), and as such was referred to by Jesus Himself (Matt. xxiii. 7, 8 ; cf. John xiii. 13). Beside this, however, ῥαββουνί is used in addressing Jesus (Mark x. 51 ; John xx. 16)—both times with the variant reading ῥαββωνεί. The pronunciation of רבּוני "my lord and master," may at that time have fluctuated between *u* and *o* in the penult. The Jewish pronunciation *ribboni* (Levy, iv. 416) probably belongs to a later period. Cf. also *ZKom. Matt.* 643, A. 70. Among the Syriac versions, Sh S¹ have retained this word in John xx. 16, S¹ has רבי in Mark x. 51, Ss רבּוּלי in both passages, Sc is wanting. (2) Μεσσίας only in John i. 41, iv. 25, and then with the translation (ὁ) Χριστός = Aramaic מְשִׁיחָא, in the Targums, and especially among the Aramaic speaking Jews = הַמְּשִׁיחַ. The Syrians, without exception, have used for this word the Aramaic form, which everywhere in the N.T. is to be presupposed as the original of (ὁ) Χριστός ; Sh alone, who elsewhere also has preserved Greek forms (*e.g.* ישׁוע Jesus), wrote מסיא in John i. 42,

iv. 25, and thus it was possible for him also, in slavish imitation of the original, to add a translation, a thing which Ss Sc S¹ declined to do. The view of Lagarde (*Verhältnis des deutschen Staats*, etc., 1873, S. 29; *Semitica*, i. 50; *Symmicta*, ii. 92; *Übersicht über die Bildung der Nomina*, 1889, S. 93–95; *Register und Nachträge*, 1891, S. 62 f.), that Μεσσίας goes back to a מְשִׁיחָא, which, according to him, was originally Assyrian or Babylonian, later Nabatæan, *i.e.* trans-Jordanic, and means "the repeatedly anointing one," has justly met with no favour. It is beyond belief that the original meaning of the Aramaic word should have been misunderstood, not only by John, who was the first to transliterate it into Greek, and by all Greek speaking Christians, who called their Lord ὁ Χριστός even before the year 43–44, during which the name Χριστιανοί arose in Antioch (§ 40, n. 9), but also by the Jews, who long since had used it in the sense of "the anointed, the promised king" (*e.g.* also Onkelos, *Gen.* xlix. 10). The double σσ for single שׁ, especially in the middle of a word, has analogies enough : Αβεσσα, Cod. B, 1 Sam. xxvi. 6; Jos. *Ant.* xvii. 1. 3; Αβεσσαλωμ, LXX 2 Sam. iii. 3, xiii. 1 ff., which also has some attestation in 1 Macc. xi. 70; Jos. *Ant.* vii. 14; Ελισσαιος, Cod. A, without exception after 1 Kings xix. 16, attested preponderantly in Jos. *Ant.* viii. 13. 7, and not inconsiderably in Luke iv. 27; Ιεσσαι, 1 Sam. xvi. 1 ff.; Isa. xi. 1 (א Ιεσαι); Matt. i. 5 f.; Luke iii. 32; אֲשִׁישְׁתָּא Dan. vi. 5 (*al.* 4), rendered by Jerome (Vall. v. 658) *essaitha*. If all this should be insufficient to explain the form Μεσσίας, we might regard as reproducing the original spelling the reading Μεσίας in John i. 42, iv. 25, a reading the attestation of which can hardly be called slight.   (3) Matt. xxi. 9, 15; Mark xi. 9, 10; John xii. 13, ωσαννα; Ss Sc (so far as they have these passages) and S¹ everywhere אושענא; on the contrary, Sh הושענא.   Furthermore, *osanna* occurred in the *Gospel of the Hebrews* according to Jerome, *Epist.* xx. (*GK*, ii. 650, 694), it was early received into the liturgy of the Eucharist according to *Didache* x. 6, and it was shouted by the people in Jerusalem in the year 66 according to Hegesippus (Eus. *H. E.* ii. 23. 14). The original form of this, as is also shown by the context in the Gospels, is unquestionably the הוֹשִׁיעָה נָא of Ps. cxviii. 25. Whether he knew the whole psalm or not, every Jewish child was familiar with these words, occurring as they did in the liturgy of the feast of Tabernacles,—a feast, moreover, which the palm branches would recall; cf. Delitzsch, *ZfLTh.* 1855, S. 653 ff.   The view proposed first, perhaps, by Merx in Hilgenfeld, *NT extra can.* iv. 26, ed. ii. p. 25, and adopted by Siegfried, *ZflVTh.* 1884, S. 359, and others, according to which the original form was an Aramaic הוֹשַׁע נָא "save us," is in the first place opposed to all the tradition. The Greek translators of Ps. cxviii. 25 and the ancient commentators understood σῶσον δή; cf. also Jerome, *Onomast.* 62. 29.   Good proof must then be forthcoming before we can believe that Jews by misunderstanding the Biblical form found here a suffix of the first person plural. In the second place, the dative "to the son of David" (Matt. xxi. 9, 15) or "to the God of David" (*Didache* x. 6), excludes the possibility that those who thus hailed Jesus, or those who reported this, thought of an "us" as contained in the hosanna. In the third place, there is no verb ישׁע in Aramaic at all, nor one related to this in derivation. The Hiph'il of this Hebrew verb is rendered regularly in Targ. and Pesh. by פרק. The Talmudic הושענא as a name of the festal palm

branch and (with יום) of the last day of the feast of Tabernacles, which
passed over to the Syrians as a foreign word in the form אושענא, and was
made to apply to Palm Sunday (Payne Smith, *Thes. s.v.*), can certainly
be nothing else than a shortened pronunciation of the Hebrew exclamation, a pronunciation reproduced exactly in the Gospels and in the liturgy
of the *Didache*. To Aramaic-speaking Jews this pronunciation probably
seemed an assimilation to their ordinary speech ; and when the East Syrians
Ss Sc S¹ replaced the initial ה by א (Sh retained the Hebrew spelling with
ה), this was simply a further Aramaicising of the foreign Hebrew word. An
equally superficial and specious assimilation to the Aramaic is seen in the
form *Oshaya*, the Babylonian Talmud's spelling of the name which occurs as
Hoshaya in the Palestinian Talmud (Levy, i. 48, 460), or in the variant
spellings אַנְדָה and אֲנָנְתָּא, which occur in both Talmuds along with the form
הַנְנָה, a word derived from הֵנִיד, and therefore Hebrew. By such a change
hosanna became Aramaic to just about the same extent that *Pension-irung* is
a German word. The same tendency, though in the reverse direction, is seen
in the inscription on the sarcophagus of a Jewish princess, apparently from
Adiabene (*C. I. Sem.* ii. No. 156, see n. 12), in which the Aramaic word
"queen" is written once in Syriac script correctly מלכתא, and once in the
Hebrew square characters מלכתהת, a form which appeared more Jewish. We
cannot tell from Jerome's report whether in the *Gospel of the Hebrews* the
ωσαννα began with a ה or an א, and it is still less possible to decide with how
strong an aspiration the various members of the mixed multitude on that
Palm Sunday shouted the first syllable of this word.

4. (Pp. 4, 7.) Even translators as early as the LXX (and Theodotion)
rendered אֲרָמִית in Dan. ii. 4, Ezra iv. 7 by συριστί (Vulg. *syriace*), *i.e.* gave the
name "Syriac" to the so-called Biblical Aramaic. The corresponding סוּרְיִסְקִין
and לִישׁן סוּרְסִי are the terms which the Palestinian rabbis apply both to the
Biblical Aramaic and to the colloquial speech of their time, cf. Dalman, *Gr.²* 2 ;
Levy, i. 168, ii. 529, iii. 495. According to Sotah, 49*b* (cf. Baba Kamma, 83*a*),
Judah the "nasi," the editor of the Mishnah, who lived in Palestine *c.* 200,
says : "What business has the Syriac language in the land of Israel? Let
us have either the sacred tongue or the Greek, none other." A rabbi, Joseph,
living in Babylonia, recast this as follows : "What business has the Aramaic
language in Babel? Let us have either the sacred tongue or the Persian,
none other." On the other hand, according to Jerus. Sotah vii. fol. 21*c*,
Samuel bar-Nachman says in the name of rabbi Jochanan : "Let not the
Syriac speech be of small account in thine eyes; for it is spoken in the
Torah, the Nebiim, and the Kethubim," which he then verifies by quoting
Gen. xxxi. 47 ; Jer. x. 11 ; Dan. ii. 4 ; cf. the Midrash on Gen. xxxi. 47,
translated into German by Wünsche, S. 364. Then follows in Jerus. Sotah
vii. fol. 21*c* : "Jonathan of Bethgubrin (*i.e.* a South Palestinian) saith : Four
languages are adapted to be of service to the world, namely, the Greek for
song, the Roman for war, the Syriac for lamentation, the Hebrew for oratory,
and certain say : the Assyrian also for writing." In *Dial.* ciii. Justin, who
was born in the colony Flavia Neapolis in Samaria, calls the speech of the
non-Greek inhabitants of Palestine ἡ Ἰουδαίων καὶ Σύρων φωνή, and distinguishes it, so far as can be made out from the corrupt text, from ἡ Ἑβραίων
φωνή. Eusebius of Cæsarea was bishop of a city, the non-Jewish inhabitants

and neighbours of which were called Syrians by Josephus, *Vita*, 11 ; *Bell.* ii. 18. 1 f., and he could not have remained ignorant of the language of the country. Moreover, he had acquired also some knowledge of Hebrew, probably even in his early years under Dorotheus in Antioch (Eus. *H. E.* vii. 32. 2), and often showed it in his exegesis ; yet he applied the name "Syriac" not only to the language of Edessa, from which he translated into Greek the legend of King Abgar (*H. E.* i. 13. 5, 20, iv. 30), but also to the vernacular of Palestine, into which the several parts of the Greek service had to be translated orally by interpreters in polyglot Churches, such as those at Jerusalem and Scythopolis, for the benefit of those who did not understand Greek (Syr. text of the *Book of the Martyrs of Palestine*, ed. Cureton, p. 4 ; cf. the Latin and Greek excerpts published by Violet in *TU*, xiv. 4, S. 7, 110). Just so *Silviæ peregrin. Itin. Hieros.*, ed. Geyer, 99, 14–24 ; Jerome, *Epist.* cviii. 30 ; *Vita Hilarionis*, cc. xxii. xxiii. (Vall. i. 723, ii. 25); Marci, *Vita Porphyrii Gaz.* (Bonn, 1895), pp. 55–57. What is meant is the language of the so-called *Evangeliarium Hierosolymitanum.* Cf. in general *Forsch.* i. 18–44, 268–272, ii. 292–299 ; *GK*, i. 43, ii. 659 f. Moreover, Eusebius has no hesitation in calling the mother tongue of the Galilean apostles Syriac : *Demonstr. ev.* iii. 7. 10, ἄνδρες τῇ Σύρων ἐντραφέντες μόνῃ φωνῇ, cf. iii. 4. 44 ; *Theoph. syr.*, ed. Lee, iv. 6, v. 26, 46, partly also in Greek in Mai, *Nova p. bibl.* iv. 1. 118, 120. So *Quæst. ev. ad Steph.* in Mai, 270 (probably words of the Julius Africanus who wrote at Nicopolis in Palestine a hundred years before Eusebius, *Forsch.* i. 40, n. 4, ὁ Ματθαῖος Σύρος ἀνήρ. In this sense Lucian, whose mother tongue was the Syriac spoken in Samosata (*Forsch.* ii. 297), called Jesus the well-known Syrian of Palestine, who is a good hand at healing demoniacs (*Philopseudes*, 16) ; and the Alexandrians derided the Jewish king Agrippa as a Syrian by hailing him as מרי, a term about equivalent to *monseigneur* (Philo, *c. Flaccum*, vi. Mangey, ii. 522 f. ; cf. Dalman, *Gr.*[2] 152, A. 3). The "five-tongued" Epiphanius (Jerome, *c. Rufinus*, iii. 6) was a Palestinian by birth, indeed, according to a not very trustworthy tradition, a Jew, and brought up by a rabbi (*Opera*, ed. Dindorf, v. p. 5 f.) ; but when he seeks to speak with precision (*Hær.* lxix. 68, above, p. 15), he calls the Aramaic words spoken by Jesus on the cross "Syriac," in distinction from the Hebrew words joined to them in Matt. xxvii. 46. Jerome in his explanation of the Hebrew names in the Bible regularly appends to the words and names in the N.T. which he regards as Aramaic the phrase *Syrum est* (*Onomastica*, ed. Lagarde, 62. 19 ; 63. 3, 13 ; 64. 27 ; 65. 12 ; 66. 14, 28 ; 67. 27 ; 71. 7 ; 73. 24 ; 75. 25), frequently with the further addition *non hebræum* (60. 18, 21, 25, 29 ; 61. 23 ; 63. 17 ; cf. the passage concerning Mammonas above, p. 18, and the clear distinction between Hebrew and Syriac in *Quæst. hebr. in Gen.*, ed. Lagarde, 22. 11 ; 50. 29). When the distinction between the Hebrew and the Aramaic form is insignificant, or one part of a compound word seems to admit of a Hebrew meaning, he expresses this also, though often rather unclearly. *Onom.* 60. 22 : "' *Barjona*,' filius columbæ, syrum est pariter et hebræum, '*bar*' quippe lingua syra filius, et '*jona*' columba utroque sermone dicitur"; cf. 65. 30 f.; 67. 22, 28 ; *comm. in Matth.* x. 13 (Vall. vii. 60 ; cf. the text-critical note appended) : "Quod enim græce dicitur χαῖρε et latine '*ave*,' hoc hebraico syroque sermone appellatur '*Salom lagh* (*lach?*')' sive '*Saluma luch*' id est '*pax tecum*'"; *comm. in Gal.* ii. 11 (Vall. vii. 409) : "Quod quam nos latine et grœce petram vocemus, Hebræi et Syri propter linguæ inter se viciniam Cephan nuncupent." On the other hand, Jerome when thinking of Dan. ii. 4 chose to call the Biblical Jewish Aramaic *sermo chaldæus* or *chaldaicus* (*Præf. in Dan., Tob., Judith*, ix. 1361, x. 2 f., 22), even though in his translation of Dan. ii. 4 he had used *syriace*. This explains, then, the combination *Syrorum et Chaldæorum lingua* in the *Prol. galeatus in libros Regum* (Vall. ix. 454), and the statement about the *Gospel of the Hebrews* (*c. Pelagium*, iii. 2 Vall. iI. 782) : "Chaldaico quidem syroque sermone, sed hebraicis literis scriptum est"; cf. *GK*, ii. 659 ff. Theodoret, who was acquainted with Syriac (cf. *Forsch.* i. 39–43), recognised no distinctions of dialect within that language as it was spoken in Palestine, in Phœnicia, on the Euphrates, and in Edessa, but such as according to Judg. xii. 6 existed within ancient Israel (*Opp.*, ed. Schulze, i. 347). To this may be added the opinion of a modern philologist (Sachau, on the Palmyrene tax law of 137 A.D. in *ZDMG*, 1883, S. 564 : "The language on no other monument is so closely related to Biblical Aramaic as that in this Palmyrene tax inscription. . . . It is the language which was spoken in Palestine at the time of the composition of Chronicles (*circa* 200 B.C.) and of Daniel (167–166 B.C.), as well as at Palmyra in Hadrian's time. . . . It is the language of Christ and His contemporaries." The ancient Syrian translators of the Gospels recognised their own tongue in the Aramaic words and sentences written in Greek letters, and transcribed them in Syriac letters either altogether unchanged (Mark v. 41), or with merely a slight change of form (Mark xv. 34), so that it was possible for them to dispense with almost all the remarks in the Gospels referring to translation. S[1], who was later than Ss Sc, was the first who quite often, *e.g.* Mark xiv. 36, John xx. 24, took the needless trouble of preserving for the Syrians these remarks so superfluous for them.

5. (P. 4.) The *Treasure Cave* (Syriac and German by Bezold, German part, p. 29, also on the margin of the Syriac text) names as the original language of mankind "the Syriac tongue, which is the Aramaic ; for this tongue is the king (ܡܠܟ being masc.) of all tongues . . . for all tongues on the earth have sprung from the Syriac, and commingled with it are all discourses in books." Cf. the Syrian Tatian's opinion of Greek, *Oratio ad Græc.* i. 26, and the writer's explanation of this, *Forsch.* i. 271 f.

6. (P. 5.) Concerning Aramaic in the Persian period, cf. Nöldeke, *Die semitische Sprachen, eine Skizze*, 2te Aufl. 1899, S. 34. Among other proofs are the Aramaic inscriptions and papyri from Egypt beginning with 482 B.C. (*C. I. Sem.* ii. No. 122). Cf. Ezra iv. 7.

7. (Pp. 5, 7.) The heathen woman from the region of Tyre and Sidon is called by Matthew (xv. 22), in accordance with his antique style (cf. ii. 20 f. γῆ Ἰσραήλ, and also the saying of Judah quoted above, p. 22, n. 4), a Canaanite woman ; in Mark vii. 26 she is called, with reference to her heathen religion, Ἑλληνίς (see § 2, n. 2), to which, however, Συροφοινίκισσα is added in order to denote that she was a Phœnician by birth and a Syrian in speech,—certainly not in order to tell, superfluously enough, in what country Tyre (vii. 24) was situated ; cf. Lucian, *Deor. concil.* 4, where Συροφοίνιξ in contradistinction to Ἕλλην denotes those Phœnicians who spoke Syriac. The earliest writings in which Συροφοινίκη is found are those of Justin ; he uses it when referring to an administrative measure which had been passed shortly before, but which

probably remained in force only temporarily, saying (*Dial.* lxviii.) of the Damascus of his time as contrasted with that of the time of Christ's birth : νῦν προσνενέμηται τῇ Συροφοινίκῃ λεγομένῃ (cf. Spart. *Hadrianus*, 14, and Tertullian, *c. Marc.* iii. 13, who is here dependent upon Justin). Archæologists fail to give this sentence due weight when they put the first establishment of a province of this name as late as *circa* 194 ; see the summary in Marquardt, *Röm. Staatsverw.*[2] i. 423 f. Cf. also the inscriptions from the time of Aretas (Haritat) iv. published by Euting, *Nabatäische Inschriften* (1885), Nos. 1–20, or *C. I. Sem.* ii. No. 196 ff. Perhaps even as early as Nehemiah's time Aramaic in various dialects was spoken in Moab and in Ashdod, so that the speech contrasted with the "Jews' language" in Neh. xiii. 24 is essentially the same as that in Isa. xxxvi. 11.

8. (P. 6.) Even as late as the times of the Hasmonæan princes, John Hyrcanus (135–105 B.C.) and Aristobulus (105–104), the language on the coins is pure Hebrew (Madden, *Coins of the Jews*, 1881, pp. 76–83). Moreover, when Alexander Jannæus (104–78) ventured to have stamped, not only coins with a Hebrew inscription, on which he designated himself as high priest, but also coins inscribed in Greek on the one side and in Semitic on the other, on which he assumed the title of king, he used in both cases a purely Hebrew expression (Madden, pp. 83–90). Even his Aramaicised name יני is replaced by the original Hebrew forms יהונתן or ינתי, more rarely יונתן.

9. (P. 6.) Aids to the elementary study of the Modern Hebrew of the learned class : Geiger, *Lehr- und Lesebuch zur Sprache der Mischnah*, 2 parts, 1845 ; Siegfried and Strack, *Lehrbuch der neuhebräischen Sprache*, 1884. Since the Greek ἰδιώτης, pronounced הדיוט by the Jews, denotes the uncultured in contrast to the scholar, *i.e.* to the scribe among the Jews (Acts iv. 13, ἀγράμματοι καὶ ἰδιῶται, cf. Artemid. iv. 59 = ἀπαίδευτοι), לשון הדיוט primarily forms the contrast to the "tongue of the learned" (לשון חכמים) or the "tongue of our teachers." When contrasted with the Aramaic vernacular, this learned tongue and the Biblical Hebrew were regarded as forming a single language ; so that the tongue of the "sacred language," or "Sursi" (p. 22, n. 4), which is but another designation of the same language, came to be contrasted with the "sacred tongue" in like manner (Jerus. Sanhed. 25d, line 8). At other times, however, the "tongue of the learned" was in its turn distinguished from the "tongue of the Torah," or Biblical Hebrew.

10. (P. 7.) We must not form our judgment of the actual relation between Hebrew and Aramaic even among learned circles from such dictatorial words as those of Judah the "nasi" (above, p. 22, n. 4). Among the good works by which a man earns eternal life, one is for an inhabitant of the land of Israel to speak the sacred tongue (Jerus. Shekalim iii. 47c, line 2 from bottom), which shows that this was no insignificant task. A very ancient commentary (Sifre, in Ugolini, *Thes.* xv. 581) emphasises the fact that Deut. xi. 19 speaks only of sons, not of daughters, and appends the remark of a rabbi, Jose ben Akiba (this should read probably Akabja, see Strack, *Einl. in d. Talmud*, 84) : "Therefore it is said, When the boy begins to speak, the father should speak the sacred tongue with him and teach him the Torah. If he neglects this, he might as well have buried him." A learned Jew in Palestine confessed to Origen that he did not trust himself to give the Hebrew names of things not mentioned anywhere in the Holy Scriptures, and that

the most learned were in no better case ; but he held that it was over hasty to make use of the Syriac tongue instead of the Hebrew in such cases (Orig. *Epist. ad Afric.* vi. Delarue, i. 18).

11. (P. 7.) Josephus, who employs πάτριος γλῶσσα (*Bell.* v. 6. 3) and πατρίως (*Bell.* v. 2. 1), uses also not infrequently and with propriety ἡ ἐπιχώριος γλῶσσα. According to him, *Bell.* iv. 3. 5, the name of a certain Jew in this language meant δορκάδος παῖς, "Son of the Gazelle"; hence the Aramaic must have been קבצה בר : cf. Acts ix. 36 ; Levy, ii. 134. Cf. *Bell.* v. 4. 2, ἐκλήθη δ᾽ ἐπιχωρίος Βεζεθᾶ τὸ νεόκτιστον μέρος ὃ μεθερμηνευόμενον Ἑλλάδι γλώσσῃ καινὴ λέγοιτ᾽ ἂν πόλις. This name has been transmitted in very manifold forms here and in ii. 15. 5 ; 194 ; v. 5. 8 ; see below, n. 15.

12. (Pp. 8, 10.) The Aramaic or Syriac (above, p. 4 f.), spoken by the Jews of Palestine, is called ἑβραϊστί in John v. 2, xix. 13, 17 ; for whatever the decision as to the correct reading in v. 2, there are Aramaic word forms in all three passages (n. 15). It is most natural, then, to assume that the same was true of the title on the cross, xix. 20. The ἑβραϊστί in John xx. 16, if its genuineness may be considered established, refers to a late Hebrew form. Josephus, too, applies the term Hebrew to both Hebrew and Aramaic forms without distinction : *Ant.* iii. 10. 6, πεντηκοστή, ἣν Ἑβραῖοι ἀσαρθᾶ καλοῦσι, Heb. עצרת, Aram. עצרתא, a form which first occurs in this signification of Pentecost. Although the distinction between Hebrew and Syriac must have been perfectly clear to him from the studies of his youth as well as from the O.T. (*Ant.* x. 1. 2, cf. iii. 7. 2), he substitutes without ceremony Aramaic for Hebrew forms not only in σάββατα, πάσχα, where he had been preceded by the LXX (above, p. 18 f.), but also on his own responsibility, as, *e.g.*, when he says of the priests, *Ant.* iii. 7. 1, οὓς χαναναίας (better χααναίας) καλοῦσιν = כהניא ; cf. Siegfried, *ZfATW*, 1883, S. 50. If, according to him, ἀδώμα = "red," is Hebrew (*Ant.* ii. 1. 1), χαγίρας or ἀγίρας, "lame" (*Bell.* v. 11. 5), can also be called Hebrew. The "tongue of the Hebrews," in which a freedman of King Agrippa i. announced to that monarch in Rome the death of Tiberius (*Ant.* xviii. 6. 10), can surely be none other than that from which the Alexandrians borrowed the derisive term *Mari* for the same Agrippa (above, p. 23). It is the πάτριος γλῶσσα of the Jerusalemites (*Bell.* v. 6. 3 ; 9. 2 ; cf. *c. Apion.* i. 9), to use which is termed ἑβραΐζειν (*Bell.* vi. 2. 1). In this language Josephus had originally written his work upon the Jewish War, so that the Jews throughout the whole East might read it (*Bell.* i. procem. 1 f.). In that very passage he designates the readers for which this first draft was intended primarily as οἱ ἄνω βάρβαροι by way of contrast to the domain of Greek literature (§ 1) ; and it is not until § 2, where he speaks of them as dwelling in the remotest parts of Arabia and also in Parthia, Babylonia, and Adiabene, that he incidentally drops the hint that he really has in mind only his own people in those regions. But this implies also that the living language which he calls his πάτριος γλῶσσα (his mother tongue, as we would say) was in the main the common language of the whole territory described. To be sure, king Izates of Adiabene, a convert to Judaism, sent five of his sons to Jerusalem in order that they might learn there the language and culture accurately (γλῶτταν τὴν παρ᾽ ἡμῖν πάτριον, says Jos. *Ant.* xx. 3. 4) ; but all that follows from this is that a Syrian from Adiabene did not speak Aramaic quite so accurately as it was

spoken "among us" in Jerusalem, to use Josephus' phrase. Upon the sarcophagus of a princess, probably of this royal house, is a double Aramaic inscription (*C. I. Sem.* ii. No. 156, cf. Schürer, iii. 121 (Eng. trans. II. ii. 310, n. 287); above, p. 22, line 17). This, then, was the πάτριος γλῶσσα of Josephus, which not infrequently he calls Hebrew. The same term was used also by those Church Fathers whose knowledge of the facts cannot be denied. Eusebius, or perhaps Julius Africanus (above, p. 23), calls Matthew in the same breath a Syrian man and "a Hebrew as to his speech." The same writer calls the Aramaic *Gospel of the Hebrews*, which he had in his hands and from which he made intelligent excerpts, "the Gospel which among the Jews is in the Hebrew tongue" (*Theoph.* iv. 12). Jerome, who by copying this Gospel and by translating it twice had become thoroughly acquainted with it, and who has indicated with precision the character of its language (above, p. 23), calls it very frequently a Hebrew Gospel, or the Hebrew Matthew (*GK*, ii. 651 ff.). Moreover, the same Aramaic words and names in the N.T. which in the *Onomasticon* and elsewhere he declares to be not Hebrew, but Syriac, are yet called Hebrew by him quite frequently in other passages (above, p. 18, line 35 f. ; *GK*, ii. 660). Epiphanius, who, as was shown above, p. 15, line 38, was quite able to distinguish between Hebrew and Syriac, nevertheless in the same passage in which he expresses the distinction, and immediately before he does so (*Hær.* lxix. 68, Dind. iii. 221. 26), classes both languages under the concept of the ἑβραϊκὴ διάλεκτος. Likewise in *Hær.* xxvi. 1 he reckons the Syriac נורא "fire," primarily as belonging to the Hebrew tongue, but adds immediately that it is not the "deep," *i.e.* ancient tongue of this name, in which the name for fire is quite different, but the Syriac dialect to which it bears this relation. Nevertheless he asserts elsewhere (*Ancyr.* 2) that βάρ is a Hebrew word. As late as 600 A.D. or thereabouts, Joannes Moschus used ἑβραϊστί of the vernacular of Palestine (*Prat. spir.* 136, Migne, 87. 3000, in the old translation *syriace*). From all of which it follows that in the whole realm of N.T. and ancient Church literature the word "Hebrew" denotes the Aramaic tongue of the Oriental Jews quite as much as it does the original language of the O.T. and the learned language of the rabbis.

13. (P. 9.) According to the corrected text of Mark xiv. 70, the way in which Peter's Galilean origin was discovered is not expressly stated, since Roman readers, for whom this Gospel was probably intended, were unacquainted with linguistic conditions in Palestine ; yet it is presupposed. And Matt. xxvi. 73 says explicitly, for the benefit of its Palestinian readers, καὶ γὰρ ἡ λαλιά σου δῆλόν σε ποιεῖ. This word is not like διάλεκτος in the ancient sense of that word (Acts ii. 6, 8); it denotes, not a grammatically and lexically separate language or dialect, but the manner of speaking (cf. also John viii. 43), and has reference to accent and pronunciation. Variations of this kind had existed from time immemorial (cf. Judg. xii. 6, and Theodoret's comment upon it, Schulze, i. 337). The anecdotes in which the Galilean "dialect" is ridiculed in the Talmud, especially Erubin, 53b, concern the pronunciation of consonants of similar sound (Neubauer, 51 ; Dalman, *Gr.*[2] 57 ff.; for illustrations see Fischer in his revision of Winer's *Chald. Gram.* 31 ff.). There is not a hint in the New Testament that Jesus caused any surprise in Jerusalem by His pronunciation, although, like Peter, He was

looked upon askance as an unlearned man (John vii. 15) and as a Galilean (John vii. 41). With all due respect for the learning and thoroughness with which of late Dalman has been at pains to distinguish Judean from Galilean Aramaic, one may question whether the separation of the sources which underlies this work furnishes a sufficiently secure foundation for such an undertaking.

14. (P. 9.) The Aramaic dialects spoken by non-Jews (East Syriac, West Syriac, Nabatæan, Palmyrene), which exerted an unavoidable influence upon the speech of Aramaic-speaking Jews also, are one language in spite of their differences, as can be seen clearly upon comparison with the High German dialects (Alemannic, Swabian, Bavarian, Franconian, etc.). Similarly a certain idea of the relation of Hebrew to Aramaic may be gained by one not versed in those languages, if he contrasts High German with Low German. In both cases there is a correspondence between certain sibilants in the one language and certain dentals in the other (High Ger. Zeit = Low Ger. *Tíd*, lassen = *láten*, beissen = *biten*, muss = *möt* ; in like manner, Heb. זהב gold = Aram. דהב, צור rock = טור, אשׁור Assyria = אתור). The difference is much greater, however, in the case of Hebrew and Aramaic, for the reason that Aramaic has no article, and possesses only an imperfect substitute for it in its *status emphaticus* with termination in *á* (טניא).

15. (P. 9.) In John v. 2 the name of the pool at the sheep-gate, which the MSS. give in such various forms, is not indeed translated, as in ix. 7 ; yet the remark is made that it is a Hebrew word, which shows that the evangelist reflected upon its meaning. But there would be reason and sense in his doing so only in case he wrote Βηθεσδα and meant this to be understood as בֵּית חִסְדָּא "house of grace," "mercy." By a deed of gracious love, in imitation of His Father who is ever working (v. 17–21), and in spite of the Sabbath, Jesus gave true meaning to the name of the place, while His opponents, who lacked the divine love (v. 42), accuse Him on account of this as a Sabbath-breaker, but for this very reason shut themselves out from the sphere of His quickening activity (v. 40). This reading, which is supported by the Greek MSS. (with the exception of D and the closely related אBL), was understood as above by the ancient Syrians (Sc Sh S¹, Ss is wanting here), and was so transcribed. Concerning the variants in text, and the attempts, continued to the present time, to give other meanings to the names, see *ZKom. Joh.* (*ad loc.*). In any case, then, the name would be Aramaic. Likewise Ακελδαμα (so most authorities, חקל דמא S¹, Ακελδαμαχ B, Αχελδαμαχ D, Ακελδαμακ E), which according to Acts i. 19 belongs to the language of those in Jerusalem (S¹ "in the language of the place "), and in agreement with Matt. xxvii. 8 is translated χωρίον αἵματος. The first part of the compound name חקל, used in the Targums to translate the Heb. שָׂדֶה, has no essentially identical Hebrew word corresponding to it. Klostermann, *Probl.* 1–8, refers the second part to the Syriac דמך "to sleep," and accordingly translates the word "field of the dead." But such an interpretation seems to have insufficient grounds from an exegetical standpoint, cannot be regarded as corresponding to Palestinian usage, and even though the χ at the end is probably genuine, cannot be established on the strength of that. Dalman, *Gr.²* 202, A. 3, cites as parallels Ἰωσήχ, Luke iii. 26, for יוסי, the abbreviated Joseph, and Σειράχ for סירא. Γαββαθα, John xix. 13 (written also, though

less accurately, Γαβαθα, Sh גיבחא, S¹ נפיפהא, Ss Sc are wanting), is probably גִּבְּתָא (Neubauer, 56 ; Dalman, *Gr.*, 1te Aufl. 108, A. 1, but נבחתא 2te Aufl. 160, A. 4 ; *Worte Jesu*, 6 [Eng. trans. 7, n. 2]). Alongside of this the evangelist puts λιθόστρωτος (or -ον), pavement, especially mosaic pavement ; and though, indeed, he does not give it as the translation of Gabbatha, he remarks that the Jews in their language call this particular mosaic pavement in the prætorium at Jerusalem, or any pavement of that kind, " gabbatha " ; so that he must have in mind a derivation which explains this. He cannot, then, have been thinking of גב, גַּבָּא (masc.) " ridge," " hillock," or גִּבְּבָא " summit," or of גַּבַּהְתָּא " baldness " (Dalman, *Worte*, 6 [Eng. trans. 7, n. 2]), but probably rather on גבב (to pick up, rake together straw, wood, vegetables, etc.), and substantive גבבה, גבבא (small sticks of wood and the like ; examples in Jastrow, 204 ; Levy, i. 291). The signification " parquet or mosaic floor " would be natural enough. Γολγοθα, Matt. xxvii. 33 ; Mark xv. 22 ; John xix. 17 ; in Sh גולגלתא, written exactly as in Targ. Onkelos *Ex.* xvi. 16, the stat. emph. of גולגלא " skull," corresponding to the Heb. גלגלת, rendered easier of pronunciation in Greek by omission of the second ל, and in Ss S¹ by omission of the first. The localities near Jerusalem, Βηθφαγη, Matt. xxi. 1, Mark xi. 1 (?), Luke xix. 29 (Sh בית פגאי, Ss S¹ without א, written by the Jews also בית פאגי, literally " house of the unripe figs "), and Γεθσημανει (-νι, -νη), Matt. xxvi. 36, Mark xiv. 32 (misunderstood by all the Syriac versions ; it is גת שְׁמָנֵי, literally " press of the oils "), are by no means Hellenised by the appending of a termination, like so many names in Josephus, but are exact reproductions of Aramaic plurals in ē, or ī for īn, and are treated as indeclinable ; cf. Dalman, *Gr.*² 191. Moreover, Ὀφλᾶς, Jos. *Bell.* ii. 17. 9, v. 4. 2, is Aramaicised. Of course, in addition to these there remained in use time-honoured names such as שׁלֹח Isa. viii. 6 in LXX (א also in Neh. iii. 15) ; Luke xiii. 4 ; John ix. 7, 11, Σειλωάμ or Σιλωάμ, probably written by Josephus regularly Σιλωᾶ, so that he could decline it, *Bell.* v. 4. 1. 2. As for the name of the Holy City itself, the Jew, and especially the Palestinian Jew, save when he wished to adapt it to the Greek by transforming it into Ἱεροσόλυμα, probably never pronounced it otherwise than *Yerushalem*, and certainly in no case said *Urishlem*, the pronunciation in Edessa.

16. (Pp. 9, 12.) No onomasticon of the N.T. can be given here, yet certain remarks can be made which will be in part pertinent to later detailed investigations. We find old Hebrew names, such as Jacob, Jochanan, Joseph, Judah, Simon, among Galileans as well as in Jerusalem and Judea. It may be that people in Jerusalem, like the historian Josephus, preferred the full form יוסף (Jos. *Vita*, 1; *Bell.* i. procem. 1, Ἰώσηπος, like the patriarch, *Ant.* i. 19. 7, the high priest Joseph Caiaphas, *Ant.* xviii. 2. 2 ; Joseph the son of Kami, *Ant.* xx. 1, 3 ; the father of Jesus, a Judean, in the N.T. invariably written Ἰωσήφ) ; and that, on the other hand, the abbreviated יוסי (Dalman, *Gr.*² 106, 175, A. 2) was more usual among the Galileans (Mark vi. 3, probably also Matt. xiii. 55, a brother of Jesus, Mark xv. 40, 47 ; Matt. xxvii. 56 another ; Jos. *Bell.* iv. 1. 41, 9, probably Ἰωσην should be read, a Jew in Gamala ; among the great rabbis " Jose the Galilean "; but there are many others also who were not Galileans in the lists given by Strack, *Einl. in d. Talmud*, 77–93, about a dozen). The Heb. שׁמעון is written Σίμων as early as Sir. l. 1 ; 1 Macc. ii. 3 (alternating with Συμεων, ii. 1, 65), and regularly so in Josephus and

the N.T., a form identical with a Greek name of even classical times (Pape-Benseler, *Wörterbuch der griech. Eigennamen*, s.v.; Fick - Bechtel, *Griech. Personennamen*, 251), and which, therefore, could not have sounded so strange to a Greek as Συμεών. This latter form was used regularly in the LXX, is the only form to be found in many passages in 1 Macc., and was used sometimes by Josephus also, *Ant.* xii. 6. 1 (along with Σίμων); *Bell.* iv. 3. 10; used in the N.T. of the old man in Luke ii. 25, 34; put in the mouth of James, Acts xv. 14, and used by Peter himself, 2 Pet. i. 1, with reference to Simon Peter; used of a teacher in Antioch, Acts xiii. 1; of the Israelitish tribe, Rev. vii. 7; and once in the genealogy, Luke iii. 30. This form sounded more ancient and more genuinely Jewish. The ε in it was an attempt to reproduce the sound of the ע, as in 'Ελ-ε-άζαρος, and the υ served the same purpose as in Συχέμ, Gen. xxxiv. 2, along with which occurs Σίκιμα, Gen. xxxiii. 18.   In a family in Jerusalem the husband bore the Heb. name Chananyah, the wife the Arm. Shappira or Shafira (Acts v. 1).   In the home in Bethany we find together names of most various kinds, viz. first מרים, which the Massoretes (Ex. xv. 20) intended should be read *Miryam*, but which seems to have been pronounced commonly *Maryam* in N.T. times, and even long before that; for the LXX everywhere has Μαριαμ; and Josephus, after his fashion of adding an ending so as to decline it in Greek, has everywhere Μαριάμη (probably it is to be spelled thus with a μ throughout), only once Μαρία, *Bell.* vi. 3, 4 (Niese, vi. 201).   The name of Jesus' mother, as one might expect from the antiquated Hebraic style of the stories of the infancy, which are the only passages where that name occurs frequently (elsewhere only in Matt. xiii. 55; Mark vi. 3; Acts i. 14), is in the nominative (v. 1; Luke ii. 19), accusative (also Matt. i. 20), and vocative Μαριάμ; in the genitive, however, Μαρίας, in the dative once Μαρία (Acts i. 14), and once Μαριάμ (Luke ii. 5).   Only once elsewhere do we find the latter form attested as the name of a Christian woman of the East (Rom. xvi. 6; see below, § 23, n. 1).   All other Marys of the N.T., including her of Bethany, are always called Μαρία. Cf. Bardenhewer, *Bibl. Stud.* i. 1. 1–17, especially also 9, n. 1, 2.   Second, the sister Martha bears an Aram. name which is quite common even in Talmudic literature (Zunz, *Ges. Schr.* ii. 14; Levy, ii. 234, 251), but which is not Hebrew at all, מרתא, "the lady"; cf. also Orig. *c. Cels.* v. 62; Epiph. *Hær.* xix. 2.   Third, the brother has the ancient Heb. name אלעזר in an abbreviated form then common, Λάζαρ (-ος), John xi. 1; cf. Luke xvi. 20; Jos. *Bell.* v. 13. 7; Jastrow, 72.   It is also indicative of the language then in use that in the N.T. there are numerous patronymics beginning with *Bar-*, but not one beginning with the corresponding Heb. *Ben-*.   In Josephus, indeed, except for Barnabazos, which was probably the Jewish way of writing the Persian Pharnabazos (*Ant.* xi. 6. 4), Bar- is altogether lacking also; but this is simply because he translates it by υἱός or παῖς, or else substitutes the genitive of the father's name.   The Simon whom he calls the son of Gioras, *Bell.* ii. 19. 2, 22. 1, had, according to Dio Cass. lxvi. 7; Tac. *Hist.* v. 12, the good Aram. name of בר גיורא, *i.e.* "son of the proselyte."   Like this Simon, most if not all the bearers of such patronymics probably possessed in addition personal names of their own; see above, p. 16, concerning Simon Peter.   This must have been the case with the many who were called *Bar-abba*, "son of the father" (*C. I. Sem.* ii. No. 154, and the list of the Talmudic teachers in Strack's *Einl. in d.*

Talmud, 2te Aufl. S. 88, 90). Thus the name of the Bar-abba in Matt. xxvii 16–26, Mark xv. 7–15, Luke xxiii. 18, John xviii. 40, was Jesus, according to very ancient tradition, which has been confirmed recently by the reading of Ss in Matt. xxvii. 16 (*Forsch.* i. 105, 108 ; *GK*, ii. 699 ; this treats also of the misinterpretation of the name traceable to the *Gospel of the Hebrews* to the effect that it meant "son of their teacher "). So the Barsabbas of Acts i. 23, who bore the particular name Joseph, and in addition to this the Latin cognomen Justus ; so also the other Barsabbas of Acts xv. 22, whose particular name was Judah. Aside from the cases, which are quite frequent, where the former person is confounded with Joseph Barnabas of Acts iv. 36 (*GK*, ii. 562), the reading in both passages of Acts, just as in Papias (Eus. *H. E.* iii. 39. 9), fluctuates between -σαββας and -σαβας. The former reading suggests שבתא (= שבתא Sabbath and week, see above, p. 19), to which Hitzig, Merx' *Archiv*, i. 107, called attention (though he himself preferred צבא host) ; the latter, סבא "the old man," as Theodoret translated it even when a proper name (*Hist. Rel.* 2, Schulze, iii. 1119). Other instances in Dalman, *Gr.²* 180, A. 2. Opinions still differ widely about the second element of Bar-nabas also (Hitzig, *op. cit.* 106 ; Klostermann, *Probleme*, 8–14 ; Deissmann, *Bibelstud.* 177 ; *Neue Bibelstud.* 16 ; Dalman, *Gr.*, 1te Aufl. 142, again differently 2te Aufl. 178 ; *Worte Jesu*, 32 (Eng. trans. 40 f.) ; Nestle, *Phil. sacra*, 19 f.), and the meaning of Bar-timai (Mark x. 46) has not been cleared up yet even by Nestle, *Marginalien*, 83–92. The evangelist, who here, contrary to his custom, mentions by name a person healed by Jesus, plainly because he was known by this name in Christian circles (cf. Mark xv. 21 and Klostermann, *Das Markusevangelium*, 222, 292), does not show the slightest interest in the meaning of Timai. Otherwise he would have translated it. He might have contented himself with ὁ υἱὸς τοῦ Τιμαίου, just as Ss does on the other hand with Bar-Timai, except for the simple reason that such an expression instead of an individual proper name would have been as strange to Greek readers in a prose narrative as it would have been natural to Jews or Syrians ; hence after the Greek words he puts the Aram. form with a Greek ending, thus making clear that this was a proper name or the ordinary substitute for such. Moreover, we do not know the particular name of the Apostle Βαρθολομαῖος (Matt. x. 3 ; Mark iii. 18 ; Luke vi. 14 ; Acts i. 13, Ss S¹ בר תולמי, Sh בר תולמאי, which may mean "son of Ptolemy," but which can just as well go back to a Semitic name, Dalman, *Gr.²* 176. In the writings of the oldest Syrians, Aphraates, 65, and the translator of Eus. *H. E.* i. 12. 3, ii. 1. 1, iii. 25. 6, 29. 4, 39. 10, the name Matthias, Acts i. 23, is supplanted by Thulmai). It is therefore very possible, indeed,—and a very simple putting of facts together makes it also probable,—that he was called Ναθαναήλ = נתנאל (John i. 46–50), an ancient Heb. name (Num. i. 8 ; 1 Chron. ii. 14, xv. 24, xxiv. 6 ; in later times, Ezra x. 22 ; Neh. xii. 36 ; also Jos. *Ant.* xx. 1, 2 ; Jerus. Hagiga, 77a, line 8 from bottom). If this name was rare in N.T. times, as seems probable, it is the more easily explained why Nathanael, like Barabba, Barnaba, Bartimai, was, as a rule, called by his father's name or his surname. Σιλᾶς, also, Acts xv. 22 ff., is an Aram. name. Especially to be rejected is the idea that it is a contraction from Σιλουανός or Σιλβανός (so B in 1 Pet. v. 12), which would be rather Σιλουᾶς or Σιλβᾶς (Jos. *Bell.* vii. 8. 1, a Φλαουιος Σιλβας, whose name, according to inscriptions and writers, **is** spelled now Silva, now Silvanus (see *Prosopographia*, ii. 75, No. 243). If the names Silas and Silvanus in the N.T. denote the same person (see below, § 13, n. 1), it is one of the many cases in which a Jew bore, besides his name in his native tongue, a Greek or Roman name of similar sound. It seems doubtful whether there was a Greek name Σίλας. The writer finds it only in *C. I. Græciæ sept.* No. 1772. On the other hand, it is quite common among Syrians and Jews. It occurs in the form שׁילא on an East Aramaic inscription as early as the fifth century B.C. (*C. I. Sem.* ii. No. 101, there derived from שׁאל) ; in the form שׁילא on a Palmyrene inscription cited by Dalman, *Gr.*² 157, A. 5 ; several Rabbis with the name שׁילא Jerus. Shabbath, 5*a* ; Sanhed. 26*a* ; Tosefta Berach. ii. 10 ; Midrash on Cant. viii. 10, and on Ruth ii. 18 ; cf. also the proverb on Ruth i. 1 (trans. by Wünsche, S. 12). Σίλας is written thus in Acts by S¹. It is the name of a Jew from Babylonia, Jos. *Bell.* ii. 19. 2, iii. 2. 1 f.; of other Jews, *Ant.* xiv. 3. 2, xviii. 6. 7 ; *Vita*, 17, 53 ; of a Syrian in Emesa in the year 78 A.D., Le Bas-Waddington, iii. No. 2567, Σαμσιγέραμος ὁ καὶ Σειλᾶς. But in seeking for the derivation of this Aramaic name we are not to think of שׁלח "to send," with Jerome on Gal. i. 7 (Vall. vii. 374, and *Onomast.*, Lagarde, 71. 16, 72. 25 ; cf. also the Greeks in the same work, pp. 198. 61, 199. 70), nor of שֵׁלַה Gen. x. 24 ; 1 Chron. i. 18, 24 (LXX and Luke iii. 35 Σαλα), with Zimmer (*JfPTh.* 1881, S. 723), but of שׁאל, "to ask, inquire."

17. (P. 9.) Since names of parties, like most names of peoples, are regularly used first in the plural and only after that in the singular, this reason alone should lead us to say that οἱ Φαρισαῖοι is the stat. emphat. plur. פְּרִישַׁיָּא = Heb. הַפְּרוּשִׁים, and not that Φαρισαῖος is the stat. emphat. sing. פְּרִישָׁא = פְּרִישׁ = הַפָּרוּשׁ. This latter assumption is unlikely even for grammatical reasons, since the numerous names in αιος (᾿Αγγαῖος, ᾿Αλφαῖος, Βαρθολομαῖος, Ζακχαῖος, Ζεβεδαῖος, Θαδδαῖος, Λεββαῖος, Ματθαῖος), and also the national and local names ᾿Αριμαθαῖος, Γαλιλαῖος, ᾿Ιουδαῖος, Ναζωραῖος, are always based upon Heb. or Aram. forms which already have at least *i* and more often *ai* or *ay* as their final sound, so that the appended Greek ending is not ιος, as Dalman, *Gr.*² 157, A. 2, thinks, but ος. On the other hand, a form based upon Perisha or Pherisha must have been Φαρισας, like Γιωρας from גיורא, Χαγιρας from חגירא (above, p. 26, n. 12 ; p. 30, line 45); cf. Messias, Kaiaphas, Kephas, Sabas, etc. Inasmuch, then, as no Greek form of the party name but Φαρισαῖοι is to be found, we must assume that the Jews of Palestine, among whom the name arose perhaps *circa* 150–130 B.C., never applied to the party either then or later any but the Aram. form of the name. Essentially the same is true of Σαδδουκαῖοι and Καναναῖος (if in Matt. x. 4, Mark iii. 18 we are to read this latter word = ζηλωτής, Luke vi. 15; Acts i. 13), likewise of ᾿Ασιδαῖοι, which does not occur in the N.T. (1 Macc. ii. 42, vii. 13 ; 2 Macc. xiv. 6), and of the oft-quoted ᾿Εσσαῖοι. To be sure, in the Talmudic literature, which emanated from the circles of the former Pharisaic party, the name regularly has the Heb. form פְּרִישִׁין; but this is an affectation of antiquity which proves nothing when set over against such witnesses for the usage in the living language of the Pharisee Paul, the evangelists, and Josephus. Concerning the Aram. forms Μεσσίας, κορβανᾶς, χααναίαι, ἀσαρθᾶ, πάσχα, σάββατα, which relate to the life of religion and worship, see above, pp. 18, 19, 20, 26.

18. (P. 10.) With regard to the three letters of Gamaliel, cf. Derenbourg, *Hist. et geogr. de la Palestine*, 241–244. In Jerus. Sanhedrin i. 18*d* (the meaning

is essentially the same, though the order is different, in Jerus. Maaser sheni v. 56c and elsewhere), after some introductory words, it runs, literally translated : " Rabban Gamliel said unto him (Johanan, the priest and secretary): Write to our brethren the sons of upper Doroma and to our brethren the sons of nether Daroma : May your peace increase. I make known unto you," etc. The salutation אנסי שלבכמ=ἡ εἰρήνη ὑμῶν πληθυνθείη is repeated in all these letters, cf. 1 Pet. i. 2 ; 2 Pet. i. 2. It is only in the third letter that Gamaliel speaks of the elders (הזקנים), who had been mentioned also in the introduction, as joint authors with him of the resolution and decree. Dalman in *Dialektproben*, 3, gives a pointed text of this among other ancient documents.

19. (P. 11.) Aram. sayings of Hillel : Pirke Aboth i. 13, ii. 6. In Jerus. Sotah ix. 24b (cf. Jos. *Ant.* xiii. 10. 3) a supernatural voice which the high priest Johanan (John Hyrcanus, 135–105 B.C.) heard, is given in Aramaic, and on the same page it is expressly said of a word which Rabbi Samuel the Less uttered when dying, that this was spoken in the Aramaic tongue. Cf. the Midrash on Cant. viii. 10, translated into German by Wünsche, 188.

20. (P. 11.) With regard to the relation of Gamaliel the elder and the younger to the Targum of Job, see Derenbourg, 241, 243. Concerning oral translation in the synagogue, see for brief discussions Zunz, *Die gottesdienstlichen Vorträge der Juden*, 2te Aufl. 9 ; Schürer, ii. 457 (Eng. trans. II. ii. 81) ; König, *Einl. in das Alte Testament*, 99 ; more details in Hamburger, *RE für Bibel und Talmud*, ii. 1167–1174. Even if the rules of the Mishnah (Megillah iv. 4) had been in force as early as Jesus' time, such a short pericope from the prophets as the single sentence which he read in Nazareth (Luke iv. 18–19 ; Isa. lxi. 1–2a) would have been read through in Hebrew without interruption on the part of the $m^e thurg^e man$ (also $thorg^e man$=dragoman), or interpreter, and only after that was done would have been interpreted, either by the same person who had read it or by someone else. The narrator had no occasion to mention the latter proceeding, since it always took place. If Jesus omitted translating the text Himself, so long as He stood with the roll in His hand (Luke iv. 16), He probably combined the interpretation with the sermon, which He gave sitting (Luke iv. 20). For later times, cf. Joel Müller, *Masechet Sopherim Einl.* 24 ; *Kommentar*, 256. Naturally the meaning of John vii. 15 is not that Jesus had not learned to read and write (cf. the ancient apocryphon, John viii. 6), but that He had received no classical education, which, in the case of other men, was the presupposition of their public activity as teachers. Men wondered in Jerusalem as in Galilee (Luke iv. 22 ; Matt. xiii. 54 ; Mark vi. 2), though with very mixed feelings, at this gifted, self-taught man. There would have been no occasion for such wonder if His knowledge of the Scriptures had been as scanty as A. Meyer, *Jesu Muttersprache*, 54 f., is disposed to represent it in view of the discourses in the Gospels, excluding the fourth and even such passages as Matt. iv. 1–12, xxiv. 15 ; Luke xxiv. 27. The question, "Where did He get this learning or technical knowledge?" we cannot answer by precise biographical statements. The narrative in Luke ii. 46 justifies the assumption that from youth up Jesus took advantage of every opportunity to acquire knowledge of the Scriptures with uncommon zeal. In the judgment of those who heard His discourses, and in the recollection of His Church, He was not inferior in this respect to the teachers who had the regular rabbinical training.

§ 2. THE GREEK LANGUAGE AMONG THE JEWS (N. 1).

That Greek was a cosmopolitan language at the time when the N.T. books were written, was due primarily, of course, to the rapid conquests of Alexander, and the long continued existence of the great empires of his successors; but it can be fully understood only when due recognition is given to the fact that the Romans, themselves nourished by Greek culture, united east and west in a world-empire. According to a law, the working of which may be observed in a variety of instances, great political changes work their effect upon language only gradually. In Gaul, *e.g.*, complete change from the Celtic vernacular to Latin was not effected under the Roman emperors, but took place later under the Frankish kings. In the same way the Hellenisation of Asia Minor, which had been prepared for so long in advance, made its most rapid progress under the Roman rule, and the process was not concluded until the time of the Empire. Under the Seleucidæ and the Ptolemies the transformation of Syria and Egypt went on even more slowly than that of Asia Minor during the same period. In fact, Aramaic spread more widely and took deeper root during the period of the Diadochi than in the Persian period. It was not until now, indeed, that Aramaic became the common language of the "Hebrews" and the vernacular of Palestine; and even so late as the Roman period it maintained its position as the distinctively national language through the whole of the Seleucidan empire. Before the Gates of Antioch, "the beautiful city of the Greeks," as it is called in the fifth century by the Syrian poet Isaac, the common people continued to speak Syriac until the triumph of Islam. While the uneducated peasantry in general remained entirely unacquainted with Greek, many of the inhabitants of the cities had some knowledge of the vernacular. The farther we go from the capital, the port cities, and the highways of commerce, the less disturbed do we find the sway of Aramaic and the more superficial the influence of Greek culture.

Under the dominion of the Ptolemies and, afterward, of the Seleucidæ, conditions in Palestine were somewhat different. In these times the Jewish community was like a small island which was not only girt about by Greek influence, but frequently also flooded by waves from the two great Greek powers between which it lay. The community was isolated from its countrymen in Galilee and Berea, and surrounded by a circle of Gentile cities, some of which offered very little resistance to the inroads of the Greek language and culture, and others of which were founded or colonised for the very purpose of Hellenising the land. Names of Macedonian cities, such as Pella and Dion, recall the times of Alexander himself, while names like Ptolemais (Accho) on the coast and Philadelphia in the east take us back to the reign of the Ptolemies. South and south-east from the Lake of Gennesaret, the regions occupied by the non-Jewish cities, Hippus, Gadara, Scythopolis, and Pella, formed an organised district, which, in Mark v. 20, vii. 31, Matt. iv. 25, is called ἡ Δεκάπολις, from the fact that originally it was a confederation consisting of ten autonomous cities. In ancient Samaria, Alexander himself had settled Macedonian colonists ; and it was made still more a Gentile city, speaking the Greek language, by Herod the Great, who rebuilt it when it was falling into decay, calling it Sebaste, in honour of Augustus, and colonising it in part with discharged soldiers. Of similar character were the cities Antipatris (Acts xxiii. 31) and Phaselus, north of Jericho, both of which were founded by Herod. Of course, one must not be misled into the error of concluding, from the names of cities found in Greek authors, from inscriptions on coins, and from traces of Greek religious worship, that the Greek language was universally spoken in the cities mentioned and in others like them, *e.g.* in Cæsarea (Strato's fortress) on the coast and its environs. Unless it is further defined, the expression πόλις ἑλληνίς cannot be taken to mean a city in which the Greek language is spoken ; because to the Jews, who had been exposed to the seductions and then to the threats and violence of Greek heathenism since the third century B.C., "Hellenic" was synonymous with heathen (n. 2). Among the inhabitants of the cities so designated by Josephus there were strong Jewish minorities, and of the non-Jewish population the majority were "Syrians" by birth and language. *E.g.*, centuries later in the Christian era we find large numbers of people in and about Gaza and Scythopolis who not only spoke Syriac, but who were even unacquainted with Greek. This was due not to a reaction from Greek conditions, but simply to a continuation of the conditions that existed before and during the time of Christ; and only because the old Semitic names of cities survived after they were given Greek names was it possible for these Greek names to be displaced again, as was done so largely in the centuries after Christ. In the thought of the Palestinian Jews, Greek remained a foreign language, or rather "the foreign language" (n. 3). But, in spite of this feeling, how profoundly were the Jews influenced by it and by the culture which came with it, even as early as 170 B.C. ! High priests borrowed their names from the Greek legends, as in the case of a certain Jesus, who gave up his Hebrew name and called himself Jason ; and of a certain Menelaus, whose Hebrew name we do not know. It was upon this disposition and tendency manifesting itself among the best classes in Jerusalem that Antiochus Epiphanes relied in his attempt to destroy Judaism. The Maccabean revolt showed that there was still vitality in the faith and institutions of the Jews, but nevertheless it was not possible longer for the Jews to keep themselves aloof from Hellenism. Men might fight for religious freedom with prayer and sword, but the measure of political independence necessary for the maintenance of this religious freedom could not be won and retained without the use of diplomacy. The ambassadors of Judas Maccabeus who appeared in the Roman senate in the year 161 B.C. could not use in that place any other language than Greek. These enemies of the Greeks, whose fathers were still known by the Hebrew names Jochanan and Eleazar, were called Eupolemos and Jason, and the former was probably one of the first Jews to write Jewish history in Greek (n. 4). As evidenced by their coins, the Hasmonean high priests, as they developed into worldly princes, allowed their government to become more and more Hellenised.

The first of them, Aristobulus (105–104 B.C.), who styled himself a king, and who was known also as a Philhellene (Jos. *Ant.* xiii. 11. 3), calls himself on his coins simply "Juda the high priest." In the case of his successor, Alexander Jannai (104–78 B.C.), part of the coins have only the Hebrew inscription, "Jonathan the high priest," while others are inscribed in Greek, "King Alexander," having on the reverse side the words "Jonathan the king" in Hebrew. From Herod the Great and his successors only Greek coins have come down to us. The founder of this foreign dynasty, which came into power by the favour of the Romans and through his own cunning and violence, made no concealment of the fact that he felt himself more a Greek than a Jew (Jos. *Ant.* xix. 7. 3). His first minister, Nicolaus of Damascus, was a Greek man of letters, and his court consisted of men of the same stamp. His sons he had educated in Rome. His army consisted largely of foreign mercenaries, Gauls, Germans, and Thracians, who would not have been at home in any other than a Greek command. In the theatres, amphitheatres, hippodromes, and all those heathen institutions established by Herod in and about

Jerusalem, in Jericho, and in all the cities of the land, predominantly Gentile, as Cæsarea (n. 4), Greek was practically the only language spoken. If the Jewish tragic poet Ezekiel, whose old Hebrew name suggests that he was a native of Palestine rather than of Alexandria, really wrote his poems for presentation on the stage, his use of Greek iambics would show that all his conceptions of the drama were Greek. Even the rabbis were of the opinion that Greek was the proper language for "Song" and all poetry intended for entertainment and amusement (above, p. 22, n. 4). The system established in 6 A.D., by which Judea and Samaria were put directly under Roman rule, and, with a brief interruption, governed by Roman procurators residing in Cæsarea until the fall of Jerusalem, far from checking further inroads of the Greek language, tended rather to increase its influence. According to Josephus (c. Apion. i. 9), he himself was the only man in the Roman army at the time of the Jewish War who understood the Jewish deserters. While the Herodian princes were Jews, at least to the extent that they understood the vernacular, the Roman officials, changing frequently as they did, never took the trouble to familiarise themselves with the language of the people. Here, as everywhere else in the East, they used Greek in their official relations. Many Latin names of objects may have been more commonly used in Palestine than previously, and may have passed over into the vernacular as foreign words. Undoubtedly also, out of deference to the ruling nation, public notices were sometimes written in Latin as well as Greek (n. 5). But this had no more practical use in Palestine than did the Latin inscriptions upon monuments and milestones in Asia Minor and other lands in the East. Greek was the only language that could be used as a medium of communication among the different bodies of soldiers who maintained the Roman authority in Palestine, representing as they did such a variety of nationalities (n. 6). Though the tax-gatherers and their subordinates may have been native Jews in the Roman districts (Luke xix. 2–9 ; Jos. *Bell*. ii. 14. 4) as well as in the domain of Herod Antipas (Mark ii. 14 ; Matt. ix. 9), all their business intercourse with their superiors in Cæsarea had to be carried on in Greek.

But foreign rule, which in one form or another had burdened the land of the Jews for centuries, was not the only agency by which Greek thought and life were introduced. Jerusalem was the metropolis of Judaism the world over, including the " Greek diaspora." Among the embassies who brought tithes and offerings to the temple at Jerusalem from all parts of the world, and among the pilgrims who streamed thither of their own accord, especially at the time of the great pilgrim feasts, there were not a few Jews who, during their long residence abroad, had entirely or largely forgotten their native tongue. Among these pilgrims there were also Greeks and Hellenised barbarians, who, though they had not espoused Judaism formally and fully by accepting the rite of circumcision, were nevertheless attracted by its faith and worship, and attended the temple services in so far as these were open to them (n. 7). There were also a great many Jews from outside Palestine who had come to reside permanently in Jerusalem in order that they might be near the temple, and that they might end their days in the holy city, and be buried in the "land of Israel." Those who had grown accustomed to use the Greek language found no occasion in Jerusalem to give it up. Jews of this sort were called "Hellenists" in contrast to the "Hebrews," *i.e.* those who remained in the land of their birth and retained the Aramaic vernacular (n. 8). This unwillingness on the part of the Hellenists to give up their language is the chief reason why they had their own synagogues in Jerusalem. Two such are fairly distinguished in Acts vi. 9, — one whose adherents were

Hellenists from Alexandria, Cyrene, and Rome; the other made up of Jews from Asia Minor, especially from the provinces of Cilicia and Asia (n. 8). They would not have grouped themselves together in this way according to the countries from which they came, nor would they have been called Hellenists, if they had not insisted upon the retention in these synagogues at Jerusalem of the Greek form of worship and the Greek translation of the O. T., the Septuagint, to which they had become accustomed in the foreign lands in which they had made their homes. The Pharisees and rabbis could make no objection to this use of a foreign language, because these Hellenists, whose settlement in Jerusalem was due mainly to their genuine Jewish piety, were among the most zealous members of the community in the fulfilment of their religious and ceremonial obligations. The useless zeal of the rabbis for the sacred language was directed not against Greek, but against Aramaic as used by the common people (n. 9). Greek was spoken even in the more prominent rabbinic families; and the law at one time enacted, that sons should not be taught Greek, was one of those renunciations which betray the peculiar earnestness of the times and the anxiety to preserve everything essential to the national good.

This leads to the consideration of the question, how far knowledge of Greek had spread among the middle and lower classes. That the majority of Palestinian Jews who came in contact with public life and were engaged in business generally had some acquaintance with Greek, is clear from the historical facts and conditions already mentioned. That this must have been the case becomes evident, when it is recalled how small the region was which was occupied more or less exclusively by Jews. It required only a day's journey, or a little more, in almost any direction from Jerusalem, to reach cities where more Greek than Aramaic was spoken. And in Galilee the same conditions must have existed all the way from Cæsarea on the coast to Cæsarea Philippi, which are to be met anywhere to-day near the language boundaries, where numbers of people are to be found who, though otherwise uneducated, are able to make themselves fairly well understood in two languages. And it is hardly necessary to appeal to similar conditions in modern times to prove that the cosmopolitan language, without which no Jew belonging to the better social classes could get along, had everywhere an advantage over the Aramaic vernacular, which no Greek or Roman needed to take the trouble to learn. Representatives of the common people, like the apostles Andrew and Philip, must have been called by these Greek names in ordinary life ; otherwise the Hebrew names by which also they may have been known would somewhere crop out (n. 10). The Aramaic vernacular and the Hebrew used by the learned classes were full of words borrowed from the Greek, and included also the Latin terms with which the Jews in Palestine became familiar through contact with Greeks and with Greek-speaking officials, countrymen, and neighbours. In particular, technical terms of a legal character were very generally Greek, but in everyday life and social intercourse also objects and relations were very commonly designated by Greek and Latin words. By reason of the ability of the Jews to adopt these foreign words into their speech through various devices, and even to form new verbs, Semitic in form, from Greek substantives, the common people were not at all conscious that these new elements in the language were foreign. Undoubtedly there were many such foreign words in the Aramaic spoken by Jesus. Words like $\sigma\nu\nu\acute{\epsilon}\delta\rho\iota o\nu$, $\delta\iota a\theta\acute{\eta}\kappa\eta$, $\pi a\rho\acute{a}$-$\kappa\lambda\eta\tau o\varsigma$, $\kappa\acute{\nu}\rho\iota\epsilon$ (as address), $\delta\eta\nu\acute{a}\rho\iota o\nu$, $\grave{a}\sigma\sigma\acute{a}\rho\iota o\nu$, $\kappa o\delta\rho\acute{a}\nu\tau\eta\varsigma$, $\pi a\nu\delta o\kappa\epsilon\acute{\nu}\varsigma$, $\pi a\nu\delta o\kappa\epsilon\hat{\iota}o\nu$, $\lambda\epsilon\gamma\epsilon\acute{\omega}\nu$, and many others which we find in the discourses of Jesus, are not translations made by the evangelists, but were spoken by Jesus Himself,

modified as they would be by a Jew, the evangelists
simply restoring the original sounds and characters
(n. 11). Besides, Jesus and His disciples must have
been able when occasion required to reply in Greek when
they were addressed in this language. Persons who
would hardly have been called Greeks if they had spoken
Aramaic like the Jews, make their request to see Jesus
personally, directly of the two disciples with Greek names
(John xii. 21). Of Pilate's transactions with the representatives of the Sanhedrin who remained outside the
pretorium, and with Jesus who was taken inside the
pretorium, we have different and comparatively full
accounts. If, as certainly was the case, Greek was used
in the first transaction, there could not fail to be some
hint of the fact if, in the intercourse between Pilate and
Jesus, they had difficulty in understanding each other, or
if an interpreter had been necessary. While the commander of the Roman garrison was surprised because
Paul, whom he took for an uneducated Egyptian, understood Greek, the populace were surprised when Paul
addressed them in their native Aramaic (Acts xxi. 37–
xxii. 2 ; cf. above, p. 11). Even before he began to speak
an expectant stillness fell over the crowd. Had he
spoken Greek, as the crowd expected he would, it would
not have been altogether without point ; he would have
been understood not only by the pilgrims of the Greek
diaspora who had come to the feast (xxi. 27), but also by
many of the natives of Jerusalem. But it is easy to
understand why attention increased when Paul addressed
them in the vernacular as " brethren and fathers." Even
visiting Hellenists and Hellenists settled in Jerusalem
who understood only with difficulty, some of them not
at all, must have been touched sympathetically by this
expression of genuine Israelitish thought and spirit. If
only it be kept clearly in mind that Aramaic was the
language ordinarily used by the Jews living within the

bounds of Palestine proper, one can hardly go too far in the assumption of a certain practical familiarity with Greek, not only in Galilee, but also in Jerusalem ; not only among the better classes, but in the middle and lower ranks of society as well (n. 9, end).

In this regard, the position of the early Church in Jerusalem was a peculiar one. According to the notices of Acts, which are the only sources we have, the membership of the Church from the start consisted predominantly of Hellenists (n. 8, 12). The first three thousand converts (Acts ii. 41) to gather about the personal disciples of Jesus, who were mainly Galileans, were not natives of Jerusalem and Palestine. From the names of their home countries one must infer that the language " in which most of them were born " was Greek. It is probable that the later accessions to the Church were largely from the native population, and that the Hellenists were already in the minority when they made complaint that their widows were not treated in the same way as the widows of the Hebrews (Acts vi. 1). But that they still constituted a considerable portion of the Church it is fair to infer from the fact that, of the seven men who as a result of this complaint were intrusted with the care of the funds for the widows and the poor, one was a proselyte from Antioch, and that no one of the seven has a Hebrew name. Though the Church was scattered after the death of Stephen, as soon as peace was restored, and the Church could reassemble in Jerusalem, many of the refugees came back ; and then, as before, the Jerusalem Church was the mother Church of Christianity. And in this Church more than one language was and continued to be used. Of the fugitives who testified their faith wherever they went, and gathered the nuclei of new Churches, persons from Cyrene and Cyprus are distinguished as the most courageous (Acts xi. 19–21). The fact that it was in Antioch that they first ventured to preach the gospel to the Greeks as well as to the Hebrews, is proof that they themselves were Hellenists, or, to put it less strongly, Jews who were familiar with the Greek language.   In the most important cities lying on the route from Jerusalem to Antioch, where primarily as a result of this dispersion Jewish Christian Churches were established, as in Cæsarea (Acts viii. 40, x., 1 ff., xxi. 8), Ptolemais, and Tyre (xxi. 4–7), though the members were Jewish Christians, Greek was spoken quite as much as was Aramaic (Syriac).   In the cities of Cyprus and in Antioch, Greek was universally used.   So that, even before the beginning of Paul's missionary work, Greek had a wide use in the Church, in spite of the fact that as yet its membership consisted very largely of native Jews.   Nor is there any reason to assume, what is not suggested in the tradition, that at that time the Hebrews opposed this development, which had its origin in the nature of existing conditions, and which was destined to become more and more marked with the growth of the Church.   People who boasted proudly that they were Hebrews (2 Cor. xi. 22) nevertheless found shortly afterwards a fruitful field for their propaganda in the Greek Churches of Asia Minor and Greece.   It was not until after the last struggles with the Romans in 66–70, 116, and 133, that the Palestinian Jews made serious efforts to get rid of the Greek language (above, p. 40 ; below, n. 9).   Likewise the strenuousness with which the Ebionitic communities, described to us by Epiphanius and Jerome, restricted themselves in life and worship to national customs and the national language (above, p. 13), is to be explained from circumstances connected with the final catastrophe in the history of Jerusalem and of the Jewish nation.   Their exile from the city was due to the enactments of Hadrian, who transformed Jerusalem into a heathen city, calling it Ælia Capitolina.   In order to retain their nationality, they tore themselves away from Jerusalem, thereby severing all connection not only with the Gentile Christian Churches, but also with the Hellenistic branch of the Jewish Christian Church. But in the apostolic age the Church in Jerusalem and throughout Palestine was comprised to such an extent of both Hellenists and Hebrews, and these were so closely united, that the only evidences in our sources of the existence of this difference of language are incidental references to the fact. It is clear that the leaders and teachers of the Palestinian Church were the ones who were most concerned with this condition of affairs. Men like James, who for at least twenty years presided over the bilingual mother Church, and Philip, residing permanently as he did in Cæsarea, the population of which was principally Gentile and half Greek, also the apostles Peter and John, who at first served both the Hellenists and the Hebrews in the Jerusalem Church as preachers and as ministers to the poor, and who laboured later as superintendents of the Churches scattered throughout the regions around Jerusalem, and as missionary preachers in Palestine and adjoining districts (Acts ii. 42, vi. 2, viii. 14–25, ix. 32–xi. 18, xii. 17 ; Gal. ii. 11 ; 1 Cor. ix. 5),—no one of these could have fulfilled even the immediate duties involved by his office, to say nothing whatever of that extension of their apostolic work which they had in view outside of their own country and nation, without a good deal of readiness in speaking Greek. How much knowledge of Greek they had before they became disciples of Jesus and entered the service of the Church, how much ability they had for acquiring language, which ability may have differed in the individual cases, and whether they made special effort to perfect themselves in the language, we do not know. But the supposition that twenty or thirty years after Jesus' death these men were still the purist "Hebrews," unable to read a Greek book, to write a letter in Greek, or to address Greeks or Hellenists without the aid of an interpreter, has against it both the general conditions existing in Palestine at the time, and the peculiar position that these men occupied.

Reference has already been made more than once to the language conditions of the Jewish diaspora in the apostolic age. There is no doubt that the Jews in Egypt, where their number was estimated at a million, in Asia Minor, in the European provinces, and in Rome, used the Greek language in their daily intercourse and in their religious services, and that this was really the only language with which they were familiar. For proof we have only to remind ourselves of the Alexandrian translation of the O.T., which from the legendary accounts of its origin is called the Septuagint; of such pieces of writing as the preface with which the grandson of Jesus Sirach introduced the Greek translation which he had made of his grandfather's proverbs to the Jews in Egypt; of an author like Philo of Alexandria, who considered himself a Greek in language and training, contrasting himself in this regard with the Hebrews; and of the inscriptions found upon Jewish tombs in Rome (n. 13). The Hellenisation of the "diaspora of the Greeks," which was now practically complete, and which had taken place in many cases with surprising rapidity, will seem less strange when we recall that the vast majority of Jewish emigrants did not leave the "land of Israel" until after Aramaic had displaced the old sacred language in Palestine. Certainly the Jews in Alexandria who translated the O.T. into Greek still retained a respectable linguistic knowledge of the original; but that their native tongue was not the Hebrew of the O.T., which they could read tolerably well, but Aramaic, which they found used also in several chapters of the O.T., is proved by their transcriptions of Hebrew technical terms and not a few translations of single words. What was true of these scholars must have been much more true of the uneducated mass of the Jews in the diaspora. Their knowledge of Hebrew was originally limited to their recollection of a number (certainly of many) of liturgical passages which they understood only imperfectly. By the second generation this knowledge was likely to have dwindled to a few Hebrew words such as are found upon Jewish gravestones, the inscriptions otherwise being in Greek. The Aramaic colloquial, which the first generation brought with them from Palestine, was all the more easily and completely exchanged by the second generation, born abroad, for the cosmopolitan Greek without which they could not get along, because even among Jews in the East, who used Aramaic as their regular language and continued to do so, it was not regarded with any special reverence (above, pp. 5 f., 22). Aramaic was not a sacred language through which the pious Jew could gain access to the sources of his religion, and it was only in the far East that it was a language of common intercourse. Now essentially the same causes which led to the substitution of Aramaic for Hebrew among the Jews in the East, produced the Hellenisation of the Jews in Egypt, Asia Minor, and Europe. But, owing to the intercourse that was kept up between the homeland and the Greek cities abroad, the return of Jews to Palestine (above, p. 39 f.), and the constant migrations from Palestine abroad, the extent to which Jews in the diaspora forgot their native tongue and came to use Greek in its stead, naturally varied very much in individual cases. The Oriental Jew who settled in Ephesus or Rome may very quickly have mastered Greek enough for practical purposes, but he could not at once forget his native tongue, and it would not be easy for him to learn to think and pray in Greek. This came with the next generation. One of the seven synagogues in Rome, the existence of which has so far been proved from inscriptions, was a synagogue of the Hebrews (n. 14). There can be little doubt that its adherents were Jews who had recently come from the East, and who in Rome were unwilling to give up the Hebrew O.T., the Aramaic oral translation and interpretation to which they had been accustomed in their synagogues at home. This synagogue of the Hebrews in Rome was the counterpart of the synagogues of the Hellenists in Jerusalem (above, p. 39 f.).

One case of the retention of the national language in the diaspora, and one of great interest to us, is that of Paul the apostle. To think of him as a Hellenist contradicts not only what is said in Acts xxi. 40, xxii. 2, xxvi. 14, but also his own very clear testimony. Twice with emphasis he calls himself a Hebrew (2 Cor. xi. 22; Phil. iii. 5). He cannot have reference to his pure Jewish origin, since in both passages this is sufficiently described by other expressions (cf. Rom. xi. 1). Quite as little can he refer to the thoroughly Israelitish spirit or bent with which he grew up; Ἑβραῖος is never used in that sense, and in Phil. iii. 5 f., Gal. i. 13 f., his strong Jewish bias is denoted by other expressions, particularly by the reminder that he belonged to the party of the Pharisees. The only possible meaning left is that of Acts vi. 1, where the word is used in contrast to the Hellenists. In the Philippian passage, Paul calls himself a Hebrew when contrasting himself to the wandering Jewish Christian teachers against whom he warns the Philippians; and in the Corinthian passage when comparing himself to the followers of Peter who had come to Corinth from Palestine. He is a Hebrew in the same sense that they are Hebrews. The language in which he threatens them (1 Cor. xvi. 22, above, p. 13) is his own mother-tongue, and therefore also the language in which he was accustomed to pray. This is perfectly clear from Gal. iv. 6; Rom. viii. 15. The only word adequate for the natural expression of his consciousness of divine sonship, as this consciousness expresses itself in prayer before God, is the Aramaic *abba*. He could expect only a few Christians in Rome, and fewer still in Galatia, to understand really what this prayer word meant; in

both passages he adds a Greek translation. This makes
it all the more certain that when he wrote the *abba* it
was not with his readers in mind, but because, without
reflection on his part, that word welled up with irresistible
force out of the depths of his own heart. But the antithesis in both the passages where he so emphatically speaks
of himself as a .Hebrew is to be explained by the fact
that it was with Paul's case in view that his opponents,
especially those in Corinth, were boasting that they were
Hebrews. In general, the Palestinians were disposed to
look a little askance at their countrymen in the Greek
diaspora, and the chief point of difference was that of
language. So it is easy to see how the followers of Peter
in their narrowness may have cast reflections upon Paul,
suggesting that he was born in Tarsus, and that his many
years of travel in Greek lands had thrown him out of
touch with genuine Israelitish life, thus at the same time
emphasising the fact that they had come to Corinth
directly from the native land of Israel and of Jesus, and
spoke the same language that Jesus spoke. So then, far
from contradicting the statement of Acts that Paul was
born in Tarsus, the emphasis and antithesis with which
Paul calls himself a Hebrew goes rather to confirm the
statement that he was born in the Greek diaspora, and
that on this account his Hebrew character could be called
in question (n. 15). In the same way his designation
of himself as ῾Εβραῖος ἐξ ῾Εβραίων can be explained from
the biographical notices of Acts. Inasmuch as he was
brought to Jerusalem at an early age, there to be educated
under Gamaliel for a rabbi (Acts xxii. 3), it was possible
to explain the knowledge of Aramaic which he really did
possess, and which could not be denied by anyone of his
opponents, as one of the acquisitions of his student days
in Jerusalem, while in reality he was the son of a Hellenistic household. But this is not a true representation of
the case. His Hebrew character was rather an inherit-

ance from his fathers. Aramaic was the language spoken in his father's house in Tarsus, the language in which his mother taught him to pray. There are other things also which confirm the opinion that his home was of this character. For one thing, his membership in the Pharisaic party was not merely in consequence of his training under the Pharisee Gamaliel, but an inheritance from his father and grandfather (n. 15). To be sure, Pharisees, like other Jews, sometimes made journeys abroad on various errands (*e.g.* Matt. xxiii. 15); but it is inconceivable that a Jewish family living in the Greek diaspora should continue for generations to count itself a member of the Pharisaic party. This party was kept up largely by its opposition to the party of the Sadducees, *i.e.* the high priestly aristocracy and their following. The seat of both parties was Jerusalem, and individual members of either who went abroad must soon have lost their distinctively Pharisaic or Sadducaic character. This shows that Paul's family had emigrated from Palestine only recently, and that it cherished zealously its connection with the home land. The first statement is supported by an apocryphal tradition (n. 16), the second by Acts. The father had given his son the old Hebrew name Saul (n. 16), and had sent him to Jerusalem in his boyhood to be instructed by the most distinguished Pharisaic teacher of the time. He had a married sister living in Jerusalem, and her son saved the life of his uncle by disclosing to the Roman commandant a plot against the apostle's life (Acts xxiii. 16–22). And later, in frequently interrupting his widely extended missionary labours in Gentile lands by journeys to Jerusalem, Paul remained loyal to the traditions of his family. It is very improbable that during the years of his residence at Jerusalem the young Hebrew, Saul, attached himself to the synagogue of the Hellenists from Cilicia and Asia (Acts vi. 9, above, p. 40; below, p. 60 f.). On the contrary, it may be considered certain that under the instruction of Gamaliel he became a more confirmed Hebrew, and made his acquaintance with the Hebrew O.T. Certainly there is nothing in his letters to prove the contrary (n. 17).

But even after full weight has been given to Paul's own testimony that he was a Hebrew, to the statements of Acts which agree with this testimony, and to the apocryphal tradition, the mastery of language and the breadth of view disclosed in his letters are by no means fully explained. He does not write Greek as a person would who had acquired the language with effort late in life (n. 18). Although he makes no claims to be an orator (2 Cor. xi. 6 ; 1 Cor. i. 17), and pays little attention to the purity of his diction, he does know how to use the language with versatility and effect. Paul was a man whose heart was easily moved and often deeply stirred, and there is no emotion which he is not able to express to his readers, as occasion may require, by delicate sug- gestion, in sharp tones of bitter irony, or in a full stream of irresistible eloquence. The most uninteresting material, such as the tedious details about a collection, disagreeable facts involved in cases of discipline, or the rebellious suspicions of persons greatly his inferiors, he is able to treat in so broad a manner that the reader is amply repaid for his effort to understand them correctly, although the matters referred to are no longer of interest. And when one takes into consideration also the dialectical skill which Paul shows when he attempts to teach, to argue, or to refute objections, it must be admitted by unfriendly modern readers, as by his ancient opponents, that " his letters are weighty and strong " (2 Cor. x. 10),—an estimate which is just as applicable to a short note like Philemon as it is to a lengthy Epistle like Romans. Paul had indeed a habit of frequently repeating certain words and phrases within a comparatively short passage, but this is not due to poverty of language ; it is to be explained

rather by his indifference to elegance of style.   In short,
taking into survey all his writings left to us, the wealth of
his vocabulary and the versatility of his grammatical
constructions are astonishing.   In comparison with his
letters, considered simply from a literary point of view,
the Fourth Gospel is monotonous and the Epistle of
James is barren.   From the Epistles, from the narratives
in Acts, and from the discourses which the latter puts
into Paul's mouth, we get uniformly the impression that
Paul was a finely cultured man, thoroughly acquainted
with the usages of Greek educated society.   There is
apparently no good reason for assuming, as some are fond
of doing, that the knowledge of the poetical literature of
the Greeks, of which there are traces here and there in the
letters, was picked up from hearsay, and not derived from
his own reading (n. 19).   The manner in which he introduces the verse from Epimenides in Tit. i. 12 shows,
better than would any mention of the poet by name,
and of the work from which the verse is taken,
Paul's familiarity with the traditions about this writer.   It
cannot be proved that the verse of the Attic comic poet,
Menander, of which he makes use in 1 Cor. xv. 33, was a
widely used proverb.   In Acts, Paul is represented as
knowing that the poetical quotation which he uses in his
speech on the Areopagus (Acts xvii. 28) occurred not
simply in *one* poet, Aratus, but in essentially the same
form in another, Cleanthes, *i.e.* "in several poets," and
these poets of the Stoic school.   Whether he was familiar
at all with the philosophical literature, and if so to what
extent, it is difficult to say.   Certainly he studied the
Greek O.T. with far more zeal than he did the heathen
poets and philosophers.   He is perfectly familiar with the
LXX, and follows it in most of his quotations from the
O.T.   Indeed, he makes use of his knowledge of the
Hebrew original so rarely that some have gone so far as to
deny his acquaintance with it altogether (n. 17).

The question whence the Hebrew Saul derived all this wisdom it is not difficult to answer from the story of his life. Since his father could hardly have sent him to Jerusalem, to be educated in the principal school of the Pharisees, before he was twelve, and since also there is other evidence to show that he passed his childhood in Tarsus (n. 15), there is hardly any doubt that besides learning Aramaic at home he acquired at an early age a practical knowledge of Greek as it was spoken in the streets of his native city. He could not have failed to have occasion to use it even in Jerusalem. During his first visit there after his conversion—a visit lasting only fifteen days—he immediately had personal dealings with the Hellenists (Acts ix. 29), from which we may assume that even before the event which took place on the road to Damascus he had had relations with his Jewish country-men from Cilicia (Acts vi. 9), although he did not belong to their synagogue. Being a Hebrew who knew Greek, he occupied a mediating position between those Hebrews who understood little or no Greek and the Hellenists who understood little or no Aramaic. But the most important factor in the development of this culture of which we find Paul possessed, is the fact that between his conversion and the beginning of his Christian ministry he spent at least five years (38–43 A.D.) in his native city, Tarsus, before Barnabas brought him to Antioch to assist in the work there (see Chronological Survey, part xi. vol. iii.). Since during this long period Paul was waiting for a new divine commission to preach the gospel to the Gentiles (Acts xxii. 21), undoubtedly he prepared himself for this new work. He had received scholarly training along the lines of Judaism, and nothing was more natural than that he should pursue such studies in the literature of the Greeks, among whom he expected to labour in the future, as seemed best suited to fit him for this work. For this purpose Tarsus was admirably adapted (n. 20). It was a prominent centre for the study of philosophy and rhetoric, and the citizens of Tarsus, unlike those of Athens, Alexandria, and other famous centres of learning, are praised for the very lively interest which they took in the sciences taught in their schools. Only rarely did students from abroad resort to Tarsus ; while, on the other hand, many of the native students, not satisfied with the opportunities afforded them in their own city, completed elsewhere the education begun at home. In Paul's case Tarsus offered quite enough of literary information and stimulus to enable him to become a Greek to the Greeks, just as his rabbinic training received at home and in Jerusalem enabled him to be a Hebrew to the Hebrews (cf. 1 Cor. ix. 19–23).

The purpose of this text-book does not call for a historical, grammatical, and lexical investigation of N.T. Greek. At the present time, researches relating directly and indirectly to this subject are being so vigorously prosecuted, and consequently are in a condition so incomplete, that I would not venture in a compendium like this to set forth any definite results. Still a few remarks may be in order, so that statements about the language made in connection with the separate writings may not seem entirely arbitrary. As is well known, after the time of Alexander the Great there grew up a popular Greek, which in distinction from the various dialects, spoken and literary, into which the Greek of classical times had separated, was called ἡ κοινή or ἡ ἑλληνικὴ διάλεκτος. This language, based upon the later Attic, was used in literature and among the educated classes. The old dialects held their sway in the regions where they had been in use earlier ; but there grew up also, as an offshoot from the literary language, a language used in daily life, varying greatly in the different lands in which it was spoken, but nevertheless taking its place along with the common literary language as a medium of general intercourse.

Only by artificial effort could its impure grammatical forms and mixed vocabulary be kept out of literature permanently. With this end in view the Greek stylists and their docile pupils had been endeavouring, ever since the beginning of the Christian era, to restore the use of the language in its Attic purity. There were those, however, more concerned about what they said than how they said it, who persisted in writing practically as they spoke. Such were the writers of the N.T. One principal cause for the continuous development of this living language after the time of Alexander, was the fact that of those speaking the Greek language there were ten non-Greeks to every genuine Greek, and of the former very many continued to make more or less use of their native tongues. In Egypt and Syria, there were some who spoke a mixture of Greek and their own language in their intercourse with Greeks and Romans (μιξοβάρβαροι). Others spoke Greek and even wrote it when necessary, but in both cases with gross violations of grammatical usage (solecisms). Then there were Syrians whose Greek style was not inferior to that of any native-born Athenian, *e.g.*, that of Lucian of Samosata, whose native tongue was Syriac. Between these extremes were almost as many intermediate stages as there were individual writers. There was never any language that could be called distinctly Syrian or Egyptian Greek, although, just to the degree that Greek was a foreign language to the barbarian, the characteristics of his national language cropped out. This is true also in the case of the Jews. Certainly the manner in which they wrote Greek calls for special notice. For, although the Jewish Aramaic spoken at the time was not very different from the Aramaic spoken by Gentile Syrians, the effect of the O.T. literature and of the religious life inseparably connected with it was always to make the Jew look at things from a point of view distinctly national, and so gives an unmistakable character to his Greek style.   And this was particularly the case when he dealt with subjects relating to his own history and religion.   Even so we may not speak of the Greek written by Jews as if it were something uniform.   For this reason the term *dialectus hellenistica*, which did not come into use until after the beginning of the seventeenth century, is not an adequate expression with which to describe the very complex facts in the case; and the number of different meanings which the word can have has given rise repeatedly to all sorts of misunderstandings (n. 21). The extremes of Jewish Greek are represented, on the one hand, by the LXX, including post-canonical books translated from Hebrew or Aramaic, such as 1 Macc., Sirach, Psalms of Solomon, etc.; and, on the other, by the writings of Philo.   The latter wrote the current literary language, and wrote it just as well as did Clement of Alexandria who was born in Athens.   So also Josephus' writings, thanks to the help of Greek correctors of whom he made use in editing his works, approach the κοινή of the educated classes.   On the other hand, the Alexandrian translators in their effort to render literally the holy original, used language which was altogether inadmissible, and indeed impossible, in the speech of common life.   Still even they did not try the patience of their readers with such absurdities as those of Aquila in the Christian era, who, in order to reproduce the two meanings of the Hebrew את, translated Gen. i. 1, Ἐν κεφαλαίῳ ἔκτισεν ὁ θεὸς σὺν τὸν οὐρανὸν καὶ σὺν τὴν γῆν (Field, *Hexapla*, i. 7).   Between these extremes, the Greek of the Alexandrian translators and that of Philo, were as many gradations of style as we find between the barbarous Greek of numerous inscriptions in Asia Minor and of various Egyptian papyri, and the Greek of the Syrian Lucian—with this difference, however, that in the case of Jewish literature it is possible to trace some little development.   The language of the LXX must have exerted on the language of those who heard it from Sabbath to Sabbath a strong influence, comparable to that of the Luther Bible upon the language of the German people. The sermon which followed the reading and the synagogue prayers based upon the Greek Bible could not have been in language wholly different from that Bible. It was not without reason that R. Simon spoke of *le Grec de la synagogue*. Moreover, it is self-evident that native-born "Hebrews" who did not become acquainted with Greek until late in life would always have had to make an effort to think in Greek, and it is a question to what extent they really made such an effort. If a man like Paul, who was far more than a "Hebrew," continued to use Aramaic, even in his old age, when he wished to express his deepest emotions (above, p. 49), we must assume that the same was true of the disciples of Jesus. The use of the term "Jewish Greek" has some justification, though the idea may be exaggerated by association with the modern expression "Jewish German." Possibly there was a language actually spoken among Jews and Jewish Christians which with propriety could be so designated. But the writings which have been gathered up in the N.T. were all written under circumstances and conditions so complex, that the language of no one of them can properly be described by the single word Jewish Greek. And, on the other hand, there is no one of them, not even the two parts of the work of Luke, born a Gentile, the language of which is not consistent with the Jewish origin of every one of the N.T. writings.

1. (P. 34.) With regard to the penetration of the Greek culture and language into Judaism, cf. SCHÜRER, ii. 21–175, iii. 304–562 (Eng. trans. II. i. 11–148, II. iii. 156–381). A bibliography of the extensive literature on the character of the Greek written by Jews on the diffusion of the knowledge of the Greek language in Palestine at the time of Jesus and similar facts, is given by SCHMIEDEL in his revision of Winer's *Grammatik des neutestamentlichen Sprachidioms* (8th ed. part i. 1894), in the notes to §§ 2–4 and the addenda, p. xiii. f. Here belong also some works cited above, p. 14. Of more recent treatises may be mentioned : E. HATCH, *Essays in Bibl. Greek*, Oxford, 1889 ; J. VITEAU, *Étude sur le Grec du NT* (2 parts), Paris, 1893,

1896; DEISSMANN, *Bibelstudien*, Marburg, 1895; *ibid.*, *Neue Bibelstudien*, 1897 (Eng. trans., Edinburgh, 1901); *ibid.*, "Hellenistisches griechisch," *PRE*,[3] vii. 627–639; KENNEDY, *Sources of N.T. Greek; or, the Influence of the Septuagint on the Vocabulary of the N.T.*, Edinburgh, 1895; BLASS, *Grammatik des neutestamentlichen Griechisch*, 2te Aufl. 1902 (Eng. trans., London, 2nd ed. 1905); *ibid.*, *Philology of the Gospels*, London, 1898. Cf. also the brief remarks of Schlatter, *Geschichte Israels von Alexander bis Hadrian*, 2te Aufl. 1906, S. 22–28; *ibid.*, *Sprache und Heimat des 4 Ev.* S. 7 ff. J. Voss, in his *De septuaginta interpr. dissertationes*, 1661, p. 76 ff. cc. xxiv, xxv, had contented himself simply with establishing the authority of the LXX by its use on the part of the apostles and the evangelists. But in his treatise, *De Sibyllinis*, Oxon. 1679, he went much further. He now made Christ Himself the witness for the authority of the LXX, p. 75 ff., believed that by Hellenists and Hebrews in Acts vi. 1 should be understood friends of Greek culture and genuine national Jews, p. 92 f., held that it was owing to a preconceived opinion that Christ and the apostles were supposed to have spoken Hebrew constantly and exclusively, p. 96, and in general unfolded a picture of the linguistic conditions of Palestine, according to which, except for a scanty knowledge of Hebrew among the learned (nor did he deny this wholly to Jesus, p. 94) and a mixed jargon of Syriac and Greek among the peasants, the ordinary language of everyone, Jesus included, was Greek. A hundred years later appeared D. DIODATI, *J. C. Neapolitani de Christo Grœce loquente dissertatio*, Neap. 1767, against whom de Rossi wrote (above, p. 14), and a hundred years later still in a similar vein A. ROBERTS, *Discussions on the Gospel* : I. On the Language employed by our Lord and His Disciples (ed. 2), Cambridge and London, 1864. Such exaggerations are refuted simply by the facts adduced in § 1.

2. (P. 36.) 2 Macc. vi. 8, with reference to the time of Antiochus Epiphanes, speaks of τὰς ἀστυγείτονας πόλεις ἑλληνίδας, along with this vi. 9, xi. 24 of τὰ ἑλληνικά as heathen religion and custom ; cf. iv. 10, ὁ ἑλληνικὸς χαρακτήρ ; iv. 13, ἑλληνισμὸς καὶ ἀλλοφυλισμός. Jos. *Vita*, 13, uses the term ἔλαιον ἑλληνικόν of oil prepared by Gentiles in distinction from that which was ceremonially clean ; cf. *Ant.* xii. 5. 1, 5, xv. 9. 5. He designates Gadara, Hippos, Scythopolis, Gaza as πόλεις ἑλληνίδες (*Bell.* ii. 6. 3; *Ant.* xvii. 11. 4, αἱ ἐν τῇ Συρίᾳ δεκαπόλεις over against πόλεις Ἰουδαίων, *Vita* 65, Niese 341, 349), meaning in every case simply that the majority of the inhabitants were non-Jews, and that the form of government was modelled after that of Greek communities. According to him, at the beginning of the Jewish War 20,000 Jews were slain by non-Jews in Cæsarea (*Bell.* ii. 18. 1), 13,000 in Scythopolis (ii. 18. 3), 2500 in Askalon, 2000 in Ptolemais (ii. 18. 5). It was said of the Jews in Scythopolis (= Bethshan, Baishan) that in their pronunciation they interchanged certain Hebrew consonants (Levy, *Lex.* i. 224), hence they must have used "Hebrew," *i.e.* Aramaic, frequently, to say the least, when speaking to one another and to their fellow-countrymen. Josephus, in a passage where he has in mind the distinction between heathen worship and Judaism, calls the non-Jews in Cæsarea Hellenes, *Bell.* ii. 13. 7, 14. 4, but remarks at the same time, ii. 13. 7, that the Roman troops in Cæsarea, which for the most part were levied in Syria, and hence were composed of Syrians by birth and language (see above, p. 7), were of the same race as these "Hellenes";

indeed, he distinctly calls these non-Jews of Cæsarea Syrians in *Ant.* xx. 8. 7, 9 ; *Bell.* ii. 18. 1 ; *Vita*, 11 ; cf. above, pp. 22, 24, n. 7. With regard to the survival of the Aramaic language in Scythopolis and Gaza in Christian times, see p. 22. The Greek names of many of the "Hellenic cities," such as Gadara, have not been handed down with any certainty ; others, such as Abila, Gerasa, bear their Greek names only on coins and isolated inscriptions.

3. (P. 36.) The subst. לעז (related to the Heb. and Syr. verb לעז Ps. cxiv. 1) when used alone denotes any foreign language, but in the Palestinian Talmud, in the passage about the four languages cited above, p. 22, and elsewhere (see Levy, ii. 515), it denotes without further modification the Greek tongue, so that the part. לועז and subst. לעז (properly = βάρβαρος, 1 Cor. xiv. 11) denote simply a Greek-speaking person. In intercourse with Greeks and in books intended for Greek readers, the Jews were obliged to reverse the proceedings and to call themselves and their fellow-countrymen, so far as these spoke Aramaic and were unacquainted with Greek, βάρβαροι (Jos. *Bell.* i. procem. 1). A native of Jerusalem like Josephus could not indeed attain to such a degree of self-effacement as the Alexandrian Philo, who reckons himself among the Greeks when he treats of the contrast between the Hebrew language and the Greek (*De conf. ling.* 26, ἔστι δὲ ὡς μὲν Ἑβραῖοι λέγουσι Φανουήλ, ὡς δὲ ἡμεῖς ἀποστροφὴ θεοῦ), and who highly praises among the merits of Augustus that he enlarged Greece by adding to it many Greeces, and that he thoroughly Hellenized the most important parts of the land of the Barbarians (*Leg. ad Cai.* xxi, ἀφελληνίσας). Yet even as early as Aristotle's time there were fully Hellenised Jews (Jos. *c. Apion.* i. 22, Ἑλληνικὸς οὐ τῇ διαλέκτῳ μόνον, ἀλλὰ καὶ τῇ ψυχῇ). Cf., on the other hand, Jos. *c. Apion.* i. 11, and quite frequently.

4. (Pp. 37, 38.) Concerning Eupolemos, see the statement in Schürer, iii. 351 f. (Eng. trans. II. iii. 203 f.). The identity of the historian with the one in 1 Macc. viii. 17 is opposed by Willrich, *Juden u. Griechen*, 1895, p. 157. The coins are found most conveniently classified in Madden, *Coins of the Jews*, 1881. Concerning Herod's troops, see Jos. *Bell.* i. 33. 9, 15. 6, 20. 3, 22. 2 ; *Ant.* xvii. 8. 2 ; concerning his military colonies, see *Ant.* xv. 8. 5, xvi. 5. 2 ; *Bell.* i. 21. 9. Concerning theatres, etc., in and near Jerusalem, see *Ant.* xv. 8. 1 ; cf. Schürer, i. 387 f., ii. 46 (Eng. trans. I. i. 432 f., II. i. 32 f.) ; in Jericho, *Bell.* i. 33. 6, 8 ; *Ant.* xvii. 6. 3, 5, 8. 2. Concerning the tragedian Ezechiel (Clem. *Strom.* i. 155 ; Eus. *Præp.* ix. 28 ; 29. 4–12), see in brief Schürer, iii. 373 f. (Eng. trans. II. iii. 225 f.).

5. (P. 38.) An instance in point is the title on the cross, John xix. 20 (Luke xxiii. 38 ?). Mention is made of bilingual inscriptions from the times just before Christ in Askalon, Tyre, and Sidon, Jos. *Ant.* xiv. 10. 2, 3, 12. 5. The case is different, however, with the inscriptions, partly Latin and partly Greek, which were placed upon the stone wall separating the inner from the outer court of the temple, and which forbade every non-Jew to advance further on pain of death, Jos. *Bell.* v. 5. 2, vi. 2. 4. The purpose here was a very practical one. The Latin inscriptions were to warn the Roman officials and soldiers. A Greek inscription of this kind was found in 1871, *Survey of Western Palestine*, vol. iii. (Jerusalem) 423.

6. (P. 39.) While an Alexander Jannæus was willing to have Pisidians

and Cilicians but no Syrians in his army of mercenaries (Jos. *Bell.* i. 4. 3), the Roman garrison of Cæsarea, *circa* 66 A.D., consisted largely of native Syrians (*Bell.* ii. 13. 7 ; cf. iv. 1. 5, above, n. 2).   A cavalry troop of the Augustans is mentioned repeatedly (*Bell.* ii. 12. 5 ; *Ant.* xx. 6. 1 ; cf. xix. 9. 2, according to which men of Cæsarea also served in it).   We are not accurately informed as to the composition of the infantry in Cæsarea (5 cohorts, *Ant.* xix. 9. 2), in Jerusalem (John xviii. 3, 12 ; Acts xxi. 31 f., xxii. 24 ff., xxiii. 17–33), and elsewhere.   The name σπεῖρα Σεβαστή (*cohors Augusta*) in Acts xxvii. 1 gives no information as to the origin of the soldiers that served in it.   On the other hand, σπεῖρα ἡ καλουμένη Ἰταλική, Acts x. 1, certainly denotes a band the nucleus of which consisted of Italian volunteers.   Schürer's argument, i. 462 f. (Eng. trans. I. ii. 51–54), against the historicity of the statement that such a band was stationed in Cæsarea at that time (perhaps *circa* 35–40) is based upon an unwarranted combination of data.   The statement in Jos. *Ant.* xx. 8. 7, according to which in the year 66 not only the cavalry troop mentioned, but the whole Roman garrison of Cæsarea, was made up largely of men from Cæsarea and Sebaste, is in itself improbable, cannot be maintained in view of the obviously more exact statement in *Bell.* ii. 13. 7 (see above), and would prove nothing about the earlier time of Acts x. 1.

7. (P. 39.)   Philo, who calls Jerusalem the μητρόπολις of all Jews on earth (*c. Flacc.* vii ; *Leg. ad Cai.* xxxvi), and who had visited it at least once himself (Fragm. in Eus. *Præp. ev.* viii. 14. 64, Mangey, ii. 646), speaks probably without exaggeration of the pilgrimages thither by Jews of all lands, *de Mon.* ii. 1, and of the bearing of tribute and gifts to that city, *Mon.* ii. 3 ; *Leg. ad Cai.* xxiii, xxxi, xl; cf. Jos. *Ant.* xiv. 7. 2, xvi. 6. 2–7, xviii. 9. 1 ; Cicero, *pro Flacco*, xxviii.   Turning to the N.T., we find in John xii. 20 certain Greeks ; in Acts viii. 27, an Ethiopian who apparently spoke Greek and read the Septuagint ; in Acts xxi. 27, Jews from the province of Asia.   *Vice versâ*, the central authority in Jerusalem, later in Jabne and Tiberias, kept in touch with all the Jews in foreign countries, and likewise with the διασπορὰ τῶν Ἑλλήνων, John vii. 35 = ןיד אתולג, as it is called in one of the letters of Gamaliel mentioned above, pp. 10, 33 (Jerus. Maas. sheni, 56c).

8. (Pp. 40, 43.)   In Acts vi. 1 we find the division into Ἑλληνισταί and Ἑβραῖοι within the community of Christians at Jerusalem ; in Acts ix. 29, where the reading Ἕλληνας is not to be considered, Jews in Jerusalem hostile to Christianity are called Ἑλληνισταί.   S[1] was right in the main in translating Acts ix. 29, "with the Jews who understood Greek" ; Chrysostom was more exact in *Hom.* xiv on Acts vi. 1 and in *Hom.* xxi on Acts ix. 29 (Montfaucon, ix. 111, 169). The same name would form a contrast to Ἰουδαῖοι in Acts xi. 20, if it were to be read there ; but for that very reason it is incredible that such is the reading. In Acts vi. 9 it is uncertain whether the author, in consideration of the fact that Λιβερτίνων was a Latin word, prefixed to it τῶν λεγομένων, or whether we should read τῆς λεγομένης, which is supported by the most authorities. In the latter case it would be certain that two groups were meant to be distinguished.   In the former case also this is the only thing probable, for otherwise simply καὶ τῶν ἀπὸ Κιλ. κτλ. would have been written instead of καὶ Κιλίκων καὶ Ἀσιανῶν.   A synagogue of the Alexandrians in Jerusalem is mentioned also in the Jerus. Talmud (Megilla, 73d).   Nothing seems more natural than that Cyrenians, like the Simon mentioned in Mark xv. 21, should

have connected themselves with this synagogue. Allied to them also were the Libertines, *i.e.* descendants of Jews who had been brought to Rome by Pompey as prisoners of war and sold as slaves, but who afterward had been manumitted and made Roman citizens (Philo, *Leg. ad Cai.* xxiii; Schürer, iii. 84 (Eng. trans. II. ii. 276). The thousands of Acts ii. 5 ff. also belong to the number of foreign Jews who had taken up residence in Jerusalem ; for κατοι-κοῦντες, ii. 5, 14, not to be confused with παροικοῦντες (Luke xxiv. 18), signifies that they were permanent residents of Jerusalem (iv. 16, vii. 4, ix. 35, xiii. 27). This interpretation is but confirmed by the use of the same word in ii. 9. With reference to the language in the midst of which they had grown up, the Jews from Mesopotamia, etc., are called "dwellers in Mesopotamia" instead of "Mesopotamians," so as not to weary by an uninterrupted series of names of nations. The idea that at this time their fixed abode was still Mesopotamia, etc., is a misunderstanding, and is excluded by vv. 5, 14. Moreover, ἐπι-δημεῖν (ver. 10), not to be confounded with παρεπιδημεῖν (1 Pet. i. 1, ii. 11, below, § 38, n. 4), denotes not a visit at a feast, but very commonly, as every lexicon shows, residence at home and return home, in contrast to a passing sojourn in a strange place. The attempt of Blass (*NKZ*, 1892, S. 826 ff., and in his *Acta Apostolorum*, Acts ii. 5) to omit the Ἰουδαῖοι in ii. 5 (following ℵ), and thus to transform the witnesses of the miracle at Pentecost into "God-fearing" Gentiles, *i.e.* so-called proselytes of the gate, is to be rejected. In ver. 10 it is said expressly of the "Romans" that they were partly Jews, partly proselytes (*i.e.*, according to the usage of the N.T., of Josephus, and of the Early Church, circumcised proselytes of righteousness) ; but this also implies that all the rest were Jews by birth, and that it was only among the Romans that there were also certain proselytes. Without a hint being given of a change in the circle of hearers, Peter addresses them in a body as Jews and Israelites (vv. 14, 22, 36, 39), as inhabitants of Jerusalem (vv. 14, 29, ἐν ἡμῖν = in Jerusalem), as representatives of the Jewish people, among whom and upon whom Jesus had done His works (ver. 22), and who by the hand of the Gentiles had slain Him (ver. 23). For the author of Acts it would have been an insupportable thought that the hearers of the first preaching of the apostles should have been uncircumcised Gentiles (i. 6, 8, ii. 39, iii. 26, xiii. 46, etc.). Further, it is not demonstrable that εὐλαβεῖς, ii. 5, ever denotes, like φοβούμενοι or σεβόμενοι τὸν θεόν, proselytes of the second degree. These Jews who had returned from a foreign land to the home of their fathers are called "Romans, Parthians, Arabians," etc., just as the Jew Aquila is called Ποντικός, and the Jew Apollos Ἀλεξανδρεὺς τῷ γένει, Acts xviii. 2, 24. It is not their parentage which is stated in ii. 5 (this would have been expressed by ἐκ παντὸς ἔθνους or γένους, Acts xv. 23 ; Rev. v. 9, vii. 9 ; Gal. ii. 15 ; Phil. iii. 5 ; Rom. ix. 24), but the fact that they had come from the most various lands ; cf. with reference to ἔθνος, § 21, n. 2. They were therefore native Jews throughout, and only in the case of the Romans is it remarked that there were also some proselytes among them. The only difficulty in this text arises from Ἰουδαίαν, ver. 9, for which Bentley, (*Crit. sacra*, ed. Ellies, p. 22) suggested Λυδίαν or Ἰδουμαίαν, the present writer Ἰνδίαν. For one of the motives for their return hinted at above, p. 39, namely, the wish to be buried in the Holy Land, see the instances in Weber, *System der altsynag. Theol.* 64, 352 ; for other instances of high regard for the Holy Land, 62 f., 192, 200 ff.   All that has been said of the Hellenists in Jerusalem naturally has its exceptions ; and it is also probable that Hellenist families in Jerusalem in the second and third generation again came to receive a Hebrew education.   The family of the Bœthusians, *e.g.*, which came from Alexandria (Jos. *Ant.* xv. 9. 3), and from which five or six high priests arose during the last century of the temple, bears in its male and female members nothing but Hebrew and Aramaic names : Simon, Joazar, Eleazar, Eljonai, Marjam (Jos. *Bell.* i. 28. 4 ; *Ant.* xvii. 4. 2), Martha (Mishna, Jebam. vi. 4).   See the list in Schürer, ii. 216-220 (Eng. trans. II. i. 197-202).

9. (Pp. 40, 43.) For the preference of Greek to Aramaic on the part of Judah the Nasi, see above, p. 22. In the portion of the Mishna edited by him, Megillah i. 8, we read : "There is no difference between the (holy) writings (on the one hand) and the Thephilin and Mesusoth (on the other), except that the writings may be written in any desired language, whereas the Thephilin and Mesusoth may be written only in Assyrian" (*i.e.* Hebrew). Rabbi Simeon son of Gamaliel (the younger), says : "Also with reference to the writings, it has been permitted that they be written only in Greek." Connected with this in Jerus. Megillah, 71c, is the following : "Search was made, and it was found that the Torah cannot be translated satisfactorily into any language but Greek." In the same passage it is stated that the Greek translation of the Bible by Aquila had met the approval of the most celebrated rabbis of his time (*circa* 100–130). The fact that this slavishly literal translation was preferred to the Septuagint as well as the origin of this translation itself, rests in part upon the opposition to Christianity. There were no objections to the use of Greek in worship. There was seen in this rather a fulfilment of the prophecy in Gen. ix. 27 (Jerus. Megillah, 71b), and by a play upon words Ps. xlv. 3 was applied to Aquila, the most accurate translator of the Torah into the language of Japhet (*op. cit.* 71c). Although in Cæsarea the so-called Schema, the basal creed of Judaism (Deut. vi. 4–9, xi. 13–21 ; Num. xv. 37–41), was said in Greek, no serious objection was made to this (Jerus. Sotah, 21b, moreover the Mishnah itself, Sotah vii. 1 ; Megillah ii. 1). According to the express testimony of rabbi Ishmael (Shekalim iii. 2), Greek letters were inscribed on the chests used for the offerings in the temple ; while, according to Shekalim v. 3, certain tokens which served as receipts for gifts offered on the altar bore Aramaic inscriptions, cf. Joel, *Blicke in die Religionsgesch.* ii. 170 f. With reference to the Greek inscriptions of the Herodians in the Hauran (especially Waddington, No. 2329), cf. Schlatter, *Gesch. Israels von Alexander bis Hadrian,*[2] S. 26, 317, and also Sifre on Deut. § 33 (*Sprache und Heimat des 4 Ev.* S. 128), "Everbody runs to read a new διάταγμα (edict)."   In Sotah ix. 14 we read : "In the war of Vespasian the crowns of the bridegrooms were forbidden, and the drums.   In the war of Titus the crowns of the brides were forbidden, nor was anyone allowed to teach his son Greek.   In the last war the bride was forbidden to go about in the midst of the town in a sedan chair."   It is now probably universally recognised that instead of Titus we are rather to read Quietus, and hence to think of the Jewish revolt under Trajan, *circa* 116 (Schürer, i. 667 [Eng. trans. I. i. 286]).   It is only of the ordinance which it was claimed arose in the last war, *i.e.* that of Hadrian, that the Mishna says expressly that it was repealed

by the rabbis. But the prohibition with reference to the Greek language likewise failed to be maintained. In true rabbinic fashion, later writers used the letter of the ordinance, which speaks only of sons, not of daughters, in order to set it aside as far as possible. A rabbi Abbahu (*circa* 300) declares in the name of his teacher Johanan (died 279) : "A man is permitted to teach his daughter Greek, since it is an ornament unto her" (Jerus. Shabbath, 7*d* ; Sotah, 24*c*). To be sure, this Abbahu, who lived in Cæsarea, shows himself to an unusual degree to have been conformed to the world and open to Greek influences (Hamburger, *RE*, ii. 4-8 ; Levy, *Verhandlungen der 33 Versamm. deutscher Phil.* 1879, S. 81). The family of Gamaliel, which after the year 70 occupied an almost princely position for a number of generations, was pardoned for its diligent cultivation of Greek as a colloquial language just because of its social standing. Tradition is probably right in this particular, that the reaction against the adoption of the Greek language and culture is connected with the last spasmodic struggles of the nation to assert its independence. Even from the historical accounts all signs of this are absent before the year 66. Josephus, born 37 A.D., the son of an eminent priestly family, but not belonging to the aristocracy proper, had acquired, in addition to the rabbinic learning of which he could boast when only fourteen (*Vita*, 2 ; *Ant.* xx. 12), so great a knowledge of Greek in Jerusalem, that when twenty-six years old, without ever having been out of his country before, he could undertake a mission to Rome, and could mingle with the highest circles of society there, advocating his cause with zeal and success before the wife of Nero, *Vita*, 3. He also endeavoured to learn Greek from books, receiving instruction in grammar ; but he confesses that the use of his mother-tongue hindered him from acquiring a correct pronunciation of Greek. In preparing the Greek revision of his work on the Jewish War, and probably also in writing the *Antiquities*, he availed himself of the assistance of several Greek literati, *c. Apion.* i. 9. In *Ant.* xx. 12 he explains that his education was lacking on this side, because among his countrymen a knowledge of foreign languages was not highly prized. Such knowledge was in their eyes something vulgar, being easily attainable, not only by any free man, but also by every slave who had a liking for it. It was only knowledge of the Law and ability to explain the O.T., in which few accomplish anything, that gave one a reputation for learning. According to this, it is a mistake to think that a knowledge of Greek was limited to the aristocratic circles in Jerusalem, much less to the scholars. Many a merchant and artisan probably excelled famous rabbis in this respect. Among the women, knowledge of Greek was at any rate much more common than knowledge of the sacred language (see above in this note, also pp. 7, 25, n. 10). Nevertheless it was expedient that Titus, when seeking to induce the besieged Jews in Jerusalem to surrender, should have treated with them through an interpreter (Jos. *Bell.* vi. 6. 2), just as it was also perfectly natural that Josephus should have used his mother-tongue when commissioned by Titus to address them (v. 9. 2, vi. 2. 1).

10. (P. 41.) Among the apostles, only Andrew, whose father and brother bore Hebrew names, and Philip have Greek names. Every one of the seven names in Acts vi. 5, among which also the name Philip occurs (cf. viii. 5, xxi. 8), is Greek ; but this is explained by the occasion for the appointment of these seven men. "Hebrews" probably always had along with their

Greek names Hebrew or Aramaic names, like the later Hasmoneans Johanan-Hyrkanos, Juda - Aristobulos, Jannay - Alexandros, Salome - Alexandra. So a Nicodemus (Jewish *Nakdimon*), perhaps identical with the one mentioned in John iii. 1, is said to have been called originally Bunay (Bab. Taanith, 20*a*). Latin names also were very common along with the Hebrew : Johanan-Marcus, Acts xii. 12, 25 ; Joseph-Barsaba-Justus, Acts i. 23 ; Jesus-Justus, Col. iv. 11 ; Shimon-Niger, Acts xiii. 1 ; Shila-Silvanus, above, p. 32, line 6. Even when we know only of the Latin name, as in the case of Niger, Jos. *Bell.* iv. 6. 1, Justus Julius Capellus or Capella and Crispus, Jos. *Vita*, 9, a Jewish name besides was probably not lacking. The Greek name Petrus (Phlegon, *de Longævis*, 3 ; in Josephus xviii. 6. 3 poorly attested for Πρῶτος) occurs even in the case of Palestinian Jews (Jerus. Moed Katon, 82*d*, line 9 from bottom), but belongs to the apostles only as a translation of the surname Kepha given him by Jesus, above, p. 16, *ZKom. Matt.* 537.

11. (P. 42.) Concerning foreign words from the Greek and Latin in Jewish literature : J. FÜRST, *Glossarium Græco-hebraicum oder der griech. Wortschatz der jüdischen Midraschwerke*, 1890 ; KRAUSS, *Griech. u. lat. Lehnwörter im Talmud, Midrasch u. Targum*, 2 vols. 1898–1899 ; SCHÜRER, ii. 44–67 (Eng. trans. II. i. 31–47), gives a selection from the Mishnah arranged according to subjects, and DALMAN, *Gr.*[2] 182 ff., presents from the grammatical point of view examples drawn from the literature claimed to be Palestinian Aramaic. Greek and Latin words probably used by Jesus are, συνέδριον, Matt. v. 22, x. 17 ; Mark xiii. 9 ; in the LXX nine times, also in Ps. Solomon iv. 1 ; 2 Macc. xiv. 5, Jewish סַנְהֶדְרִין court of justice, especially the highest at Jerusalem ; also title of a tractate of the Mishnah. Whether we should include here ἀντίδικος, Matt. v. 25 ; Luke xii. 58, xviii. 3, which is quite common in the Midrash literature, but which does not seem to occur in the Talmud and Targum, is doubtful. On the other hand, there is little doubt that he used παράκλητος, John xiv. 16, 26, xv. 26, xvi. 7 ; 1 John ii. 1 ; *Didache*, v. 2, πλουσίων παράκλητοι, πενήτων ἄνομοι κριταί ; Clem. *Quis dives*, xxv, τὸν τῆς σῆς συνήγορον καὶ παράκλητον ψυχῆς ; Heb. פְּרַקְלִיט Pirke Aboth iv. 11, "advocate." Here, as in the Targum of Job xxxiii. 23, the word is used in opposition to מְקַטְרֵג = κατή-γορος, or rather κατήγωρ, Rev. xii. 10, a form which probably belonged to the Greek colloquial ; a similar form is συνήγωρ (= συνήγορος), סַנֵּיגוֹר, which in Jewish literature forms the contrast to *kategor* much oftener than does *peraklit*, e.g. Jerus. Joma, 44*b* ; cf. Krauss, *BZ*, 1893, S. 526. Among the Jews the meaning of the more infrequent *peraklit* has become broadened and is plainly treated as active = παρακαλῶν. In the Targum of Job xvi. 20, xxxiii. 23, the Aram. פְּרַקְלִיטָא corresponds to the Heb. מֵלִיץ, which in both passages, even in xvi. 20, where it does not suit, the translator has taken in the sense of "interpreter, representative of another before a third party, mediator." Two Jewish translators, Aquila and Theodotion, render Job xvi. 2, מְנַחֲמִים "comforters," by παράκλητοι, where the LXX has παρακλήτορες and Symmachus παρηγοροῦντες (Field, *Hexapla*, ii. 30). Thus Philo, *Opif. mundi*, 6, expresses the thought that God, without having been persuaded or exhorted thereto by anyone, bestowed the riches of His goodness upon His creatures, οὐδενὶ δὲ παρακλήτῳ—τίς γὰρ ἦν ἕτερος—μόνῳ δὲ ἑαυτῷ χρησάμενος ὁ θεὸς ἔγνω κτλ. Less characteristic is *Vita Mosis*, iii. 14. Likewise Origen, *de Orat.* 10, treats the παράκλητος πρὸς τὸν πατέρα in 1 John ii. 1 as active, among other

things paraphrasing it συμπαρακαλῶν τοῖς παρακαλοῦσι. Originally the word was not construed actively, but such a meaning grammatically is by no means impossible. To the examples in Kühner-Blass, ii. 289, should be added λαλητός, "speaking, able to speak," Iren. *Fragm.* xiv., Stieren, 833. Tertullian, who translates παρακαλεῖν by *advocare, c. Marc.* iv. 14, p. 191, παράκλησις by *advocatio, Pud.* xvii, and παράκλητος by *advocatus, Prax.* ix, found it necessary to form *advocator, Marc.* iv. 15, p. 193 ; Greeks, however, and Jews who used the foreign term παράκλητος, could dispense with the other form παρακλήτωρ found in the LXX. Jesus, who in John xiv. 16 applied the term to Himself primarily, had been up to that time not the advocate called to the aid of the disciples, but the teacher speaking to their hearts in the name of God, the interpreter through whom God spoke to them. After His departure this is the office of the Spirit, xiv. 26. On the other hand, it is the ascended Jesus who, in the name of the disciples and for their advantage appeals to the heart of God, intercedes for them, 1 John ii. 1. The extent to which the meaning of the word can vary is just the same in the N.T. as in Jewish writings. διαθήκη, Matt. xxvi. 28 ; Mark xiv. 24, Luke xxii. 20, cf. xxii. 29, διατίθεσθαι, of testamentary disposal, very common in the form רייתיק or רייאתיק, in the sense of a testamentary disposal of one's property in the event of death, as distinguished from מתנה, a gift during one's lifetime, Jerus. Pea, 17d ; on the other hand, διάθεμα, which was uncommon even among the Greeks, or the verb διεθέμην (according to JASTROW, 294), which occurs in a saying of Simon the son of Gamaliel, was unintelligible to a later rabbi Joshua (Jerus. Baba Bathra, 16c, lines 17–19). κύριε as a form of address to a superior, Matt. vii. 21 f., xiii. 27, xxi. 30 ; John xiii. 13 f.; also the numerous cases where in the narrative Jesus is thus addressed. How common the Greek word was among the Jews is shown by the fact that קירי is adduced as an example of the corrupt pronunciation of the Galileans, in whose mouth it became כירי (allegedly = χείριε ?), b. Erubin, 53b ; moreover, in b. Chullin, 139b, we have even the doubling of קירי, which goes to show that in Matt. vii. 21 we have not a translation, but merely a transcription. Outside of the Targums, which are acquainted also with קריס ὁ κύριος, and use it even of God (Levy, *Targ. Wörterbuch,* ii. 360 ; Dalman, *Gr.*[2] 186), we meet with קירי almost exclusively, and that, too, in the vocative ; but this is explained by the fact that the form of address κύριε was more frequently to be heard than the other case forms, and was the first to become common among the Jews (cf. *Monsieur* and *le Sieur*). In this it is like the Greek proper names, which as spoken by the Syrians were often in the vocative form (Nöldeke, *Syr. Gr.* § 144). However, what is found in the lexica under כירי (also = χαῖρε, χαρά, or χάρις), קירי, קירים, is still very much in need of sifting. πανδοχεύς, or more correctly πανδοκεύς, and πανδοκεῖον, Luke x. 34, 35, the former as פונדקי (yet it also has the spelling of the latter in the Mishnah, Gittin viii. 9 ; Kidd. iv. 12), the latter as פונדק, פונדקיה, פונדקא, were very common, as is especially evident from the further fact that even the feminine פונדקית = πανδοκεύτρια occurs not infrequently in the Mishnah (*e.g.* Jebam. xvi. 7), Targums, etc. δηνάριον, Matt. xviii. 28, xx. 2–13 ; Mark xii. 15 ; Luke vii. 41, x. 35, xx. 24, in the mouth of the disciples, Mark vi. 37, xiv. 5 ; John vi. 7, xii. 5. The transliteration דינר is at least as common in the Mishnah as the Heb. equivalent ni (examples in Schürer, ii. 54, A. 162 [Eng. trans. II. i. 39, n. 164]) ; in the Jerus. Talmud (also רינא in an Aram. context), Targ., and Mid. the proportion is probably about the same.   Also ἀσσάριον, Matt. x. 29, Luke xii. 6, which as איסר (אִסָּר) is very common in the Mishnah (Erubin vii. 10 ; Kidd. i. 1, etc.) and in all Jewish literature, was probably used by Jesus in this form ; probably also κοδράντης, Matt. v. 26, Latin *quadrans* in the form קרדיונטס. It is not necessary to suppose that Mark of Jerusalem, who in xii. 42 writes for his Roman readers λεπτὰ δύο ὅ ἐστι κοδράντης, did not learn this last expression until he came to Rome, for we read almost exactly the same thing in Jerus. Kidd. 58*d*, שני פרוטות קרדיונטס. But, in any event, Luke, who in the parallel passages, xii. 59, xxi. 2, uses the purely Greek λεπτόν, which had not made its way into the Jewish vernacular at all, has not preserved for us, as Schürer, ii. 55, A. 169 (Eng. trans. II. i. 40, n. 171), thinks, the wording of the original written source used also by Matthew ; for this was written not in Greek, but in Aramaic. Elsewhere, also, Luke has substituted the genuine Greek word for the Latin term used by the Jews of Palestine ; thus φόρος, xx. 22 (xxiii. 2), instead of κῆνσος, Matt. xxii. 17 ; Mark xii. 14 (Matt. xvii. 25, xxii. 19).   How completely the latter word had become naturalised is seen from the fact that קנס, קנסא occurs mostly in the later and secondary sense of " mulct, fine," that a denominative verb קנס was in use, and that a Greek derivative form κήνσωμα, קיסומא, which cannot be pointed out elsewhere, occurs (Krauss, *Lehnwörter*, ii. 534, 554). λεγιών, λεγεών, Matt. xxvi. 53, cf. Mark v. 9, 15 ; Luke viii. 30, לגיון, plur. לגיוני and לגיונות. Levy in both his lexica maintains that this has a second meaning, "commander"; and on the basis of that A. Meyer makes bold assertions concerning Mark v. 9, 15 ; but such a meaning is incredible at the outset, since the Romans had no title of an officer that was formed from *legio*. When the word denotes an individual, we must either alter לגיון into לגינא (*legatus* ; Fürst, *Gloss.* 130) or understand a soldier (*miles legionarius* ; Krauss, ii. 305).   A verb corresponding to ἀγγαρεύειν in Matt. v. 41 (xxvii. 32 ; Mark xv. 21 ; cf. Hatch, *Essays in Biblical Greek*, 37 ; DEISSMANN, *Bibelst.* 81 [Eng. trans. 86 f.]) has not been pointed out as yet in Jewish literature ; but the substantive אנגריא = ἀγγαρεία (Epict. *Diss.* iv. 1. 79 ; Artemid. *Oneirocr.* v. 16) is very common, and the Jews appropriated ἀγγαρευτής also, which shows that these words, though derived from the Persian (Herodot. viii. 98), did not become naturalised among the Jews until Hellenistic times.   The people were for the most part not conscious that such words were foreign, as is shown by the remark of the linguist Epiphanius that φοῦρναξ = *fornax* = κάμινος, belonged to the vernacular of Palestine (*Hær.* xxx. 12).   The Latin *furnus*, or even *furna*, in the form פורנא, פורני, was common among both Jews and Syrians ; cf. Krauss, *BZ*, 1893, S. 524 ; *Lehnwörter*, i. 72, ii. 434.

12. (P. 43.)   Concerning Acts ii. 5 ff., see above, p. 61.   The half foreign character of the young Church in Jerusalem is confirmed by iv. 36 (Barnabas from Cyprus), vi. 1-5 (above, p. 63, n. 10), xi. 20 (Κύπριοι καὶ Κυρηναῖοι), xxi. 16 (Mnason, a disciple from the early days of the Church, from Cyprus).   Perhaps we may reckon with these the family of Simon of Cyrene (Mark xv. 21 ; Rom. xvi. 13 ; below, § 22).   The further growth is given in iv. 4, without a statement of their origin ; v. 16 mentions people from the towns in the neighbourhood of Jerusalem ; vi. 1 refers to the increase of the Church as occasioning the complaint of the Hellenists, in so far as they seem to have been forced by it into the background ; vi. 7 speaks of many priests, or more

probably according to א*S¹ ὄχλος Ἰουδαίων, *i.e.* Judeans, cf. Klostermann, *Probleme*, 13 ; further, Pharisees are mentioned xv. 5, *i.e.* certainly genuine "Hebrews," even if zeal for the law was common to all Jewish Christians in Palestine, whatever their origin or language, xxi. 20. What was said above, p. 44, of Cæsarea, Ptolemais, and Tyre, is probably not true of Damascus. Although belonging to the Decapolis, it had received no Greek name, but had, on the contrary, a large Jewish population ; according to Jos. *Bell.* ii. 20. 2, almost all the wives of the Gentiles were attached to Judaism, and in the war 10,500 Jewish men were slain in one day. The names Hananyah and Judah in Acts ix. 10 f. are Hebrew.

13. (P. 46.) Concerning Philo as a Hellene, see above, p. 59, n. 3. The question to what extent he and other Jews of the diaspora were acquainted with Hebrew (answered in very different ways, *e.g.*, by Frankel, *Vorstudien zur Septuaginta*, S. xv. 45 f., who denies him all such knowledge ; and by Siegfried, *Philo*, 142 ff.) may be allowed to remain unanswered all the more since the point at issue as between "Hebrews" and Hellenists is not a scholarly knowledge of Hebrew, but the practical use, either of Greek or of Aramaic, inaccurately called Hebrew (above, p. 46 f.). Philo, *c. Flacc.* vi, states that the Jews in Alexandria and in Egypt, as far as the Ethiopian border, were no fewer than a hundred myriads (1,000,000). Among perhaps a hundred and fifty Jewish epitaphs from Rome, there are, according to A. Berliner, *Gesch. der Juden in Rom*, i. 53, only forty in Latin, the rest—indeed, all those dating from the first three centuries A.D.—are in Greek. It is only seldom that the word "Peace," or "In peace," or "Peace upon Israel," is added in the Hebrew language and character. See the list in Berliner, i. 71–92, which is convenient, even if not satisfactory in every respect. For Aramaic forms in the LXX, see above, p. 18 f. No. 13. Here belongs also γειώρας for the Heb. גר = προσήλυτος, Ex. xii. 19 ; Isa. xiv. 1 ; cf. above, p. 30, line 45. The translation νικήσῃς in Ps. li. 6, cf. Rom. iii. 4, gives to the Heb. זכה ("to be pure") the meaning of the Aram. זכא ("to conquer"). Other examples in Frankel, 201.

14. (P. 47.) *C. I. G.* No. 9909, also Schürer, *Gemeindeverfassung der Juden in Rom*, 35, No. 8—epitaph of a certain Salome, daughter of Gadia, who bears the title of a πατὴρ συναγωγῆς Αἰβρέων = Ἐβραίων. Another epitaph, first brought to light by Derenbourg in *Mélange Renier*, 1887, p. 439, calls this same Gadia "father of the Hebrews" (πατρὸς τῶν Ἐβρέων). For the interpretation given in the text, cf. Schürer, *ibid.* 16 ; *ibid. Gesch.* iii. 46 (Eng. trans. II. ii. 248) ; still more definitely Berliner, 104, who cites Neubauer also in support of this ; while Derenbourg, who appeals to Jos. *Ant.* xi. 8. 6, etc., tries to make out that the Hebrews in and about Rome were Samaritans. Gadia (Jastrow, 211, גדיא II. ; Berliner, 55) and Salome were ordinary names among Palestinian Jews.

15. (Pp. 49, 50, 53.) With this and the following note, cf. the writer's essay, "Zur Lebensgesch. des Paulus," *NZK*, 1904, S. 23 ff. (among others against Mommsen, *ZfNTW*, 1901, S. 81 ff.) and S. 189 ff. ; also *PRE*,³ xv. 61–88. Acts xxii. 3 tells unequivocally in what sense Paul is called Ταρσεύς in xxi. 39, cf. ix. 11, 30, xi. 25. It was a needless supposition of Fabricius, *Cod. apocr. NT*, iii. 571, that on account of the tradition to be cited in n. 16 Jerome must have read in Acts xxii. 3 with Cod. A, γεγενημένος (simply

"having been "). The contrast between the birthplace and the place of education was unmistakable. Starting with the fact that Paul was born in Tarsus, the Ebionite work entitled ἀναβαθμοὶ 'Ιακώβου (Epiph. Hær. xxx. 16, 25) asserts that he was a Hellene on both his father's and his mother's side. Paul would not have called himself a citizen of Tarsus if he and his father had not really possessed, in addition to the *civitas Romana*, municipal citizenship in his native town (cf. a number of inscriptions in *JHSt.* 1889, p. 50 ff., Nos. 12–20, 'Ρωμαῖος καὶ Λυδάτης, and similar expressions). The fact that Paul spent the first part of his youth in another city than Jerusalem and among a population differing in race from him, is attested also in Acts xxvi. 4; for there is no doubt of the genuineness of the τε (אABES[1]), and certainly not of the τὴν ἀπ' ἀρχῆς, which Blass strikes out; and, moreover, ἐν τῷ ἔθνει cannot mean "among the Jewish people," which in any case would be a singular mode of expression in an address to the Jew Agrippa (cf. *contra* ἡμετέρα, ἡμῶν, xxvi. 5–7), but = ἐν τῇ πατρίδι μου. For this use of ἔθνος, cf. below, § 21, n. 2. He says in this address that all the Jews know how from his youth up he has led a life of strict conformity to the law, and this, too, not merely as a result of his rabbinic training, but "from the beginning," in his native city of Tarsus, as well as later in Jerusalem. This piety, inherited as it was and early instilled into him in the home before ever he sat at Gamaliel's feet (cf. 2 Tim. i. 3), is defined more closely in xxvi. 5 as Pharisaic piety ; cf. Phil. iii. 5; Acts xxiii. 6, where we are certainly to read Φαρισαίων, not Φαρισαίου. For several generations the family had belonged to that party. Moreover, in Gal. i. 14 (τῶν πατρικῶν [not πατρῴων] μου παραδόσεων) Paul is thinking of his father, as in Gal. i. 15 of his mother ; and one can hardly avoid the conjecture that he uses the words ὁ ἀφορίσας με (Gal. i. 15), ἀφωρισμένος (Rom. i. 1), as a play upon the name of the Pharisees,—a name which earlier he had borne with pride, but which now he can employ in an altogether different sense ; cf. Clem. *Hom.* xi. 28, τῶν Φαρισαίων . . . οἵ εἰσιν ἀφωρισμένοι. Cf. Orig. *in Matt. serm.* 20 (Delarue, iii. 843, cf. 835 f. 847). Epiph. *Hær.* xvi. 1 ; Jerome, *Interpr. hebr. nom.* (Lagarde, *Onom.* 61. 20, 69. 6 ; also 204. 47).

16. (P. 50.) Jerome in *Ep. ad Philem.* 23 (Vall. vii. 762): "Quis sit Epaphras concaptivus Pauli, talem fabulam accepimus : Ajunt parentes apostoli Pauli de Gyscalis regione fuisse Judææ, et eos, quum tota provincia Romana vastaretur manu et dispergerentur in orbem Judæi, in Tharsum urbem Ciliciæ fuisse translatos ; parentum conditionem adolescentulum Paulum sequutum. Et sic posse stare illud quod de se ipse testatur ' Hebræi sunt,' etc. (2 Cor. xi. 22), et rursum alibi ' Hebræus ex Hebræis ' (Phil. iii. 5), et cetera, quæ illum Judæum magis indicant quam Tharsensem." *Ibid.,Vir. Ill.* v: "Paulus apostolus . . . de tribu Benjamin et oppido Judææ Giscalis fuit, quo a Romanis capto cum parentibus suis Tarsum Ciliciæ commigravit." From this latter passage the story passed over into Latin Bibles, cf. Card. Thomasius *Opp.*, ed. Vezzosi, i. 382 (*ex oppido Judææ Egirgalis*). The fact should not have been overlooked that the tradition which is given in full in the commentary on Philem. 23 (written A.D. 387) is essentially altered through careless abbreviation in the later work, *Vir. Ill.* v. The tradition, in the only form in which it needs to be considered, does not say that Paul emigrated with his parents from Gischala to Tarsus, but means that his parents, on the

occasion of a capture of Gischala by the Romans, were (taken prisoners of war, and thus, perhaps having been sold as slaves, involuntarily) removed to Tarsus, and that Paul (inherited and) shared in his youth this condition of his parents. It surely goes without saying that Jerome learned about this *fabula* not through hearsay, but from an older commentary. Probably his source is Origen's commentary on Philem., cf. *GK*, ii. 1002. Photius draws his similar statements (*Quæst. Amphil.* 116, 117, Migne, 101, col. 688 f.; perhaps also the further statements in *Quæst.* 211, col. 965) from the same source, and by no means from the Greek translation of Jerome, *Vir. Ill.*, though he often shows dependence upon this elsewhere (*Forsch.* ii. 8, iii. 35; Wentzel, *Die griech. Übers. der viri ill.* 1895, S. 1 ff.). The τῷ Ῥωμαϊκῷ δόρατι of Photius, *e.g.*, corresponds to the *Romana manu* of Jerome. Although the Coptic fragments of the *Acts of Paul* have furnished no verification, the supposition remains probable, that this legend, which was quite highly esteemed by Origen (*GK*, ii. 865 f.) is the ultimate source of the tradition. The *fabula* of Jerome, hardly worthy of notice, is in keeping with his attitude toward apocryphal writings, which differed from Origen's; and the *Acts of Paul*, which was written *circa* 170, represents its hero as a Hebrew. Prayers spoken in Hebrew are represented as being the apostle's last words before his execution (*Acta Petri, Pauli*, etc., ed. Lipsius, p. 115; *GK*, ii. 875, 877). In any case this tradition, which does not contradict Acts, and yet cannot by any possibility have been derived from it, is too definite to have been invented. Hero Krenkel, *Beiträge z. Gesch. des Paulus*, 8 ff., is right as against Hausrath, *Neutest. Zeitgesch.*[1] ii. 404; Schenkel's *Bibellex.* iv. 408. The criticism of neither, however, is satisfactory, since both confuse the careless version in *Vir. Ill.* v with the original tradition, and overtax our credulity by the assumption that there existed in Gischala until Jerome's time a true (so Krenkel) or false (so Hausrath) tradition of this purport. The tradition that Paul's parents lived in Gischala in Galilee (see Buhl, *Geogr. Palästinas*, 233; Schürer, i. 616 ff., ii. 445 f. [Eng. trans. I. ii. 226 f., II. ii. 70 f.]) before they removed to Tarsus, where their son was born, is one that probably dates from the second century, is independent, and supplements the NT statements in a most satisfactory way. If the first person who recorded this tradition, very probably Jerome, regarded the taking of Gischala by the Romans in 67 A.D. (Jos. *Bell.* vi. 2. 1–5), *i.e.* perhaps about the year of Paul's death, as the occasion of the captivity of Paul's parents, it was certainly a gross error on his part. But aside from the fact that we do not know this certainly, such an error on the part of this reporter would not prejudice much the essential truth of the tradition worked over by him. The event might very easily have taken place in the year 4 B.C., when Galilee suffered severely at the hands of the legions of Varus and his Arab auxiliaries; and among others the inhabitants of Sepphoris were made captives and slaves (Jos. *Ant.* xvii. 10. 9; *Bell.* ii. 5. 1; cf. the allusion in Keim, *Gesch. Jesu*, i. 318, A. 1 [Eng. trans. ii. 15, n. 1]). The story thus corrected deserves credence for the added reason that in this way it becomes explicable why such a strict Pharisaic family should have come to Tarsus; they came to Tarsus, just as the original contingent of the Roman Jewish population came to Rome, in the condition of prisoners of war and then slaves. As the latter for the most part obtained their freedom and at the same time Roman citizenship (above, p. 61), so Paul's father must have done, and that, too, before Paul's birth, for Paul was born a Roman citizen (Acts xxii. 25–28, cf. xvi. 37 f., xxiii. 27). As such he must also have had a Roman prænomen, nomen, and cognomen in this general form : (*Marcus Claudius*) *Paulus*. In the interpretation of a hideous dream, Artemidorus says (*Oneirocr.* v. 91) : "The slave receives at his emancipation three names instead of the one which he has borne hitherto, taking two names from the master who gives him his freedom. The view that Paul took this name in honour of his convert Sergius Paulus, was known even to Origen (*com. in Rom.*, præf., Delarue, iv. 460), was spread especially by Jerome (*Vir. Ill.* v ; *ad Philem.* 1, Vall. vii. 746 f.), and of late has been defended by Krenkel (18) ; but this view finds no support in Acts xiii. 9, where it is said simply that in addition to his Jewish name Saul, Paul bore the Roman name Paulus, the name which Luke uses thenceforth. Cf. Ἰανναῖον τὸν καὶ Ἀλέξανδρον, Jos. *Ant.* xiii. 12. 1 ; also Σίμων ὁ καὶ Πέτρος (*Alexandrin. Inschr. Bull. di arch. crist.* 1865, p. 60). Concerning this formula in general, see the writer's note on Ign. *Eph. Inscr.*, or Deissmann, *Bibelst.* 182 (Eng. trans. 313). It is still more improbable that the apostle exchanged the name Saul for Paul after his conversion ; for Luke applies the Hebrew name to him after that event as well as before it. It was natural that a Pharisee who, since his son was born a Roman citizen, had to give him Roman names, should have given him also a Heb. name, and that Paul should have ordinarily borne the latter name as a disciple of the rabbis and a persecutor of the Christians in Jerusalem, and on the other hand his Roman cognomen as a missionary to the Gentiles. The doubts of Krenkel (20 f.), that an orthodox Pharisee should have called his son after king Saul, the persecutor of David, are not sufficient to cast suspicion upon the statement of Acts. Many contemporaries of the apostle in Palestine were called Saul (*Bell.* ii. 17. 4, a relative of the house of Herod ; *Bell.* ii. 18. 4, a prominent man in Scythopolis) ; Abba Shaul is a rabbinic authority of the second century (Strack, *Einl. in d. Talmud*, 84) ; moreover, the female name Shaulah occurs in rabbinic circles (Levy, *Neuhebr. Lex.* iv. 491). The question whether the fathers who bestowed these names thought more of king Saul, who was by no means a monster, and who like Paul belonged to the tribe of Benjamin (Rom. xi. 1 ; Phil. iii. 5), or of the meaning of the word ("the one asked for"), need not be considered. Conjectures as to why the particular name Paul was chosen are to be found in a letter of Levy to Delitzsch, *ZfLTh.* 1877, S. 12.

17. (Pp. 51, 52.) The question as to what extent Paul shows a knowledge of the Hebrew O.T. is in no wise settled by the work of KAUTZSCH, *De VTi locis a Paulo apostolo allegatis*, 1869, or of VOLLMER, *Die alttest. Citate bei Paulus*, 1895. At the same time, isolated remarks in reply, for which alone there would be room here, would not help in its solution. Cf. König, *ThLb*, 1896, No. 14.

18. (P. 51.) E. CURTIUS, *Sitzungsber. der Berliner Akad.* 1893, S. 934 : "Paul did not acquire Greek as a missionary acquires the language of the natives, in order to make himself understood by them as far as might be necessary. Paul did not acquire the language for missionary purposes at all, but grew up in it." With the qualification made above in the text, this is correct. Blass, *Gr. des neutest. Griech.*[2] 5 f. (Eng. trans. 2nd ed. 5), finds in Paul's speech before Agrippa, which he regards as "very accurately repro-

duced," signs that Paul was in a measure familiar with the finer Attic forms, and made use of them when before a select audience.

19. (P. 52.) Even in early times attention was paid to Paul's quotations from profane literature, Clem. *Strom.* i. 59 (cf. *Pæd.* ii. 50; Epiph. *Hær.* xlii., ed. Pet. p. 362; Jerome, *Ep.* lxx *ad Magn.*; *comm. in Gal.* iv., *Eph.* v., *Tit.* i. (Vall. i. 426, vii. 471, 647, 706); Socrat. *H. E.* iii. 16; pseudo-Euthalius (Zacagni, *Mon. coll.* i. 420, 543, 545, 558, 567). Concerning Tit. i. 12, see below, § 35, n. 1. The verse from the Thais of Menander (*Fragm. com. gr.*, ed. Meineke, iv. 132), or, according to the Church historian Socrates, from a tragedy of Euripides (cf. Clem. *Strom.* i. 59), which Paul appropriates in 1 Cor. xv. 33, is not, to be sure, quoted by him as the saying of a poet. But, on the other hand, we are not to conclude from the fact that the Pauline text as handed down is without the metrical form (χρήσθ’, as Lachmann printed it, instead of χρηστά, the form handed down), that Paul dictated the word in unmetrical form, and was not conscious that he was quoting poetry. Copyists have very frequently destroyed the metrical form of such quotations (*e.g.* Just. *Apol.* i. 39, γλῶσσα ὀμώμοκεν for γλῶσσ’ ὀμώμοχ’ in a verse of Euripides). In a sacred text, which was to be read in church, anything that would remind of a comedy would be disturbing rather than pleasing. Yet in later times verses from Menander were inscribed even on Christian tombstones (*C. I. G.* No. 3902r; Ritter, *De compos. tit. christ.* 27; de Rossi, *Inscr. christ.* ii. 1, procem. viii.). In Acts xvii. 28, where ποιητῶν is an addition to fit the facts which does not make its appearance until the second recension of the text, the idea expressed in any case is that several writers have said essentially the same thing. The quotation agrees literally with Aratus, *Phainom.* v. 5; as also Acts xvii. 25 corresponds to the preceding sentence in Aratus, πάντη δὲ θεοῦ κεχρήμεθα πάντες. Cf. also the citation of the Jew, Aristobulos, in Eus. *Præp.* xiii. 12. 6; but a quite similar thing is said by Cleanthes, *Hymn. in Jovem*, v. 4 (Mullach, *Philos. græc. fragm.* i. 150), ἐκ σοῦ γὰρ γένος ἐσμέν. Aratus of Soloi in Cilicia, whither his family probably moved from Tarsus, is thought to have composed his *Phainomena* in Athens (see in brief, Knaack in *Pauly-Wissowa*, *RE*, ii. 394); Cleanthes was for years a disciple of Zeno in Athens, and then head of the Stoic school there until his death. Paul could therefore reckon them both among the Athenian poets. Since both were Stoics, he could also say with reference to the Stoics present (xvii. 18), τινὲς τῶν καθ’ ὑμᾶς ποιητῶν.

20. (P. 53.) With the statement in the text concerning Tarsus (above, p. 54), cf. Strabo, xiv. p. 673. That writer also mentions a considerable number of well-known Stoics and other philosophers also and of philologists who came from Tarsus. Cf. Lightfoot, *Ep. to the Phil.*, 3rd ed. p. 301 ff., *ibid.* 308; *Bibl. Essays*, 205 f. Concerning the time of waiting in Tarsus, cf. the Chronological Survey, Part XI., and also *Skizzen*, 67, 69.

21. (P. 56.) Jos. SCALIGER, who in his *Animadv. in chron. Eusebii* after the *Thes. temp.* 1606, p. 124, ed. 1658, p. 134, reproduced correctly the ancient interpretation (above, p. 60) of Ἑλληνισταί, Acts vi. 1, nowhere to my knowledge speaks of Hellenistic language. On the contrary, JOH. DRUSIUS, *Annot. in NT*, 1612, on Acts vi. 1 (*Critici sacri*, Frankf. 1696, tom. iv. 2193) writes: "Hi græca biblia in synagogis legebant et græce sciebant, *peculiari dialecto* utentes, quam *hellenisticam* vocant, cujus frequens mentio in his libris." On the analogy of

οἱ σοφισταί (sc. τέχνη, ἐπιστήμη), derived from ἡ σοφιστική, we might have had οἱ Ἑλληνισταί, formed from ἡ ἑλληνιστικὴ διάλεκτος; but such is not the case. Further, since Luke, who in the extant literature is the first writer and the only one for a long period to use this word, unquestionably understands by Ἑλληνισταί Jews, it did not seem unfitting to call the Greek used by such Jews Hellenistic. But this limitation of the concept lies merely in the historical setting here. In itself the word Ἑλληνισταί refers to all non-Hellenes who speak Greek or who in general have adopted Greek customs and ways of thinking. Indeed, the intrans. ἑλληνίζειν taken alone means simply "to speak Greek," and in general "to appear as a Greek"; yet it lies in the nature of things that it is used only where there is a contrast to other languages (Luc. *Philopseudes*, 16, ἑλληνίζων ἢ βαρβαρίζων), and hence as a rule only of non-Greeks (Xenoph. *Anab.* vii. 3. 25 ; Æschines, *c. Ctesiph.* 54 of Demosthenes with reference to his Scythian grandmother, βάρβαρος ἑλληνίζων τῇ φωνῇ), just as ῥωμαΐζειν denotes Roman ways of thinking on the part of non-Romans (Jos. *Bell.* ii. 20. 3), and ἰουδαΐζειν Jewish manner of life on the part of non-Jews (Gal. ii. 14). Moreover, the transitive and occasionally passive ἑλληνίζειν (Thuc. ii. 68 ; Jos. *Ant.* i. 6. 1) and ἀφελληνίζειν (Philo, above, p. 59, n. 3) must everywhere mean simply to make Greek a person or thing that is not Greek ; cf. "Germanise," "Anglicise," and similar terms. So also ἑλληνισμός means, as a rule, Greek ways adopted by non-Greeks. We are not justified by such passages as 2 Macc. iv. 13 (above, p. 58, n. 2, line 4) in limiting this concept to Greek language, culture, and customs only so far as they were appropriated by Jews ; we must rather apply the term Hellenism to all the Greek culture spread abroad since Alexander's time among the barbarian peoples, and thereby modified according to their individual peculiarities. On the same principle, *dialectus hellenistica* must denote all Greek spoken by barbarians (Egyptians, Syrians, Jews, Phrygians, Scythians) with its consequent modifications in each case. As a matter of fact, the term "Hellenistic" has often been used in this sense, and, what is altogether confusing, the Hebraistic colouring of the Greek written by Jews has even been contrasted with Hellenistic, and in the works written by Jews in Greek the Hebraisms as a rule have been distinguished as exceptions from the Hellenistic used elsewhere in them. If a writer is unwilling to give up the unfortunate concept of the *dialectus* or *lingua hellenistica*, he should state clearly in the preface to the work in which he is going to use the term whether he employs it in the narrow sense which Drusius gave it, or in the wider sense so common to-day. In the former case, Hebraisms would be just the characteristic marks of that *peculiaris dialectus*. In the latter case, the Greek written by Jews would be a variety within that species of Greek speech which people choose to call "Hellenistic." Likewise this variety, in distinction, say, from the Greek which Copts (Egyptians) wrote, would be recognised by its Hebrew or Aramaic colouring ; for in proportion as Jews have been able to divest themselves of their national peculiarities in the use of the Greek, they have approached or fully adopted the common Greek, whether that was the cultured literary language or the vulgar colloquial of their time.

II.

THE EPISTLE OF JAMES.

§ 3. THE DESTINATION OF THE LETTER INDICATED BY THE GREETING.

REGARDING the origin of this Epistle, there is no tradition whose certain age or apparent originality makes it of use as a guide in the investigation. Though the document itself is in the form of a letter, it contains very little which can be connected with events of which we have knowledge from other sources. With the exception of the author (i. 1), mention is made of no person living at the time when the letter was written; nor is there notice of any historical event which had taken place in the immediate past, nor reference to any event that had happened in the life of the author or of the readers (n. 1). Nothing is said which indicates the abode of the author or the place where the readers lived. Here, as in the case of all the N.T. Epistles, the address placed on the outside of the letter, and designed to assist the messenger in delivering it into the proper hands, has not been preserved (n. 2). On the other hand, unlike some of the N.T. Epistles (1 John, Heb.), James does retain the salutation at the beginning of the letter, which in ancient literature contained both the address to the reader, as is customary in modern letters, and as a rule also the writer's signature. Doubtless in many instances it happened that persons receiving letters did not know from whom they came until they opened them and saw the writer's name in the

greeting. On the other hand, as a general rule, the address
to the reader served no such practical purpose, but, like the
greeting proper with which the superscription was generally concluded, it could be used to express in various
ways the esteem in which the person addressed was held
and the way in which the writer felt toward him. Consequently, in greetings of this kind, we generally find,
in addition to the mention of the person addressed by
name, and where necessary of his place of residence also,
elements of a purely ideal character (n. 3). There are
instances in the N.T. of greetings where the designation
of the person addressed is altogether of this kind, as, in
fact, is the case with Jas. i. 1.

Hopeless as the undertaking may seem in the absence
of every other clue, we are compelled, provisionally at least,
to seek a historical and geographical background for the
letter by an exegetical discussion of the words ταῖς δώδεκα
φυλαῖς ταῖς ἐν τῇ διασπορᾷ. Taken alone, the words αἱ
δώδεκα φυλαί can hardly mean anything but the Jewish
people, and the Jewish people in their entirety (n. 4).
But throughout the entire letter it is clearly presupposed,
both by implication and by express statement (ii. 1), that
the readers as a body accept Jesus as the Messiah. Even
if this were not so, it hardly needs proof that what we
have here is not an epistolary address to the entire Jewish
nation (n. 5). Naturally, therefore, one looks to the
accompanying ταῖς ἐν τῇ διασπορᾷ to supply the exacter
definition which the conception requires. That this modifying phrase gives a characterisation of the readers'
situation which cannot be logically dispensed with, and
which is by no means unimportant for the determination
of the conception itself, is clear from the conditions
existing in apostolic and post-apostolic times (n. 6). At
that time no one could say that the Jewish nation as such
was living in a dispersion, either as regards its condition
or its location, nor is any such statement made. No

matter how largely the Jews were living outside of Palestine, and no matter how widely they were scattered, the
nation retained its fatherland.   Long after Jerusalem was
destroyed, and even after the still more stringent measures
adopted by Hadrian, Jews and Jewish Christians called
Palestine "the land of Israel," and so it is spoken of
to-day (n. 7).   Jews living abroad, such as Philo, for
example, nevertheless considered Jerusalem, "where stood
the temple of the Most High God," their capital (c. *Flacc.* vii;
Leg. ad Cai. xxxvi).   The high priests ruling in Jerusalem
treated Palestine, with its land and people, as their domain
(John xi. 48), and Jews living in Palestine were accustomed
to speak of their countrymen living abroad as the diaspora
among the Greeks (John vii. 35), as the exiles in Babylon
and other lands, in contrast to themselves who lived in
the land of their fathers and constituted the nation (n. 7).
Consequently no author informed at all as to the facts
could say that the Jewish nation was living in the diaspora.
On the other hand, if it is assumed that someone hostile
to the Jewish nation made use of this exaggerated and
awkward expression (instead of some such phrase as ταῖς
κατὰ πᾶσαν τὴν οἰκουμένην διεσπαρμέναις) in order to direct
attention to the sorry plight into which the Jews had
fallen, one is still at a loss to understand why he makes
it include his Christian readers also, and how he could
have omitted to indicate by a word the religious condition
which distinguished his readers from Israel as a whole.
These objections retain their full force also against the
interpretation, often attempted, by which it is maintained
that, so far as the words are concerned, James does address
the Jews living outside of Palestine, but really means
the Jewish Christians living outside of Palestine (n. 8).
And besides, this construction stands in absolute contradiction to the idea of the "Twelve Tribes" which indicates
specifically the Jewish people with special emphasis upon
their entirety.   The interpretation is right only in its

recognition of the fact that ταῖς ἐν τ. δ. is one of those appositives or attributes which complete the idea and at the same time express a contrast to another determination of it which might be possible, or which is assumed to be known (n. 6). Here the contrast is not between individual Jews, or single tribes of Israel, and the remaining Jews or tribes, but between the "Twelve Tribes" which live in the dispersion, so constituting a homeless diaspora, and another "Twelve Tribes" of which this is not true. It is only by such an assumption that we get a natural explanation of the omission of the usual τοῦ Ἰσραήλ after ταῖς δ. φ. (n. 4). This phrase is replaced by one which, while on the one hand retaining the comparison with the Jewish people, on the other brings the object which it describes into sharp contrast with the Jewish people. Unlike the twelve tribes who have Palestine for their native land, Jerusalem for their capital, and the temple as a centre of religious worship, the twelve tribes addressed in the letter have no earthly fatherland, nor any capital upon earth, but always, no matter where they may be settled, live scattered in a strange world, like the Jewish exiles in Mesopotamia or Egypt. It is no new doctrine concerning a twofold Israel which James develops here ; this would be entirely out of place in a greeting. He assumes that his readers are familiar with the general thought which he has in mind ; and more than this, that the language which he uses to express the idea will be understood at once. It is not likely that he was mistaken (n. 9). It is only for us moderns, before we have made a careful examination of the historical conditions under which the letter was written, that the greeting can have a double meaning. The expression, the twelve tribes in the diaspora, may mean *either* the entire body of Christians living at the time, the sense in which Peter and Paul use practically identical expressions, *or* it may mean the believing Israel, the entire body of Jewish

Christians,—a sense in which Paul sometimes uses expressions of this kind. Between these two meanings the letter itself must decide. It is to be remembered, however, that there was a time when such an alternative did not exist, because the believing Israel constituted the entire Church (n. 10).

1. (P. 73.) Some writers have thought that they found in Jas. v. 11 a reference to the death of Jesus as an event that had taken place before the eyes of the readers. This is the view of as late a writer as W. Schmidt, *Lehrbegr. des Jakobus*, 76. But since in the same verse ὁ κύριος undoubtedly refers to God, κύριος without the article, occurring as it does just a few words before, cannot possibly mean Jesus. Where there is a distinction, it is in the reverse direction, κύριος meaning God, and ὁ κύριος, Jesus (Jas. v. 8, 10, 14, 15). If the death of Jesus is to be understood, then we must remember that this was in no way witnessed by "the twelve tribes in the dispersion," that no one at all saw the resurrection, and that only a few beheld the ascension. There is no intelligible reference to the patience of Jesus or to His blessed departure contained in τὸ τέλος. In fact, the juxtaposition of ὑπομονή and τέλος (cf. Matt. x. 22, xxiv. 13 ; Jas. i. 4) makes it clear that what is meant is the end in keeping with Job's patience and constancy, the end which God the Lord put to His testing of Job. On logical grounds the reading ἴδετε has much to commend it ; and if this is the true reading, there should be a heavy mark of punctuation before it. It was so understood even by Greek commentators : Leontius, c. *Aphthardoc. et Nestor.* iii. 13 ; Cramer, *Cat.* viii. 35. Among more recent writers, see Hofmann, *ad loc.*

2. (P. 73.) The salutations which stand at the head of most letters of antiquity preserved to us in literature are not to be confused with the address of the letter, the inscription written upon the outside of the sealed Epistle. Among the *Ägypt. Urkunden aus den berliner Museen*, which have been appearing in parts since 1892, as in other collections of similar content, there are not a few letters, mostly of a business character and dating from the first century A.D., which illustrate this relation, and which are instructive in other ways also. No. 37 of the 15th Aug. 51 (*i.e.* about contemporaneous with James) has at the top of the enclosed letter Μυσταρίων Στοτόητι τῷ ἰδίῳ πλεῖστα χαίρειν, and on the outside has the address Στοτόητι Λεσώνῃ εἰς τὴν νῆσον τ . . . No. 93, Πτολεμαις (*sic*) Ἀβοῦ(τι) τῷ τιμιωτάτ(ῳ) πατρὶ πλ(εῖστα) χαίρειν, the outside address Ἀβοῦτι οὐετρανῷ χ(αίρειν) π(αρὰ) Πτολ(εμαίου) υἱοῦ. Sometimes the address on the outside names also the place of destination : No. 423, εἰς Φιλαδελφίαν Ἐπιμάχῳ ἀπὸ Ἀπίωνος υἱοῦ. After this a still more precise direction to the bearer, introduced by ἀπόδος ("to be delivered at"). This form of the address is particularly common : Nos. 38, 164, 261, 332, 435, 523, 530. Near as address and salutation often stand to one another, yet these examples confirm the fact that there is a distinction—and that a self-evident one—between the two, the address being primarily a direction for the bearer, though occasionally informing the receiver from whom the letter comes before he opens it, the salutation, on the

other hand, being an address and greeting directed to the recipient of the letter. Chrysostom (Montfaucon, iii. 55) remarks that on receiving a letter one is not wont to read immediately what is within, ἀλλὰ πρότερον τὴν ἔξωθεν ἐπιγραφὴν ἐπερχόμεθα καὶ ἐξ ἐκείνης μανθάνομεν καὶ τὸν πέμψαντα καὶ τὸν ὀφείλοντα ὑποδέξασθαι. Since the address served its purely practical purpose at the moment of delivery, it is not to be wondered at that it fell away in the literary transmission of letters. Especially with more voluminous letters consisting of several sheets, in ancient as in modern times, the address, together with the enfolding sheet (envelope) on which it was written, in most cases probably was soon destroyed. The salutation, on the other hand, which in case of proper delivery of the letter served no practical end, and hence occasionally could even be omitted altogether, was regularly transmitted in the literature together with the other essential and constituent parts of the letter. Of the three letters in the Aristeas legend (Jos. *Ant.* xii. 2. 4–6), the first has only an address, the second and third have only a salutation. Of the three regular parts of ancient salutations (name of the writer of the letter in the nominative, name of the recipient in the dative, and greeting), the third had among the Greeks from ancient times usually the form χαίρειν, the form employed in Jas. i. 1, but only twice elsewhere in the N.T., Acts xv. 23, xxiii. 26 ; cf. the six letters of king Philip (*Epistologr. gr.*, ed. Hercher, 461 ff.). The remark of Artemidorus, *Oneirocr.* iii. 44, ἴδιον γὰρ πάσης ἐπιστολῆς τὸ χαῖρε καὶ ἔρρωσο (cf. Acts xv. 23, 29), is not to be taken literally with reference to the opening salutation ; for unless the greeting took the form of a grammatically independent sentence, the writer's designation of himself in the third person required, instead of the χαῖρε usual in oral address (seldom so in letters, Barn. *Epist. ; Berl. äg. Urk.* 435, 821 ; *Oxyrh. Pap.* i. 189, No. 122 ; *Fayûm towns*, p. 285, No. 129), the elliptical infinitive χαίρειν dependent on λέγει, εὔχεται understood (cf. 2 John 10, 11) and often strengthened by πλεῖστα, cf. *Berl. äg. Urk.* 37, 93, 623 ; Ign. *ad Polyc.* (address) ; in the other letters of Ignatius except *ad Philad.* there are Christian embellishments. Other Greek forms, such as εὖ πράττειν, preferred by Plato to χαίρειν, it is alleged, and employed in the pseudo-Platonic letters (Hercher, 492 ff., especially *Ep.* 3, p. 496 ; cf. Plato, *Charmides*, 164), and ὑγιαίνειν (*Berl. äg. Urk.* 775, 794), which writers as early as Pythagoras and Epicurus are said to have used commonly (Lucian, *de lapsu in salut.* 4–6, cf. Pearson, *Annot. in epist. Ign.*, ed. Smith, 6 ; Bernays, *Lucian und die Kyniker*, 3 f., 88 f.), did not pass over into common Christian usage ; cf., however, Acts xv. 29, εὖ πράξετε, and 3 John 2, εὐοδοῦσθαι καὶ ὑγιαίνειν, also as early a passage as 2 Macc. i. 10.

3. (P. 74.) We find prosaic mention of place united to ideal elements in all Epistles addressed to local Churches, *i.e.* in those of Paul except the private letters and Eph., also in Rev. i. 4 ; 1 Pet. ; Clem. 1 *Cor.* ; in the letters of Ignatius, of Polycarp, and of the Churches of Smyrna (*Mart. Polyc.*) and of Lyons (Eus. *H. E.* v. 1. 3). Every external indication of the recipient, such as would have been necessary for the address of a letter, is lacking in Eph. i. 1 (§ 28, n. 4) ; 2 Pet. i. 1 ; Jude 1 ; 2 John 1, and probably also Rom. i. 7.

4. (Pp. 74, 76.) Usually we find (τοῦ) Ἰσραήλ or words of similar meaning appended to αἱ δώδεκα φυλαί : Ex. xxiv. 4 ; Matt. xix. 28 ; Luke xxii. 30 ; Rev. xxi. 12 ; *Protev. Jac.* 1. 1 ; cf. Acts xxvi. 7, τὸ δωδεκάφυλον ἡμῶν ; Clem. 1 *Cor.*

lv. 6, τὸ δωδεκάφυλον τοῦ Ἰσρ.; *Protev. Jac.* 1. 3, τὴν δωδεκάθυλον τ. Ἰσρ. (see the variants in Tischendorf, p. 3; Thilo, *Cod. ap.* 166); *Test. patr. Napht.* 5, τὰ δώδεκα σκῆπτρα τοῦ Ἰσρ.; Clem. 1 *Cor.* xxxi. 4, τὸ δωδεκάσκηπτρον τοῦ Ἰσρ.; Just. *Dial.* cxxvi, ὑμῶν αἱ δώδεκα φυλαί. The context alone can render such an addition unnecessary, *e.g.* Ex. xxxix. 14; *Sibyll.* iii. 249. This is not practicable, however, at the beginning of a letter, especially of such a one as James, which at all events is not addressed to the Jewish people. Consequently Jas. i. 1 is distinguished from all the other passages cited by its lack of a genitive with αἱ δ. φ. Further, it must be borne in mind that since the political separation of the Israelitish people and State, and especially since the return of but a fraction of the nation from the Exile, αἱ δώδεκα φ. τ. Ἰσρ. was synonymous with an emphatic πᾶσαι αἱ φ. τ. Ἰσρ. (Josh. xxiv. 1; Judg. xxi. 5–8) or πᾶς Ἰσραήλ (2 Chron. xxix. 24, cf. xxx. 1, 5; Rom. xi. 26), cf. Ezra vi. 17 or 1 Kings xviii. 31 with xiv. 21, or Ezek. xlvii. 13 with xlviii. 19, or Sir. xxxiii. 11 (συνάγαγε πάσας φυλὰς Ἰακώβ) with xliv. 23, or Rev. xxi. 12 with vii. 4. Over against the statement "All Israel (כל ישראל) has a share in the future world" (Mishnah Sanhedrin x. 1), Rabbi Akiba declared: "The ten tribes will not return," in reply to which Rabbi Eliezer, plainly in dependence upon Isa. viii. 23–ix. 1, asserted that at last the light would arise again upon them also (Sanh. x. 3). It goes without saying that it would have been quite impossible for a Jew and Christian of ancient times to designate as the people of the twelve tribes a part of the Jewish people, such as the Jews of the diaspora; and even if this were not self-evident, it would be proved most clearly by the Apocalypse of Baruch, written probably *c.* 80 A.D. Viewed from the standpoint of the time after the first destruction of Jerusalem, the nation divides itself into three parts: (1) the two and a half tribes of the former kingdom of Judah, which were deported to Babylon; (2) the nine and a half tribes of the former northern kingdom, which were deported farther toward the north-east; and (3) the few from all twelve tribes who remained behind among the ruins of Zion (lxxvii. 1–19, lxxviii. 1, lxxx. 4 f., cf. i. 2, lxii. 5, lxiii. 3, lxiv. 5). Including these three divisions, Baruch writes, lxxviii. 4: "Ecce colligati sumus nos omnes duodecim tribus uno vinculo." On this point cf. the fantastic speculations about the lost ten, or nine and a half, tribes in 2 Esdr. xiii. 40 ff., and in the writings of the Christian Commodianus, *Instr.* ii. 1, *Apol.* 941–998, ed. Dombart. See also Zöckler, *Bibl. und Kircheng. Studien,* v. 74–114.

5. (P. 74.) This was the view of M. Baumgarten, *Apostelgesch.* ii. 2. 121. So far as the formal correctness of the exegesis of Jas. i. 1 is concerned, this is certainly to be preferred to the view of H. Grotius on Jas. i. 1 and of Credner, *Einl.* 595, that the letter is addressed to "Jews outside of Palestine" quite aside from their division into Christian and unbelieving Jews; and also to the view of Spitta, that the letter was written by a Jew and addressed to the Jews in the diaspora who had not been touched at all by Christianity as yet; see n. 8 and § 8. But what was said above in the text is a sufficient answer to Baumgarten as well.

6. (Pp. 74, 76.) The history of the interpretation of Jas. i. 1 compels us to recall some rather trivial considerations. We must decide whether ταῖς ἐν τῇ διασπορᾷ belongs to that class of appositives and attributives which could be omitted without impairing the logical and grammatical completeness of the

concept, or whether we have here really a closer definition and limitation of the concept, a contrast being thus expressed to something else under the more general class to which the concept might be referred if it were not for this closer specification. Examples of the first kind are Jas. ii. 25, ἡ πόρνη, Matt. i. 6, τὸν βασιλέα ; Matt. xxi. 11, ὁ ἀπὸ Ναζαρέθ ; Acts xxiv. 5, πᾶσιν τοῖς Ἰουδαίοις τοῖς κατὰ τὴν οἰκουμένην ("all Jews" are nothing more nor less than "the Jews in the whole world ") ; Mark iv. 31, in like manner, πάντων τῶν σπερμάτων τῶν ἐπὶ τῆς γῆς. Examples of the second kind are Rom. x. 5, τὴν ἐκ τοῦ νόμου (cf. Phil. iii. 9) ; 2 Cor. i. 1, τῇ οὔσῃ ἐν Κορίνθῳ ; Acts xi. 22, xv. 23, τοῖς ἐξ ἐθνῶν, in contrast to the writers and their Jewish fellow be-lievers. In many cases, such as Gal. i. 22 (Is ταῖς ἐν Χριστῷ in contrast to unbelieving Jewish communities ?), the decision may remain doubtful, but not so in Jas. i. 1.

7. (P. 75.) In the *Pesachhaggadah* (ed. D. Cassel, 5): " Here this year, next year in the land of Israel." So in Matt. ii. 20 f., and very commonly in the Mishnah, *e.g.* Baba Kamma vii. 7 ; Jebamoth xvii. 7, and above, p. 22, n. 4. Also in direct contrast to the diaspora in Babylonia, *e.g.* Bab. Sanhedr. 38a. Διασπορά, like the corresponding הָלוּג, גּוֹלָה, גַּלְוָתָא (Levy, *Neuhebr. Lex.* i. 332, Jastrow, 221, 247), had originally the abstract meaning "act or state of dis-persion, banishment from home" (Jer. xv. 7 ; Dan. xii. 2 ; LXX Ps. Sol. ix. 2 ; Clem. *Hom.* iii. 44 ; so also 1 Pet. i. 1, § 38, n. 5) ; it then came to mean "the territory in which the banished ones are dispersed" (Judith v. 19 ; so also Jas. i. 1 and John vii. 35, since we should there read not εἰς, but πρὸς τὴν διασπορὰν τῶν Ἑλλήνων ; cf. *Paralip. Jeremiæ* : Βαρούχ ἀπέστειλεν εἰς τὴν διασπορὰν τῶν ἐθνῶν, cited by Wetstein, i. 888, on John vii. 35, not to be found in Ceriani, *Monum.* v. 1–18) ; finally, it meant "the Jews dwelling in scattered communities outside the home land (Deut. xxviii. 25, Cod. B, ἔσῃ διασπορά ; Isa. xlix. 6 ; 2 Macc. i. 27 ; Ps. Sol. viii. 34 f.), the same who in Gamaliel's letters are called "sons of the diaspora," above, pp. 10, 33.

8. (P. 75.) This was probably the meaning of Didymus (Migne, xxxix. 1749), " Judæis scribit in dispersione constitutis," with the note appended that this could be interpreted also of the spiritual Israel. Most significant is the way in which pseudo-Euthalius, in order to gain the desired meaning, improves upon the clumsy author (Zacagni, *Coll. mon.* i. 486), τοῖς ἀπὸ τῶν δώδεκα φυλῶν διασπαρεῖσιν καὶ πιστεύσασιν εἰς τὸν κύριον ἡμῶν Ἰ. Χρ. Even apart from this additional assumption that they were Christian Jews, the mode of expression presupposed in James would be hardly more sensible than ex-pressions, say, like this : "that German nation which lives in America." If he had been speaking of real Jews, James must have written τοῖς ἐν τῇ διασπορᾷ Ἰουδαίοις or ἀδελφοῖς ; cf. 2 Macc. i. 1 (also i. 10), τοῖς ἀδελφοῖς τοῖς κατ' Αἴγυπτον Ἰουδαίοις ; *Apoc. Baruchi*, lxxviii. 2, "fratribus in captivitatem abductis" ; see also the letters of Gamaliel, above, pp. 10, 33. To this day the expression used by James as a rule is grossly misinterpreted : (1) αἱ δ. φ. = "the Jewish people in its entirety " ; (2) as limited by ταῖς ἐν τ. δ. = the Jews dwelling outside of Palestine ; (3) = Christians, but only as determined from the contents of the Epistle. Cf. the commentaries of Kern, 79 ; Wiesinger, 49 ; Beyschlag, 43. This seems to be the view of Mayor also, who, in his introduction, cx., refers us to his comment on Jas. i. 1, p. 30, and in his comment on that passage refers to the introduction, without, in either place,

going into a very thorough discussion of the concepts. Recently (1896) this position has been taken by Spitta with the greatest frankness, *Zur Gesch. u. Literatur des Urchristentums*, ii. 14, though he abandons the idea that either author or readers are Christians ; see below, § 8.

9. (P. 76.) Since this idea is important in several questions of N.T. introduction, its development must be set forth briefly here. Even the Baptist, gathering suggestions as he did from O.T. prophecies, conceived at least as possible a future race of Abraham, into which non-Jews would be received in place of unworthy Israelites (Matt. iii. 9 ; Luke iii. 8). In the mouth of Jesus this thought became the prediction of a future actuality (Matt. viii. 11 f., xxii. 9 f. ; Luke xiii. 28 f., xiv. 21 f. ; John x. 16, xii. 32, cf. xii. 20 ; also on the negative side, John viii. 33–40 ; Matt. xv. 13). Jesus spoke of this future fellowship as of another ἔθνος in contrast with the Jewish people led by the high priests and rabbis (Matt. xxi. 43). There is, of course, no need of proof to show that He meant His readers to understand by this, not some other particular nation, the Greek, *e.g.*, in which case all non-Greeks, His own disciples at that time among the rest, would have been excluded from it, but rather the same people of God whom He elsewhere called His Church, and represented as a house to be built by Him (Matt. xvi. 18, xviii. 17). The thought that the Christian Church, composed of men of various nationalities, and based not on birth at all, but on faith in Jesus, was a new people of God, the true race of Abraham, or a spiritual Israel, was consequently implanted in His Church from the beginning, and was developed by it in manifold directions. Indeed, an instance of this is the frequent likening of Christ's redemption of mankind or of His Church to the deliverance of Israel from Egypt (1 Cor. v. 7, x. 1 ff. ; Rev. i. 5 f., v. 9 f. ; 1 Pet. i. 15–20 ; Jude 5), a comparison which found expression also at every celebration of the Lord's Supper, this feast serving as the antitype of the Passover meal. Paul especially developed the thought that the Church, composed of believing Jews and Gentiles, was the legitimate continuation of the people of God which began with Abraham (Rom. 4 ; Gal. iii. 7–29 ; 1 Cor. x. 1) ; or, to put it in another way, that the Gentiles, who before were excluded from citizenship in Israel and from the sphere of saving revelation, were now, so far as they had become believers, incorporated into the holy people (Eph. ii. 11–22), or, like wild olive branches, were grafted into the good olive tree (Rom. xi. 17–24). While in these passages Paul represents Christianity as the continuation of the O.T. Church, being simply an enlargement of Israel through the reception of believing Gentiles, in other passages, written from a different point of view, the great schism which Jesus produced in His own nation finds its appropriate expression. It is, after all, not the Jewish nation, but only a small fraction of it, which has united with the believing Gentiles to form a new people of God. In contrast to the Jewish people, the vastly greater part of which will have nothing to do with the gospel, and, like Ishmael, is begotten according to the flesh, since it is connected with Abraham only through bodily descent and other externalities. Christianity is like Isaac, who was begotten according to the promise, *i.e.*, according to the Spirit, but was persecuted by his brother (Gal. iv. 21–31). The thought that the Christian Church, in contrast to the Jewish people, is the spiritual Israel, is so usual with Paul, that he once tacitly presupposes it, and quite incidentally calls the Jewish people

with its cultus "Israel according to the flesh" (1 Cor. x. 18; cf. Buttmann, *Neutest. Grammatik*, 81 [Eng. trans. 92]). This spiritual Israel also has its metropolis, which likewise can be termed Jerusalem. It lies, however, not in Palestine, but in heaven, where the ascended King of the spiritual Israel is enthroned (Gal. iv. 26, cf. Heb. xii. 22). There the members of the true Israel are enrolled, even while still living upon earth (Phil. iv. 3, cf. Luke x. 20); there is the proper seat of the commonwealth, of which they are citizens even here (Phil. iii. 20), and there they are received if they die before the return of the Lord (2 Tim. iv. 18). The reverse side of this view is that Christians here have no sure and abiding dwelling-place (Heb. xiii. 14) and no citizenship. Peter gave especial prominence to this idea, not only transferring to the Gentile Churches all Israel's titles of honour (1 Pet. ii. 9 f., cf. i. 15), but also likening their condition in the world to that of those Jews who are scattered abroad far from their native land, calling them sojourners in distinction from the citizens of the cities and lands in which they dwelt, or strangers who tarry only for a time, in contrast to those who live upon this earth as if they could remain here always (i. 1, 17, ii. 11; cf. § 38). It is to Peter that most of the later Church usage with regard to παροικεῖν, παροικία is related : Clem. 1 *Cor.* (address); 2 *Cor.* v. 1, 5; Polyc. *ad Phil.* (address); *Mart. Polyc.* (address); Dion. Corinth. in Eus. *H. E.* iv. 23. 5; *Epist. Lugd.* in Eus. v. 1. 3; Apollonius in Eus. v. 18. 9; Irenæus in Eus. v. 24. 14. Indeed, the connection is traceable even down to our attenuated use of "parish." Moreover, the concept of the διασπορά is further developed in Iren. i. 10. 1 (διεσπαρμένη); iii. 11. 8; Can. Mur. 77 (*GK*, ii. 7, 142). Hermas, *Sim.* ix. 17, in a manner quite characteristic of him and yet often misunderstood, applied the figure of the twelve tribes to all mankind as the field of mission work and the source of the materials for the building of the Church; cf. the writer's *Hirt des Hermas*, 223-232. On the other hand, Hermas represents the Church as the true Israel, making Michael Israel's guardian angel, the chief overseer of the Church, *Sim.* viii. 3. 3; cf. the writer's *Hirt des Hermas*, 230 f., 264 f. But the thought of the spiritual Israel was developed in still another direction; and here again we must look to the many-sided apostle. Inasmuch as Paul did not abandon his belief in the ideal continuance and future revival of his nation in its calling as leader in religious history, he was forced to inquire after a real ground and pledge of this belief. He found the answer in the fact that God, in accordance with the O.T. promise, has even yet left to His people a remnant in which the people as a people is preserved for this its calling (Rom. ix. 29). Every single Israelite who is converted to Christ is a practical proof of the fact that God has not cast off this people for ever; and there are thousands of such Jews. The seven thousand of Elijah's time is a typical expression for their numbers, but falls far below the reality (Rom. xi. 1-7, cf. Acts xxi. 20). These Jews who believe in Christ, who through the Spirit have received a circumcision of the heart, are the real Jews (Rom. ii. 29, cf. Phil. iii. 3), the "Israel of God," which, when Christians in general are referred to, can be especially singled out as a narrower circle (Gal. vi. 16). Corresponding to this, the spiritual fatherhood of Abraham in its relation to Christianity is twofold; he is the father of all believing Gentiles, but in an especial and more limited sense by reason of circumcision he is the father of Christian Jews (Rom. iv. 11 f.). Whether this thought is expressed also in

Rev. vii. 1–8 (xxi. 12) is not so easy to determine. There is no need of proof, however, to show that it must have been an exceedingly natural thought for every Christian of Jewish birth who was as lovingly attached to his people as were Paul and James.

10. (P. 77.) An essentially correct interpretation of the "address" is to be found in Thiersch, *Die Kirche im apost. Zeitalter*, 3te Aufl. 109 ; a more thorough demonstration is given by Hofmann, vii. 3. 8 ff., 159 ff.

§ 4. THE CIRCUMSTANCES OF THE READERS.

There is no reason to doubt that the readers whom James addresses were, without exception, Christians. In ii. 1 they are exhorted to hold their faith in Christ without respect of persons ; and there is nothing to indicate that this exhortation is intended for only a part of those to whom he is writing. The confession which James makes so frankly for himself at the very beginning of the letter (i. 1) is likewise their confession ; the only question is whether they are willing to live in accordance with it. They have implanted in them the word of truth, by which God has begotten them and the author alike to a new life (i. 18, 21). How long they had been Christians, and through whose influence they had been converted, is not indicated.

Even with the exact meaning of the salutation left undecided (§ 3, p. 76 f.), it is yet clear from it that the letter was not intended for a single local Church, but for a large number of Churches, widely separated. Where the author speaks of elders of *the* Church, he does so only as an example, and means the elders of the particular Church where a case of serious illness, such as he has in mind, may occur (v. 14). If, as is perfectly possible, συναγωγὴ ὑμῶν in ii. 2 means a building and not the coming together of the congregation for worship, or the congregation as gathered from time to time for worship (n. 1), the omission of the article shows that a number of such buildings belonged to the readers. As a matter of fact, the plural κριτήρια in ii. 6 indicates that in the region where the readers lived there were a number of tribunals.

Some of the readers lived in cities, others in the country. Besides wealthy landowners and the day labourers in their employ (v. 1–6), there were merchants among them whose business took them from city to city, often requiring a residence of a year or more (iv. 13–17). On the other hand, without assuming at all that James meant his reproofs to apply alike to all his readers, one does get from the letter the impression that the readers were a homogeneous body, representing about the same grade of intelligence, having similar tastes, and exposed to the same moral dangers. Theoretical knowledge of the way of salvation is everywhere presupposed (i. 18, 21, ii. 1, iv. 17), and no effort is made to instruct them further in this regard. Many of them boast their faith, make capital of their religious knowledge (ii. 14, iii. 13), exhibit a passionate zeal for teaching others, and give free rein to their tongues, even yielding to crude curses in their anger at those who prove to be unteachable (i. 18 f., 26, iii. 1–18, n. 2). In fact, among themselves they are more inclined to revile and curse than they are to help one another by prayer and loving admonition (iv. 11 f., v. 16, 19 f.). At the same time they are zealous in the fulfilment of formal religious duties (n. 3). There is no want of prayer, but an entire lack of the energy of faith and sincerity of motive, without which prayer works no outward effect and brings no inward peace (i. 6–8, iv. 3, 8, cf. v. 15–18). The most serious defect which the author discovers, however, is the want of a proper correspondence between their conduct and the vital content of the word which they have heard and know (i. 22–25); the faith which they confess with their lips, they do not manifest in a life that evidences its truth and vitality (ii. 14–26); particularly do they fail in works of mercy and love (i. 27, ii. 13, 15 f.), in bridling the tongue (i. 26, iii. 2 ff.), and in being patient in suffering (i. 3 f., 12, v. 7–11). Many of those who boast about their

faith could well be put to shame by the good conduct of
the confessor of another religion—doubtless a Jew. With
good reason such a one might compare the dead faith of
the Christian with the involuntary recognition of the
existence of God by evil spirits (n. 4). The readers are
constantly charged with prizing too highly the things of
this world. Among those engaged in commerce this
tendency manifests itself in utter disregard of all religious
restraint (iv. 13–17); those who are landowners rob
their labourers without mercy (v. 4–6); while such as
have no property are full of vain longings for better
conditions (iv. 2), and give way constantly to impatient
sighs and complaints, not only against their oppressors
(v. 7–11), but even against God (i. 13, iv. 7). This same
spirit leads to contemptuous treatment of the poor and
cringing politeness toward the rich (ii. 1–9). The author
brands them all "adulteresses," unfaithful to their covenant vow to God, and forgetful that in and of itself the
love of the world is enmity against God, and that the
Spirit which God has sent to dwell in them is a Spirit of
jealous love, whose presence precludes all division of the
heart (iv. 4 f.). They all need to be reminded of the
transitoriness and worthlessness of the things which they
overvalue (i. 10 f., iv. 14, v. 2 f.), and to be made to feel
the incomparably greater value of the things which God
gives and promises to them as Christians (i. 9, 12, 17 f.,
21, ii. 5, iv. 6, v. 7 f.). A feeling of general discontent
seems to have taken possession of the readers, as appears
from the fact that immediately following the χαίρειν of the
greeting, indeed with this very word, James begins his
exhortation that they count it pure joy when they fall
into all sorts of trials, and that they never on any account
regard God as the author of the temptation to sin that
may be involved in such trials (i. 2, 13). The expression
shows clearly that the author is not referring to some
single great distress and danger which affects or threatens

all the readers, but to trials as varied as are their own separate conditions or personal aptitudes.

According to i. 9–11, one principal cause for the state of affairs described was the sharp distinction made between rich and poor. It is clear also from the same passage that these distinctions were made within the Church; for, in his exhortation to the readers, James urges that instead of complaining about the difficulties of his lot, and asking God's help only in a half-hearted way, the Christian re-joice with a certain feeling of pride; if in humble circum-stances, let him remember the high place that belongs to him as a child of God (i. 18); if he is rich, let him glory that in spite of wealth he is privileged to be reckoned among the poor and lowly to whom the grace of God is given (n. 5). In the same way the severe reproof which in v. 1–6 is administered to the rich for their luxurious living, and to landowners for their heartlessness, is meant for con-fessors of the Christian faith. In and of itself it is hardly conceivable that James should have directed such an earnest and such a practical reproof to non-Christians whom he knew it would never reach; in fact, such a supposition is ruled out altogether by the clear parallelism between the two paragraphs beginning with ἄγε νῦν (iv. 13, v. 1); inasmuch as iv. 15 shows that the merchants of whom he is speaking (iv. 13–17) must have been mem-bers of the Church. Moreover, when it is recalled that v. 7–9 not only follows the reproof of the landowners, but is also a consequence of it (v. 7, μακροθυμήσατε οὖν), and when it is further remembered that the suffering which the readers are exhorted to endure with patience is the oppression of the field labourers just described, the brethren mentioned in v. 9 (μὴ στενάζετε κατ᾽ ἀλλήλων, ἀδελφοί) must have included the oppressors among the readers as well as the oppressed. James does not address the rich any more than the covetous merchants as brothers, but reserves this epithet until he comes to speak words of comfort to the oppressed (v. 7). He calls the oppressed labourer "the righteous," in contrast to his oppressor whom he calls a murderer (v. 6). This is a severe judgment, but it is in keeping with the entire character of the reproof, which is designed to awaken terror. Moreover, the exhortation to lament in view of the impending judgment, which we have in v. 1, is found also in iv. 9, where without any question the persons addressed are Christians, though they are called sinners, not brethren. And in a still earlier passage (iv. 2) the readers as a body are charged with committing murder through their contentions about worldly possessions. Of course, this is not to be taken literally, any more than the epithet μοιχαλίδες in the immediate context (iv. 4) applies to a few of his women readers and not to all the readers. As the context shows, the expression is certainly employed in the well-known figurative sense in which it is used in the O.T. and by Jesus (*e.g.* Matt. xii. 39). The strong expression in v. 6 is anticipated by what is said in v. 4. Because the landowners withhold or reduce the lawful wages of their harvesters while living themselves in luxury, they are held like unjust judges to have deprived them of their rights, and like murderers to have taken their very life. The same strong comparison is to be found also in Sir. xxxi. 21 f. (*al.* xxxiv. 25), a book which seems to have been carefully read by James (§ 6, n. 10). These charges of murder and adultery were perfectly intelligible to readers acquainted with the circumstances here alluded to, and who knew how Jesus had interpreted the Decalogue.

The reference in ii. 1–7 is different. Here a case is assumed in which two persons come into the place of assembly together, the one well dressed and prosperous, the other a poor man in soiled garments. Neither of them is described as a Christian. The author simply pictures the different way in which these two persons are received by the Christians as they assemble for worship. The one is politely shown to a comfortable place, while the other is told in a contemptuous manner to remain standing, or to occupy one of the poorer seats. The description suits only such visitors at the Christian services, who are not members, or not yet members of the Church (n. 6). The readers are not reproved because they show preference to wealthy non-Christians over poor Christians, but simply because the poor man is mistreated on account of his poverty and shabby dress (ii. 6), while the rich man is treated with obsequious politeness for no other reason than his fine appearance. Such "respect of persons" is inconsistent with faith in the exalted and glorified Christ (ii. 1), as well as with God's stated attitude toward the poor and the general conduct of the rich toward the Christian (ii. 5–7). "Hath not God chosen those who are poor so far as this world is concerned and in the judgment of the world, to be rich in faith, and heirs of the kingdom which He has promised to them that love Him?" (n. 7). So God had actually treated the poor as a class since the days of Jesus. In every sense of the word the gospel had been preached to the poor. On the other hand, when he describes the rich as a class, James appeals to the daily experience of the readers. It is by the rich that they are oppressed and dragged before judgment-seats, and it is the rich who blaspheme that worthy name by which they are called. Both from the illustration with which this whole discussion is introduced (ii. 2), and from the reminder that God has chosen His Church chiefly from among the poor (ii. 6), it is entirely natural to suppose that the comparatively few rich persons in the Church are here left out of account. While these latter may have manifested more the spirit of the wealthy than of the Christian (i. 10, iv. 16, v. 1–6), making their poor fellow-Christians feel the superiority of their social position (καταδυναστεύουσιν), and while in isolated cases contentions about property (iv. 1 f., v. 4, 6) may have led them to prefer charges against their poorer brethren before secular magistrates (cf. 1 Cor. vi. 1 ff.), here, where the author is describing the treatment which Christians were accustomed to receive at the hands of wealthy men as a class, the description gets its colour not from the conduct of wealthy Christians, but of wealthy non-Christians. Only of such could it be said that the chief reason why Christians should dislike and not honour them was the fact that they blasphemed the name of Jesus, which was borne not by themselves, but by the Christians (n. 8). Although there is no statement directly to that effect, it is easy to see how this blasphemy was uttered in connection with the civil processes, in which a malicious hint to the effect that the accused belonged to the sect of the Nazarenes or Christians must have prejudiced their case in the eyes of a non-Christian judge. If such was actually the case, no explanation is necessary why it is the *rich* non-Christians who are charged with such blasphemy. It is also easy to see how in common life men of wealth and position would be likely to express their contempt for the Nazarene and His poverty-stricken Church more frequently than would the poor (cf. John vii. 48 f. ; Luke xvi. 14.— Acts iv. 1, 5 f., v. 17.—Acts iii. 6, xi. 29; Gal. ii. 10; 1 Cor. xvi. 1 ; 2 Cor. viii. 9 ; Rom. xv. 25–31).

That the readers were Jews is proved neither by ii. 21 (ὁ πατὴρ ἡμῶν; cf., however, Rom. iv. 1 ff. ; 1 Cor. x. 1 ; Clement, 1 *Cor.* xxxi. 2) nor by the greeting (above, p. 76 f.) ; nor does it follow certainly from the use of συναγωγή (n. 1), and the employment of the expression " Lord of Sabaoth" (v. 4) in a passage where even a Gentile Christian, if he were familiar with the Scriptures, would recognise an echo of Isa. v. 9. It is proved rather by the general impression which the letter gives of the character of its readers. Though its purpose throughout is practical, the letter contains no warning against idolatry

and the evils associated with it (n. 9), nor against unchastity, a subject dwelt upon at such length and with
such emphasis in all letters written by Christians to
Gentile Christians and Christians living among the
Gentiles.   Nothing is said which indicates the proximity
of the readers to Gentiles and their contact with Gentile
institutions.   Furthermore, there is no mention of the
relations of slaves to their masters,—relations, the significance of which was altogether different among Gentile
Christians from what it was among Jews and Jewish
Christians in Palestine.   The non-Christians with whom
the readers come in contact are Jews, not Gentiles.   In ii.
18 f. this is self-evident (n. 5), and in ii. 6 f. it is the only
natural inference ; since it is necessary to assume the
peculiar relations existing between Jewish Christians in
Palestine and their chief opponents in order to explain
naturally why it is just the upper classes who profane the
name of Jesus by their treatment of those who bear his
name (see above).   Moreover, the sins and weaknesses
which James denounces are the very ones for which Jesus
scourged His countrymen, particularly the Pharisees.
What James wants his readers to get rid of are the
remnants of inherited faults (n. 2 end).   Among these
are the superficial hearing of God's word instead of that
living of it which shows that it has been inwardly
appropriated ; pious prattle and profession instead of the
practice of what they believe (Jas. i. 19–26, ii. 14–26, iii.
13 ; cf. Matt. vii. 21–27, xiii. 19–22, xv. 8, xxi. 28–31,
xxiii. 3) ; the disposition to dogmatise and proselytise (Jas.
i. 19 f., iii. 1–18 ; cf. Matt. vii. 3–5, xv. 14, xxiii. 4, 15 f. ;
Rom. ii. 19–24) ; the failure to fulfil the real requirements
of the law, mercy, love, and justice, while paying devotion
to its letter (Jas. i. 26 f., ii. 8–12, 15 f., v. 4–6 ; cf. Matt.
xii. 7, xv. 2–9, xxiii. 23–33 ; Mark xii. 40) ; the getting
of wealth without any thought of God, with the impossible attempt to divide their affections between God

and earthly possessions (Jas. iv. 4, 13, v. 2 ; cf. Matt. vi. 19–24 ; Luke xii. 15–34, xvi. 13) ; the exercise of prayer without faith in God (Jas. i. 5–8, xiii. 16 f., v. 16 f. ; cf. Matt. vii. 7–11 ; Luke xi. 5–13, xviii. 1–8) ; the judging, slandering, and cursing of their neighbours (Jas. iii. 9, iv. 11 f. ; cf. Matt. v. 22, vii. 1) ; and the taking of oaths too lightly. The examples of oath formulæ in Jas. v. 12 are such as were in use among the Jews, not among the Greeks and Romans (n. 10) ; while the numerous references to objects in nature are at least suited to conditions in Palestine (n. 11).

If from what has been said above it is reasonably certain that the body of the readers to whom the letter was addressed were Jewish Christians living among their countrymen, this by no means precludes the possibility of there having been among them a number of native Gentiles and proselytes. Hofmann (vii. 3. 81–84, 159) held with good reason that there is reference to these in Jas. ii. 25 ; the lesson from Abraham's example is developed to its completion and finally stated in ii. 24 ; then follows the example of the heathen woman Rahab, which neither substantiates what has been said before nor develops a new phase of the truth, and appears to be dragged in without purpose. It does have point, however, if referring to a number of Gentiles who had been received into the Jewish Christian Churches, and if designed to say : the example of Rahab has the same lesson for them that the history of Abraham has for his descendants.

This being the case, we are able to determine when the letter was written, and to answer the question left unanswered above (p. 76 f.). If by the twelve tribes in the dispersion James meant the entire Christian Church, then the letter must have been written at a time when as yet there were but few Gentile converts, and while these were still members of Churches which otherwise were composed of Jewish Christians, *i.e.* before Paul's missionary labours had resulted in the organisation of a number of Churches composed mainly of Gentile Christians, and before the Gentile Church began to develop along lines independent of the Jewish Christian Church. The same conclusion holds also if we assume that James intended by the expression to designate the Jewish Christian as the true Israel; for in the membership of the Churches organised in Asia Minor, Macedonia, Greece, and Rome, there was included among the Gentiles a considerable number of Jews who had accepted Christ. These James could not ignore when speaking of the twelve tribes in the dispersion. Nor if his letter was meant for them could he have remained so entirely silent concerning the very peculiar position which they occupied in relation to the Gentile majorities in the Churches where they were; neither could he have ignored so completely all those questions arising out of this situation, which since the first missionary journey of Paul and Barnabas had agitated the minds of Jewish and Gentile Christians alike, and occupied the attention of leaders on both sides. If it be assumed that the letter was written after the time when a faction of the Jewish Church undertook to force the observation of the Mosaic law upon the newly formed Gentile Church as a means and condition of the acceptance of the Gentiles with God, it is impossible, in view of the historical situation, to understand the entire silence of the letter about the question of the obligatoriness of the Mosaic law upon all Christians. Equally difficult of explanation is the simple way in which the author speaks, on the one hand, of the word with its life-begetting power and of the law of liberty (i. 18–21, 25, ii. 12); and, on the other hand, of justification by works (ii. 14–26), without in any way suggesting in contrast the bondage of the law. If, now, as is probable, the Gentile Christian Churches in Lycaonia were not organised before the year 50 or 51 (Chron. Survey, Part XI.), we have the latest date at which

James could have addressed his letter to the Church while
it was still entirely Jewish, and confined to Palestine and
the regions immediately adjoining. Only thus does the
designation of the readers in Jas. i. 1 become perfectly
clear. Although the idea expressed in this address can be
traced back to the preaching of Jesus, and even to that of
the Baptist (above, p. 81), the definite form which it here
assumes, if it is to appear natural at all, must have some
historical explanation. The Churches organised in various
parts of Palestine and Syria prior to the year 50 were
colonies of the mother Church in Jerusalem. Up to the
time of Stephen's death Jerusalem was practically the
only centre which the Church had ; by the persecution
of 35 the Christians were driven from Jerusalem and
scattered beyond the bounds of Palestine, with the result
that many of the ties which had bound them to the
Jewish nation while they remained a part of it, were
severed. Wherever these Christians went they became
the nuclei of new Churches, and we know that they
travelled as far as Cyprus and Antioch. The journey of
Peter and John to Samaria (Acts viii. 14–24), the more
extended journeys of Peter (Acts ix. 32–xi. 2), the sending
of Barnabas to Antioch (Acts xi. 22), and the visits to
this city of other Christians like Agabus and John Mark
(xi. 27, xii. 25), show that effort was made to hold the
scattered members of the Church together. And this was
the purpose for which the Epistle of James was written.
Under these conditions, how natural that the feeling
should grow that the Church was another people of God,
chosen by God through Jesus, the true Israel ! How
natural also that existing conditions should suggest a term
which should fittingly express the relation of the spiritual
Israel both to the Jewish nation and to God's heavenly
kingdom (n. 12). So James did not employ an obscure
allegory, which was arbitrarily invented by himself, and
afterwards spun out by other authors, and applied in a

different direction, but actual conditions in the Church at the time became of themselves a symbol perfectly intelligible to James' contemporaries who found themselves in this situation.

1. (Pp. 83, 89.) According to א*BC, we should read in Jas. ii. 2, εἰς συναγωγήν without the article. For this reason, if for no other, we must reject the assertion that, in inconceivable contradiction to the salutation, the real destination of the Epistle is evidently "a single narrowly exclusive conventicle of Essene Jewish Christians" (Brückner, *Chronol. Reihenfolge*, 293). Further than this, ὑμῶν, following as it does an address to the readers which plainly characterises them as Christians, just as certainly excludes the view that what is referred to is a Jewish synagogue, which these Christians yet occasionally visit. Something regarding συναγωγή may be found in Harnack on Herm. *Mand.* xi. p. 115, and in the writer's *Forsch.* ii. 164. It denotes originally, and in profane Greek usually, (1) the act of collecting and assembling the meeting, Ex. xxiii. 16, xxxiv. 22 ; Deut. x. 4 ; Sir. xxxiv. 3 ; Ps. Sol. xvii. 50 (cf. xvii. 48, x. 8) ; of the meetings of Christians for worship, Ign. *ad. Polyc.* iv. 2 ; Dionys. Al. quoted in Eus. *H. E.* vii. 11. 17, cf. 9. 2. Also in a heathen inscription published by Foucart, *Assoc. relig.* 238, not a corporation, but a "réunion en l'honneur de Zeus" ; (2) concretely : the assembled congregation, commonly for עֵדָה Ex. xii. 3 ; Num. xiv. 7, 10, xvi. 19, not infrequently also for קָהָל Num. x. 7. As in our "meeting," this second meaning cannot always be distinguished clearly from the first, *e.g.* Acts xiii. 43 ; Herm. *Mand.* xi. 9, of Christian meetings : ὅταν ἔλθῃ . . . εἰς συναγωγὴν ἀνδρῶν δικαίων, and *ibid.* §§ 9, 13, 14, three times more ; cf. also the Gnostic *Acts of Peter* (ed. Lipsius, p. 56. 23, cf. p. 53. 17) and ἐπισυναγωγή, Heb. x. 25. So probably is it to be understood in our passage, though it is not impossible that we have here the third meaning, namely, place of meeting, Matt. vi. 2, 5 ; Luke iv. 16, vii. 5 ; John xviii. 20 ; Acts xviii. 4, 7, xxiv. 12. Whereas in these and other passages συναγωγή, without any modifying word, denotes Jewish meeting-places, the ὑμῶν here would seem to indicate that the Christians addressed had their own particular places of worship by themselves. An inscription of 318 A.D. (Le Bas-Waddington, iii. No. 2558) designates a building as συναγωγὴ Μαρκιωνιστῶν. It does not seem to me at all certain that the African Commodian, *Instr.* i. 24. 11, understands by *synagoga* a Christian church. (4) Even aside from the meeting at a particular place and time, it may mean in general the religious community, association of those with common interests, for עֵדָה Ex. xii. 19, 47, xvi. 22 ; Num. xvi. 24 (the company of Korah) ; Ps. xxii. 17 ; for קָהָל Ex. xvi. 2, 3 ; Num. xv. 15, xvi. 47 (*al.* xvii. 12) ; cf. 1 Macc. ii. 42 (συναγ. Ἀσιδαίων), vii. 12 (συναγ. γραμματέων). Quite early, however, συναγωγή was used as the specific designation of the Jewish religious community in contrast to the Christian ἐκκλησία. We see this usage at least in process of formation in Rev. ii. 9, iii. 9 ; Just. *Dial.* cxxxiv (Λεία ὁ λαὸς ὑμῶν καὶ ἡ συναγωγή, Ῥαχὴλ δὲ ἡ ἐκκλησία ἡμῶν). We see it fully established in Commod. *Instr.* xxxix. 1-4 ; *Apol.* 253. Eusebius lays stress upon the fact that Jesus called His Church, not συναγωγή, but ἐκκλησία (*Theoph. syr.* iv. 12). On the other hand, the Ebionites in East

Palestine called their Church community συναγωγή, and seem also to have retained the title ἀρχισυνάγωγοι (Epiph. *Hær.* xxx. 18). The *Evang. hieros.* translates ἐκκλησία in Matt. xvi. 18, xviii. 17 by כנשׁתא, *i.e.* συναγωγή (*Forsch.* i. 372, n. 1). The Christian compiler of the *Testaments of the Twelve Patriarchs* (Benjamin, 11) terms the Church and the individual congregations of the Gentile Christians συναγωγή and συναγωγαὶ τῶν ἐθνῶν. But we find the word sometimes used of the Christian Church and its individual congregations even where we may not assume a direct connection with Palestine and Judaism : Just. *Dial.* lxiii ; Theoph. *ad Autol.* ii. 14 (τὰς συναγωγάς, λεγομένας δὲ ἐκκλησίας ἀγίας) ; Iren. iii. 6. 1 (here in an interpretation of Ps. lxxxii. 1) ; Iren. iv. 31. 1 and 2 (αἱ δύο συν., the Jewish and the Christian, suggested by the story of Lot's daughters), a combination like that of Victorinus on Gal. iv. 24 (Mai, *Script. vet. coll.* iii. 2. 38), who, however, uses the opposite term : "ecclesiis Judæorum et Christianorum." In the discussion of our passage, we may leave out of account the common Greek usage under No. 1, and we should notice that James by no means avoids the word ἐκκλησία when he wishes to designate the Church as a corporate body (v. 14). When, then, he designates the Church assembly (or place of assembly) by συναγωγή instead of by ἐκκλησία (cf. *per contra* 1 Cor. xi. 18, xiv. 28, 35 ; 3 John 6 ; *Didache*, iv 14), and this, too, not in a theological discussion or in rhetorical speech, but in the simple description of an external event, this may be considered good evidence that we are here on Jewish soil or near it. This view is confirmed by the Ebionites of Epiphanius, by the *Evang. hieros.*, which arose in Palestine and exhibits many other Jewish expressions, and by the compiler of the Testaments, who, whether by nature or by design, wrote Greek just like a Jew (under No. 4). Hermas (under No. 2) shows by his speech that he is a Jew by birth or education (cf. the writer's *Hirt des Hermas*, 485–497). It should also be noted that Justin was born in Palestine ; that Theophilus (under No. 4) and Ignatius (under No. 1) were bishops of the Syrian capital, and that the Marcionite "synagogue" referred to was some miles south of Damascus. Cf. also *Epist. Hadriani* given in Vopiscus, *Saturninus*, viii. 2, "Archisynagogus Judæorum . . . Christianorum presbyter"; Lampridius, *Alex. Sev.* 6, "Syrum archisynagogum." With regard to the failure to distinguish between Syrians and Jews, cf. Origen on Job xlii. 18 in Pitra, *Analecta*, ii. 390 f.

2. (Pp. 84, 90.) The continuity of thought in iii. 1–18 is unbroken, and this fact determines the meaning of particular sentences in it. The cursing, iii. 9, can hardly have reference to fellow-Christians, for in that case they would have been designated as such (cf. *per contra*, iv. 11) ; it refers rather to men whom the Christian, obtrusively desirous of being a teacher (iii. 1), would like to instruct and convert, so that James is calling to mind simply the dignity common to all men by virtue of their creation in the image of God. Moreover, in iii. 13–18, the matter under discussion is not, as it is from iv. 1 on, the behaviour of Christians one toward another, but rather the demeanour of the one who, lifted up by the consciousness of his own religious knowledge, desires to teach others, and thus falls into a bitter, disputatious tone, failing, however, for that reason to achieve the desired result, namely, the righteousness of the person to be instructed (cf. i. 20). The πραΰτης, which is the proper disposition for the reception of the word, is the very attribute

which is indispensable in the teacher also (Matt. xi. 29 ; 2 Tim. ii. 24 f.; 2 Cor. x. 1 ; Gal. vi. 1 ; 1 Pet. iii. 15, towards non-Christians ; Tit. iii. 2, "toward all men" ; Ign. *Trall.* iii. 2 ; *ad Polyc.* ii. 1). In all probability μὴ ψεύδεσθε κατὰ τῆς ἀληθείας in iii. 14 is not an idle pleonasm, but (like Xenoph. *Apol. Socr.* 13, οὐ ψεύδομαι κατὰ τοῦ θεοῦ) = καταψεύδεσθαί (τι) τινος, "to make a lying statement about a thing or person " (cf. Ign. *Trall.* x.; Herm. *Vis.* i. 1. 7 ; Jos. *c. Apion.* ii. 10 beginning, 13 end ; *Ep. ad Diogn.* iv. 3 ; *Ep. Lugd.* in Eus. *H. E.* v. 1. 14 ; Hippol. *Refut.* vii. 20 in. ; Eus. v. 28, 6 and 16 ; Plutarch. *de Superst.* 10 end). If this is so, the warning here is not simply against lying, but it is presupposed that the person in question is speaking about the truth, *i.e.* saving truth, but that in so doing he makes statements that are in contradiction to that very truth. On this view, κατακαυχᾶσθε also, which further is modified by κατὰ τῆς ἀληθείας, is not any boasting in general, but a boasting specifically with reference to the truth, a bragging about the truth, which, however, at the same time contradicts it. This untruthfulness is not, however, a theoretical departure from Christian doctrine, but is rather practical, consisting in the fact that one who claims to be a knower and teacher of revealed truth opposes himself to others, thereby showing a lack of the wisdom and gentleness which necessarily flow from the real possession of the truth. Jas. i. 20 bears upon this very point. At all events, the translation, "The wrath of man doeth not what is right before God," is incorrect ; for (1) the connecting link between i. 17 and i. 18–25 is plainly the concept λόγος ἀληθείας. Consequently the subject treated in i. 19 f. cannot be talkativeness and passionateness in general, but rather the evil disposition to teach others the word of God instead of allowing oneself to be instructed, thus becoming angry instead of waiting for God to give His blessing. (2) The thought involved in such a translation would require ὁ ὀργιζόμενος instead of ὀργή, if the passage were to be measurably clear. (3) Such a general statement would be very incorrect, for there is an anger which is righteous. (4) The evidently intended contrast between ἀνδρός and θεοῦ does not, on this view, receive its proper emphasis. We are not indeed to read with the later MSS. κατεργάζεται, yet neither is ἐργάζεται to be taken in the sense of ποιεῖ, as in Jas. ii. 9 ; Acts x. 35 ; Matt. vii. 23 ; rather, as in John vi. 27 ; 2 Cor. vii. 10, it has the meaning of κατεργάζεται (Jas. i. 3). The object of the verb is the thing produced. A man's anger does not bring about God's righteousness (cf. Matt. vi. 33, and below, § 7). This is a fruit which is sown in a peaceable spirit, and the growth and ripening of which must be waited for with patience (Jas. iii. 18). No man can come to believe that he himself can achieve righteousness through angry speech ; yet, on the other hand, nothing is more common than for heralds of the truth to imagine that they should convert their hearers by passionate zeal. It can be therefore only the latter error that James is opposing ; cf. Schneckenburger, *Beiträge z. Einl.* 199 ; Hofmann, vii. 3. 35. In Jas. i. 21 περισσεία is used unquestionably in the sense of περίσσευμα (Rom. v. 17), and hence cannot mean excess (Matt. xii. 34) ; for a man should lay aside not only a certain excess of wickedness, but all wickedness. The only meaning possible is therefore "residue, remainder" (Mark viii. 8). The writer means the old hereditary faults which still cling even to those born of God,—the first-fruits of His creatures (i. 18),—in other words, the evil Jewish nature, the "leaven of the Pharisees and Sadducees" (Matt. xvi. 6–12, xv. 1–20).

3. (P. 84.) Jas. i. 26 f., θρησκός θρησκεία, θρησκεύειν denotes not the pious disposition (εὐσέβεια, ὁσιότης, also θεοσέβεια, though this concept inclines towards θρησκεία; cf. Seeberg, *Forsch.* v. 264 f.), but the outwardly displayed religion, worship, ceremonies (Philo, *Quod deterior*, vii, Mang. i. 195, πεπλάνηται γὰρ καὶ οὗτος τῆς πρὸς εὐσέβειαν ὁδοῦ, θρησκείαν ἀντὶ ὁσιότητος ἡγούμενος καὶ δῶρα τῷ ἀδεκάστῳ διδούς; cf. Wis. xi. 15, xiv. 16, 18, 27; Jos. *Ant.* ix. 13. 3; Col. ii. 18, 23; Clem. 1 *Cor.* xlv. 7); so that it also comes to mean not infrequently a publicly-professed religion together with its worship in distinction from other religions and forms of worship: Acts xxvi. 5; *Ep. ad Diogn.* i.; Melito quoted in Eus. iv. 26. 7; *Ep. Lugd.* in Eus. v. 1. 63.

4. (P. 85.) The words in Jas. ii. 18, ἀλλ' ἐρεῖ τις, at any rate do not introduce an objection to the author's preceding statements to be expected from one of the readers or from a like-minded Christian, as is the case in 1 Cor. xv. 35, cf. Rom. ix. 19, xi. 19; for the person speaking in ii. 18, 19 agrees with James in requiring works and in condemning faith without works; and the people characterised in ii. 14–17 are the ones who are taken to task in ii. 18, 19 also. On the other hand, James cannot introduce himself, or a Christian who agrees with him, as speaking in this way (cf. Rom. x. 18, 19); for what reason would there be in introducing a third person, when that person has nothing to say which James himself could not say just as well? Further, it is hard to understand how James could assert of himself so confidently, even though in the disguise of a third person, that he, in distinction from the one addressed, had works to show; cf. *per contra*, iii. 2. Then, too, it would be quite uncalled for on James' part to defend himself against the charge that he lacked the faith of which the person addressed boasted. This charge is implied in the speaker's offer through his works to prove his faith, thus called in question by his opponent. Finally, in recognising the formal orthodoxy of the Christians addressed, James could not possibly have limited their creed to their confession of monotheism. For these outwardly professing Christians are not content simply to acknowledge the unity of God, which the devils also do, or even to bless God as their Lord and Father (iii. 9), which the devils do not do, they confess their faith in Christ (ii. 1). From all of which it follows that the ἐρεῖ τις of ii. 18 is not an empty and purposeless phrase; rather there is thus introduced into the discussion between James and the τις of ii. 14 a speaker who is represented as really a third person, and that, too, of another faith. But this third person must be a Jew, not a pagan; for the speaker praises the Christian addressed, even if in a sarcastic tone, for confessing monotheism, the fundamental dogma of Judaism. Not only is it evident that the Jewish Christians, following the example of Jesus (Mark xii. 29), held fast to the doctrinal content of the "Schema" from Deut. vi. 4–9, which every Israelite repeated morning and evening daily; but there is also no reason to doubt that as persons "zealous for the law" (Acts xxi. 20), they repeated it with their fellow-countrymen after their conversion as well as before it. Later Jewish Christians emphasised the μοναρχικὴ θρησκεία so much, that the distinguishing mark of Christianity came to be regarded as of less importance than the fundamental dogma common to Jews and Jewish Christians (Clem. *Hom.* vii. 12, v. 28;

Ep. Petri ad Jac. 1). But besides this, James would have defeated his own purpose if he had made the Jew introduced by him speak of the doctrinal difference between Judaism and Christianity. Lastly, as to the form of the introduction, it goes without saying that the Jew does not begin to speak until after ἐρεῖ τις, and hence that the ἀλλά is spoken by James himself. After giving his own judgment, he uses ἀλλά to introduce as something new and startling the doubly humiliating judgment of the Jew—ἀλλά, even without καί, being adapted to this purpose (cf. John xvi. 2 ; 2 Cor. vii. 11). That it is not James himself who is speaking in ii. 18, 19, follows also from the fact that in these sentences not a single thought from ii. 14–17 is developed further. It is not until ii. 20 that James begins to speak again, and resumes the thought of ii. 17. The assumption of Spitta, *Z. Gesch. u. Lit.* ii. 79, that an objection of the man of faith without works, who has been attacked by James, has fallen out after ἐρεῖ τις, and that James begins to answer this with σὺ πίστιν ἔχεις, is not called for by the text, and for positive reasons is inadmissible.

5. (Pp. 86, 90.) Since ὁ ταπεινός and ὁ πλούσιος in i. 9 f. form an antithesis, the former cannot be a lightly accented epithet of a merely explanatory character (the brother, who by very reason of being a brother, is, as everybody knows, always poor likewise); it is rather within the class denoted by ὁ ἀδελφός (perhaps better without ὁ, following Cod. B) that the poor is contrasted with the rich. On the view that the rich non-Christian is contrasted with the poor Christian, the ground upon which the rich man should boast remains unclear. If ταπείνωσις denotes the exact opposite of ὕψος, *i.e.* lack of moral and religious worth, or even lack of the riches of the rich man,—an interpretation which has no usage at all to support it,—then the same καυχάσθω, which is meant very seriously when used with its first subject, must, when used with the second, have the sense of a mocking challenge : "Let the rich man boast, if he likes, in his baseness or his miserable riches." Such a rendering is impossible, for the added reason that the argument which follows presupposes not an ironical challenge to sinful boasting, but an earnest exhortation to glory only in the possessions that endure. Nor indeed can ταπείνωσις denote the attitude of humility (cf. Jas. iv. 6–10 ; Sir. iii. 18), for to glory in this would be the worst kind of pride ; it denotes rather, as might be expected from its position in antithesis to ὕψος, the rank and condition of lowliness (Luke i. 48 ; Phil. iii. 21). If the rich man is a Christian, of course he also possesses the exalted station of which the poor Christian should rest assured ; but as it is fitting for the latter to emphasise just that side of his condition as a Christian which forms a contrast to his outward situation, so likewise is it for the former (cf. 1 Cor. vii. 22 with reference to slaves and free). We need only recall Matt. xix. 23–26 ; Luke vi. 24, xvi. 14 f., 19–31, to see that the rich man is the very one who should be glad and thankful to belong among the confessors of Jesus, those who were called οἱ μικροί by Jesus Himself, and who are despised by the world. The reason added in i. 10*b*–11 is intended primarily to enforce the warning to the rich man implied in 10*a*, but it thus bears at the same time upon the positive exhortation. This reason agrees with the context; for just as poverty is a temptation to the poor man, so are riches for the rich man. It is also very applicable to the Christian who is rich ; for since he

is rich, indeed since he is a man living in the flesh, he is actually like the fast fading flower; cf. Jas. iv. 14; 1 Tim. vi. 6–10, 17–19; Ps. xc. 5 f., ciii. 15.

6. (P. 88.) We have evidence that Christian preaching was permitted temporarily in Jewish synagogues (Acts ix. 22, xviii. 4–6, xix. 8), and that Jewish Christians in Palestine visited the synagogues, the Jews on their part resorting to prohibitive measures in order to exclude them (cf. Derenbourg, *Hist. et géogr. de la Palestine*, 354 f.). The perfectly reasonable inference, then, is that the reverse was true, and that Christian services were visited by non-Christians. Quite aside from such an inference, however, we have direct proof in 1 Cor. xiv. 23–25 that this was the case. Whether this was done from a religious desire, or from curiosity, or even with hostile intent, is indifferent in this supposed case.

7. (P. 88.) It will not do in Jas. ii. 5 to connect πλουσίους κτλ. with τοὺς πτωχούς as its attribute; for (1) a δέ or ἀλλά would be necessary with πλουσίους; (2) the men whom God has chosen are not rich in faith before and apart from their being thus chosen, and are certainly not heirs of the kingdom; it is only through being chosen that they become so. Consequently what we have here is the good Greek usage of ἐκλέγεσθαι with a double accusative, the εἶναι (Eph. i. 4) not being necessary in such a construction, cf. Mayor, 79 f. It stands to reason that James does not say here that all the poor and none of the rich find grace before God, any more than we may infer from Matt. xi. 25 that all uncultured people and none of superior culture attain to a knowledge of salvation. The self-evident meaning of general statements such as these, which briefly sum up a multitude of individual experiences (1 Cor. i. 27 f.), is clearly expressed by Paul in 1 Cor. i. 26 (οὐ πολλοί).

8. (P. 89.) The blaspheming in Jas. ii. 7 is not an indirect dishonouring of the name of God or of Christ through the unworthy behaviour of those who confess Him; for (1) this could not well have been left unexpressed (cf. Eus. *H. E.* v. 1. 48, διὰ τῆς ἀναστροφῆς αὐτῶν βλασφημούντων τὴν ὁδόν); (2) the blasphemers must have been designated as themselves bearers of the name of Christ (ἐπ' αὐτούς instead of ἐφ' ὑμᾶς; cf. Herm. *Sim.* viii. 6); (3) such indirect blasphemy of God or of Christ is always expressed in the passive form elsewhere: Rom. ii. 24 (Isa. lii. 5); 1 Tim. vi. 1; Tit. ii. 5; 2 Pet. ii. 2; Clem. 1 *Cor.* i. 1 (xlvii. 7); Clem. 2 *Cor.* xiii. 1–4; Ign. *Trall.* viii. 2; Polyc. *ad Phil.* x. 2. "The honourable name," judging simply from the O.T. parallels, from which the expression is borrowed (Isa. xliii. 7; Jer. xiv. 9, xv. 16; Amos ix. 12; cf. Acts xv. 17), can be none other than the name of God or of Christ. In what form the readers bore this name, whether as μαθηταὶ τοῦ Ἰησοῦ (John vii. 3, xviii. 25; Acts iv. 13), or as Ναζωραῖοι (Acts xxiv. 5, following the usage Ἰησοῦς ὁ Ναζωραῖος, Matt. xxvi. 71; John xviii. 5; Acts xxvi. 9; cf. *GK*, ii. 662 f., n. 2, where there is reference also to the reviling of the Nazarenes on the part of the Jews), or as Χριστιανοί (Acts xi. 26, xxvi. 28; 1 Pet. iv. 16; cf. Mark ix. 41), is as impossible to conclude from the expression used by James as to gather from the above O.T. passages in what form Israel bore Jehovah's name. In this passage, which would lend itself most inappropriately to such a reference, there is no trace of any government persecution of the Christians because of their

confession, as there is none in other passages (*e.g.* i. 2–12) where such reference would be quite in place.

9. (P. 90.) In the matter of worship and similar topics, cf. Acts xv. 20, 29, xxi. 25 ; 1 Cor. v. 10 f., viii. 1–xi. 1, especially viii. 10, x. 7, 14–22 ; 2 Cor. vi. 15 ; Gal. v. 20 ; 1 John v. 21 ; Rev. ii. 14, 20, xxi. 8, xxii. 15 ; *Didache*, iii. 4, v. 1, vi. 3 ; Herm. *Sim.* ix. 21. 3. Cf. also the reminder of the readers' former worship, 1 Cor. vi. 9, 11, xii. 2 ; 1 Thess. i. 9 ; Gal. iv. 8 ; 1 Pet. iv. 3 ; Clem. 2 *Cor.* i. 6, iii. 1, xvii. 1, and the parallels, Col. iii. 5 ; Eph. v. 5 ; Herm. *Mand.* xi. 4 ; Polyc. *ad Phil.* xi. 2. In the matter of πορνεία, cf. Acts xv. 20, 29, xxi. 25 ; 1 Cor. v. 1–13, vi. 9–11, 13–20, vii. 2, 9, x. 8 ; 2 Cor. vii. 1, xii. 21 ; Gal. v. 13–21 ; Eph. iv. 19, v. 3–14 ; Col. iii. 5 ; 1 Thess. iv. 3–5 ; 1 Tim. i. 10 ; 2 Tim. ii. 22, iii. 6 ; Rom. i. 24–27, vi. 19–21, xiii. 13 ; 1 Pet. iv. 3 ; Rev. ii. 14, 20–24, xiv. 8, xvii. 1 ff., xix. 2, xxi. 8, xxii. 15 ; *Didache*, ii. 1, iii. 3, v. 1 ; Herm. *Mand.* iv. 1 ; Clem. 2 *Cor.* iv. 3, viii. 6–ix. 4, xii. 5, xiv. 3–5 ; Pliny, *ad Traj.* xcvi. 7. On the other hand, James speaks in general only of worldly luxury, i. 27, iv. 1–4 (as to μοιχαλίδες, see above, p. 87), iv. 9, v. 1–3, 5. Perhaps in ii. 11 there is a testimony to the prevailing honourableness of the readers as regards the conjugal life. The command μὴ μοιχεύσῃς was generally observed, the command μὴ φονεύσῃς often through hard-heartedness transgressed, cf. iv. 2, v. 6. In the matter of the life among the Gentiles, cf. 1 Cor. v. 1, 10 ff., ix. 24, x. 32, xv. 33 ; 2 Cor. vi. 14–18 ; Eph. iv. 17 ff. ; 1 Pet. ii. 12–17, iv. 3 ff. ; Rom. xii. 2, xiii. 1–7 ; 3 John 7 ; Ign. *Trall.* iii. 2, viii. 2 ; Herm. *Mand.* x. 4 ; *Sim.* i. 10, viii. 9. 1. In the matter of slaves, cf. 1 Cor. vii. 21 f. ; Eph. vi. 5–9 ; Col. iii. 22–iv. 1 ; 1 Pet. ii. 18–25 ; 1 Tim. vi. 1 f. ; Tit. ii. 9 f. ; Philem. 10–21 ; *Didache*, iv. 10 f. ; Ign. *ad Polyc.* iv. 3 (1 Cor. xii. 13 ; Gal. iii. 28 ; Col. iii. 11) ; also the writer's *Skizzen*, 93–115, especially 102, also 136 ff., 350, n. 17.

10. (P. 91.) For the form of oath, cf. Matt. v. 34–37, xxiii. 22, and in addition Lightfoot, *Op.* ii. 2, 93, 359 ; Schöttgen, *Hor. Hebr.* 1733, pp. 48, 202. It is characteristic of the Jewish, in distinction from the Gentile oath, that it avoids the name of God. In place of such a sacrilegious formula, Philo recommends swearing preferably by the Earth, Sun, Stars, Heaven, and the Universe entire (*Leg. Spec.* i, ed. Mangey, ii. 271).

11. (P. 91.) The scorching wind, i. 11 (Luke xii. 55), the early and the latter rain, v. 7 (providing ὑετόν be an essentially right completion of the passage, cf. Deut. xi. 14), fig, olive, and vine culture (iii. 12) in addition to considerable agriculture (v. 4, 7), salt springs (iii. 12), unless in the obscure and most uncertainly traditioned text there be a reference to ἡ θάλασσα ἡ ἁλυκή— the Dead Sea (Num. xxxiv. 3, 12 ; Deut. iii. 17 ; Josh. xv. 2, 5 ; cf. Gen. xiv. 3 ; Ezek. xlvii. 9 ff.). On the other hand, we can understand the Mediterranean as the source of the conceptions in i. 6, iii. 4, without assuming that James, at the time he wrote, was resident in Joppa—a view that Hitzig at one time expressed ; cf. for additional points, Hug, *Einl.* ii.[3] 511.

12. (P. 93.) Acts viii. 1, πάντες διεσπάρησαν ; viii. 4, οἱ οὖν διασπαρέντες διῆλθον κτλ.; xi. 19, οἱ μὲν οὖν διασπαρέντες διῆλθον ἕως . . . 'Αντιοχείας. The connection of Jas. i. 1 with these facts I find first noticed by Georgius Syncellus, *ad A. M.* 5537, ed. Bonn, i. 623. Accordingly we are to consider as included in this greeting the communities in Judea, Samaria, and Galilee,

Acts viii. 1, 14, 25, 40, ix. 31, 32, 36, x. 24, xxi. 8 ; Gal. i. 22 ; 1 Thess. ii. 14 ; further, those at Ptolemais and Tyre, in Cyprus, and at Antioch, Acts xi. 1–26, xiii. 1, xxi. 3, 7, and then the one at Damascus, where it would seem that, even before the death of Stephen, there were disciples, Acts ix. 2–25. In fact, the community which reassembled in Jerusalem after the persecution that followed Stephen's death is not to be excluded. To be sure, without taking into account the half-Jewish Samaritans, Acts viii. 14, and such isolated cases as Acts viii. 27, x. 1–11, 18 ; cf. xv. 7, there were, even previous to the first mission tour, not a few Gentile Christians in Antioch. But supposing that they numbered into the hundreds, their proportion to the many myriads of Jewish Christians (Acts xxi. 20) was never more than 1 to 100, and the way in which James gives passing notice to this exceptional class (above, p. 91) and then pays no further attention to it, is in perfect keeping with the relations existing in the Church up to 50 A.D.

§ 5. THE PERSONALITY OF JAMES.

The author introduces himself to his readers by the simple mention of his name, which was a very common one among the Jews, and by the modest designation of himself as a Christian (i. 1). The omission of all reference to the occasion for his writing is not explained entirely by the fact that what he writes is not a letter, but an address thrown into the form of a letter in order the more easily to reach his readers, who were widely scattered (n. 1). There is no indication as to the grounds on which James based his right to address his opinions in any form to the entire Church of his time with so much earnestness and with so little regard to personal feelings. The tone of the letter is not overbearing ; James calls his readers *brethren*, and reckons himself among them, not only when he is referring to their experience of divine grace (i. 18), but also when speaking of their moral weaknesses and actual failures (iii. 2, 9). But he speaks as an older brother accustomed to receive attention from his brothers when he gives advice, and unquestioning obedience when he rebukes them (n. 2).

Who is this James whose authority is so widely acknowledged ? The opinion that he was the Apostle James, the son of Zebedee, is of late origin, and was not very generally held (n. 3). On account of the obvious connection between the number of the apostles and the twelve tribes of Israel, one would expect that an apostle, in addressing the twelve tribes of the spiritual Israel, would indicate the fact that he was one of the twelve apostles. Although James the son of Zebedee, who was executed very early in the history of the Church, in the year 44 (Acts xii. 2), was one of Jesus' intimate disciples, there is no evidence that his position was so commanding as to render unnecessary any explanation on his part why he, and not one of the other apostles, should write his opinions to the entire Church. In Acts i.–xii. only Peter and John are prominent. Moreover, when this James is mentioned, he is always spoken of as one of the sons of Zebedee, or as a brother of John (Matt. iv. 21, x. 2, xvii. 1, xx. 20, xxvi. 37, xxvii. 56; Mark i. 19, iii. 17, v. 37, x. 35; Luke v. 10; John xxi. 2; Acts xii. 2), or this relation is indicated by the context (Mark i. 29 cf. i. 19, ix. 2, x. 41 cf. x. 35, xiii. 3 cf. iii. 16–18, xiv. 33; Luke vi. 14, viii. 51, ix. 28, 54; Acts i. 13). What has just been said argues also, and in some respects with even greater force, against the assumption that the letter was written sometime after the death of James the son of Zebedee by the Apostle James the son of Alphæus; unless this second James of the apostolic circle is artificially identified with a third person of the same name. Where the name of this second Apostle James actually occurs he is always spoken of as the son of Alphæus (Matt. x. 3; Mark iii. 18; Luke vi. 15; Acts i. 13). On the other hand, in spite of the frequency of its occurrence, the name James is always deemed a sufficient designation of the James who at the latest from the year 44 on was the head of the Jerusalem Church and the leader of Jewish Christianity: Acts xii. 17, xv. 13–21, xxi. 18; Gal. ii. 9—according to the correct reading, James is mentioned before Peter and John; Gal. ii. 12.

That, among the Christians of the apostolic age, there was *one* James distinguished above all his contemporaries of the same name is strongly attested by Jude 1. This is the James who, according to the tradition of the second century, was the first bishop of Jerusalem. Although the accounts of Hegesippus, Clement of Alex., and later authors are partly legendary, so much may be regarded as historical: this James never ceased to love his countrymen and to pray for their conversion; on account of his strict observance of the law and otherwise ascetic manner of life, and on account of his faithful attendance upon the temple worship, he was held in high esteem, even among non-Christian Jews, and, among other titles, bore that of "the Just." Shortly before the outbreak of the Jewish War, probably at the time of the Passover in the year 66, because of his public confession of Jesus, he was hurled from the top of the temple by fanatical Jews, stoned, and finally clubbed to death (n. 4). In this account the subordination of the distinctively Christian to the Jewish elements in the description of James' character impresses one as being original. It was just because of this disposition of his that the orthodox rabbis and Pharisees tried to induce him openly to deny that Jesus was the Messiah. His unhesitating confession left no doubt as to where he stood. Similarly for the Ebionitic account which makes James the head of all the Churches centring in the Hebrew Church at Jerusalem, there must be some historical basis (n. 5). So long as the Church was composed only of congregations whose charter members had been members of the Jerusalem Church before they were scattered abroad by persecution, and before the missionary work among the Gentiles, which began from Antioch, made this city a new centre of church life independent of Jerusalem, the man at the head of the mother Church must have had authority throughout the entire Church. Until this independent movement developed, his name was a power even in Antioch, and could be used to intimidate even a man like Peter (Gal. ii. 12 ; regarding the time, cf. Chron. Survey, Part XI.).   Such a position on the part of the writer is presupposed in this letter, which tradition has always ascribed to James, the head of the Jerusalem Church.

Tradition is just as unanimous in identifying this "bishop" James with James "the brother of the Lord." There is little doubt, therefore, that the writer of this letter is the James referred to by Paul in Gal. i. 19 (n. 6). As to the sense in which he was called a brother of the Lord, there has been difference of opinion ever since the beginning of the second century, and after the fourth century the question was warmly debated.   But it is easy to see that it was dogmatic and æsthetic rather than historical considerations which prevented a general accept- ance of the facts as stated in the Bible and in the earliest traditions of the Jerusalem Church.   It is shown else- where (*Forsch*. vi. 328–363) that this James, his brother Jude (Jude 1), together with a Simon and a Joseph, all younger brothers of Jesus, were real sons of Joseph and Mary (Mark vi. 3 ; Matt. xiii. 55).   After the death of their father they lived with their mother (Mark iii. 21, 31–35 ; Matt. xii. 46–50; Luke viii. 19–21), without, however, keeping themselves entirely apart from their brother's public work.   When Jesus selected Capernaum as the centre of His prophetic work in Galilee, His brothers removed thither with their mother (John ii. 12 ; cf. Matt. iv. 13); while their sisters, who were probably married, continued to reside in Nazareth (Matt. xiii. 56 ; Mark vi. 3).   Still, Jesus' brothers were never among His intimate disciples. We learn from John vii. 3–10 that six months before Jesus' death His brothers did not believe in Him.   But the words which this remark of the evangelist is intended to explain, bitter as they may seem, are very far from betraying in- difference, and certainly do not show any hostility.   Since

Jesus' influence on the people in Galilee was already on the wane, and the ranks of His faithful followers were growing constantly thinner (John vi. 60–71), the brothers impatiently urge the Lord to go back now to Jerusalem, which He had avoided for a long time, and there at the centre of Jewish life, where He had won considerable following earlier (John ii. 23, iii. 22–iv. 3), to remove all doubt, particularly their own doubt, regarding His high calling by there performing miracles such as He had been doing in Galilee since His withdrawal from Jerusalem. Jesus did not follow their suggestion, or, at least, He followed it in such a way as to teach them that they ought to accommodate their ideas to His. We are unable to trace accurately the development of their relation to Him. We only know that at the latest within a few days after the Resurrection they had decided for Jesus; for on the day of the Ascension we find them gathering for prayer with their mother and the apostles (Acts i. 14), and we have the record of a separate appearance of the risen Jesus to James, the brother of the Lord (n. 7). In the year 57, Paul mentions the brothers of the Lord and the apostles as being married missionaries. Jude was a married man, for tradition mentions his grandsons; and this may have been true also of Joseph and Simon. Paul could hardly have meant to include James; for though the tradition has more to say about James than about any other of Jesus' brothers, it makes no mention of descendants of his; only distant relatives are spoken of. The picture of James as a stern ascetic, so deeply impressed upon the memory of the early Church, favours the view that he remained unmarried. And then, according to all the evidence which we can gather from the N.T. (Acts xii. 17, xv. 13, xxi. 18; Gal. i. 19, ii. 9, 12), from the tradition of the Church, and from the Ebionitic literature, James was a resident of Jerusalem, whereas the persons referred to in 1 Cor. ix. 5 were itinerant teachers.

In order thus to overshadow every contemporary of
the same name in the early Church, from the death of
James, the son of Zebedee, in 44 to the time of his own
death in 66, James must have occupied a very prominent
place in Jerusalem ; and it is to be remembered that
this list includes not only a certain James the Less (Mark
xv. 40), but also the Apostle James, the son of Alphæus.
Whether the latter died undistinguished at an early date,
or whether his influence was never widely exerted, we do
not know, but the fact that his position in the early
Church was an · entirely subordinate one must simply be
recognised. Just as the bare name Simon stands for
Simon Cephas, even under circumstances where the
Apostle Simon the Zealot seems to be present (Luke
xxiv. 34 ; Acts xv. 14), so from 44 to 66 and long afterward the name James was always understood as referring
to the eldest of Jesus' four brothers.

1. (P. 101.) As regards the authoritative tone in which the author speaks,
there is a general resemblance between the Epistle of James and the communications of Jewish patriarchs (above, pp. 10, 33), the Easter letters of the
Christian patriarch of Alexandria (*GK*, ii. 203), or even the Lenten pastoral
letters of bishops in our own time. In these cases, ecclesiastical custom,
or the recognised official character of the authors, is sufficient occasion for
writing. On the other hand, compare the explanations or even apologies in
Rom. i. 1–16, xv. 14 ff. ; 1 Cor. i. 11 ; 2 Cor. ii. 3, 9, iii. 1, vi. 11–13, vii. 8 ff.,
xi. 1 ff., xiii. 10 ; Eph. iii. 3 f. ; Col. ii. 1–5 ; Phil. iii. 1 ; 1 Pet. v. 12 ; 2 Pet. i.
12; Heb. xiii. 18, 22; Ign. *Rom.* iv. 3 ; *Eph.* xii. 1; *Trall.* iii. 3; Polyc. *ad Phil.*
iii. 1, xii. 1. The only remains of early Christian literature which are
comparable with James in this regard are the Johannine Epistles.
2. (P. 101.) Change of tone is reflected in change of address. ἀδελφοί μου
ἀγαπητοί, i. 16, 19, ii. 5 ; ἀδελφοί μου, i. 2, ii. 1, 14, iii. 1, v. 12, 19 ; ἀδελφοί, iv.
11, v. 7, 9, 10. Until, finally, the name of brother is omitted altogether, iii. 13,
iv. 1, 13, and the tone becomes that of severest rebuke, ii. 20, iv. 4, v. 1.
3. (P. 102.) The old Latin translation, the latest and best edition of which
is that of J. Wordsworth (*Stud. bibl. Oxoniensia*, i. 113–123), based on the only
existing MS. (ninth or tenth century), has this note at the end, "explicit
epistola Jacobi filii Zæbedei" (*sic*). A trace of this same view, for which
Wordsworth in another passage, i. 144, probably by an oversight, makes
Jerome responsible, is to be found in the confused lists of the twelve apostles
and seventy disciples known as those of Hippolytus and Dorotheus, where it is
said of James the son of Zebedee, that he preached the gospel "to the twelve
tribes of Israel in the diaspora." Then either no other James is mentioned

among the apostles, while James the brother of the Lord is mentioned among the seventy disciples without any suggestion that he wrote the letter (*Chron. pasch.*, ed. Bonn, ii. 122, 136; cf. Cave, *Hist. lit.* 1720, p. 107), or, without his being made the son of Alphæus, his name is found among the apostles between "Judas of James" and "Thaddæus Judas" on the one hand, and Simon Zelotes and Matthew on the other (Lagarde, *Const. ap.* p. 283). In the first printed edition of the Syriac N.T. (ed. Widmanstad, Viennæ, 1555), the following is found in Syriac on a title-page just before the Catholic Epistles: In the name of our Lord Jesus Christ we print three Epistles of James, Peter, and John, who were witnesses of our Lord's revelation, when He was transfigured before their eyes on Mount Tabor, and when they saw Moses and Elias, who talked with Him. Until it is proved that this statement is found in ancient MSS. the entire title must be regarded as the work of the Jacobite bishop Moses of Mardin, who furnished the MS. for the edition of 1555. Of an entirely different character is the frequent designation of the writer of the letter as an apostle. Thus, *e.g.*, in the sixth century MSS. of the Pesh. in Wright's *Catal. of Syr. MSS.* pp. 80, 81, 82, and in the Latin versions of Origen, cf. ed. Delarue, ii. 139, 158, 671 ("apostolus est qui dicit"), but never in the writings which are extant in Greek. This may be due to Jerome's identification of the bishop James with James the son of Alphæus, or simply to the fact that in ancient times the apostolic title was quite freely used (cf. *Skizzen*, 341, n. 12)—being given to the seventy disciples (Iren. ii. 21. 2; Tert. *c. Marc.* iv. 24 in.)—but especially to authors whose writings were regarded with more or less unanimity as belonging in the N.T., as Luke (Hippol. *De Antichr.* 56), Barnabas (Clem. *Strom.* ii. 31 and 35), Clement of Rome (Clem. *Strom.* iv. 105). In modern times the authorship of the Epistle by James the son of Zebedee has been defended by G. Jäger, *ZfLTh.* 1878, S. 420 ff.

4. (P. 103.) Cf. the treatise on "Brüder und Vettern Jesu," *Forsch.* vi. 225–363. The title ὁ δίκαιος was given him not only by Christians, such as the redactor of the *Gospel of the Hebrews* (*GK*, ii. 700, Frag. 18), Hegesippus (Eus. ii. 23. 18, iv. 22. 4), Clement (Eus. ii. 1. 3 f.); but, according to Hegesippus, by all from the time of Jesus (Eus. ii. 23. 4), particularly by the unbelieving Jews (Eus. ii. 23. 6, 15–17). Probably by the event which followed shortly after the death of James, Hegesippus did not understand the siege and capture of Jerusalem by Titus (A.D. 70), but the outbreak of the Jewish war under Vespasian in the spring of A.D. 67 (Eus. ii. 23. 18, καὶ εὐθὺς Οὐεσπασιανὸς πολιορκεῖ αὐτούς). A war which not only ended with the siege and capture of Jerusalem, but which in its previous conduct had been characterized mainly by the investment and capture of fortified places (Jotapata, Gamala, Tabor), might very appropriately be described as a πολιορκεῖν τοὺς Ἰουδαίους; cf. 2 Kings xvii. 4, 5; Eus. *H. E.* iv. 5. 2 and 6 title; cf. also *Chron. ad a. Abrah.* 2039 of the entire Hadrianitic war. This statement of Hegesippus is our only authority, since the passage in Josephus (*Ant.* xx. 9. 1) where it is said that "James the brother of Jesus, the so-called Christ," along with several others, was condemned to be stoned for breaking the law by a court appointed by the high priest Ananus, in the year 62, shows unmistakable signs of interpolation by a Christian hand. Besides this passage, which is accurately quoted in *H. E.* ii. 23. 21, Eusebius cites another statement of Josephus (ii. 23. 20) which

represents the destruction of Jerusalem as a penalty for the killing of James. This statement is not to be found in any of the extant MSS. of Josephus, but is given in essentially the same form by Origen, c. Cels. i. 47 (cf. ii. 13), and is elsewhere referred by him to the *Antiquities* of Josephus (*Com. in Mt.* xiii. 55, ed. Delarue, iii. 463). Since Eusebius cites the passage in direct discourse, while Origen gives it only in indirect discourse, it is highly improbable that Eusebius took it from Origen. More likely both read it in their Josephus, but not in the twentieth book of the *Antiquities* cited by Eusebius in the context, but in the *Jewish War*, in the fifth book of which something similar was found by later readers (*Chron. pasch.*, ed. Bonn, i. 463). Origen, quoting from memory, made a slight mistake in citing his authority, as he does in making other quotations from Josephus (*e.g.* on Matt. xvii. 25; Del. iii. 805). This passage, which is not to be found in existing MSS. of the *Jewish War*, is even more open to suspicion than *Ant.* xx. 9. 1, which is extant. It is on the authority of the latter passage that the *Chronicle* of Eusebius fixes the date of James' death (*a. Abrah.* 2077, in the redaction of Jerome 2078, *i.e.* 61 or 62 A.D.), while the date given in the *Paschal Chronicle* (ed. Bonn, i. 460), 69 A.D., is based upon the other apocryphal Josephus passage, or upon a wrong interpretation of the statement of Hegesippus. The statements of Jerome, *Vir. Ill.* ii (cf. xiii), which depend upon Eusebius and which are very confused, are worthless. While Jerome seems to think that the gravestone of James, erected on the spot where he was executed, beside the temple, remained there only until the time of Hadrian, Hegesippus, who did not write before 180, says, ἔτι αὐτοῦ ἡ στήλη μένει παρὰ τῷ ναῷ. Andreas Cretensis, who lived in Jerusalem in 680, says of James (*op. cit.* p. 12), λαβόντες αὐτὸν ἔθαψαν ἐν τόπῳ καλουμένῳ Καλῷ πλησίον τοῦ ναοῦ τοῦ θεοῦ. In Jerome's time (*Vir. Ill.* ii end) it was a matter of common belief that he was burned on the Mount of Olives.

5. (P. 103.) *Ep. Petri ad Jac.* 1 ; *Clementis ad Jac.* 1 ; cf. *Skizzen*, 64 f., 342, n. 17. Nothing is said in Acts concerning the beginning of the "episcopate" of James. Just as we learn in Acts xi. 30 without any previous notice of the existence of presbyters in Jerusalem, so in Acts xii. 17 we learn that "James and the brethren" means the entire Jerusalem Church. Though not an apostle, he stands in close relation to the presbyters (Acts xv. 6, 13, 22 f.), and the latter are represented as gathering to him (Acts xxi. 18). Clement makes the vesting of James with the episcopate follow immediately upon the ascension (see Eus. ii. 1–3, and *Forsch.* iii. 73, 75, n. 1). Hegesippus says that James assumed the leadership of the Jerusalem Church, not like the bishops of other Churches who became the successors of the apostles who founded the Churches, on the death of the latter, but in conjunction with the apostles while these still remained for the most part in Palestine (Eus. ii. 23. 4, μετὰ τῶν ἀποστόλων, not *post apostolos*, as in Jerome, *Vir. Ill.* ii). More trustworthy seems the statement of Eusebius (ii. 1. 2), which probably rests back upon other passages in Hegesippus, that he became bishop after the death of Stephen. The changes in the organisation of the Jerusalem Church, which we observe from Acts xi. 30 on, were probably the result of the temporary dissolution of the Church in the year 35 (Acts viii. 1–4), not of the events recorded in Acts xii. As late as the fourth century, in Jerusalem was shown the seat in which James was accustomed to sit (Eus. vii. 19.

32. 29). Gregorius Barhebr. (*Chron. Eccl.*, ed. Abbeloos et Lamy, i. 62), who could not have derived his information from Eusebius, testifies that this was true in the time of Timæus (called by him Timothy), 270–280 A.D. While the principal reason for James' promotion to a place of commanding influence may have been his personal integrity, there was another influence that helped to bring it about. After his death, Simeon, another relative of Jesus, was chosen bishop (Heges.; see Eus. iv. 22. 4). The grandchildren of Judas the brother of Jesus were considered by non-Christians to be of the line of David, and until the time of Hadrian occupied prominent positions in the Palestinian Church (Heges.; see Eus. iii. 20. 1–8, 32. 6, cf. iii. 11. 12, 19). As late as the third century there were still kindred of Jesus in Palestine and outside who were honoured with the title δεσπόσυνοι (belonging to the family of the δεσπότης, *i.e.* Christ. Cf. 2 Pet. ii. 1; Jude 4), and who boasted about their nobility (Africanus; see Eus. i. 7. 11, 14). According to the same writer, they had spread from Nazareth and Kokaba throughout the world. According to the Syrian tradition, three successive bishops of Seleucia, in the third century,—the third a contemporary of Porphyrius, the opponent of Christianity,—were descendants of the carpenter Joseph (Greg. Barh. *Chron. Eccl.* iii. 22 f.; Assemani, *Bibl. Or.* ii. 395). With these traditions compare the fact that after the destruction of the temple and of the high priesthood, which had always had a certain show of princely dignity (Acts xxiii. 5), the Jews called the Rabbi who, after seventy, stood at the head of the highest rabbinic school and court, a prince (נשיא), regarded the office as hereditary, and laid emphasis upon the descent of Hillel and his posterity, from David on the maternal side; cf. Hamburger, *RE für Bibel und Talmud*, ii. 401, 838 ff. One is reminded also of the so-called exiliarch, the "head of the diaspora" in Babylon, and of the Jewish ethnarchs of Alexandria. James, and after him Simeon, was such a *Nasi* of the Christian twelve tribes. So, when in Clem. *Recogn.* i. 68, James is called *episcoporum princeps* in contrast to Caiaphas, the *princeps sacerdotum*, it is not out of keeping with the view current in the earliest Jewish Christian Church.

6. (P. 104.) C. Wieseler's hypothesis (*ThStKr.* 1842, S. 80 ff., cf. his *Kom. zum Galaterbrief, ad loc.*), that the brother of Jesus mentioned in Gal. i. 19 was not an apostle, while the James referred to in Gal. ii. 9, 12 is James the son of Alphæus, scarcely requires refutation to-day. It would be easier to believe that two different persons are referred to in Gal. i. 19 and Gal. ii. 9, 12, if in the former passage mention were made simply of a James, and then later of a James further distinguished as ὁ ἀδελφὸς τοῦ κυρίου. Gal. i. 19 deals with an event which took place while James the son of Zebedee was still alive, and in the connection it was natural to note that the James in question was not an apostle. On the other hand, the events mentioned in Gal. ii. 9, 12 took place subsequent to the death of the son of Zebedee.

7. (P. 105.) From 1 Cor. xv. 7 it is not clear whether the James referred to is an apostle or not. Nor is the statement of the Hebrew Gospel decisive; for, on the one hand, it represents the James to whom the risen Christ appeared as the brother of Jesus, known as "The Just"; but, on the other hand, it speaks of him as partaking of the Last Supper with Jesus, apparently regarding him as an apostle (Fragment 18, *GK*, ii. 700). This Gospel contradicts both Paul and the canonical Gospels when it speaks of the appearance as if it were the

very first that occurred in the early morning. According to 1 Cor. xv. 7, the appearance to James occurred toward the end of the forty days (Acts i. 3, xiii. 31), and so must have taken place in Galilee, where Jesus appeared to more than five hundred brethren before He appeared to James. There is nothing to indicate that the brothers of Jesus were present at the Passover during which Jesus was put to death. John xix. 26 f. is more easy to understand if they retained their critical attitude and at the time remained away from Jerusalem. Although the Hebrew Gospel varies from the true tradition at this point, it does not impress one as being a mere idle tale. It is supported by 1 Cor. xv. 7. The saying of Jesus to James, " My brother, eat thy bread, for the Son of Man is risen from the dead," is beautiful. The vow of James which the saying presupposes, namely, that he will eat no more bread until he sees the Lord risen, is not only thoroughly Jewish (Acts xxiii. 14), but quite in keeping with the personal character of James, who was a Nazarite (Heges.; see Eus. ii. 23. 5), and there is no reason for questioning its historicity. The sentiment expressed in such a vow is not unlike that of Thomas (John xx. 24-29, xi. 16). In the very unbelief there is a longing to behold what it is not yet possible to believe.

§ 6. THE AUTHOR'S TRAINING AND HABITS OF THOUGHT.

Better acquaintance is to be had with James from his own letter than from the scant remains we have of trustworthy tradition. It is due quite as much to James' way of looking at things as to the circumstances of the readers to whom he wrote, that he does not feel it necessary to develop the faith confessed by him and his readers (i. 1, ii. 1) in any of its theoretical aspects, but insists as strenuously as he can that they make their lives conform to the orthodox faith which they profess. That he had a profound and vital opinion concerning the cardinal doctrines of the Christian faith, is proved by incidental references to the glory of Christ (ii. 1), to sin and the deep roots which it has in human nature (i. 14 f., iii. 7 f.), and to the power of God's word, once rooted in the Christian's heart, to create new life and to save. This word is a law of liberty which the Christian can and ought to obey (i. 18, 21, 25, n. 1). It is shown further by references to the Spirit which God has sent to dwell in the hearts of Christians (iv. 5), to the still greater

boon which Christians are finally to receive (iv. 6),—
the heavenly kingdom to be ushered in with the parousia
of the Lord, of which they are heirs, and to the new
creation of which they, the children of God begotten by
the word of His truth, are the first-fruits (i. 12, 18, ii. 5,
v. 8 f.). While a man like Paul, even in cases where the
application of religious truth to life was direct, always
sought to show the relation between the content of the
Christian faith and its practical application by recalling
the facts of the gospel history and showing the natural
development of the practical application from these facts,
James always begins at once with practical exhortation.
He is not so much a teacher who develops the truth, as
he is a preacher who speaks like a prophet (n. 2). A
man of the logical type of mind and a teacher who had
been trained in the schools could hardly have failed, in
a discussion as elaborate as that in Jas. i. 2–17, to make
clear to the readers the distinction between the two ideas
in the word πειρασμός. Nor would such a person have
been likely to cite Gen. xv. 6 without stating in what
sense he understood the reckoning of faith there spoken
of to be righteousness, and without showing wherein this
idea here expressed differed from his own conception of
δικαιοῦσθαι.

Without any extended discussion or argument, James
shows that he has a vital grasp of the truth, in language
which for forcibleness is without parallel in early Christian
literature, excepting the discourses of Jesus. We have
here the eloquence that comes from the heart and goes
to the conscience, a kind which was never learned in a
school of rhetoric. The flow of words (n. 4) seems to be
just as natural as the succession of ideas (n. 3). Several
words do not occur in literature before James. Whether
some of these were coined by the author or whether all
of them were in common use in the locality where he lived,
we do not know. But it is very clear that the author

got his facility in the use of Greek, not in some rhetorical school, but from life. His language is comparatively free from gross mistakes, and even shows some feeling for the euphony and rhythm of the Greek tongue (n. 5). And yet on the whole how limited is his command of this foreign language. In the entire Epistle there is scarcely one periodic sentence, the language used consisting for the most part of short sayings, questions, and exclamations. There is no good reason for denying that James wrote Greek by assuming that the letter was written originally in Aramaic (n. 6); nor is it right to make his inability to do so an argument against the historical character of the tradition concerning James. If the membership of the mother Church consisted from the beginning in large part of Hellenists who kept on using the Greek language after their settlement in Jerusalem (above, pp. 39 f., 42 f.), the same is likely also to have been the case in the Churches colonised from this centre. Then, besides the native Jews, who were called Hellenists, in Cæsarea (Acts x.), certainly also in Ptolemais and Tyre (above, p. 44), there must have been added to the Church a number of Gentiles and prose-lytes, who had no more occasion after than before their conversion to familiarise themselves with the Jewish vernacular, Greek being the language of common intercourse in those cities; and in Antioch this number must have been very large. Now, if an author wanted to be understood by these Greeks and to reach the heart of these Hellenists, it was necessary to address them in Greek. And he could do so in the confidence that he would be understood by much the larger part of the "Hebrews" living in this extended region. The latter were certainly to be found not only in Jerusalem, but also in Lydda, Joppa, Damascus, and elsewhere (above, p. 66, n. 12). But, writing from Jerusalem in the circumstances that he did, while not formally excluding the Christians near him from the address, he must have had these far less in mind than the more remote Churches, including those as far away as Antioch, who could not have the benefit of his oral instructions. We saw, moreover, that James took account of the Gentiles who were among his readers (above, p. 91). What was there, then, to prevent him from adapting the form of his letter to the large number of Hellenists among his readers by writing in a language which was certainly intelligible to all, and which it did not greatly inconvenience him to use? Even the greeting, i. 1, shows conscious adaptation to the habits of these Greeks and Hellenists; for, without obscuring the sense at all, James could have used a Jewish greeting, as do Paul and the other apostles, translating it into Greek and adapting it for Christian use (n. 7).

To assume that from the position which James occupied in Jerusalem he would have had no opportunity to acquire the facility in the use of Greek which the author of this letter had, or that he lacked the ability to acquire it, is entirely arbitrary (above, p. 45). Assuming that the letter was written between 44 and 51, the author had been from fifteen to twenty years a member, and for a number of years the official head, of this Jerusalem Church, which very early in its history had more Hellenists than Hebrews in its membership. As the head of this Church, James must have been familiar with the Greek O.T. (above, p. 40), so that it would be entirely natural in writing a Greek letter that he should make his quotations from the LXX (n. 8). Still the letter is not altogether without traces of the author's familiarity with the original text. James lives and moves in the atmosphere of the O.T. Besides the few instances where the O.T. is quoted directly (ii. 8, 11, 23, iv. 5, 6) and specific references to individuals and facts in the O.T. (ii. 21, 25, v. 10 f., 17 f.), there are numerous passages where the author's thought seems to flow unconsciously in the mould of O.T. language (i. 10 f., ii. 7, iii. 9, v. 4, 20). One of his quotations is

from a writing unknown to us (n. 9).　While the Book of
Proverbs, written by the Palestinian Jesus the son of
Sirach, is not quoted, the letter does show familiarity with
a number of his sayings (n. 10), though it would be going
too far to say that there was any particular mental affinity
between this author and James.　On the other hand, there
is a resemblance both in thought and in language between
James' letter and the discourses of his brother Jesus which
have come down to us, which is all the more natural if James
was not directly under Jesus' influence during the latter's
public ministry, and if the resemblance is due neither to
artificial imitation of nor to conscious dependence upon
the discourses of Jesus.　There is not a single word of
Jesus' quoted, much less anything from the Gospels.　And
yet, although none of the sayings of Jesus are reproduced
in exactly the form in which they have come down to us,
it is possible to fill the margin of the Epistle with
parallels of Jesus' discourses which resemble James more
closely in thought than the parallels from Jewish literature, some of which are closer verbally (n. 11).　Though
James may have become acquainted with most of the words
of Jesus preserved in the oral tradition of the Church by
hearing them from others, still there were not a few of
these sayings which he had heard from Jesus' own lips,
though often with doubt and disapproval (above, p. 104 f.).
After he became a believer, what he learned from others
and what he had heard himself fused together in his
thought, and the impression of the personality of Jesus,
under the influence of which he had been ever since his
childhood, made the tradition so vital that it developed
in him a Christian character which in the early Church
made him seem all but superior to the apostles themselves.

　　Unlike his brothers, he felt no call to engage in missionary work (1 Cor. ix. 5 ; above, p. 105).　Here also the
letter is in keeping with James' character, for there is

very little of the gospel in it, and of all the N.T. writings it is the one least adapted to give us an idea of the sort of preaching by which converts were made. It does, however, presuppose this preaching. It is also in keeping with the description which we have of the character of James of Jerusalem, that his letter, while presupposing the Christian faith, pays little attention to forms of statement specifically Christian, and that its teachings have the O.T. and Jewish stamp. If this were not the case, we should have to deny that the Epistle was written by James, for he was a man who was looked upon as an authority by the Jews of his own time and by the Ebionites of a later period, such a man that, as he was being stoned, Jewish priests are said to have exclaimed, "Stop! what do ye? the Just is praying for you." It was possible to be deceived into supposing that James' Christian confession was only an adjunct of his Jewish piety, which could be cast off without changing his character. But this supposition he proved to be mistaken (above, pp. 103, 107).

1. (P. 110.) From the connection of i. 18, 21, 22, 25 it appears that the law, whose continued contemplation and fulfilment is urged upon the readers, is identical with the word of truth, through which God has given them their religious life, making it thus an "implanted word," or at least is included as an essential element in it. Now, if it is self-evident that i. 18, 21 f. refer not to O.T. revelation but to the gospel of Christ, it is also plain that i. 25, ii. 9–12, iv. 11 f., refer not to the Mosaic law as such, but to the law contained in the gospel. When it is characterised, then, as a "perfect law," the epithet is not loosely applied to divine law in general (Ps. xix. 8), but marks the law which is binding upon the newborn, and is implanted in them as a perfect law in distinction from another which is imperfect. This distinction is made still clearer by the added phrase, τὸν τῆς ἐλευθερίας. But since "freedom" is not regarded, in the common experience and usage of any age, as a natural attribute of "law," but rather as its contradiction, it is plain that James meant his readers to feel in the very form of his expression (cf. Rom. ix. 30) the contrast between this law and another to which the phrase could not apply. There is a law of bondage, also, which for that very reason is imperfect. By this can be meant no other than the Mosaic law, which was not implanted in the heart, but inscribed on tables of stone (Jer. xxxi. 31–34 ; Heb. viii. 7–13 ; Rom. viii. 15 ; Acts xv. 10), and which, particularly in the hands of the Rabbis, had become a heavy yoke of slavery (Matt. xxiii. 4,

cf. xi. 29 f., xii. 7); while by the same treatment, on the other hand, it was reduced in fact and impoverished in spirit (Matt. v. 21–48, xv. 1–20). The law contained in the gospel demands not less, but more, than the Mosaic law as expounded by the Pharisees. At the very point, therefore, where James reminds his readers of the increased responsibility of Christians and the seriousness of the judgment which awaits them (ii. 12), he dwells once more upon the character of Christian law as a law of liberty. In this he is quite in accord with the preaching of Jesus. The fact that this new and perfect law of liberty includes commandments from the Decalogue also, and that special stress is laid (ii. 8–11) upon the law of love to one's neighbour, which is likewise an O.T. command, is again in agreement with the preaching of Jesus, and with the teaching of Paul as well (Rom. ii. 23–27, viii. 4, xiii. 8–10; Gal. v. 14, vi. 2). When James calls the law of love a "royal law," he cannot mean simply that it was given by a king, for that is true of all commands of God and Christ. Nor is there any usage to justify the interpretation, "a law royally superior to all others, an all-inclusive law." He means rather that it is a law for kings and not for slaves. In Philo, *de creat. Princ.* iv, Mangey, ii. 364, βασιλικὴ ὁδός denotes the manner of life and conduct which befits a king. It would seem that James was so understood by Clement (*Strom.* vi.—not vii.—164, vii. 73, cf. *GK*, i. 323; Mayor, 84). How admirably this suits the context is apparent. The heirs of the kingdom (ii. 5), who are themselves kings (Rev. i. 6, v. 10; 1 Pet. ii. 9), ought to be ashamed to meet the rich with fawning politeness, offered under pretext of due brotherly love, and at the same time dishonour the poor. The reverse legalistic attitude accordingly is closely related to the idea expressed in ἐλευθερίας. As a king's sons, the disciples of Jesus are free, just as He Himself was; and if as members of the pre-Christian people of God they perform what is there required of them, they are still free nevertheless (Matt. xvii. 24–27).

2. (P. 111.) The distinction between διδάσκαλος and προφήτης is by no means absolute. In Acts xiii. 1 it is hardly permissible to arrange the various names under the two titles separately. By the transition to the first person plural in iii. 1, James intimates that he is one of the διδάσκαλοι in the broader sense. But the difference between διδαχή and προφητεία was clearly felt in the life of the Church till well into the second century, cf. 1 Cor. xii. 8–10, 28, xiv. 6, 26; Eph. iv. 11 (cf. ii. 20, iii. 5); Herm. *Mand.* xi.; *Didache*, x. 7; xi. 3, 7–12; xiii. 1–4, cf. *Forsch.* iii. 298–302; Ign. *Philad.* vii. Although 1 Cor. xiv. 3, 24 f. deals with quite another distinction between prophecy and the gift of tongues, its characterisation of the prophetic type of discourse is of general validity, and is applicable to James. Andrew of Crete calls James a προφήτης (iii. 7, xiv. 3); and in referring to the Epistle, from which he makes extended extracts, he speaks repeatedly of its prophetic style (iv. 31, v. 24, vii. 28). Luther did not, as is commonly said, call James "a straw Epistle" outright, but, contrasting it with John, Romans, Galatians, and 1 Peter, he wrote in 1522 what he did not reprint in later editions of his Bible: "Therefore St. James' Epistle is a right strawy Epistle *as compared with them;* for it has no real gospel character" (Erlangen, ed. 63. 115). There is, nevertheless, both here and in the introduction to James and Jude (63. 156 ff.), a degree of unfairness, which is as easily accounted for as it is re-

grettable. Cf., further, Kawerau, "Die Schicksale des Jas. in 16 Jahrhundert" (*ZfKW*, 1899, S. 359 ff.).

3. (P. 111.) Χαίρειν, i. 1, is echoed immediately in πᾶσαν χαράν, the opening words of the *first section*, i. 2–18, which set forth and urge the right attitude toward the assaults of temptation. The special mention among God's gifts of the regenerative word (i. 18) forms the transition to the *second section*, i. 19–27, which calls for the right acceptance of this word in heart and life. Care for widows and orphans, which is mentioned (i. 27) as an example of the proper activity of the word, leads on to the reproof of a wrong attitude toward both rich and poor in the *third section*, ii. 1–13. The contrast between believing and doing, pointed out in the very beginning of this section, becomes the theme of the *fourth section*, ii. 14–26. As this passage censures the dead faith, which expresses itself in words and not in deeds (ii. 14, 16, 19), it is naturally followed by the *fifth section*, iii. 1–18, rebuking the tendency to instruct others (cf. i. 19), and pointing out the danger of sins of the tongue (cf. i. 26). In the description of true and false wisdom (iii. 13–18), James does not lose sight of its immediate occasion (see above, p. 95 f., n. 2); but the description becomes so comprehensive, and passes finally into so urgent a commendation of peaceableness, that it brings to mind in contrast the many disputes among the readers, which are dealt with in the *sixth section*, iv. 1–12. The desire for the betterment of external conditions, which is noted as the chief ground of these dissensions, appears most markedly among the merchants and the landowners, but also among the farm hands, who complain against them. To these classes the *seventh section*, iv. 13–v. 12, with its three subdivisions, refers. Not only Job, however, but Elijah is an example to be considered. The Christian is not simply to endure in patience what is well-nigh unendurable; prayer offers to the individual and to the Church a means for the relief of earthly suffering and the cure of moral hurt which transcends even the natural order. This is pointed out in the *eighth section*, v. 13–20. Thus, at the close, as at the beginning of his Epistle, James treats of earthly suffering, patience, and prayer.

4. (P. 111.) Mayor, clii–cciv, presents a comprehensive examination of the language of James, and concludes, not improperly, that it contains fewer formal violations of good usage than any other N.T. book, except perhaps Hebrews. This is by no means to assert, however, that Paul had not far greater facility in the use of Greek, or that the style of James could be confused with that of a classical writer. There are only three periodic sentences of any extent in the whole letter (ii. 2–4, 15–16, iv. 13–15). The first two are similarly arranged; the third (and perhaps the second also) is not correctly carried out. The genitive absolute participle, the accusative with infinite, and the optative, are entirely lacking. The use of the particles is exceedingly limited, e.g. ἄν (iii. 4, v. 7, spurious; only iv. 4, ὃς ἐάν), μέν (only iii. 17; never μέν—δέ), ἄρα, ἐπεί, ὥστε, do not occur, ἵνα appears but twice (i. 4, iv. 3). Rare words are ἀνέλεος, ii. 13 (instead of ἀνελεήμων, LXX), altered to ἀνίλεως by the Antiochians; ἀνεμίζεσθαι, i. 6; ἀπείραστος, i. 13, of persons = untested, or above temptation (differently, Jos. *Bell. Jud.* v. 9. 3, vii. 8. 1), next again in Clem. *Strom.* vii. §§ 45, 70, *Const. Ap.* ii. 8, in an apocryphal citation; ἀποσκίασμα, i. 17,—it is perhaps a matter of chance that this is not found till the later Church

Fathers, for Plutarch has ἀποσκιασμός ; δαιμωνιώδης, iii. 15, first reappearing in the Jewish Christian Symmachus, Ps. xci. 6, δίψυχος, i. 8, iv. 8 ; Clem. 1 *Cor.* xi. 2, also in an apocryphal citation, xxiii. 3, cf. Clem. 2 *Cor.* xi. 2 (διψυχεῖν and διψυχία some twenty times in Hermas) ; θρησκός, i. 26, only in grammarians and lexicographers ; πολύσπλαγχνος, v. 11, recurring for the first time with its derivatives, Herm. *Vis.* iv. 3. 5 ; *Sim.* v. 7. 4 (cf. the writer's *Hirt des Hermas*, 330, 399, 487), and Clem. *Quis Dives*, xxxix ; προσωπο-λημπτεῖν, ii. 9 (together with the more common προσωπολημψία, ii. 1, cf. Rom. ii. 11 ; Col. iii. 25 ; Eph. vi. 9) ; χαλιναγωγεῖν, i. 26, iii. 2, cf. Herm. *Mand.* xii. 1. 1 ; Polyc. *ad Phil.* v. 3 ; Lucian, *Tyrannic*, 4 ; χρυσοδακτύλιος, ii. 2, otherwise unknown.

5. (P. 112.) With regard also to paronomasia, alliteration, rhythm, etc., Mayor, cxcv ff., is well worth reading. In many passages he finds something of a "Miltonic organtone," and in others a volcanic fire glowing through the words. It is still a question whether πᾶσα δόσις ἀγαθὴ καὶ πᾶν δώρημα τέλειον, i. 17, is an hexameter, known and quoted by James, as, for example, Ewald, *Das Sendschr. an die Hebr. u. Jak. Rundschreiben*, 190, and Mayor, 53, think probable, or one accidentally formed with a permissible use of the short final syllable of δόσις in the arsis. The analogy of Heb. xii. 13 (cf. Winer, § 68. 4) favours the latter view, as does the circumstance that the line contains only a subject and no predicate. The conjecture that it was a one line adage, "Every gift is good, and every present perfect," in the same sense as "Don't look a gift horse in the mouth" (H. Fischer, *Philologus*, 1891, p. 378), needlessly charges James with a decidedly ill-timed use of a somewhat flippant proverb.

6. (P. 112.) The almost forgotten hypothesis of an Aramaic original (Berthold, *Hist. krit. Einl.* vi. 3033 ff.) has been revived by J. Wordsworth (*Stud. Bibl. Oxon.* i. 141–150). He does not base the theory upon an enumeration of errors and obscurities in the Greek text which would be explained by the reference to an Aramaic original, but on the Latin translation of the Cod. Corb., which presupposes, he says, a Greek original very different from the text otherwise transmitted. Then the existence of two Greek texts so divergent is to be explained on the ground that they are two independent versions of an Aramaic original, and this in turn is confirmed by corre-spondences between the Latin Corb. and the Pesh. Now, these correspond-ences amount to no more than those between Corb. and other versions and Greek MSS. (cf. *e.g.* Tischendorf on Jas. ii. 25), and would be significant only in case one could assert and prove that the Pesh. contained not a translation of James but the original. The only point which might demand attention, namely, the translation of ἱμάτια by *rcs*, Jas. v. 2, as an indication that the Syriac word used in the Pesh. was here the underlying term, is after all of no consequence ; for, as Mayor, ccvii, shows, Rufinus, Eus. ii. 23. 18, translates ἱμάτια in the same way. The originality of the Greek text is established not only by the lack of proof to the contrary, but by the unconstrained manner of the Epistle, which, if it were not in the original language, would imply a mastery of the translator's art unparalleled among the ancients. In i. 1, 2 the paronomasia between χαίρειν and χαρά, so essential to the thought, would have to be ascribed to the translator. For nothing could have stood in an Aramaic original but the שלם of the Pesh., which excludes the possi-

bility of assonance, and which, in connection with the usual N.T. salutation, would have been rendered by εἰρήνη, and not χαίρειν, by any ancient translator ; see the following note.

7. (P. 113.) The Jews of the Hellenistic period considered the Gentile χαίρειν an equivalent for the Semitic salutation of peace ; cf. Jerome, p. 23 above, n. 4. This appears even in the LXX, Isa. xlviii. 22, lvii. 21, cf. Luke i. 28 ; then at the opening of letters, not only those from Gentile rulers to Jews (ad Est. vi. 1, Fritzsche, 62 ; 1 Macc. x. 25, xi. 30), but also letters from Jewish high priests to Gentiles (1 Macc. xii. 6 ; Jos. Ant. xii. 2. 6, according to Aristeas). 2 Macc. i. 1 shows a combination of Jewish and Greek forms in the intercourse between the Jews of Palestine and those of Egypt, first χαίρειν and then εἰρήνην ἀγαθήν (more skilfully in Barn. i. 1, χαίρετε . . . ἐν εἰρήνῃ). In the second letter, 2 Macc. i. 10, a thoroughly Greek expression, χαίρειν καὶ ὑγιαίνειν, see above, p. 78, n. 2. The Semitic greeting, Dan. iii. 31, vi. 25 (cf. Ezra v. 78), which Gamaliel also uses (see above, p. 33, n. 18), is translated by LXX and Theodotion pretty literally εἰρήνη ὑμῖν πληθυνθείη, cf. 1 Pet. i. 2 ; 2 Pet. i. 2 ; Jude 2. εἰρήνη alone in closing, 1 Pet. v. 14 ; 3 John 15. There are also strictly Jewish expansions, like that of ap. Baruchi, lxxviii. 2, in the letter to the nine and a half tribes beyond the river (Ceriani, Monumenta S. et Prof. v. 2. 168) : רחמא נ שלם אא שלם נהוא לבן, cf. Gal. vi. 16 ; Jude 2, ἔλεος καὶ εἰρήνη. After χάρις, with its resemblance in sound to χαίρειν, had established itself in connection with εἰρήνη, ἔλεος might still be added, 1 Tim. i. 2 ; 2 Tim. i. 2 (Tit. i. 3 ?) ; 2 John 3. James contents himself with the simplest, because he knows that the more ceremonious greeting of the Israelite may degenerate into empty formality (cf. John xiv. 27), and that the Greek salutation, though not exactly the expression of a serious conception of life, may be lifted to a higher plane of thought. John, who incidentally assumes the customary use of χαίρειν in the spoken intercourse of Christians (2 John 10 f.), does not hesitate to appropriate the specifically Epicurean form, 3 John 2, cf. p. 78, n. 2. Bengel, Gnomon on Acts xv. 23, " Non semper utuntur fideles formulis ardentissimis." It is noteworthy that, except for the letter of a Gentile, Acts xxiii. 26, this χαίρειν occurs elsewhere in the N.T. only in Acts xv. 23, in a document sent at James' suggestion to the Gentile Christians of Antioch, Syria, and Cilicia. Other resemblances between Acts xv. 13–29 and James have been noticed (Schneckenburger, Beiträge zur Einl. 209 ; Mayor, iv), e.g. Acts xv. 13, ἄνδρες ἀδελφοὶ ἀκούσατέ μου, cf. Jas. ii. 5 ; Acts xv. 17 (Amos ix. 12), ἐφ' οὓς ἐπικέκληται τὸ ὄνομά μου ἐπ' αὐτούς, cf. Jas. ii. 7 ; Acts xv. 29, ἐξ ὧν διατηροῦντες ἑαυτούς, cf. Jas. i. 27, ἄσπιλον τηρεῖν ἑαυτὸν ἀπὸ τοῦ κόσμου. Such similarities tend constantly to confirm the tradition, which ascribes the origin of both letters to the same period and the same circle.

8. (P. 113.) In Jas. ii. 23, Gen. xv. 6 is cited according to the LXX with the passive ἐλογίσθη, and not the active construction of the original. The connective δέ, which is well attested, also, in Rom. iv. 3, and recurs in Clem. 1 Cor. x. 6, Just. Dial. xcii, appears as early as Philo, de Mut. Nom. xxxiii, Mangey, i. 605, and then in the text of Lucian, ed. Lagarde. Lacking א and B for Gen. xv. 6, it is hard to say whether καί or δέ is original in the LXX. Jas. ii. 8 = Lev. xix. 18, LXX ; but this could scarcely have been translated otherwise. One can hardly determine from Jas. ii. 11 the arrangement of the Decalogue to which James was accustomed. The order of the command-

ments as James uses them is based upon their content (see above, p. 100, n. 9), μή instead of οὐ, Ex. xx. 13 ff., was an amendment of style, cf. Luke xviii. 20. καθ' ὁμοίωσιν θεοῦ γεγονότας, Jas. iii. 9, is derived from Gen. i. 26, LXX. Jas. iv. 6 = Prov. iii. 34, but differs materially from the Hebrew, to which the substitution of θεός for κύριος brings it no nearer. If we grant that Jas. i. 10 f. is manifestly based on Isa. xl. 6–8, ἄνθος χόρτου is an agreement with the LXX against the Hebrew ("flower of the field"). The same is true of Jas. v. 4, if Isa. v. 9 is, in the main at least, its foundation. But in one passage, at any rate, and perhaps two, the case is different. Jas. v. 20 (cf. 1 Pet. iv. 8) has affinities with the Masoretic text of Prov. x. 12, but none with the LXX.   Jas. ii. 23, καὶ φίλος θεοῦ ἐκλήθη, does not indeed purport to be part of the citation from Gen. xv. 6, but it is introduced as an undoubted fact, that is, as one to be found in the O.T. It is derived from the original of Isa. xli. 8 ; 2 Chron. xx. 7, whereas the LXX in both passages, in different forms, makes the one "loving" God into one "loved" by Him. Still the application of this term to Abraham need not necessarily be accounted for by personal acquaintance with the original text.   James might also have learned it in the synagogue, like Philo, who, in quoting Gen. xviii. 17 (de Sobr. xi. ed. Mangey, i. 401) inserts after Abraham's name τοῦ φίλου μου, to which there is nothing in the Hebrew to correspond.   In another citation of the same passage (Leg. All. iii. 8 M. i. 93) he has, instead of this, τοῦ παιδός μου, like the LXX. The epithet occurs also in the Book of Jubilees (xix. 20, xxx. 21, ed. Rönsch, xxiv. 25, 420 f.), which was probably written in Palestine in the first century. It is doubtful whether this term was in the thought of so early a writer as Apollonius Molon (circa 80 B.C., according to Schürer, iii. 402 [Eng. trans. II. iii. 252]) when he explained the name Abraham etymologically as πατρὸς φίλος (Eus. Praep. ev. ix. 19. 2, cf. Hilgenfeld, Einl. 542). Symmachus, at a later period, translated Isa. xli. 8, τοῦ φίλου μου (Field, Hexapla, ii. 513), and seems then to have been followed by the Antiochian recension of the LXX (Holmes-Parsons on 2 Chron. xx. 7).

9. (P. 114.) The formula ἡ γραφὴ λέγει (without ὅτι, moreover), as well as the fragmentary and obscure form of the saying Jas. iv. 5, forbid the view of Hofmann, vii. 3. 111 f., and Mayor, 131, that this is simply a free combination of O.T. ideas (Ex. xx. 5, xxix. 45 ; Deut. xxxii. 21 ; Isa. lxiii. 10). The saying does indeed ally itself with that O.T. line of thought (cf. 1 Cor. x. 22 ; Rom. x. 19) of which μοιχαλίδες, iv. 4, is already just a suggestion, but in such a way that we recognise that it must have been taken from a connection unknown to us. " Enviously (jealously) does that spirit long (love its object) which He (God) has made to dwell in us." Spitta, 117–123, conjectures that the saying is taken from the Book of Eldad and Modad cited by Hermas, Vis. ii. 3. 4. Resch, who does not consider it an anachronism that James should already quote gospels as Scripture, is positive that we have here a citation from a Hebrew gospel (Agrapha, 256). It is to be hoped that Spitta's proposition (118 f.) to connect πρὸς φθόνον with ἡ γραφὴ λέγει in the sense of περὶ τοῦ φθόνου (!) will not meet with approval. Kirn, ThStKr. 1904, S. 127 ff., would read πρὸς τὸν θεόν, cf. Ps. xlii. 2 ; Eccles. xii. 7. The change of subject between ἐπιποθεῖ and κατῴκισεν need not surprise us in a quotation thus removed from its context. Otherwise we should not hesitate to read κατῴκησεν with the Antiochians.

10. (P. 114.) Jas. i. 5=Sir. xli. 22, μετὰ τὸ δοῦναι μὴ ὀνείδιζε, cf. xviii. 17, xx. 14, always of human beings. Jas. i. 13 f.=Sir. xv. 11-20. Jas. i. 19= Sir. iv. 29, μὴ γίνου ταχὺς (al. τραχὺς, θρασύς) ἐν γλώσσῃ σου (in contrast with slothfulness in works); v. 11, γίνου ταχὺς ἐν ἀκροάσει σου καὶ ἐν μακρο-θυμίᾳ φθέγγου ἀπόκρισιν (and gentle in answering), cf. vi. 33-36. Jas. i. 20 (p. 96 above)=Sir. i. 19 (al. 22), οὐ δυνήσεται θυμὸς ἄδικος δικαιωθῆναι κτλ., Jas. i. 25=Sir. xiv. 23. Jas. ii. 1-6=Sir. x. 19-24 (22, ἀτιμάσαι πτωχόν= Jas. ii. 6). Jas. iii. 2=Sir. xiv. 1, μακάριος ἀνὴρ ὃς οὐκ ὠλίσθησεν ἐν στόματι αὐτοῦ; cf. xxv. 8, xix. 16, τίς οὐχ ἥμαρτεν ἐν τῇ γλώσσῃ αὐτοῦ. Jas. iii. 9 (to be considered with its context)=Sir. xvii. 3, 4. Jas. v. 3=Sir. xxix. 10, 11 (ἀργύριον μὴ ἰωθήτω . . . χρυσίον), cf. xii. 10. Jas. v. 4, 6=Sir. xxxi. (xxxiv.) 22 f. (al. 25 f.), cf. iv. 1-6. Jas. v. 13 ff.=Sir. xxxviii. 9-15. There is not enough material to determine whether James had read the Hebrew original of Sirach, still extant in Jerome's time, or the Greek translation, or both. The parallels from Wisdom, and those from Philo diligently collected by Schneckenburger, *Annotatio in Epic. Jac.* 1832 (in his comments on the several passages); Siegfried, *Philo,* 310-314; Mayor, 1, are useful for illus-tration, but are by no means sufficient to show that James was acquainted with these writings. With regard to Philo, cf. Feine, *Jakobusbrief,* 142-146. Parallels from Greek philosophical literature, especially that of Stoicism (Mayor, lxxix ff.), are even less pertinent. One might rather undertake to show that Epictetus had read James. Hilgenfeld, 539, A. 2, saw in Jas. iii. 6 (τὸν τροχὸν τῆς γενέσεως) a "conclusive" proof that James was familiar with the conceptions of Orphic mysticism. In that case, as it was the progress of souls contemplated in the doctrine of metempsychosis which was spoken of in Orphic phraseology as κύκλος γενέσεως, and occasionally also (with a reference to the wheel of Ixion) as τροχὸς γενέσεως (Lobeck, *Aglaophamus,* 798 ff.), we must suppose that James seized upon a phrase which he did not understand, without making the least use of the correspond-ing idea. But James uses γένεσις here just as in i. 23, and he compares human existence to a wheel, because he is thinking of it in its constant activity. The tongue, though itself a very unstable member (iii. 8), stands amid the members (καθίσταται ἐν τοῖς μέλεσιν) as the centre of the body, and in relation to it may be likened to the hub or axle of a wheel which con-tinually revolves about it. Cf. in addition also the gloss after Sir. xx. 30 (in Fritzsche on margin) ἀδέσποτος τροχηλάτης τῆς ἰδίας ζῆς. It is remark-able that, in connection with the Orphic suggestions in James, no one has adduced also the line in Clem. *Strom.* v. 127, δαίμονες ὃν φρίσσουσιν (Jas. ii. 19), and the oracle of Apollo of Miletus in Lact. *de Ira,* xxiii, and the Egyptian incantations (*Pap. mag. Lugd.,* ed. Dieterich, *JbfKPh.,* Supplement, Bd. xvi. 800; *Neue griech. Zauberpap.,* ed. Wessely, *Denkschr. der Wiener Ak.* xlii. 2. 65).

11. (P. 114.) James' affinity with the discourses of Jesus can be but imper-fectly indicated by means of figures. The less immediate parallels are placed in parentheses. Jas. i. 2=Matt. v. 12 (Luke vi. 23 is further removed on account of ἐν ἐκείνῃ τῇ ἡμέρᾳ). Jas. i. 4=Matt. x. 22, xxiv. 13. Jas. i. 5 f., 17=Matt. vii. 7 (αἰτεῖτε καὶ δοθήσεται ὑμῖν)-11, xxi. 21 (μὴ διακριθῆτε)-22 (Luke xi. 9-13; Mark xi. 23). Jas. i. 22-25=Matt. vii. 21-27; Luke vi. 46-49. Jas. i. 26 f.=Mark xii. 40 (Matt. xii. 7, xv. 2-9, xxiii. 2-4, 23-26).

(Jas. ii. 1–4 = Mark xii. 38 f. ; Matt. xxiii. 6–12.) Jas. ii. 5 = Luke vi. 20, 24,
xii. 21 ; Matt. v. 3. (Jas. ii. 8, 10 f. = Matt. v. 19 ff., xix. 18 f., xxii. 36 ff.,
with the synoptic parallels, and with reference to the conceptions ἐλευθερία
and βασιλικός, p. 116, note 1, above.) Jas. ii. 13 = Matt. v. 7, xviii. 23–37 ;
Luke vi. 33. (Jas. iii. 1 = Mark xii. 40, λήμψονται περισσότερον κρῖμα.) Jas.
iii. 10–12 = Luke vi. 43–45. (Jas. iii. 18 = Matt. v. 9.) Jas. iv. 4 = Matt. vi.
24 ; Luke xvi. 13 ; and for μοιχαλίδες, Matt. xii. 39 ; Mark viii. 38. Jas. iv. 9
= Luke vi. 25. Jas. iv. 10 = Matt. xxiii. 12 ; Luke xiv. 11, xviii. 14. Jas. iv.
11 = Matt. vii. 1 ; Luke vi. 37. Jas. iv. 12 = Matt. x. 22. (Jas. iv. 17 = Luke
xii. 47.) Jas. v. 2 f. = Matt. vi. 19. (Jas. v. 8 f. = Matt. xxiv. 33 ; Mark xiii.
29.) Jas. v. 12 = Matt. v. 33–37, xxiii. 16–22. Jas. v. 17 = Luke iv. 25 (with
regard to the note of time, which is not to be traced directly to the O.T.,
cf. Hofmann, vii. 3. 143). The correspondence between Jas. v. 14 and Mark
vi. 13 indicates a close connection with the earliest days of Christianity. We
have nothing to do here with the sacramental use of oil in the ancient Church ;
James stands, like Jesus, on the soil of Judaism, cf. Spitta, 144 f. Those
sayings deserve special consideration, to which certain of James' readers
appealed in a way that he disapproved. Since προσωπολημπτεῖτε, Jas. ii. 9,
maintains the connection with ii. 1, we are to infer from ii. 8 that to justify
obsequiousness toward persons of prominence, in spite of their own generally
hostile attitude, appeal was made to Lev. xix. 18, that is, of course, to its
meaning as interpreted by Jesus, Matt. v. 43–47, according to whom the
command is not rightly fulfilled till it includes love to enemies. In Jas.
ii. 14 it is implied that the persons whom the writer would oppose fall back
upon the proposition ἡ πίστις μου σώζει (σώσει, σέσωκεν) με, cf. Matt. ix. 22 ;
Mark v. 34, x. 52 ; Luke vii. 50, viii. 48, 50, xvii. 19, xviii. 42 (viii. 12).
It has been repeatedly pointed out that those elements in James which
remind us of the Gospels are closely related to Luke (Nösgen, ThStKr. 1880,
S. 109 ; Feine, Vorkanonische Ueberlieferung des Lucas in Ev. u. der AG, 132 ;
the same, Jakobusbrief, 70 ff., 133 f.), but it cannot be said that the points
of contact with Luke outnumber those with Matthew. The only inference
which can be drawn is that Luke, even in what is peculiar to his Gospel,
follows early Palestinian tradition. The same is true of the Fourth Gospel,
for James presents noteworthy resemblances to this Gospel also ; cf. P. Ewald,
Hauptproblem der Evangelienfrage, 58–68 ; Mayor, lxxxiv. ff. Jas. i. 18 =
John iii. 3 [ἀποκυεῖν = γεννᾶν, which even in John iii. 4 is applied primarily
to the function of the mother ; βουληθείς, cf. John iii. 8, ὅπου θέλει, and the
denial of any other θέλημα, John i. 13. ἄνωθεν καταβαῖνον, Jas. i. 17, may
also remind us of John iii. 3, 13 (vi. 33, 50), and λόγῳ ἀληθείας of John xvii.
17]. Jas. i. 25 = John viii. 31 f. [Jesus' word, or the truth contained in it,
is the means of freedom to him who abides in it ; add the blessing of the
doer, John xiii. 17.] Resch, Agrapha, 131 ff., 255 ff., claims to have found
extra-canonical sayings of Jesus in Jas. i. 12, 17, iv. 5, 6, 7, especially Jas.
i. 12, on account of the alleged formula of quotation. But as James left
ἐπηγγείλατο without an expressed subject, and ὁ κύριος or κύριος or ὁ θεός was
plainly inserted later by way of supplement, it is impossible to assume that
Jesus, of whom, except for i. 1, he has not yet spoken, is the intended subject.
Cf. rather Jas. ii. 5 and Zec. vi. 14 LXX, ὁ στέφανος ἔσται τοῖς ὑπομένουσιν
αὐτόν. The crown of life, like the crown of righteousness (2 Tim. iv. 8) and

the crown of glory (1 Pet. v. 4), is a general term for the reward of the persistent and victorious fighter. The assertion that, because this phrase appears also in Rev. ii. 10, James must have read the Apocalypse, or that he refers directly to the promise of Jesus found in that passage (Pfleiderer, *Urchristentum*, 867), needs no further refutation. Brückner, who declares this to be unquestionable (*Chronol. Reihenfolge der Briefe des NT*, 289), adduces even more trivial resemblances. All we can say is that James and Revelation show a certain similarity in their point of view ; cf. Spitta, *Offenbarung des Johannes*, 521 ; Feine, *Jakobusbrief*, 131. According to Brückner, 291, and Pfleiderer, 867, James' dependence on Hebrews is also indisputable, since Jas. ii. 21, 25 = Heb. xi. 17, 31, and Jas. iii. 18 = Heb. xii. 11 ; further parallels in Mayor, cii. According to Holtzmann (*ZflVTh.* 1882, S. 293), James more than once presents itself as a direct answer to Hebrews. Cf., further, M. Zimmer, "Das schriftstellerische Verhältnis des Jakobus zur paulin. Lit.," *ZflVTh.* 1893 (year 36, vol. ii.), 481–503 ; and again, on the other hand, Feine, *NJbfDTh.* iii. 305–334, 411–434. On the Epistle's relation to Romans and to 1 Peter, see § 7.

§ 7. THE EXTERNAL EVIDENCE.

Between the time of the composition of the letter, as determined in the preceding paragraphs, and the time when James came to be recognised generally as a part of the N.T. Canon, there is an interval of more than three hundred years, cf. *Grundriss*,[2] S. 21, 43, 45, 53, 56, 61, 68, 70, and below nn. 4–6. The Latin Church did not receive it into its N.T. until after the middle of the fourth century, and then only gradually. The Churches in Mesopotamia and adjoining regions did not include any of the so-called Catholic Epistles in the Syriac Bible which they used. In the Peshito, James takes its place in the Canon for the first time along with 1 Peter and 1 John. The recollection of this fact still survived in the time of Theodore of Mopsuestia, who, against the authority of his own Church, the Greek Church of Antioch, went back to the original Syriac Canon, claiming that James and the other Catholic Epistles ought not to be included in the Canon. The Alexandrian Church is the only one which, as far as the sources enable us to determine, can be proved always to have included James in the Canon along with a number of other Catholic Epistles on a basis of equal authority with the rest. In the case of the Churches in Jerusalem and Antioch, this can be shown to be probable. All this is not so strange, if the fact is taken into consideration that the N.T. Canon was composed of the books coming down from the apostolic age which were adopted as lectionaries in the religious services of the *Gentile-Christian* Church, and if it is admitted that James was addressed to the Church in the year 50, while its membership was still almost entirely *Jewish*.

That this is the right date for the composition of the letter, is confirmed by the clear traces of its influence upon the Christian writers of the period immediately following the year 50. Assuming that the letter reached Antioch while Paul and Barnabas were still engaged in teaching there, or during their first missionary journey, it is not likely that Paul would have failed to read the letter of a man of such recognised authority as James. And it can be proved that he had read it with care. It has, of course, been very often claimed that Jas. ii. 14-26 was written in opposition to Paul's doctrine of justification by faith, or to counteract the degeneration of Christian life resulting from teaching of this kind. But, in order to maintain the first position, it is necessary to assert that James misunderstood Paul's doctrine in a way almost incredible, or that he perverted it wilfully, and then undertook to refute it by a cowardly trick (n. 1). But such a supposition contradicts the impression which every unprejudiced reader gets from the letter regarding the intellectual and moral character of the author. What James opposes in ii. 14-26 is not a doctrine, but a religious profession which was unhealthy and not genuine. Equally untenable is the other assumption, that what is here said is directed against a practical abuse of Paul's doctrine of justification. It is a well-known fact that the effect of the gospel preaching in the apostolic age, as well as later, among those superficially affected by it, was to produce moral apathy rather than to stimulate moral energy. All the apostles sounded a note of warning against it, or testified against it (Gal. v. 13 ; 1 Pet. ii. 16 ; Jude 4 ; 2 Pet. ii. 1 ff., cf. 1 John i. 6, ii. 4 ; Rev. ii. 14, 20–24 ; 1 Cor. vi. 9–20), defending Christianity against the charges made on this ground by non-Christians (Rom. iii. 8, cf. vi. 1). It is true that at different times Paul's letters have been misinterpreted and misused (2 Pet. iii. 16), particularly by Valentinus and his school. That, however, these Gnostics paid little attention to the doctrine of justification by faith, is proved by the conceited way in which they despised those who were no more than believers. We know that Marcion, who professed to be a faithful disciple of Paul, combined with his fanatical hatred of the O.T. ethical views of an ascetic kind. But how could either the error of Valentinus or of Marcion have induced a man in his senses to write what we have in Jas. ii. 14–26 ? That neither Marcion nor any of the great Gnostic teachers could have taken such an attitude, goes without saying. The tendencies which they represented had nothing whatever to do with Paul's doctrine of justification on the ground of faith ; and, besides, it cannot be proved that it was Paul's particular doctrine, and not the common Christian teaching about redemption by grace and the consequent freedom of the Christian, which was abused by thoughtless believers and slandered by non-Christians. Finally, what James opposes is not libertinism, but the moral indolence which went along with the consciousness of faith and of orthodox profession. According to James, his readers were convicted of the worthlessness of their faith and their confession not by the immorality of their living, but by their lack of good works. When he represents them as speaking (ii. 14), it is not a Pauline formula which he puts into their mouth ; he makes them say, rather, that they have faith, meaning that their faith saves them. If this was based upon any formula at all, it must have been some such saying as the one used so often by Jesus, "Thy faith hath saved thee" (above, p. 122, n. 11).

Although, in view of what has been said, opposition to Paul's doctrine of justification, and opposition to any tendency supporting itself by false appeals to Paul's teaching, is out of the question, it is not to be denied that a relation exists between Jas. ii. 14–26 and Rom. iv. 1 ff. (n. 2). The statement in Rom. iv. 2, that Abraham was justified by works, thereby obtaining something of which he could boast, is introduced as the opinion of someone else. The statement contradicts Paul's conclusion that the manner in which Christians obtain righteousness and life excludes all boasting (iii. 27). Or if Paul held both views to be correct, then Abraham must have had a religion different from the Christian's. But if this be the case, then the question is raised whether Paul and the readers who have agreed with him in the preceding exposition are not forced to admit that they are apostates from the religion of Abraham, and without any vital relation to him. Moreover, there is nothing in the preceding context which leads up to this statement, to the discussion of which the whole of chap. iv. is devoted. It is not one of those apparent conclusions from the preceding discussion, which Paul so often introduces in order to strengthen the position already developed by refuting supposed inferences from it. Neither is it a familiar sentence taken from the O.T., for the statement is contrasted emphatically with Scripture (iv. 3). From what source, then, was this proposition taken? In Jas. ii. 21 we have the statement that Abraham was justified by works, and in ii. 23 the title of distinction which Abraham thereby obtained is given. In the same passage, Gen. xv. 6 is quoted just as it is in Rom. iv. 3, with the same text and at the same length (above, p. 119, n. 8). Paul does not dispute the application which James makes of Gen. xv. 6, nor does he question directly James' thesis. But from the Scripture passage which James had used incidentally, and left without definite explanation, he develops his own thesis, namely, that Abraham's significance for the history of religion rests upon the fact that in the Genesis account his righteousness is reckoned as faith, and so his justification is on the ground of faith. There is no conflict at all between Paul and James; Paul takes up the thought where James left it, and develops it further. The conception δικαιοσύνη θεοῦ (Rom. i. 17, iii. 21, x. 3, cf. 2 Cor. v. 21; Phil. iii. 9) did not originate with Paul. It goes back to Jesus (Matt. vi. 33), starting from his description of the difference between true righteousness and the human makeshift for it, the righteousness of the Pharisees. James uses the same contrast (i. 20, above, p. 96). Paul merely puts emphasis upon the thought suggested in θεοῦ, and so develops a new idea. Is it merely by accident that δικαιοσύνη θεοῦ (Rom. i. 17) occurs for the first time just after Paul has called the gospel a δύναμις εἰς σωτηρίαν (Rom. i. 16), and that it is just before he makes the statement that the word of the Christian proclamation is τὸν δυνάμενον σῶσαι (i. 21), that James speaks of the δικαιοσύνη θεοῦ (i. 20)? There is also a very close connection between Rom. v. 3 f. and Jas. i. 2–4, especially if καὶ καυχώμεθα ἐν ταῖς θλίψεσιν be taken as a hortative. Not only is there exact verbal correspondence between Paul's εἰδότες (Jas. γινώσκοντες) ὅτι ἡ θλῖψις ὑπομονὴν κατεργάζεται and Jas. i. 3, but the passage in Romans throws light upon the meaning of James' somewhat obscure language. The expression, "ways by which your faith is tested," must certainly mean the same as "manifold trials," or, according to Paul, "tribulations." Finally, the question is raised in the mind of a thoughtful reader by Jas. i. 4, how the ὑπομονή is to persist to the end and to be made perfect. It was this that suggested to Paul the writing of Rom. v. 4 f. Even the word δοκιμή

is a reflection of James' δοκίμιον. Anyone's character may
be described as tested or proved when the means of
testing it are rightly and patiently endured. Furthermore, although the thoughts expressed in Rom. vii. 23,
ἕτερον νόμον ἐν τοῖς μέλεσίν μου ἀντιστρατευόμενον τῷ
νόμῳ κτλ., and Jas. iv. 1, ἐκ τῶν ἡδονῶν ὑμῶν τῶν στρατευομένων ἐν τοῖς μέλεσιν ὑμῶν, show differences, they
are essentially the same, and neither of them is obvious.
Now, if these parallels prove that Paul had James in
mind when he wrote Romans, then it may be the
more readily admitted that there are indications of a
use of the same in other passages where the dependence
cannot be absolutely proved (n. 2). Altogether, a letter
which left Paul unsatisfied with its conclusion about
Abraham's justification, and which influenced him to take
up the passage Gen. xv. 6 and discuss the subject with
far greater thoroughness (Rom. iv. 3–24) than he had
done heretofore (Gal. iii. 5–7), must have made a deep
impression upon him.

But it is important to bear in mind that Romans is
the only one of Paul's letters which shows traces of
James' influence. 1 Peter was written in Rome, probably
in the year 63 or 64 (§ 39). Granted that the resemblance
between this letter and James is such as to necessitate
the assumption that one of them depends upon the other,
it is easy to see that throughout it is Peter who elaborates
James' short suggestions, expands his pithy sentences, and
tones down the boldness and abruptness of his thought
(n. 3). Chronologically, the next document which shows
clear traces of the influence of James is the letter, sent
probably about the time of Domitian's death (Sept. 96),
from the Roman Church to the Corinthian Church, which,
according to ancient and unanimous tradition, was written
by Clement, the head of the Roman Church (n. 4). In
the *Shepherd*, written during Clement's lifetime by
Hermas, a lay member of the Roman Church, there are

a number of passages from James which are made, as it were, texts for extended remarks (n. 5). If we leave out of account those parts of the Church where James was early accepted into the Canon, and the later periods when James was commonly quoted, these are all the clear evidences which we have of the influence of the Epistle upon Christian literature (n. 6). Not only do these references to James in Romans, and its use in 1 Peter, confirm the conclusion already arrived at, that James was written in or before the year 50 ; but if the organisation of the Roman Church was due in no small measure to the influence of Jewish Christians who came from Palestine and settled in Rome, and if during the first decades of its history its membership was composed largely of Jewish Christians (§ 23), then there is nothing strange about the fact that it is this series of writings prepared in Rome in the years 63–64 and 96–100 which betray acquaintance with James, and that it is in Romans that Paul refers to this Epistle. It was among the Christians there that he could assume acquaintance with James' teaching, and he is wise in making the reference that he does to his Epistle.

1. (P. 124.) It is well understood that Paul developed and defended his doctrine that men are justified not by the works of the law, but through faith in Christ, in opposition to the Judaistic demand that the Gentiles should submit to circumcision, and with it to the whole Mosaic law, if they would become Christians in full standing, and partakers of salvation. For anyone who knew anything whatever of the great struggle of the decade 50–60, this position defined with historical precision the works of the law, to which Paul denied justifying efficacy. On the other hand, the faith to which Paul does ascribe this efficacy is more fully defined in his designation of it in his most polemic Epistle (Gal. v. 5, cf. Tit. iii. 8), as the faith which works itself out through love. All misunderstanding as to the ethical consequences of his teaching is precluded by his unconditional requirement of the observance of God's commands (1 Cor. vii. 19 ; cf. Rom. viii. 4) or the fulfilment of the law of Christ (Gal. vi. 2), by his insistence on the avoidance of all vicious life as a condition of blessedness (1 Cor. vi. 9 f. ; Gal. v. 21 ; Rom. viii. 5–13), and by his expectation of a judgment awaiting Christians, when inquiry shall be made into their actual conduct (2 Cor. v. 10 ; Rom. ii. 6 ff., xiv. 10 ; 1 Cor. iv. 3–5). The faith, however, to which James denies saving efficacy is

not only not the faith which he praises elsewhere (i. 6, v. 13–18) as the vital strength of prayer, unfailing in its operation, and for which he claims that its possessor is rich in the midst of outward poverty (ii. 5). To James' mind the "empty" man (ii. 20, κενός, contrasted with πλούσιος, ii. 5, cf. Luke i. 53) is rather the man who *says* he has faith, while at the same time he has no works to show for it. It is true that James calls this inactive faith faith also, but only in the way in which the speaking of charitable sounding phrases is called love in 1 John iii. 18, that is to say, a love with word and tongue as over against love in deed and in truth. James neglects here, as in the similar instance in which the words πειρασμός, πειράζεσθαι denote very different things (i. 2–15, see p. 111 above), to distinguish with precision between true and false faith. But he is careful not to deny saving power to all faith. The question μὴ δύναται κτλ., ii. 14, like the question τί τὸ ὄφελος, is dependent upon the particular conditions stated, as indeed αὐτόν for ἄνθρωπον shows. Moreover, he puts it beyond question that this λεγομένη πίστις has nothing in common with what he himself considers faith, further than the name. It is an intellectual conviction, which even the devils may possess. It is to true faith what sympathising words are to really helpful love (ii. 15 f.), what the corpse is to the body (ii. 17–26). Now, just as this faith to which James denies all saving efficacy bears no resemblance to that which Paul sets forth as the condition and means of justification, so is it too with the works which James represents as the basis of justification and those works of law to which Paul denies any such value. The offering of Isaac and the reception of the spies by Rahab are anything but the fulfilment of legal requirements ; rather are they heroic acts of faith ; and James expressly emphasises (ii. 22) the fact that faith was involved in them, and in them found its realisation. On the other hand, he makes not the slightest attempt to represent them ingeniously as works of law, by characterising them, for example, as the fulfilment of some exceptional command of God, and thus the rendering of obedience. How could a man of sound intelligence imagine that ii. 14–26 was any refutation of Paul ? Even the fact that James makes use of the very passage (Gen. xv. 6) with which Paul supports his doctrine of justification, is no proof that he was familiar with the latter's treatment of it. On the contrary, it would then be incomprehensible that James should not have made an attempt, at least, by a different exposition of the passage, to invalidate Paul's very obvious deductions. James gives no interpretation of the passage at all, but is satisfied to represent the fact to which it testifies as a presage of Abraham's subsequent justification by his works, without so much as hinting what he understands by this imputation of faith as righteousness. We may conclude, however, from the context that James was not in the habit of designating this imputation (which he himself adduces from Gen. xv. 6 without any modifying addition) as δικαιοῦσθαι. It was absolutely wrong to infer from the mere use of δικαιοῦσθαι ἔκ τινος by both James and Paul, that one was dependent upon the other. Neither of them invented the verb, and the prepositional connection is the most natural one ; cf. Matt. xii. 37, and similarly κρίνεσθαι, Rev. xx. 12 (Luke xix. 22). Certainly James conceives the good conduct, which he considers indispensable, as a fulfilment of law (i. 25, ii. 8–11, iv. 11 f.). But, in the first place, Paul does so also, and, in the second place,

James characterises the law he has in mind, in direct contrast to that given by Moses and interpreted by the rabbis, as the law of liberty, the law implanted in Christians in and with the gospel, to be fulfilled by them in kingly freedom (above, p. 115 f.). How could a James, or a pseudo-James, imagine that to demand the fulfilment of such a law was to oppose Paul? To the question at issue between Paul and the Judaisers with regard to the attitude of Gentile Christians toward the Mosaic law, James does not devote a single word, even where he refers to the Gentiles among his readers (ii. 25, above, p. 91). As little does he touch upon the closely related question, how far Jewish Christians were under obligation to observe the Mosaic law, or were justified in so doing. The only passage which could possibly be referred to Jewish ceremonial (i. 26 f., p. 97, n. 3) criticises all over-rating of ritual piety. To infer from this that this James, utterly unlike the James of history, was opposed to the continued participation of Jewish Christians in the temple services and to the Mosaic regulation of life, would be as preposterous as to ascribe a like attitude to Jesus on the ground of His denunciations of the Pharisees. Nor does it need to be proved that James could not have directed a polemic against the legal observance of the Jewish Christians in this indirect and casual way. For him and his readers it was a matter of course, and was assailed by no one, not even Paul. A polemic against those δοκοῦντες θρησκοὶ εἶναι is entirely consistent with legal observance on one's own part, cf. Matt. xxiii. 23, iii. 15. If, as tradition tells us (above, p. 103), James' manner of life was strictly, even exaggeratedly, legal, and he was himself, therefore, a θρησκός, this only gives the more weight to his warning against the over-estimation of θρησκεία, just as Paul's argument against the over-estimation of the gift of tongues is emphasised by the fact of his own facility in that particular (1 Cor. xiv. 18). That the author of James was an enthusiast for the law of the same type as the Judaisers of Galatians, is certainly unthinkable; but neither does the James of history occupy any such position. With regard to his attitude toward missionary work among the Gentiles, Paul (Gal. ii. 4, 9) distinguishes him as clearly from the false brethren whose proceedings made the action of the council necessary, as does the account in Acts xv. 13–29. Any reasonably careful exegesis of Acts xv. 21 shows that James sets aside effort for the extension of the Mosaic law and of the legal manner of life as a task which has no claim upon him and the mother Church. Μωϋσῆς . . . τοὺς κηρύσσοντας αὐτὸν ἔχει does not mean simply κηρύσσεται, but calls for a corresponding clause in contrast, as in John v. 45, ἔστιν ὁ κατηγορῶν ὑμᾶς Μωϋσῆς, cf. John viii. 50. It is as unsafe to conclude from Gal. ii. 12 that James would have disapproved Peter's participation in the meals of Gentile Christians (though Feine, ii. 89, is still of this opinion), as to hold Peter responsible for the conduct of his partisans at Corinth. The disinterested wording of the statement made by the elders gathered with James in Jerusalem (Acts xxi. 20, ὑπάρχουσιν, not ὑπάρχομεν), suggests that in their judgment the legalistic zeal of Jewish Christians was a one-sidedness which should be treated with forbearance, rather than that the speakers themselves occupied that standpoint. Even in Hegesippus' account there is no hint which might be interpreted as Judaistic in the historic sense of the word.

2. (Pp. 126, 128.) The present writer presupposes as the reading of Rom.

iv. 1 f., τί οὖν ἐροῦμεν; εὑρηκέναι 'Αβραὰμ τὸν προπάτορα ἡμῶν κατὰ σάρκα—εἰ γὰρ 'Αβραὰμ ἐξ ἔργων ἐδικαιώθη, ἔχει καύχημα—ἀλλ' οὐ πρὸς θεόν; with v. Hengel, v. Hofmann, and others, I hold that τί οὖν ἐροῦμεν undoubtedly constitutes an independent question, as in vi. 1, vii. 7, ix. 14 (cf. iii. 5, vi. 15, viii. 31 ; 1 Cor. x. 19), and that, taken with the following question, which requires a negative answer, it yields this meaning : " Are we, then, compelled by the foregoing discussion to adopt some such conclusion as follows ? " The sense is not substantially altered by the omission, with B, of εὑρηκέναι (to which supply "we" as subject). Klostermann, *Korrekturen zur bisherigen Erklärung des Römerbriefs*, 1881, S. 121, 129, made a decided advance in the interpretation of the passage by pointing out the parenthesis indicated above. But the question whether Paul and his readers who followed him must now admit that Abraham was indeed their physical but not their spiritual ancestor, was possible only in case the readers were, like the writer, actually sons of Abraham κατὰ σάρκα (see § 23 below). I agree with Spitta, 209–217, in the opinion that Paul has James in mind; but I fail to find any satisfactory evidence that Paul could have assumed such an attitude only toward a Jewish writing, and therefore that he knew James as the work not of a Christian, but of a Jew (210, 211, 217). The way in which James is referred to in Rom. iv. 2 presupposes that the readers, or many of them at least, knew and esteemed the authority which had put forward this proposition. How could Paul assume this in the case of an obscure Jew whose private composition had by chance come to his notice ? Why does he avoid combating the statement outright as erroneous, and let it stand as in some measure valid, or at least uncontradicted, unsatisfactory as he regards it ? In Rom. iii. 28, too, we can find no polemic against James, for James had by no means ascribed justifying efficacy to the ἔργα νόμου with which Paul was dealing. In spite of his acquaintance with James, Paul could, here as in Gal. ii. 15–21, express the conviction that a man becomes just through faith independently of works of law, as the outcome of the common experience of all sincere Christians of Jewish origin. In so doing he by no means asserted that this thesis was continually on the lips of all Jewish Christians, a Peter or a James ; in that case he would have had no need to write Romans. He lays down his proposition in Rom. iii. 28 not as a generally recognised Christian doctrine, but as a conclusion reached by elaborate arguments and deductions. It is the conclusion at which he himself has arrived, and every reader who has followed him with assent thus far must finally come to the same. It is the same "we" as in Rom. iii. 9, iv. 1, vi. 1, etc. According to this view, Rom. iv. 2, not iii. 28, is the point at which we may trace Paul's reference to James. In addition to the passages already mentioned, compare Rom. ii. 1, xiv. 4 with Jas. iv. 11 ff. ; Rom. ii. 13, 21–29 with Jas. i. 22–25, ii. 9, iii. 1, iv. 11 (ποιητὴς νόμου); Rom. viii. 2 ff., 15 with Jas. i. 25, ii. 12 (law of liberty); Rom. viii. 7, 8 with Jas. iv. 4–7 (ἔχθρα τοῦ θεοῦ . . . τὸ πνεῦμα ὃ κατῴκισεν ἐν ὑμῖν . . . ὑποτάγητε τῷ θεῷ); Rom. xii. 8 (ὁ μεταδιδοὺς ἐν ἀπλότητι) with Jas. i. 5. M. Zimmer (*loc. cit.*) and Mayor, xcii.–xcv., give more than exhaustive lists of points of contact between James and the Pauline Epistles. Von Soden in his guarded treatment (*JbfPTh*. 1884, S. 163) mentions as indications of the writer's literary acquaintance with the Pauline letters, only Jas. i. 13 = 1 Cor. x. 13 (where, however, ἀνθρώπινος has by no means a contrasted θεῖος), and Jas. ii. 5 =

1 Cor. i. 27, in addition to passages from Romans. Spitta, 217–225, concludes that aside from Romans there are but few passages in Paul's letters which could suggest any direct dependence upon James, but does not account for this marked difference between Romans and the other Pauline Epistles.

3. (P. 128.) Spitta (183–202) is the latest writer to maintain the dependence of 1 Peter upon James. Brückner, *ZfWTh*. 1874, S. 530 ff., *Chronol. Reihenfolge*, 60–66 ; Pfleiderer, 868, and others, have attempted to prove the converse. We may decide confidently for the first-mentioned view, if for no other reason than that the author of 1 Peter, in his attitude toward other N.T. books as well, particularly toward Romans and Ephesians, shows himself as one whose tendency is to appropriate the ideas of others without possessing any marked literary individuality of his own (see § 40 below). No one can deny that James has a consistent style, with a bold and even rugged character of its own. To come to details, a superficial comparison of 1 Pet. i. 6 f. with Jas. i. 2–4 shows unmistakable similarities : 1. ἀγαλλιᾶσθε = πᾶσαν χαρὰν ἡγήσασθε ; 2. λυπηθέντες ἐν ποικίλοις πειρασμοῖς = ὅταν ποικίλοις περιπέσητε πειρασμοῖς ; 3. τὸ δοκίμιον ὑμῶν τῆς πίστεως. But while James, following Jesus' example (Matt. v. 12 ; Luke vi. 22 f.), calls upon those who suffer to regard their still continuing trials even now as a matter for rejoicing, 1 Peter, at least in the beginning (for contrast iv. 13a, 16), tones down the thought to this, that, over against the tribulations which seem now to have their right, there will be joy for the Christian at the Parousia. For the connection of ἐν ᾧ with ἐν καιρῷ ἐσχάτῳ, the contrasted ἄρτι, and the comparison of i. 8 and iv. 13b, make it certain that ἀγαλλιᾶσθε, i. 6 and ver. 8, have a future sense, even if it may not be permissible to construe ἀγαλλιᾶσθε directly as an Attic future = ἀγαλλιάσεσθε (cf. Schmiedel-Winer, *Gramm*. § 13, A. 5 ; but also A. Buttmann, *Ntl. Gramm*. S. 33 *end* [Eng. trans. p. 38]). Note, further, the difference in the use of τὸ δοκίμιον. James used it, as Paul also understood him to do (p. 128 above), in the sense of a means of testing (= δοκιμεῖον, cf. Orig. *Exh. ad Mart*. 6, ed. Berol. viii. 1, δοκίμιον οὖν καὶ ἐξεταστήριον τῆς πρὸς τὸ θεῖον ἀγάπης νομιστέον ἡμῖν γεγονέναι τὸν ἑστηκότα [al. ἐνεστηκότα] πειρασμόν). In 1 Peter, on the other hand, the word is treated as the neuter of the adjective δοκίμιος = δόκιμος (cf. Deissmann, *N. Bibelst*. 86–90 [Eng. trans. 259–262]), "the tested, genuine," and so practically = δοκιμή, "approvedness." But if 1 Peter is convicted here of dependence upon James, one cannot escape the feeling that James was before the writer's thought from the very beginning. It is not that the word διασπορά, 1 Pet. i. 1, Jas. i. 1 is peculiarly significant, but the constant transfer to the Christian Churches of the characteristics of Israel, and especially of the Jews living in the diaspora (§ 38), seems like an amplification of the thought suggested in three words in Jas. i. 1. The idea of being born of God (Jas. i. 18) reappears in more detail in 1 Pet. i. 23–25, and in addition the passage Isa. xl. 6–8, which is only hinted at in Jas. i. 10 f., is utilised here in more extended quotation. As Jas. (i. 19 ff.) follows the mention of new birth with the exhortation to attend repeatedly to the word whose quickening power has been thus experienced, so we find in 1 Peter. Cf. Jas. i. 21, διὸ ἀποθέμενοι πᾶσαν . . . τὸν δυνάμενον σῶσαι with 1 Pet. ii. 1, ἀποθέμενοι οὖν πᾶσαν . . . εἰς σωτηρίαν. While James speaks of this constant need of receiving the word in terms which would apply equally well to the first acceptance of the gospel,

Peter takes pains to bring out the distinction by adding to James' figure of birth through the word a reference to the readers as newborn babes. Even the admonition to put in practice that which has been heard (Jas. i. 22–25) follows soon enough, in 1 Pet. ii. 11 ff. It is applied by Peter in substance only, with entire independence and in a way adapted to the circumstances of his Gentile readers, but there are echoes of James even here : 1 Pet. ii. 16, ἐλεύθεροι=Jas. i. 25, τῆς ἐλευθερίας ; 1 Pet. ii. 11, ἀπέχεσθαι τῶν σαρκικῶν ἐπιθυμιῶν αἵτινες στρατεύονται κατὰ τῆς ψυχῆς=Jas. iv. 1, ἐκ τῶν ἡδονῶν ὑμῶν τῶν στρατευομένων ἐν τοῖς μέλεσιν ὑμῶν. Prov. iii. 34 is cited in 1 Pet. v. 5 precisely as it is in Jas. iv. 6 (ὁ θεός instead of κύριος, LXX) ; with it is connected (1 Pet. v. 6) the admonition to humility which follows more briefly in Jas. iv. 10, and finally in 1 Pet. v. 8, 9 the exhortation to resistance of the devil, which Jas. iv. 7 inserts between the quotation and the admonition just mentioned. Thus we have again quite a complex of ideas and expressions in which the two Epistles coincide. If Jas. v. 20 follows in the main the Hebrew text without regard to the LXX (above, p. 120), the similarity of 1 Pet. iv. 8 cannot be accidental. 1 Peter, however, which adopts from the original the ἀγάπη omitted by James, has again (as in i. 24) gone back directly to the O.T. passage suggested by James' reference, and thus given a different turn to the thought. It is plain that the author of 1 Peter was well acquainted with James, and had read the letter reflectively. The fact that he often alters its antiquated—strictly speaking, its primitive Christian—style to the more developed modes of expression current in the Churches founded, and thus far trained, by Paul and his associates, does not justify Spitta's argument (201) that he knew James only as a Jewish, not as a Christian, writing. The absence of all allusion to the section Jas. ii. 14–26 no more calls for explanation than does the fact that 1 Peter has no echo of the thundering rebukes addressed to the merchants (Jas. iv. 13–17) and the landowners (Jas. v. 1–6). It is perfectly evident that not everything that James had to say to believers of his own race (e.g. v. 12) would apply to the Gentile Christians of Asia Minor. For these the section ii. 14–26 was quite useless ; it could not be transformed into the language of the Pauline Churches without perverting it to its opposite, while the appropriation of it but in part could only have confused such readers, and frustrated the main object of the Epistle as set forth in 1 Pet. v. 12.

4. (P. 128.) Clem. 1 Cor. x. 1, Ἀβραὰμ ὁ φίλος προσαγορευθεὶς πιστὸς εὑρέθη ἐν τῷ αὐτὸν ὑπήκοον γενέσθαι τοῖς ῥήμασιν τοῦ θεοῦ. 17. 2, ἐμαρτυρήθη δὲ μεγάλως Ἀβραὰμ καὶ φίλος προσηγορεύθη τοῦ θεοῦ. The mere designation of Abraham as a "lover of God" would not show that Clement had read Jas. ii. 23 (above, p. 120 f.); but, like James, he speaks (twice, indeed) of the bestowment of this title as an historical event, and emphasises the proof of Abraham's faith through acts of obedience (x. 1), while in the same connection (x. 7) he cites Gen. xv. 6 quite as it appears in Jas. ii. 23, and recalls similarly the offering of Isaac (x. 6). When Clem. xxx. 2, like Jas. iv. 6 and 1 Pet. v. 5, quotes Prov. iii. 34 with ὁ θεός, instead of κύριος as in the LXX, there is, besides a dependence on James or 1 Peter, still a third possibility, namely, that in early times there may have been a text of the LXX with ὁ θεός. That in reality Clement followed James appears from the fact that immediately afterward in xxx. 3 he writes ἔργοις δικαιούμενοι, καὶ μὴ λόγοις ; and it is the more

certain that this goes back to Jas. ii. 21, 24, since there, too, works are contrasted with a λέγειν, Jas. ii. 14, 16. The same contrast is drawn in Clem. xxxviii. 2 (ὁ σοφὸς ἐνδεικνύσθω τὴν σοφίαν αὐτοῦ μὴ ἐν λόγοις, ἀλλ᾽ ἐν· ἔργοις ἀγαθοῖς) in a way which reminds us of Jas. iii. 13, cf. iii. 1 ff. That an admirer of Paul acquainted with his Epistles should venture at all to speak of justification through works, could hardly be explained unless he were emboldened by another authority. Clement was aware, too, of the difference between Paul's type of teaching and James', for it cannot but appear that he was undertaking to reconcile the two when, shortly after the reference to James (xxx. 3), he attributes Abraham's blessing to the fact that he exercised righteousness and fidelity through faith (xxxi. 2, cf. Jas. ii. 22, ἡ πίστις συνήργει τοῖς ἔργοις αὐτοῦ), then maintains that the devout of all ages have been justified not of themselves, but by the will of God ; not through their works, but through faith (xxxii. 3 f.) ; and, finally, in setting forth the necessity of works arrives at the formula (xxxiv. 4): προτρέπεται οὖν ἡμᾶς πιστεύοντας ἐξ ὅλης τῆς καρδίας ἐπ᾽ αὐτῷ, μὴ ἀργοὺς μηδὲ παρειμένους εἶναι ἐπὶ πᾶν ἔργον ἀγαθόν. Cf. Lightfoot, St. Clement, ii. 100. Similarly Clement combines the πίστει of Heb. xi. 31 with the ἐξ ἔργων of Jas. ii. 25 when he writes (xii. 1), διὰ πίστιν καὶ φιλοξενίαν ἐσώθη Ῥαὰβ ἡ πόρνη. The like could be said of Clem. xlix. 5 (ἀγάπη καλύπτει πλῆθος ἁμαρτιῶν, ἀγάπη πάντα ἀνέχεται, πάντα μακροθυμεῖ κτλ.) as compared with Jas. v. 20 and 1 Cor. xiii. 4, 7, were it not that the word ἀγάπη points primarily to 1 Pet. iv. 8 (p. 134 above). But it is highly probable that Clement was influenced at the same time by Jas. v. 20 also, since in l. 5 he mentions love, as James does, as a means of obtaining forgiveness of sins for oneself.

5. (P. 129.) On Hermas and James, cf. Schwegler, Nachapost. Zeitalter, i. 339 ; the writer's Hirt des Hermas, 396–409 ; GK, i. 962 ; Hofmann, vii. 3. 175 f. ; Taylor, JPh. xviii. 297 ff. As early as in one of the Greek catenæ (Cramer, viii. 4), Herm. Mand. ix. is quoted in connection with Jas. i. 6. The assertion often heard, that the proofs of the dependence of Hermas upon James are not forthcoming, is valueless so long as one will not take the trouble to refute the thorough presentation of the actual facts, which cannot well be repeated here, and whose place, moreover, cannot be supplied by a table of citations (like that in Feine, 137). In answer to Pfleiderer's verdict (868) that Hermas is the earlier of the two, it is quite sufficient to remark with Mayor (cxliii. f.) that one might with as good right declare Quintus Smyrnæus older than Homer, or any present-day sermon older than its text.

6. (P. 129.) We are probably to assume that James was known to Irenæus (GK, i. 325) ; the Marcosians (Iren. i. 13. 6), whose leader belonged in Syria, and was principally active in Asia Minor (GK, i. 729, 759) ; Justin (GK, i. 576; Mayor, lxi.), who became a Christian in Ephesus and wrote in Rome. It is possible, too, that the echoes of James found in the old sermon known as Clem. 2 Cor. are not all to be accounted for by the large dependence of the preacher on Clem. 1 Cor. and on Hermas, but are derived from an independent acquaintance with James. Clem. 2 Cor. iii. 4–iv. 3 is quite in James' spirit. Further, cf. Clem. 2 Cor. xv. 1, xvi. 4, and ii. 5–7 with Jas. v. 19 f. In the case of xvi. 4, however, 1 Pet. iv. 8 and Clem. 1 Cor. xlix. 5 (see above, n. 4) come still closer. Cf. also Clem. 2 Cor. xx. 3 with Jas. v. 7. Mayor, liv.–lvi., gives a long list of correspondences between Test. XII Patr. and James. Nothing is absolutely

conclusive, and until greater certainty is attained with regard to the time and place of this book in its present form, more definite testimony, even, would be of little value. In the pseudo-Clementine literature, which esteems the bishop James so highly (above, pp. 103, 108 f. n. 5), we look for more points of contact with James than we find. Kern, 56–60, and Schwegler, i. 413, 424, have decidedly exaggerated the kinship of ideas which they maintain. Even Feine, too (81 f.), adduces parallels, which on closer examination show only the radical difference between James' thinking and this Ebionitic tendency (see also § 8, n. 4). The chief points deserving consideration would perhaps be these : the modification of Matt. v. 37 in conformity with Jas. v. 12 in Clem. *Hom.* iii. 55, xix. 2—especially iii. 55 (cf. xvi. 13), the mention of those who say ὅτι ὁ θεὸς πειράζει, and appeal to the Bible for support, with which cf. Jas. i. 13. Further, in *Hom.* v. 5 it is said of the demons, that they, when exorcised by the names of the higher angels, φρίττοντες εἴκουσιν ; cf. Jas. ii. 19 and p. 121, n. 10. Reminders of Jas. i. 18 may perhaps be found in *Hom.* ii. 52 ; iii. 17, of Adam, ὁ ὑπὸ τοῦ θεοῦ κειρῶν κυοφορηθείς.

§ 8. DIVERGENT VIEWS.

Of those who accept this as the letter of James the Just, there are always some who hold that he wrote it toward the end of his life, somewhere about the time of Paul's imprisonment in Rome (n. 1). But the chief ground on which this assumption rests, namely, James' supposed polemic against Paul, or against an abuse of Pauline doctrine, is itself an untenable hypothesis (above, p. 125 f.); while, if it be held that the letter was addressed to the entire Church at a time when the Church was still almost entirely Jewish (above, p. 92), it is absolutely necessary to give up the hypothesis with the dating of the Epistle that it involves. Even granting that it is possible exegetically to take Jas. i. 1 as an address to Jewish Christians outside of Palestine, there is no reasonable explanation of the entire absence of reference in the letter to the relation which in the year 60 many, in fact most, of these Jewish Christians sustained to their more numerous Gentile Christian neighbours and to their Gentile surroundings. Equally inexplicable is the letter's entire silence about the significance of the Mosaic law, a question which, if the testimony of the times can be trusted, was still agitating the minds of all affected by it

(n. 2). That all these great questions should be passed over in a letter written in the year 60, particularly in a letter in which the fulfilling of the law, and of the entire law, is repeatedly spoken of, and the proposition polemically maintained that men are justified by works and not by faith alone, in which, moreover, there is shown a grasp of the readers' practical situation, is historically impossible, to say nothing of the cowardice it would evidence on James' part to ignore so completely the well-known author of the principles which he combats. In fact, it is impossible to explain how such Pauline watchwords and interpretations of particular passages of Scripture (Gen. xv. 6) could come to exert such a dangerous influence among James' immediate associates, among men who were zealous for the law (Acts xxi. 20 ; Gal. ii. 12), and in circles which mistrusted Paul, and sought everywhere to arouse the same mistrust in others. If, on the other hand, contrary to his agreement with Paul (Gal. ii. 9), James presumed to warn Gentile Christian Churches quite outside his own acknowledged sphere of influence against misunderstanding or abuse of Pauline formulæ, he must at least have done so directly by a fundamental setting forth of the true doctrine, and not by a few incidental, furtive hints.

Such a halting, weak, and cowardly polemic would be more comprehensible if it had come from someone who, unwilling in his own name to vouch for his convictions, preferred to assume deceptively the mask of James, long since dead. For this reason the majority of those who hold James to be the product of the post-Pauline development of the Church, admit frankly that it is pseudepigraphic. The earlier Tübingen school dated the letter about 150. They explained it as growing out of opposition to Paul's doctrine of justification, leading it to place a construction upon this doctrine as injurious to practical Christianity, and to discover in it a toned-down Jewish

Christianity, whose tendency was to become more catholic (n. 3). But a Jewish Christianity of this sort is a phenomenon, the reality of which cannot be proved historically; it is wholly imaginary, constructed from writings declared to be pseudonomous without any careful investigation of their historical character. The real Jewish Christianity of the post-apostolic age, the Jewish Christianity which, according to the testimony alike of Ignatius, Barnabas, and Justin, and of the Ebionitic literature, concerned itself about Paul and the general progress of the Church, never ceased to insist that Gentiles should observe the Jewish law, with allowances, to be sure, but always this particular law, and the Jewish manner of life determined by it. Nor did this Jewish Christianity ever cease to hate and to persecute Paul on the ground of his hostility to Jewish institutions, and on the ground that he taught men to disregard the law, at the same time ignoring his doctrine of justification, which was looked upon as a harmless theory. These objections hold also against the theory of Weizsäcker, who dates the letter after the death of James, assigning it to the time when the Church was leaving Jerusalem. He regards it as a product of Palestinian Jewish Christianity at the time when this had begun to develop in the direction of Ebionitism; Jewish Christianity, "shut up against Gentile Christians," "with no course open but that of resignation," takes up Paul's teaching, adopts very essential ideas from it, and at the same time subjects its principal doctrine to "a mild, almost conciliatory criticism," but nevertheless rejects it most decisively (n. 4). According to Pfleiderer (865–880), James has very close affinities with the *Shepherd of Hermas*, both being products of the "practical catholicism" of the post-Hadrianic age; it combats the intellectualism of the Gnostics or pneumatics (Jas. iii. 5), the antinomianism of Marcion (iv. 11), and the tendency to worldliness on the part of the more well-to-do Christians. In view of the situation in the Roman Church, the condition of which he had primarily in view, but in view also of the general situation in the Church at large, to which the letter was addressed, the author condemns Paul himself with those who had fallen into all sorts of errors, ostensibly because of the emphasis they put upon the idea of faith and upon Paul's doctrine of justification (above, p. 125 f.). While Pfleiderer very quietly passes over all those facts, which, as we saw, point to the Church of Palestine and the adjoining regions as the home of author and readers, von Soden (*HK*, iii. 2. 160 ff.) contends there are things in the letter which indicate the Jewish origin of author or readers.

There is thus great diversity of opinion as to the conditions actually presupposed by the letter; but all who believe that it could not have been written by the distinguished James of Jerusalem are very generally agreed that it was meant to pass as his work. The perfectly artless way, however, in which the author introduces himself is very much against this assumption that the letter is a literary fiction. A later writer, passing himself off for James the Just, if he were like other writers of this kind whose work is preserved in literature, would certainly have called himself the brother of the Lord, or the head of the Jerusalem Church, or have indicated in some way that he was the great contemporary of the apostles. He would have been all the more likely to do so, because there was more than one James of distinction in the early Church (n. 5). Such a writer would never have begun his letter with an address so simple and so nearly like those used in secular literature, when he had before him apostolic writings of earlier date in which was a fixed model for the sort of greeting which might be appropriately used by an apostle or by one of apostolic rank. In keeping also with the simple dignity of its beginning is the entire literary character of the letter, the peculiarity of its style, and the clear impression which it gives of the character of the writer. In the literature of the early Church, admitted to be pseudepigraphic, there is nothing that can be even remotely compared with James. And in cases where opinion is divided as to whether a writing is spurious or genuine, the characteristics mentioned always argue strongly in favour of genuineness. A class of pseudo-writers possessing originality and genius, and able to write in a dignified, crisp, and pithy style, has never existed. Nor, as a rule—certainly not in the literature of the early Church—are these pseudo-writings without some discernible purpose, which explains why a particular rôle is assumed. If, for the purpose of teaching or rebuking his contemporaries, someone found it advantageous to pass himself off as the distinguished James, then the end which he had in view must have been such that the personality of James, as the recollection was retained in the tradition, would have lent especial weight to what he said. But the contents of the Epistle are absolutely against this presupposition. It does not bring out a single one of those characteristics by which James is distinguished in history and legend ; there is nothing to suggest the brother of the Lord, the first bishop of Jerusalem, the Israelite clinging with tenacious love to his people and to the temple, the strict observer of the law who was in high favour with the Judaistic party, and the ascetic, severe beyond what the law required of him. All that does appear is the strong personality of an earnest Christian who *might* have had these peculiarities. Moreover, ancient pseudepigraphic writings are never free from tell-tale anachronisms, things which can be avoided only through the aid of archæological science, which at that time was unknown. No anachronisms have been discovered in James (n. 6). The thing which strikes one as peculiar about the Epistle is not the evidence of its late date, but the absence of clear indication that the author and readers had drunk of the new wine of the gospel at all.

This impression is at the basis of the hypothesis recently advanced by Spitta, which he thinks solves all the difficulties. According to Spitta's theory, James is a purely Jewish writing, dating from either the first century after or the first century before Christ, and given the superficial appearance of a Christian writing simply by the later addition of the phrases καὶ κυρίου Ἰησοῦ Χριστοῦ (i. 1) and ἡμῶν Ἰησοῦ Χριστοῦ (ii. 1, n. 7). This letter has come down to us only through Christian channels, and in Christian circles has always passed as the work of a distinguished Christian of the apostolic age. Moreover, according to the text of the letter as we have it, the author calls himself a servant of the Lord Jesus Christ, indicating also that a belief in the same Lord Jesus or in His glorification is an essential part of his readers' faith. For these reasons it has always been regarded as a product of Christian thought. If Spitta is right, it simply shows how little real progress the art of criticism has made in spite of its long history; but when he (p. 8) calls the opinion which heretofore has prevailed a *hypothesis built upon rotten foundations*, it only goes to show how far he himself is from standing upon the foundation of a criticism that is sound and just. Anyone trying to judge from the point of view of sound criticism can readily see that this new hypothesis, supported as it is by exegesis for which the word bold is mild, has not been worked out by its author into a clear, historically grounded view. If it were, how possibly could Spitta compare the work of this supposed Christian interpolator with the interpolations and verbal changes in Jewish writings known to have been introduced by Christian hands (p. 56)! Books like the Jewish *Sibyllines*, the *Testaments of the Twelve Patriarchs*, the *Ascension of Isaiah*, and many others which have been handled in this way, were originally written with a view to easily deceiving the credulous.   It was the honourable names of remote antiquity and of Israel's past that made these works interesting, and made them seem credible, first to Jews and then to Christians; and it was this that brought about their adaptation to the changed conditions and the different religious point of view of the Christian reader.   No attempt was made to give them the appearance of Christian writings, but the design was, rather to make these supposed representatives of bygone ages and of different stages of religious development prophets of Christian truth.   Or, take the case of a work by an author of distinguished name, such as the author of the Jewish James is supposed to have been.   The person who changed Josephus' *Antiquities* so as to make it a witness for Christ, apparently inserting also the remark about the death of James, the brother of Jesus, was not foolhardy enough to attempt the making of the Jew Josephus over into a Christian.   On the contrary, everything depended upon Josephus' remaining a Jewish historian of the time of Jesus, whom by his insertion the interpolator designs to make an impartial witness of the wonderful greatness of Jesus.   The interpolator was careful to make Josephus retain his historical Jewish character.   This manifest intention on his part is not affected in the least by the fact that he did not understand that character better, and that he was not able permanently to deceive persons trained in methods of historical criticism.   The Latin writer who slipped the name *Jesus* into the place of the original *Christ* in the Jewish apocalypse known as the Fourth Book of Ezra (vii. 28), had no idea of making this alleged Ezra a disciple of Jesus in spite of the distinguished name which he bore, and in spite of the chronology; he simply meant to make a work which passed for that of the original Ezra still more beautiful and still more edifying to Christian readers, by putting into Ezra's mouth an unmistakable prophecy concerning the Jesus whom the Christians accepted as Messiah. The procedure of the Christian interpolator of James would, however, have been just the reverse. For by the insertion of seven words he is assumed to have deceived the Christian world in all ages, learned as well as unlearned, concerning the religious character of James. Taking the work of a Jew named James, a person entirely undistinguished in history, and inserting these seven words, but leaving it otherwise unchanged, the interpolator leads every unsuspecting reader to say at once, as a matter of course, "This was written by a Christian." If the writing seemed to him to be good reading for Christians, as it was, why did he treat it in a manner different from the way in which the *Proverbs of Jesus Sirach* or the *Wisdom of Solomon* were treated in the early Church? If he felt it necessary to subject it to a Christian revision, why did he content himself with adding to it two Christian confessions which only serve to make its pre-Christian or un-Christian character all the more glaring? The work of this supposed interpolator is as inconceivable as it is unparalleled. Indeed, the character of the entire hypothesis may be judged from the fact that its author does not feel under any necessity whatever to tell us the motives for the interpolation, nor to indicate the conditions under which it was made.

If Paul was acquainted with James when he wrote Romans in Corinth at the beginning of the year 58, and if Peter was familiar with the work when he wrote from Rome to Christians in Asia Minor in 63 or 64, at that time the letter must have been already widely circulated in the Church. But this makes it extremely improbable that a Christian interpolation made subsequently should have had the general acceptance in the Church which, from all we know of the history of James in the Church, must have been accorded it. Moreover, the manner in which Paul refers to James shows that it was known by him and by the Roman Christians of that time to be the work of a distinguished Christian teacher (above, p. 126 f.). But the assumption that this Christian interpolation was made as early as 50–60, during the lifetime of James of Jerusalem, and the supposition that even Paul was deceived by it, hardly requires refutation. Furthermore, the impression which we get of the Jewish writing and of its author after these seven words are stricken out, is in the highest degree fantastical. Without any apparent authority for doing so, a Jew addresses the entire Jewish nation, or, as Spitta understands the "address," all the Jews in the dispersion, in the superior tones of fatherly advice and of prophetic condemnation. Possibly before the destruction of the temple this might have been done by a high priest in Jerusalem, or, after the year 70, by the recognised head of one of the schools, as Gamaliel the younger. Earlier than this, such a letter might have been sent in the name of the whole body of Jews in Palestine, represented by the Sanhedrin, through the autocratic head of this body (n. 8). But for a Jew named James, with no other credentials than the claim to be the servant of God, to have written such a letter, would have been to expose himself to ridicule. Generally, persons not in any recognised position of authority who felt called upon to preach to their fellow-countrymen in this way, preferred to suppress their own names entirely, and to write in the name of Solomon, or Enoch, or Ezra, or Baruch, or even of the Sibyl or Hystaspes. Moreover, it is an error to suppose that a letter with *these contents* could have been addressed by a Jew to his countrymen. To begin with, there were no twelve tribes in the dispersion, so that the words ταῖς ἐν τῇ διασπορᾷ (i. 1) must also be a Christian interpolation (above, pp. 74 f., 79). The idea of divine birth through the word of truth, *i.e.* through the soul-saving word of divine revelation read

and preached in religious services (i. 18–21, n. 7), made
its first appearance upon Christian soil. So also did the
conception of a moral law, which, as distinguished from
the imperfect law that had been in force heretofore, is
perfect; and in contrast to a law which compels and
enslaves, is a law of liberty; which, finally, in view
especially of its principal commandment—love for one's
neighbour, is called a law for kings (i. 25, ii. 8, 12; above,
p. 115 f.). Although it is true that quite independently
of Christianity the Jews esteemed faith very highly, the
thought that one may be rich in such faith even in this
world, and an heir through faith of the promised kingdom
of God, is a Christian thought (ii. 5). It needs also to
be proved that, before Jesus' time (Matt. v. 12), and independently of Him, a Jew could have exhorted his readers
not only to endure suffering and temptation with patience
and hope, but to discover in them as well a source of pure
and proud rejoicing (Jas. i. 2, 9). But, what is most
significant, the folly combated in Jas. ii. 14–26 of supposing that faith of itself, without being manifested or
proved by works, can save, is a possibility only as the
preaching of Jesus is presupposed; while the careful proof
of the proposition that a man is justified in consequence
of works and not of faith alone, by which this folly is
combated, would have been superfluous for Jewish
readers. So, then, the entire result of this bold attempt
to interpret James as the product of Judaism before it
came into contact with the gospel, is simply to re-emphas-
ize the thought how deeply this first piece of Christian
literature is rooted in the soil out of which it sprang
originally, namely, the Jewish Christian Church of Palestine. Its genuinely Israelitish character, and the absence
from it of that ecclesiastical language with which we are so
familiar, and which was a development out of the Pauline
gospel, are the strongest possible proofs of the correctness
of the interpretation which led us to assign the letter to

a time prior to the apostolic council, and of the truthfulness of the tradition which ascribes its composition to James of Jerusalem.

It was at the suggestion of this same James that the apostles and elders of the mother Church, gathered in Jerusalem in the winter of 51–52, sent the communication preserved in Acts xv. 23–29 to the Gentile Christians in and about Antioch. It is of interest to note that the discourse of James, preserved in this passage, which resulted in the communication to the Churches, shows very striking resemblances to the letter which James had written in his own name only a few years—perhaps only a single year—before (above, p. 119, n. 7). Regarding the genuineness of this document, it will be necessary to inquire in connection with the question about the sources of Acts. All the other writings originating in the Palestinian Church and meant for this Church belong to a date considerably later, and take for granted the independent development of the Gentile Christian Church concerning which we get our information from the letters of the great apostle to the Gentiles (n. 9).

1. (P. 136.) For example, Kern, *Kommentar*, 65 ff., 82 ff.; Wiesinger, 36 ff.; Feine, 57 ff., 89 f. The last named, without entering on a discussion of the idea and wording of the salutation, claims that the Epistle was originally a discourse addressed by James to "the Palestinian Church" (the local Church of Jerusalem, more properly), a homily which he afterwards allowed to circulate in the form of a letter among "the believing Jews of the dispersion," or also among the mixed congregations, in Syria probably, composed of both Gentile and Jewish Christians (95, 97, 99). The local colour would thus be explained by the original destination of the document, and the alleged inappropriateness of its "address" by its subsequent use. But how shall we explain the thoughtless indolence which led James to set down his opinions in a form quite unsuited to the wider audience, or, if the homily was already in writing, to have it copied mechanically without adding a few words at least to indicate to the new readers that he was submitting to their consideration a discourse originally intended for quite different people? Other letters, indeed, were soon enough current beyond the circle to which they were first addressed, without the addition of a new heading (cf. Col. iv. 16 ; Polyc. *ad Phil.* xiii. 2). But in this case we are asked to suppose that James confined his efforts in a new edition to the preparation of an address which, in its general terms, as Feine himself holds (97), did not correspond at all to

the actual destination of the Epistle now in view. Compared with this it would be almost preferable to accept Harnack's bold hypothesis (*TU*, ii. 2. 106–109), that in this, as in other general Epistles, the salutation is a false heading attached later, because the authority of the old writing could be maintained only by connecting it with the name of an apostle. Apart from the absence of positive proof of such a state of affairs, this conjecture must be set aside, first, because the celebrated James was not considered an apostle in the second century or for some time thereafter. In the second place, whoever sought to preserve or heighten the dignity of the Epistle by attaching the false heading, would either have pointed to the well-known James by describing him as the brother of the Lord, or bishop of Jerusalem, or the like, or else have assigned the authorship to one of the two apostles of that name, in which case he would have had to designate him as such. In the third place, the connection between χαίρειν, Jas. i. 1, and πᾶσαν χαράν, i. 2 (see p. 117, n. 3 above), shows that both greeting and text are from the same hand; cf. Spitta, *Der zweite Brief d. Petrus*, 26–30, 475. The attempt to evade this difficulty by declaring (Harnack, 108) that in this instance only the words Ἰάκωβος . . . δοῦλος are a later insertion, and what follows is genuine, cannot be justified by the bold assertion that a greeting which does not mention the writer's name is just as complete as the opening of the *Epistle of Barnabas* or the *Didache*, which have no greeting at all. Harnack has recently (*Chron.* 485–491) declared the entire greeting to be a label attached towards the close of the second century, and the whole letter a compilation, prepared probably before 150, from various discourses of an unknown but "vigorous" teacher.

2. (P. 137.) From the period following the apostolic council and the heated controversy in Galatia, indications of the continued friction between Jewish and Gentile Christianity in many various forms are to be found in such passages as 1 Cor. xvi. 22 (i. 12, iii. 16–23, ix. 1 f., xv. 11 ; cf. § 18) ; 2 Cor. ii. 17–iv. 6, v. 11–16, xi. 1–xii. 13 ; Rom. ii. 11–iii. 8, iii. 29–viii. 17, xiv. 1–xv. 13, xv. 25–33, xvi. 4 ; Col. ii. 6–iii. 11, iv. 10 f. ; Phil. i. 14–18, iii. 2 ff. ; 1 Tim. i. 3–11 ; Tit. i. 10, 14, iii. 9.—Acts xxi. 18–26.—Ign. *Magn.* viii–x ; *Philad.* vi–ix ; *Smyrn.* i (cf. the writer's *Ignatius v. Ant.* 359 ff.) ; Barn. iii. 6, iv. 6, ix.–x. 15 ; Just. *Dial.* xlvi–xlviii (*GK*, ii. 671) ; the Anabathmoi of James, Epiph. *Hær.* xxx. 16 = Clem. *Recogn.* i. 55–71, and the whole pseudo-Clementine literature.

3. (P. 138.) Baur, *Paulus*,[2] ii. 322–340 (all thought of genuineness already set aside on account of the writer's familiarity with the Greek language and modes of thought, 335) ; *Christentum der drei ersten Jahrh.* 122 f. (somewhat earlier than the Pastoral Epistles). Schwegler, i. 418 : "In any case it was not written earlier than the Clementine homilies " [which cannot be shown to have existed before the third century]. Schwegler's remark (i. 437), that the view that James was not opposing Paul directly, but a misconception of the Pauline doctrine, was "in itself a most absurd hypothesis," did not deter Baur from adopting that view in his presentation of the subject.

4. (P. 138.) A more definite impression than that outlined above cannot be gained from Weizsäcker's shifting and altogether inconclusive reasonings (*Apost. Zeitalter*, 364–369, 671). When we read that Jas. iii. 6 shows the writer's acquaintance with Greek literature, and that iii. 1 ff. warns "against

all sorts of wisdom-teaching" (366), Hilgenfeld's treatment of the passage (*Einl.* 535 f., 539, n. 2, see p. 121 f. above) seems to be regarded as an adequate exegetical foundation. Yet Weizsäcker goes even beyond Hilgenfeld, in his claim (368) that not merely false wisdom is combated in Jas. iii. 1–13, but all striving after wisdom of any sort. It would be folly to argue against such wisdom as this, and useless to point to Jas. i. 5, iii. 17. It is alleged further (367), that James' attitude toward rich and poor is Ebionitic, and presupposes that Ebionite modification of the first part of the Sermon on the Mount which, we are told, appears in Luke. Now the cardinal principle of Ebionism is (Clem. *Hom.* xv. 9) πᾶσι τὰ κτήματα ἁμαρτήματα, whereas James follows Jesus (Matt. xiii. 22) in considering the cares of poverty no less a temptation than the deceitfulness of riches, and urges the wealthy Christian not to dispose of his goods, but to make his boast of lowliness (i. 2–11, see p. 86). In Jesus' usage the conception of πτωχοί is derived, as we know, from Isa. lxi. 1 ; cf. Luke iv. 18, vii. 22 ; Matt. xi. 5 ; also Matt. v. 3 ; Luke vi. 20, and accordingly, even without the explanatory τῷ πνεύματι, Matt. v. 3, it corresponds to the Hebrew עֲנָיִים, cf. *ZKom. Matt.*[2] 177 ff. Those who cannot see this should at least take account of the fact that the Ebionites saw fit to substitute πένητες, a word of quite different signification, for the scriptural πτωχοί, and then again, afterward, were obliged to guard by arbitrary additions against too gross a misconception (Clem. *Hom.* xv. 10, ὁ διδάσκαλος ἡμῶν πιστοὺς πένητας ἐμακάρισεν). Again, we are told (366) that the Epistle has no "dedication,"—in spite of the opening greeting,—because "the address mentions only an ideal body like the one hundred and forty and four thousand of Rev."! In this way the "address," which may not be counted a "dedication," is left without any explanation whatever; and, further, Weizsäcker overlooks the fundamental difference, that James addresses the twelve tribes of his people as his brethren, and discusses with no little thoroughness their social, moral, and religious condition, with which, of course, Rev. vii. 1–8 has nothing to do. Neither Weizsäcker nor Hilgenfeld, whose view is that the letter was written by an Eastern Jewish Christian in the reign of Domitian (540 f.), explains why the "facile" use of Greek (which, in their judgment, makes the composition of the letter by James impossible) should be more conceivable in the case of a Jewish Christian of Palestine in the episcopate of Simeon than it would be some twenty to forty years earlier, *circa* 45–50 A.D.

5. (P. 139.) We have a spurious letter of James (translated from the Armenian by Vetter, *LR*, 1896, S. 259), which begins, "James, bishop of Jerusalem, to Quadratus," etc. ; cf. also Clement, ed. Lagarde, 3, Πέτρος Ἰακώβῳ τῷ κυρίῳ καὶ ἐπισκόπῳ τῆς ἁγίας ἐκκλησίας κτλ. ; 6, Κλήμης Ἰακώβῳ τῷ κυρίῳ καὶ ἐπισκόπων ἐπισκόπῳ, διέποντι δὲ τὴν Ἱερουσαλήμ ἁγίαν Ἑβραίων ἐκκλησίαν κτλ., and the other recension (*Patr. Ap.*, ed. Cotelerius-Clericus, 1724, i. 617), "Clemens Jacobo, fratri Domini et episcopo episcoporum," etc. Cf. also the spurious letters of Paul, *GK*, ii. 584, 600, and the letter of John in the writer's *Acta Jo.* lxiii. 2. On the curious self-concealment of the author of *Protevang. Jac.* see *GK*, ii. 775.

6. (P. 140.) It is hardly necessary to say anything about the comfortably arranged meeting-places (ii. 2) and the Church organisation (v. 14) which, we are sometimes told, shows an advanced stage of development ; see Hofmann's

brief and excellent remarks, vii. 3. 157 f. In particular, the confidence with which healing efficacy is attributed to prayer, without leaving a place for the physician, as in the parallel passage Sir. xxxviii. 9–15, points to high antiquity. As to the use of oil, above, p. 122, n. 11. The opinion repeatedly expressed that such distressing conditions as James censures might indeed appear in Christian communities thirty, sixty, or one hundred, but not twenty years after Jesus' death, cannot be historically substantiated. We have no right to think of the Jewish Christians, among whom even before 35 there were such murmurings as are reported in Acts vi. 1, and such occurrences as that described in Acts v. 1–11, as above all need of serious reproof. Certainly not, when perhaps only a few months after the composition of this letter, men among them were asserting themselves to whom Paul denied all right to be in the Church (Gal. ii. 4), and whom James disowned as unwarranted disturbers (Acts xv. 19, 24). If the errors which James rebukes are thoroughly Jewish (p. 90 f.), then, as uneradicated vestiges of pre-Christian thinking, they are most comprehensible at an early period. Paul found more practical heathenism to correct in the newly founded Church at Corinth than the leaders of the post-apostolic time found in their Churches. The historical picture of the early Churches, whether of Jewish or of Gentile origin, becomes unintelligible only when the rebukes administered to individuals and for individual misdeeds are generalised, and we assume in preachers of such deep moral earnestness as James or Paul, Isaiah or Jesus, the equanimity of an ethical statistician.

7. (P. 141.) Spitta supports his hypothesis in a commentary on James (14–155), the value of which lies in its citation of parallels from Jewish, especially Jewish-Greek, literature, not in its interpretation of the text. The latter can be illustrated here in a few examples only, but in passages which are fundamental to the conception of the book as a Jewish product. With regard to the "address," see above, pp. 73, 80, n. 8. Spitta understands i. 18 not of the new birth of the Christian, but of the creation of mankind (45). But that the creative word of God should be referred to as "a word of *truth*" instead of being characterised in accordance with the *power* which is shown in creation (cf. Heb. i. 3; Wis. xviii. 15; Clem. 1 *Cor.* xxvii. 4; Herm. *Vis.* i. 3. 4), is hardly credible in itself, and is contrary to the usage both of the Old Testament, where the "word of truth" signifies the revelation given to Israel (Ps. cxix. 43, cf. vv. 30, 86, 138, 142, 160), and of the New (Eph. i. 13; 2 Tim. ii. 15; John xvii. 17; cf. Clem. *Hom. Epist. Petri*, ii.). The impossibility of this interpretation appears from the context, since the word spoken of in i. 18 must be identical, as Spitta himself recognises (48, 50), with that which is read and heard in public worship, i. 19–25. But the assertion that James tacitly identified this soul-saving word with the word of creation, is one which the exegete should not venture, unless the text somehow indicated this mistaken conception; and even then the choice of phrase in i. 18 would be as unmeaning as it is unparalleled. In order to make it possible to refer ii. 14–26 to controversies within Judaism, and to prepare for that conception of πίστις as Jewish orthodoxy, which in commenting on ii. 14 (72) is put forward as a matter of course, we are asked to understand the word in the same sense in i. 6, where it plainly denotes the spiritual attitude of the worshipper (cf. v. 15), against

whose lack of childlike trust in God even i. 5 is directed. For proof of the incredible we are pointed to i. 7, according to which the doubter also expects to receive something from God,—as if one who was certain that he should obtain nothing from God by prayer could be called a doubting petitioner, or would still pray at all. The very fact that he wavers between fear and hope, between desire and distrust, makes him a διακρινόμενος. With regard to ii. 14–26, exegetical agreement is practically out of the question, as Spitta (79) without sufficient reason assumes a lacuna at an important point (see p. 98 above). But he has not succeeded in finding in Jewish literature a single example of the view opposed by James, that faith saves of itself apart from works. Even in the passages from 4 Esdr. which he cites (75), which indeed have sometimes been taken as showing traces of contact with Christian thought, there is nothing in the least similar —not so much as an antithesis between works and faith. While Spitta (54) explains τέλειος as an attribute of the law, i. 25, in contrast with the laws of heathen nations, he overlooks the contrast much more sharply emphasised by the very wording of the passage, which calls this law the law of freedom, and thinks he has accounted for this Christian idea as Jewish by referring to the well-known Stoic phrases about the wise and virtuous which are found in Philo, and to the saying of a certain rabbi Joshua of the third century after Christ in the Appendix to the Pirke Aboth vi. 2 : "No one is free but him who devotes himself to the study of the *Thorah.*" So also does he fail to comprehend the use of the same term in ii. 12 ; for the idea that the law is there spoken of as a law of liberty because it puts forward no impossible requirements, and in order to represent the judgment as reasonable or lenient (70), is plainly at variance with the phraseology of ii. 13 (ἡ γὰρ κρίσις ἀνέλεος κτλ., not ἡ δέ, or, better, ἀλλά). Then, too, aside from the possibility of explaining the contents of James from the Jewish standpoint which he claims to have established in his commentary, Spitta holds that the seven words which mark the writer as a Christian may be recognised as disturbing interpolations. Though Christians are often enough referred to in the N.T. now as servants of God (1 Pet. ii. 16 ; Tit. i. 1 ; Rev. xix. 2) and now as servants of Christ (Gal. i. 10 ; 1 Cor. vii. 22 ; Rom. i. 1 ; Phil. i. 1 ; Rev. i. 1, ii. 20), the combination of the two terms in Jas. i. 1, being a solitary instance, is said to be suspicious. But if Paul and the author of Revelation used the two conceptions interchangeably, why might not James combine them, just as in 2 Pet. i. 1 we find the two titles servant and apostle of Christ united ? These latter Paul commonly uses by turns (Gal. i. 1, 1 Cor. i. 1 on the one hand, Phil. i. 1, Tit. i. 1 on the other), in combination but once (Rom. i. 1), and even then in a form unlike that of 2 Peter. We see from 1 Cor. viii. 6 and Eph. iv. 5 f. how little fear the early Christians had that they might appear either to be serving two masters or obliged to choose between two, God and Christ. In faith, in worship, and in service, God and Christ for them were one. This finds striking grammatical illustration in 1 Thess. iii. 11 ; Rev. xxii. 3 ; and for the same reason ὁ κύριος is not infrequently a title which stands above the distinction between God and Christ, 1 Thess. iii. 12 ; Rom. x. 9–15. Until examples are brought forward, we cannot believe that a Jew without office or honours would have introduced himself to his readers as a "servant of God"; and no one will find passages like Ezra v. 11, or the use of the formula " thy servant" in prayer, Ps. xix. 12, Luke ii. 29, at all comparable. In Spitta's opinion (4 f., cf. Vorrede, iv), the difficulty which ii. 1 has presented to expositors arises from the fact that the original text τὴν πίστιν τοῦ κυρίου τῆς δόξης (to be understood of God) has been obscured by the interpolation of ἡμῶν Ἰησοῦ Χριστοῦ (in the sense of 1 Cor. ii. 8). But how are we to conceive that an interpolator, whose important object was to make a Christian book out of a Jewish writing, which, according to Spitta, had already been read and highly esteemed by Paul and Peter, should have used no other means to that end than the introduction at one point of four words which make the passage "unique" in early Christian literature, and at the other point of three words which constitute a *crux interpretum*, when it would have been child's play to avoid both? Here, too, the difficulty of the text is an indication of its originality. Moreover, we cannot see why the words should not be translated, as by the Peshito, Grotius, and Hofmann, "the faith in the glory of our Lord Jesus Christ." For the order of words, cf. Jas. iii. 3 (τῶν ἵππων . . . στόματα) ; Acts iv. 33 (according to B and Chrysost., ἀπεδίδουν τὸ μαρτύριον οἱ ἀπόστολοι τοῦ κυρίου Ἰησοῦ [Χριστοῦ] τῆς ἀναστάσεως) ; and for πίστις τῆς δόξης, cf. εὐαγγέλιον τῆς δόξης, 2 Cor. iv. 4 ; 1 Tim. i. 11 ; ἐλπὶς τῆς δόξης, Col. i. 27.

8. (P. 144.) In addition to the writings of Gamaliel, which have been mentioned several times (p. 33, n. 18), cf. 2 Macc. i. 1 and 10 ; also a communication which the Jews of Jerusalem at the time of Simon ben Shetach and king Alexander Jannai (104–78 B.C.) addressed to the Jewish community of Alexandria in order to bring about the return of Judah ben Tabai (reputed to be the Nasi of that period) who had fled thither, Jer. Chagigah, 77d ; Sanhedrin, 23c ; and in the same connection Joël Müller, *Briefe u. Responsen in der vorgenäischen jüdischen Literatur*, Berlin, 1886, S. 7, 21— a book in general well worth reading. See above also, p. 106, n. 1.

9. (P. 146.) The letters of recommendation, by means of which the Petrine party introduced themselves in Corinth (2 Cor. iii. 1), would be properly considered, if they were extant, among the literary products of Jewish Christianity. Of the documents which have been preserved, 2 Pet., Jude, and Matt. belong here, but probably not Heb.

III.

THE THREE OLDEST EPISTLES OF PAUL.

§ 9. PRELIMINARY CRITICAL REMARKS.

It is impossible to investigate the letters commonly attributed to Paul without discussing a great many different opinions. It seems best, therefore, in order to avoid repetition, to preface the investigation proper by a general survey of the history of the various attempts which have been made to criticise the Pauline letters (n. 1).

As early as the year 150, Marcion (*GK*, i. 585–718, ii. 409–529), who held that Paul was the only one of those called apostles who really preached an uncorrupted gospel, found the collection of Pauline letters in use by the Church at that time to be in need of a thoroughgoing criticism. There is no hint, however, that Marcion's view regarding the origin of any one of these letters differed from that of the Church, or that he regarded any one of them as wrongly attributed to Paul, or as an intentional forgery in Paul's name. Besides the nine letters addressed to Churches, he included in his *Apostolicon*, or collection of Pauline letters, designed for use in the independent Church which he organised, the Epistle to Philemon. The Epistles to Timothy and to Titus were not in this collection. Whether Marcion was familiar with them, and for some reason rejected them, is a disputed question. But we do know, from the form which he gave the ten letters that he did accept, as well as from the statements of his opponents, that he held the form of the Pauline letters current in the Church at that time and later to be the result of a systematic interpolation, Jewish in spirit, and made after the Church had been degenerated by Jewish influences. He undertook to restore the genuine text by cutting out a number of longer sections and shorter paragraphs, by the addition of a few sentences and words, most of which were taken from other passages of Paul's letters, and by slightly emending the text in numerous places. Marcion was in possession neither of the sources nor of the historical information necessary for such a critical operation ; nor did he profess to be. The only criterion which he used, and which sufficed for his Church several centuries afterwards, was his preconception of what was genuinely Christian and so genuinely Pauline.

It is readily seen how it was easier for the Church to refute Marcion's criticism of the Pauline documents, lacking as it did all historical basis, than it was for it to get rid of the fundamental idea upon which this criticism was based, namely, the irreconcilable contradiction between Christianity and Judaism,—an idea which has since come to the front more than once in a variety of forms. What critical investigations of Paul's letters were made by the early Church was not the result of historical or linguistic inquiry into the letters themselves, but simply of the fact that the differences in tradition and opinion which had long existed in different parts of the Church entered gradually into the consciousness of the Church at large. Thus from the third century we have such a process taking place with reference to the Epistle to the Hebrews, which was regarded as Pauline and canonical in some sections, but not by any means in all. So also in the fourth century a similar process took place with reference to Philemon, which was not included in the collection of Pauline letters used by the Syrian Church (*GK*, ii. 997–1006). Whether or not the appearance of spurious

Pauline letters, two of which are mentioned in the Muratori Canon, particularly whether the acceptance and subsequent rejection of an apocryphal Third Epistle to the Corinthians in the Syrian Canon, occasioned critical discussion, we do not know. Though in discussions of this kind occasional reference was made to the style and contents of the questionable letters, the discussion of such references belongs rather in the history of the Canon than in a history of the theological investigation of the Pauline letters; still more so the statement of the conclusion with which the entire Church was finally satisfied.

The tradition regarding the Pauline letters, which in its essential points existed even before Marcion's time, which was substantially accepted by him, and which, after some question had been raised with reference to a few points, finally prevailed through the entire Church, remained practically unquestioned up to the beginning of the last century. The question of origin, sources, and authenticity of the Gospels had been heatedly discussed for decades before there was the least question about the genuineness of any of the Pauline Epistles. Doubts expressed by Evanson in his critique of the Gospels in 1792 made little impression (n. 2). When, in 1807, Schleiermacher asserted with great positiveness that 1 Tim. was spurious, serious-minded people asked "whether perhaps the whole was not a mere *lusus ingenii*, a game of wit and ingenuity, just to see how far critical Pyrrhonism could be carried and still retain a semblance of truth" (n. 3). When, however, F. Chr. Baur, a man whom no one could suspect of joking about things scientific, subjected all the extant Pauline letters to criticism in the light of his new and comprehensive theory about the development of Christianity in the apostolic age, concluding that only Gal., 1 and 2 Cor., and Rom. (excepting chaps. xv. and xvi.) were genuine, the whole Pauline question became one of the utmost importance (n. 4). It was a great mistake on the part of those who found that they could not follow Baur in his rejection of Pauline Epistles, or who could not accept his results regarding them all, that they raised no question about the genuineness of the Epistles which Baur did accept, although Baur and his followers never attempted any proof for their positive critical conclusions.   Since no effort was made by critics to set forth the reasons which compelled historical investigators to accept some of Paul's letters as genuine historical documents, or to show the scope of these reasons, we are not surprised when Bruno Bauer declares that all the Pauline Epistles are spurious, written between the years 130 and 170 ; and when a later school of Dutch critics, working independently of Bauer, question and finally deny the genuineness of all the Pauline writings (n. 5).   The position of the critic is not an enviable one, who, by denying the genuineness of all the documents associated with a distinguished name, and the essential trustworthiness of all the early traditions concerning these documents, deprives himself of a fixed and common standard by which he may test what seems doubtful.   What is spurious can be tested only with reference to what is acknowledged to be authentic, and if criticism is to obtain any positive results, it must be based upon historical data acknowledged to be trustworthy. We need not inquire whether it is from this consideration primarily, or because of the irresistible impression that the character of the life portrayed in the Pauline letters is such as could not have been produced second-hand, that criticism of the sort which simply denies everything is not making headway at the present time.

Consequently, at the present time all the more attention is being paid to that type of criticism of which Marcion is still the best example.   When in doubt about any point, the critic satisfies his own mind by assuming an interpolation, and so avoids depriving himself of the necessary basis for the critical process, as he would do if he denied the genuineness of all his traditional sources and facts. Attempts in this direction were made by Herm. Weisse and F. Hitzig in Germany. More recently this method has been pursued chiefly in Holland (n. 6).

Another method followed by many is that suggested first by J. S. Semler. Certain inequalities which are thought to exist between different parts of the same letter, it is assumed, can be explained by supposing that when the separate letters were first copied, or when they were gathered into a collection, either by oversight or intention, parts became dislocated and confused, so that sections were united in a single document which originally did not belong together. Inasmuch as we have not the means at our command for restoring the text of Paul's letters, and the N.T. text generally, so that every sentence and every word is established beyond all doubt, the process of text criticism is largely identical with the process of the higher, literary, and historical criticism.

The more important of the critical attempts made along these various lines we shall have occasion to notice in connection with the investigation of the separate Epistles. Here a few considerations of a more general character may be stated briefly.

1. The early date of all Paul's Epistles, except that of the Epistles to Timothy and Titus, is comprehensively and strongly attested by Marcion's *Apostolicon*. That Marcion, who withdrew from the Roman Church and became the head of a separate organisation, probably in the year 144, did not himself write any one of the Pauline letters in his collection, is clear from the fact that, in the year 180, the Catholic Church accepted all the ten documents in Marcion's *Apostolicon* as Pauline, and used them in their religious services. Now it is simply impossible to suppose that any of these could have been borrowed from this " firstborn son of Satan " by a Church whose bishops and their faithful followers summarily

rejected Marcion's teaching and treatment of the apostolic
writings.   The probability is that Marcion accepted these
ten letters as Pauline from the Church in which he grew
up, and, after making some changes in them, adopted
them in his own Church.   His acceptance of the Pauline
origin of these letters, his criticism of single points in the
tradition regarding them, *e.g.* regarding the traditional
address of the Ephesian letter (§ 28), the belief which led
him to make a new recension of the text, namely, that all
the copies of the Pauline letters extant in his time contained a text which had been corrupted by the Church, all
go to show that in 140–150 there was no suspicion in the
Church of the recent date or sudden appearance of any of
the Pauline letters.   That these Epistles should have been
written during Marcion's lifetime, or after the year 110, is
therefore out of the question.

2. A comparison of Marcion's text of the Pauline letters
with the text used in the Church, shows that Marcion
found a number of readings which, in the course of the
transmission of the text in the Church, have been replaced by other readings.   But, leaving this difference
out of account, it is clear that in plan, general contents
and compass, the Pauline letters which Marcion had before
him were substantially the same as the letters which
have come down to us.   He found chaps. xv. and xvi.
already a part of Rom., and chaps. i.–xiii. of 2 Cor. forming a single letter.   Hence it follows that all important
changes in the order and structure of the letters must
have been made before the year 110.

3. Difference of opinion still exists regarding the date
of a great many early Christian writings, *e.g.*, that of the
letters of Ignatius, the *Epistle of Polycarp*, the *Epistle
of Barnabas*, the *Shepherd of Hermas*, and the *Didache*.
Even a work which is so thoroughly attested, and which
can be so definitely dated as Clement's so-called *First
Epistle to the Corinthians*, is sometimes brought down

to a later period. But, allowing for this uncertainty, we have still a sufficiently large number of Christian writings, admittedly belonging in the period between 90 and 170, from which to form a definite idea as to the thoughts which were uppermost in the mind of the Church during this period, and the spiritual forces which were at work. Perhaps it would be too much to say that this literature shows a general decline from the high standard of apostolic Christianity, especially from the strikingly original teachings of Paul. But so much is clear, that there is nothing in the literature of 90–170 comparable in character to what we find in the letters of Paul accepted by Marcion, or to the ideas which these letters were meant to refute. How little this age was in a position even to understand Paul's thoughts, is quite as evident in the case of Marcion and of the school of Valentinus as in the writings of the Apostolic Fathers and the earlier apologists, such as Aristides and Justin. It is absurd to suppose that a Christian living in the year 100 or 130, with interests so different from those of his age, and so superior to his contemporaries in the compass and depth of his thought, should have given no expression to his ideas except under a false name, and in letters dated back into the past. The Pauline letters must therefore have been written prior to the period of transition between the first and second centuries.

4. Before a denial of the genuineness of this collection of letters, or of separate parts of the same, can command general assent, it must be shown to be made in agreement with the principles derived from a careful study of the literature of the early Christian Church, which is acknowledged to be pseudepigraphic. Here we have, besides the apocryphal letters of Paul already mentioned, some other letters (n. 7), some fragments of the ancient "Preaching of Peter," the apostolic legends of the second and third centuries, and the pseudo-Clementine literature. All

these are similar in character to the pseudo-Pauline litera-ture. The conclusion of an unbiassed comparison must always be, that even the least important and the most suspected of Paul's letters show characteristics altogether the opposite of those in this literature, which leave no intelligent reader in doubt as to its fictitious character.

5. It has not always been clearly realised what diffi-culties are in the way, not so much of the composition of letters of this kind, as of their successful forgery and circulation. From 2 Thess. ii. 2, iii. 17, it may be inferred that even in Paul's lifetime letters were put into circulation which were falsely attributed to him ; but it is to be remembered at the same time that the forgery was almost immediately detected (§ 15). Then, as now, spurious letters, if written with any expectation of permanently deceiving people, could not be put into circulation until after the death of the alleged author and readers. With the exception of Philem., 1 and 2 Tim., and Tit., however, Paul's letters are addressed to Churches which had a continuous life. Though there is proof enough of the fact, if it were necessary to adduce it (n. 8), it goes without saying that up to the close of the first century there were Christians living in Corinth and else-where who had been members of the Church during Paul's lifetime. I confess that I cannot conceive how a letter, purporting to be Paul's, and addressed to the Corinthians, the Thessalonians, the Philippians, or the Colossians, could have been actually written and put into circulation between the year 80 and the year 100, and yet have been received and accepted in these various localities. Then the older members of these Churches must have made themselves believe that the letter, which now came to light, had been sent to them by the apostle himself thirty or forty years before, and yet had been entirely lost sight of up to this time.

Special difficulties arise from the occurrence in many

of these letters of a great many significant personal references (1 Cor. i. 14–16, xvi. 15–17 ; Col. iv. 9–17 ; Philem.
1 f., 10 ; Phil. ii. 25–30, iv. 2 f., 18 ; Rom. xvi. 1–23).
Even if, as is extremely improbable and contrary to what
is usual in pseudepigraphic literature, the forger was well
enough acquainted with conditions in the several Churches
to employ only names of persons who were actually
members of these Churches during Paul's lifetime, and to
assign them their proper rôles, such very personal remarks,
greetings, warning exhortations, and injunctions of the
apostle, which never reached the persons for whom they
were intended, must have been read by these persons,
or if they were dead, then by their relatives, with the
greatest interest and with no little astonishment. Every
mistake which the writer made in these matters—and a
person writing thus in Paul's name could hardly have
avoided making some — tended during the generation
after Paul's death to make the forged letter appear in the
highest degree ridiculous, at least in the Church to which
it was addressed, and so absolutely to preclude its acceptance by such a Church. And as a matter of fact, so far
as we know, this was actually the fate of the spurious
letters put out in Paul's name. And these spurious
letters were certainly written later than the canonical
letters of Paul, even assuming that the latter are spurious,
at a time when one might expect the Churches to which
these letters are alleged to have been sent by Paul to be
more easily deceived. The third letter to the Corinthians
never found acceptance in Corinth, but only in the far
East, among the Syrians and Armenians. Early Christians in Alexandria and Asia Minor seem never to
have known anything about the spurious letters to the
Laodiceans and Alexandrians. The first mention made of
them is by a Roman writer, and in the case of the letter
to the Alexandrians this is the only mention. Such compilations could never be widely accepted, for the reason

that the Churches to which they are alleged to have been sent, and from which alone they could be successfully circulated, never did and never could accept them.

6. The same reasons which make it improbable that the spurious letters to the Churches purporting to be from Paul were put into circulation between the time of the apostle's death and the time of Marcion, argue just as strongly against the assumption that the letters which Paul did write to the Churches were materially altered during the same period. Such alterations are usually associated with the gathering up of Paul's letters into a collection, and changes generally supposed to have been made in the text are explained as due to the fact that the letters were circulated only in the form of a collection. Such a hypothesis presupposes that up to the time when the letters were collected, and so passed into general circulation, they remained quite unnoticed and were not much copied. But this in turn, an assumption of itself, is improbable, and contrary to plain facts. That Paul's letters made a profound impression at the time when they were written, and did not remain without influence until they were accepted by the Church as Holy Scripture, is clear from the N.T. itself. Besides Paul's own hints (2 Cor. x. 9–11) and that of 2 Pet. iii. 15 f.,—a passage generally assigned to a much later date (§§ 42, 44),—we have as proof the fact that the author of 1 Peter, which was written in Rome, certainly before the close of the first century and probably in 63 or 64, had read Ephesians and Romans, and was influenced by them in the composition of his own letter (§ 40). What is expressly enjoined in one case in Col. iv. 16 must have happened in other cases where there was no express direction, and Churches which were in communication with one another must have exchanged the apostle's letters very soon after they were received. It is hardly likely that Paul's letters

created less interest than the hastily written Epistles of Ignatius to the Churches in Asia Minor, for which request was made of the bishop of Smyrna by the Church in Philippi shortly after the martyr passed through that city (Pol. *ad Phil.* 13).   Moreover, we know that in the post-apostolic age Churches made a great deal of any special relations they had had with particular apostles, and letters addressed to them were regarded as being of special importance (n. 8).   An idea like this, which determined the whole development of the Church, could not have grown up suddenly, nor could it have been the immediate effect of the introduction of a collection of the letters of Paul or of any apostolic writings.   If, as is more probable, the making and general circulating of such collections presuppose an interest in the apostles and the writings they left behind them, then there is no reason to doubt that before the collection was made, which Marcion found in existence, Paul's letters to the Churches had been much copied and circulated.   In particular, there is no reason to doubt that in the Churches which could boast that they had been the first to receive them, such letters were not forgotten.   But in that case it is next to impossible that in the process of gathering Paul's letters to Churches into a collection, which afterwards passed into general circulation, material changes should have been made in the text.   Such alterations must have been made before the letters began to be copied and circulated in this way ; but at that stage in their history such alterations are not at all likely to have been made.

In making these general statements, the purpose has been to establish a certain degree of confidence in the tradition according to which nine of the N.T. writings are letters of Paul addressed to different churches, and to create a general mistrust of attempts of one sort and another to replace this tradition by theories which do not themselves hang together.

1. (P. 152.) The writer has discussed several aspects of the matter more fully in the *ZfKWuKL*, 1889, S. 451–466, "Die Briefe des Paulus seit fünfzig Jahren in Feuer der Kritik."

2. (P. 154.) E. EVANSON (*The Dissonance of the Four Generally Received Evangelists and the Evidence of their Authenticity Examined*, Ipswich, 1792,—a work not to be found in Erlangen or Munich, but cited on the authority of Hesedamm,—cf. n. 6, p. 1) accepted of the Gospels only Luke, omitting chaps. i. and ii. ; and of Paul's letters rejected Rom., Eph., Col. as spurious, questioning also Titus, Phil., Philem.

3. (P. 154.) With regard to SCHLEIERMACHER, see below, § 37, n. 1. The opinion quoted in the text was expressed by H. PLANCK (and in the name of other scholars also), *Bemerkungen über den ersten paulin. Brief an Tim.*, Göttingen 1808, S. 256.

4. (P. 154.) F. CHR. BAUR (1792–1860) began his critical work on the N.T. with an essay on the Christ party in Corinth (*TZfTh.* 1831, S. 61 ff.). A criticism of the Pastoral Epistles followed (1835, see § 37, n. 1), and various essays which are to be regarded as preliminary studies for his *Paulus* (1845, 2nd ed. in 2 volumes, published by Zeller, 1866–1867). H. THIERSCH in his *Versuch zur Herstellung des histor. Standpunkts für die Kritik der ntl. Schriften*, 1845, a work issued at about the same time, and still worth reading, could not, of course, take Baur's *Paulus* into consideration, and touched upon the criticism of the Pauline Epistles only in his chapters on the heresies mentioned in the N.T. and on the Canon. J. CHR. K. v. HOFMANN, however (1810–1877), in his last and unfinished work, *Die heilige Schrift NT's zusammenhängend untersucht* (i.-ii. 3, 1862–1866, 2nd ed. 1869–1877 ; iii.-viii. 1868–1878 ; ix.-xi. published by Volck, 1881–1886), chose as the starting-point in his historical and exegetical investigations of the N.T., primarily the Pauline Epistles, in opposition to Baur (i.[2] 60).

5. (P. 155.) BR. BAUER, *Kritik der paul. Briefe*, 3 parts, 1850–1852 ; *Christus u. die Cäsaren, der Ursprung des Christentums aus dem römischen Griechentum*, 1877, S. 371 ff. Doubts of the authenticity of Galatians were expressed by A. PIERSON in Holland, *De Bergrede*, etc., 1878, p. 99 ff. A. D. LOMAN, *Quæstiones Paulinæ* in *ThTjd.* 1882 ff., and R. STECK, *Der Gal. nach seiner Echtheit untersucht nebst krit. Bemerkungen zur den paul. Hauptbriefen*, 1888, followed with greater confidence and more detailed argument, with some dependence also on Bauer. In opposition to Steck, cf. J. GLOËL, *Die jüngste Kritik des Gal. auf ihre Berechtigung geprüft*, 1890, and the writer's essay (S. 462–466), mentioned in n. 1 above.

6. (P. 156.) CHR. H. WEISSE, *Beiträge zur Kritik der paul. Briefe an die Gal., Röm., Phil., Kol.*, published by Sulze, 1867. F. HITZIG, *Zur Kritik paul. Briefe*, 1870, belongs here also, on account of his hypothesis with regard to Col. and Eph. (S. 11–33, see § 29 below). The same PIERSON who gave the first impulse in Holland to the denial of the genuineness of all the Pauline Epistles (n. 5), had at the time remarked on the possibility that their difficulties were to be ascribed to an interpolator. While LOMAN went further in the first-named path, Pierson, in collaboration with the philologist NABER, pursued the second : *Verisimilia. Laceram conditionem NTi exemplis illustrarunt et ab origine repetierunt A. Pierson et S. A. Naber*, 1886. The obscurities and contradictions of this account of the origin of the Epistles,

as based upon able Jewish writings appropriated and redacted by an ignorant Churchman, may be due in part to the fact that two different minds were at work in this critical effort, as well as (supposedly) in the writings with which it deals. Cf. in opposition KUENEN, *Verisimilia? ThTjd.* 1886, S. 491-536, and the writer's essay (S. 458 ff.) mentioned in n. 1 above. Another work to be mentioned here is D. VÖLTER's *Die Komposition der paul. Hauptbriefe, I. Röm. u. Gal.*, 1890, in which a genuine Romans (i. 1a, 7, v. 6, 8-17, v. and vi., xii. and xiii., xv. 14-32, xvi. 21-23) is extracted from the shell of the traditional Epistle, which is held to have acquired its present form by a fivefold interpolation and the addition of a letter addressed to Ephesus, Rom. xvi. 1-20. Galatians, according to this critic, has suffered only minor interpolations; but even so is the work not of Paul himself, but of a Paulinist of a later period. On Völter's treatment of Philippians see § 32. C. CLEMEN, *Die Einheitlichkeit der paul. Briefe an der Hand der bisher mit bezug auf sie aufgestellten Interpolations- und Kompilationshypothesen,* 1894, gives an outline of all attempts in this direction. Worth reading, also, is the pseudonymous essay of an American theologian, *Der Röm. beurteilt u. gevierteilt, eine krit. Untersuchung von* CARL HESEDAMM, 1890 [*Romans Dissected,* by E. D. M'Realsham = Charles M. Mead].

7. (P. 158.) With regard to spurious letters by James and to James, see above, p. 148, n. 5; spurious Pauline Epistles, *GK,* ii. 565-621. The principles referred to above the writer has already developed, and supported by examples, in his *Ignatius,* 529 ff., especially 537-541; and to some extent, indeed, in his *Hirt des Hermas,* 70-93.

8. (Pp. 159, 162.) Clem. 1 *Cor.* xliv. 3-6, the presbyters appointed by the apostles at Corinth, some of them still living. Fortunatus. chap. lxv. = 1 Cor. xvi. 17, see § 18, seems to have been one of these. On the relations of the several Churches to the apostles and on apostolic letters, see Clem. 1 *Cor.* xlvii.; and on chap. v. see § 36 below; also Ign. *Eph.* xi. 2, xii. 2; *Rom.* iv. 3; Polyc. *ad Phil.* iii. 2, xi. 3; cf. *GK,* i. 807, 811 ff., 839.

§ 10. THE HISTORICAL PRESUPPOSITIONS AND THE OCCASION OF THE EPISTLE TO THE GALATIANS.

Since it is impossible to determine beforehand what is understood by Γαλατία, to the Churches of which the letter is addressed (i. 2, iii. 1), the only thing to do is to gather from the letter itself what historical information it has to give with reference to the origin and early development of the Churches to which it was sent, the relation Paul sustained to these Churches, and the occasion which led to the composition of the letter.

These Churches had been established by Paul's own preaching (i. 8). From him they received the gospel

(i. 9). He recalls now with sorrow the labour he had bestowed upon them (iv. 11), and remembers with a feeling of sadness the joyful reception he had had among them when for the first time he came to them with the preaching of the gospel (iv. 13–15). He calls them his own children, whom he, like a mother, had born with travail (iv. 19); speaking manifestly in the same sense in which, addressing another Church, he speaks of himself as their father who had begotten them (1 Cor. iv. 15). This does not, of course, preclude the possibility of Paul's having had the support of one or more helpers in his work among the Galatians (cf. 2 Cor. i. 19). That this was actually the case is proved by the plural εὐηγγελισάμεθα (i. 8, n. 1). When in iv. 13 f. Paul says that it was on account of physical illness that he first preached the gospel among the Galatians,—an illness that might have made him repulsive to those who heard his preaching,—of course he does not mean to say that this was the primary motive of his preaching, but only that it was this circumstance that kept him in this region for a sufficient length of time to preach the gospel to these particular persons (n. 2). From this same passage we learn also that Paul afterwards revisited the Galatian region and preached the gospel there a second time. In those instances where Paul reminds the Galatians of something that he had said to them previously, there is no way of determining absolutely whether it is to be referred to the first or to the second visit. On the first visit he must certainly have declared that scandalous living excluded one from the kingdom of God (v. 21, cf. 1 Cor. vi. 9 ; 1 Thess. iv. 2, 11 ; 2 Thess. iii. 10). But he preached the gospel also on his second visit, and so had occasion to re-emphasise this primary rule. It may not have been until his second visit to the Galatians that he had occasion to warn them against permitting themselves to be circumcised, and against preachers of a false gospel (n. 3). Even if he did warn them on the second visit, the occasion for it could not have been the condition of the Galatian Churches, still less so if the warnings are to be referred back to the earlier visit; for the letter begins with a strong expression of surprise that the Galatians had turned away so quickly from the real and the only gospel of Christ, and had suffered themselves to be persuaded by certain troublesome preachers to accept a caricature of the gospel. This introduction and the tone of the Epistle throughout show that shortly before writing Paul had been surprised by the report of the first appearance of these teachers, and of the rapid success of their work. Consequently they must have come among the Galatians in the interval between Paul's second visit and the writing of this letter, and they must have been still at work when he wrote. This latter point is proved by the use of present tenses in i. 6, 7, v. 10–12, vi. 12 f. Throughout the letter these false teachers are distinguished from the members of the Churches addressed, and charged with being their seducers (i. 7, iii. 1, iv. 17, 29–31, v. 7, 10, 12, vi. 12 f.). There is no hint anywhere that they belonged in the Galatian Churches (for this distinction cf. 1 Cor. xv. 12; Acts xx. 30 with Acts xx. 29). Paul does not resist them as if they were settled teachers, who as members of the Churches were doing things which to him seemed injurious, but he treats them as if they were preachers of a false gospel, i.e. missionary preachers who dogged his steps and invaded the Churches which he founded. In the Galatian Churches, as in all the Pauline Churches of which we know anything, there were some native Jews, a necessary assumption if Gal. iii. 26–29 is to have a natural explanation. But, he is writing with the large majority of the members in view, and with reference to the character which he himself had impressed upon them, so that he treats them throughout as Gentile Christians. Not only is this clear from single passages

such as iv. 8 f., ii. 5 ($\pi\rho\grave{o}s$ $\dot{v}\mu\hat{a}s$, cf. ii. 2, $\grave{\epsilon}\nu$ $\tau o\hat{i}s$ $\ddot{\epsilon}\theta\nu\epsilon\sigma\iota\nu$; ii. 8,
$\epsilon\grave{\iota}s$ $\tau\grave{a}$ $\ddot{\epsilon}\theta\nu\eta$), iii. 29, v. 2, vi. 12, but it appears also from
the character of the questions discussed throughout the
letter.   On the other hand, the preachers of what can
only falsely be called a gospel are Jews, by birth, through
circumcision, and in spirit (iv. 29–31, v. 12, vi. 12–17).
The comparison which Paul makes in iv. 21–31 between
his opponents and himself by contrasting the spiritual
with the fleshly descendants of Abraham, referring to the
earthly Jerusalem as the home or mother of the latter,
and to the heavenly Jerusalem as the home or mother of
the former, is very far-fetched, unless these Jewish Christian missionaries had come into Galatia from this earthly
Jerusalem.   This supposition is favoured by what we
know of similar disturbances in the Gentile Christian
Churches (Acts xv. 1, 24 ; Gal. ii. 12 ; 2 Cor. iii. 1, § 18).
As indicated by the plurals in i. 7, iv. 17, v. 12, vi. 12 f.,
there were certainly a number of these missionaries who
came to the Galatians, so that in all probability they had
a prearranged plan, entering the various Churches simultaneously, and doing their work in concert.   That one
of their number acted as a leader is not unlikely ; but
there is no hint of it in the letter, and it certainly cannot
be inferred from the one singular $\acute{o}$ $\tau a\rho\acute{a}\sigma\sigma\omega\nu$ $\dot{v}\mu\hat{a}s$ in v. 10,
much less from the form of the questions in iii. 1, v. 7.

From *the first main division of the Epistle*, i. 11–ii. 14,
which is *principally historical and apologetic* in character, we learn that these Jewish missionaries had criticised in an unkindly manner his missionary work and
his life history since his conversion, hoping thereby to
undermine the confidence of the Galatian Churches in
their founder, and so to gain foothold for their own
teaching, which they represented as a more perfect form
of the gospel.   They must have made it appear that
immediately after his conversion Paul accepted a position
quite subordinate, and entirely dependent upon the earlier

apostles, and also that at the so-called apostolic council he submitted to the decision of his superiors in Jerusalem. So, they argued, the independence with which Paul worked among the Gentiles was an unjustifiable pretension on his part, while the radical departure from the practices of Jewish Christians in Palestine, which Paul not only permitted in the Churches under his influence, but for which he himself was directly responsible, was nothing less than a degeneracy from Christianity as originally taught. It is implied in i. 10 that in his effort to please men, *i.e.* to make the gospel palatable to the Gentiles, and to make as many converts as he could in his missionary work, Paul abridged the gospel in some of its essential points, and preached it to the Gentiles only in a mutilated form.

What it was that Paul's opponents wanted to substitute for the gospel, parts of which they claimed Paul had left out, we learn from the *second main division of the letter* (ii. 15–iv. 11), in which Paul develops his own doctrine, and from certain portions of the *third main division* (iv. 12–vi. 18), which is *largely hortatory.* They insisted that the Mosaic law, which they regarded as God's chief revelation, was to be for all time the rule of faith and practice in the Church of God. Therefore, if they were to be saved, Gentile Christians must submit to its demands. First of all they must be circumcised (v. 2, vi. 12 f.); and, in order to become real Christians, sanctified and fully qualified members of the Church of Jesus, they must become proselytes of righteousness and accept Judaism. This was the position taken by those Pharisaic Jewish Christians from Palestine, the coming of whom to Antioch made necessary the apostolic council (Acts xv. 1, 5 ; Gal. ii. 4). At the time when this letter was written, the persons holding similar views who had gone among the Galatians do not seem to have succeeded in inducing a single Gentile Christian to accept circum-

cision, though they had made a deep impression. All
the Churches seem to Paul to have been bewitched (iii. 1),
and their prosperous growth interfered with (v. 7). All
the Galatians have suffered themselves to be disturbed
(i. 7, v. 10), and are even on the point of turning away
from the only gospel of Christ (i. 6, iii. 3). Their confidence in Paul is shaken (iv. 12–20). The observance
of Jewish holy days and feasts seems to have become
quite general (iv. 9 f.). Many, at least, were contemplat-
ing further steps in the same direction (iv. 21). Although
these foreign Judaisers were wise enough to assume a
certain appearance of liberality by not demanding at
once from the Gentile Christians a complete observance
of the law, so that Paul himself was compelled to call
attention to this inevitable consequence (v. 3), yet with
regard to one point, namely, the necessity of being circumcised, they made no concessions. The worst was to be
feared.

Since Paul does not seem anywhere to be uncertain
with regard to the facts and conditions among the
Galatians which are presupposed and discussed by him,
it is hardly possible that his information was derived
solely from private sources, letters and oral statements
of individual Christians (cf. 1 Cor. i. 11, xi. 18). On
the other hand, also, nothing in the letter gives evidence that it is an answer to a writing sent to Paul in
the name and by direction of the Churches, cf. *ZKom.
Gal.* 8. It is much more probable that accredited representatives of the Galatian Churches had come to Paul to
obtain a decision on the question, which had not yet been
decided. Of them he could have inquired also concerning
everything which they had not reported to him of their
own accord. Otherwise he could not have written this
Epistle without first asking for an explanation of the
surprising things that were going on, or without expressing doubt as to the truthfulness of the reports that had

come to him. The *quæstio facti* between him and his readers is settled. Therefore, assuming the facts, he proceeds at once (i. 6) to pass judgment upon them, beginning with a passionate remonstrance in which attack and defence are almost inseparably blended. Although, as we learn in this Epistle, he was in the habit of dictating his letters, this one was written by his own hand, a fact to which he calls his readers' attention (vi. 11, n. 4). On this occasion, when he needed to throw the entire weight of his personality into the wavering balance, to address them through another seemed like erecting a barrier between himself and the hearts of the children for whom he had been in travail. And even when he wrote himself, words seemed wooden and unsuited to his purpose. Best of all would it be if he could be present in person and with the emotion of his voice win their half-estranged hearts back again to himself and to the truth for which he stood (iv. 20). It is necessary to assume that he was at such a distance from the Galatians that a journey to them in the near future was out of the question. Otherwise in this passage he must have stated in so many words that at the time a journey was out of the question, with the reasons why it was impossible. From what is said in other letters, one would at least expect him to say something about coming to them in the more remote future (1 Thess. ii. 17–iii. 11 ; 1 Cor. iv. 18–21, xi. 34, xvi. 2–7 ; 2 Cor. ix. 4, x. 2–16, xii. 20– xiii. 10). How long a period had elapsed since his last visit we are not able to determine from the letter (n. 5), nor is there any indication as to the place where it was written, except that from i. 2 f., and the entire absence of special greetings, it may be inferred that no one of the persons who assisted in the organisation of the Galatian Churches was with Paul at the time. The fact that he represents the letter as being from all those about him (i. 2), does no more than produce the impression that what Paul says in this letter, where his position is that of an advocate in a process affecting his own person and moving him deeply, is, by the unanimous judgment of all unbiassed persons capable of judging the matter, correctly said.

1. (P. 165.) That "we," i. 8 and i. 9 (where reference is had probably to two distinct incidents, § 11), is to be taken literally, follows from the otherwise constant use of "I" throughout the Epistle. Special proof of this interpretation is afforded by ἄρτι πάλιν λέγω, which stands in immediate sequence to the plural in i. 9. In spite of the inclusion with him in the address of all the brethren in his company (i. 2),—which cannot be looked upon as a joint authorship,—Paul is the sole speaker throughout the Epistle, as in 1 Cor., in spite of the mention of Sosthenes, 1 Cor. i. 1.

2. (P. 165.) It is not necessary to prove that δι' ἀσθένειαν τῆς σαρκός (iv. 13) cannot designate merely an accompanying situation, as though it read either δι' ἀσθενείας or ἐν ἀσθενείᾳ σαρκός. The text will hardly support the hypothesis of Ramsay (The Church in the Roman Empire, 2nd ed. 1893, pp. 62–65 ; St. Paul the Traveller and Roman Citizen, 1896, pp. 92–97) that the apostle is here referring to an attack of fever to which he fell a victim in the heated regions of Pamphylia, and on account of which he felt constrained to travel northward to the cooler mountain region of Pisidian Antioch. An attack of malaria must certainly incapacitate one for strenuous exertions of any sort. But when one has recuperated to such a degree as to enable him to preach successfully as Paul did among the Galatians, his convalescence cannot make him an object of aversion, either natural or religious, as was the case with Paul in his first preaching in Galatia (iv. 13 f.). The reference here, as in 2 Cor. xii. 7–9, is rather to another malady, incurable in its nature, and reappearing from time to time. Against Ramsay, but especially in opposition to Krenkel's assumption (epilepsy), see the medical opinion of Professor W. Herzog (RKZ, 1899, Nos. 10, 11), who thinks it most likely to have been "neurasthenic conditions in consequence of repeated over-exertions and an excessive strain upon the nerve system, combined with periodic nervous pains." τὸ πρότερον (iv. 13), used as it is with a verb expressing definite action (aorist), cannot designate simply the past, as in John vi. 62, ix. 8, but involves, by way of comparison, a πάλιν or τὸ δεύτερον εὐαγγελίζεσθαι. At the same time, however, it can have no reference to the composition of Galatians so long as εὐαγγελίζεσθαι retains the meaning which it has throughout the N.T., namely, "to bring the message of salvation to those who do not yet know it, or have not yet received it." The objection that εὐαγγελίζεσθαι, in the strict sense of the term, could not be directed twice to the same persons, is without point, since Paul in Galatia addressed a number of persons, or rather of congregations—a large circle, in which some heard the gospel during his first and others during his second visit to the province. Even in a local congregation like that at Corinth, we find some who were brought to the faith by Paul and others after Paul's departure by Apollos (1 Cor. iii. 5).

3. (P. 165.) πάλιν in v. 3 implies contrast to a declaration of the truth here expressed made before the writing of the Epistle ; for in the Epistle itself

there is no expression of this truth before this passage. This is even clearer in the case of ἄρτι πάλιν of i. 9, especially since we find the plural προειρήκαμεν displaced by the immediately following singular λέγω. Whom Paul includes with himself in i. 8, 9 depends upon a determination of the exact meaning of Γαλατία (see § 11). It has been incorrectly inferred from iv. 16 (Wieseler, Sieffert, ad loc.; Godet, Introd. i. 270) that Paul was compelled to utter bitter truths or earnest warnings as early as his second visit to the Galatians,—a conclusion which led to the further assumption that by that time the Judaistic movement had already taken root among the Galatians. In iv. 15-20 Paul sketches his *present* relationship to the Galatians as contrasted with his *first* contact with them described in vv. 13, 14, and again alluded to in the intermediate sentence of ver. 15. In reviewing the letter, which at this point would seem to have reached its conclusion, he discusses the existing state of affairs. The Galatians have forgotten with what enthusiasm they received him when he first came to them (ver. 15a), and how earnest was the expression of mutual love between himself and them as long and as often as he was in their midst (ver. 18). Instead of this now, they permit his opponents to court their favour (ver. 17). Paul, who as he writes feels again the birth throes which the conversion of the Galatians had cost him, stands pen in hand at a loss what to advise them, since he cannot now realise his desire to treat with them in person (vv. 19, 20). He seems now to be their enemy, because he writes them the truth. It is not to the point to say that the Galatians knew nothing of this enmity before reading the Epistle; for with ἐχθρὸς ὑμῶν γέγονα—ὠδίνω—ἀπορούμαι Paul describes his present relation to them, as he himself feels it at this particular moment, and not as they look at it. ὥστε refers back beyond the parenthesis to the question: "Where is then that gratulation of yourselves?" The question has the force of a demonstrative referring to ὥστε (Kühner-Gerth, ii. 502). So thoroughly has their relationship to Paul been disturbed, that his fearless declaration of the truth in this letter has made him seem their enemy. This is the picture he presents to himself, while at the same time he is conscious of striving for their spiritual life with a maternal love. Cf. 2 Cor. xii. 11, γέγονα ἄφρων. The present ἀληθεύων cannot possibly refer to the past of his second visit, as if Paul meant to say that he became their enemy on account of the censures uttered at that time; for it is connected with the present perfect, and follows the question ver. 15a, also in the present, upon which the clause introduced by ὥστε is dependent. Such reference Paul must have expressed by ἐγενόμην or ἐγενήθην (cf. Isa. lxiii. 10, ἐστράφη αὐτοῖς εἰς ἔχθραν,—a passage which otherwise perhaps he had in mind). It would have been also necessary for him to distinguish this second sojourn from the first (τὸ πρότερον, ver. 13). Instead of this, he passes from the first visit (vv. 13, 14) directly to the present moment of his writing (vv. 15-20).

4. (P. 170.) The ἴδετε πηλίκοις ὑμῖν γράμμασιν ἔγραψα τῇ ἐμῇ χειρί of vi. 11 is certainly not, with Jerome (Vallarsi, vii. 529) and Theodore (Swete, i. 107), to be confined in its reference to the immediately following conclusion of the Epistle which Paul is supposed to have written in larger characters on account of its importance, or in order to show the fearless spirit with which it was written. Such a limitation would have been expressed as in 1 Cor. xvi. 21; 2 Thess. iii. 17; Col. iv. 18. Moreover,

the aorist ἔγραψα is never employed—at least in the N.T.—to refer to something which the author is about to write; rather does Paul look back upon the entire letter which is just being closed, cf. Rom. xv. 15, xvi. 22. In the same way we conclude from Philem. 19 that the apostle wrote all of this short letter with his own hand. Anyone accustomed to dictate, and not hindered from so doing by external circumstances, when he deviates from this course, does so because he desires to give to his writing the highest possible personal character. Cf. Ambrosius, *Ep.* i. 3 (ed. Ben. ii. 753 to the Emperor Gratian) : "Scripsisti tua totem epistolam manu, ut ipsi apices fidem tuam pietatemque loquerentur." Herein lies the explanation of the πηλίκοις γράμμασιν in this instance. Hofmann, i. 2. 205, has not succeeded in justifying, from linguistic usage, his translation : "Such a large, explicit Epistle I have written to you." Cf. *per contra* Acts xxiii. 25 ; 2 Pet. iii. 1, ἐπιστολήν ; Eph. iii. 3, ἐν ὀλίγῳ ; 1 Pet. v. 12, δι᾿ ὀλίγων ; Heb. xiii. 22, διὰ βραχέων ἐπέστειλα ; Eus. *H. E.* i. 7. 1, δι᾿ ἐπιστολῆς Ἀριστείδῃ γράφων περὶ κτλ. ; Ign. *Rom.* viii. 2, δι᾿ ὀλίγων γραμμάτων αἰτοῦμαι ὑμᾶς, likewise *ad Polyc.* vii. 3 with παρεκάλεσα. In case the helplessness of the writer, which showed itself in the unusually large characters of his writing, was caused by Paul's constant manual labour, or by his continuous bodily suffering, or by a recent injury, the reference to the roughly formed large letters, supplemented by τῇ ἐμῇ χειρί, was, at the same time, a proof of the self-sacrificing labour it had cost him to approach as near and as personally as possible to the readers, cf. *ZKom. Gal.* 277.

5. (P. 170.) It cannot by any means be inferred from i. 6 that only a brief period had elapsed since Paul's last visit to Galatia—certainly not since the founding of the Galatian Churches, for only when a distinct point of time, from which the rapid introduction of an event is measured, is either distinctly expressed or implied in the statement, does ταχέως acquire the meaning "soon," *e.g.* with ἔρχομαι, ἐλεύσομαι, in which the present moment of the statement is the point of time after which the coming is to follow promptly, without delay and at once (1 Cor. iv. 19 ; Phil. ii. 19, 24). It would not indeed be specially strange if Churches just established and consequently immature, or if Churches that had just been visited by their founder, allowed themselves to be estranged by false teachers ; but such a situation would become intelligible only if we were here reminded of the apostle's last visit, and of the favourable state of affairs which he found. As a matter of fact, however, Paul represents himself as astonished and incensed at the situation, and says merely that the Galatians have so impulsively allowed themselves to be turned in a false direction, and that the Judaists have needed but little time to secure such a dangerous influence over them. The original sense of ταχύς, ταχέως, ταχινός is frequently preserved, *e.g.* 2 Thess. ii. 2 ; Jas. i. 19 ; Mark ix. 39 ; John xx. 4 ; 2 Pet. ii. 1.

§ 11. GALATIA AND THE GALATIANS (N. 1).

In order to connect the statements of Galatians with what is said elsewhere about Paul, it is necessary to decide

what is meant by ἡ Γαλατία in i. 2 (cf. iii. 1), a question
which comes up again in connection with 1 Cor. xvi. 1
and 1 Pet. i. 1 (n. 2). According to the older view,
which distinguished scholars still hold, Galatia means the
region about Ancyra, Pessinus, and Tavium, which, after
the incursions of Celtic warriors in the third century B.C.,
was called Γαλατία. By others, Γαλατία, in i. 2, is understood as referring to the Roman province of that name,
which was organised in 25 B.C., after the death of Amyntus,
the last king of the Galatians. From the time of its
establishment, the province, the boundaries of which
fluctuated greatly, included besides the Galatian region
the greater part of the region of Pisidia, Isauria, and
Lycaonia, also a portion of eastern Phrygia, though the
greater part of Phrygia belonged to the province of Asia.
In Asia Minor, as elsewhere, the organisation and marking
out of Roman provinces, though furnishing new names,
did not by any means displace the old territorial designations. Roman writers, such as the elder Pliny (died 79) and
Tacitus (*circa* 115), also the geographer Ptolemy (*circa* 150),
understood by Galatia the entire Roman province, which,
besides other districts, included Galatia proper (n. 3).
The question as to which usage is followed by Paul would
not for so long a time have been given such different
answers, were it not for a tendency, on the one hand, to
let Paul's usage be determined by that of Acts, and, on
the other, to interpret the statements of Acts in the light
of the Pauline usage. There is all the less excuse for this
confusion, since the name Γαλατία does not occur in Acts
at all, while the meaning of the peculiar expression (ἡ)
Γαλατικὴ χώρα, which is twice used by Luke (Acts xvi. 6,
xviii. 23), can be determined only from the context of
these passages and from Luke's usage elsewhere. Now it
is clear that, when speaking of Asia Minor and other
districts, Luke employs the old territorial names, which
do not correspond at all with the divisions and names of

the Roman provinces, whereas Paul never uses any but the provincial name for districts under Roman rule, and never employs territorial names which are not also names of Roman provinces (n. 4). So that the natural supposition is that ἡ Γαλατία in Gal. i. 2, 1 Cor. xvi. 1, means the Roman province of Galatia. And this judgment is but confirmed by the fact that in an Epistle written in Rome (§ 39), in 1 Pet. i. 1, the name Galatia occurs in a list of names which otherwise consists entirely of names of Roman provinces (n. 3, end). Even admitting that by Galatia Paul could have meant the entire province of that name, some have had difficulty in understanding how the readers could be addressed as Galatians in iii. 1 when the majority of them were not Galatians at all, *i.e.* of Celtic stock. But it is to be noticed that both Paul and Luke speak elsewhere of all the inhabitants of a given city or district without making ethnographical distinctions, *e.g.* between Jews and Greeks, Romans and non-Romans ; thus, Corinthians (2 Cor. vi. 11), Philippians (Phil. iv. 15), Macedonians (2 Cor. ix. 2, 4 ; Acts xix. 29), Pontians (Acts xviii. 2), Asians (Acts xx. 4), Alexandrians (Acts xviii. 24), Romans (Acts ii. 10). To take a modern example, no one hesitates at all to call the inhabitants of the regions about Nuremberg and Würzburg Bavarians, although the original stock was Frankish, and although the political union of these people with peoples of Bavarian stock is not much older than the political union of Lycaonians and Galatians in the province of Galatia at the time when this letter was written. The greater the diversity of nationality in a Christian community, the more natural it was in addressing them to designate them by the customary name of the political division where they lived, which was a neutral term.

The question, what is meant by the name Galatia in Gal. i. 2 ? must be decided ultimately by a comparison of the historical facts involved in each of these views with the text of the letter itself. If by Galatia the Roman province is meant, then, of those addressed, the most important, if not the only, Churches are the four which were founded by Paul and Barnabas on Paul's first missionary journey, at Antioch in Pisidia, at Iconium, Lystra, and Derbe (n. 5). Concerning the first preaching among the readers, mentioned in Gal. iv. 13, we should have a more detailed account in Acts xiii. 14–xiv. 23, and the second preaching of the gospel in Galatia, indirectly but certainly attested by Gal. iv. 13, would be evidenced in reference to these Churches by Acts xvi. 5. For as a result of the visit of Paul and Silas to the Churches founded in South Galatia during the first missionary journey (xvi. 1–5), these Churches were not only confirmed in the faith, but their membership was also increased. With these Churches Paul (Gal. i. 2) must have included also the other Churches which had been organised in other parts of the province in the interval preceding the writing of the letter; provided there were such Churches in existence at that time, and provided they were established by his preaching. But both are very ·doubtful. Certainly the second visit to South Galatia was followed at once by a tour through the regions of Phrygia and Galatia, which Paul had not succeeded in reaching on his first journey (Acts xvi. 6); and when it is said that this route was chosen because the Spirit forbade them to preach in Asia, this command did not hold for the regions through which in obedience to this direction they actually passed. It could be taken for granted, therefore, in spite of the silence of Acts, which in xvi. 6 mentions merely a journey of the missionaries through these regions, that Paul and Silas on this occasion preached in Phrygia and a portion of North Galatia; and that the disciples (not Churches, as in xv. 41, xvi. 5, cf. xiv. 23) whom Paul met on the third missionary journey to several places of the same regions (Acts xviii. 23) had been converted by the preach-

ing of Paul and Silas on the second journey. But everyone feels the uncertainty of these combinations.

And yet, if one connects the name Galatia with the
northern portion of the province, the region inhabited by
the Celtic tribes, the account of the founding of all the
Churches addressed in Galatians must be read between
the lines of Acts xvi. 6, and the second visit must be
identified with that mentioned in Acts xviii. 23. But
this in itself is a serious objection to the latter hypothesis.
We do not lay great stress upon the fact that Gal. iv. 13
presupposes not only a second visit, but also a second
preaching of the gospel in Galatia, and that, on the contrary, in Acts xviii. 23 there is no more reference to a
second than in xvi. 6 to a first preaching in those
regions. The thing that makes the hypothesis improbable is especially the fact that, assuming it, the Churches
in Derbe, Lystra, Iconium, and Antioch in Pisidia, whose
importance is evidenced by the account of their organisation (Acts xiii. 14–xiv. 23 ; 2 Tim. iii. 11), and by the
fact that from them come several of Paul's helpers (Acts
xvi. 1, xx. 4), would be left with scarcely a trace of
their subsequent development in the N.T. On the other
hand, the Churches in the northern part of the province
of Galatia, of whose founding we can read something
between the lines of Acts, would have in Galatians, in the
greeting of 1 Peter, and in the mention of 1 Cor. xvi. 1,
witnesses of an ecclesiastical importance, of which the
author of Acts could have had no idea whatever. Furthermore, it would be strange if Jewish teachers from Palestine
passed by such important cities as Iconium and Antioch,
where there were Jewish synagogues (n. 6), and where there
would certainly be some native Jews in the local Christian
Churches, without starting a movement considerable
enough to leave some traces of itself in our sources, and
still more strange if they made their way to the more
remote Galatian region, the Churches of which, according

to statements of Acts, were not important, in order to oppose Paul's gospel and influence. This hypothesis also involves difficulties as to the time and place of the composition of Galatians, which disappear when the other hypothesis is accepted (§ 12). Besides, it has against it Paul's assurance (Gal. ii. 5) that, in the transactions of the so-called apostolic council in Jerusalem, he had in mind the readers addressed in Galatians, endeavouring to retain for them the truth and freedom of the gospel (n. 7); moreover, at the time when the events described in Acts xv. took place, the winter of 51–52, Paul as yet had not even visited Galatia proper, the first indication of such a visit being that in Acts xvi. 6. This of itself is sufficient proof that the "Churches of Galatia," to which the letter is addressed, were primarily at least the Churches of the southern part of the province of Galatia, which were organised prior to the apostolic council on the first missionary journey.

This hypothesis (§ 12) gets positive confirmation from a comparison of Galatians with the accounts in Acts, which under this presupposition are to be taken into consideration. If without question in Gal. i. 8 Paul is speaking primarily of the preaching of the gospel which led to the organisation of the Churches of Galatia, i.e. to the εὐαγγελίζεσθαι τὸ πρότερον of iv. 13, then the helper to whose assistance he refers is Barnabas. In so far, however, as there is a reference to the second visit, on which occasion also the gospel was preached with good success, Silas is to be thought of as the fellow-worker (Acts xv. 40–xvi. 6). Only Silas is referred to in Gal. i. 9, since on the first missionary journey which Paul made in company with Barnabas there would hardly have been as yet any occasion for warnings against a false gospel, particularly against a gospel distorted by requirements of a legalistic kind (cf. Gal. v. 3). The condition of the Churches in the early stages of their development furnished no occasion for such

warnings (above, p. 171 f. n. 3); while, on the other hand, it
was perfectly natural that on the second journey, which he
made in company with Silas, after the experiences which
he had had in Jerusalem and Antioch (Acts xv. 1–29 ;
Gal. ii. 1–10) in the interval between the first and second
visit to the province of Galatia, Paul should warn the
newly organised Churches in Lycaonia against the false
brethren and their legalistic Christianity. According
to Acts xvi. 4, the missionaries communicated to the
Churches of Lycaonia also the decisions of the apostolic
council which were intended only for the Christians in
Antioch in Syria and the neighbouring regions, who had
been disturbed by the Judaisers (Acts xv. 23). In this
way they were prepared for the attacks of the Judaisers,
xvi. 5, which were to be expected. Similarly, the repeated
reference to Barnabas by name (ii. 1, 9, 13) is especially
appropriate if Paul is here writing to Churches the most
important of which were organised with Barnabas' help.
While, to be sure, it does appear from 1 Cor. ix. 6, Col.
iv. 10, that Barnabas was known as a distinguished
missionary even in Churches which he had not visited in
person, in both these cases there were special reasons for
the mention of his name. In 1 Cor. ix. 6 he is mentioned
because Paul wants to say that from the beginning of his
missionary work, when he was associated with Barnabas,
he had followed the principle under discussion ; while in
Col. iv. 10 it is necessary because in commending Mark,
who was entirely unknown to his readers, to the kindly
reception of the Church, he has occasion to say that he is
a relative of a distinguished missionary. In Gal. ii. no
special reasons of this character are discernible, and if the
threefold mention of Barnabas is to be explained naturally, it must be assumed that Barnabas assisted in the
organisation of the most important of the Churches which
he was addressing. That in thinking over his first and
second visits in Galatia, Paul should occasionally at least

think of his helpers Barnabas and Silas (i. 8 f.), and at the same time consistently represent himself to be the organizer and head of the Galatian Churches (iv. 11–20, v. 2 f., 21), is consistent with the accounts in Acts. Even on the first missionary journey which was made in company with Barnabas, Paul was the spokesman and principal preacher (Acts xiii. 16, xiv. 9, 12). In this connection attention is called to the noteworthy incident in Lystra (Acts xiv. 11–14), of which there is a reflection in Gal. iv. 14. While in their excitement at the case of miraculous healing, the Lycaonians thought they recognised in Barnabas Zeus; they took Paul, to whose preaching they listened, to be Hermes, the messenger and interpreter of the gods; so it is with deep emotion that Paul looks back to the day when they received him as "a messenger of God"; indeed, as the son of God. This was, to be sure, only an outburst of naïve popular superstition, which the missionaries repudiated with indignation ; but in the case of those who were afterwards taught and converted, this heathen superstition, in which their enthusiasm found expression at first, gave place to a feeling of grateful joy that not the gods of Olympus, but "the living God, who made heaven and earth," had sent His "messenger" to them, and that Christ Himself had visited them in the gospel which Paul preached. If Acts xvii. 16–34 gives an historical picture of the apostle to the Gentiles, which statement no one has as yet disproved, it is perfectly conceivable that Paul should see a connection between the worship which the Gentiles rendered to the unknown gods and their enthusiastic love for the God whom he preached (Acts xvii. 23), and for God's messenger. Unless this coincidence between the hints in the letter and the account in Acts is a tantalising accident, it must be admitted that there is an echo of this same event also in Gal. i. 8, where likewise Paul is looking back to the first preaching in Galatia, and where we have the strange combination of two ideas, in themselves quite foreign to each other,—" we or an angel from heaven." In the ancient legend of Thecla, which begins with the flight from Antioch in Pisidia (Acts xiii. 50–xiv. 1; *Acta Theclæ*, i.), the impression which Paul made at that time upon the impressionable mind of one of the citizens of Iconium is thus described, evidently with the words of Galatians in mind : "How he seemed like a man, and again he had the face of an angel" (chap. 3 ; *GK*, ii. 904).

Regarding the illness of Paul, which was the occasion of his first sojourn and so of his first preaching among the Galatians (iv. 13, above, p. 171, n. 2), there is no direct information in Acts. Perhaps, however, Paul's statement offers some explanation of the unusual route chosen by the missionaries. The direction which they took from Perga to Antioch (Acts xiii. 14) would seem to indicate their intention of pressing their way from Antioch northward or westward into the valleys of the Lycus and of the Meander, where there were numerous cities, and of making their way thence to the large cities on the western coast of Asia Minor. When, instead of following out this plan, the missionaries turn toward the south-east from Antioch, returning shortly from this same point by the route over which they had come, though no statement is made as to the reasons for the change (cf. Acts xvi. 6–10), it may have been an attack of his malady that led Paul for the time being to give up the carrying out of this more extended plan.

Naturally, to us, who are able only to infer the facts presupposed in the letter from allusions which Paul makes for the benefit of those who were already acquainted with them, much must remain obscure. But this itself is the very strongest proof that we are not dealing with a literary fiction, but with a genuine letter, which had its occasion in circumstances connected with real life. One of the most obscure of these passages is v. 11, and obscure it will remain unless we are allowed to explain the letters of Paul from Acts. It appears that the opponents of Paul had called the attention of the Galatians to the fact that even Paul, the man of progress, could, like the older apostles, when occasion demanded, preach circumcision. So, they argued, it would be no serious rupture with their past Christian experience, which had been formed under Paul's influence, if now the Galatians permitted themselves to be circumcised. Basing their argument on Paul's conduct, the errorists could make it appear to the Galatians that Paul might be easily convinced, and in the end allow the Galatians to be Judaised. How untrue this representation of his attitude was, Paul shows by pointing out that it was just because he was so unyielding of this point that he was hated and persecuted by the Judaisers (διώκομαι, v. 11, to be understood in the same sense in which the word is used in iv. 29). It was in opposition to insinuations of this character that in v. 2–4 he solemnly avowed that his judgment regarding the unreasonable demands of the Judaisers was unalterable. It must have been some recent event, which had come within the observation of the Galatians, which enabled the Judaisers to represent with some show of plausibility that Paul could περιτομὴν ἔτι κηρύσσειν. This event is the one recorded in Acts xvi. 1–3, none other than the circumcision, at Paul's suggestion, of Timothy, a native of Lystra in the province of Galatia, whose father was a Gentile and whose mother was a Jewess.

Assuming that this is the right reconstruction of the facts, the appearance of the Judaisers at this time is most natural. Their defeat at the apostolic council did not discourage them permanently. It was only in Antioch and the Churches of which Antioch was the centre (Acts xv. 23) that they seem not to have ventured a second attack; for what is narrated in Gal. ii. 11–14 probably took place earlier (§ 11). When they learned that Paul

had gone over to Europe on his second missionary
journey, and was kept there by the success of his work,
they thought it an opportune time to attack the Churches
in Galatia, which had been founded before the apostolic
council, and in the absence of their founder to induce
them to accept a legalistic form of Christianity. As soon
as Paul heard of their move, he hastened to meet the
threatening danger by sending this letter.

1. (P. 173.) On Galatia, cf. PERROT, *Die Galatia provincia Romana*, 1867 ;
also his *Exploration de la Galatie*, 1872, pp. 173–206 ; SIEFFERT, *Galatien und
seine ersten Christengemeinden*, 1871 ; MARQUARDT, *Röm. Staatsverwaltung*,[2]
i. 358–365 ; RAMSAY, *Historical Geography of Asia Minor*, 1890, pp. 252 ff.,
375, 453, and his *Church in the Roman Empire*, 2nd ed. 1893, pp. 8–15,
25–111 ; see also n. 2. The view the present writer has taken of the destination of the Epistle would justify him, if such justification were necessary, in
leaving out of consideration the question, in any case so unimportant for the
understanding of the letter, as to the nationality of the tribes which gave the
district of Galatia its name, the Tectosages, Trocmi, and Tolistobogii. Their
Germanic origin has been argued with unwearied zeal by WIESELER in his
Komm. zum Gal. S. 521–528, and in special monographs : *Die deutsche
Nationalität der kleinasiatischen Galater*, 1877 ; *Zur Geschichte der kleinas Gal.*
1879 ; *Untersuch. zur Geschichte und Religion der alten Germanen*, 1881, S.
1–51. Among those who have combated his theory are W. GRIMM, *ThStKr.*
1876, S. 199–221, and HERTSBERG, *ibid.* 1878, S. 525–541.

2. (P. 174.) According to J. D. Michaelis, *Einl.*, 4th ed. 1199, the view
which is adopted above was first put forward by J. J. SCHMIDT, rector of
Ilfeld, and was afterward defended by him against the criticisms of Michaelis.
The contributions made to the subject by MYNSTER, *Kleinere Schriften*, 1825,
and BÖTTGER, *Beiträge*, 1837, pt. iii. 1–5, and Suppl. 32–47, produced no particular impression, nor did the agreement with the view by THIERSCH, *Die
Kirche im apost. Zeitalter* (1te Aufl. 1852, 3te Aufl. 1879), 123. It was not till
after the appearance of Perrot's works (see n. 1) that this view began to win
more numerous adherents, as RENAN, *St. Paul*, 1869, pp. 47–53, and HAUS-
RATH, *Ntl. Zeitgesch.* ii. (1872) 528 ff. In more recent times its most prominent
advocate has been RAMSAY, *Church in the Roman Empire*, 8–15, 59–111 ;
Stud. Bibl. et Eccl. iv. (Oxford, 1896) 15–57, and *A historical comm. on St.
Paul's Ep. to the Galatians*, 1899. Cf. also V. Weber, *Die Addressaten
des Gal. Beweis der rein südgal. Theorie*, 1900 ; J. Weiss, *PRE*,[3] x. 554 ff., and
others. Of the representatives of the older view, according to which
"Galatia" in the N.T. always denotes the country of the Galatæ, we may
mention WIESELER, *Komm. zum Gal.* 530 ff. ; LIGHTFOOT, *Galatians* (4th ed.),
19 ; HOFMANN, i. 149 ; SIEFFERT (see n. 1), also in the revision of Meyer's
Commentary, 7th ed. 1886, S. 6–15 ; SCHÜRER, *JbfPTh.* 1892, S. 460–474 ;
ZÖCKLER, *ThStKr.* 1895, S. 51–102.

3. (Pp. 174, 175.) Pliny understands by "Galatia" the whole Roman

province, when he refers (*Hist. Nat.* v. 27. 95) to *Ide* (Ύδη), a city of eastern Lycaonia, as lying "in confinio Galatiæ atque Cappadociæ"; again, when in v. 32. 147 he assigns the Lycaonian cities, Lystra and Thebasa (cf. v. 27. 95), to Galatia ; and when in the same passage he speaks of Galatia as bordering on the districts of Cabalia and Milyas, which at that time belonged to the province of Pamphylia. These were separated by some distance from the country of the Galatæ, whereas Galatia, in the meaning of Pliny and the Romans generally, and Pamphylia were actually adjoining provinces. To them Tacitus refers, *Hist.* ii. 9, "Galatiam ac Pamphyliam provincias Calpurnio Asprenati regendas permiserat Galba." That Galatia here does not mean the country of the Galatæ proper, but the whole of the province organised *c.* 25 B.C., appears not merely from the fact that only on this assumption should we have a connected administrative district, but even from the word *provincias* itself, for the several districts of which provinces were composed were not themselves called provinces. The same usage, therefore, must underlie *Ann.* xiii. 35, "habiti per Galatiam Cappadociamque dilectus" ; xv. 6, "Galatarum Cappadocumque auxilia." The assertion, repeated with strange persistency, that only those of Celtic birth, or residents of Galatia proper, could be termed Galatæ, and not all the inhabitants of the province called Galatia by Pliny and Tacitus, has already been refuted from the N.T., p. 175 above ; cf. *ZKom. Gal.* 11. Ramsay discusses this point fully and conclusively, *Stud. Bibl. et Eccl.*, Oxford, 1896, pp. 26–38, and in his *Hist. Comm.* Ptolemy describes Asia Minor essentially and at the outset quite clearly in accordance with the Roman provincial divisions : (*a*) v. 1. 1, Pontus-Bithynia (in viii. 17. 1, Bithynia for brevity); (*b*) v. 2. 1, ἡ ἰδία or ἡ ἰδίως καλουμένη or ἡ ἰδίως Ἀσία (cf. viii. 17. 1, 8), to which belonged Greater Phrygia, with Eumeneia, Philomelion, and Hierapolis (v. 2. 22–26) ; (*c*) v. 3, Lycia ; (*d*) v. 4, Galatia, with which he reckons parts of Lycaonia, Pisidia, and Isauria, and among other cities Pisidian Antioch, § 11, and Lystra, § 12. Following another authority, he assigns the Antioch situated "in Pisidian Phyrgia" to the province of Pamphylia, v. 5. 4, and Iconium and Derbe to Cappadocia, v. 6. 16 ff. The latter agrees with his statement regarding the στρατηγίαι of Cappadocia, which is somewhat obscure and at all events depends on antiquated sources ; cf. Ramsay, *Hist. Geog.* 283 f., 310, 336. Furthermore, the inscriptions, rightly understood, confirm the usage of Pliny, Tacitus, and Ptolemy. An honorary inscription set up in Iconium to an imperial administrator of domains or revenue officer (ἐπίτροπος Καίσαρος) of the time of Claudius and Nero (*C. I. Gr.* 3991) designates his administrative district as Γαλατικῆς ἐπαρχείας. The city of Iconium, which, having been made a Roman colony under Claudius (see below, n. 5), honoured this official as its founder and benefactor, belonged to what they called simply the Galatic province (cf. Ramsay, *Church*, etc. 56 ; Marquardt, i. 364, n. 11). Provinces formed by the union of two districts originally separate might bear a double name, like Bithynia-Pontus (see the reference to Ptolemy above, and Marquardt, i. 351), as we have in Bavaria "Schweben and Neuburg." But, on the other hand, it is quite incredible that the name commonly applied in official business to the great province which was erected out of the kingdom of Amyntas should have consisted of an enumeration of all the districts which composed it. Even if one concluded from a few inscriptions dealing with Galatia, that official usage described the united province thus circumstantially and reserved the term Galatia for the region of the Galatæ proper, that would be, in the first place, of no consequence to our inquiry ; for Paul had even less occasion than Pliny, Tacitus, Ptolemy, and the municipality of Iconium in its inscription, to employ the legal style. And, in the second place, the reasoning itself is as incorrect as if we should undertake to determine our own official usage from the so-called great titles of our German rulers, which even in the official publication of laws are usually omitted altogether or abbreviated by an "etc." An inscription (found in Pisidian Antioch and dating from the end of the first century) in honour of a certain Sospes—not Sollers—governor of Galatia (*C. I. L.* iii. No. 291, corrected Suppl. No. 6818), designates his administrative territory by nine names, beginning *provinc. Gal. Pisid. Phryg.* etc. (similarly in Suppl. No. 6819, except that *Phryg.* precedes *Pisid.*). If we read *provinc(iarum)*, then Pisidia, Phrygia, and the rest, which at that time were not separate provinces, are inaccurately so called, and this Sospes is represented as in charge of nine provinces at once. More probably we are to read in this as in similar inscriptions *provinc(iæ)*, which applies only to *Galatiæ*, while the eight following names are connected with it by apposition, to describe the great province as impressively as possible. In other inscriptions in which we are really to read *provinciarum*, *e.g.* on two milestones from Ancyra from the years 80 and 82 (*C. I. L.* Nos. 312, 318), the names of actual provinces come first, *Galatiæ, Cappadociæ,* and not till afterward such districts as Pisidia and Lycaonia, which are already involved in the larger titles. We have further to consider those enumerations which would be unintelligible if we could not assume that by the term *Galatia,* as by *Asia,* all the sections belonging to these provinces were intended. When we read in *C. I. L.* iii. No. 249 (Ancyra), the following, *inter al.,* "proc. fam. glad. per Asiam. Bithyn. Galat. Cappad. Lyciam. Pamphyl. Cil. Cyprum. Pontum. Paflag.," we are taken the rounds of all Asia Minor together with Cyprus. Consequently Lycaonia and Pisidia, which are not mentioned, must be included in Galatia, and Phrygia, also not mentioned, partly with Galatia and partly with Asia. This is true also in 1 Pet. i. 1. There all the Roman provinces of Asia Minor are enumerated with the exception of Lycia-Pamphylia, where there can hardly have been any Christians (Acts xiii. 13, xiv. 25), and of Cilicia, where Christianity seems to have been introduced not by Paul and his helpers, but from Antioch, so that from the beginning the Cilician Churches were grouped ecclesiastically with those of Syria (Acts xv. 23, 41). As Phrygia and Mysia are not explicitly named, the Phrygian Churches, Colossæ, Laodicea, Hierapolis (Col. i. 1, ii. 1), the Church at Troas (Acts xx. 6–12), and the six Churches besides Laodicea mentioned in Rev. i. 11, so far as they were in existence at the time of 1 Peter, were evidently included in Asia ; that is, the name was used in its Roman sense. The like holds true, then, of the word Galatia in the same passage (1 Pet. i. 1); the term includes Lycaonia and Pisidia also. Indeed, it would be impossible to conceive why Peter should exclude from his greeting the Churches of that region, belonging historically with the Churches of the province Asia, and take up instead of them the much less important Churches in Galatia proper.

4. (P. 175.) Paul uses Ἀχαία, Rom. xv. 26 ; 1 Cor. xvi. 15 ; 2 Cor. i. 1, ix. 2,

xi. 10 ; 1 Thess. i. 7, 8, and Μακεδονία, 1 Cor. xvi. 5 ; 2 Cor. i. 16, ii. 13, vii. 5, viii. 1, xi. 9 ; Rom. xv. 26 ; 1 Thess. i. 7 f., iv. 10 ; Phil. iv. 15, evidently in the sense of the Roman provincial divisions. Along with τὸ Ἰλλυρικόν, Rom. xv. 19, we find in 2 Tim. iv. 10 the term Δαλματία also used by the Romans of that time ; cf. Marquardt, i. 299. Ἰουδαία, Gal. i. 22 ; 1 Thess. ii. 14 ; 2 Cor. i. 16 ; Rom. xv. 31, is not used, as the first-named passages show, in contradistinction to Galilee, Samaria, and Perea, for there were Christians in these districts also (Acts viii. 5–25, ix. 31–xi. 1) whom Paul could not exclude in this connection ; but he uses the term in the Roman sense = Palestine, cf. Tac. *Hist.* v. 9 ; Ptol. v. 16. 1 on the one hand, and v. 16. 6–9 on the other. Ἀραβία, Gal. i. 17, iv. 25, is a political term ; it stands for the Nabatæan kingdom of Aretas (2 Cor. xi. 32), which at that time was still independent of Rome. Syria and Cilicia, Gal. i. 21, were then politically united ; cf. Marquardt, i. 387. Of the divisions of Asia Minor, Paul names only Ἀσία, 1 Cor. xvi. 19 ; 2 Cor. i. 8 ; Rom. xvi. 5 ; 2 Tim. i. 15 ; and Γαλατία, Gal. i. 2 ; 1 Cor. xvi. 1 ; and it is unlikely that he meant by these anything else than the Roman provinces so called, for the very reason that he mentions no districts of Asia Minor whose names do not at the same time denote such provinces. This corresponds with the terminology of 1 Pet. i. 1 (see the preceding note) and of Revelation ; for all the seven Churches of Asia (Rev. i. 4, 11), even the Phrygian city of Laodicea on the Lycus, were in the province of Asia. In the same way Polycrates of Ephesus in his letter to Victor of Rome (Eus. *H. E.* v. 24. 2–5) uses Ἀσία of the whole extent of the Roman province, including Hierapolis, Eumeneia, and Laodicea. Luke, however, as a rule expresses himself differently. Of course the Roman nomenclature is not unknown to him, and he uses it where it seems to him necessary or appropriate ; but usually in his geographical references he follows the other usage, and employs the names of the several sections. So Ἰουδαία stands (*a*) in Luke i. 5 for the whole country of the Jews, or Palestine, even without the πᾶσα, ὅλη, which he adds elsewhere to make sure that the term shall have its widest significance (Luke vi. 17, vii. 17, xxiii. 5 ; Acts x. 37) ; (*b*) in Luke iii. 1 for the territory governed by the Roman procurator, which in addition to Judea proper included Samaria and the coast district to Cæsarea and beyond ; (*c*) but otherwise regularly for Judea proper as distinguished from Galilee and Samaria, Luke ii. 4 ; Acts i. 8, viii. 1, ix. 31, xi. 1, xii. 19. Luke knows Ἀχαία, and uses the term to denote the Roman province where reference is made to its prefect, Acts xviii. 12, and twice besides, xviii. 27, xix. 21, where he mentions journeys to Corinth, its capital city. But he uses Ἑλλάς in xx. 2, and, according to the more ancient text of xvii. 15, probably Θεσσαλία also, both of them names which have no place in Paul's nomenclature. It is just so with regard to his references to Asia Minor. True, it is of no moment that after Pamphylia he mentions Lycia also (xxvii. 5, cf. ii. 10, xiii. 13, xiv. 24, xv. 38), and Pontus (ii. 9, cf. xviii. 2) as well as Bithynia (xvi. 7), for in each of these instances the official usage of the Romans also retained the names of the two sections which were united to form the province. But Luke also uses the names of smaller districts in Asia Minor which at that time did not constitute provinces, but were distributed among various Roman provinces of other names, namely, Lycaonia (xiv. 6, cf. xiv. 11), Pisidia (xiv. 24, cf. xiii. 14), Mysia (xvi. 7, 8), and Phrygia (ii. 10, xvi.

6, xviii. 23). Since he also speaks of Asia (ii. 9 f., xvi. 6-8) along with Phrygia, Mysia, and Troas, and in the same connection, it follows that Asia, too, does not mean for him the whole Roman province of that name, cf. Winer, *RIV*,[3] i. 97 ; Wieseler, *Chronol.* 34. For at that time Mysia and the greater part of Phrygia belonged to the province of Asia, and the city of Troas was also situated in it. For the boundaries of the province of Asia, the Asia propria of Ptolemy (above, p. 184), see Waddington, *Fastes des prov. Asiat.* 25 ; Ramsay, *Hist. geogr.* 172, and the map in his *Church in the Roman Empire.* We are not dealing here, however, with a peculiarity of Luke. The Church at Lyons, intimately connected with the Churches of Asia Minor, writes in the year 177 (Eus. *H. E.* v. 1. 3), τοῖς κατὰ τὴν ᾿Ασίαν καὶ Φρυγίαν . . . ἀδελφοῖς. So Tertullian, *c. Praxean,* i, "ecclesiis Asiæ et Phrygiæ." Asia and Phrygia are here, as with Luke, mutually exclusive or supplementary terms, and Asia has a narrower meaning than in Roman official usage. It is the same region which Irenæus (*Epist. ad Flor.* in Eus. *H. E.* v. 20. 5, cf. Pausanias, i. 4. 6) calls ἡ κάτω ᾿Ασία, that part of the province Asia which lay nearer the coast, in distinction from the parts which lay farther inland (Acts xix. 1, τὰ ἀνωτερικὰ μέρη ; cf. Acts xviii. 23 ; Clearchus in Jos. *c. Ap.* i. 22. 180, Niese ; Epiph. *Hær.* xlv. 4, ἐν τοῖς ἀνωτάτω μέρεσιν). This more restricted use of the name corresponds to some extent with older boundaries (Marquardt, i. 334) and divisions (Plin. *H. N.* v. 27. 102), and to some extent also with Diocletian's arrangement, which returned in so many particulars to older groupings (Marquardt, i. 348). Luke appears, however, to use the term consistently in its narrowest sense. At least there is no necessity of supposing that in Acts xix. 10 the Phrygian cities, Laodicea, Hierapolis, and Colossæ (Col. ii. 1, iv. 13) are also intended, or of thinking of the entire province in Acts vi. 9, xix. 22, xx. 4, 16, 18, xxi. 27, xxiv. 18, xxvii. 2. Only in the mouth of Demetrius (xix. 26, 27) is it likely that the term, which is strengthened, moreover, by the addition of ὅλη and πᾶσα (cf. Judea above), is used in its wider application. In Acts xvi. 6 this is quite excluded by the accompanying and contrasted Φρυγία. Both recensions (אABCE and D with the old versions against HLP) agree on the main point in the reading of xvi. 6 f. : διῆλθον δὲ τὴν Φρυγίαν καὶ Γαλατικὴν χώραν . . . ἐλθόντες (or γενόμενοι) δὲ κατὰ τὴν Μυσίαν. The article before Γαλ. (EHLP) is to be suspected as a simplification, and the reading *Galatie* (sic) *regiones* (cf. Acts viii. 1), preserved only in one Latin authority (Blass, ed. min. 53), seems to be an arbitrary substitution for an unusual expression. If we compare xviii. 23, διερχόμενος καθεξῆς τὴν Γαλατικὴν χώραν καὶ Φρυγίαν, it would seem that the construction of Φρυγίαν as an adjective (Lightfoot, *Galatians,* 22 ; Ramsay, *Church in Roman Empire,* 78 ff.), which is quite impossible there, is out of the question in xvi. 6. If the analogy of xv. 41, where the article before Κιλικίαν is of very doubtful authenticity to say the least, or of Luke v. 17 ; Acts i. 8, ix. 31, or (to meet perfectly Ramsay's requirement, *Stud. Bibl. et Eccl.,* Oxford, 1896, p. 57) Luke iii. 1 (τῆς ᾿Ιτουραίας καὶ Τραχωνίτιδος χώρας ; cf. also Winer, *Gr.* § 19. 3-5 [Eng. trans. pp. 126-130] ; A. Buttmann, *Gr.* 85 ff. [Eng. trans. p. 97 ff.] ; Blass, *Gr.*[2] § 46. 11 [Eng. trans.[2] § 46. 11]), did not suffice to excuse the anarthrous Γαλ. χ. in xvi. 6, one might find in it an expression of the idea that this through-journey did not touch everything that fell within the term Γαλ. χ. from beginning to end ($\kappa\alpha\theta\epsilon\xi\tilde{\eta}s$, xviii. 23), but only some "Galatian country" among other regions. But the choice of the unusual geographical term can itself be explained naturally only on the ground that Luke, in deliberate consideration of the usage by which the whole great province, including the Lycaonian cities, and the so-called Pisidian Antioch and other Phrygian cities, was styled $\dot{\eta}$ $\Gamma\alpha\lambda\alpha\tau\acute{\iota}\alpha$ or $\dot{\eta}$ $\Gamma\alpha\lambda\alpha\tau\iota\kappa\dot{\eta}$ $\dot{\epsilon}\pi\alpha\rho\chi\acute{\iota}\alpha$, meant by $\Gamma\alpha\lambda\alpha\tau\iota\kappa\dot{\eta}$ $\chi\acute{\omega}\rho\alpha$ to indicate the country of the actual Galatæ, which was absolutely distinct from the districts of Phrygia and Lycaonia from which Paul came to it. The attempt of Renan, *St. Paul*, 52, and the still more ingenious attempt of Ramsay, *Church in Roman Empire*, 77 ff., to interpret Luke's $\Gamma\alpha\lambda$. χ. as also referring to the Roman province, go to pieces first of all on the connection of the narrative. The journey was from Syrian Antioch first through Syrian and Cilician territory (xv. 41), but this only in passing. According to xv. 36 the first object was to visit the four Churches which had been founded in the three Lycaonian cities and Pisidian Antioch on the first missionary journey (xiii. 14–xiv. 23). This visit is reported xvi. 1–5. The journey, proceeding from south-east to north-west, brought Paul first to Derbe and then to Lystra. Here the narrative pauses in order to relate something of Timothy, who lived there. That the journey was continued to Iconium and Antioch is not expressly stated, not even with regard to Iconium, which is mentioned in xvi. 2 for an incidental reason only. But in view of xv. 36 it goes without saying that Iconium and Antioch were not omitted, and that xvi. 4, 5 refers to all four cities and their Churches. Not till the missionaries had reached Antioch, a meeting-place of the roads leading west and north, did the question arise whether they should continue their journey in a westerly direction, *i.e.* to Asia, or northward. A revelation from "the Spirit" decided the question. The negative expression employed by the narrator shows that the intention and inclination of the missionaries themselves had been to proceed, after the visitation of the four Churches, to "Asia," to the large cities on the coast,—Ephesus, Smyrna, etc.,—and to preach there. In this, however, they were hindered by the Spirit; and this decision, according to the clear construction of the best-attested text, gives the reason why the missionaries now, instead of journeying westward from Antioch toward Asia, turned northward rather, and proceeded through Phrygian territory, on which they had already entered just before reaching Antioch, and then through a part of Galatia proper, until they reached the borders of Bithynia. Thus the order of events and of the geographical terms shows clearly that by $\Gamma\alpha\lambda$. $\chi\acute{\omega}\rho\alpha$ Luke did not mean the province of Galatia, within which the missionaries already were during their stay in Derbe, Lystra, Iconium, and Antioch, but the country of the Galatæ. It is in vain that Ramsay (77 f.) undertakes to persuade us that xvi. 6*a* is to be carried back to the journey already described by its content, and to be understood in some such way as this : "On the tour of visitation described in xvi. 4 f. they traversed a region which, with respect to its population, may be called Phrygian, and with respect to the Roman provincial divisions, Galatian." In the first place, the account of the tour of visitation is entirely finished in xvi. 1–5. In the second place, $\delta\iota\tilde{\eta}\lambda\theta\sigma\nu$ has for its temporal and logical presupposition the decision of the Spirit, which would be communicated only at the close of the visitation and as they were on the point of departure

from Pisidian Antioch, *i.e.* διῆλθον can only refer to a farther journey
which followed the completed tour of visitation. In the third place, as has
been shown, we are to understand by the cities of xvi. 4, 5 not only Iconium
and‘ Antioch, to which if necessary Ramsay's elaborate paraphrase of the
simple words might be applied (see n. 5), but Lystra and Derbe as well.
These, however, were not Phrygian but Lycaonian cities—particularly according to Luke's own usage, Acts xiv. 6, 11. Further, according to Ramsay (76)
we are to understand Acts xvi. 6*b*, 7*a* as stating : "The Spirit forbade their
preaching in Asia, but by no means forbade travelling through ; accordingly
they proceeded through a part of the province of Asia also as far as Bithynia,
but without preaching." But, in the first place, it follows from Acts xx. 18,
(cf. xix. 8–10, xx. 31) that before Paul's first arrival in Ephesus (xviii. 19),
and therefore before his first activity in Macedonia and Greece (xvi. 11–xviii.
17), he had not been in the region which Luke calls Asia at all. Furthermore, the unprejudiced reader finds in the text no suggestion of an antithesis
between "preaching" and "travelling," or of a journey through part of
"Asia," but sees only the contrast between the mutually exclusive geographical
references. Because they may not preach, and consequently may not travel,
in Asia, where they wished to go as missionaries, they go through Phrygia
and through Galatian country, not forgetting, of course, that preaching was
their commission. Since an intelligent narrator in such a connection would
have made explicit reference to the contrary condition, we must assume that
the missionaries, as they continued their journey from Antioch, tried to
apply themselves to their vocation. The difficulties which Ramsay (81 ff.)
urges against what is shown by Acts xvi. 6*a* to be the fact, namely, that
Paul then passed through a part of the Galatian region preaching, rest upon
the arbitrary assumption that when he set out from Pisidian Antioch or from
Iconium he already had Bithynia in view as his objective, and that until
he reached this goal he wished to refrain from preaching (84). In that case,
certainly, he would have had no occasion to touch Galatian cities like Pessinus,
the capital of the Tolistobogii, or the colony Germa. He would have gone
more directly to Nicæa and Nicomedia by way of Cotiæum or by Nacoleia
and Dorylæum. But the second assumption has no foundation in the text,
and the first contradicts the text. But the purpose to push forward into
Bithynia was first conceived when Paul stood not far from its border, and
at the same time at a point where another road struck off toward Mysia
(xvi. 7). The phrase ἐπείραζον εἰς τὴν Βιθυνίαν πορεύεσθαι does not at all
suggest that the missionaries had now attained a long-sought-for goal, but,
on the contrary, rather that, having arrived at this point, they were trying
to decide in which direction they should turn next. We do not know their
route in detail ; it may have been a zigzag course, as the hope of finding
somewhere a favourable soil for their preaching drew them now this way
and now that. A side trip into Galatia proper may have ended with a
return to Phrygia, as on the first journey the side trip from Antioch
(which was not originally intended) returned to that city (xiv. 21). The
summary account in xvi. 6–8, especially the union of Phrygia and the
Galatian country under one article, leaves the utmost freedom to fancy.
The present writer does not know what objection there would be to
supposing that the missionaries, setting out from Armarium, say, under-

took to preach in Pessinus and Germa, and finding the conditions there unfavourable or their success small, turned to Dorylæum, where, then, it was necessary to decide whether they should proceed to Bithynia or to Mysia. Again, Acts xviii. 23 raises difficulties not for us, but for Ramsay. Though he claims that in Acts xvi. 6 the vicinity of Iconium and Antioch is styled "the Phrygian and at the same time Galatian country," he interprets (93) quite differently the double term in xviii. 23, which except for the relative position of the two members is precisely similar. Here, he tells us, τὴν Γαλατικὴν χώραν by itself denotes the district so enigmatically referred to in xvi. 6, but with the addition of Derbe and Lystra; and Φρυγίαν, beside it, denotes the region usually so called, to which Paul betook himself after visiting the Churches which had been organised on the first journey. This of itself is a good deal to ask the exegete to believe; but it ought besides to be shown, by examples or credible conjectures, that the southern part of the province of Galatia may conceivably have been called ἡ Γαλ. χ. (note the article), or why Luke, if he merely wished to say that at some point Paul passed through the province, did not write τὴν Γαλατίαν, to be sure, leaving the reader to guess what route he followed. Differing from his earlier view, Ramsay (*Historical Comm.* 209) finds the expression xviii. 23 only shorter than that in xvi. 6, and in spite of the arrangement of the words assures us that in xviii. 23 "the Phrygian region" is mentioned. But if, on the contrary, Luke here, too, meant by ἡ Γαλ. χ. the northern part of the province, the country of the Galatæ,— Galatia, strictly speaking,—then it follows first from the order of the districts named that Paul on this occasion, as compared with xvi. 6, was travelling in quite a different direction, not from the south toward the north and north-east, but from east to west. Further, καθεξῆς indicates that he did not visit merely individual towns in the two districts as on the former journey, but that he traversed both quite extensively. Also the fact that there is no mention here of Churches, but only of disciples (see above, p. 176), does not agree well with the opinion that it has to do with a visit to the great Churches which Paul himself had established in the Southern part of the province. The expression πάντας τοὺς μαθητάς does not at all allow one to think of a great number, but is to be explained by the number of the places where Paul met disciples. The route this time may have been from the Cilician Gates by way of Tyana, Archelaïs, Ancyra, Pessinus, and on through northern Phrygia to Ephesus. The journey did not bring him (cf. Col. ii. 1) to the valley of the Lycus and the Meander, which would have been the natural way if he had occasion to go from Iconium and Antioch to Ephesus. The support which Ramsay (*Stud. Bibl. et Eccl.*, Oxford, 16 ff.) finds for his view of Acts xviii. 23 in a homily of Asterius (Migne, xl. 294), which he claims as evidence of an old tradition, appears weak. Asterius' homily, like an essay on Paul's journeys falsely ascribed to Euthalius (Zacagni, *Coll. mon.* 426), took the Antioch of Acts xviii. 22 to be the Pisidian Antioch. Asterius, sharing this undoubtedly traditional error, is reminded, probably without looking up the references, of the narrative, Acts xiii. 14–xiv. 7, and then tacitly assumes Λυκαονίαν instead of Γαλατικὴν χώραν as the text of xviii. 23. Since Ramsay also (*Historical Comm.* 209 f., 314 ff.) is unable to adduce one satisfactory proof for his ever varying interpretation of (ἡ) Γαλατικὴ χωρα, he has deprived himself of all right to lay stress upon the lack of examples elsewhere of this designation of the Galatian country proper, as a determining reason against this interpretation (namely, the country inhabited by Galatians). In itself, indeed, the expression is anything but striking. Cf. e.g. 1 Macc. viii. 8 (χώραν τὴν Ἰνδικήν), x. 38, xii. 25 ; Jos. Bell. iii. 3. 4 (ἡ Σαμαρεῖτις χώρα), and the innumerable instances, where an adjective formed from the name of a people with the ending -ικος in the feminine, designates the country inhabited by the people concerned, also without χώρα which is to be understood, as ἡ Κελτική, Ἰσαυρκή, Ἰνδική, Περσική.

5. (Pp. 176, 177.) ANTIOCH, on Phrygian soil, near the border of Pisidia, hence Ἀντιώχεια πρὸς Πισιδίᾳ, Strabo, 557, 569, 577, less exactly Ἀντ. Πισιδίας, Ptol. v. 4. 11, or Ἀντ. ἡ Πισιδία (v.l. τῆς Πισιδίας), Acts xiii. 14, now Yalowadi, the most important military colony of Augustus in that region, founded probably in 6 B.C. (Marquardt, i. 365 ; Ramsay, Hist. Geogr. 398, 396, 391 ; Church in Roman Empire, 25–27). ICONIUM, the most south-easterly city of Phrygia (Xen. Anab. i. 2. 19), still called a Phrygian city about 160 by a Christian who was born there (Acta Justini, chap. iv. ed. Otto, ii. 3. 274), and again a century later by bishop Firmilianus, who attended a synod there (Cyprian, Ep. lxxv. 7), and distinguished from the Lycaonian cities in Acts xiv. 1, 6 also (cf. Ramsay, Church in Roman Empire, 37 ff.), was nevertheless commonly reckoned with Lycaonia (Cic. Ep. xv. 4. 2 ; Strabo, 568 ; Plin. Hist. Nat. v. 27. 95), in fact was considered its chief city, a Roman colony under the emperor Claudius (contrary to Ramsay, Hist. Comm. 123, who disputes this, see ZKom. Gal. 13), and at that time attached to the province of Galatia (C. I. Gr. 3991, see p. 184 above). LYSTRA, a colony of Augustus, see Sterrett, The Wolfe Expedition, p. 142, No. 242 (by which the situation is determined also), p. 219, No. 352 ; Ramsay, Hist. Geogr. 332, 390, 398 ; Church in Roman Empire, 48. DERBE, probably near the modern Gudelissin, between one and two days' journey from Lystra, farther west and nearer the Isaurian mountains than was formerly supposed, probably made a colony under Claudius, and named Claudio-Derbe, cf. Sterrett, 20 ff. ; Ramsay, Hist. Geogr. 336; Church in Roman Empire, 54, 69. All four of the cities, then, in which we are to look primarily for "the Churches of Galatia," were half Roman cities like Philippi and Corinth. The more natural is it therefore that the "Roman" Paul (Acts xvi. 37) should address these Christians not as Lycaonians and Phrygians, but as Galatians, from the province to which they belonged. When we come to inquire whether these four Churches or the Christians of Galatia proper, who are not so much as called Churches in Acts xviii. 23, are the ἐκκλησίαι τῆς Γαλατίας referred to in Gal. i. 2 ; 1 Cor. xvi. 1 ; 1 Pet. i. 1, we must further take into consideration the fact that in the post-canonical literature, also, the Lycaonian Churches occupy a much more prominent place than the north Galatian. In the Thecla legend we find Iconium, Lystra, Antioch, and perhaps, in the perverted form Daphne, Derbe as well, GK, ii. 908. In the passage already mentioned, Cypr. Ep. lxxv. 7, Firmilian says : " Quod totum nos iam pridem in Iconio, qui Phrygiæ locus est, collecti in unum convenientibus ex Galatia et Cilicia et ceteris proximis regionibus confirmavimus," etc. As the reporter himself was bishop of Cæsarea, Cappadocia was also represented in the synod

in addition to the districts mentioned by name. Iconium was a centre of ecclesiastical life. Contemporaries of Origen speak of a bishop Celsus of Iconium and a bishop Neon of Laranda (in Eus. *II. E.* vi. 19. 18) ; a little later Nicomas of Iconium is mentioned as a noted bishop, Eus. vii. 29. 2. On the other hand, Church history has little to say of the cities in the Galatian region. We know from Eus. *II. E.* v. 16. 4 that there was a Christian Church in Ancyra about 192 A.D. The next witness is the Synod of Ancyra in 314, at which Marcellus of Ancyra probably presided ; cf. the writer's essay on Marcellus, 8 f. ; Hefele, *Konziliengesch.*[2] i. 221; *Stud. Bibl. et Eccl.*, Oxford, iii. 197, 211. Lequien, *Oriens Christ.* i. 489 f., could not discover any bishop of Pessinus earlier than the fifth century.

6. (P. 177.) Furthermore, if the appearance of Judaisers in Galatia pre-supposes the presence of Jews and Jewish Christians as a natural point of connection, we know from Acts xiii. 14–51, xiv. 19, that Antioch had to all appearances a prominent and influential body of Jews. In Iconium, too, there was a synagogue largely attended by Jews and God-fearing Gentiles (xiv. 1), and in Lystra (or Derbe ?), the home of Timothy, who was of Jewish descent on his mother's side, there were at least individual Jews (xvi. 1–3 ; 2 Tim. i. 5, iii. 15). On the other hand, even in rhetorical accounts like that of Philo, *Leg. ad Cai.* xxxvi, one hears nothing of Jews in the Galatian country. In Acts ii. 9–11, Galatia is not included. That Jews had gone to Ancyra is a pure conjecture of Scaliger's in connection with Jos. *Ant.* xvi. 6. 2 ; and even if the conjecture were right, it would point to the Ancyra in the province of Asia, and not to the Galatian city of that name ; cf. Mommsen, *Res. Gestæ D. Aug.* ed. 2, p. x ; Waddington, *Fastes des prov. Asiat.* 102, whose con-jecture is Pergamus. An epitaph (*C. I. Gr.* No. 4129), which is possibly Jewish, and which was not found in the Galatian region, but near its western boundary, and another, discovered on the road between Germa and Pessinus, and probably from a somewhat later period (*Bull. de Corresp. hellén.* 1883, p. 24), do not prove that there were Jews in the Galatian region in the first century. Cf. *ZKom. Gal.* 13, A. 12. We are by no means to infer from Acts xiii. 43 that any considerable number of Jews in Antioch became adherents to Christianity, for it is not said that the admonitions of the missionaries were accepted by the Jews, who were at first favourably inclined toward them. According to xiii. 45–51, for which we are already prepared by xiii. 41, the contrary is more probable. In xiii. 48 f. it is only said of a number of Gentiles in and about Antioch that they really became believers and so continued. In Iconium it seems not to have been very different (xiv. 1–7), even if the success among the Jews was perhaps some-what greater there than in Antioch. From the reports concerning Lystra and Derbe, aside from the supplementary notice of Timothy's Jewish mother (xvi. 1), and the intimation of an influence exercised upon the citizens of Lystra and Derbe by the Jews of Antioch and Iconium (xiv. 19), one receives nothing more than the impression that the missionaries were dealing with Gentiles, xiv. 6–18. The fact that Paul constantly deals with the readers of Galatians as Gentile Christians (see p. 166 f. above) is consequently no obstacle to the assumption that it was primarily these four Churches for which Galatians was intended. It is impossible to say with Wieseler (*Komm.* 533) that Paul in ii. 15 ff., iii. 13, 23–25, iv. 3 groups himself and his readers together as

Jewish Christians. The readers, the great majority of whom were of Gentile origin, understood readily enough that in these passages Paul was associating with himself in a "we" not themselves, but others who like him were of Jewish birth. In ii. 15 this is perfectly clear from the context, ii. 11–14, even if one does not take ii. 15 ff. as a continuation of the address to Peter. In iii. 13, 14 the distinction between ἡμᾶς, to whom Paul belongs, and τὰ ἔθνη, to whom the readers belong, is unmistakable. So is the transition from the Jewish Christians in whose name Paul speaks to the Gentile Christians whom he addresses, iii. 23–25 to iii. 26–29, and iv. 1–7 to iv. 8–11. Only it follows from the otherwise superfluous πάντες, iii. 26, and ὅσοι, iii. 27, and especially from iii. 28, that there were also some of Jewish birth among the readers themselves ; for only on this supposition could the idea that in Christianity distinctions between Jew and Gentile, like those between man and woman, or between slave and freeman, are ideally abolished, be expressed in the form of the direct address, "*you all*" (instead of, we all, *i.e.* we Jews and you Gentiles) "are one in Christ." These four Churches were composed of a few full-born Jews, a number of proselytes of different grades (Acts xiii. 43, xiv. 1, xvi. 1), and a much larger number of Gentiles, and they received through Paul the stamp of law-free Gentile Churches (cf. Acts xvi. 4). According to Galatians, the same was true of the Churches of Galatia. The two groups are identical.

7. (P. 178.) Hofmann, i. 93, thought it permissible to interpret ὑμᾶς, Gal. ii. 5, of the Gentile world not yet affected by the gospel ; Sieffert, finding this at variance with the text, understood Gentile Christians at large. But comparison with Eph. ii. 11 or Eph. iii. 1 f., by which one or the other view is to be supported, shows that Paul would have indicated it by an appositional phrase like τὰ ἔθνη if he meant to take the readers as representatives either of Gentile Christians at large or of the Gentile world. In the latter case one ought also to expect that he would have referred to the former status of his readers as a condition now past, as in Eph. ii. 11 f. (ποτὲ . . . τῷ καιρῷ ἐκείνῳ); 1 Cor. xii. 2. Moreover, the translation "for you" cannot be defended ; the phrase presupposes, rather, that the readers had already received "the truth of the gospel." The use of πρός is not more remarkable than in ἐπιμένειν πρός τινα, Gal. i. 18 ; 1 Cor. xvi. 7, cf. Buttmann, *Gram.* 292 [Eng. trans. 339 f.]. διαμένειν in such a connection only intimates with especial emphasis that the relation in which the true gospel had already stood to the Galatians was to continue uninterrupted for all time.

§ 12. TIME AND PLACE OF THE COMPOSITION OF THE EPISTLE TO THE GALATIANS.

On the supposition that the Galatians addressed in this letter are to be sought in the northern part of the province of that name and only there, the *terminus a quo* of the Epistle is fixed as the settlement of Paul in Ephesus at the beginning of the year 55 (Acts xix. 1). The second visit implied in Gal. iv. 13 will then be the one referred to in Acts xviii. 23 ; and even when the error is avoided of supposing that ταχέως in Gal. i. 6 implies that the danger which was threatening the Galatian Churches at the hands of the Judaisers, and which occasioned this letter, arose immediately after this second visit of Paul, the advocate of this theory will be inclined to place the composition of the letter in the period of $2\frac{1}{4}$ years ending at Pentecost 57 (n. 1), during which Paul was at work in Ephesus (Acts xix. 8–10). But this time and place seem to be ruled out by the fact that in Gal. iv. 20 it is taken for granted that Paul is at such a distance from the readers that it is impossible for him to make a journey to them in the near future (above, p. 170). Yet at any time during the year it was quite possible to make the journey from Ephesus to Pessinus or Ancyra. Furthermore, if the letter was written in Ephesus, the expression in Gal. iv. 20, of a desire to visit them which could not be fulfilled, is very strange, in view of the fact that during this period Paul did visit the Church in Corinth (§ 17).

If, on the other hand, it be accepted as proved that the letter was meant for the Churches in South Galatia which were founded on the first missionary journey, every reason for supposing that the letter was written in Ephesus between the beginning of the year 55 and Pentecost 57 disappears. Then the *terminus a quo* is the second visit to the Churches in Lycaonia (Acts xvi. 1–5) in the spring of 52. Any reference of the letter to an earlier date (n. 2) is at once precluded by the chronological and historical data of Gal. i. 15–ii. 10. The apostolic council, to which reference is made in Gal. ii. 1–10 (cf. Acts xv. 1–29), took place during the winter of 51–52. It was not until after this council that Paul and Silas set out upon the second missionary journey, and visited the Churches in Lycaonia a second time. Similarly the *terminus ad quem* of Galatians is the beginning of Paul's two imprisonments in Cæsarea and Rome (Pentecost 58), which together lasted for at least five years. The hypothesis that Galatians was written while Paul was a prisoner in Rome is of long standing (n. 3), but quite untenable. All the letters which Paul wrote while in prison, or which he is supposed to have written in prison, disclose this fact unmistakably and in various ways (Col. iv. 3, 10, 18, cf. i. 24 ; Eph. iii. 1, iv. 1, vi. 20 ; Philem. 1, 9, 10, 13, 22, 23 ; Phil. i. 7, 12–17, cf. ii. 23, iv. 10–18 ; 2 Tim. i. 8, 16, ii. 9, cf. i. 12, ii. 10, iv. 6–18). But in Galatians there is no hint that at the time of writing Paul's free movements were hindered, or that he was being persecuted by the civil authorities on account of his missionary activity. If he had been in prison at the time, he could hardly have failed to make some reference to the fact in the passage where he expresses his earnest wish, impossible of fulfilment, that he might be present among the Galatian Churches in person, and that they might hear his trembling voice (iv. 20). Nor, when speaking of his preaching as still being carried on, ii. 2, v. 11, also i. 8, 16, could he have remained entirely silent about his captivity had he been a prisoner. While, to be sure, he is being opposed, iv. 29, v. 11, his persecutors are Judaising Christians, and the means employed are not violence, but slanders and insinuations. When he does speak of bodily injuries inflicted upon him on account of his Christian faith or on account of his missionary activity (vi. 17), they are not referred to, as in the letters of his imprisonment, as something being endured at the time ; he simply mentions the marks of injuries received some time before, which he still bore and could show. In view of the infrequency of references of this kind in Paul's letters, it is very improbable that he is referring to the marks of ill-treatment which he had borne for years, such as an ineffaceable scar on his forehead, or the maiming of a limb caused by a stone thrown at the time when he was organising the Church in Galatia (Acts xiv. 19, cf. xiv. 5), or on some other occasion about which we are not definitely informed (2 Cor. xi. 23–25 ; 1 Cor. xv. 32 ?). The mention of the fact, τὰ στίγματα τοῦ ᾽Ιησοῦ ἐν τῷ σώματί μου βαστάζω, and the peculiar expression used, are natural here only if the wounds, marks of which were still visible when Galatians was written, had been in‧flicted not very long before. They are the same as those clearly referred to in 1 Thess. ii. 2 (προπαθόντες καὶ ὑβρισ‧θέντες ἐν Φιλίπποις). That on this occasion Paul and Silas were not only insulted, but also roughly handled, is clear from Acts xvi. 22–24, 33, 37–38.

But this evidence may be left quite out of account; for if, as has been shown, dates previous to the spring of 52 (Acts xvi. 1–5), and subsequent to Pentecost 58 (Acts xx. 16 ff.), are precluded, and if the letter could not have been written during the 2¼ or, reckoned from the first arrival of Paul in Ephesus, the three years' stay in that city, i.e. between Pentecost 54 and Pentecost 57 (Acts xviii. 19, xix. 1, 8–10, xx. 18, 31), then it must have been written shortly after the events described in Acts xvi. 22 ff. After Paul's second visit to the Churches in Lycaonia during the summer of 52, and his preaching tour through several parts of the province of Galatia, where he had not been before (Acts xvi. 1–6, cf. second preaching presupposed in Gal. iv. 13), at least several months must have elapsed before Galatians was written. Besides, it required time for the Judaisers to reach Galatia, as they did in the interval, and for them to secure the wide influence which they contrived to win, and for this state of affairs to be reported to Paul, who had gone over to Europe. Before the close of the year 52, Paul had settled in Corinth for a stay of eighteen months (Acts xviii. 11), lasting up to the summer of 54. Galatians was written during this time, and more probably in the first half of the period than in the second. A company of

believers was already gathered about Paul in the place
where he was staying (Gal. i. 2), but no one of these
appears to have been closely associated with the Galatian
Churches. If we were right in concluding (above, p. 170)
that Paul could not have addressed a letter to Churches in
Timothy's home (Acts xvi. 1), and to Churches which he
had visited in company with Silas some time before, and
warned against the Judaistic propaganda (Gal. v. 3,
i. 9), without sending greetings from both these persons,
so well known among the Galatians, if they were with
him at the time, then it follows that Galatians could not
have been written when Silas and Timothy were with
Paul in Corinth, when the two letters to the Thessalonians were written in his own name and theirs. The
letter must be dated either before or after this time,
either while he was waiting for them in Corinth (Acts
xviii. 1–5), or after the two helpers had left Corinth
again, a period the length of which cannot be definitely
determined. The former is the more probable. At the
time of the first letter to the Thessalonians, shortly after
Timothy's arrival in Corinth (1 Thess. iii. 6), he had
already had occasion to learn from Christians, who did
not belong in Macedonia or Achaia, or anywhere in
Europe, that they were familiar with the organisation of
the Church in Thessalonica (1 Thess. i. 8 f. ; see below,
§ 13). When Paul had been on the point of informing
them of the cheering successes in Macedonia, they had
replied that this was no news to them, or they had anticipated his account by expressions of joy at the triumph of
the gospel in Macedonia. The persons referred to must
have been Christians, who came to Paul in Corinth from
Asia, before the time indicated in Acts xviii. 5 and 1 Thess.
iii. 6. And they must have come directly by sea ; for
if they had come by the land route through Macedonia,
visiting the Churches in Philippi and Thessalonica which
lay on their way, Paul could not have related to the Thessa-

Ionian Church what these Christians from abroad had said to him, in the manner that he does in 1 Thess. i. 8 f. If, now, we ask where these Christians from Asia got their information about the circumstances under which the Church in Thessalonica was organised, the source could not possibly have been any written communication of Paul's; on the contrary, Paul is agreeably surprised by their voluntary expression of gratification at the entrance of the gospel into Thessalonica, and tells the Christians there about it in order to encourage them. So it must have been another Christian who had witnessed the progress of the gospel in Macedonia, and who at the same time was intimately associated with the Churches in Asia from which these Christians had come to Paul, who had sent reports of the missionary work in Macedonia to these Churches or to individual members of the same. What more natural than to suppose that this person was Timothy, who could hardly have failed to inform his mother, in Lystra, and through her the Churches in Galatia, what happened to him and his companions on their missionary journey through Macedonia? So these Christians from outside of Europe, who, according to 1 Thess. i. 8 f., did not need to be informed by Paul about the organisation of the Church in Thessalonica, because they had already heard about it in detail, were none other than the representatives of the Galatian Churches who brought the report of the incursion of the Judaisers in Galatia to Paul in Corinth (above, p. 169). In view of the condition of things in Galatia, Paul did not dare wait, so he sent the messengers from the Galatians home again as quickly as he could with a letter written by his own hand. When Silas and Timothy arrived, Galatians was already written and sent.

If this putting together of very simple exegetical observations is not altogether wrong, Galatians is the earliest of Paul's letters that has come down to us. At the time when it was written the marks of the blows which he had received in Philippi, possibly some eight or nine months before (Gal. vi. 17 ; 1 Thess. ii. 2), could very well have been still visible. If the intercourse between the Galatian Churches and Paul in Corinth took place by sea, as seems to be the case, Galatians was written some time after the opening of navigation, *i.e.* after March in the year 53, not very long before the arrival of Silas and Timothy in Corinth and the writing of 1 Thessalonians.

1. (P. 193.) As early as 370, Victorinus (Mai, *Script. vet. n. Coll.* iii. 2. 1) mentions as traditional the view that Galatians was written in Ephesus at the time of Paul's ministry there. The old prologues affirm the same (Cod. Fuld. 248 ; Amiatin. 296 ; Card. Thomasius, *Opp.* i. 402, 421, 433, 451). In more recent times this has been the prevailing view among those who understand by Galatia the country of Galatæ, *e.g.* Hug, *Einl.*[3] ii. 351 ; Wieseler, *Chronol. des apost. Zeitalters,* 285 ; *Komm. zum Gal.* 541 ; Hofmann, ii. 1. 1 ; Meyer-Sieffert, 24 ; Godet, *Introd.* i. 269. Confirmatory evidence has been sought in the fact that, according to Jewish tradition, the year from the autumn of 68 to the autumn of 69, and therefore also the year 54–55, were Sabbatical years (Anger, *Ratio Temporum,* 38 ; Wieseler, *Chronol. Synopse,* 204 ; *Komm. zum Gal.* 356, 542, cf. the summary in Schürer, i. 35 ff. [Eng. trans. I. i. 41–43]), and it has further been supposed that this was referred to in Gal. iv. 10 (ἐνιαυτούς). But if this, the last of the seasons there enumerated, had an actual significance for the readers at that time, we should expect a more explicit emphasis upon it. Chronologically, too, this supposition, if all its premises were valid, would still be highly improbable. If the two and a quarter years, Acts xix. 8–10, ended with Pentecost 57, Paul must have begun his stay in Ephesus somewhere near the last of February 55. But since several months must have elapsed between his arrival there (which followed directly upon his second visit to the Galatian region, Acts xviii. 23) and the writing of Galatians, it appears that the Sabbatical year ending in the autumn of 55 was already past when the Epistle was sent. Moreover, it was half gone when Paul last visited the Galatians without his noticing then any signs of Judaistic tendencies (see p. 165 f. above). But it is exceedingly improbable that the Judaisers from Jerusalem, arriving among the Galatians in the latter half of the Sabbatical year, should have come out at once with the recommendation of the legal provisions in this particular, and have succeeded with them before the expiration of the year. We must note, besides, that the Sabbatical year in any case was observed only in Palestine and the neighbouring districts, and then not with the same exactness in all parts of the Holy Land (Mishna, Shebiith vi. 1, ix. 2 ; cf. A. Geiger, *Lesestücke aus der Mischna,* 75 f., 78 f.), a fact which Clemen, *Chronol. der paulin. Briefe,* 204, presents with quite arbitrary inadequacy. Of the representatives of the old idea of "Galatia,"

Gal. i. 2, Bleck (*Einl.* 1862, S. 418) and Lightfoot (*Galatians*, 36–56) assigned the Epistle to a period between 2 Cor. and Rom., both on account of the affinity in thought between Gal. and Rom., and because of the great difference between Gal. and 1 and 2 Thess. ; Gal., then, would have been written in the three months Acts xx. 3, or on the journey through Macedonia just before. Some, too, who have cut loose from the old assumption with regard to the persons to whom the letter was sent, have been so impressed with the idea of the development of Pauline thought as reflected in the succession of the Epistles, as to suppose that they must even put Galatians later than Romans. So, for example, Kühn, *NKZ*, 1895, S. 156–162, who thinks that Galatians was sent to the Lycaonian Churches during the apostle's imprisonment in Cæsarea. Clemen, too, in his altogether confused *Chronologie* (205), puts Galatians after Romans, though he cannot tell us where it was written (203). Kühn (159) and Clemen (200 ff.) see confirmation in Gal. ii. 10, which they understand as a reference to the great collection which Paul was only just ready to take to Jerusalem when Romans was written (Rom. xv. 25 ff.). But as little as the obligation which Paul assumed in the apostolic council, according to the tenor of Gal. ii. 10, looked merely to the gathering of a single money collection in specified parts of the Gentile Church, just so little did he appeal to one such collection as the fulfilment of it. He can testify, rather, that he has been zealous and diligent to meet the obligation assumed at the council, and this he could not say unless immediately upon his return from Jerusalem, in Antioch, Syria, Cilicia, and on his second missionary journey (Acts xv. 30–xvi. 5), he had stirred up the existing Gentile Christian Churches to make these collections and gifts. On the other hand, Gal. ii. 10 would be empty talk, if the contribution which he took to Jerusalem about Pentecost 58 were the first fruit of his ostensibly so zealous endeavour to carry out a pledge made some six and a half years before. We need not here concern ourselves with the question whether the Galatian and Asiatic Churches had any part in the great collection of 58, which would seem from Rom. xv. 26, 2 Cor. viii.–ix., not to have been the case, and which cannot be inferred from 1 Cor. xvi. 1 ; Acts xx. 4. Between 52 and 58 three or six contributions may have been sent to Jerusalem from the Galatian Churches and others founded and guided by Paul, just as gifts had already been sent before (Acts xi. 30). From Gal. ii. 10 we must conclude that a beginning had been made within the first year after the apostolic council. Even Ramsay (*Church in Roman Empire*, 101) seems to have been influenced to some extent by Lightfoot's discussion to put Galatians as late as his historical and geographical data would permit, and holds that the Epistle was written from Antioch in 55, at the beginning of the third missionary journey (p. 168 ; Acts xviii. 22 f.). I merely ask how Paul, who, according to Ramsay's interpretation of Acts xviii. 23 (see p. 190 above), was then on the point of visiting the Galatian Churches for the third time, could have written iv. 20, or the letter as a whole, without alluding to his impending visit. We shall never reach a chronological arrangement of Paul's Epistles which will do justice to the indications of the letters themselves and to the notices in Acts, if we assume as our underlying premise that Paul was a theological thinker and writer, who derived the essential impulse to the composition of his letters, the choice of his teaching material, and the particular manner of its treatment in the several Epistles, from the progress of his investigations. Rather was he a missionary, who was determined not only in the composition of Epistles, but in the choice of themes and treatment, by the aims of this his calling, and the requirements of the Churches which he had founded and which were under his care. Through long preparation, and longer missionary experience, he had arrived at fixed and basal principles before he wrote the first of the letters which have come down to us. The ideas of Galatians which reappear in Romans must have become perfectly clear to him, at the latest, at the time of the controversies described in Acts xv. and Gal. ii. 1–10. According to Gal. ii. 15–21, cf. i. 12–16 ; 2 Cor. iv. 6, v. 16 f.; Rom. vii. 6–viii. 2 ; Phil. iii. 5–12, they were rooted in the very experiences which made him a Christian. But in that conflict he must not only have become conscious of the contradiction between his Christianity and that of the Pharisaic Christians, he must also have learned even then to develop from Scripture and from Christian experience the arguments for his gospel and against legalistic Christianity, and to use them as weapons in the debate. That he so uses them in Galatians requires no explanation beyond the fact that these controversies in Antioch and in Jerusalem already lay behind him, and that he was now confronted by substantially the same opponents in Galatia. The fact, too, that the ideas of justification by and through faith, together with their contraries, drop into the background in Thessalonians and Corinthians, and appear more prominently again in Romans and Philippians, shows simply that Paul was not a stupid schoolmaster repeating his monotonous formulas in season and out of season. The reason why the weapons, which had already been tested more than once in combat, were brought out again from his armoury when he wrote the letter to Rome, will become clear enough in our examination of that Epistle. Occasional expressions like 1 Cor. xv. 56 or 2 Cor. v. 21 show that the whole circle of thought which meets us first in Galatians did not become unfamiliar to the apostle in the interim. If it were admissible to interpret and explain the differences in teaching in the several Epistles from the order of their composition instead of from the variety of conditions in the Churches and in the historical occasion of the letters, one might infer from a comparison of Gal. iv. 10 with Rom. xiv. 5 f. that several years of inner development lay between Galatians and Romans, and Col. ii. 16 would have to be set near Galatians in time but as far as possible from Romans. Halmel, *Über röm. Recht im Gal.* 1895, concludes from the observation expressed in the title, together with the affinity between the theological conceptions of Galatians and Romans, "that Galatians must have been written in Rome or Italy, and in any case, therefore (*sic*), was not far removed from Romans in point of time" (S. v and 30). Now, there was an interval of more than three years between Romans, which was written from Corinth at the beginning of the year 58, and Paul's arrival at the capital in the spring of 61. As Halmel, further, does not insist on Rome at all, and consequently, it would seem, does not insist that the letter was written during Paul's two years' imprisonment there (Acts xxviii. 30), the possible interval between Galatians and Romans seems to stretch out to five years or more, that is, to some period after the expiration of the two years mentioned in Acts xxviii. 30, when Paul no longer sojourned as a prisoner in Rome, but somewhere in Italy in freedom. And this, we are told, is proximity in point of time! If the introduction of provisions of Roman law "as things quite well known" were really inconceivable outside of Rome and Italy, it would not suffice to remove the author thither; but, assuming that he wished to be understood, it would be necessary first of all to look for the readers also in Italy, instead of in Galatia. If, again, we are really to presuppose in Galatians an acquaintance with Roman law specifically (cf. *ZKom. Gal.* 160 ff., 191 ff.), it is a sufficient explanation that Paul, according to the tradition of Acts, which has never been assailed with any sound objection, was born a *civis Romanus*, and that the principal Churches of Galatia were located in Roman colonies (p. 191 above). Roman citizens, who claimed the privileges of Roman law, were found everywhere in the empire; cf., for example, *Berl. äg. griech. Urk.* Nos. 96, 15; 113. 3, 6; 327. 2; 361. ii. 19; and, moreover, Roman law had had everywhere a transforming influence on the legal procedure of the ἔθνη; cf. Strabo, x. p. 484.

2. (P. 194.) Calvin, who reckoned the fourteen years of Gal. ii. 1 before Paul's conversion, and identified the visit to Jerusalem there mentioned with that of Acts xi. 30, assigned the composition of Galatians to a date before the apostolic council (*Komm. zu Gal.* ii. 1–5, ed. Tholuck, 546). This presupposes—what Calvin does not expressly say, however—that the Galatian Churches were those situated in Lycaonia.

3. (P. 195.) The view that Galatians was written by Paul during his Roman imprisonment first gained currency, somewhat late, in the Eastern Churches. In the West, before Jerome's day, a very different view prevailed (above, p. 199, note 1). Among the expositors of Galatians, Ambrosiaster, Pelagius, Ephrem Syrus, and Theodore of Mopsuestia nowhere express themselves, to the writer's knowledge, with regard to the time and place of the Epistle. Chrysostom, not in his commentary on Galatians but in the introduction to Romans, gives his opinion that Paul wrote Galatians before Romans, that is, of course, like Romans, before his imprisonment (Montfaucon, ix. 427). Eusebius of Emesa (Cramer, *Cat.* vi. 67) seems to have been the first to find in Gal. iv. 20 an indication of imprisonment. Jerome, who in the preparation of his own commentary on Galatians made free use of Eusebius' and many others (*Praef.*, Vall. vii. 370), borrowed from him this interpretation of iv. 20 (468), and again, on vi. 11 (529), alludes to the imprisonment of Paul at the time of the Epistle, whereas on vi. 17 (534) he contents himself with a vague reference to the recital of his sufferings, 2 Cor. xi. 23 ff. Galatians was first assigned to the *Roman* imprisonment by the pseudo-Euthalius (Zacagni, 624), Theodoret (Noesselt, 4), Œcumenius (Hentenius, i. 713), and a number of Greek, Syriac, and Coptic Bible MSS. Possibly the fact that Galatians was not infrequently placed after Ephesians, that is, among the Epistles of the imprisonment (*GK*, ii. 351, 358, 360), contributed to the perpetuation of the error. Thus we see to what extent Halmel (30) is justified in calling this the general opinion of the early Church, and that we are not dealing with a historical tradition, but with the spread of an error which arose from a careless reading of the Epistle.

§ 13. THE ORIGIN OF THE CHURCH IN THESSA-LONICA, AND THE COURSE OF ITS HISTORY UNTIL THE COMPOSITION OF PAUL'S FIRST EPISTLE TO THE CHURCH THERE.

It must have been somewhere about September 52 when Paul, driven from Philippi, came directly to Thessalonica (1 Thess. ii. 2 ; Acts xvi. 19–xvii. 1) along with Silvanus or Silas (n. 1), without stopping in Amphipolis and Apollonia, which were situated upon the great military road by which he travelled (Via Egnatia). His younger helper, Timothy, who had been with him only during the journey from Lystra (n. 2), and the author of the account, who by the use of "we" in Acts xvi. 16–17 indicates his presence, and in Acts xvi. 13 his participation in the teaching activity of the missionaries, seem for the time being to have been left behind in Philippi. Although Timothy is not mentioned in connection with the flight of Paul and Silvanus from Thessalonica (Acts xvii. 10), and does not appear again until after Paul's departure from Berœa (Acts xvii. 14), it is not to be inferred that Timothy had no share in Paul's work at Thessalonica, nor is it to be supposed that he journeyed from Philippi to Berœa (or Berrhœa) without stopping on the way to visit the newly made converts in Thessalonica. If it may be regarded as certain that the "we" which runs through both letters includes both the helpers mentioned in the greeting with Paul as joint writers with him of the Epistle, then Timothy is to be considered one of the organisers of this Church (n. 3). After Paul's departure from Philippi, he very soon followed him to Thessalonica and thence to Berœa.

Before Byzantium became Constantinople, Thessalonica was the largest city on the Balkan peninsula (n. 4), which, together with the fact that it had a numerous Jewish population, made it a suitable station for Paul's work ; and, had it not been that he was compelled to go, he would not have left it so soon as he did. As it was, after three weeks' preaching in the synagogue (n. 5), the Jewish majority succeeded in stirring up the populace against the missionaries to such an extent, that the latter were compelled to conceal themselves; and, after their host Jason and several of the converts were brought before the city authorities in their stead, and released only on bail, the missionaries fled for refuge to Beroea.

The original Church in Thessalonica consisted of a few Jews and a large number of Greeks, some of whom, before they became Christians, had been adherents of the synagogue. Among them were several women belonging to the upper classes. Subsequent additions to the Church seem to have been made exclusively from the Gentile population (n. 6). That the attack upon the missionaries and the persecution of the new converts immediately following (Acts xvii. 5–9; 1 Thess. i. 6) emanated from the Jews, is clear from 1 Thess. ii. 15; since, inasmuch as Paul speaks here not of himself alone, but also of Silvanus and Timothy, the reference is not to the threatening of his life in Jerusalem (Acts ix. 29), but to his expulsion from Thessalonica and Beroea. But inasmuch as the Jews succeeded at once in arousing the populace against the missionaries by charging them with teaching doctrines contrary to the State, which led the politarchs to take precautionary measures oppressive to the Christians (Acts xvii. 5–9), it is not surprising that Paul, in speaking of the persecution which the Church had endured earlier, and was still enduring (1 Thess. i. 6, ii. 14, iii. 3; 2 Thess. i. 4), does not make special mention of the fact that the persecution was begun by the Jews. This oppressed condition of the infant Church in Thessalonica made the missionaries desirous of turning back immediately after their departure (1 Thess. ii. 17 f.), i.e. while they were still in Beroea. Speaking for himself, Paul assures them that he had made still a second attempt to carry out this intention, but had been hindered as before by Satan. This effort Paul must have made at the time when he was alone in Athens, waiting for Silvanus and Timothy (Acts xvii. 16). Here, however, the accounts in Acts do not correspond entirely with Paul's statements. Although Acts xvii. 15 gives the impression that Silvanus and Timothy were to follow Paul to Athens as soon as they could, there is no report of their arrival, which omission, together with what is said in Acts xviii. 5, forces one to the conclusion that these helpers remained for a considerable time longer in Macedonia, and did not join Paul again until he had been at work in Corinth for some time (n. 7). On the other hand, according to 1 Thess. iii. 1–6, Silvanus and Timothy actually came to Athens as Paul had instructed them to do (Acts xvii. 15), from which point Paul and Silvanus sent Timothy back to Macedonia, in particular to Thessalonica (n. 3). Shortly before the composition of this letter, Timothy returned with cheering news to Paul, or rather, since the " we " is retained in 1 Thess. iii. 6 f., to Paul and Silvanus, whereupon this letter was sent to the Church in Thessalonica in the name of all three.

The letter must have been written in Corinth. Had it been written in Athens, there would be something strange even about the ἐν ᾿Αθήναις of iii. 1 (but cf. 1 Cor. xv. 32, xvi. 8). Moreover, in i. 7 f. it seems to be presupposed that the gospel had been preached with good success, not in Athens alone, but in several places in Achaia, as it had been preached earlier in Macedonia. But we have definite proof for a later date, and so for Corinth as the place of composition in the statement (i. 8 f.) that the conversion of the Thessalonians was known not only in Macedonia (Berœa and possibly also Philippi) and Achaia (Athens and Corinth), whither the news was brought by those who preached the gospel in this region, but every-

where (ἐν παντὶ τόπῳ, cf. Rom. i. 8), so that it was unnecessary for Paul to tell the story of the founding of the
Thessalonian Church, but was able to listen to expressions
of praise and joy at the entrance of the gospel into Thessalonica (above, p. 197 f.).   Since the contrast to Macedonia
and Achaia implies that the persons in question must have
been Christians from Asia, not only is it necessary to
suppose that the news of the successful preaching of the
gospel in Thessalonica had reached the Christian Churches
in Asia, but it must also be assumed that Paul had had
occasion shortly before to converse with Christians from
Asia, and to learn from them the joy which had been
awakened in their home by his successes in Macedonia.
If Paul had received his information about the joyful
interest with which his missionary work in Macedonia was
followed only through letters from Galatia or Antioch in
Syria, he could not have written the words, οὐ μόνον ἐν τῇ
Μακεδονίᾳ καὶ ἐν τῇ Ἀχαίᾳ ἀλλὰ ἐν παντὶ τόπῳ ἡ πίστις ὑμῶν
ἡ πρὸς τὸν θεὸν ἐξελήλυθεν.   The expressions which follow
(λαλεῖν, ἀπαγγέλλουσιν) prove that the intercourse between
Paul and the representatives of the Churches outside of
Europe had been rather of the nature of a conversation, in
the course of which the latter had shown that they were
familiar with the story of the founding of the Church in
Thessalonica in all its details.   We have seen above,
p. 197 f., that in all probability these persons were the
ambassadors of the Galatian Churches.   But whether this
was so or not, unless the most extraordinary circumstances
be assumed, the spread of the news of the organisation
of the Churches in Macedonia as far as the Churches in
Galatia or Syria, and the reporting of the impression
which this news made there back to Paul, who was travelling in Europe, requires an interval of several months
between Paul's flight from Thessalonica and the composition of 1 Thessalonians.   If, therefore, for chronological
reasons, we conclude that the letter was written in Corinth

and not in Athens, the use of the three names in the greeting (i. 1) would indicate a time subsequent to the event described in Acts xviii. 5, while 1 Thess. iii. 6, shows that it was written immediately after this event. Paul wrote Galatians before the arrival of the helpers in Corinth, possibly in April or May 53 (above, p. 198); 1 Thessalonians after the reunion, possibly in June of the same year.

1. (P. 203.) The identity of Silas, Acts xv. 22, 27, 32 (34), 40, xvi. 19, 25, 29, xvii. 4, 10, 14, 15, xviii. 5, and Silvanus, 1 Thess. i. 1; 2 Thess. i. 1; 2 Cor. i. 19; 1 Pet. v. 12, appears from the statements made by Paul, and in Acts with regard to the second missionary journey. As to his double name, above, p. 31 f. As Acts xvi. 37 presupposes that he, like Paul, possessed Roman citizenship, he may have been one of the " Libertines" spoken of in Acts vi. 9, above, p. 60 f. As a man of prominence in the Jerusalem Church (xv. 22), of mature years, therefore, and besides prophetically gifted (xv. 32), he was sent together with Judas Barsabbas to accompany Paul and Barnabas to Antioch, in order to explain and confirm the decision of the apostolic council by word of mouth (xv. 27, 32). This implies that Silas was, on the one hand, a man who enjoyed the confidence of the mother Church; and, on the other hand, that he was also in sympathy with the progress of the Gentile mission up to that time. Both things were important for Paul, and probably decided him, after his break with Barnabas, to choose Silas of Jerusalem as his companion on the second missionary journey (xv. 40), instead of some one of the other teachers at Antioch (xiii. 1). Let it be noted here that what is said of the dissuasion of the Spirit, Acts xvi. 6, 7 (also xvii. 15, according to Cod. D), is not to be referred to Paul as the medium, for he used rather to receive such instructions in visions at night (xvi. 9, xviii. 9, xxiii. 11, xxvii. 23, cf. xxii. 17; 2 Cor. xii. 1–4), but to Silas (xv. 32, where καὶ αὐτοί, like καὶ αὐτούς, xv. 27, is to be taken by itself, and separated from προφῆται ὄντες by the punctuation—so Blass; only Judas and Silas were prophets, not Barnabas and Paul). The account in Acts xv. 30–34, partly because of the uncertainty of the text, is by no means as clear as one could wish. First, the clause xv. 34a is to be recognised as part of the earlier text, in the form ἔδοξε δὲ τῷ Σιλᾷ ἐπιμεῖναι αὐτούς (CD*) and πρὸς αὐτούς (correction in D), αὐτοῦ (min. 13=ev. 33, Gregory, Prol. 469, 618), αὐτόθι (3 min.), ibi (many MSS. of the Lat. Vulg. and Copt., Sah. and margin of S[3]) are to be regarded as alterations with a view to an easier reading. The opinion given by the prophet Silas, in such a way as not to exclude the action of the πνεῦμα, but rather to include it (cf. xv. 28), was that Judas and Silas should remain still longer in Antioch. The clause μόνος δὲ Ἰούδας ἐπορεύθη, vouched for only by D and some Latin MSS., is then an amplifying gloss, to explain the fact that in what follows there is mention only of Silas, and nothing of Judas' remaining there, whereas the ἔδοξε applied to both men. The gloss, moreover, is clumsy enough, as it should either have said, "Judas returned to Jerusalem notwithstanding," or

else, "Silas alone, however, really remained in Antioch." On the contrary, the stubborn clause 34a, so original in form and substance, which had a wide-spread and significant currency without the addition of 34b, is not to be understood as a gloss, reconciling the apparent contradiction between vv. 33 and 40. An emendator with this in view would have written simply, "But Silas preferred (perhaps at Paul's request) to remain longer in Antioch." 34a, probably the original in both recensions, was in the one so amplified by the addition of 34b that the reader learned to a certainty what became of Judas and Silas, while in the other it was struck out on account of the apparent contradiction between it and 33. It is possible, again, that a slip of the eye from αὐτούς, 33, to αὐτούς, 34a, was responsible for the omission, and this Blass considers probable in spite of his preference for αὐτοῦ in the second passage. D illustrates the ease with which the omission might occur, for there the clause in question forms a complete line, which ends in αὐτούς, like the line preceding. If we admit 34a to the text, we have an account which is not exactly connected, but which involves no contradictions. xv. 33 does not say that Judas and Silas for their part took leave of the brethren in Antioch and set out for Jerusalem, a statement which Luke would have made outright (Luke viii. 38, 39; Acts iv. 21, 23, v. 40, 41, xiii. 3, 4, xv. 30) and without ἀπὸ τῶν ἀδελφῶν (xxviii. 25, xv. 30), but only that the Antiochians said they would not detain them longer. Silas gave a decisive reply to the effect that he and Judas ought still to remain in Antioch, and in consequence they did so remain, as Barnabas did in his time (xi. 22 ff.). Thus the way is sufficiently paved for xv. 40, whereas if 34a were rejected it would be hard to understand how the man who had just returned to Jerusalem should suddenly reappear at Antioch. The narrator could not have omitted to state that Paul summoned him from Jerusalem. Even in that case, to be sure, Luke would have left no room to doubt the identity of Silas, xv. 40, with the Silas of xv. 22, 27, 32, 34. Zimmer's attempt (ZfKW, 1881, S. 169–174, cf., per contra, Jülicher, JbfPTh. 1882, S. 538–552) to distinguish the Silas who assisted Paul on the second missionary journey from the Jerusalem envoy of the same name, has no support whatever in the only account we have of the latter. The hypothesis that Silas (=Silvanus) is to be identified with Titus, suggested in the first instance by Märcker (Titus Silvanus, 1864) and championed by Graf (Vierteljahrsschr. f. englisch-theol. Forschung, ii. 1865, S. 373–394), cannot be rescued in this fashion. Originating in a needless astonishment that Titus is not mentioned in Acts, and an effort to justify Acts in the matter, the hypothesis has simply created contradictions between Acts and Paul. Titus was an uncircumcised Gentile, whom Paul took with him from Antioch to the apostolic council (Gal. ii. 1, 3, cf. Acts xv. 2), and, of course, took back to Antioch again. Silas, on the other hand, was sent to Antioch on the same occasion by the mother Church. At that time, as for some time before, he belonged to the Church in Jerusalem, for ἐξ αὐτῶν and ἐν τοῖς ἀδελφοῖς, Acts xv. 22, have no other antecedent than the immediately preceding mention of those who sent him as "the apostles and the elders, with the whole Church," cf. xv. 4. He was a Jew, therefore, or at least a circumcised proselyte, cf. Acts vi. 5. This is true also of Paul's helper, Silas=Silvanus, according to Acts xvi. 3 (for otherwise his subsequent circumcision would have been noticed as well as Timothy's) and xvi. 20. Silvanus, Paul's colleague in the organisation of the Achaian Churches (2 Cor. i. 19, cf. Acts xviii. 5), cannot be identical with the man who in the same Epistle is constantly and exclusively spoken of as Titus (2 Cor. ii. 13, vii. 6–14, viii. 6, 16, 23, xii. 18), who first became a co-labourer with Paul in his work with the Corinthians (2 Cor. viii. 23), by his successful execution of the errand on which Paul had sent him to Corinth in the interval between the first and second Epistles, up to that time having known the Church only from Paul's laudatory accounts of it (2 Cor. vii. 14).

2. (P. 203.) From Acts xvi. 1, Timothy's home seems to have been not at Derbe, but at Lystra, the town last mentioned, and in אAB introduced with a second εἰς. It would be strange, too, if the name of his own home Church were omitted from those in xvi. 2, or, if peculiar importance were attached to the testimony of neighbouring Churches, that it should not be brought in as a more emphatic confirmation of the opinion of the home Church. The idea that he was from Derbe arose from the unnatural supposition that in Acts xx. 4 Δερβαῖος καί was to be attached to the name after it, like Θεσσαλονικέων δέ and ᾽Ασιανοὶ δέ, instead of to the one preceding, like Βεροιαῖος, the only parallel term (Wieseler, *Chron.* 26, "a Derbean also, Timothy"; for "there was also a Derbean with them, namely, Timothy"; K. Schmidt, *Apostelgeschichte*, i. 42, "from Derbe; Timothy besides," which in the first place is linguistically inadmissible; and, secondly, would tell us, contrary to the translator's intent, that Gaius also was from Derbe). For this interpretation one ought really to conjecture Δερβαῖος δέ, as does Blass, following an earlier precedent, so that Gaius would appear as a third Thessalonian with Aristarchus and Secundus, and be identical with the Gaius of Acts xix. 29. The present writer sees no necessity for this. It is true we have no right to consider Paul's companions named in Acts xx. 4 as being, all of them, representatives of the Churches which had taken part in the collection for Jerusalem (2 Cor. viii. 19, 23 ; 1 Cor. xvi. 4). Aside from the fact that the provinces of Asia and Galatia, which are represented in xx. 4, do not seem to have had any part in this collection (above, p. 200 f.), it would be strange that no Corinthian is mentioned here. But, apart from that supposition, we can easily conceive that Luke meant that the men in whose company Paul was travelling to Jerusalem should be viewed as representatives of the cities and districts from which they came, and that he arranged their names and described them accordingly. There were : 1. Sopater from Berœa (minusc. *Sosipatros*= Rom. xvi. 21, both names found in Thessalonian inscriptions, Le Bas, ii., Nos. 1356, 1357) ; 2. Aristarchus and Secundus from Thessalonica ; 3. Gaius from Derbe (a different person, therefore, from the Macedonian of Acts xix. 29, as well as from the Corinthian of 1 Cor. i. 14 and Rom. xvi. 23, but perhaps the same as the Gaius addressed in 3 John 1) and Timothy (whose Lystran extraction had been mentioned in xvi. 1, and is recalled here also by S[1]),— both these men representing the province of Galatia (1 Cor. xvi. 1, above, p. 191) ; 4. Tychicus and Trophimus from the province of Asia (according to D and Sah., and also S[3] margin, both from Ephesus, as appears in Trophimus' case at least from Acts xxi. 29).

3. (Pp. 203, 205.) Although expositors down to Hofmann for the most part paid little attention to the " we " in the Pauline Epistles, Laurent (*ThStKr.*

1868, S. 159 ff., cf. his *Neutest. Stud.* 117) tried to maintain that in 1 and 2 Thess. Paul referred to himself as "we" only when speaking in the consciousness of his official position; but as "I," on the other hand, when he spoke "more personally, confidentially, as it were." On the contrary, we must assert that there is not a passage in the Epistles where Paul uses this "we"="I" (least of all Rom. i. 5). As Paul in 1 Thess. i. 1; 2 Thess. i. 1, introduces Silas and Timothy, co-founders of the Church, as joint authors with himself of the Epistles, it goes without saying that when he proceeds to the letter itself with "we," and not with "I," as in 1 Cor. i. 4; Gal. i. 6; Phil. i. 3, he means that the two join with him in everything that he puts in this form. If this holds true without question of the thanksgivings with which both Epistles open, it is equally impossible to draw a line further on beyond which the "we" is shrunk to an "I." So, too, an express explanation of the "we" in 2 Cor. i. 19 would have been needless if Silas as well as Timothy had been included in the "we" of vv. 1-14. On the other hand, it was unnecessary in 1 Thess. iii. 1 f. to explain that the "we" was confined to Paul and Silas, because it was plain from the statement itself that when Timothy was to be sent away, Paul and Silas were the senders. That the "we" is seriously meant becomes obvious in 1 Thess. ii. 18. Paul can say of the three missionaries that after their departure from Thessalonica it was their strong desire and earnest purpose to visit the city again : he interrupts the plural with an ἐγὼ μὲν Παῦλος, because it is only of himself that he can say that the purpose was entertained, not merely once but twice. Putting forward the three missionaries as a single τύπος, 2 Thess. iii. 9 (cf. Phil. iii. 17, i. 1, ii. 20), is as natural as the similar reference to the many Thessalonians, 1 Thess. i. 7, according to the correct reading (cf. John xx. 25, and παράδειγμα, Thuc. iii. 57). Since the Church is represented as a single family made up of many children, the corresponding relation of the three missionaries to the Church can be compared to that of a nurse and again to that of a father, 1 Thess. ii. 7, 11 ; but in this very passage we are reminded by ὡς Χριστοῦ ἀπόστολοι, ii. 7, that it is more than one person whose attitude is described. That this title (ἀπόστολοι) was applicable also to Silas and Timothy is unquestionable, see p. 107, n. 3. Moreover, it accords with the nature of such descriptions of the attitude of a number of persons, that not every individual statement is equally applicable to them all. It is of no consequence, therefore, that we do not know whether Timothy and Silas shared Paul's manual labour, or to what extent they did (1 Thess. ii. 9; 2 Thess. iii. 8). On the other hand, if one is speaking for others also, but is himself the principal person, it is still permissible to let his own "I" take the place now and then of the "we" (1 Thess. iii. 5, v. 27). Hofmann, *NT*, i. 205 ff., and Spitta, *Z. Gesch. des Urchr.* i. 115, 121, are hardly correct in inferring from 1 Thess. iii. 5 that, after Paul and Silas together had despatched Timothy from Athens to Thessalonica (iii. 2), Paul alone sent still another messenger thither. To explain the singular in iii. 5, it is assumed that in the meantime Silas also had left Paul ; but to what place was this helper, who worked with Paul in Macedonia, in Athens, and afterward in and about Corinth, likely to have gone from Athens at this time? One could only conjecture a return to Macedonia, like Timothy's. In this case there would be a double sending in addition to the mission of Timothy

(iii. 2),—the sending of Silas, which is nowhere mentioned, and that of an unnamed person supposedly referred to in iii. 5. But how could Paul have been silent here regarding Silas' absence, even if the journey—no one knows in what direction—had been one of indifference to the Thessalonians? His absence would in any case have accentuated the painful sense of loneliness (iii. 1), and in that very fact would have been an accentuation of the feeling expressed in μηκέτι στέγων, iii. 1, 5, and consequently a motive for the despatch of still another messenger. And why should not Paul have named the messenger, whether it were Silas, which would be the easiest supposition, or some "quite subordinate person" (Spitta, 122)? As he was plainly careful to recount every expression of his anxious love for the Thessalonians since his departure from them, he would not only have mentioned Silas by name, if he were the messenger intended in iii. 5, but, in view of his prominence, would have referred to him at least as particularly as to Timothy (iii. 2). In the other event, however, the messenger could only have been the bearer of a letter, and the failure to mention the letter thus sent by him would be incomprehensible. The omission of the object of ἔπεμψα, iii. 5, has no justification, unless it is to be supplied from iii. 1 f. (to which the repetition of μηκέτι στέγων points every reader), and both places refer to the same occurrence ; cf. 2 Cor. ix. 3 and viii. 18, 22. Otherwise a πάλιν could hardly be omitted (Gal. i. 9), and Paul would have marked the contrast with the unemphatic "we" of iii. 1 f., not with κἀγώ, but with ἐγὼ Παῦλος (1 Thess. ii. 18 ; Col. i. 23, as opposed to the plural, Col. i. 1-9, cf. 2 Cor. x. 1 ; Gal. v. 2 ; Philem. 19). κἀγώ finds its natural explanation in a contrast with the persons addressed (cf. Phil. ii. 19, 28 ; Eph. i. 15). Paul, as is said plainly enough in iii. 2 f., was greatly troubled for fear that the Church in its distressed condition might not hold out longer without the personal encouragement of its founders, and for that very reason (iii. 5, διὰ τοῦτο) he himself could not endure it longer, and, as remarked, sent Timothy to Thessalonica, in order not only to guard the Church from the shaking of its faith, and of its confidence in its organisers (iii. 2 f.), but also to obtain for his own part the satisfying assurance that the Church had not succumbed to its temptations. This also opposed to view of Wohlenberg, ZKom. 1 & 2 Thess. 73.

4. (P. 203.) Tafel, De Thess. eiusque Agro Dissertatio Geographica, Berlin, 1839, in which the writer's earlier program, Historia Thessalonicæ, Tübingen, 1835, is incorporated ; Lightfoot, Biblical Essays, pp. 253-269. Formerly Θέρμη (Herod. vii. 123-128 ; Thuc. i. 61), or Θέρμα (Æschines, De Falsa Legatione, 31. 36), rebuilt by Cassander about 315 B.C., and named Θεσσαλονίκη, for his wife (also Θεσσαλονίκεια, Strabo, pp. 106, 330, Fragm. 21), after the battle of Philippi civitas libera (Pliny, H. N. iv. 10. 36 ; for the coinage cf. Tafel, p. xxix), hence βουλὴ καὶ δῆμος (Le Bas, Inscr. 1359) and προάγειν εἰς τὸν δῆμον, Acts xvii. 5, cf. xix. 30, 33, residence of the governor of the province of Macedonia, which after 44 A.D. was again separated from Achaia and administered as a senatorial province by propraetors with the title of proconsul (Marquardt,[2] i. 319). The title πολιτάρχαι, Acts xvii. 6, 8, though otherwise unknown in literature, is splendidly attested for just this part of Macedonia and especially for Thessalonica. The inscriptions bearing on the matter have been very fully collated and thoroughly discussed by

E. De Witt Burton, *AJTh*. 1898, vol. ii. 598–632. Of the seventeen inscriptions in which the term occurs, and two others in which it is restored conjecturally, five or six are from Thessalonica, seven or eight from other Macedonian cities, two from Philippopolis, one from Bithynia, one from Bosphorus, and one from Egypt (=nineteen in all). In addition, *Oxyr. Papyri*, iv. 225, No. 745, of about the year 1 A.D. Of the inscriptions from Thessalonica, one from the time of Augustus (Duchesne et Bayet, *Mission au Mont Athos*, 1876—separate reprint from *Arch. des Miss. Sc.*, Ser. iii. vol. iii. p. 11, No. 1) names five politarchs ; one of 143 A.D. (Le Bas, iii., No. 1359, cf. Burton, 605–608) and one not dated (*C. I. Gr.* 1967, cf. *Addenda*, p. 990 = Le Bas, No. 1357 ; Burton, 600, 607) mention six. Another of the year 46, which mentions but two politarchs, probably belongs to Pella (Burton, 611–613). With regard to the population we have only general statements, Strabo, 323 ; Lucian, *Assin*. 46 ; Theodoret, *Hist. Eccl.* v. 17. In the time of the first emperors it surely cannot have been less than at present. About 1835 it was estimated at 80,000 ; Leake, *Travels in Northern Greece*, iii. 248, considered 65,000 more exact. According to Th. Fischer in Kirchhof's *Länderkunde von Europa*, ii. 2. 180 (1893), estimates vary from 100,000 to 135,000, and the proportion of Jews is said to be nearly two-thirds. Cf. Meyer's guide-book, *Türkei und Griechenland* (1888), 357, " population 100,000 ; 60,000 Jews." The unusual reading, ἡ συναγωγή, Acts xvii. 1, would indicate that the Jews of the whole district, perhaps even those at Amphipolis and Apollonia, made the synagogue at Thessalonica their place of worship, and maintained their connection with it. According to ℵABD, however (omitting the article), it is merely stated that there was a Jewish synagogue at Thessalonica, as at Berœa (xvii. 10), unlike Philippi (xvi. 13), Apollonia, and Amphipolis. But, aside from this, the prominence of the Jews at Thessalonica is clear from Acts xvii. 4–9, 13.

5. (P. 204.) Acts xvii. 2, ἐπὶ σάββατα τρία, cannot mean " on three Sabbaths," as one might infer from the deceptive analogy of Acts iii. 1, iv. 5 ; Luke x. 35, but " for three weeks," as Luke iv. 25 ; Acts xiii. 31, xvi. 18, xviii. 20, xix. 8, 10, 34, xxvii. 20. For σάββατον and σάββατα = week, cf. Luke xviii. 12, xxiv. 1 ; Acts xx. 7, and p. 19 above. If Paul's discourses were confined to the Sabbaths, as at the beginning in Corinth (Acts xviii. 4, cf. xiii. 42, 44), the statement would have had to be made more explicitly. Meetings were also held in the synagogue on Monday and Thursday, the usual fast-days (Schürer, ii. 458, 490 [Eng. trans. II. ii. 83, 118] ; *Forsch.* iii. 317). The synagogue was open at other times as well (Matt. vi. 2, 5), and served as a meeting-place for unusual gatherings (Jos. *Vita*, 54). Nothing is said here of any other hall to which Paul removed his lectures in consequence of the opposition of the Jews (contrast Acts xviii. 7, xix. 9) ; so we are not to suppose that his stay in Thessalonica was much extended beyond these three weeks. The first remittance of money from Philippi to Thessalonica (Phil. iv. 16) may have followed immediately upon Paul's enforced departure from the former city, and the second two weeks later.

6. (P. 204.) Acts xvii. 4. According to D (πολλοὶ τῶν σεβομένων καὶ Ἑλλήνων πλῆθος πολὺ καὶ γυναῖκες τῶν πρώτων οὐκ ὀλίγαι—a reading which, as regards the καί before Ἑλλ., is confirmed by A, Copt. Vulg.), the actual Gentiles, who visited the synagogue only in exceptional circumstances and without breaking

with their heathen worship, would be distinguished from the σεβόμενοι (Acts xiii. 50, xvi. 14, xvii. 17, xviii. 7 ; cf. φοβούμενοι τὸν θεόν, Acts x. 2, 22, xiii. 16, 26), the Gentiles who, as "proselytes of the gate," regularly attached themselves to the Jewish worship. The common text, τῶν τε σεβομένων Ἑλλήνων, would be analogous to σεβομένων προσηλύτων, xiii. 43, without, however, being quite synonymous. In any case, it is clear that among the converts a small minority were Jews, and a large majority of Gentile birth. Even more, therefore, than in the case of the Galatians (above, p. 166), Paul was justified in regarding the Christians of Thessalonica as Gentile Christians ; cf. 1 Thess. i. 9. We must, nevertheless, notice here that along with the contrast with former heathenism there appears also (i. 10) a contrast with Judaism. If Jason (Acts xvii. 5-9) is the same as the Jason of Rom. xvi. 21, which seems at once probable from the fact that Sosipater (= Sopater, Acts xx. 4), another Macedonian Christian, is there mentioned with him, he too was of Jewish birth (οἱ συγγενεῖς μου). According to Clement of Alexandria, he was identical with the Jason who represents Christianity over against the Jew Papiscus in the dialogue of Ariston of Pella (*Forsch.* iii. 74, iv. 309). Secundus and Aristarchus of Thessalonica were probably Gentiles (Acts xx. 4, xix. 29, xxvii. 2 ; Philem. 24 ; Col. iv. 10) ; for Col. iv. 11 refers only to Mark and Jesus Justus, not to Aristarchus ; cf. § 27. The name Secundus (Acts xx. 4) is abundantly attested in Thessalonica (*C. I. Gr.* 1967, 1969 ; *JHSt.* 1887, p. 367, No. 10 ; Heuzey et Daumet, *Macédoine*, p. 280, No. 113, Σεκοῦνδα). The occurrence of the name Γάϊος Ἰούλιος Σεκοῦνδος in Thessalonica (Duchesne et Bayet, *Mission au mont Athos*, p. 50, No. 78) gives ground for the conjecture that the Secundus of Acts xx. 4 may be identified with the Macedonian Gaius, who in Acts xix. 29 is similarly associated with Aristarchus, and that in distinction from (Gaius) Secundus of Thessalonica the other Gaius is designated as from Derbe (Cod. A, ὁ Δερβαῖος). Origen's observation on Rom. xvi. 23 (Del. iv. 686) : "Fertur sane traditione maiorum, quod hic Gaius (Rom. xvi. 23) primus episcopus fuerit Thessalonicensis ecclesiæ," is probably an addition of the translator, Rufinus. It rests upon an arbitrary identification of Gaius, Rom. xvi. 23, with the Macedonian Gaius, Acts xix. 29, whereas Origen himself more correctly compares Rom. xvi. 23 and 1 Cor. i. 14.   Demas also (2 Tim. iv. 10 ; Col. iv. 14 ; Philem. 24) was probably from Thessalonica. If Demas = Demetrius, we may note that the name Demetrius frequently occurs in Thessalonica : *C. I. Gr.* 1967 (*bis*) ; *JHSt.* 1887, p. 360, No. 2 ; E. D. Burton, *op. cit.* 608, No. iv. Demetrius the martyr (c. 304) became patron of the city ; cf. *Acta SS.*, Oct., iv. 50–209, and also Laurent in *BZ*, 1895, S. 420 ff.   The continued existence of a Thessalonian Church is evidenced by the edict of Antoninus Pius of which Melito speaks (Eus. *H. E.* iv. 26. 10). A certain Paraskene, who erected a monument to her daughter Phœbe (cf. Rom. xvi. 1) at Thessalonica in 156, was probably, to judge from her name, either Jewish or Christian ; cf. Duchesne et Bayet, *op. cit.* 46, No. 65. Tertullian, *Præscr.* xxxvi. mentions Thessalonica among the cities in which, as he was convinced, the apostles' letters to the respective Churches were still read from the autograph originals, and their "cathedræ" were yet in use (*GK*, i. 652). A large stone pulpit (ἄμβων, βῆμα), half of which stands in the court of the Church of St. George and half in the court of St. Panteleemon's, is known to this day as

"St. Paul's pulpit," Bayet, *op. cit.* 249 ff. ; in Leake, iii. 243 ; and Lightfoot, *Biblical Essays*, 269, other accounts which do not altogether agree.   The work in question is of the early Byzantine period.   The name στοὺς ἀποστόλους, at the site of the ancient Pella, might more readily embody a genuine reminiscence ; that is, in case "the apostles" (1 Thess. ii. 6) went on from Thessalonica, not by the direct road to Bercœa, which runs through swampy country at the outset, but first by the Via Egnatia to Pella, whence a road branches off to Bercœa.

7. (P. 205.)   The reading ἕως ἐπὶ τὴν θάλασσαν, Acts xvii. 14 (cf. Luke xxiv. 50), cannot, of course, mean "they brought him clear to the sea" (Weiss, *Textkrit. Unters. d. Apostelgesch.* 210), for the sentence says nothing about "bringing," and those who accompanied Paul from Bercœa brought him rather as far as Athens (xvii. 15).   We are probably to read ὡς with HLP. Luke might also have written ὡς ἐπὶ τῆς θαλάσσης (cf. Polyb. v. 70. 3 and 12, and Kühner-Gerth. i. 496), but it was not necessary if he really wrote ὡς. Still uncertain which way he should turn, or perhaps, too, with the idea of evading possible pursuers, Paul and his companions set out at first as if they meant to go directly to the coast and take ship somewhere in the neighbourhood of Methone.   He went on by land, however, either to Dium to take ship there, or all the way to Athens.   The other recension, too, which gives us ἀπελθεῖν ἐπὶ τὴν θάλασσαν, does not exclude the meaning which the insertion of ὡς expresses even more clearly ; for even this says only that the Christians of Bercœa dismissed Paul and the companions they had provided for him (xvii. 15), with the intent and expectation that he would go to the coast.   But ver. 15 shows that the decision as to the route, and even as to the destination, was reached not in Bercœa, but only after the travellers were on their way ; for otherwise there would have been no need of new instructions to Timothy and Silas.   This appears even more certainly from the original reading, παρῆλθεν δὲ τὴν Θεσσαλίαν ἐκωλύθη γὰρ εἰς αὐτοὺς κηρύξαι τὸν λόγον ; cf. xvi. 6, 7.   Paul, then, originally intended to preach in Thessaly also, and undertook to do so (cf. xvi. 7), a thing he could not have thought of at all if he had gone from Bercœa to Methone, and thence by sea to Athens, without even approaching the Thessalian border.   This word παρελθεῖν (not παραπλεῦσαι, xx. 16) seems rather to point to a land journey, which avoided the larger places of Thessaly, or in the course of which, at all events, there was no preaching in that region.   The statement made by the bishop of Servia to the traveller Leake (iii. 330), as an undoubted fact, that Paul passed through there, is not altogether improbable.   The adjustment of the account in Acts to that in 1 Thess. may be variously conceived. If Paul came alone from Athens to Corinth (Acts xviii. 1), and Silas and Timothy came together from Macedonia to Corinth (Acts xviii. 5 ; 2 Cor. xi. 9), then Paul must have left Silas behind at Athens, as previously at Bercœa, and Silas, waiting in vain for Timothy, may on his own motion have gone to Macedonia to meet him, and then, without having gone as far as Thessalonica himself, have proceeded with Timothy to Corinth.   Even if Timothy had been alone in Macedonia, had returned from there to Athens and found Silas waiting, and then had gone on with him to Corinth, there would be no serious inaccuracy in Acts xviii. 5.   In that case, what Timothy told to Silas in Athens and to Paul in Corinth would be summed up together in

1 Thess. iii. 6.   Ephrem Syrus (according to an Armenian catena on Acts, Venice, 1839, p. 310 ; cf. Harris, *Four Lectures on the Western Text*, 25, 47) had a text of Acts xvii. 15 which made it possible for him to understand the words πρὸς αὐτὸν ἐξήεσαν (which in D form a line by themselves, and so are taken together) as referring to a journey made by Timothy and Silas to Athens.

§ 14. THE FIRST EPISTLE TO THE THESSALONIANS.

The Epistle was written shortly after the arrival of Timothy and Silvanus in Corinth (iii. 6), under the stimulus of the good news which Timothy brought back from Macedonia.   The principal occasion of the letter and its purpose we learn from its first division, which forms a complete unit, concluded by a solemn benediction (iii. 11–13).   As indicated by the introductory λοιπόν (iv. 1), the discussions which follow, and which are not very closely connected in thought, constitute a series of more incidental concluding remarks.

In the first division we have a review of the founding of the Church by the preaching of the writers (i. 2–ii. 16), and of everything which since their departure from Thessalonica had manifested their loving interest in the growth of the Church and in the continuance of its pleasant relations with its founders (ii. 17–iii. 5).   In this review a prominent place is given to statements about the persecutions which the readers had endured at the beginning, and in the face of which they had since maintained their faith (n. 1).   It was mainly this that made the missionaries solicitous and anxious to return to Thessalonica (ii. 17 f.), and which led, finally, to the sending of Timothy thither (iii. 2 f.).   Now the tone which pervades these statements is not predominantly that of consolation and encouragement, but of apology.   Of course it is for the sake of encouraging the readers that attention is called to the fact that their brave endurance of persecution has become an example to later converts in Macedonia and Achaia (i. 7) ; and this same purpose is in view when it is

said that in so doing they have followed the example of
the Christians in Judea (ii. 14), on which account the
missionaries are proud of them, and filled with grateful
joy at their conduct (ii. 19 f., i. 2 f.). In the same way
the reminder that there is no reasonable hope of improvement in the situation (iii. 4), might be understood
as an attempt to keep the readers from growing impatient.
Taken, however, in connection with other statements, its
purpose seems rather to be that of self-defence on the
part of the writers. For example, in i. 5 f., practically
at the beginning of the letter, they appeal in the same
way to their readers' knowledge of the manner in which
they had come among them, reminding them that, like the
Lord Himself, they had furnished the readers an example
of patience in enduring persecution. Especial attention
is called (ii. 2) to the insulting treatment to which they
had been subjected in Philippi, just before they came to
Thessalonica, and to the feeling of anxiety with which
they had to do their work even in Thessalonica (ἐν πολλῷ
ἀγῶνι). So that, if subsequently the readers had to endure much at the hands of their fellow-citizens, they
certainly ought not to forget that the Jews, with whom
the chief responsibility for the unfortunate condition of
affairs in Thessalonica rested, had first driven the missionaries themselves from Thessalonica, and had persecuted
them to Beroea (ii. 14–16, cf. p. 204, line 22). This same
hostility on the part of the Jews to the preaching of
the gospel among the Gentiles, which was prompted by
their hatred, the missionaries were now encountering
in Corinth, as is shown by the change to the present
tense in ii. 15 f., in the light of which passage also iii. 7
is to be understood. As a further indication of the
apologetic purpose of the Epistle, we have the statements
about the preaching and general conduct of the missionaries in Thessalonica, which manifestly are made in the
light of a different representation regarding that ministry.

They did not preach with empty words (i. 5), they did not set forth mere human doctrine, but they preached the word of God and the gospel of Christ (ii. 2, 9, 13, iii. 2), and did it with the power, and confidence, and openness which that word inspires in its true preachers (i. 5, ii. 2). It is true that their preaching made certain demands of the hearers (ii. 3, ἡ παράκλησις ἡμῶν, cf. ii. 11), but they were not those of the deceiver who flatters his hearers in order that he may make himself personally acceptable to them. They were not actuated by ambition, nor by any other unworthy motive which might have led them to employ improper means; above everything else, they had not been covetous (ii. 3–6). With the utmost effort they had supported themselves by toiling with their own hands (ii. 9), and their entire conduct had shown their complete devotion to the work with which they had been intrusted by God, and proved their unselfish, even tender love for those who heard their preaching (ii. 7–12). God as well as the Church is witness to their blameless behaviour (ii. 10, 5, cf. i. 4).

Now the Thessalonian Christians to whom Paul makes this vigorous defence of himself and of his helpers, could not have been the accusers in the case. The feeling which the authors have concerning them is uniformly that of gratitude (i. 2); and one of the items of good news which Timothy had brought back a little while before, was the information that the Thessalonians held those who had laboured among them always in kindly remembrance, and were just as anxious to see Paul and Silvanus as the latter were to see them (iii. 6). On the other hand, there is not the slightest indication that these persons who were slandering Paul and opposing his gospel were Christians from abroad like those who had appeared in Galatia shortly before. The accusations, therefore, must have been made by the non-Christian neighbours of the Thessalonian Christians. The husbands of the women converts be-

longing to the upper classes, who remained heathen (Acts
xvii. 4), and the relatives and former friends of the new
converts generally, may have represented to them that
they had been misled into a foolish superstition by self-
seeking and covetous adventurers, and in consequence
were compelled to encounter the ill-will of their neighbours
with all the unpleasant things that this involved, while
the men who had got them into this trouble had disappeared at the right time to avoid all such consequences.
It is easy to see how the flight of the missionaries from
Thessalonica, the placing of Jason and other Christians
under bail (Acts xvii. 9), the sending of money from
Philippi to Thessalonica (Phil. iv. 16), and the hostility
to the Christians on the part of their fellow-citizens
(1 Thess. ii. 14), might all be used to give colour to such
a representation of matters. That this was actually the
case is directly indicated in iii. 3 ; for the anxiety which
led to the sending of Timothy was not caused so much
by the fear that the faith of the *Church might be shaken
by persecution*, as that *individuals under the stress of
persecution might be coaxed away*, *i.e.* led to speak
disparagingly of their own conversion (n. 2). This, of
course, must result in the shaking of their faith ; for if
the organisers of the Church were deceivers, then the
faith of the Thessalonians was vain. The tempter, who
was threatening to destroy the apostle's entire work in
Thessalonica (iii. 5), assumed not only the form of a
roaring lion (1 Pet. v. 8), but also that of a fawning dog
(Phil. iii. 2) and a hissing serpent (1 Cor. xi. 3). So
also iii. 6 shows that until Timothy's return Paul and
Silvanus were very anxious for fear lest the Church had
lost confidence in its founders, and lest its love for them
had grown cold. Perhaps it may seem strange that, after
having been thus reassured by Timothy on these and other
points,—indeed, after having had his feeling changed to
one of joy,—Paul should now review the entire previous

history of his relations to the Church so earnestly, in such detail, and withal in a manner so apologetic. But, in the first place, we know from experience that when one has been weighed down for months by some great care, how difficult it is to speak of it, particularly if it be a delicate matter ; but once let the burden of anxiety be relieved, and there comes a very strong desire to give vent to one's pent-up feelings, and the recollections of the agony through which one has passed are apt to be mingled with expressions of joyful gratitude. In the second place, it was not until Timothy's return that Paul knew how much pressure was being brought to bear upon the Thessalonian Christians, and how seriously he was being slandered by their neighbours, so that up to this time he had not been in a position to set the facts in a clear light with definite reference to such slanders. In the third place, the grateful joy and the profound satis- faction for the present condition of the Church, so strongly expressed in iii. 6 f. (i. 2, ii. 19 f.), do not imply that there was nothing more to be desired. The desire to return to Thessalonica, which from the first had been prompted by a feeling of solicitude for the Church, was just as strong as ever (iii. 10, 11, cf. iii. 6). There were still defects in their faith which Paul felt could not be remedied except by his personal presence (iii. 10). In the second division of the letter there are references to moral deficiencies which from the coldly scholastic point of view may seem inconsistent with the expressions of exuberant joy which we find in the first division (i. 2, ii. 19 f., iii. 6, 9). But even in this first division the steadfastness of the Church, which is the occasion of the apostle's rejoicing, seems to be in need of fuller demon- stration in the future (iii. 8), and, as indicated by the elliptical καθάπερ καὶ ἡμεῖς εἰς ὑμᾶς (iii. 12, cf. iii. 6), the desire expressed that the Lord may make the Christians in Thessalonica abound yet more in love toward one another and toward all men, has some reference to the relation between the Church and its founders. The Church had proved itself much more steadfast than Paul had dared to hope while he was waiting for news, though the whispering of their neighbours had not left them entirely unaffected ; Timothy had discovered more than one shadow. It was not yet possible for Paul to say definitely when he could return to Thessalonica, as the Church and as he himself desired (iii. 6, 10 f.). In the meantime, how much could happen in Thessalonica ! In fact, was it not possible that this continued absence of the person who had been chiefly instrumental in organising the Church might be the very thing calculated to arouse further suspicions ? In view of all this, it is entirely comprehensible that along with the exalted expressions of joy in i. 2–iii. 13 there should appear signs not only of the anxiety of the past months just relieved, but also of solicitation for the future welfare of the Church. The perfectly spontaneous expression of this mingled feeling of joy and of anxiety was one of the best means for strengthening any good tendencies in the Church and for averting future danger. Certain specific defects in religious thought and moral conduct about which he had been informed by Timothy, Paul attempts to remedy by the suggestions of chaps. iv., v. While on the whole their conduct is recognised as altogether praiseworthy (iv. 1, 9 f., v. 11), there are a number of points in which he urges progress, referring the readers repeatedly to the instructions he had given them at the very first (iv. 1, 2, 6, 11). Warning against unchastity, which was so common among their heathen neighbours (iv. 3–5), is followed immediately by a similar warning against covetousness and dishonesty in business, to which persons living in a great commercial centre were particularly apt to be tempted (iv. 6). The commendation of their generous brotherly love prepares the way for an exhortation to improve their condition in money matters, by living a quiet, thrifty life, which will not only enable them to give more liberally (Eph. iv. 28), but which will also make them more independent of their non-Christian neighbours (iv. 9–12).

Now, inasmuch as the idleness against which these exhortations are directed is a manifestation of a general state of unrest (iv. 11, cf. 2 Thess. iii. 11 f.), and inasmuch as this warning is followed immediately by eschatological teachings (iv. 13–v. 11), we assume that under the influence of the idea that the end of the world was at hand many were neglecting their daily duties (n. 3). Another evidence of the expectancy with which the return of Jesus was awaited, is seen in the peculiar way in which the Church mourned for its departed members. This was due to the opinion that those who had died before the parousia would not immediately share the glory of the kingdom as would those who lived to witness the Lord's return. Although, the apostle argues, they should have been saved from this error by their faith in the resurrection of Jesus from the dead, because it was not possible that death should separate the Christian from Christ (iv. 14), all anxiety concerning the participation in the parousia of those who have died in the faith he sets at rest by a word of the Lord, i.e. a specific teaching consciously based upon one of Jesus' prophetic utterances (iv. 15, n. 4). In this definite form such teaching could not have been a part of the missionary preaching. While on this point Paul is inclined to enlarge upon what he had said before, another question which was occupying attention in Thessalonica, namely, as to when the end should come, and the length of time that must elapse before that event, he holds to be superfluous (v. 1, cf. Acts i. 6 f.) and without practical value. For, he argues, it is one of the simplest elements of the Christian preaching, that for those absorbed in a worldly life the coming of the day of the

Lord will be unexpected and sudden ; while, on the other hand, the Christian, who lives in constant expectation of the parousia, the time of which it was impossible to determine by natural reckoning, will be always ready, living always the kind of a life that is in keeping with this future day of the Lord (v. 2–10). With the exhortation to mutual helpfulness in regard to this matter of the parousia (v. 11), we have the transition to exhortations relating to the general life of the Church, for which its officers are primarily responsible (v. 12 f.). There seems to have been some insubordination, especially on the part of those inclined to be idle (v. 14, τοὺς ἀτάκτους, cf. iv. 8). That there was not complete harmony among all the members, seems to be implied by Paul's injunction that *all* the brethren salute one another, and with a fraternal kiss, and by his solemn command in the name of the Lord that the letter be read to *all* the brethren (v. 26, 27).

1. (P. 215.) It is wrong to assume (as does Klöpper, for example, in *Der Zweite Thess.-brief* 14, 15) that the θλίψεις spoken of in 1 Thess. belong simply to the past, and, specifically, to the time of the founding of the Church, and that a new outbreak of the once ended persecution constitutes the background of 2 Thess. The emphasis upon the sufferings endured at the first acceptance of the gospel (i. 6, ii. 13 f.) was a necessary consequence of the fact that just these beginnings of the Church demanded an apologetic interpretation. That the oppressed condition of the Church still continued after the departure of the missionaries and at the time Timothy was sent, appears from the connection of ii. 17 f. with what precedes and from iii. 3. An improvement in this condition would hardly have been passed over in silence among the good tidings which Timothy brought (iii. 6), nor would the receipt of news of renewed persecution have been similarly ignored in 2 Thess. The way in which the ὑπομονή of the Church is recalled, 1 Thess. i. 3, the occurrence of the present ἐνεργεῖται, ii. 13, among the aorists both before and after, the ταύταις in iii. 3, the summing up of all the trials of the Church hitherto in the present αἷς ἀνέχεσθε and πάσχετε, 2 Thess. i. 4 f.,—all this shows, rather, that the outward circumstances of the Church from its organisation to the sending of the second Epistle were essentially unchanged. From the altered tone in which they are spoken of in 2 Thess. i. 3–12, we can only, perhaps, infer that they were growing worse from day to day.

2. (P. 218.) If the reading μηδένα σαίνεσθαι is beyond question in iii. 3, there is also no occasion to abandon the oldest meaning of the word σαίνειν, in current use from Homer's time down to the empire, namely, "to wag the tail (of dogs)," with accusative of the person. The fawning upon one, thus indi-

cated, is often in contrast with barking and biting. For this usage, as well as for the transference of it to human beings as subjects, cf. especially Polyb. xvi. 24. 6; Artemid. *Oneirocr*. ii. 11; Hercher, p. 99. 12–20. It also means "to move," "to cause to yield," but not "to frighten" or "startle," but rather "to entice to sin" (Leont. Neapol. *Vita Sym. Sali*, Migne, 93, col. 1724). The better Greek commentators (Chrys., Montfaucon, xi. 445; Sever. Gabal. in Cramer, *Cat.* vi. 353; Theodorus, ed. Swete, ii. 17) all felt the necessity of explaining the word, which seemed strange to them here, but they missed the simple solution because they did not understand the historical situation indicated in chap. ii. What is meant is illustrated to some degree by passages like *Acta Theclœ*, x; *Mart. Polyc*. ix; *Passio Perpet*. v; *Acta Carpi*, 43, except that in these instances we are dealing with more or less genuine expressions of natural sympathy, whereas σαίνειν denotes insidious and crafty wheedling. Artemidorus, *loc. cit.*, explains: ἀλλότριοι δὲ κύνες σαίνοντες μὲν δόλους καὶ ἐνέδρας ὑπὸ πονηρῶν ἀνδρῶν ἢ γυναικῶν σημαίνουσιν.

3. (P. 221.) Hofmann, i. 230 f., rightly warns against exaggerations of this matter of indolence. Spitta, *Zur Gesch. des Urchr.* i. 131 f., exaggerating this in turn, rejects the explanation altogether, and infers from the connection of iv. 11 f. with what precedes, that "fraternal fellowship, where those who had property gladly shared of their means with those who had none, became to not a few a temptation to an indolent, unoccupied life." Such a remark, however, could not have been connected with the last preceding admonition by καί, but would have been introduced in sharp antithesis to it: "Abound still more in active brotherly love, but not so as to foster thereby the lazy man's aversion to labour"; or, "on the other hand, everyone who can work must do his part, so as not to become a burden on the generosity of the brethren." Certainly we must not conceive a fanatically excited expectation of the approaching end of the world as the prevailing temper of the whole local Church. The admonitions, iv. 3–7, v. 4–10, point to the existence of a very different attitude toward the present world. Paul even has to warn them against despising prophesyings and suppressing the prophetic spirit which stirs within the Church (v. 19 f.). But in immediate proximity there is also the caution not to accept such prophetic utterances without examination (v. 21).

4. (P. 221.) 1 Thess. iv. 15, ἐν λόγῳ κυρίου, is to be understood, as regards the significance of λέγειν or λαλεῖν ἔν τινι, in accordance with 1 Cor. ii. 7, xiv. 6; Matt. xiii. 34; and for content, in accordance with 1 Cor. vii. 10, 12, 25, ix. 14, xi. 23. The teaching thus introduced need not, therefore, be a verbal citation. If ὅτι in iv. 15 is a "because," as it probably is, the prophecy ascribed to the Lord does not come till iv. 16. And if this saying goes beyond the words of Jesus handed down to us in the Gospels, we recall that in other particulars also, Paul's information was not confined within those limits (Acts xx. 35; 1 Cor. xv. 5–7). We need not do more than mention the fact that Steck, *JlfPTh*. 1883, S. 509–524, claimed to find the λόγος κυρίου in what the angel Uriel says to Ezra (4 Esdr. iv. 1, v. 42) in answer to his question regarding the fate of those that do not live to see the end: "Coronæ assimilabo iudicium meum; sicut non novissimorum tarditas, sic nec priorum velocitas." If we bring the eschatological statements of 1 Thess. together, we shall find their essential elements, and in part their phraseology, reappearing in the

Gospels and Acts. With v. 1 cf. Acts i. 7 (χρόνοι καὶ καιροί) ; Matt. xxiv. 36 ; Mark xiii. 32. With v. 2 cf. ὡς κλέπτης ἐν νυκτί, Matt. xxiv. 43 ; Luke xii. 39 f. ; and for the expression in v. 4 cf. John xii. 35 also. With the description of false security before the parousia and the surprise of it to most, v. 3, cf. Matt. xxiv. 37–51 ; Luke xvii. 26–36. With αἰφνίδιος . . . ἐκφύγωσιν, cf. Luke xxi. 34–36, ἐπιστῇ ἐφ᾽ ὑμᾶς αἰφνίδιος . . . ἐκφυγεῖν ταῦτα πάντα. With ἡ ὠδίν cf. Matt. xxiv. 8, 19 ; Mark xiii. 8, 17. With the figurative representation of readiness and its opposite, v. 6 f., cf. Matt. xxiv. 42, 49 (μετὰ τῶν μεθυόντων), xxv. 13 ; Mark xiii. 33–37 ; Luke xii. 35, 37, 45 (μεθύσκεσθαι), xxi. 34, 36. With iv. 14–17 cf. the return of the Lord from heaven, or in the clouds of heaven, and in the company of the angels, Matt. xvi. 27, xxiv. 30, xxvi. 64 ; Mark viii. 38, xiii. 26, xiv. 62 ; Luke ix. 26, xxi. 27 ; Acts i. 11 ; the gathering of the elect by angels with the loud sound of the trumpet, Matt. xxiv. 31 ; Mark xiii. 27 (ἐπισυνάξαι, cf. 1 Thess. iv. 17 ; 2 Thess. ii. 1 [τῆς] ἡμῶν ἐπισυναγωγῆς ἐπ᾽ αὐτόν). This is the presupposition also of 1 Thess. iv. 14 (ἄξει σὺν αὐτῷ). Matt. xxiv. 31 ; Mark xiii. 27 refer to those members of the Church who at the time of the parousia are living scattered about upon earth (cf. Matt. xxiv. 22, 24 ; Mark xiii. 20, 22). That the departed members, also, would share in the glory of the kingdom as it should then be realised, is not, indeed, handed down to us in the immediate context of the eschatological discourses, but is elsewhere abundantly attested as Jesus' promise. When He intimated that some of His disciples would witness His return (Matt. xvi. 28 ; Mark ix. 1 ; Luke ix. 27), it was also implied that others of them would die before that time (cf. also Matt. xx. 23 ; Mark x. 39 ; John xiii. 36, xxi. 18 f.). But all are to share in the kingdom which appears in glory (Matt. xxvi. 29 ; Mark xiv. 25 ; Luke xxii. 30),—all who have not despised its invitation, or by their conduct subsequently become unworthy of it (Matt. xxii. 9–14 ; Luke xiv. 12–24 ; John xii. 26), and the O.T. righteous as well (Matt. viii. 11 ; Luke xiii. 28). That the dead must be awakened at the end is self-evident, and is shown in many ways (Matt. xxii. 23–32 ; Mark xii. 18–27 ; Luke xx. 27–38 ; John v. 25–29, vi. 39, 40, 44, 54, xi. 24). Only, if the resurrection of the righteous dead is generally set at the end of time, without being put, like the gathering of the living on earth, in a closer connection with the parousia, it must still be conceived as simultaneous with the parousia, since it is the condition of participation in the kingdom. Of the distinction in time between the resurrection of believers and the general resurrection, which is attested in apostolic literature as a general Christian belief (1 Cor. xv. 23–28 ; Rev. xx. 4–6), and which appears also in 1 Thess. iv. 16, we have at least a hint in Luke xiv. 14.

§ 15. THE SECOND EPISTLE TO THE THESSALONIANS.

This briefer letter, which, like the longer one that stands just before it in the Canon, is addressed to the Church in Thessalonica not in Paul's name alone, but in the name also of Silvanus and Timothy (i. 1), shows striking resemblance to the other in its general plan. Here, as in the first letter, there is one principal section (chaps. i., ii.) concluding with a solemn benediction (ii. 16 f.). To this is attached a shorter section, which, as indicated by the introductory τὸ λοιπόν (iii. 1, cf. I. iv. 1), is made up of a series of more incidental remarks. In this case the letter does not begin with a joyful expression of thanks for the Church, but with the assurance that the writers feel under obligation at all times to render such thanks to God, even at times when, if they followed their inclinations, they might express other emotions (i. 3). How indicative this is of the situation of the writers when they wrote, and of their feelings at the time, is shown by the recurrence of the phrase at the end of the first section, ii. 13. For the attentive reader the impression made by this expression is still further strengthened by the explanatory statement (καθὼς ἄξιόν ἐστιν) that such constant thanksgiving on the part of the writers is only appropriate in view of the growth of the Church in faith and love, especially in view of the patience they had shown in all their persecutions and afflictions. About this patience the writers do not need to be informed by others; but, having themselves been the founders of the Church, they take occasion of their own accord, in their intercourse with other Churches, to point with joyful pride to this Church (i. 4). This patience, which the readers have shown in enduring such constant sufferings, ought to be a source of comfort also to themselves, inasmuch as it is at once the token and the warrant that as believers they shall have part in the glory of the kingdom of God at the righteous judgment to be established at the return of Christ, when their persecutors shall be given over to eternal destruction (i. 5–10). That the readers may be made more and more ready for the decision of that great day, is the constant prayer of the founders of the Church (i. 11, 12).

With these verses we have the transition to the teachings of chap. ii., for the development of which the letter
seems mainly to have been written. The Church needed
to be warned against the error of supposing that the day
of the Lord had already come or appeared. The disturbance which existed in the Church was due partly to prophetic utterances by its own members, partly to oral and
written statements in which this opinion had been falsely
represented as that of Paul and his helpers (ii. 2, n. 2).
Further deceptions in the same direction were to be feared
(ii. 3). This error Paul meets not by proclaiming a new
revelation, but by reminding his readers of the things
they had heard him say when he first preached the gospel
to them,—things which, therefore, they ought not only to
know, but also to use as a means of defence against such
a misleading claim as this (ii. 5, 6, n. 3). This explains
why, in what is said later about the forms which the
unfolding of the closing events of the present age is to
assume, as also about the parousia of Christ and the union
of Christians with Him, the definite article is used (ii. 1,
cf. I. iv. 14–18), it being assumed that these terms were
familiar to the readers. "*The* Day of the Lord," Paul argues,
cannot have come already; for, according to what he had
said earlier, it could not come before "*the* falling away"
and the revelation of "*the* man of lawlessness," whom
Christ is to destroy at His second coming. Similarly, the
readers must have known what the power was which for
the present was restraining the "man of lawlessness," which
power had to be set aside before the "man of lawlessness"
could appear. Although Paul does not use these particular words, this "man of lawlessness" is described, on
the one hand, as an ἀντίθεος whose hostility to all that is
called God, and to the worship of God, will reach the point
where he will declare himself to be God and take his
place in the temple of God, *i.e.* in the place where the
true God is worshipped, demanding such worship for

himself (ver. 4). He is described, on the other hand, as ἀντίχριστος. That this man of lawlessness was to be a Satanic caricature of Christ, one infers from the occurrence three times of the word ἀποκαλυφθῆναι (vv. 3, 6, 8), from the description of his coming as a παρουσία (ver. 9), and from the contrast between his deceiving and destroying activity, which is to be promoted by Satanic wonders, and the saving power of the gospel (vv. 9–14). Very essential elements in this picture, which is so clearly outlined, are to be found in the prophecies of the Book of Daniel, in the descriptions in 1 Maccabees of the attack made by Antiochus Epiphanes upon the religion of the Jews and upon their temple, and in the prophetic discourses of Jesus (n. 4). But these sources could hardly have supplied those teachings about the end of the world which, as we have seen, Paul presented in essentially the same form as that in which they are written here, when he first preached the gospel in Thessalonica. Still less can we suppose that this Christian statement of the doctrine which goes back through the prophecy and life of Jesus to Daniel, first appeared essentially as we have it here in some Jewish apocalypse now lost, which Paul had read and believed (n. 5). Only single features of the same could have been derived from such a source. The combination of these various elements, some of which may be found here and there in earlier sources, into a new and vivid picture, and the confidence with which the whole is presented, are quite incomprehensible—all the more so if it is Paul who is speaking—unless it be assumed that what was found in the sources mentioned had been further developed by Christian prophecy, and that Paul, who entertained a high opinion of such prophecy, made use of it, and, after testing it, adopted such parts of it into his preaching as seemed to him to be of value (cf. 1 Thess. v. 21, n. 6). In order, therefore, to comprehend Paul's words historically, and so to understand them clearly, we need to know

what was spoken in the Churches by Silvanus, the prophet
who accompanied Paul on his journeys, and what generally was said by Christian prophets in the Churches during
the reign of the emperor Caligula (37–41) and Claudius
(41–54). For to this source is to be traced back Paul's
firm conviction that the last potentate hostile to God was
not only to desecrate the temple of God, but also to
establish himself there as the one to be worshipped.
Events which took place under Caligula, in whose reign
the prophet Agabus from Judea predicted in the Church at
Antioch the coming of a general famine, which occurred in
the reign of Claudius (§ 11), led almost inevitably to the
development of prophecy of this kind (n. 7). Moreover,
Jesus had spoken repeatedly of ψευδόχριστοι, although, so
far as we know, He kept these predictions distinct from
His prophecies about the final affliction to result from the
desecration of the holy place, so that nothing was more
natural than that the Church should expect the appearance
of a single false Christ, and that it should identify this
false Christ with a world-ruler hostile to God, who was to
desecrate the holy place, and bring the final affliction upon
the Church (n. 8). So then, in a word, when Paul describes
the ἀντίθεος as being also ἀντίχριστος, this identification is
not to be regarded as simply Paul's own opinion, but in the
light of 1 John ii. 18, iv. 3 is to be taken as the common
belief of the Church ; for, in using the name ἀντίχριστος,
which occurs here for the first time in the N.T., and only
here, John means to describe an individual who was to
appear in the future, not only hostile to the true Christ,
but also His rival, whose appearance was to mark the beginning of the end of the world. But just as John, speaking with this general expectation of the Church in view,
makes mention of a *spirit* of antichrist which is already
at work in the world, which expresses itself through men,
and of the numerous forerunners of the antichrist who
may also be called antichrists (1 John iv. 3, ii. 18–22 ;

2 John 7), so Paul speaks of a *mystery* of lawlessness at work prior to the revelation or appearance of the man of lawlessness (ii. 7). In this way he justifies and explains his statement about the power which as yet restrains the revelation and appearance of the "man of lawlessness." The expression κατέχειν would be inappropriate if the object restrained were simply the lawless person who was to appear in the future, and not rather the principle which this person was eventually to embody, as it already existed and was at work in the world in its impersonal form. While the idea in κατέχον and κατέχων is not without parallel in Daniel (n. 9), here it is so definitely represented as something which was known, consequently as one of the elementary things taught in the early Christian Church, that we must assume that this, too, was a thought that had been developed by the Christian prophets of the time. While the man of lawlessness is described throughout as a person, being only once referred back to the impersonal principle of which eventually he was to become the embodiment, the restraining power is designated first by a neuter form and then by a masculine, both, however, being used to describe an existing thing. The restraining power is an impersonal something, which nevertheless has complete embodiment in personal form. From the contrast with ἀνομία, which is used three times to characterise the "antichrist" (vv. 3, 7, 8), it is clear that this restraining power was the system of laws then in operation in the world, which for the present was repressing the powers of lawlessness that had already begun to work, and was keeping them from manifesting themselves with full force, thus preventing the revelation of the mystery, the appearance of lawlessness in personal form, *i.e.*, the restraining power is the Roman empire. For its system of laws, which, in spite of the unrighteousness and unprincipled character of individual representatives, was magnificent, its strict administration of justice

and its broad tolerance made the empire a τὸ κατέχον, and the emperor a ὁ κατέχων (n. 9). If this was really Paul's view, it is a grave error to suppose that ὁ κατέχων is meant to designate a particular emperor, *i.e.* the reigning emperor, and if the Epistle was written prior to 54, the emperor Claudius ; because the setting aside of the κατέχων is the necessary precondition of the revelation of the man of lawlessness only in so far as that involves at the same time the setting aside of the κατέχον. There is no evidence, however, that Paul nor anyone else prominent in the early Church associated the breaking up of the empire and of the entire system of Roman government with the death or deposition of any reigning emperor. And this belief is less probable in view of the fact that neither the personal character nor the government of any of the emperors from Tiberius to Domitian was such as to render them the particular champions of that which made for moral order in the State (n. 10).

The description which follows of the deceiving and destructive influence of the man of lawlessness upon unbelievers (ii. 9–12), determines the manner in which the writers, passing now to the conclusion of the letter, mention again, as they had done in i. 3, the duty which they feel of giving thanks for the condition of the Church, for the grace shown it in the past, and for its hopeful future (ii. 13, 14). This is followed immediately by an exhortation to hold fast the teachings and advice which had been given them by oral instruction and by letter, and by a benediction (ii. 15–17). Here the Epistle might have been concluded, but some supplementary matter is added. On account of the opposition which the writers were encountering at the time from the unbelievers in the place where they were working, more prominence is given in this Epistle (but cf. I. v. 25) to the request for the prayers of the Church, and they are asked for with more feeling (iii. 1, 2). This request replaces for the time being some command which had been given them earlier, and which apparently he was on the point of mentioning in ii. 15. This renders necessary the transition in iii. 4, 5, which would have been unnecessary directly after ii. 15–17. In spite of the opposite example and the express advice of the missionaries, the disposition to unruly idleness (I. iv. 11, v. 14) had developed in the case of many members of the Church into a condition of chronic disorderliness (iii. 6–11). While these individuals are earnestly urged to resume their ordinary occupations (iii. 12), at the same time the Church is advised to mark those who disregard this exhortation of the letter and to break off intercourse with them until they reform, but not to give up the hope of helping them (iii. 14, 15, cf. iii. 6). The special attention which Paul calls in this letter to the fact that he had added the concluding benediction by his own hand, and his affirmation in this connection that the benediction by his own hand was the sign by which the genuineness of every one of his letters might be determined (iii. 17 f.), are explained by the facts hinted at in ii. 2 (n. 2).

Assuming that both the Epistles to the Thessalonians are genuine, there is no doubt (n. 11) that the shorter of the two was written last. In I. i. 2 ff. he gives thanks for the founding of the Church; in II. i. 3 ff. for the entirely gratifying character of its growth. Since there is no indication in 2 Thess. of any intention, nor even of any longing, on Paul's part, to return to Thessalonica, the letter could not have been written in the interval between the flight of the missionaries from Thessalonica and the sending of Timothy back from Athens, nor immediately after the arrival of Timothy in Corinth. The latter date is impossible, because 1 Thess. was written at that time (I. iii. 6); the former, because a letter with the contents and in the spirit of 2 Thess. written at practically the same time as 1 Thess. would prove all the touching expressions in the first letter, I. ii. 17–iii. 5, of desire to visit the Church again, to be insincere. Moreover, if 2 Thess. had been written first, Paul could hardly have failed to mention it in 1 Thess. as a strong proof of the interest which he and his helpers had in the welfare of the Church. Furthermore, the fact that this strong desire to revisit the Thessalonian Church continued, I. iii. 6–11, excludes the possibility of 2 Thess., in which there is no evidence of any such desire, having been written at an interval of only a few weeks from 1 Thess. There was an interval of several months between them. And during this time there seems to have been no direct intercourse, either in person or by letter, between the Church and its founders. II. iii. 14 has reference to I. iv. 11 f., and the more indefinite reference of II. ii. 15 to instructions by letter is based on 1 Thess. (n. 12). Still less probable is it that in the interval Paul or one of his helpers had visited Thessalonica. In ii. 5, iii. 10, Paul speaks of the occasion when he had been with them, but without distinguishing different times when he had been there. Developments had also taken place in the Church which required time. Nothing is said of the slanders which he had found it necessary to refute in 1 Thess., nor is there any reference to the necessity of confirming the confidence of the Church in its founders. There had been time for information, not from Paul, to be sure, but from the vicinity where he was, to reach Thessalonica by letter, and for the news of the injurious effect of these communications to come back to Paul (II. ii. 2, above, p. 226 and n. 2). Furthermore, from some source unknown to us, he had received more recent news concerning the condition of the Church (II. iii. 11). A number of Churches seem already to have been organised in and about Corinth (cf. 2 Cor. i. 1 ; Rom. xvi. 1), among which it was possible for Paul and for Silvanus and Timothy to

spread the good reports about the Church in Thessalonica
(II. i. 4). What is suggested with regard to the opposition which was rendering the work in Corinth difficult
and hindering its progress (II. iii. 2), is confirmed by Acts
xviii. 6–17, in that this opposition is represented as
emanating from persons who, having been offered the
choice between faith and unbelief, had refused to believe
the gospel, and if the hints of 1 Thess. also be taken into
account, from Jews (I. ii. 16, iii. 7, above, p. 216, line 31).
But it is hardly likely that, after having been so decisively repulsed by the proconsul (Acts xviii. 14–17),
the Jews could have interfered further with the growth
of the Christian Church in Corinth. The exceptionally
favoured situation of the Church, as regards its relation to
the authorities, disclosed in the Corinthian letters, was
a result of this favourable decision of Gallio; so that
2 Thess. must be dated before Acts xviii. 12. There is no
hint of any immediate intention on Paul's part of changing his field of labour. When he went to Ephesus at the
beginning of summer 54, after 1½ years of work in
Corinth (Acts xviii. 18), Silvanus and Timothy did not go
with him,—indeed, they do not seem to have been in
Corinth at the time. But when 2 Thess. was written
they were still with him (i. 1). Without, of course,
attempting to speak with absolute certainty or with
perfect accuracy, we shall be in agreement with all the
statements and hints of the letters, and with the accounts
in Acts, if we distribute the three oldest Epistles of Paul
in the period of his residence in Corinth (Acts xviii. 11,
approximately from Nov. 52 to May 54) as follows : Gal.
somewhere about April 53, 1 Thess. in May or June,
2 Thess. in August or September of the same year.

1. (P. 225.) " I," designating Paul, is distinguished three times in 1 Thess.
from " We," ii. 18, iii. 5, v. 27. In only one of these cases is the "I" further
explained by the addition of the name, ii. 18. The same distinction occurs
in 2 Thess., once without, ii. 5, once with the name, iii. 17. While in I. ii. 18,
II. iii. 17 the addition of the name is natural because of the character of the

statements made, in the three other passages it is assumed that the simple "I" is sufficient to designate Paul, who is named first in both the greetings, and whose importance is far greater than that of his two helpers. Spitta's hypothesis (122 ff.) that Timothy is meant by "I" in II. ii. 5 is untenable, for the reason that this is the only case where "I," which occurs five times altogether,—three times where the proper name is omitted because superfluous, —is made to refer to Timothy. The unnaturalness of the hypothesis is not lessened by assuming that the contents of ii. 5 may have given a clue as to which one of the three writers of the letter it was who thus suddenly spoke in his own name. In that case there was all the more reason why the youngest of them should have added ἐγὼ Τιμόθεος, and if, at the same time, he was acting as 'Paul's amanuensis, ὁ γράψας τὴν ἐπιστολήν (Rom. xvi. 22), if he did not want the readers to think that Paul was speaking—or Silvanus, if what was said did not sound like the apostle—until they finally convinced themselves that the youngest of the three missionaries was so stupid as, without previous notice and as a matter of course, to introduce himself in such a way as to make him appear the principal one of the three! Spitta is not justified in supporting this hypothesis (125) by claiming that the readers would distinguish the hand of Timothy, who wrote the letter, from that of Paul in iii. 17 f., because, when this letter was written, Paul was already in the habit of dictating, adding only a farewell greeting in his own hand. Cf. above, p. 170. He does not say in iii. 17 that henceforth he will do this, but that it is his custom in every letter. So, if Paul dictated 1 Thess., and, as is quite likely, dictated it to Timothy, then, according to Spitta's theory, the reader must have concluded from the handwriting that "I" in I. iii. 5, as distinguished from "I" in I. v. 27, referred to Timothy, not to Paul. Similarly, the personal acquaintances of Tertius (Rom. xvi. 22) among the Roman Christians must have concluded from his writing that he was the person designated by "I" in Rom. i. 8–xvi. 21, and the real author of Romans. According to Spitta, Timothy was not only the amanuensis to whom Paul dictated 2 Thess., but the real author of the letter, which he himself composed at the direction of Paul and Silvanus. This, he thinks, enables us to explain its many variations from Paul's style and doctrine, which have caused the letter to be suspected, particularly the Jewish apocalyptic views which Paul did not hold. Without correcting the composition of his follower, or making him responsible for it, or even so much as hinting that Timothy had a large share in its preparation (cf. 1 Pet. v. 12, § 38), the apostle, who was very much preoccupied at the time, subscribed his name to this letter, which varied so much from his own writings both in style and contents, just as if it had been his own (iii. 17)! That was certainly the best way in the world to perpetuate the fraud referred to in ii. 2.

2. (Pp. 226, 231, 232.) If πνεῦμα, ii. 2, means, as it clearly does, the prophetic spirit uttering itself in human speech (I. v. 19 f. ; Acts xiii. 2, 4, xx. 23, xxi. 4, 11 ; Rev. ii. 7), then διὰ λόγου does not stand alone in contrast to διὰ πνεύματος, but the whole clause taken altogether, μήτε (D* μηδέ) διὰ λόγου μήτε δι' ἐπιστολῆς ὡς δι' ἡμῶν, so that ὡς δι' ἡμῶν is to be taken with λόγου as well as with ἐπιστολῆς, like ἡμῶν in ii. 15. Oral as well as written reports had come to Thessalonica, which made it appear that Paul and his helpers shared these views. To us, who are not acquainted with the facts in the case, the

language of the passage leaves it somewhat doubtful (1) whether actually false appeals to alleged statements of the apostle and to a letter forged in his name are meant ; or (2) whether oral and written reports had reached Thessalonica from the region where Paul was, which, because they came from this region and without any fraudulent intention on the part of those who gave them out, gave rise to the erroneous opinion that the view which they represented had the authority of the apostle, or (3) whether actual written and oral statements of Paul were so misinterpreted. In the last mentioned case these statements would naturally be sought in 1 Thess., but this letter does not lend itself to such misinterpretation. It contains no language such as that found in Jas. v. 3, 5, 8, 9 ; 1 John ii. 18. Moreover, we should expect Paul to correct such misinterpretation (cf. 1 Cor. v. 9–11). Finally, on this view it is impossible to explain iii. 17 as due to what is said in ii. 2. The first of the three possible meanings mentioned explains best the connection between these two passages. But it is to be observed that there is no expression of anger at this insolent deceit. Furthermore, in this case we should expect to read not ὡς δι' ἡμῶν, but ὡς ἡμετέρων or ὡς παρ' ἡμῶν (Cod. P., cf. Hippol. in Dan. iv. 21, ed. Bonwetsch, 236. 15, ὡς ἐξ ἡμῶν), or, if the reference were to a letter, ὡς ὑφ' ἡμῶν γραφείσης. Moreover, in this passage nothing is said about the origin of the oral and written statements in question, but all we have is a protest against the inference that they express the apostle's views. This agrees only with the second meaning suggested. Since, however, Paul saw that all sorts of such deceptions might develop in the future (ii. 3, κατὰ μηδένα τρόπον), he took occasion to call attention to the fact that only letters coming directly from him and specifically subscribed by his own hand could be regarded as expressions of his opinion (iii. 17). The rendering of ἐνέστηκεν, "is immediately at hand," or "is beginning" (so still Schmiedel HK, ad loc.), should be abandoned, because unsupported both by grammar and by usage. As is well known, the present is called by the grammarians ὁ ἐνεστὼς χρόνος, and in business transactions ἡ ἐνεστῶσα ἡμέρα was the regular name of "this day," e.g. Berl. äg. Urk. Nos. 394. 19 ; 415. 18, 30 ; 536. 6 ; 883. 3 ; 891 verso, line 15.

3. (P. 226.) The ἔτι, ii. 5, which does not occur in iii. 10, indicates nothing as to the length of time that had elapsed since the Thessalonians had been reminded of the things in question, cf. Luke xxiv. 6 ; Rom. v. 8 ; Heb. vii. 10. It is only intended to emphasise the fact that these teachings were not an afterthought, of which the readers were informed by a subsequent letter from the apostle, or by Timothy at the time when he was sent back to Thessalonica, but a part of the missionary preaching, and so an original part of the Christian message. That the Thessalonians missed entirely the point of these teachings, or immediately forgot them, is unlikely. When, therefore, notwithstanding this message, many had fallen into the error opposed in ii. 2, the natural supposition is that it had been represented to them that the man of lawlessness, who after the casting aside of all restraints was to set himself up as God, had already come, doubtless in the person of Caligula. But if the "antichrist" made his appearance in Caligula (n. 7), then with Caligula's death (Jan. 24, 41) began "the Day of the Lord," which naturally was not thought of as a day of twelve or twenty-four hours' length, but as the epoch during which constantly—almost hourly—the visible return of Christ was to be expected.

If, now, Christian prophets declared Caligula to be the expected man of law-lessness ; if Paul and his helpers saw in this figure of the recent past, whom all remembered, a foreshadowing of the antichrist, and pointed to it as a proof that the μυστήριον τῆς ἀνομίας was already working ; and if, as was un-doubtedly the case, the missionaries in Thessalonica spoke of the present as the end of the age, as is everywhere done in the N.T. (1 Cor. x. 11 ; Jas. v. 3, 5, 8, 9 ; 1 John ii. 18 ; 1 Pet. i. 20 ; Heb. i. 1 ; Acts ii. 16 ff.),—nothing is more natural than the rise of such errors and delusions as Paul here opposes. But there was no event corresponding to the prophesied falling away (below, nn. 4, 9). If, moreover, the readers really knew from the earlier teaching who and what the κατέχων and the κατέχον were, then they must understand that the power which is keeping back the full manifestation of the man of lawlessness is not yet set aside, but is still in active operation, so that the time characterised by the reign of this power (νῦν τὸ κατέχον, ver. 6 ; ὁ κατέχων ἄρτι, ver. 7) continues, and the time of the "antichrist" has not yet come. Finally, the detailed description of the activity of the lawless one, and, above all, the fact that Paul refers to the destruction of the same by the returning Christ, made it impossible to suppose that the antichrist was Caligula, or any other person who had lived and disappeared. There is no philological reason why νῦν, ii. 6, cannot be connected with κατέχον, cf. John iv. 18 ; νῦν ὅν ἔχεις, cf. 1 Cor. vii. 29 ; Xen. Cyrop. i. 4. 3, ἀεὶ τοὺς παρόντας ; Hell. ii. 1. 4, ἀεὶ ὁ ἀκούων, especially numerous in designations of time, cf. Kühner-Gerth, i. 617 ; Winer, 561. 4 ; but also in numerous other cases, where, for the sake of stronger emphasis, objects and other modifiers precede the par-ticiple and its article (Epitaph. Avercii, i. 19, Forsch. v. 71, ταῦθ' ὁ νοῶν) or the conjunction which governs the sentence, cf. A. Buttmann, 333 (Eng. trans. 388). Even if we translate as if the reading were τὰ νῦν, "As for the present, ye know the power restraining," the logical necessity of connect-ing νῦν with κατέχον still appears, (1) from the analogy of ὁ κατέχων ἄρτι in ii. 7 ; (2) from the contrast running through the entire context of the present (νῦν, ἤδη, ἄρτι), not to the past, when Paul was in Thessalonica, but to the future revelation of the man of lawlessness ; and, finally, (3) from the fact that the νῦν gives no clear sense when taken with οἴδατε, from which, moreover, it is unnaturally separated.

4. (P. 227.) With ii. 1 (ἐπισυναγωγῆς) cf. Matt. xxiv. 31 ; Mark xiii. 27 ; 1 Thess. iv. 14, 17, above, p. 223 f. With ii. 2 cf. Matt. xxiv. 6 ; Mark xiii. 7 (μὴ θροεῖσθε) ; Luke xxi. 9. With ii. 3a cf. Matt. xxiv. 4, 23, 26 ; Mark xiii. 5, 21 ; Luke xxi. 8, xvii. 23. With ἡ ἀποστασία, which appears partly to precede the appearance of the "antichrist" (ver. 3), and partly to be the result of the same (vv. 9–11), cf. for the first aspect Dan. viii. 12, 23, xi. 30, 32 ; 1 Macc. i. 15 (ἀπέστησαν ἀπὸ διαθήκης ἁγίας) ; for the second, 1 Macc. i. 41–53, ii. 15 (οἱ καταναγκάζοντες τὴν ἀποστυσίαν). Also for the first aspect, Matt. xxiv. 10-12, and for the second, Matt. xxiv. 21-24 ; Mark xiii. 19-21. With ὁ ἄνθρωπος τῆς ἀνομίας, ver. 3 (אB, cf. among other authorities also Just. Dial. xxxii ; still τῆς ἁμαρτίας has strong support), and ὁ ἄνομος, ver. 8, cf. Dan. vii. 25 (ἀλλοιῶσαι καιροὺς καὶ νόμον), xi. 37 f. ; Matt. xxiv. 12 ; Didache, xvi. 4 ; Barn. xv. 5. With ver. 4a (ὁ ἀντικείμενος—σέβασμα) cf. Dan. vii. 7, 11, 20, 25, xi. 36 (LXX ὑψωθήσεται ἐπὶ πάντα θεόν, καὶ ἐπὶ τὸν θεὸν, τῶν θεῶν ἔξαλλα λαλήσει) ; 1 Macc. i. 24. No entire equivalent to ver. 4b is to be found in Dan. viii.

11–13, ix. 27, xi. 31, xii. 11 ; 1 Macc. i. 54–61, iv. 38, 43–45, vi. 7 ; 2 Macc. vi.
1–7 ; Matt. xxiv. 15, still less Isa. xiv. 13 f. ; Ezek. xxviii. 2. In Mark xiii.
14, the only thing that would seem to indicate that the evangelist thought of
the "desolating abomination" as a man who set up himself or his image in the
holy place, is the grammatically abnormal reading ἑστηκότα (אBL), if indeed
this reading be correct.   The deification and self-deification of the monarch
which reached a high point in Antiochus IV., the θεὸς ἐπιφανής (e.g. Jos. Ant.
xii. 5. 5), did not come to the climax which is indicated in 2 Thess. ii. 4
until Caligula ; cf. below, n. 7.   With ver. 8 cf. Isa. xi. 4 (from which the
expression is borrowed) ; Dan. vii. 11, 26, viii. 25, xi. 45. With ver. 9 cf.
Dan. viii. 25 ; Matt. xxiv. 24 ; Mark xiii. 22. With ver. 11 cf. Isa. xix. 14 ;
Jer. iv. 11 (especially if the apocryphal form of this verse which Hippol.
de Antichr. 57 on Dan. iv. 49, quotes is ancient).   In all these parallels it is
to be remembered that Paul was not confined to the Sept. version of Daniel,
much less to the translation of Daniel by Theodotian which was sometimes
used in the Church instead of the LXX.   Hence, e.g., he might well have translated פשע Dan. viii. 12 (ix. 24) by ἀποστασία, and פשעים (viii. 23) by ἀποστάται.

   5. (P. 227.)   According to Spitta (139), Timothy, the alleged author of
2 Thess., here gives out as his own opinion what he learned from his source,
which was a Jewish apocalypse of the time of Caligula, of which apocalypses
Spitta has discovered no less than three (137 f., cf. also his Offenb. des Joh.
498).   Such an apocalypse, he thinks, was among the "sacred writings," the
contents of which Timothy under the direction of Eunice "piously absorbed"
from his youth up (129, 139, cf. 2 Tim. i. 5, iii. 15).   In this way he came
to have eschatological views which Paul did not share (above, n. 1), although
later in his life Paul directs him to those (τὰ) ἱερὰ γράμματα which were
γραφὴ θεόπνευστος, points out that this is the right source from which
Timothy is to draw instruction both for himself and others (2 Tim. iii. 15 f.) ;
and, on the other hand, warns him against unholy and Jewish fables (1 Tim.
i. 4, iv. 7 ; 2 Tim. iv. 4 ; cf. Tit. i. 14).

   6. (P. 227.)   Paul never claimed to be a prophet, although he could boast
of having received revelations (2 Cor. xii. 1–4 ; Gal. i. 12–16, ii. 2), and did
declare that he had other charismata (1 Cor. xiv. 18 ; 2 Cor. xii. 12 ; Rom.
xv. 19).   But from the very beginning of his ministry he had about him men
who in their own circles were regarded as prophets (Acts xi. 27, xiii. 1, 2, 4, xx.
23, xxi. 9–11.   Thus, both at the time when the letters to the Thessalonians
were written and when the Church in Thessalonica was founded, he had with
him the prophet Silas (above, p. 207, n. 1).   That in their preaching there
Paul and Silas emphasised strongly the kingship of Christ and hence the
eschatological elements in the gospel, is attested by Acts xvii. 17.   The fact
that, so far as we know, none of the discourses of the Christian prophets was
written down, does not prove that they had no influence upon the development of the beliefs of the Churches.   How highly they were valued by Paul
appears from 1 Cor. xii. 10, 28 f., xiv. 1–39 ; Eph. ii. 20, iii. 5, iv. 11 ; Rom.
xii. 6 ; 1 Thess. v. 20 ; 1 Tim. i. 18, iv. 1, 14.

   7. (P. 228.)   For the decrees of Caligula relating to the Jews, cf. Schürer,
i. 495–505 (Eng. trans. I. ii. 90–103) ; for the Jewish traditions, cf. Derenbourg,
Hist. de la Palestine, 207 ; for its influence in Christian circles, cf. the writer's
essay, ZfKW, 1885, S. 511 f., also the writer's Ev. des Petrus, 41 f.   The prin-

cipal event is the decree of Caligula of the winter of 39–40, in which he ordered that a colossal statue of himself be set up in the temple at Jerusalem, which, notwithstanding long preparations, was never accomplished ; cf. Philo, *Leg. ad Cai.* xxx. ; Jos. *Ant.* xviii. 8. 2 ; *Bell.* ii. 10. 1.   Still this is only the climax—to Jews and to Christians most horrible climax—of this emperor's unlimited contempt for everything moral and religious, and his mad self-deification (Suet. *Calig.* xxii, " Hactenus quasi de principe, reliqua ut de monstro narranda sunt," which occupies the narrative up to chap. lx. ; Dio Cassius, lix. 4, 26–28).   H. Grotius (*Annot. in NT*, ed. Windheim, ii. 715 ff., 721 ff.) was the first definitely to connect this passage with Caius Caligula.

8. (P. 228.) ψευδόχριστοι is used in two senses. For the wider meaning— any assumed authority over Israel—cf. John x. 8 with reference to the past, John v. 43 with reference to the future.   For the stricter meaning—any deceptive counterpart of the returning Jesus Christ—cf. Matt. xxiv. 5, 23 f. ; Mark xiii. 6, 21 f. ; cf. Luke xvii. 23.

9. (Pp. 229, 230.) For the analogues of κατέχων and κατέχον in Dan. x.–xii., cf. Hofmann, i. 319–326, also his *Schriftbeweis*, i. 330–335, iii. 671.   Both the words themselves and Paul's manifest didactic purpose indicate clearly that the reference is not to those preservative forces which lie in the background of national life operating in the spirit world, but to something that is manifest, from the existence of which it is possible to discern that the "antichrist," and so "the day of our Lord," has not yet come.   Neither does Hofmann offer any adequate explanation of the interchange between κατέχων and κατέχον (*NT*, i. 326 ; *Schriftbeweis*, iii. 672).   It is evident that the view of the emperor and of the empire expressed in these words is in perfect agreement with Rom. xiii. 1–7, and that it had then or afterward the corroboration of Paul's own personal experience, cf. Acts xiii. 7–12, xvi. 35–39, xviii. 12–17, xix. 31 (the asiarchs were the priestly representatives of the imperial idea), xxi. 32–40, xxii. 24–30, xxiii. 16–30, xxiv. 22–26, xxv. 4–12, 16–27, xxvii. 3, xxviii. 16, 30 f. ; Phil. i. 13.   The general friendly judgment of the Roman State by Clemens Romanus, Melito, Irenæus, and others, does not signify a falling away from Paulinism.   This interpretation of 2 Thess. ii. 6 f. is the oldest that we have.   We do not find it definitely stated by Irenæus,—indeed, not until Hippol. *in Dan.* iv. 22 ; Tert. *Resurr.* xxiv.   But the general eschatological views of these writers, which agree in their main features and many of their details, are evidence enough that the reference of κατέχον to the Roman empire was from the first common to them.   The empire must be rent in pieces before the " antichrist " can come (Iren. v. 26. 1, 30. 2 ; Hippol. *Antichr.* 25, 27, 43, *in Dan.* iv. 5–6, 14 ; Tert. *Resurr.* xxiv.   Tertullian (*loc. cit.*) translates 2 Thess. ii. 6 f. " nunc quid teneat " (*al.* " detineat "), and "qui nunc tenet", which makes it appear as if the reference to the Romans in Irenæus by the phrases "qui nunc tenent " (Iren. v. 30. 3) and "qui nunc regnant " were suggested by 2 Thess. ii. 6 f., if indeed in both passages the original reading was not οἱ νῦν κρατοῦντες, as in Hippol. *de Antichr.* 28, cf. 43, 50, *in Dan.* iv. 5, 9, 17 (ed. Bonwetsch, pp. 196. 2, 206. 16, 228. 20 f.).   This does not exclude the possibility of a certain connection between the empire of the antichrist and the Roman empire.   Irenæus (v. 30. 3) declares it possible that the number 666 may mean Λατεῖνος, and the empire of the antichrist may bear this name, although

he prefers the interpretation which makes it mean Τείταν, an old discarded name which was borne by none of the Roman emperors. Hippolytus regards the world-empire which had existed since the time of Augustus as a Satanic imitation of the world-rule of Christ (*in Dan.* iv. 9), and thinks that the antichrist will return to the form of government existing under Augustus (*Antichr.* 49). Accordingly, in clear distinction from Irenæus, Hippolytus prefers to all others that interpretation of the number 666 which makes it mean Λατεῖνος (*Antichr.* 50). On the other hand, Hippolytus agrees with his master Irenæus in the opinion, which is certainly much older than either of these writers, that the antichrist is to be a Jewish pseudo-Messiah of the tribe of Dan (Iren. v. 30. 2, cf. v. 25. 4 ; Hippol. *Antichr.* 6, 14–15, 54–58, *in Dan.* iv. 49 ; Theophil. *Lat. in Evv.* i. 29, iii. 7 ; *Forsch.* ii. 58, 71 ; *ZfKW*, 1885, S. 570). It is probable that even Marcion interpreted 2 Thess. ii. as referring to a pseudo-Messiah of the God of the Jews (Tert. *c. Marc.* v. 16 ; *GK*, i. 589). In a peculiar form this idea is to be found in Ephrem (*Comm. in Epist. Pauli*, 193 f.). The man of sin is a circumcised Jew of the tribe of Judah, who sends his apostles or false prophets before him who bring about a "falling away" (2 Thess. ii. 3), but when the man of sin himself comes he does not connect himself with a sect, but appears in the holy Church, declaring himself to be God. According to this interpretation, the power which at the time of Paul was restraining his appearance was the continuance of the Jewish temple and worship, and the fact that the conversion of the Gentiles was not yet complete. The theory of a Jewish anti-Messiah, which, *mutatis mutandis*, has been advocated even in modern times by many (*e.g.* Schneckenburger, published by Böhmer, *JbDTh.* 1859, S. 405 ff. ; B. Weiss, *ThStKr.* 1869, S. 22 ff. ; Spitta, *Z. Gesch. d. Urchr.* i. 140 ff.), is as difficult to maintain as the theory that the man of lawlessness was a Roman emperor. The latter theory does not agree with the opinion mentioned above held by Paul and the ancient Church concerning the emperor and the empire. Neither can it be maintained on the ground that the insane acts of the emperor Caligula were really due to the conception which Paul and his contemporaries had of the man of lawlessness. Still less does it follow from the fact that in the conception of the man of lawlessness there are certain parallelisms with Christ which were afterwards stereotyped in the expression ἀντίχριστος (not ψευδόχριστος), that Paul thought of him as a ψευδόχριστος of Jewish origin. Against this view (1) argues the fact that the lawless one, following in the footsteps of Antiochus and Caligula, is to desecrate the temple of God by idolatrous deification of himself. Even assuming that "temple" is here used in a figurative sense, there is nothing which connects this picture with the Christ-hostile Judaism of the apostolic and post-apostolic periods. In general, it may be said that the antichrist as here described by Paul, and the unbelieving Judaism as elsewhere depicted by him, have no points in common. (2) According to Paul's view, the opposition of the majority of his nation to Christ had already reached its climax. The wrath of God, which was to visit upon them outward punishment, had already attained its object and would soon abate (1 Thess. ii. 16 ; see below, § 16, n. 4). That inward judgment to which they are now exposed, namely, the hardening of heart against the gospel, makes the Jewish nation during the whole period of the preaching of the gospel to the Gentiles a fossil

capable of practically no change. This state of things is to be ended not by
the revival and increase of hostility to Christ, but by the conversion of
Israel to Christ. This is not a passing fancy of Paul's in some moment
when his feelings were conciliatory, but is stated by him as a truth of
revelation in line with the prophecies of Jesus and based upon the O.T. as
he understood it (Rom. xi. 25–32). (3) The term ἀντίχριστος, which is not
used by Paul, although in content its meaning corresponds to Paul's description, does not by any means justify the conception of a Jewish pseudo-
Messiah ; for, in the thought of the apostle, Christ is not simply a Jewish
Messiah, but also the second Adam, who unites the whole world under His
headship as its Lord and King because He is the incarnation of that human
righteousness which comes from God. For that reason the man who represents the incarnation of all human lawlessness and of all human opposition
to God, and who with Satanic power subjects mankind under his sway, is a
caricature of Christ, an "antichrist," whatever his origin may be. The
ἀνομία, from which his name is derived, exists naturally wherever sin exists
(1 John iii. 4), and so even among the Jews (Rom. ii. 23–27 ; Acts xxiii. 3 ;
Matt. xxiii. 28). But the characteristic of Jewish hostility to God and
Christ is neither lawlessness, nor idolatry, nor self-deification, but false zeal
for God and His law (Rom. ix. 31–x. 3 ; Gal. i. 13 f. ; Phil. iii. 6). On the
other hand, ἀνομία is such a characteristic feature of heathen life and of sin
in the heathen world (Rom. ii. 12 ; 1 Cor. ix. 21 ; 2 Cor. vi. 14), that it is
necessary to think of the lawless one as springing out of the heathen world.
When in ii. 4 he is declared to be the foe of all religion, it does not follow
that he might not assume the forms of existing religions. On the contrary,
Caligula's attempt at self-deification connected itself with the emperor
cult, that of Antiochus with the worship of Zeus, and both these forerunners
of the antichrist undertook by force to identify these heathen cults with
that of the Jews, thereby destroying the latter. But even Christianity is
not free from lawlessness. Just as the confessors of Christ are not free from
ἀνομία (1 Cor. vi. 7–20 ; 2 Cor. xii. 20–xiii. 2 ; Matt. vii. 23, xiii. 38–42), so
there are points of connection between the lawless one and the Church. On
the basis of the prophecies of Jesus (Matt. xxiv. 10–12, 24 ; cf. Luke xviii. 8),
and following the prophecies in Dan. and the history of Antiochus (above,
p. 236, n. 4), the Christian prophets announced a falling away within the
Church as one of the characteristics of the last days (1 Tim. iv. 1–4 ; 2 Tim.
iii. 1–5 ; Acts xx. 29–31 ; 2 Pet. ii. 1, iii. 4 ; *Didache*, xvi. 4), and both Paul
and John directed attention to the signs of the same in their own time
(1 Tim. i. 19, vi. 5 ; 2 Tim. ii. 16–18, iii. 5–9 ; 1 Cor. xi. 19 ; 1 John ii.
18–23, iv. 1–3). Of this character must be the falling away which in 2 Thess.
ii. 3 is referred to as something specifically known. It could not be some
sort of a political revolution, a revolt against the Roman authority established
by God, or a falling away on the part of the Jews from the law of their
fathers, since for Paul and the Christians of that age and of the ages following, the holy people, who at the end of the days will have to endure in
increased measure what Israel suffered at the time of Antiochus, are not the
Jewish people who owed their obligations to Moses, but the Church of Jesus.
To what extent this falling away conditions the appearance of the antichrist
it is not possible to determine from Paul's brief reference to what had

been said about it in his earlier preaching. In view of the ἐκ μέρους προφητεύομεν in 1 Cor. xiii. 9, we have no right to assume that the elements and fragments of Christian prophecy that here come to view formed in Paul's mind a finished and completed picture.

10. (P. 230.) It is a noteworthy fact that, with the exception of Luke ii. 1, iii. 1, Acts xi. 28, where mention of the emperor could not be avoided, no name of an emperor is to be found in the N.T. Very little thought was devoted to Tiberias or Caligula, Claudius or Nero, reference being made simply to the emperor who was reigning at the time (Matt. xxii. 17–21 ; Mark xii. 14–17 ; Luke xx. 22–25, xxiii. 2 ; John xix. 12, 15 ; Acts xvii. 7, xxv. 8–12, xxvi. 32, xxvii. 24, xxviii. 19 ; Phil. iv. 22 ; 1 Pet. ii. 13, 17). So we have mentioned the government of the empire and its agents (Rom. xiii. 1–7 ; 1 Pet. ii. 13, 17) or different classes of kings (Matt. x. 18, xvii. 25 ; Luke xxii. 25 ; Acts iv. 26, ix. 15 ; 1 Tim. ii. 2, vi. 15 ; Rev. i. 5, vi. 15).

11. (P. 231.) Grotius (*Ann. in NT*, ed. Windheim, ii. 715 ff.), Ewald (*Sendschreiben des Pl.* 17 f.), Laurent (*Ntl. Studien*, 49 ff.), on the presupposition that both Epistles are genuine, declare 2 Thess. to be the older of the two. Baur reaches the same conclusion, on the assumption that both are spurious (*Paulus*, ii. 368 f.). Grotius thinks that 2 Thess. was written as early as 38 A.D., before Paul visited Thessalonica, to certain Jewish Christians there. Ewald and Laurent make Berœa the place of composition (Acts xvii. 10), and think that it was written during the weeks immediately following the founding of the Church. Here again reference must be made to II. i. 4 in addition to what has been said above, p. 231. It is not a question here as in I. i. 8 f. of personal contact of Paul and his helpers with Christians from outside of Europe (above, p. 205 f.), but of reports spread by the missionaries in a number of Churches where they had sojourned since their flight from Thessalonica, or where they were sojourning at the time when the letter was written. Hence they must have gone at least as far as Berœa and Athens and Corinth. The language used would still seem unnatural if it referred simply to reports made in the preaching that gathered congregations in Berœa, Athens, and Corinth. The reference is to conditions in Churches already existing. During the eighteen months of continuous " residence " in Corinth (Acts xviii. 11), Paul may have made an occasional visit to other Churches, but only to such as that in the port town of Cenchrea (Rom. xvi. 1). This is not the case, however, with Silvanus, and Timothy, in whose name II. i. 4 is also written. The latter, upon his return from his mission in Thessalonica, certainly stopped in Berœa and probably also in Athens, and so had opportunity to do what in II. i. 4 is declared to have been done by all three missionaries. From II. iii. 17 it is not to be inferred that the Church had never before received a letter signed by Paul's own hand. Notwithstanding the fact that the Corinthians had previously received a letter from him (1 Cor. v. 9), he calls attention to the concluding greeting in his own hand (xvi. 21) ; while the fact that in 2 Thess. iii. 17 he calls attention even more expressly to the form of his own handwriting, stating in addition that it is the same in every letter, is fully explained by the circumstance that henceforth the ending of the letter in his own hand is to be regarded by the Church as a proof of genuineness. A point in the tradition which tends to confirm the priority of 1 Thess. is the fact that the two letters were not arranged in the Canon according to the

principle which came into use comparatively late and which is still in vogue, namely, the determining of the order of the writings in accordance with their respective lengths. They had their present order as early as the Canon of Marcion, who knew nothing of the later principle of arrangement, from which we may assume that they were always circulated in their present order.

12. (P. 232.) If II. iii. 14 stated simply the possibility that someone might disregard the exhortation of iii. 6–13, the language would be different, reading somewhat as follows : ἐὰν δέ τις οὐχ ὑπακούσῃ τούτοις τοῖς λόγοις ἡμῶν ; while, apart from its character as a conditional sentence, it would be compared not with I. v. 27, but with I. iv. 18. Paul refers to a definite passage in an earlier letter (cf. 1 Cor. v. 9), I. iv. 11 f., and on the basis of reports received (II. iii. 11), declares that the exhortation of the letter is now actually being disregarded. The language in II. ii. 15 is less definite : "oral or written." Hence it may refer to something in the letter in which it occurs. Since, however, there are to be found in this letter no new instructions and directions supplementing the missionary preaching, such as I. iv. 13–18 certainly is, and possibly also such detached sentences as I. iv. 1–8, 11 f. ; v. 12–22 (cf. *per contra* I. iv. 9, v. 1), II. ii. 15 also is to be taken as a reference to 1 Thess. In particular does II. ii. 1, ὑπὲρ τῆς . . . ἡμῶν ἐπισυναγωγῆς ἐπ᾽ αὐτόν, sound like a recollection of I. iv. 14, 17.

§ 16. THE GENUINENESS OF THE FIRST THREE EPISTLES.

These three Epistles, which, if written by Paul at all, were all composed within a single year at intervals of from one to three months (above, p. 233), are all entitled to the benefit of the critical principles laid down above (pp. 156–162). The difficulties which are always in the way of getting forged letters of apostles into circulation in Christian Churches (p. 159, paragr. 5) are enormously increased in the case of 2 Thess., the genuineness of which has been far more seriously questioned than that of the other two letters, because of what is said in the Epistle itself about possible or actual forgeries (ii. 2, iii. 17). Remarks of this kind would at once call for criticism on the part of the original readers, and it is difficult to see how within thirty or forty years after Paul's death the Thessalonian Church could have been made to believe that this Epistle had been received from Paul during his lifetime, unless it contained at least a fragment that looked like an original document, and unless it were signed in a peculiar hand in characters distinctly different from those appearing in the body of the letter. In view of what is said in 2 Thess. ii. 2, iii. 17, it is quite out of the question, not only for us modern readers, but also for those readers from whom the letter passed into circulation and for whom it was intended originally, to suppose that 2 Thess. is a more or less harmless forgery " in the spirit of Paul " ; simply because this passage raises the question in the mind of every reader, no matter how unsophisticated, whether it is a genuine writing of Paul's that he has before him, or some document that has been forged in a manner the boldness of which is unparalleled (n. 1). In addition to this, more traces are to be found of 2 Thess. than of either 1 Thess. or Gal. in the Church prior to the time of Marcion and outside of his *Apostolicon* (n. 2).

The questions discussed in Galatians had less general interest for the Church of the second century than had the statements of eschatological doctrine and the practical advice of 1 and 2 Thess. Only Marcion is an exception. After his fashion he values Galatians very highly, and in testimony of this esteem places it first in his collection of Pauline letters, calling it *principialem adversus Judaismum epistolam*, and making it the starting-point for his criticism of the entire tradition (Tert. *c. Marc.* iv. 3, v. 2). So also the comprehensive critique of the Pauline Epistles and of the entire N.T., begun by Baur, started by assuming that Gal. was a source the genuineness of which did not need to be proved in order to show, on the basis of the clear and fundamental opposition between Jewish and Pauline Christianity which comes out in this Epistle, that Acts and most of the Epistles which bear Paul's name are the product of a biassed (*tendenziös*) attempt to tone down this opposition, and are consequently spurious. Perhaps this is the chief reason why, by the latest critical method popular in Holland, it is customary to begin with the discussion of Gal. (n. 3).

The arguments advanced by these critics against the genuineness of Gal., and by the critics of the older school against that of 1 Thess. (n. 4), have made a lasting impression only upon very few. Not so, however, in the case of 2 Thess. Assuming the genuineness of both Gal. and 1 Thess., it must be admitted that Paul was able, as occasion demanded, in the course of a single year to write letters very different both in thought and spirit. This renders all the more striking the resemblance in plan (above, p. 224 f.), thought, and language of 1 and 2 Thess., which were written with scarcely a longer interval than that between Gal. and 1 Thess. There is only one very obvious difference, namely, 2 Thess. is far inferior to 1 Thess. in freshness of emotion, in vividness of language, and in the winsome expression of friendly fellow-feeling. It is this difference principally, taken along with the fact of the great similarity of the letters in plan and language, that has given rise to the suspicion that someone familiar with 1 Thess. used it as a model by which to compose 2 Thess. Still this observation has less weight critically than the similarity of the two letters. What contrasts of feeling and expression do we find, for example, in a single letter of Paul's like 2 Cor. ! 1 Thess. was written under the immediate stimulus of the extremely gratifying news brought by Timothy, which had revived the apostle's spirits that had been so long depressed by heavy cares. The news which led to the writing of 2 Thess. was less cheering. The exhortations of 1 Thess. had been entirely disregarded by some, and had to be repeated with severity (iii. 6–16). The teachings about the parousia of Christ and the events connected with it (ii. 5, 15), which he had recalled to their minds and enlarged upon in 1 Thess., had not been effective in putting a stop to certain misleading reports. Moreover, means were being used for the circulation of these reports which, to say the least, were hardly honourable (ii. 2, cf. iii. 17). Of course, the steadfastness of the Church, in spite of constant suffering (i. 3 f.), was something to be thankful for, though for Paul there was something depressing in the thought that the only prospect of a change in this condition of affairs was that offered by the hope of the judgment connected with the return of Christ. When one takes into consideration also the opposition with which Paul had to contend in the place where he was (iii. 2), and the missionary work in Corinth which claimed his entire attention (iii. 1 ; Acts xviii. 5–17), it it quite easy to understand the spirit and tone of this letter. On the other hand, it is hardly likely that a person forging such a letter would have put into Paul's mouth twice a sentence like this : " We are under obligation at all times to give thanks for you " (i. 3, ii. 13, above, p. 225), which is not to be found elsewhere in Paul's letters, genuine or spurious (n. 5), instead of imitating 1 Thess. i. 2 and other similar sentences at the beginning of Paul's letters (Rom. i. 8 ; 1 Cor. i. 4 ; 2 Cor. i. 3 ; Eph. i. 3, 15 f.; Col. i. 3 ; Phil. i. 3 ; Philem. 4 ; 1 Tim. i. 3). On the other hand, the similarity of the two letters is quite natural in view of the fact that they were written within a comparatively short time of each other to the same Church, that conditions were such that it was necessary in part to write about the same things (the sufferings of the Church, eschatological questions, and unruly idleness), and, finally, that there were definite reasons for back references in 2 Thess. to the former letter (ii. 15, iii. 14). If the claim was being made in Thessalonica on the basis of oral and written communications from the vicinity where Paul was, that Paul himself held the opinion which in this letter he feels called upon to pronounce absurd (ii. 2, above, p. 226), it is perfectly

natural that he should recall what he had written to
the Church a few months before, and that in dictating
2 Thess. he should have in mind the argument and the
language of the former letter (n. 6).

Of course, 2 Thess. could not have been written by
Paul if 2 Thess. ii. 3–12 is based upon the legend of
the return of Nero as antichrist from Parthia or from
the dead, still less if it presupposes the description of
antichrist in Rev. xiii. and xvii. 8 (n. 7).   The latter
assumption is purely arbitrary, because the most distinctive feature in Paul's description, which it is impossible to derive from Dan. or 1 Macc., and which
certainly cannot be referred to Matt. xxiv. 15, Mark
xiii. 14, namely, that the antichrist is to set himself up
in the temple of God and demand that he be worshipped,
is not to be found at all in Rev.   On the contrary, it is
to be explained as a prophetic reflection of historical
events which took place in the reign of Caligula (above,
pp. 228, 237, n. 7).   There is not the slightest suggestion
in ii. 3–12 of Nero's conduct nor attitude toward the
Roman Christians.   If, as is at least doubtful, we really
have here a description of the miraculous return to life of
some historical personage (n. 8), this personage cannot
be Nero.   For, so far as our knowledge goes, the idea that
Nero was to come back from the dead could not and did
not originate until through the lapse of time it was no
longer possible to retain the older notion that he was
hidden somewhere among the Parthians, i.e. the idea did
not originate until the beginning of the second century.
As a matter of fact, we know that it was not until 150
that the legend was adopted from the Jewish into the
Christian Sibyllines with some other material taken from
the Johannine apocalypse, and that it was not until the
third century that the legend secured wide circulation in
the Church (n. 9).   But there is absolutely no trace in
2 Thess. of this older view, that Nero, who was still living

in the far East, was to reascend the imperial throne by the help of the Parthians and by the general aid of the powers of this world.   Least probable of all is the supposition that the rise of some pseudo-Nero, due to the influence of this superstition, furnished the motive for the writing of 2 Thess. (n. 10).   The fact that elsewhere in his letters Paul does not refer to the man of lawlessness, is no reason for suspecting 2 Thess., unless a passage can be pointed out elsewhere where he had the same occasion to refer to him which according to 2 Thess. ii. 2 he has here.   No inconsistencies between the eschatological views set forth here and those developed elsewhere in Paul's writings, and no peculiarities of style, can be pointed out which make improbable the identity of the authorship of this Epistle and of the other Epistles of Paul (n. 11).

1. (P. 243.) While the majority of critics up to the time of Schmiedel, *HK*, ii. 1, 12, are content merely to cite imperfect analogies, Weizsäcker, 251, admits that it " really is not easy to get over " 2 Thess. iii. 17, but makes not the slightest attempt to remove the difficulties suggested above.   As even Baur admits, ii. 105, these words are of just the character to betray a forgery, not only because so manifestly designed, but also because the motive for the subscription in Paul's own hand is different from that in 1 Cor. xvi. 21 ; Gal. vi. 11 (not really a comparable case, see above, p. 170 ; *per contra*, Col. iv. 18).   It is wrong to say that Paul did this always " in order to give his readers direct proof of his affection for them " (Baur, ii. 105) ; in 1 Cor. xvi. 21 it is used to introduce an anathema.   Even more arbitrary is the claim that 2 Thess. iii. 17 is meant to explain this custom of Paul's.   Confessedly in all the realms of nature and of art, where distinctions are possible, a phenomenon which recurs regularly under given conditions is a characteristic, even when no reason is given for the distinction and no explanation of its origin offered.   Even if, as Weizsäcker suggests, II. ii. 2 be a " hypothetical explanation of the meaning of this genuine Epistle " (*i.e.* of 2 Thess.), that does not make it any more credible that an interpolator should be so utterly shortsighted as to lay himself open to criticism by referring so blindly to alleged utterances of Paul's without any indication of their historical setting. Hilgenfeld's theory, *Einl.* 646, that II. ii. 2 was written in order to cast suspicion upon 1 Thess., which is genuine, while not so meaningless as Weizsäcker's statement, is not more credible.   For (1) there is no reference here to a spurious Pauline Epistle (above, p. 235) ; (2) this theory does not harmonise with the fact that in II. ii. 15, iii. 14 (above, p. 232), 1 Thess. is referred to as a genuine Epistle ; (3) to cast suspicion upon a recognised work of Paul's was the worst possible way in which to introduce a forgery which had to establish its own claims.

2. (P. 243.) For traces of Gal. in Clemens Rom. (?), Ignatius (?), Polycarp, Justin, cf. *GK*, i. 573 f., 828, n. 2. For traces of 2 Thess. and fainter traces of 1 Thess. in the same authors, cf. *GK*, i. 575, 815, 826, n. 1.

3. (P. 244.) The attacks made heretofore on Gal. are of so little significance that it is sufficient in a handbook like this merely to mention them, above, p. 163, notes 5 and 6.

4. (P. 244.) Baur, ii. 94, in proof of his contention that in the originality and importance of its contents 1 Thess. is inferior to all the other Pauline letters, makes the statement that with the exception of iv. 13–18 "it does not contain a single dogmatic idea of special importance." But what dogmatic idea of special importance is to be found in 1 Cor. i.–xiv. or 2 Cor. i., ii., vi.–xiii. ? Only when the apologetic purpose of the first main section of the letter is denied (above, p. 215 f.), and the strong emotion which it reveals ignored, is it found to contain simply superfluous reminders of things already known. It is also wrong to affirm that the historical material is taken from Acts (Baur, ii. 95, 97). On the contrary, the facts that come to light in 1 Thess. ii. 17–iii. 5 are new, and not always easy to reconcile with Acts (above, pp. 204 f., 214 f.). Where their agreement is apparent (ii. 2 = Acts xvi. 22–40), there is no trace of the dependence of the one upon the other. Resemblances between 1 Thess. and 1 and 2 Cor. Baur felt to be particularly open to suspicion (95 f., 342 ff.). So long as barren and ineffective words continue to exist in the world, the contrast between λόγος and δύναμις is natural (1 Thess. i. 5, cf. 1 Cor. ii. 4, iv. 20) ; its occurrence in 1 Thess. is certainly very inadequate proof for the statement that 1 Thess. "emphasises the more general ideas that are to be found specifically applied in 1 Cor." (343). This is not the case, for 1 Thess. i. 5 has reference only to the preaching in Thessalonica, while in 1 Cor. iv. 20 (cf. i. 18 ; Rom. i. 16) a general proposition is in mind, and even in 1 Cor. ii. 4 f. the method of preaching in Corinth is brought under a general principle. The expressions ἐν βάρει εἶναι (1 Thess. ii. 7), ἐπιβαρῆσαι (ii. 9, cf. II. iii. 8), suggest 2 Cor. xi. 9, xii. 16 ; but the resemblance is not verbal, consequently the words are not copied from 2 Cor. Baur contends (345) that what we have here is only a generalisation of what is said in 1 and 2 Cor. with reference to special conditions in the Corinthian Church. But here again it is to be observed that in 1 Cor. ix. 6–18 Paul speaks of his refusal to avail himself of that right of the evangelist, of which he and Barnabas had regularly availed themselves ever since the beginning of the first missionary journey ; whereas in 1 Thess. ii. 7, 9 ; 2 Thess. iii. 7–9, reference is had only to his conduct in Thessalonica. Of like value with these observations are those of Holsten (*JbfPTh*. 1877, S. 731), that in 1 Thess. i. 3 the Pauline trilogy "faith, hope, and love" (1 Cor. xiii. 13) is confused with the trilogy of the Jewish Apocalypse, ἔργα, κόπος, ὑπομονή (ii. 2), and that the pseudo-Paul, who wrote this letter, like the one who wrote Phil., did not venture to speak of Paul in the greeting as an apostle. As if a forger, who depended for the acceptance of his work upon readers who held the apostle and the genuine Epistles in high regard, would not be tempted to imitate, even to outdo, the genuine letters (Gal. i. 1 ; 1 and 2 Cor. i. 1 ; Rom. i. 1) in emphasising as strongly as possible Paul's apostleship. Then this theory overlooks the emphatic Χριστοῦ ἀπόστολοι in 1 Thess. ii. 7. Baur thought the chief objection to the letter

lay in its recognition of the Christian Church in Judea (ii. 14), notwithstanding the fact that their Christian standing is fully admitted in Gal. i. 22–24 (cf. 2 Cor. viii. 13 f.; Rom. xv. 27; indirectly also 1 Cor. xiv. 36). Had Paul in this passage, as Baur thinks he ought to have done (97), said something about his participation in the persecution of the Jewish Christians on the part of the Jews, it would be a stronger reason than anything Baur has suggested for suspecting an imitation of 1 Cor. xv. 9; Gal. i. 13; since such a reference would have been out of place in this connection, where the point of comparison between the persecution of the Thessalonians and of the Jewish Christians was the fact that by their Christian confession both had incurred the bitter hatred of their own countrymen.   It is possible to speak of the vague polemic against the Jews (Baur, 97, 347) only when the fact is overlooked that the persecution of the Thessalonians began with the attack of the Jews upon the missionaries (above, p. 203 f.), and that shortly after the arrival of Timothy and Silas in Corinth, *i.e.* about the time 1 Thess. was written, Paul was compelled by the opposition of the Jews to separate himself from the synagogue (Acts xviii. 5 f.).   Of course, the letter is spurious if ii. 16 refers to the destruction of Jerusalem as already past.   But this is so evident a blunder that even Baur (97, 369) does not venture to make the forger directly responsible for it.   The avenging wrath of God has reached the rebellious nation, but the cloud has not yet broken.   Having rejected both the testimony of Jesus and of the apostles, Israel is fallen and rejected (Rom. xi. 11–15), and the judgment of hardening has already been visited upon them, which must and will soon show itself in judgment of a more external character (Rom. xi. 7–10, cf. ix. 32 f.).   There is no reference to present internal conditions in Palestine, nor any indication of the banishment of the Jews from Rome by the emperor Claudius (as held by Paul Schmidt, *Der Erste Thessaloniker-Brief*, 87; cf. below, XI. [Chron. Survey]). Only in a very young Church could the deaths which thinned their ranks be felt to be irreconcilable with the word of life received by faith; presumably this would be felt most strongly in the case of the first deaths, cf. also 1 Cor. xi. 30.   Positive proof of the genuineness of the Epistle is to be found in iv. 15–17; for no one ascribing a letter to Paul after his death could have made him say—more definitely here than in any passage in the unquestioned letters of Paul —that he himself expected to experience the parousia.   Moreover, the particular kind of grief for the dead which appears in iv. 13 ff. is inconceivable in a Church which for decades had been losing its members by death one after the other.   Consequently Baur (99, cf. 94) is wrong when, in the eschatological teaching of the Epistle, iv. 13 ff., which has not even first place among the discussions in the passage appended to the main section of the Epistle, beginning with λοιπόν, iv. 1 (above, p. 220 f.), he discovers the purpose which, after Paul's death, led to the composition of the entire letter.

5. (P. 245.)   Even the apocryphal *Epistle to the Laodiceans*, ver. 3, reproduces the usual Pauline formula, *GK*, ii. 584; while the *Third Epistle to the Corinthians*, ver. 2, ed. Vetter, p. 54, is dependent upon Gal. i. 6.   On the other hand, the καθὼς ἄξιόν ἐστιν of 2 Thess. i. 3 has a parallel in Phil. i. 7.

6. (P. 246.)   Ability to reproduce from memory what has been written or spoken earlier, naturally varies greatly with different individuals.   The question recurs in connection with 1 Cor. v. 9–11; 2 Cor. i. 13, and all the references

of 2 Cor. to 1 Cor. But to the author it seems unlikely that the letters of Paul were sent to the Churches in the form in which they were written down by the amanuensis from dictation. Generally it would be necessary to revise the letter after it was dictated, and to prepare a new copy. This was sent to its destination, while the original copy might remain for some time in the hands of Paul or of his amanuensis. Cicero usually treated his letters in this manner; cf. H. Peter, "Der Brief in der röm. Literatur," 1901 (*Abh. der Sächs. Ges. d. Wiss. phil. hist. Kl.* xx. 30), S. 29 f., 35. Now, busy as Paul was, and knowing as he did his emotional temperament, nothing was more natural in the circumstances than for him to read over again the original copy of 1 Thess., if he still had it, before dictating 2 Thess.

7. (P. 246.) Since Kern, *TZfTh.* 1839, ii. 145–214, and Baur, ii. 351–364 (Baur asserts more positively than Kern the dependence of 2 Thess. on Rev., which has since been generally accepted; cf. Weizsäcker, 503, and Hilgenfeld, 647, who holds an entirely different view regarding the date and purpose of 2 Thess. Schmiedel, however, *HK*, ii. 1. 43, holds that literary dependence cannot be proved),—since Kern and Baur, many have been inclined to regard 2 Thess. ii. 3–12 as a reproduction of the popular superstition concerning *Nero redivivus.* Nero is held to be the "mystery of lawlessness," active in the present, secretly preparing for his own return (Baur, 354, and Kern, 205, "the continued longing for this prince after his downfall," cf. Tac. *Hist.* i. 78). The κατέχων, on the other hand, is Vespasian (Kern, 200, "with his son Titus"), or Otho, or even Galba (Schmiedel, 43); in any case "the emperor reigning at the time when the letter was written" (Baur, 355). This is the πρῶτον ψεῦδος held in common by these critics and numerous defenders of the Epistle's genuineness (*e.g.* Döllinger, *Christent. u. Kirche zur Zeit der Grundlegung,* 2te Aufl. 288). Since, in ii. 4, the existence of the Temple at Jerusalem seems to be presupposed (Kern, 157, 207; P. Schmidt, 119; Baur undecided on this point, 358), on this view 2 Thess. must have been written between June 68 and August 70. According to Baur (356), the occasion for the forgery was the appearance of the first pseudo-Nero in 69 A.D. (see below, nn. 9, 10). In order to explain the address of the forgery, Baur (357) assumes gratuitously that not only the provinces of Achaia and Asia (Tac. *Hist.* ii. 8), but also Macedonia, were set in commotion by this adventurer. Furthermore, the champions of this so-called historical interpretation, which, according to Schmiedel (39), is the only scientific one, pass over very lightly the fact that the pre-existence of the expected antichrist is not by any means so clearly affirmed as in Rev. xvii. 8, 11. It is impossible to find in 2 Thess. a single characteristic feature of the brief history of the pseudo-Nero in question, nor of the real Nero (comparison of Suet. *Nero,* lvi, with 2 Thess. ii. 4, only serves to reveal the extremity to which this theory is reduced), nor of the representative of the *Nero redivivus* (n. 9) in the Sibylline books. It has not been shown how, after the pseudo-Neronic movements were passed and before 120,—to judge from the literature of the time,—when Gentiles and Jews alike looked only for a restoration of the Neronic rule through political means, a Christian could have formed the conceptions which are to be found in 2 Thess. This difficulty is somewhat lessened by Hilgenfeld's suggestion that "in the end 2 Thess. proves to be a short Pauline apocalypse written in the last years of Trajan's reign" (*Einl.*

642, old paragraphs). But this hypothesis is not advanced save as a conjecture (650). It is difficult to understand how Christians who, with the emperor's approbation, were condemned to execution, and, according to Hilgenfeld, led, by this constant persecution, to entertain false hopes concerning the parousia, could come to regard Trajan not as the *Nero redivivus*, but as the κατέχων (651) ; particularly so if, as is suggested by Hilgenfeld, the *Nero redivivus* of this apocalypse is not the historical matricide or the persecutor of the Christians, but the leader of the falling away of which there were already signs in the Church in the current Gnosticism. With this interpretation of the mystery of lawlessness is severed the one slender thread by which 2 Thess. ii. 3–12 can possibly be connected with the legends concerning Nero. Bahnsen (*JbfPTh.* 1880, S. 681–705) still feels it necessary to retain the connection, although he too understands by the mystery of lawlessness the rising Gnosticism as he finds it described in the Pastoral Epistles. He, however, interprets the κατέχον as the spiritual office, and makes the κατέχων refer either to one distinguished ἐπίσκοπος, or the ἐπίσκοπος of the Ignatian Epistles, who occupied a position of authority over the other ἐπίσκοποι = πρεσβύτεροι. To such vagaries the theory of Kern is preferable. P. Schmidt (127) endeavours to relieve the theory of a number of fatal objections by assuming—but without giving his reasons—that ii. 2b–12 and several expressions in chap. i. were introduced into the Epistle, which is otherwise genuine, sometime between 68 and 70. Klöpper justly remarks (56) that nothing has caused more confusion in connection with the question regarding the origin of 2 Thess. than its association with the person of Nero.

8. (P. 246.) With praiseworthy impartiality, Hofmann (i. 331–334, cf. *Schriftbeweis*, ii. 2. 674) admits that, strange as it may seem to us, Paul does conceive of the entrance of the lawless one into the world after the analogy of the return of Christ from the other world, as a return from the dead. And certainly the threefold occurrence of ἀποκαλύπτεσθαι (iii. 6, 8, cf. i. 7), followed immediately by παρουσία (viii. 9), used of the coming of Jesus and of the lawless one, does give the coming of the antichrist the appearance of a caricature of the parousia of Christ, preceding this latter event. But it is to be observed that the meaning of μυστήριον (7) is the same here as in other passages (1 Cor. ii. 7, 10, xiv. 2, 6 ; Rom. xvi. 25 ; Eph. iii. 3–12 ; Col. i. 26 f. ; 1 Tim. iii. 16), there being an implied contrast to the ἀποκαλύπτεσθαι which precedes and follows, and that the "mystery of lawlessness" means—admitted even by Hofmann (i. 329, 331)—not the person of the lawless one, but the increased spirit of lawlessness which is an active force even in the present. Consequently it would seem as if it were this impersonal power which is now concealed, but is to be revealed in the person of the lawless one. That the passage speaks not of the revealing of this impersonal power, but of the man of lawlessness, is sufficiently explained : (1) by the fact that the latter is presented as a caricature of the returning Christ ; (2) by the fact that the spirit of lawlessness assumed personal form for the first time not in the "antichrist," but in all his forerunners (Antiochus, Caligula). In this way the conception was reached of a pre-existence of the lawless one not purely ideal. He, *i.e.* the personal ἀνομία, has existed again and again, but, before the complete development and revelation of his character, he is to be set aside, that he may operate for a time only as an impersonal power, eventu-

ally finding his complete personal manifestation, and so, his revelation in the man of lawlessness whose appearance immediately precedes the parousia of Christ. A partial analogy is to be found in the sayings about the coming Elias, Matt. xi. 14, xvii. 10–13, not all of which, however, indicate a personal return (cf. Matt. xiv. 2, xvi. 14, but are to be understood in the sense of John i. 21 ; Luke i. 17).

9. (P. 246.) Cf. the writer's essay, *Nero der Antichrist, ZfKW*, 1886, S. 337–352, 393–405. Nero (born December 5, 37 ; died June 9, 68) himself believed, because of certain predictions, that he would lose his throne, but rise to power again in the East, and live until his seventy-third year, *i.e.* until 110 A.D. (Suet. *Nero*, xl). Up to about this time the popular belief seems to have survived that he was still alive, and would regain his power (Dio Chrys. *Or.* 21). This led to the rise of a pseudo-Nero, who established himself on the island of Cythnus in 69 A.D., but was soon easily overpowered and beheaded by Asprenas, who had been appointed governor of Galatia, and stopped at the island on his way thither (Tac. *Hist.* ii. 8. 9 ; Dio Cass. lxiv. 9 ; Zonaras, xi. 15). A second pretender, Terentius Maximus by name, appeared under Titus (79–81 Zonaras, 11. 18), if, indeed, he be not identical with a third, who in 88 came near causing a Parthian war (Suet. *Nero*, lvii ; Tac. *Hist.* i. 2). The spread of this belief, which led to these political uprisings among Hellenistic Jews of the time, is indicated by *Sibyll.* v. 137–178, 361–385 (71 A.D.) and *Sibyll.* iv. 117–139 (80 A.D.). It is not until we come to the Sibyllines written between 120–125 (v. 28–34, 93–110, 214–227) that we find the return of Nero represented as supernatural in character, and himself described as an ἀντίθεος whom the Messiah is to destroy. About 150 this last prophecy was worked over in connection with others of earlier date in *Sibyll.* v. by a Christian. About the same time, either by this Christian, or by one of kindred mind (*Sibyll.* viii. 1–216), these conceptions were fused with important features of the Johannine Apocalypse. Cf. also the picture of the Antichrist, supplied with the features of Nero, *Ascensio Isaiæ*, chap. iv. 2. The *Sibyllines*, which date from the first century, and with which alone 2 Thess. can be compared in point of time, reproduce simply the historical picture of Nero, the matricide, the stage-hero who celebrated his own burning of Rome, and the builder of a canal through the isthmus of Corinth. Though, in punishment of his own misdeeds, compelled to flee beyond the Euphrates, the missing one is to return from Parthia with a great army as a scourge to Rome. The Jewish conception of Nero during the first decades after his death shows no trace of an antichrist and of a mysterious supernatural being.

10. (P. 247.) Assuming that the Christians in Thessalonica were stirred up by the appearance in 69 A.D. of the pseudo-Nero whom they regarded as the antichrist,—though 2 Thess. ii. 2 assigns an entirely different reason,—this excitement must have been thoroughly allayed by his immediate downfall. The opinion that the day of the Lord had already come because the antichrist had appeared, would then have disappeared of itself, for the reason that the pretender perished miserably before he was able to extend his authority over the little island of Cythnus, and to do anything that could establish his character as the antichrist. The only conceivable effect of disillusionment would be doubt as to the nearness of the parousia, or as to the truth of the

prophecies concerning the event. Furthermore, an author, sharing all the essential presuppositions of his deluded readers, who desired to prevent a recurrence of such deceptions and disillusionments, must have indicated the signs by which a false Nero, or antichrist, might be distinguished from the true one. But there is no trace of this antithesis in the letter. On these presuppositions reference to the κατέχων would be without point; for, as each new pseudo-Nero appeared, there was nothing to prevent the expectation that he would replace the reigning emperor and remove all other hindrances to his power.

11. (P. 247.) For example, P. Schmidt (111) and Schmiedel (*HK*, ii. 1. 9) find a contradiction in the fact that in I. v. 1 the time of the parousia is left undetermined, the Lord coming as a thief in the night ; whereas, according to II. ii. 1–12, the approach of the parousia is indicated by numerous signs, many of which are to be observed even in the present. But the same contradiction can be said to exist between Matt. xxiv. 7–33 (Mark xiii. 9–29 ; Luke xxi. 10–31) and Matt. xxiv. 35–44 (Matt. xiii. 32–37 ; Luke xvii. 20–30, xxi. 34–36 ; Acts i. 7), or between Rev. iii. 3, xvi. 15, and other parts of Rev. In reality there is no contradiction, only the same difference that existed between Noah and the men of his time. To those absorbed in the present earthly life the day of the Lord will come as a snare and the Lord as a thief ; the disciples of Jesus are to watch, be sober and ready in order that He may not so come to them. They are to give heed to the signs of the times which portend the end ; not to pay overmuch attention to those that are remote from the event, but not to overlook those that are near. If they are to avoid the latter mistake, they must know what those signs are to be ; if the former, they must have a general idea of what is to happen before they appear. But since it is fundamentally impossible to know when the end will come and when the signs immediately preceding will appear, it is the part of wisdom as well as the natural impulse of love to live in constant readiness for the approaching end. The genuine prophecy of the apostolic age retains these fundamental features of the eschatological teaching of Jesus (cf. Rev. xix. 10). So does Paul. The impossibility of determining when the end would come (I. v. 1–3), and the knowledge that the man of lawlessness had not yet appeared, and could not appear until the existing government, the Roman empire, had given place to a different order of things (II. ii. 3–7), did not prevent him from believing that the parousia was near (I. iv. 17 ; cf., however, II. i. 5 ff.), though he does not assert this belief dogmatically (I. v. 10 ; cf. Rom. xiii. 11–14, xiv. 7–9 ; 1 Cor. xv. 51 f.). On the other hand, his attention to existing signs of the coming end (II. i. 5, ἔνδειγμα, ii. 7a, ἤδη ἐνεργεῖται), and to the events which had happened since he had become a Christian (above, p. 237, n. 7), saved him from an error such as he opposes in II. ii. 2, and from making a prophecy which would be proved false by the next succession to the throne at Rome. 2 Thess. i. 5–10 has been proved un-Pauline ; indeed, it is said to breathe a spirit of revenge quite unchristian (Kern, 211, cautiously ; more strongly stated, *e.g.*, by Schmiedel). But of the general principle of the retributive righteousness of God (Rom. ii. 2–10), Paul very often makes severe application (Rom. iii. 8, xi. 9 f., xvi. 20 ; 1 Cor. iii. 17, xvi. 22 ; 2 Cor. xi. 15 ; Gal. i. 8, v. 10, 12 ; Phil. iii. 18 f. ; 2 Tim. iv. 14 ; 1 Thess. ii. 16), and in addressing those who were afflicted, with whom he does not identify

himself, he could without objection say things which would be more objectionable if said by themselves.　　Without parallel in Paul's other writings is the
use of κλῆσις, in i. 11, in the sense not of a call to martyrdom (Hilgenfeld,
647), nor of the future glory (Klöpper, 23), but of a forthcoming invitation
to enter into the possession and enjoyment of the promised glory.　This
meaning is particularly clear, if we follow Hofmann's suggestion and connect
ἐν τῇ ἡμέρᾳ ἐκείνῃ with ἀξιώσῃ.　But Paul uses κλῆσις only once (Rom. xi.
29) of the call of the Israelitish nation which was involved in the call of
Abraham.　　In the first passage the meaning approaches that of οἱ κεκλημένοι
in Matt. xxii. 3, 4, 8 ; Luke xiv. 17, 24 ; in the latter, that of καλέσαι, Matt.
xxii. 3, the object of the verb being those long since called (cf. Matt. xxv. 34 ;
Rev. xix. 9).　The usage in Rom. xi. 29 departs much farther from Paul's
customary usage than 2 Thess. i. 11 ; since the call of the gospel has much
more direct reference to the future glory of Christians (1 Thess. ii. 12, v. 23f.;
2 Thess. ii. 14 ; Eph. i. 18, iv. 4 ; Phil. iii. 14) than to the call of Abraham
and of Israel.　　It is claimed that the use of κύριος for God instead of
Christ (Hilgenfeld, 646),—a use which occurs only in quotations from the O.T.
(1 Cor. i. 31), and in passages suggested by the O.T. (2 Cor. viii. 21 = Prov. iii.
4),—that this use is un-Pauline.　But in I. iii. 12, ὁ κύριος, which occurs in a
context where the distinction is twice made between God the Father and
"our Lord Jesus" (I. iii. 11, 13), cannot mean Jesus in distinction from the
Father, but only the Lord who, according to the Christian conception,
has been revealed as "God and Father" and "our Lord Jesus."　Hofmann
(i. 214) compares Rom. xiv. 1–12 (3 ὁ θεός, 4–8 ὁ κύριος, 9 Χριστός), and the
usage is to be constantly observed where Paul makes O.T. passages refer to
Christ, when he knows as well as we do that the anarthrous κύριος means
Jahveh and not Jesus, e.g. Rom. x. 9–15.　Why should ὁ κύριος be understood
differently in II. iii. 3, 5 and I. iii. 12, especially in view of the numerous
resemblances between these passages, e.g. αὐτὸς δέ, I. iii. 11, II. ii. 16 ;
κατευθύναι, I. iii. 11, II. iii. 5 ; στηρίξαι, I. iii. 13, II. ii. 17, iii. 3 ?　It is true
that Paul, who in II. i. 7–ii. 14 has constantly before him the Christ who is
to return in glory, when he comes to speak of God and Christ together in
II. ii. 16, places Christ's name first (in contrast to I. iii. 11), and that in II. i.
12 he calls Christ "our Lord and God" (cf. Rom. ix. 5 ; Tit. i. 3).　It is also
true that in this Epistle ὁ κύριος occurs in combinations where analogy might
lead one to expect ὁ θεός (πιστὸς . . . ὁ κύριος, II. iii. 3, cf. per contra, I. v.
24 ; 1 Cor. i. 9, x. 13 ; 2 Cor. i. 18 ; ἠγαπημένοι ὑπὸ κυρίου (al. τοῦ κυρίου
and θεοῦ), II. ii. 13, cf. per contra, I. i. 4 ; ὁ κύριος τῆς εἰρήνης, II. iii. 16, cf.
per contra, I. v. 23 ; Rom. xv. 33, xvi. 20 ; 2 Cor. xiii. 11 ; Phil. iv. 9 ; also
Heb. xiii. 20 ; 1 Cor. xiv. 33).　This usage can be considered un-Pauline only
if, in striking contrast to other Christians of his time, Paul did not recognise
Christ as the Faithful One (2 Tim. ii. 13), the Redeemer through His love
(Gal. ii. 20 ; Rom. viii. 37 ; Eph. v. 2, 25), the Bringer of Peace (Eph. ii.
14–18 ; Col. iii. 15, with Phil. iv. 7 ; "peace from God and Christ" in the
greetings).　It is evident, on the other hand, that a forger would not have replaced an expression like "The God of Peace," which occurs so frequently
in Paul's writings, by the unusual "The Lord of Peace."　The same is true of
the use of ἐγκαυχᾶσθαι between two ἐν's, in II. i. 4, instead of the single verb
which occurs more than thirty times in Paul's writings, and which a copyist

of an early date thought ought to be inserted here.   It is asserted also that having used ἐξελέξατο in two passages of his letters (1 Cor. i. 27 f. ; Eph. i. 4), Paul could not have written εἵλατο in a third, II. ii. 13, although naturally he is familiar with the word (Phil. i. 22), and although the word is excellently chosen in this passage, where there is a contrast implied to the destruction of unbelievers over whom the Christians have the advantage.   ἡ ἐπιφάνεια, which is not at all superfluous, along with τῆς παρουσίας, but, like the expression, "the breath of his mouth," indicates the outward manifestation of the coming of Christ (II. ii. 8, cf. i. 7-10), cannot be considered un-Pauline simply because it is used in a similar connection in Tit. ii. 13 and elsewhere with reference to the return of Christ, 1 Tim. vi. 14 ; 2 Tim. iv. 1, 8.   It is quite without point to reject as un-Pauline the phrase ἀπὸ τῆς δόξης τῆς ἰσχύος αὐτοῦ, II. i. 9, from Isa. ii. 10, because used instead of δυνάμεως αὐτοῦ, which it is alleged is the only expression Paul uses (cf. *per contra*, Eph. i. 19, vi. 10), and the word ἐπισυναγωγή, II. ii. 1 (cf. I. iv. 14, 17 ; Mark xiii. 27), for which no genuine Pauline equivalent can be named.   The difficult construction of sentences in the first main division of the letter, amounting in several passages (i. 10-12, ii. 3-9) to anacolutha, and the succession of short sentences at the end (iii. 2b, with the contrast in iii. 3 ; the sentence, iii. 10 ; antithesis, ii. 11b ; all from iii. 13 on), are signs of genuineness.

IV.

THE CORRESPONDENCE OF PAUL WITH THE CORINTHIAN CHURCH.

§ 17. THE EARLY HISTORY OF THE CHURCH.

THE city of Corinth, which was destroyed and depopulated by Mummius in the year 146 B.C., and rebuilt by Cæsar and made a Roman colony ("Laus Julia Corinthus"), was the capital of the province of Achaia, which since the year 27 B.C. had been separate from Macedonia, and which in size corresponded practically to the modern kingdom of Greece. Here resided regularly the proprætor, who had the rank of proconsul. After its restoration Corinth developed rapidly into a flourishing city, and at this time was the principal city in the province in point of population, industry, and commerce. The celebration there of the Isthmian games made it a centre of Greek life in spite of the mixed character of its population, though after its restoration, as before, Corinth was a "city of Aphrodite" (n. 1).

Paul came to Corinth from Athens in November 52 (Acts xviii. 1). As the result of eighteen months of labour there, the Corinthian Church was organised. Of this Church Paul declares himself to have been the sole founder with an exclusiveness and an emphasis which would have been out of place in the case of the Thessalonians, and there is nothing in Acts nor in Paul's own writings which calls for any dispute of his right to this position (n. 2). If, as seems to be the case, there were already in existence

at this time a number of small Churches in the vicinity of
Corinth, there is no necessity for assuming that Paul
himself had taken an active part in their organisation.
More probably the same plan was adopted that was
followed later in Ephesus.   While the apostle remained
in the capital and bent all his energies to kindle a central
flame of Christian life, sparks from this fire were scattered
in every direction through the province.   In Corinth, as
in Ephesus, Paul's helpers did valiant service in spreading
the gospel in localities which the apostle did not visit in
person.

The circumstances under which Paul came to Corinth
were peculiar.   For whatever cause, whether on account of
the experience which he had had in Athens, or on account
of continued anxiety about the Thessalonian Church, he
was in an unusually discouraged state of mind when he
began his Corinthian work.   As he himself intimates, it
was for this reason that in Corinth he confined himself so
strictly to the simple preaching of the cross, refusing more
than at other times and in other places to make the foolishness of the gospel attractive to his hearers by the use of
rhetorical art and of learning (1 Cor. ii. 1–5 ; cf. Acts
xviii. 9).   The manner in which he lived in Corinth was
also such as to foster this feeling.   While in Athens, he
made no attempt to earn his living by working with his
own hands, a course of action which was natural in those
surroundings, and quite possible on account of contributions sent by the Macedonian Churches (Phil. iv. 15 ;
2 Cor. xi. 8 f.).   As a result, he not only preached on the
Sabbath in the synagogue of the Jews and proselytes, but
also sought opportunities on week days to converse in the
public places with those who resorted thither.   In Corinth,
on the other hand, after he obtained quarters in the house
of Aquila and Priscilla, the Jewish couple who from this
time on were associated with him closely and constantly,
he worked for wages during the week in their tent shop,

so that his religious activity was confined to the Sabbath and the synagogue (n. 3). The relief which came with the good news brought by Timothy from Thessalonica (1 Thess. iii. 6), and the encouragement which naturally resulted from reunion with his two trusted helpers, stimulated him to preach with greater energy, in consequence of which the opposition of the Jews became more pronounced, and Christian preaching was forbidden in the synagogue (Acts xviii. 5–7). It was a triumph for Paul when Crispus, the ruler of the synagogue, and his entire family were baptized by him, an example which was followed at once by a considerable number of the Corinthians. In this manner originated the Church, which continued to assemble in the house of an uncircumcised proselyte adjoining the synagogue. During the succeeding months its membership was materially increased by the addition of Gentiles from all classes (n. 4).

Having now succeeded in establishing a Church separate from the synagogue, Paul might have considered his work in Corinth at an end. And he seems actually to have had it in mind to leave Corinth at this time, lest the continuation of the preaching should lead to further outbreaks of fanaticism on the part of the Jews. But, encouraged by a dream vision, he remained at this post longer than at any of the mission stations where he had worked heretofore. This period was not altogether without opposition (2 Thess. iii. 2); but an attempt on the part of the Jews to charge the apostle, before the proconsul Gallio, with teaching a religion contrary to the laws of the State, was frustrated by this statesman's ability to see at once that it was a question of differences about Jewish doctrine, and by his determination to have nothing to do with such matters (n. 5). The Jews gave vent at once to the indignation which they felt at this miscarriage of their plans upon Sosthenes, the ruler of the synagogue, before the tribunal from which the accusers were driven by

Gallio, *i.e.* as the accusing party were leaving the judg-ment-hall, doubtless because, as their spokesman, he had not shown positiveness nor tact enough in presenting their case. If this is the same Sosthenes who is men-tioned in 1 Cor. i. 1, this painful experience probably helped him to decide fully in favour of a cause which previously he had not had the requisite hostility and decision to prosecute (n. 6). As will be presently shown, the development of the relation between the synagogue and the Church was not yet at an end when Paul left Corinth, at Pentecost 54, and went to Ephesus.

With this departure begins a period of three years devoted mainly to the spread of Christianity in Ephesus and the province of Asia (Acts xx. 31). It was toward the end of this period that the first of the Corinthian letters preserved to us was written. Plans had been under consideration for some time for making a journey in the near future to Corinth. This purpose was now on the point of being carried out, since the route, by way of Macedonia, and the time of departure, Pentecost, had been already determined upon (1 Cor. iv. 18–21, xi. 34, xvi. 2–9). Timothy and, according to Acts xix. 22, a certain Erastus, who apparently was the treasurer of the city of Corinth (Rom. xvi. 23, cf. 2 Tim. iv. 20), had been sent on by the same indirect route which Paul intended to take (1 Cor. iv. 17, xvi. 10). It is assumed that on account of the indirectness of the route through Macedonia and the commissions to the Churches there which they had to fulfil, Timothy will arrive in Corinth somewhat later than the letter, which has been sent directly by the sea route. He therefore gives the Church certain instructions as to how Timothy is to be received when he arrives (1 Cor. xvi. 10). At the same time he makes request that Timothy be sent back at once from Corinth to Ephesus, where he plans to await his arrival. When the cause which was keeping Paul in Ephesus until Pentecost (xvi.

9) is also taken into account, we must assume that the letter was written from four to eight weeks before this date. This makes it very probable that the figurative language used in 1 Cor. v. 7 f. was suggested by the Jewish passover, which was being celebrated about the time when the letter was written (n. 7).

Of the things affecting the relation of the Church to Paul which happened between his departure from Corinth at Pentecost 54 and the composition of 1 Cor. at Easter 57, there are some which without difficulty may be determined. The immediate presupposition of 1 Cor. is a letter from the Church to Paul (1 Cor. vii. 1). From the apostle's expression of joy in xvi. 17 at the arrival of Stephanus, Fortunatus, and Achaicus (n. 8), who in large measure made up to him for the deficiencies of the Church toward him, and from the request that the Church recognise these men and follow their advice (xvi. 15–18), we ascertain what did not need to be told the readers, that these three Corinthians had come recently to Ephesus and were now returning to Corinth. It is therefore very probable that they had brought the communication of the Church to Ephesus, and were about to take Paul's answer back with them to Corinth. Assuming that vii. 1 refers expressly to written opinions and questions of the Church, it may be inferred from the formulæ by which the several topics are introduced in vii. 25 ($\pi\epsilon\rho\grave{\iota}$ $\delta\grave{\epsilon}$ $\tau\hat{\omega}\nu$ $\pi\alpha\rho\theta\acute{\epsilon}\nu\omega\nu$), viii. 1 ($\pi\epsilon\rho\grave{\iota}$ $\delta\grave{\epsilon}$ $\tau\hat{\omega}\nu$ $\epsilon\grave{\iota}\delta\omega\lambda o\theta\acute{\upsilon}\tau\omega\nu$), xii. 1 ($\pi\epsilon\rho\grave{\iota}$ $\delta\grave{\epsilon}$ $\tau\hat{\omega}\nu$ $\pi\nu\epsilon\upsilon\mu\alpha\tau\iota\kappa\hat{\omega}\nu$), xvi. 1 ($\pi\epsilon\rho\grave{\iota}$ $\delta\grave{\epsilon}$ $\tau\hat{\eta}s$ $\lambda o\gamma\acute{\iota}\alpha s$), xvi. 12 ($\pi\epsilon\rho\grave{\iota}$ $\delta\grave{\epsilon}$ $'A\pi o\lambda\lambda\hat{\omega}$), which are similar to the formula of vii. 1, only abbreviated, that all the discussions introduced in this way, namely, chaps. vii., viii.–x., xii.–xiv., xvi. 1–12, are in reply to this communication of the Church. This conclusion is confirmed by the observation that in these connections Paul repeatedly states principles and then proceeds at once to limit their application (vii. 1 f., viii. 1, x. 23 ; cf. § 18, n. 1). This is true even in the

case of the commendation in xi. 2, to which the following
context is only a contrast.   Paul quotes these statements
from the letter of the Church, and appears for the time
being to give his assent to them, but only in order at once
to qualify them, xi. 16 f.   The expression used in xi. 34 is
natural only if the Church had asked some questions or
expressed some opinions about the celebration of the
Lord's Supper.   Thus also chap. xi. is in answer to questions asked by the Church in their letter, which does not
exclude the possibility of Paul's having taken account
here (xi. 18), as in other passages after vii. 1, of separate
oral reports.   But there are traces of the letter of the
Church even before vii. 1.   The principle stated in x. 23,
of which Paul admits only the general truth, pointing out
its limitation as applied to the practical question in hand,
is to be found also at the beginning of vi. 12–20.   So in
v. 9–13 he corrects a misinterpretation of instructions
which he had given the Church in an earlier letter, without
mentioning the source of his information or without any
suggestion of doubt as to the fact of the misinterpretation.   Consequently this misinterpretation of his earlier
advice must have been found in the letter of the Church.
We have therefore to assume that, with the exception
of certain chapters and passages, the whole of 1 Cor.
is a reply to a letter of the Church which itself in turn
had been written with reference to an earlier letter of Paul
to the Corinthians, in fact was a direct answer to such
a letter.   The chapters excepted are i.–iv., the occasion
and material for which were supplied by particular information, probably oral, coming to him from the members
of the household of a certain Chloe (i. 11); the passages
are v. 1–8, possibly also vi. 1–11, and probably chap. xv.,
in which Paul seems to speak of his own initiative about
things that had happened in the Church, with regard to
which he had been definitely informed, though not by the
Church itself.

While this lost correspondence (n. 9) is to be dated only a few weeks or at most months before the writing of 1 Cor., the coming of Apollos to Ephesus is to be placed a few weeks or a few months after Paul's first departure from Corinth. According to Acts xviii. 24 ff., Apollos (n. 10) was an Alexandrian Jew distinguished for his Greek culture and rhetorical training (λόγιος), as well as for his Jewish learning. Though when he came to Ephesus he had not been baptized and so received into the membership of the Christian Church, he not only possessed a fairly accurate knowledge of the facts about Jesus, but also entered into the synagogue in Ephesus and taught with enthusiasm a form of Christianity which was not current in the Church. This brought him into contact with Aquila and Priscilla, who had come to Ephesus with Paul, and who remained there during the several months while Paul was absent on his journey to Palestine and Antioch, attending the synagogue services as Paul did when he first came to Ephesus (xviii. 19), and for the first months after his return (xix. 8). After Apollos had been instructed by this couple in the form of Christianity taught in the Church, he was all the more anxious to continue his preaching journey. So, when he came to Corinth bearing letters of recommendation from Aquila to the Christians there, it was not primarily in the rôle of a teacher in the Christian Church, but as a missionary preacher among the Jews in Corinth. And it was chiefly through his success among this class that he contributed materially to the growth of the Church (n. 11). This does not, of course, preclude the possibility of Apollos' having been a very acceptable teacher in the Christian gatherings; indeed, it is most natural to assume that it made him more so. How long he remained in Corinth we do not know. When 1 Cor. was written, he had been for some time with Paul in Ephesus. But he had not been forgotten in Corinth. From 1 Cor. xvi. 12

we learn that in their letter the Church had expressed to Paul the desire that Apollos might return to Corinth. Although he was strongly urged by Paul to comply with this request and to go back with the messengers from the Corinthian Church, for the time being Apollos steadfastly refused to do so.

Some time after Apollos' appearance in Corinth, but apparently a considerable time before the correspondence with the Church which took place just before 1 Cor. was written, the apostle himself had made a visit to Corinth. No mention of this visit is made in Acts, which gives very few details of the period of three years when Paul was engaged chiefly in organising the Ephesian Church, and which here as elsewhere omits all reference to the intercourse which took place between Paul and the Churches that had been already organised. Nor is anything said about it in 1 Cor. (n. 12). On the other hand, there are several passages in 2 Cor. where it seems to be presupposed that Paul had been in Corinth twice before the visit that he was now on the eve of making (n. 13). If, now, as will be shown, it is impossible to assume that the second visit took place in the interval between 1 and 2 Cor., we must suppose that prior to the correspondence of which we get information, partly from the remains of it which we have and partly from the testimony of 1 Cor., Paul had interrupted his work in Ephesus by a visit to Corinth, which presumably was short (n. 14). The impressions which he had received on his visit were thoroughly depressing. He had been humiliated to find that not a few of the members of the Church which he had spent so much effort in organising were living as unchastely as their heathen neighbours (2 Cor. xii. 21, ii. 1). He had exhorted them very earnestly, but had refrained from employing disciplinary measures of a severer kind (2 Cor. xiii. 2). He had given them instructions with reference to this matter in the letter of his mentioned in 1 Cor. v. 9. The communication from the Church, in which, among other things they had replied to this letter of the apostle's, together with the numerous oral reports that had recently come to him concerning the condition of the Church and events that had taken place (n. 15), had pressed the recollection of this short visit into the background, and had created a condition of affairs which called for the writing of 1 Corinthians.

1. (P. 256.) MARQUARDT, *Röm. Staatsverw.*[2] i. 321–333 ; MOMMSEN, *Röm. Gesch.*[2] v. 234 ff.; BRANDIS in *Pauly-Wissowa RE*, i. 190 ff. From the days of Augustus, Achaia was a senatorial province ; and again, after a temporary union with Macedonia under Tiberius and Caius, it held this position at the time of Claudius. It is with the period of Claudius that we are concerned. Regarding Corinth see CURTIS, *Peloponnesos*, ii. 514–556, 589–598. On account of its former glory it was termed " lumen totius Græciæ " (Cic. *pro lege Manl.* 5, cf. *de Nat. Deor.* iii. 38). This " bimaris Corinthus " (Hor. *Od.* i. 7. 2), on account of its location on the isthmus between the ports of Κεγχρεαί and Σχοινοῦς on the Saronic Bay and Λέχαιον on the the Bay of Corinth, soon reassumed its importance as a commercial centre for the trade between Asia Minor and Italy (Strabo, p. 378 [here also the proverbial οὐ παντὸς ἀνδρὸς ἐς Κόρινθύν ἐσθ' ὁ πλοῦς], 380 ; Aristides, *Or.* iii., Dindorf, i. 37). In view of the dangers attending the voyage around Cape Μαλέαι and the difficulties involved in transporting wares and ships *via* the " Diolkos," which crossed the isthmus from Schœnus (Strabo, 335, 380 ; Plin. *H. Nat.* iv. 4. 10), there were repeated attempts to cut a channel through the isthmus, the last of these being made by the emperor Caligula (Suet. *Calig.* xxi ; Plin. i. 1). The channel was not completed until 1893. The management of the Isthmian games (cf. 1 Cor. ix. 24–27), which had been transferred to Sicyon during the time when Corinth was in ruins, was afterwards intrusted again to the latter city (Pausan. ii. 2. 1). Among the sanctuaries in and near the city were those of Isis, Serapis, and Melikertes (Pausan. ii. 1. 3, ii. 3, iv. 7). Like Argos and Athens, Corinth was a residence place of Jews (Philo, *Leg. ad Cai.* xxxvi, cf. Justin. *Dial.* i). It was an ambition of students also to see Corinth (Epict. *Diss.* ii. 16. 32), although as an educational centre it was not to be compared with Athens. Here near together lay the graves of the philosopher Diogenes and of the famous courtesan Lais (Pausan. ii. 2. 4).

2. (P. 256.) Paul was the sole founder of the Corinthian Church, 1 Cor. iii. 6–10, iv. 15, cf. ix. 2, xi. 23, xv. 1 ff. This is not contradicted by 2 Cor. i. 19 ; for 2 Cor. is not directed exclusively to the Church in Corinth, as in 1 Cor., but to the Christians of all Achaia (2 Cor. i. 1). There is consequently to be considered as included in the address primarily both Corinth and Athens, where Paul had tarried for some time with Timothy, in whose name also 2 Cor. was written, and where he had also spent some time with Silas (1 Thess. iii. 1–5, above, p. 205 f.). The broad term used (πᾶσιν, ὅλῃ) permits us, however, to include a number of places in the province

where there were Christians. According to the reading of Codex D, Acts xviii. 27 would seem to indicate that immediately after the departure of Paul there were several ἐκκλησίαι in and near Corinth. According to 2 Thess. i. 4 (above, p. 241, n. 11), such ἐκκλησίαι existed as early as the middle of Paul's sojourn in the city. But only at a somewhat later date (Rom. xvi. 1) is reference made to a particular ἐκκλησία, namely, that at Cenchrea. From 2 Cor. i. 19 we infer that Timothy and Silas, who, according to 1 Cor., could have had no appreciable share in the founding of the local Corinthian Church, laboured successfully in the vicinity of Corinth. Nor is this assertion contradicted by Acts. Just as Paul had prosecuted his labours at Corinth for some time before his assistants arrived (xviii. 1–4), so when he leaves Corinth nothing is said about them (xviii. 18). Even after their arrival at Corinth, allusion is made only to Paul (xviii. 5–17, cf. *per contra*, *e.g.* xvii. 1–15). It does not follow because Timothy and Silas were with Paul when 1 and 2 Thess. were written, that they remained in Corinth continuously even for several months. While Paul "dwelt" in Corinth alone for eighteen months (Acts xviii. 11), Timothy and Silas were probably engaged in missionary activities in the province, working from Corinth as a centre.

3. (P. 258.) Acts xviii. 1–4. Concerning the edict of Claudius, see § 11. The fact that Priscilla, or Prisca (according to the decisive testimony of Rom. xvi. 3 ; 2 Tim. iv. 19—perhaps also 1 Cor. xvi. 19), is regularly mentioned along with Aquila and more than once before him (Rom. xvi. 3 ; 2 Tim. iv. 19 ; Acts xviii. 18, perhaps also xviii. 26), permits the supposition that she was the more important of the two. Because Aquila (Acts xviii. 2) is designated as a certain Jew of this name, and because Paul's introduction into his household is due merely to the fact : ἦσαν γὰρ σκηνοποιοὶ τῇ τέχνῃ (xviii. 3), we are not to imagine that they were already Christians, or had been previously acquainted with Paul. Paul "found" Aquila in looking for lodgings and opportunity for work. It is easy to understand why in such commercial centres as Thessalonica (1 Thess. ii. 9 ; 2 Thess. iii. 8) and Corinth (2 Cor. xi. 7–12, xii. 13–18 ; 1 Cor. iv. 12, ix. 4–18) Paul should not desire his missionary activity to be looked upon as a money-making pursuit. On the other hand, this humble character of his daily work was in keeping with the spirit in which he came to Corinth. His occupation also was an ἑαυτὸν ταπεινοῦν, 2 Cor. xi. 7.

4. (P. 258.) Paul himself baptized Crispus (Acts xviii. 8), and also a certain Gaius (1 Cor. i. 14). There is no good reason for doubting that the Crispus mentioned in the two passages is the same person, nor for questioning the accuracy of the statements concerning him (Heinrici, *Comm.* i. 1880, p. 10 ; Holsten, *Ev. des Pl.* i. 186). In 1 Cor. Paul had no occasion to mention his Jewish origin, or the fact that he was a ruler of the synagogue, or even to refer to the time of his baptism. The objection that the representation of Acts xviii. 1–17 is constructed after the model of Rom. i. 16, ii. 9 f. is entirely without foundation. In Thessalonica and Berœa, Paul preached, as a rule, only in the synagogue ; in Athens, both in the market-place and on the streets ; in Corinth, first in the synagogue, then in a private house. In Berœa, almost the whole Jewish populace, to which must be added certain proselytes, especially women, seems to have accepted the gospel (Acts xvii. 10–12). On the other hand, in Thessalonica and Corinth the opposition of

the Jews was so pronounced that the first converts were almost all Gentiles. Where, then, is the model that Luke is supposed to have followed in composing his narrative? The argument that in Corinth the gospel found its first believers in a Greek home, which Holsten, i. 187, makes from 1 Cor. xvi. 15, is based primarily upon the incredible error that Greek names such as Stephanas were borne by Greeks only and not by Jews (see above, p. 63, n. 10); and, secondly, on the further mistake of supposing that Stephanas was a Corinthian. Since the household of Stephanas is termed ἀπαρχὴ τῆς Ἀχαίας (1 Cor. xvi. 15), and since Paul before coming to Corinth was not unsuccessful in his preaching at Athens, which belonged to Achaia, Stephanas must have been converted and baptized at Athens. This is not contradicted by the fact that about the time 1 Cor. was written Crispus had come from Corinth to Ephesus (1 Cor. xvi. 17), had won credit for himself by aiding the collections in Corinth and Achaia for the Christians in Jerusalem (1 Cor. xvi. 15, cf. xvi. 1; 2 Cor. ix. 2), and very probably at that time resided in Corinth. The fact that Paul names Stephanas in such incidental way in 1 Cor. i. 14 f.—evidently bethinking himself of one whom he could name in addition to Crispus and Gaius—can be explained only on the ground that Stephanas was not one of the early converts of Corinth, to say nothing of his not being the ἀπαρχὴ Κορίνθου; though at the time the Epistle was written his relationship to the Corinthian Church was such that the failure to mention him in 1 Cor. i. 14 f. would have seemed unbecoming. It is obvious that the agreement reached by the Church at Jerusalem, Gal. ii. 9, did not prevent Paul from beginning his preaching in the synagogues wherever he had an opportunity to do so (cf. *Skizzen*, 70–76, and *NKZ*, 1894, S. 441 f.). That this was what he did in Corinth we should infer from 1 Cor. i. 22–24, vii. 18, ix. 20, even were it not reported in Acts xviii. with so many lifelike details, and consequently in a manner so worthy of credence. Whether the Gaius mentioned along with Crispus, who, according to Rom. xvi. 23, was a man of great hospitality, was a Jew or not we do not know. Titus (*al.* Titius), or Justus, or Titus Justus (Acts xviii. 7), who cannot be identified with the Titus of Gal. ii. 3; 2 Cor. ii. 13, vii. 6-xii. 18 (Wieseler, *Chronol.* 204), if the correct chronology is followed, was a σεβόμενος, *i.e.*, according to the terminology of Acts (above, p. 212, n. 6), a Gentile holding allegiance to the synagogue, not a circumcised proselyte. Aquila and Priscilla, Paul had no reason to mention in 1 Cor. i. 14 as they had permanently left Corinth, Acts xviii. 26; 1 Cor. xvi. 19; Rom. xvi. 3. They certainly were won to the faith before Crispus, and must have been baptized not later than the formation of the independent Church in Corinth. The "many Corinthians" who were influenced to a decision by the baptism of Crispus, Acts xviii. 8, must for this reason have belonged to those Hellenes who before that time had been more or less closely allied with the synagogue, Acts xviii. 4. This, however, does not hold of the λαὸς πολύς in ver. 10. At the time when 1 Cor. was written (vi. 11, viii. 7, xii. 2), the congregation was for the most part made up of native Gentiles, although later on Apollos was successful in bringing some Jews into the Church (nn. 6, 11). From 1 Cor. i. 26–31 we may infer that there were in the congregation several persons, though not many, of higher rank and of more thorough education. With regard to Erastus, see above, p. 259 (middle).

5. (P. 258.) Concerning Gallio, see XI. (Chron. Survey). It is not to be assumed that the Jews (Acts xviii. 13) accused Paul as a transgressor of the Mosaic law; for (1) there is wanting here any expression which would indicate such to be the case, as in John xix. 7, xviii. 31; Jos. *Ant.* xiii. 3. 4 (in the contest between the Jews and the Samaritans before Ptolemy Philometer, κατὰ τοὺς Μωυσέως νόμους). (2) It is self-evident that the law to which the accuser appeals is that by which the judge must decide the case. It was a principle with the Jews that in legal process appeal might be made to Gentile as well as to Jewish laws (Baba Kamma, 113a). (3) It is no objection that Gallio says, ver. 15, περὶ νόμου τοῦ καθ' ὑμᾶς. On the contrary, this pointed expression implies that this was just the opposite of that law according to which Gallio had to judge. In the accusation, which in ver. 13 is naturally presented in a very much abbreviated form, the Jews must have argued that Christianity was not to be identified with Judaism, which was tolerated by the Roman law, but that it was rather to be treated as an apostasy from Jewish law and faith. This was the basis of fact for Gallio's judgment. (4) It would have been folly, of which even blind fanaticism would be incapable (C. Schmidt, *Apostelgeschichte*, i. 533), to seek the defence of Jewish orthodoxy at the hands of a proconsul, especially outside of Palestine, where the conditions were especially adverse to the success of such a plea. It would have been more clumsy still, before a judge whose religion and worship were opposed to Mosaism, to accuse Paul of teaching mankind (not Jews) to honour God in a manner contrary to the Mosaic law. The real accusation of the Corinthian Jews was essentially the same as that in Acts xvii. 7, cf. xvi. 21; Luke xxiii. 2; John xix. 15.

6. (P. 259.) If in Acts xviii. 17, whether we read πάντες (אAB) without οἱ ῞Ελληνες (DEHLP), or the very slightly attested οἱ Ἰουδαῖοι, we can understand only the Jews who appeared before Gallio in great crowds (ver. 12, ὁμοθυμαδόν). If the ring of Hellenes on the outside were meant, statement to that effect would be necessary, and even then it would be impossible to exclude the Jews from the πάντες. If, as appears from xviii. 8, 17, and as was customary (Schürer, ii. 439 [Eng. trans. II. ii. 65]), there was only one ruler of the synagogue at Corinth, then Sosthenes was the successor of Crispus. He is not to be distinguished from the Christian Sosthenes of 1 Cor. i. 1. Paul does not usually mention the amanuensis to whom he dictates,—especially not in such a prominent place as the opening address (cf. Rom. xvi. 22). On the other hand, Sosthenes is not to be looked upon as the joint writer with him of the letter; for, from i. 4 on, Paul speaks only in his own name. The only addresses which are strictly comparable are Phil. i. 1, 3; Philem. 1, 3, and perhaps also Gal. i. 2. If, however, it carried weight with the Corinthians to know that there was with Paul a Sosthenes who agreed with what was said in the letter, this person must have been well known to them and respected by them,—a description which suits the former chief of the synagogue in Corinth. If, later, he became a Christian, and we have no reason to believe he did not, Apollos may have helped him from his attitude of opposition to the gospel, which had already begun to waver, to a condition of actual faith (see n. 11). According to Eus. *H. E.* i. 12. 1 f., Clement Alex. reckoned this Sosthenes among the seventy disciples. He clearly distinguishes him from the Sosthenes of Acts xviii. 17, just as he attempts to distinguish the Cephas of Gal. ii. 11, and also of 1 Cor. i. 12, from the

Apostle Peter. Lipsius (*Apocr. Apostelgesch.* i. 201 ; *Ergänzungsheft*, S. 3) has been misled through the careless reading of Eus. *H. E.* i. 12 into stating that the author's statement here and in *Forsch.* iii. 68, 148 is "simply untrue." Eusebius writes : "It is said that to these (seventy disciples) belonged also Sosthenes, who, together with Paul, wrote to the Corinthians. And this narrative is found in the fifth book of the *Hypotyposes* of Clement, in which he *also* says that "Cephas," etc. The "also" (ἐν ᾗ καὶ Κηφᾶν) proves that this assertion regarding Cephas was not the only thing that Clement said, and that ἡ ἱστορία refers to the preceding remark about Sosthenes (cf. Eus. *H. E.* ii. 15. 2).

7. (P. 260.) Krenkel, *Beiträge zur Gesch. u. den Briefen des Pl.* (1890, 1895[2]), 233 ff., opposes the dating of 1 Cor. at about the end of the Ephesian activity of Paul, on the ground that an inference drawn from the combination of statements in Acts, which he alleges are entirely unreliable, with those of 1 Cor. is not to be trusted. But the route taken by Paul, according to Acts, namely, by way of Macedonia and Corinth to Jerusalem (Acts xix. 21), is identical with that proposed in 1 Cor. xvi. 3-7. Nor is there any contradiction in the fact that, according to Acts xix. 21 (cf. Rom. xv. 25), Paul looks upon Jerusalem quite definitely as his goal, whereas in 1 Cor. xvi. 4 he seems to speak of it hypothetically ; for the concluding clause in this latter passage—not σὺν αὐτοῖς πορεύσομαι, but σὺν ἐμοὶ πορεύσονται—shows that it is not a question whether Paul will go to Jerusalem at all with the offering, but whether he will go in company with the delegates of the Corinthians. It is pointed out that in Acts xix. 22 mention is made of Timothy's journey only to Macedonia, not to Corinth, and that, on the other hand, it is not expressly stated in 1 Cor. xvi. 10 that Timothy was to go to Corinth by way of Macedonia. But in the latter passage this is the clear inference (above, p. 259). On the other hand, in Acts, which does not touch at all upon the relations of Paul and the Corinthian Church, there is no occasion to mention the final goal of Timothy's journey. The mention in Acts xix. 22 (cf. Rom. xvi. 23) of the Corinthian Erastus would make it seem, quite apart from 1 Cor., that the journey was to be continued from Macedonia to Corinth. It is true that we are not able to infer from 1 Cor. what actually took place after Timothy was sent, but only Paul's intention at the time of his departure. This intention is not only the same as that which, according to Acts xix. 21 f., xx. 1 f., Paul had had shortly before and at the time of his final departure from Ephesus, but it excludes every thought of a return to his labours at Ephesus after having paid his projected visit to Corinth. Had this been Paul's intention, or had he even thought of it as a serious possibility, consideration of the large opportunity afforded him of spreading the gospel in Ephesus, and the many obstacles with which he had to contend in doing this, would not have been sufficient reason for his remaining in Ephesus at least until Pentecost, instead of leaving at once (xvi. 8, 9). At all events, Paul could not have designated the limit of his stay by ἕως τῆς πεντηκοστῆς, if it had not been self-evident that he was referring to the coming Pentecost. Inasmuch as this reckoning follows the order of the Jewish festivals, he could not have expressed himself very well in this way if the Jewish "Church year," the Pentecost of which year was in question, had not yet begun, *i.e.* if the first

of Nisan were not already past,—which agrees with the apparent suggestion
in 1 Cor. v. 8, that this Epistle was written about the time of "unleavened
bread" (14-21 Nisan). The period of six to seven weeks until Pentecost was
long enough to accomplish what is suggested in 1 Cor. xvi. 9, being twice as
long as the period required for the founding of the Church in Thessalonica
(above, p. 212, n. 5). If Timothy's return was delayed (xvi. 11), it is quite
possible that the period of Paul's further activity in Ephesus was extended.
All that Paul means to say is, that in view of conditions at Ephesus, he
could not bring himself to leave until Pentecost. Then there was before
him the journey through Macedonia, which evidently he did not think of as
one that would be executed hastily, since he admits that his proposed longer
sojourn at Corinth may consume the entire winter (xvi. 6). Not before the
following spring, i.e. about a year after the sending of 1 Cor., does he
think of travelling to Jerusalem. It is true that his further intention of
going from Jerusalem to Rome is mentioned only in Acts xix. 21. But
since 1 Cor. contains no contradictory suggestion, it is hypercritical to
question the historicity of the expression in direct discourse given in Acts
xix. 21. Instead of the inference from 1 Cor. xvi. 19 that all the Christians
of Ephesus assembled in the house of Aquila, whereas in a writing alleged
to be directed to Ephesus (Rom. xvi. 5, 14 f.) reference is made to three
house congregations (Krenkel, 234), the proper conclusion to be drawn from
the accompanying greeting from all the brethren is, that the congregation in
the house of Aquila formed only a part of the brotherhood at Ephesus, as
did the congregation in the house of Philemon (Philem. 2) at Colossæ.

8. (P. 260.) Clem. 1 Cor. 65, τοὺς δὲ ἀπεσταλμένους ἀφ᾽ ἡμῶν Κλαύδιον
Ἔφηβον καὶ Οὐαλέριον Βίτωνα σὺν καὶ Φορτουνάτῳ ἐν εἰρήνῃ μετὰ χαρᾶς ἐν τάχει
ἀναπέμψατε πρὸς ἡμᾶς. If we take into consideration the distinct position
here accorded to Fortunatus, it becomes evident that he is not one of the
representatives of the Romans commissioned to the Corinthians, but merely
the one in whose company these are travelling to Corinth, and in all probability a Corinthian who made complaints at Rome concerning the disturbances
in the home Church (GGA, 1876, S. 1427 f. ; Lightfoot, S. Clem. ii. 187). If
the Fortunatus of 1 Cor. xvi. 17 was at that time (57 A.D.) a young man of
thirty, he can easily be identical with the Fortunatus of 97 A.D., being one of
the presbyters of the Corinthian Church who was installed by the apostles,
and who had grown grey in its service (Clem. 1 Cor. xliv. 3-6 ; xlvii. 6 ;
liv. 2 ; lvii. 1). If Stephanas, Fortunatus, and Achaicus are the bearers,
not only of the letter of the Corinthian Church to Paul, but also of 1 Cor.,
then they are the "brethren" in whose company Apollos might have gone
back to Corinth, 1 Cor. xvi. 12. The order of the words does not agree
with Hofmann's interpretation of the verse, according to which the Christians about Paul join with him in urging Apollos to undertake this
journey. Assuming, on the other hand, that the order of the words in
xvi. 11 does necessitate the reference of μετὰ τῶν ἀδελφῶν to the Christians
in whose company Paul will await the return of Timothy at Ephesus, they
cannot have been the three Corinthians who were not to await the return of
Timothy, but were to journey to Corinth at once (xvi. 12, νῦν) with
1 Cor. in their keeping, and, in case Apollos could be persuaded to go
in company with him. Neither can they have been the collective Christian

community at Ephesus (xvi. 20); they were rather those who were to travel with Paul *via* Macedonia to Corinth (see below, § 19, n. 6). The similarity of the expression, μετὰ τῶν ἀδελφῶν, in xvi. 11, 12, does not justify us in identifying the persons referred to in these passages. ὁ ἀδελφός or οἱ ἀδελφοί may designate very different persons, according to the context or conditions previously known to the readers (cf. 2 Cor. viii. 18, 22, ix. 3, 5, xi. 9, xii. 18; Eph. vi. 23).

9. (P. 262.) The references to the two early Epistles of Paul which are not in the collection of his letters, 1 Cor. v. 9–11, vii. 1, led in the second century to the fabrication of an Epistle from the Corinthians to Paul, and an answer from Paul to the Corinthians, both of which were embodied in the Canon of the Church of Edessa in the fourth century, bearing the common title, *The Third Epistle to the Corinthians*. From the Syrians they reached the Armenians and also some of the Latins. The best texts—Armenian and Latin, the former with a German translation—are those of P. Vetter, *Der apokryphe dritte Korintherbrief (Tübinger Programm*, Wien, 1894). Originally these pieces were a portion of the old *Acta Pauli*, as previously conjectured by the writer (*GK*, ii. 607, 611, 879), and as is now proved to be the case by the Coptic fragments (C. Schmidt, *NHJb.* vii. 122; *NKZ*, 1897, S. 937, n. 2); also *Acta Pauli*, ed. C. Schmidt, pp. 74–82.

10. (P. 262.) Ἀπολλῶς (nominative), 1 Cor. iii. 5, 22 (G incorrectly Ἀπολλω); Acts xviii. 24 (D Ἀπολλώνιος, of which the shorter form is a contraction, א Copt. Ἀπελλης); Ἀπολλῶ (genitive), 1 Cor. i. 12, iii. 4, xvi. 12; *Berl. äg. Urk.* 295. 7; Ἀπολλῶτι (dative), 811. 1, cf. 449. 1 (with a correction see also the address there; on the other hand, Greek Pap. ed. Kenyon, ii. 333, No. 393, Ἀπολλῶ, dat.); Ἀπολλῶ, acc. 1 Cor. iv. 6 (CDGLP, Απολλων א*AB*); Acts xix. 1 poorly attested also Απολλων, א Copt. Απελλην, D does not here contain the name); Tit. iii. 13 (אH have Απολλων, G Απολλωνα). The reading Απελλης seems to be of Egyptian origin (cf. besides א Copt., Ammonius in Cramer's *Catenæ in Acta*, p. 311. 1, 7, 13, apparently also Didymus, *ibid.* p. 309. 31, 312. 18), and goes back to the modest question of Origen (Delarue, iv. 682), whether Apelles, Rom. xvi. 10, be not identical with Apollos, Acts xviii. 24, as Didymus (*loc. cit.*) asserts. This was claimed also by those who made Apelles = Apollos, a bishop of Corinth. In commenting upon Acts xviii. 24, Blass suggests the Doric form Ἀπέλλων for Ἀπόλλων. Though not so strongly attested as Ἀπολλώνιος, there is abundant proof of this abbreviated form in Egypt, the home of the Apollos of Acts (see the indices of vols. i. ii. iii. of the *Berl. äg. Urk.*). We find that even down to the present, German scholars of distinction write the name of the man *Apollo*. This, as is well known, is the Latin form of the name of the god, Ἀπόλλων, and it is therefore necessary in a text-book to warn against this mistake. Or shall we soon read and hear *Mino, rhinocero*, etc.?

11. (P. 261.) The scene of the public disputations, Acts xviii. 28 (δημοσίᾳ, to which E alone adds καὶ κατ' οἶκον), was certainly not the assembly of the Christians, nor a public place, but the synagogue, in which Apollos held forth at Corinth as he had done previously at Ephesus (Acts xviii. 26). The connection between Acts xviii. 28 and 27 leaves no doubt that the advantage of which Apollos proved himself to those who were already believers (or, according to another text, to the congregations of Achaia) was due to his

frequent triumphs in these disputations with the Jews. The use of the strong word διακατηλέγχετο points likewise to actual results. From 1 Cor. iii. 5 we learn specifically that part of the Christians who composed the Church at the time of 1 Cor. owed their conversion to Apollos (ἐπιστεύσατε). It is therefore wrong to interpret the figure in 1 Cor. iii. 6–8 to mean that the special work of Apollos was the religious or intellectual training of those who had already been converted by Paul. It is not the individual Christians and their spiritual life, but the congregation in general, which constitutes the θεοῦ γεώργιον and θεοῦ οἰκοδομή. According to 1 Cor. iii. 10–15, the activity of those who, like Apollos, continued the work of Paul, consisted in adding further material to the building, i.e. in winning men to the faith and bringing them into the Church (cf. Eph. ii. 20–22 ; 1 Pet. ii. 5–7). According to the original text of Acts xviii. 27, certain Corinthians stopping in Ephesus heard Apollos preach and invited him to come to Corinth with them. This was the beginning of the " Apollos party " in Corinth.

12. (P. 263.) Hofmann, ii. 2. 396 (comp. also Holsten, 189, 445), was minded to find in 1 Cor. xvi. 7 reference to a former visit to Corinth. Were this the case, however, we should expect not ἄρτι, which does not mean " on this occasion," but rather πάλιν (2 Cor. ii. 1, xii. 21, xiii. 2), or, if it is decided to associate the coming again with the present, ἄρτι πάλιν (Gal. i. 9). Furthermore, the reason for this statement given in 7b would be somewhat tautological. Finally, in its present context ἄρτι must mean " even now " in contrast with a later point of time (John xiii. 7, 33, xvi. 12). There is no force in the objection that Paul could speak in this way only if he were already on the journey (Hofmann, 395), because, even in this case, ἰδεῖν would still refer to the future ; while, from the criticisms of the Atticists, we learn that ἄρτι was very commonly employed to designate the immediate future (cf. Lobeck, ad Phryn. 18 f.). What Paul says is this : He does not wish to visit Corinth at once coming directly from Ephesus, which would permit him to stop at Corinth only for a brief stay on his way into Macedonia. Then he gives as his reason for this decision not to come now, his hope of a longer visit, which, nevertheless, will have to be delayed (ver. 5), since, in any case, he must proceed soon to Macedonia.

13. (P. 263.) The testimony of 2 Cor. to a visit not mentioned in Acts is denied by Grotius (ii. 488, 539–541, with the stereotyped evasion est et hic trajectio), Reiche (Comm. Crit. i. 337 f.), Baur (i. 337–343), Hilgenfeld (Einl. 260, n. 2), Heinrici (ii. 9–13). But the only possible sense that can be given to 2 Cor. xiii. 1 is that Paul, at the time when he was writing 2 Cor., was on the point of coming to Corinth for the third time. In the light of this verse xiii. 2 must be understood ; τὸ δεύτερον is to be taken with παρών, νῦν with ἀπών, so that the προείρηκα must have taken place during the second visit. Similarly xii. 14 and xii. 21 must be taken together. There is no grammatical objection to taking τρίτον with ἐλθεῖν πρὸς ὑμᾶς, and this is the only interpretation that fits the context (cf. Krenkel, Beiträge, 185) ; for to say that this was the third time that Paul was ready to come to Corinth, even if it were possible, would be without point in connection with xii. 14. In order, with good conscience, to separate ἐν λύπῃ from πάλιν (ii. 1), which Theodoret, contrary to the word arrangement and Paul's linguistic usage (Krenkel, 202), undertook to connect with ἐλθεῖν, making it refer to Paul's return to

Corinth, in some cursives the πάλιν was placed after ἐλθεῖν, and in the Coptic, which omits πάλιν, after ὑμᾶς. But in all the other MSS. it is clearly stated that Paul had visited in Corinth once in sorrow, in fact, as the context and the comparison xii. 21, xiii. 2, show, in sorrow for the Church's condition. This can have no reference to the despondency with which Paul appeared for the first time in Corinth (1 Cor. ii. 3), but must refer to the second visit, of which we are speaking. Wrongly assuming that 2 Cor. x. 10 represents the words of one of the Jewish Christians who had come to Corinth from without (see *per contra,* below, § 18, n. 8), Krenkel (210) finds in this passage also definite reference to the second visit. If, however, the speaker is rather a native Corinthian, his words may well represent the impression which Paul made at the time of his first visit. If the second visit is also included, no conclusion can be drawn regarding the time of the same.

14. (P. 264.) Krenkel, 154–174, thinks he proves that 1 Cor. itself excludes the assumption of a second visit to Corinth prior to the time when 1 Cor. was written. If this visit occurred in the first year of his work in Ephesus—say in the summer or fall of 55 or in the spring of 56—the *argumentum e silentio* (n. 12) is particularly weak. We are unable to determine all that took place in Corinth in the twelve or twenty months which elapsed between this time and that of the writing of 1 Cor., and all the transactions between Paul and the Church. But the character of the facts that do come to light in 1 Cor., the immediately preceding correspondence which has not been preserved to us, and the reports concerning the factional differences, and various other disorders in the Church (1 Cor. i. 11, xi. 18), make it clear that Paul has no more occasion to speak of that visit. In the letter spoken of in 1 Cor. v. 9, and in numerous other letters of which we know nothing, he may have spoken of it. It is argued that there is no expressly stated distinction in 1 Cor. ii. 1–5, iii. 6–10, xv. 1 ff. between the first and second visits (as in Gal. iv. 13) ; but this is true also of 2 Cor. i. 19, xi. 8 f. The only inference to be drawn from all these passages is that, on his second visit to Corinth, Paul did not carry on a missionary activity as he had done during his second visit in the province of Galatia (above, p. 171, n. 2). This, however, would need no explanation if Paul interrupted his fruitful missionary activity at Ephesus for only a brief time in order to visit the Corinthian Church. The instructions, exhortations, and discussions with the believers which took place at that time do not come properly under the idea of an ἐποικοδομεῖν (1 Cor. iii. 10–15, above, n. 11). To the view advanced first by Baronius and most recently by Anger, *de Temp. in Actis Ratione* (73), that the second visit to Corinth was only a return from a short excursion made during the eighteen months of his residence there (Acts xviii. 11), the following objections may be made : (1) the use of the word ἐκάθισεν (see above, p. 263 f., n. 2), to which there is nothing analogous in the report of his stay in Ephesus ; (2) such a resumption of labours after a brief interruption could not be classed as a second visit along with his first appearance in Corinth and his last visit, which was months in preparation. Still less, since 2 Cor. is addressed to the Christians of entire Achaia, could it be compared to a journey to that region. Even more questionable is the suggestion of Neander (*Pflanzung und Leitung,* 5te Auf. 320), that we read into Acts xix. 1 a journey to Achaia.

15. (P. 263.) Since the persons who brought the Epistle of the Corinthians were in entire harmony with Paul, at least at the time when they started back to Corinth (1 Cor. xvi. 17, above, p. 260 f.), there is no doubt that of their own accord, or in response to his questions, they reported many things to him which were not in the communication of the Church. From them he may have learned the facts touched upon in iv. 18, v. 1 ff., vi. 1 ff., xi. 18, xv. 12. Inasmuch, however, as it was not from them but from those of the household of Chloe that Paul learned of the strifes mentioned in i. 11–iv. 6, it is evident that these "members of Chloe's family" must have reached Ephesus before the bearers of the Epistle from the Church. On the other hand, the information brought by the members of Chloe's family must have concerned events which had just occurred ; for manifestly in i. 11 ff. Paul is speaking of the conditions in question for the first time. This situation must have been as yet unknown to him when he wrote his previous letter (v. 9), for otherwise he would have discussed it, and from the tone of i. 11–iv. 6 it is evident that he did not. Still less, then, could Paul have noticed these discords at the time of his visit to Corinth. The only respect in which he compares the impressions which he received on this second visit with those which he fears he will receive when he comes again, is that of sorrow (2 Cor. ii. 1, xii. 21). He clearly distinguishes, however, between the unchastity which had caused him sorrow then (II. xii. 21, xiii. 2), and the factional strifes which he fears he shall now find (II. xii. 20).

§ 18. THE CONDITION OF THE CORINTHIAN CHURCH AT THE TIME WHEN FIRST CORINTHIANS WAS WRITTEN.

In striking contrast to the situation of the Christians in Thessalonica, the Church in Corinth was enjoying a condition of undisturbed peace. There are a number of things which account for this condition, e.g. the mixed character of the population of a great commercial city, where men are constantly coming and going from all parts of the world, the great number of different religious cults tolerated in Corinth, the impartiality in religious matters of the proconsul in whose term of office the Church became established (above, p. 267, n. 5), the social standing of some of the members of the Church, and the prominent place of others even in the government of the city (above, pp. 258, 265 f., n. 4). But, as indicated by the ironical comparison which the apostle makes between the situation of the Corinthians, who were living in this world as if it

were the millennium (iv.8–13), and that of himself and
his fellow-missionaries, this condition of peace had been
secured at too great cost. The word of the Cross, the
sharp contrast which it implies to all natural wisdom
with the practical inferences therefrom (i. 17–31 ; Gal.
vi. 14), had not made an impression sufficiently deep.
They need to be reawakened to a sense of the fact that
they were a body of persons separated by faith and
baptism from the world about them, and from their
own past (i. 2, iii. 17, vi. 11). Members of the Church
were actually bringing suit against each other in heathen
courts (vi. 1–8). No scruples were felt about maintaining
friendly and social intercourse with the heathen (x. 27).
Many even went so far as to take part in festivities connected with idolatrous worship, in the banquets held in
heathen temples (viii. 10, x. 21). Although this dangerous
approach to the worship of idols which had been so recently
abandoned was not approved by all, so that, as may be
inferred from the detail with which it was answered
(viii. 1–x. 33), the question was submitted to Paul in
the communication of the Church whether it was permissible to use meat that had been offered to idols, it
was the opinion of the majority, expressed in the communication from the Church, that this liberal attitude
toward heathen worship was entirely justifiable. Because
every Christian knew that the heathen conception of the
gods was entirely false, it was argued, everyone was free
to consider everything associated with heathen worship
an adiaphoron so long as he did not engage in the worship
itself. Indeed, it was said, to act with this freedom was
an obligation, in fulfilling which an encouraging example
might be given to such of their fellow-Christians as were
still undeveloped in knowledge and in the sense of moral
freedom. By this it was hoped they might be raised to a
level with themselves (n. 1). Without disputing at all
the theoretical presupposition of this position, but rather

himself affirming repeatedly the nothingness of the gods believed in and worshipped by the heathen (viii. 4, x. 19), Paul combats such an employment of their Christian knowledge and such a use of their Christian liberty. The principle advocated by the Church, πάντα ἔξεστιν (x. 23, cf. vi. 12), he holds, must be limited in two directions. In the first place, not everything permissible is advantageous to one's neighbour. Out of tender regard for a fellow-Christian less developed than himself, particularly for the sake of the conscience of such a person, the Christian must stand ready to give up his undoubted rights and liberties (viii. 1–3, 7–12), an example which had been set by Paul himself in the conduct of his ministry (viii. 13–ix. 22). In the second place, not everything permissible is best for the Christian himself the use of whose freedom is in question. Just as the apostle for his own spiritual good foregoes many things in themselves pleasant (ix. 23–27), so for their own sakes the Corinthians ought to avoid dangerous contact with heathen worship (n. 2). The history of Israel in the wilderness proves by terrible example that wantonly to long after the pleasures enjoyed in the old life before conversion, to incline toward the use of heathen forms of worship, and to indulge in the practice of heathen unchastity, is to tempt God, and to bring down destruction even upon the redeemed (x. 1–11). In order to correct the spirit of false confidence with which many of the Corinthians had been treading upon this slippery ground (x. 12, 22), the apostle insists that, quite apart from the question whether or not there is a Zeus or an Apollo, an Aphrodite or an Isis, there are evil spirits which work in connection with the worship of these so-called gods, to whose influence everyone is exposed who has anything to do with heathen worship, even though so indirectly as was the case among the Corinthians (x. 15–21). From x. 13, taken in connection with x. 14 (διόπερ), it appears that the Church had argued that it was impossible to cut themselves off entirely from contact with heathen life, because it would only be to subject themselves to greater temptations than it was possible for human powers to endure (cf. Hofmann, ii. 2, 207, and the similar line of thought in 2 Cor. vi. 14–18). Similarly, the casuistic questions which Paul was required to answer in x. 25–30 were asked for the purpose of showing that in the intercourse of daily life it was quite impossible to avoid eating εἰδωλόθυτα. This same principle, the necessary limitations of which Paul here points out, the Church had applied also to questions about sexual relations (vi. 12). In view of the manner in which Paul replies, it is very probable that the Church had represented the gratification of sexual desire to be a natural function, like the satisfaction of hunger, although we are no longer able to determine how far the comparison was carried and how much it was made to cover. Certain it is, however, that the Church had not agreed with what Paul had said on this subject. An exhortation in his previous letter to refrain from intercourse with wicked persons, particularly with unchaste persons, had been misunderstood, or, as Paul hints when making his transition to this subject in v. 8, unfairly misconstrued. He was represented as demanding an impossible avoidance of all contact with immoral persons, whereas his exhortation was meant to apply only to immoral *members of the Church* (v. 9–13). It was the general opinion in Corinth that Paul, being himself unmarried, had been too rigorous in his demands affecting this side of the natural life. So in their letter the Church had taken him to task for holding that entire abstinence from all sexual intercourse was something to be commended. Paul confesses this to be the principle upon which he stands, and makes various applications of it (vii. 1, 8, 26–35, 40), but in such a way as to make it appear

that marriage is to be the rule, the right to remain
single being conditioned upon personal possession of the
charismata requisite thereto (vii. 2, 7, 9).   At the same
time we learn that there were some in Corinth who
were opposed to the position taken by the majority, and
treated marriage contemptuously, possibly on the strength
of what Paul had said, recommending or even insisting
that married persons should refrain altogether from sexual
intercourse or even dissolve their marriage relation altogether, particularly in cases where husbands remained
non-Christians ; also rejecting as sinful marriage subsequent to conversion, particularly the re - marriage of
widows (n. 3).   Although Paul tells this minority
quietly and earnestly that marriage is a natural right
(vii. 3–5), reminding them of the command of Jesus
by which the marriage bond is declared to be inviolable
(vii. 10 ff.), against the majority, whose opinion was
expressed in the letter, he defends his point of view
not without some show of irritation.   Where the case
is not covered by an express command of Jesus, while
not speaking with apostolic authority, he does speak as
one who has been given the grace to become a faithful
Christian (vii. 25).   He thinks that he has the spirit of
God quite as much as this self-sufficient Church (vii. 40).

This feeling on the part of Paul was due as much as
anything else to the concrete case with the discussion of
which this second section of the letter (chaps. v.–vii.) begins.
He does not need to mention the source whence he had
derived this information ; for this case of one of their own
members who was living in incestuous relations, or in
relations of concubinage, with his father's wife, i.e. with
his step-mother, was talked of quite publicly, more openly
than was customary in such cases even among the heathen
(n. 4).   The haughty manner in which the Church had
written the apostle, not about this particular case, to
be sure, but about kindred questions (v. 9 ff., vi. 12 ff.,

vii. 1 ff.), and the general moral condition of the Church
(v. 6), show that there was no feeling of shame about the
matter, and that nothing had been done to remove the
scandal. As shown by the relation of v. 2, 13 to Deut.
xvii. 7, 12, xxiv. 7, the only atonement which Paul
deemed adequate was the extermination of the offender
at the hands of the Church. He had decided at once how
this requirement of God's law could be carried out consistently with the nature of the Church of the new
covenant; and since he could not, nor would not, act
alone in the matter, he communicated his view to the
Church, with the suggestion that they adopt it and unite
with their absent founder in carrying it out. The apostle
in Ephesus proposes that the Church in Corinth join with
him in the name of Jesus and in the confidence that Jesus'
miraculous power will be vouchsafed to them (cf. Matt.
xviii. 19 f.), to constitute a court which shall deliver the
offender over to Satan in bodily death, in order that his
spirit may be saved in the day of judgment. It is not to
be an act of excommunication by the Church, but a judgment of God, a miracle in answer to prayer, in which Paul
and the Church are to unite, and for which a definite day
and hour are to be arranged.

While the two sections chaps. v.–vii. and chaps. viii.–x.
show that the moral life and the moral judgment of
the Church were imperilled by lack of separation from
the customs and ideas of their heathen neighbours, from
chap. xv., particularly from the poetical quotation xv. 33,
we learn that in the case of some (xv. 12, 34, τινές), things
had reached the point where their judgment about matters
of faith was being formed under the influence of heathen
conceptions. As Paul's argument shows, the contention
of some of the Corinthians, "There is no resurrection of
the dead," was not intended to refer to the resurrection of
Christ. In this case, on account of Christ's exceptional
character and the close relation in time between His death

and resurrection, those denying the resurrection of the dead would necessarily have had to make an exception of this event of gospel history. What they did mean to deny was only the Christian's hope of a future bodily resurrection. But this denial was so radical in character, and so fundamentally connected with the belief that the bodily resurrection of the dead was impossible and inconceivable, that Paul felt it necessary first of all to show that the resurrection of Christ, denial of which was after all involved in their premises (xv. 13, 16), was a fact amply attested, and an essential element not only in the gospel which Paul preached and upon which the faith of the Corinthians was based, but of all the apostolic preaching (xv. 1–11).

Another source of degeneracy was the unusually rich endowment of the Church with χαρίσματα, especially with various forms of inspired speech (n. 5). Not only did this increase the feeling of self-importance on the part of the Church as a whole, but the pride felt by individuals because of their special gifts, and the preference for one gift above another, produced discord and disorder in public worship. The Church had asked particularly for Paul's opinion about the so-called speaking with tongues (n. 5). Here, too, as in the case of questions about marriage and sacrifices made to idols, there was an opposing minority view, as is evidenced by the two principles which Paul lays down at the beginning of his discussion (chaps. xii.–xiv.). While to some the ecstatic and unintelligible utterances of those who spoke with tongues seemed like the outbursts of enthusiasm heard in heathen worship, and while in general these opposed the use of tongues for fear of the utterances of blasphemies in connection with it, the majority showed an abnormal, or, as Paul expresses it in xiv. 20, a childish preference for tongues, regarding this gift as the strongest possible proof of the overwhelming power of the Spirit in the Church,

which feeling on their part was due to the associations of
heathen worship quite as much as were the exaggerated
fears of the minority (xii. 2). These fears Paul sets at
rest by the assurance that no one speaking by the Spirit
of God can call Jesus accursed. On the other hand, in
order to guard against an over-valuation of the gift of
tongues, he lays down the principle that even the simplest
confession of Jesus as Lord cannot be made without the
Holy Spirit. Exclusive preference for a single charisma,
no matter which one it was, and the giving of prominence
to those possessing it, is contrary to the divine purpose in
bestowing a diversity of gifts, and is inconsistent with
the nature of the Church (xii. 4–30). The necessary condition for the proper valuation of the different charismata
is the insight that it is in no sense these spiritual en-
dowments and extraordinary powers which in this world
bring human and even inanimate nature into the service
of the Church, that give men value and insure their
salvation, but only conformity of the heart to God, faith
in the gospel, and hope in everlasting life, and above
everything else love (xii. 31–xiii. 13). But love also
teaches the proper valuation and right use of the charismata (xiv. 1–40). Judged by this standard, the prophet
who, while speaking to the Church with enthusiasm and
in the belief that he has a revelation, yet retains self-
consciousness and self-control, who is able also when
occasion offers to reach the heart and conscience even of
unbelievers who come into the Christian religious services,
stands infinitely higher than the person who speaks with
tongues, and in a state of ecstasy gives utterance to unintelligible prayers and praise. Because love does not seek
its own, but the good of its neighbour and the prosperity
of the whole Church, it supplies also the practical rules
regulating the use both of tongues and of prophecy in the
services of the Church. It was lack of discrimination in the
use of this talent which led even women, as the connection

shows, especially those who possessed the gift of glossolalia (speaking with tongues) or of prophecy, to speak openly in the public services of the Church (xiv. 33–35). Since Paul discountenances this practice altogether, what is said in xi. 3–16, where prayer and prophecy on the part of women are spoken of as if entirely allowable, objection being made only to the custom that had been introduced in Corinth of allowing the women to remove their veils, must refer to services held in private houses. It is quite easy to see how the woman who was capable and felt called upon to act as priestess or prophetess in her own household, perhaps because her husband was not a Christian or not especially gifted, might feel that she ought to bear witness to this equality between man and woman in the eyes of men and of God, also by appearing in public and speaking (n. 6).

Besides the arguments against this disposition on the part of the women to be independent, suggested by the nature of the subject in hand, Paul reminds the Corinthians twice that in permitting such practices they are acting contrary to the custom of all the other Churches (xi. 16, xiv. 33). Their conduct is such as would become them if they were the oldest Church in existence, when the fact that the gospel had gone out from them might give them a certain authority in matters of custom in the Church; or if they were the only Church in the world, with no need whatever to consult the judgment and practice of other Churches (xiv. 36). This same thought is the conclusion also of the discussion about idolatrous sacrifices. The Corinthians need to be careful, lest in deciding these questions arbitrarily they offend Jews and Gentiles and the Church of God, i.e. the entire community of Christians (x. 32, n. 7). Even more clearly than by the passages cited and other hints less strong (iv. 17, vii. 17), the supreme contempt with which the Church seemed to Paul to treat its relation to all the rest of the Church is brought out in the greeting of the letter, in which at the very start Paul endeavours to bring the readers to the realisation that they constitute a society of persons called to be saints not in and of themselves, but only as they stand related to all other persons in the world who call upon the name of Christ (n. 8). The same exaggerated sense of independence which influenced individuals to assert their personal views or preferences without regard to anyone else, even at the cost of sacrificing order and unity in the life and worship of the Church as a whole, threatened also to sever its connection with all the rest of the Church.

This danger was all the more imminent, because at this time the Church was in peril of losing its respect for the authority of its founder and its reverence for him. This affected their relation to other Churches, because it was Paul's personal influence, with the doctrinal traditions and the rules regulating practical life which they had received from him, that from the beginning constituted the bond of union between them and the rest of the Church (vii. 10, xi. 23, xv. 3, 11), particularly the Churches in the Gentile world, which like themselves had been organised by Paul, and of which also he was the head (iv. 17, vii. 17, xi. 16, xiv. 33, xvi. 1, 19). Consequently, when the apostle, moved by the insolent manner in which he had been talked about and criticised behind his back (iv. 3, 7, 19, ix. 3), and by the way in which the Church had taken him to task in their communication (v. 9 ff., above, p. 276), affirms very positively his general authority as an apostle of recognised position (i. 1, 17, ix. 1, xv. 10), and his special authority as the organiser of the Corinthian Church (iii. 10, iv. 15, ix. 2), far more is involved than his own honour or a specific obligation of reverence on the part of the Church.

The existence of cliques in the Church, of which Paul had learned recently (above, p. 273, n. 15), and on the

basis of which information he discusses at length the
question of factionalism at the very beginning of the letter
(i. 10–iv. 6 ; n. 9), must have imperilled both the pleasant
relations between the Church and its founder and its own
inner harmony.   Nothing could be more erroneous than
to suppose that either in Paul's thought, or in fact, the
Church was divided into four factions or even sects.
One party is not set over against another, *e.g.* the professed followers of Paul over against the followers of
Apollos, and the Cephas party over against the party of
Christ.   But he is simply speaking of a deep-seated habit
which more or less all the Corinthians had, namely,
that the individual, without reference to others of like
opinion, called himself the personal follower of Paul, *i.e.*
he made Paul his hero, in contrast naturally to others
who affected a like relation to Apollos, Cephas, or Christ
(i. 12, iii. 4, 22, iv. 6).   If a leader is at all essential to a
party, then, so far as we are able to ascertain, these alleged
parties in Corinth had no leaders.   Certainly the men whom
individuals in Corinth professed to follow had no purpose
of being such leaders.   Paul does not simply find fault
with those who were using his name as if that which
they were doing was only an exaggeration of something in
itself justifiable, or an awkward defence of his interests ;
but, specifically, in connection with his own name, he
shows the foolishness and unchristlikeness of such talk,
thereby condemning in the severest terms the persons by
whom his name was so used (i. 13).   That Apollos also
condemned the persons in Corinth who were using his name,
is very clear from iv. 6, xvi. 12, above, p. 262 f.   It is self-
evident that Paul assumes that Christ cannot approve
what His apostle condemns, along with the other formulæ
expressing this folly.   The same is true with reference to
the relation of Peter to the followers of Cephas, as is especially evidenced by the fact that elsewhere Paul speaks
of him only in terms of respect (xv. 5, 11, ix. 5, iii. 22 ;

Gal. ii. 6–9). Consequently the men whose followers the Corinthians were fond of calling themselves had either already disowned their admirers, or, Paul thinks, would have done so had they been asked about the matter. It is impossible, therefore, to suppose that the question here is one with reference to parties which relatively were clearly defined. In this case the difference of opinion which came out in the course of the letter regarding the relation of the sexes, sacrifices to idols, speaking with tongues, and the resurrection, would have to be referred necessarily to one or another of the four alleged parties, something quite impossible to do. If it were a question of distinct parties, it is also hard to understand why, after chap. v., Paul makes not the slightest reference to any of the four watchwords. Still less can we suppose that the reference is to sects which held their own religious services, having separated themselves in this way from the body of the Church. The communication which Paul had received shortly before, to which 1 Cor. is the apostle's answer, had been written, and the messengers bearing it sent not by individual Christians in Corinth, but by all the readers, *i.e.* by the Corinthian Church (vii. 1, xvi. 17 f., above, p. 261 f.). The whole Church was in the habit of assembling to celebrate the Lord's Supper and for other religious services (x. 17, xi. 17–22, xiv. 4, 5, 19, 23–25, 33 f.). In view of disorders of all kinds, and even of σχίσματα (xi. 18), in connection with these services, it is probable, at least there is nothing in what Paul says which excludes it, though he does not say it in so many words, that those whose views were expressed in the various watchwords sat together in groups. Only upon this supposition—and not by supposing that these groups were formed purely on the basis of kinship or on a social basis (xi. 22, 33)—can we understand how the apostle foresaw that inevitably the outcome of such manifest divisions in the religious service, which was still

one, must eventually result in the formation of distinct
parties, and the breaking up of the Church into a number
of sects (xi. 19, αἱρέσεις).

In a Church which had been founded by Paul there
was no occasion for anyone to affirm that he was a
follower of Paul with an emphasis implying opposition to
someone else, unless some other teacher had made an
impression in Corinth by which Paul was likely to be
overshadowed.   That this teacher was Apollos, and that
it was his successful work as a teacher in Corinth (above,
p. 262 f.) that gave rise to the use of the two watchwords
first mentioned in i. 12, does not require proof.   Moreover, from iii. 4–8, iv. 6 it appears that up to iv. 6 the
discussion is concerned mainly with the differences between
the followers of Paul and of Apollos.   What these differences were we ascertain from i. 17b–iii. 2.   The purpose
of the whole passage is to justify the way in which Paul
had preached in Corinth during the eighteen months of
his residence there (Acts xviii. 11) in the face of hostile
criticism, and to show that his preaching was free from
certain pretensions which were contrary to his principles.
Paul's statements could not well be more entirely misunderstood than by Hilgenfeld (*Einl.* 267), when he assumes
that Paul is here replying to the criticisms of Jewish
Christians, who represented his successes as due to the
use which he made of Greek culture, since it is not the
fact that he had refrained from the use of these means
which Paul proves.   On the contrary, always simply
stating this fact or assuming it (i. 17, οὐκ ἐν σοφίᾳ λόγου,
i. 23, ii. 1, 4, iii. 1 ; 2 Cor. xi. 6), he justifies his action at
length by setting forth his reasons and objects.   Consequently the objection which he is meeting must have been
to the effect that his preaching showed a lack of requisite
learning and of convincing eloquence.   In reply to this
criticism, he develops the principles which he regarded as
rightly determining the method of preaching the gospel

in missionary fields, the method required by the nature of
the gospel. Both in its essential content, as presenting
the cross of Christ, and in its consequent character, as a
foolish preaching, missionary preaching—and that is the
only commission that he has received from Christ—is
inconsistent with the use of rhetoric and of other forms
of learning (i. 17–31). While Paul's refusal to use these
means in the presentation of his message, and his strict
confinement of himself to the essentials of the gospel, was
very natural in view of his state of mind when he came to
Corinth, it was nevertheless in keeping with the principles
which he regarded as regulative of the missionary preaching (ii. 1–5). Nor does he omit to say that for those whose
self-denying faith has led to their salvation through the
gospel, this sharp distinction between the foolish gospel
and the natural mind both of Jews and of Greeks largely
disappears ; since for Christians Christ comes to be also
the only wisdom (i. 24, 30). He points out also that it is
not the office of Christian teachers to be continually
repeating the word of the cross to those who have been
converted and are of mature spiritual understanding, but
also to develop those conceptions of divine truth, which,
being fully realised in the glory of the world to come, will
bring the reconciliation of all contradictions in the nature
of things and of all differences between faith and reason
(ii. 6–12). But even if it were untrue that the things
which he taught them could not be set forth in the
categories of human culture, but from their nature demanded a method all their own (ii. 13), the immaturity of
his hearers made it impossible for Paul, while he was
engaged in organising the Church, to employ this method
of teaching (iii. 1 f.). It is clear, therefore, that the difference between the followers of Paul and of Apollos was
not one affecting the essentials of the word of the cross
and of the " wisdom of God," any more than the difference between Paul and Apollos themselves, but only

involved the question as to how these should be presented, and a difference of opinion as to the value of rhetoric and logic in setting them forth.   Many of the Corinthians seem to have been so carried away by the brilliant discourses of the eloquent Alexandrian, that thereafter the unadorned preaching of the " plain " (2 Cor. xi. 6, ἰδιώτης) Paul seemed in comparison very deficient.   It was not until it had been presented to them by Apollos' logic, so they thought, that they had come to have a true understanding of Christianity.   When Apollos was talked about in this way, it is easy to see how some would regard such remarks as disparaging to the founder of the Church, and the less such persons approved of the method of Apollos, the more earnest they would be in their championship of Paul.   Instead of all judging these two men at their real value, in the light of what they had actually done for the Church and in accordance with their respective gifts, individuals formed their own estimates in accordance with their own feelings, with the result that they vied with each other in their championship of one or the other of these two men (iv. 6).   That they believed such championship gave them a better hold upon Christianity is indicated by Paul's question, whether Christ is divided so that they possess Him in greater or less degree according as they follow one or the other of their teachers (i. 13). Paul condemns their procedure, not only because it involves presumption in the formation of their judgments, but also because, in a manner inconsistent with the dignity of a Christian, it involves submission to men who are no rivals of God and of Christ in the work of redemption and in the bestowment of pardon upon the individual (i. 13b, iii. 4–7, 22).

This condemnation applies also to those who called themselves followers of Cephas.   Inasmuch as it is impossible to suppose that at this time Peter had been in Corinth in person (n. 10), we must assume that Christians

who had been converted through his influence, perhaps
also baptized by him (n. 11), but who in any case had
had personal relations with him, had come from their own
home to Corinth, and had increased the existing confusion
by their ἐγὼ δὲ Κηφᾶ. This is confirmed by the conclusion
of the letter. As he is on the point of adding the parting benediction in his own hand, Paul stops suddenly to
insert an anathema against everyone who does not love
the Lord (xvi. 22), before putting down the benediction
which he had already started to write. In this way he
means to indicate that the persons referred to are excluded from his greeting to the Church, and so from
the Church itself, to which he gives assurance of the grace
of Jesus and of his own love (xvi. 23 f.). When to this
anathema he adds a significant phrase in the language of
the Palestinian Jews, it is clear that the persons whom he
has in mind are Christians who had come from Palestine
(n. 12). That iii. 16–20 is directed against the followers
of Peter, we must infer from the fact that the name of
Peter occurs again in iii. 22 along with those of Paul and
Apollos, in striking contrast to iii. 4–8, and in seeming
contradiction to the reference in iv. 6 to an earlier passage.
After speaking in iii. 10–15 of those who, like Apollos, with
good intentions, but in a way not altogether skilful, had
built upon the foundation of the Church in Corinth laid
by Paul, in iii. 16–20 Paul turns to those who, though
engaged upon the same structure, had done their work in
such a way that, in an outburst of anger, he feels constrained to call it not the building but the destroying of
the temple of God. He trusts, however, that God will
frustrate their evil designs and overwhelm them with
destruction.

It was impossible for anyone to boast with pride that
he was a follower of Peter in a Church founded by Paul,
without at the same time belittling Paul, the inevitable
result of which, especially where opposition already

existed between the admirers of Paul and of Apollos, must have been an increase of the confusion and the insubordination to Paul of which there were already tokens enough. These followers of Peter were responsible, at least primarily, for the aspersions against which Paul defends his apostolic dignity, even in i. 1, more clearly in ix. 1–3, and in somewhat different tone in xv. 8–10. It was argued that a man who had never seen the Lord Jesus, the Redeemer, in the flesh, could not rank as an apostle in the full sense in which this title belonged to Peter and to the other disciples whom Jesus Himself had called and trained for their mission. But by placing the appearance of Jesus, to which was due his conversion and call, on the same level with the personal intercourse between Jesus and His disciples (ix. 1), especially with the appearances of the risen Lord to His disciples (xv. 5–8), Paul claims for himself the full apostolic title and all the rights which belonged to the other apostles. Inasmuch, however, as he aims to avoid any protracted argument on this point with these opponents who had come from abroad, simply insisting that the Corinthians shall recognise him as their apostle (ix. 2, cf. iii. 10, iv. 15), he makes in this letter only a few pointed remarks about these followers of Peter. One observes that Paul knows more than he writes, and fears more than he knows. Possibly he found it advisable, before saying any more, to wait until he saw the effect of the threatening hint which he makes in this letter, perhaps also until he was more accurately informed as to what these persons were doing.

He does say more in 2 Cor., and such parts of this letter as bear upon this subject may be discussed here, though there is no doubt that in the meantime not only had Paul learned more about these persons, but also their work in Corinth had assumed larger proportions. If the followers of Peter mentioned in 1 Cor. were Jewish Christians who had come from Palestine, and were exert-

ing a very active and in Paul's judgment destructive
influence in and over the Church in Corinth, then they
can be no other than the persons against whom Paul
directs his attack in 2 Cor. ii. 17 ff., v. 12, xi. 1–12, 18.
They had come to Corinth with letters of recommendation
from outside authorities (iii. 1), and on the basis of these
letters they claimed to possess authority at least equal to
that of Paul.   They boasted the purity of their Judaism,
and made the Gentile Christians in Corinth feel the
superiority which this gave them (xi. 18–22); to which
Paul objects that the assumption of this air of superiority
on their part only shows that the advantages which they
claimed were merely external and borrowed, and not
based upon their consciousness of personal merit and
personal service (v. 12, cf. iii. 2).   In preaching the word
of God, they employ all the tricks which the salesman uses
to get rid of his wares (ii. 17, cf. iv. 2, xi. 13, ἐργάται
δόλιοι, cf. Phil. iii. 2).   They were travelling preachers,
and had therefore the same formal right to call themselves apostles as Barnabas, Silas, and Timothy, and they
thought also the same right as Paul (cf. *Skizzen*, 53–65).
They accepted the hospitality of the Corinthian Church,
and took advantage of their position as evangelists to
claim support from their hearers.   Paul's refusal to do so
they declared to be proof of lack of faith in his calling
and of want of love for the Church ; it was only a shrewd
device on his part, they said, to get the Church more
entirely under his control (xi. 7–12, xii. 13–18).   These
facts make it very clear why he discusses this topic in
1 Cor. ix. 1–18 with a detail which, considering the
particular theme of 1 Cor. viii.–x., is out of all proportion.
He does it because even here in the first letter he has in
view these followers of Peter who refused to admit that he
had the same apostolic rights as the Twelve (1 Cor. ix. 1).
It is for this same reason that he makes special mention of
Cephas among the brethren and apostles of the Lord in

1 Cor. ix. 5. To a certain extent Paul recognises the
formal right of these wandering preachers to call themselves apostles, when with "foolish boasting" he compares himself to them (2 Cor. xi. 21 ff.), and calls them
"the very chief apostles" (xi. 5, xii. 11, cf. xi. 23, n. 13).
But he does not hesitate at all to express his real opinion
of them, comparing them to the serpent who deceived
Eve, and calling them false apostles and servants of
Satan, who make pretence of being apostles of Christ and
servants of righteousness (xi. 3, 13–15). It was because
their only purpose was to deceive that they made no
direct attack upon the gospel which Paul had brought to
Corinth.   That they did not is proved absolutely by
the fact that, while these persons are condemned in the
strongest possible terms by Paul, there is not a single
passage in either of the letters in which he opposes or
warns his readers against "another gospel" (Gal. i. 6), or
even against doctrine inconsistent with the one gospel of
Christ (contrast with Col. ii. 6–8, 20–23 ; Eph. iv. 14 ;
Heb. xiii. 9).   It was just because these teachers from
abroad had no Jesus and no gospel to preach other than
those which Paul had preached before them, and no Holy
Spirit to offer their hearers other than the one they had
received when the gospel was preached to them for the
first time, that it seemed to Paul so incomprehensible and
so uncalled for that the Corinthians should receive these
intruders, and allow themselves to be alienated from their
own apostle by their influence (2 Cor. xi. 4, n. 13).   Paul
is certainly afraid that they may succeed in accomplishing
more, by their cunning devices depriving the Church
altogether of its simple and primitive Christian faith
(2 Cor. xi. 3).   That, of course, would involve subsequent
corrupting of the gospel which the Corinthians had
believed (1 Cor. xv. 1).   There could be no doubt as to
the direction which this falsification would take.   By
boasting the purity of their Judaism (2 Cor. xi. 22), these

persons had made an impression upon the Gentile Christians which amounted virtually to moral influence over them, and the Gentile Christians had allowed themselves to be imposed upon by them (cf. 1 Cor. vii. 18 f., above, p. 265 f., n. 4). Hence to the apostle, who saw in the indirectness and deceitfulness of these persons only proof that their false Jewish ways had not been overcome by the life-giving truth of the new covenant and by the liberating spirit of Christ (2 Cor. ii. 14–iv. 6), it must have seemed that the only possible outcome of ,the unhealthy development of things in Corinth, which he was striving to check, was a form of Christianity corrupted by Jewish influences. But at the time when 2 Cor. was written, and less so when 1 Cor. was written, there were no positive indications that this was to be the outcome.

It is only from the way in which they are contrasted with each other that we are able to understand the three watchwords in which the names of Paul, of Apollos, and of Cephas were misused ; the same is true of the fourth, ἐγὼ δὲ Χριστοῦ, which Paul condemns quite as much as he does the others (1 Cor. i. 12). Since taken by itself no fault can be found with the expression Χριστοῦ εἶναι, which simply expresses the fact that to be a Christian means to belong to Christ (1 Cor. iii. 23 ; 2 Cor. x. 7 ; Rom. viii. 9 ; Mark ix. 41), what was to be condemned was the way in which individuals claimed this prerogative of belonging to Christ for themselves in opposition to the other members of the Church, instead of endeavouring, as Paul did, to impress upon the mind of the Church, so rent by factions, the fact that they all belonged to Christ, and that it was in the one indivisible Christ that they were to find their own unity and at the same time the bond between themselves and all other Christians (1 Cor. i. 2, 13, iii. 11, 23). Even if the Christ party had opposed their ἐγὼ δὲ Χριστοῦ to the other watchwords, thinking that thereby they raised themselves above the petty

squabbling of the rest, they could not have expressed
it in this way if they were endeavouring to defend the
authority which Paul and Apollos possessed through their
connection with the history of the Church, against the
misuse which was being made of their names and against
the despicable criticisms of the followers of Peter, as Paul
himself was doing, and as he insisted the Church ought to
do (1 Cor. iii. 5–iv. 5, ix. 1–6 ; 2 Cor. iii. 2 f., v. 12, xii. 11).
As contrasted with the tendencies represented by the other
watchwords, the ἐγὼ δὲ Χριστοῦ represents a conscious and
studied indifference to all human authority, an insolent
ignoring on the part of those who used it of all dependence for their Christian faith upon things historical.   If,
now, it is clear from the way in which the Church expresses
itself in the letter to Paul and from the way in which
Paul addresses the Church in his reply, that the Corinthians had an exaggerated sense of their independence of
all authority, this watchword which some individuals were
using can only be taken as an extreme expression of this
feeling of independence to which the Church as a whole
was inclined.   Just as the self-consciousness of the Church,
which was so inconsiderately expressed in their communication to Paul, was based upon the exceptional endowment of its members with natural and Christian gifts,
so it is impossible to conceive of anyone as saying ἐγὼ δὲ
Χριστοῦ unless he were possessed of exceptional ability, or
thought that he was.   If Paul charges the Church with
being conceited (v. 2, cf. viii. 1 f., xiii. 4), even more
emphatically does he accuse individuals of so being (iv.
18 f.).   It was presumptuous enough for individuals to
take sides with Apollos or Cephas against Paul, and *vice
versâ* (iv. 6), but this was not to be compared with the
presumption of the individual who, from an exaggerated
sense of his own independent knowledge, met these
expressions of some particular human authority with the
assertion that he belonged to Christ.   Consequently Paul

endeavours to bring not only the Church in general (xiv. 36), but also the individual who feels himself to be of importance (iv. 7, xiv. 37), to the consciousness that everything of which he boasts has been received from God through other men.

This same relation between the Church as a whole, which Paul addresses in his letter as " you," and the individuals whom he singles out as leaders in this general movement toward independence, we meet again in 2 Cor. x. 1–11. Paul makes the return of the Church to a state of entire obedience (x. 6) the condition of any action on his part against individual revolters or evil-doers ; since he cannot and will not proceed to discipline such individuals without the co-operation of the Church. If, now, it be asked why as yet the Church had not resubmitted itself entirely to Paul's authority, we have the following answer :—There was someone in the Church who believed and boasted that he belonged to Christ, as if Paul could not claim this same distinction for himself (x. 7), someone who was bold enough to talk about the apostle's egotistical letters and his unimpressive personal appearance (x. 10 f., cf. x. 1). Just as we are unavoidably reminded by the Χριστοῦ εἶναι (x. 7), for which nothing in this context calls, of the watchword in 1 Cor. i. 12, so we must assume that the strongest expressions of insubordination to Paul came from the Christ party (e.g. 1 Cor. iv. 18 ; 2 Cor. x. 9–11), and that to them more than to anyone else was due the danger of a rupture between the Church and its apostle, and so between the Corinthian Church and the whole body of Christians.

The fact that there are no long sections in either letter devoted especially to opposing the Christ followers, is explained by the relation, pointed out above, of this movement to the tendency of the Church as a whole. Very probably it was one of the Christ party who was entrusted by the Church with the preparation of the

communication sent to Paul. What Paul said in replying
to the Church he said primarily for the benefit of those
members of the Christ party who were so conscious of
their Christian knowledge and discernment with the freedom and independence which these involved.

It was high time that Paul should express his mind.
It was impossible for him to leave the settling of matters
in Corinth to Timothy, who possibly had left Ephesus
before the arrival of the latest oral and written reports
from Corinth, and who could not go to Corinth at once
on account of his errands in Macedonia (iv. 17, xvi. 10,
above, p. 259). Since, moreover, in spite of all possible
haste, the summer now beginning (above, p. 259 f.) might
end before his own arrival in Corinth (xvi. 5, iv. 19),
Paul saw that there was occasion to discuss thoroughly
in an extended letter not only the questions that had
been asked him by the Church, but also the unfortunate
condition of affairs of which he had been informed by
members of the household of Chloe and by the three
messengers of the Church. In this manner he hoped to
prepare the way for the visit which had been announced
some time before, and, so far as possible, to keep that
visit free from the painful necessity of discussing off-hand
and orally the numerous aggravated and threatening
questions arising out of the conditions in the Church
(cf. also xvi. 2). He presented himself to the Church
rod in hand, but at the same time with all the love of a
father who would much prefer to forgive than to punish;
it is for them to decide how he shall come to them
(iv. 21).

The agreement between the letter and the occasion
for it indicated in the letter itself is so entire, and, besides
this, the letter is so strikingly testified to by the letter of
the Romans to the Corinthians, written in the year 96,
that no reasonable doubt can be entertained as to the
genuineness and unity of the Epistle.

1. (P. 274.) If, with Semler and Hofmann, we read οἶδα μέν, viii. 1, we have only more definitely expressed what in any case is self-evident, namely, that πάντες γνῶσιν ἔχομεν is a proposition which Paul simply accepts—in other words, his statement is nothing more than a quotation from the letter sent him by the Church. Between this preliminary concession and viii. 7 there is no contradiction, particularly since here γνῶσις has the article. Even the "liberals," who boast about their knowledge, lack the right sort of knowledge (viii. 1-3); while, on the other hand, those who are "weak" lack that complete knowledge which everybody assumes they have, and without which action such as theirs seems to be done against conscience. Moreover, the unexampled use of οἰκοδομεῖν, viii. 10, is explained only on the supposition that Paul is ironical, flinging back at the Corinthians their own expression, as if he meant to say: "Fine edification, this!" (cf. above, p. 260 f.). It may be that i. 4–7 also are expressions quoted by Paul from the letter sent by the Church (cf. P. Ewald, NJbfDTh. 1894, S. 198–205).

2. (P. 275.) In x. 14 the correct reading is φεύγετε ἀπὸ τῆς εἰδωλολατρείας, not φεύγετε τὴν εἰδωλολατρείαν (cf. vi. 18). The latter, taken literally, would be a superfluous exhortation; and in any case an exaggerated characterisation of what had actually taken place. From x. 15–22 it is clear that Paul had in mind, primarily if not exclusively, participation in the sacred meals connected with the idol sacrifices (cf. viii. 10, x. 7). So also 2 Cor. vi. 16, which refers to nothing more nor less than an approach on the part of the Corinthians toward idolatry occasioned by too intimate social connection with their pagan environment.

3. (P. 277.) In vii. 3-6, 10-14, 27a, 28a, 36, 38a, 39, Paul combats the false ascetic tendency of a minority for whose errors the Church, in its letter, evidently had made the example of Paul and occasional opinions expressed by him responsible. This is proved by vii. 6, which, rightly understood, cannot refer to the positive commands in ver. 2 or vv. 3–5a, but only the concession (εἰ μήτι) in 5b.

4. (P. 277.) The expression γυναῖκα τοῦ πατρός, v. 1, would be inconceivably weak if by it were meant the man's own mother, not his stepmother, cf. Lev. xviii. 8 contrasted with xviii. 7. So also Sanhedr. vii. 4 (cited by Wetstein, ad loc.), where it is likewise stated that it makes no difference whether the father is still living or not. If 2 Cor. vii. 12 deals with the same case, the father was still living. A marriage contracted between a man and his stepmother, whether the father was living or not, was not admitted as legal by Roman law, and so would not be recognised in Corinth. It is clearly not such a marriage as this that is here described by ἔχειν; neither, on the other hand, is it a single lustful transgression, one adulterous act, but the relation is that of concubinage (cf. John iv. 18). The stepmother had evidently left the house of her husband and taken up her residence with her stepson, at his request, who, for this reason, is described in v. 2 as ὁ τὸ ἔργον τοῦτο πράξας; also in v. 3, particularly in view of certain aggravating circumstances unknown to us, as ὁ οὕτως τοῦτο κατεργασάμενος; and, in view of his offence against the father, in vii. 12, as ὁ ἀδικήσας (cf. § 20, n. 6). Since Paul makes no reference whatever to the guilt of the woman, who must also have been involved in the transgression, it is probable that neither she nor her

husband were members of the Church. And so Paul follows the rule laid down in 1 Cor. v. 12.

5. (P. 279.) It is a peculiar fact that thanks are given in i. 4–9 not for the religious and moral condition of the Corinthian Christians, nor for the practical proof of their faith in conduct and suffering (cf. *per contra*, 1 Thess. i. 3 ; 2 Thess. i. 3, ii. 13 ; Eph. i. 15 ; Col. i. 4 ; Phil. i. 5), but simply for their charismatic gifts, and it is specially worthy of note that in i. 5 speech of every kind is mentioned before knowledge (cf. the order of gifts, xii. 8 ff., xiii. 1, 8, and the opposite order in 2 Cor. xi. 6). If from xiv. 37 it is clear that πνευματικός does not mean simply the person who has a χάρισμα, but, like προφήτης, the one who has a special χάρισμα, and specifically, as the context shows, the person with the gift of tongues who spoke "in the spirit" in a higher degree than did the prophet and the teacher (xiv. 2, 14–19, 23), then the theme περὶ τῶν πνευματικῶν, stated in xii. 1, does not refer to spiritual gifts in general, but either to those who speak with tongues (οἱ πνευματικοί), as in xiv. 37, or, as in xiv. 1, to the gift of tongues itself (τὰ πνευματικά distinguished from προφητεύειν), of which there were several kinds.

6. (P. 281.) The principle advanced in the preaching, that no natural or social distinctions were to be recognised in the Church (xii. 13), seems to have been applied in Corinth to the question of slavery in a way not pleasing to Paul. For it will be observed that in vii. 18–23, where marriage is discussed, the example of slavery is used as well as that of circumcision ; but it is highly improbable that Paul would have expressed such decidedly though briefly stated opinions about these two relationships in a purely theoretical way, and without any practical occasion from conditions to be found in Corinth. The slave is not to think his condition inconsistent with his Christianity ; on the other hand, he is not to think that in all circumstances he must remain a slave (cf. *Skizzen*, 145, 348, A. 9–11).

7. (P. 281.) Τῇ ἐκκλησίᾳ τ. θ., x. 32, does not mean the local Church at Corinth, but, as in xii. 28, the whole body of Christians ; for there is no contrast here, as in xi. 22, between the individual members of the Church residing in different homes—some poor, others wealthy—and the assembled Church. Rather, in accordance with the general principle laid down in x. 31, is it the entire body of Corinthian Christians, who, in x. 32, are urged to conduct themselves in such a way as not to offend the non-Christians among whom they live, nor the larger Christian body of which they are only a part. Otherwise we should read not τῇ ἐκκλησίᾳ τ. θ., but τοῖς ἀδελφοῖς, τοῖς ἀσθενέσιν, ἀλλήλοις, or something of the sort. The correctness of this interpretation is confirmed also by such passages as xi. 16 (αἱ ἐκκλησίαι τ. θ.), iv. 17, vii. 17, xiv. 33, 36.

8. (P. 282.) The placing of ἡγιασμένοις ἐν Χρ. Ἰ. right after θεοῦ, i. 2, in BD*G is too original not to be genuine. If, however, we place these words after Κορίνθῳ, then the immediately following κλητοῖς ἁγίοις seems to be a needless repetition of essentially the same thought of the holiness belonging to the Corinthians as members of the Church, unless the idea of "called saints" goes with the following σὺν πᾶσιν κτλ. by which it is rounded out. In no case can σὺν πᾶσιν κτλ., following the delusive analogy of 2 Cor. i. 1 ; Phil. i. 1, be joined with τῇ ἐκκλησίᾳ . . . Κορίνθῳ as a completion of the address : for

"all who call upon the name of Christ" is the broadest possible designation for all who profess Christianity (Rom. x. 12 ; 2 Tim. ii. 22 ; Acts ix. 14, 21). Nor can the necessary restriction be secured by connecting αὐτῶν after τόπῳ with the remote κλητοῖς ἁγίοις . . . Κορινθίοις instead of with τοῖς ἐπικαλουμένοις and taking σὺν πᾶσιν κτλ. to mean the worshippers in every locality belonging to the Corinthians, i.e. in the cities belonging to Corinth. For τόπος τινός does not mean the region belonging to one, but the place which one occupies ; and, besides, the other cities of Achaia where there were Christians (Cenchrea, Athens) did not belong to the Corinthians. Holsten's view (456) that "all the worshippers of Christ in all their places" mean the Christians who had migrated to Corinth from all possible places, requires no refutation. "The Catholic idea" (Holsten, 453), which such distortions as this are intended to explain away, characterises the letter throughout (above, p. 281). To this point of view Paul commits himself personally when he adds καὶ ἡμῶν (without τε, following א*A*BD*G and the earlier translations). If αὐτῶν καὶ ἡμῶν is certainly to be taken with τόπῳ and is not a supplementary explanation of the preceding ἡμῶν—which no reader could surmise—Paul says, using a not unfamiliar form of expression (Rom. xvi. 13), that every place where there are worshippers of Christ is his own and Sosthenes' place, i.e. they feel themselves at home there. The Corinthians lack this genuinely catholic or ecumenical sense.

9. (P. 283.) Räbiger (Krit. Untersuch. über den Inhalt der beiden Briefe an die kor. Gemeinde, 2te Aufl. 1–50) gives a relatively complete summary of the various views about party conditions in Corinth. Clement's view (1 Cor. xlvii.) of the condition mentioned in 1 Cor. i. 12, διὰ τὸ καὶ τότε προσκλίσεις ὑμᾶς πεποιῆσθαι, and immediately afterwards ἡ πρόσκλισις ἐκείνη . . . προσεκλίθητε γὰρ ἀποστόλοις μεμαρτυρημένοις καὶ ἀνδρὶ δεδοκιμασμένῳ παρ' αὐτοῖς, is more correct than that of the majority of modern critics. Because Clement takes no account of ἐγὼ δὲ Χρ. as occasionally Origen (Hom. ix in Ez., Delarue, iii. 388, but not tom. xiv. 1 in Mt. p. 616) and Adamantius (Dial. in Marc. i., Delarue, 809 ; Caspari, Anecd. 12) fail to do, Räbiger, 2, ascribes to him the opinion that in Paul's time there were not four but three parties at Corinth, "who, appealing to the respective teachings of Paul and of Peter and of Apollos, opposed one another." In reply, it is to be observed (1) that the opinion that these so-called parties were founded upon special teachings of Paul, Peter, and Apollos is arbitrarily read into Clement's words, while it is just the opposite view that we find in Paul's 1 Corinthians. (2) There is no justification for saying that it would have been inappropriate for Clement, who found no corresponding party in the Corinthian Church of his time, mechanically to have repeated the fourth watchword. Certainly that does not apply to Adamantius, whose purpose was to prove to the Marcionites that men ought not, like them, to bear the name of a man (Marcion), but only the name of Christ. (3) It is taken for granted that πρόσκλισις means "party," which is refuted by the description of all these varied προσκλίσεις by the singular ἡ πρόσκλισις ἐκείνη (see just above). The term means rather an inclination toward, preference for, attachment to individuals (Clement, 1 Cor. xxi. 7, l. 2 ; 1 Tim. v. 21). In contrast to the careful language of Clement is the manner in which the elder Lightfoot (Horæ hebr. ad 1 Cor. i. 12) and Vitringa (Observ. sacræ, ed. Jenens. 1725, pp. 799–812) and also Baur (i. 292 ff.)

speak of a *schisma* in the later ecclesiastical sense of the word, and of four *sectæ* into which the congregation had been divided and which possibly held their religious services in different places (Vitringa, 812). The very first presupposition upon which a correct interpretation rests is the recognition of the fact that the situation as disclosed in i. 12 is not a sort of μετασχηματισμός, iv. 6, as was taught by the Syrian Ephrem (*Comm. in ep. Pauli*, ed. Mechith. 48), by Chrysost. (Montf. x. 16, iii. 138, 347), by Theodoret and others ; in other words, that the names there mentioned are not mere disguises for entirely different persons who were party leaders in Corinth. This is an error which Beza was the first definitely to oppose (*NT*, 1582, ii. 93). As clearly proved by the λέγω δὲ τοῦτο, which shows that the following words are explanatory, by the earnest defence of Paul's manner of preaching i. 17 ff., and by the statement in iii. 4–8, there is no question that Paul and Apollos, Peter and Christ, were the persons whose names were actually used in Corinth as party watchwords. Furthermore, it is clear beyond question that the term ἐγὼ δὲ Χριστοῦ was employed by certain Corinthians to distinguish their point of view from that of other members of the Church. Had Paul desired in this formula to set his own standpoint over against the three other views, and to recommend it to the Corinthians (as the older critics suggested, especially Mayerhoff, *Einl. in die petrin. Schriften*, 1835, S. 81) in opposition to the ἕκαστος ὑμῶν λέγει, it would have been necessary for him to say, ἐγὼ δὲ λέγω ὑμῖν, ὅτι Χριστοῦ εἰμι, or more correctly, ὅτι ὑμεῖς (ἡμεῖς) πάντες Χριστοῦ ἐστε (ἐσμεν), or ἀντὶ τοῦ λέγειν ὑμᾶς (Jas. iv. 15) ὅτι Χριστοῦ ἐσμεν. Still more preposterous is the interpretation of Räbiger (76 f.), according to which ἐγὼ δὲ Χριστοῦ is taken with each of the three other watchwords as a sort of supplement : "I belong to Paul, but in belonging to Paul I belong to Christ," etc.; for, apart from the absolute grammatical impossibility of this construction, the opinion that in these sentences we must seek the common confession of movements in all other respects divergent, rests upon a misunderstanding of ἕκαστος ὑμῶν, which here has its ordinary distributive force (1 Cor. iii. 5, 8, 13, vii. 7, 17, xi. 21, xiv. 26, xv. 23, xvi. 2), and is to be contrasted with τὸ αὐτὸ λέγητε πάντες (i. 10). Furthermore, the suggestion that the Christ party might appeal to Paul himself in justification of their watchword is without foundation ; for Paul never claimed the Χριστοῦ εἶναι for himself as opposed to other Christians ; but, on the contrary, in i. 2–10 he repeatedly speaks of "the name of *Our* Lord Jesus Christ" as the unifying term which excludes all schism, and gathers together into one all the Churches in the world and all members of the several Churches. This is referred to again in iii. 23 and in 2 Cor. x. 7, where, opposing the Christ party, Paul asserts that the Χριστοῦ εἶναι belongs to him as well as to them ; cf. 1 Cor. vii. 40, where there is the same contrast. Nor is any difficulty presented by the first question in i. 13, for it is a question in spite of the absence of μή, which is not absolutely necessary, and which is omitted here because of the repetition of the same sound that would be caused by its insertion. Certainly it is not directed against the Christ followers alone (Baur, i. 326 ; Hofmann, ii. 1, 18), but to them along with the rest. The members of the Christ party were quite like the representatives of the other movements, who, because of their attachment to Paul or Apollos or Cephas, thought themselves in possession of a better Christianity than the others, possessing as it were a

larger portion of Christ ; but without denying that the others were Christians.
Only the watchword which the Christ party adopted was the most presumptuous of all, and expressed most strongly the opinion that they had an
incomparably greater interest in Christ than all the rest. It is exegetically
and historically impossible to suppose that the Christ party was composed
of Jewish Christians from Palestine, who either boasted that they had
heard the preaching of Jesus (Grotius, ii. 366 ; Thiersch, 141 ; Hilgenfeld,
265), or who, although essentially identical with the followers of Peter, called
themselves the Christ party, because those to whose authority they appealed,
namely, the older apostles and brothers of Jesus, had been called and
taught by Christ Himself as Paul had not been (Baur, ii. 296 ff.), or because
of their attachment to James the brother of the Lord (Weizsäcker, 277). The
latter suppositions rest upon the error that Paul is merely contrasting the
other party names with his own, and so is able to put side by side all manner
of watchwords—even such as are practically synonymous—in order to present
the confusion in the Church in a realistic way. But Paul does not say "the
one says this and the other that " ; on the contrary, he introduces the watchwords in contrast to each other. In the mind of those who are here represented as speaking, the ἐγὼ δὲ Χριστοῦ stands in just as sharp contrast to the
ἐγὼ δὲ Κηφᾶ as it does to ἐγὼ δὲ Ἀπολλῶ, and as the latter expression does to
the ἐγὼ μὲν Παύλου. It is a piece of purely arbitrary criticism to reduce the
tendencies expressed in the four watchwords to two fundamental groups, a
Gentile Christian and a Jewish Christian, which divisions would again fall
into two closely related groups, the followers of Paul and Apollos on the one
hand, and of Cephas and of Christ on the other,—particularly in view of the
fact that Paul dwells at length only upon the alleged minor contrast between
the followers of Paul and Apollos. Furthermore, it is incomprehensible how
those who could boast only of their relationship to the personal disciples or
relatives of Jesus could on that basis ascribe to themselves a special relationship to Christ. They had no advantages over any of the disciples of the personal disciples of Jesus in the world (Heb. ii. 3 ; 2 Pet. i. 16 ; 1 John i. 3),
certainly none over the party of Peter, from whom they desired to be distinguished, and whom at least they tried to outdo in boasting. Most fantastic
and unhistorical of all is the idea of a Jewish Christian party which refused
to acknowledge the authority of Peter—only a party of that character could
describe itself as ἐγὼ δὲ Χριστοῦ in contrast to ἐγὼ δὲ Κηφᾶ. The Judaisers
in Galatia looked upon Peter, John, and James as being equally pillars of the
Church (Gal. ii. 9), and in spite of their high estimation of James the pseudo-
Clementine literature nevertheless chooses Peter as its hero. Finally, it
cannot be denied that the name of the Saviour, personal contact with whom
gave Peter and James an advantage over Paul and other preachers, was Ἰησοῦς
not Χριστός (1 Cor. ix. 1, xi. 23 ; 1 John iv. 3). For this reason we are not
to imagine that in 2 Cor. v. 16 Paul is referring to personal contact with
Jesus. Here, as indeed from ii. 14 onwards, Paul speaks of himself in such
a way as to include with himself Timothy (i. 1) and the others who had
laboured with him in a true Christian spirit, as opposed to the Petrine
followers who had come to Corinth bringing letters of recommendation (ii.
17–iii. 1, v. 12). Not until vii. 3 does the "I" take the place of the "we."
If Paul says of himself and of his fellow-workers, first passionately and

then more soberly (v. 13), things that sound like self-praise, the Corinthians must know that the fear of Christ before whose judgment-seat they must give account and the love of Christ who died for all men are the standards by which they judge and act toward all men, both those who are yet to be converted and those who are Christians, and the standards also for their judgment of themselves.   To do the opposite would be an εἰδέναι or a γινώσκειν κατὰ σάρκα (v. 16).   Both the order of the words and the context make it clear that this latter expression means a human judgment determined by one's inborn nature and natural powers (cf. i. 17, x. 2–4).   Before God brought Paul to a recognition and acceptance of the reconciliation in the death of Christ, recreated him in Christ, and committed to him the proclamation of the word of reconciliation, his judgment was the judgment of man, *i.e.* κατὰ σάρκα, because his estimation of Christ, of whom he had heard and whom he was persecuting, was κατὰ σάρκα.   Since his conversion and call his situation has been different.   The contrast to the party of Peter again suggested in v. 12 would clearly imply that the manner in which these missionaries judged and treated people, and the manner in which they sought to obtain favour among the Corinthians, proved that their estimation of men was κατὰ σάρκα, which in turn was due to the fact that they did not know Christ as Paul had known Him since his conversion.   It may not be possible to identify καυχᾶσθαι ἐν προσώπῳ (v. 12) with ἀνθρώπους εἰδέναι κατὰ σάρκα (v. 16), nor can we assert that Paul makes the foolish affirmation that followers of Peter are fanatical antagonists of Christ and of Christianity, as he himself was before his conversion.   Nevertheless, here as in iii. 4 ff., iv. 1 f., 5 f., there comes to light Paul's opinion that the petty, secretive, selfish conduct of these persons was due to the fact that they had not, like the true preachers of the gospel, experienced in themselves the renewing and liberating power of the revelation of God in Christ, but had retained their Jewish nature.   The principal source of the confusion which has obtained regarding these parties is the utterly untenable theory that 2 Cor. x. 7 and sentences in the immediate context are connected with the polemic against the false apostles at whom xi. 1–12, 18 and even ii. 17–vi. 10 are directed.   The latter were wandering teachers who came to Corinth from abroad, bringing letters of recommendation from the place whence they came, whom Paul everywhere distinguishes from the congregation.   In 2 Cor. they are not once included in a single "you" with the Corinthians.   If they are identical with the followers of Peter (see above, p. 288 f.), then they are included among the Corinthian Christians addressed in 1 Cor. i. 12, but nevertheless in iii. 16–20 they are distinguished from the congregation which they are represented as making the subject of their harmful work, and in xvi. 22 are expressly excluded from the Church to which Paul sends his greeting.   On the other hand, in 2 Cor. x. 1–11 Paul is dealing exclusively with the Church itself, and that, too, in its corporate capacity as it was beginning again to subject itself to his authority, without having gone far enough to lend him full support in the performance of the required act of discipline in the Church (x. 6). It is impossible to assume that the individual to whom λογιζέσθω (x. 7b) refers belonged outside the circle to whom the βλέπετε (x. 7a) applies.   Practically the same charge which Paul refutes x. 9–11, in x. 1 is assumed to be generally made throughout the Church.   If the ἐγὼ δὲ Χριστοῦ in x. 7 refers to 1 Cor.

i. 12, then the members of the Christ party were not travelling teachers from abroad, but had been members of the Corinthian Church ever since conversion. Furthermore, one of the characteristics of a false apostle was lack of genuine self-reliance (v. 12), and of that openness and boldness of which Paul boasts in his own case and in that of all true servants of the new covenant (ii. 17–vi. 10). They make boasts after a fashion, but only superficially and concerning mere externalities (v. 12, xi. 18, 22), especially about the authorities from whom they have letters of introduction (iii. 1). Their weapons are malice and hypocrisy (ii. 17, iv. 2, xi. 3, 13–15, cf. 1 Cor. iii. 19 f., above, p. 288). How is it possible to identify these people with those in x. 7–11, where we have pictured in strong, almost reckless language a self-consciousness very blunt in its expression of itself, relying not upon foreign authorities nor upon external advantages, but upon its own attachment to Christ! At any rate, the contest against these false apostles from abroad does not begin, as in xi. 1, abruptly without any previous word of introduction. In x. 12–18, especially x. 15 (καυχώμενοι ἐν ἀλλοτρίοις κόποις), there is a very clear contrast to other missionaries. The polemic against the teachers from without which extends to xii. 18 begins with the command that the Church pay heed to what is before their eyes (x. 7). Between himself and his opponents the Church shall decide from the known facts in the case, to which he proceeds immediately to call their attention—particularly from xi. 7 on. But before he begins the presentation of these facts, it occurs to him that in the Church itself which he is challenging to an impartial consideration of the respective claims of himself and the followers of Peter, there are persons who boast of their indifference to the distinctions between the followers of Paul, Apollos, and Peter, and treat with contempt any appeal whatever to the authority of these persons, saying ἐγὼ δὲ Χριστοῦ (above, p. 292 f.). Even this prevented the proper adjustment of the matter. They accused Paul of defending his personal honour, especially against the followers of Peter, in just as perverted a way as did they, and of constantly sounding his own praises in his Epistles (iii. 1, v. 12, x. 12, 18, xii. 19). For this reason Paul prefaces his polemic against the party of Peter (xi. 1–xii. 18) with his apologetic remarks addressed to the Christ party, x. 7b–18. καυχήσομαι, x. 8, 13, refers to the unavoidable self-praise beginning with xi. 1 (cf. xii. 1, ἐλεύσομαι which follows). The τινὲς τῶν ἑαυτοὺς συνιστανόντων, x. 12, can refer to none other than the followers of Peter; and so throughout the entire polemic against the followers of Peter (xi. 1–xii. 8) there are interspersed apologetic remarks directed to the Christ party (xi. 1, 16–21, 30, xii. 1, 5 f., 11, 19). Hints of a defensive character directed against the Apollos followers occur only incidentally (xi. 6). Inasmuch, however, as only a single πεποιθὼς ἑαυτῷ Χριστοῦ εἶναι is addressed in x. 7–11, whereas elsewhere the Church is addressed in quite the same apologetic tone without any such distinction of individuals, we must conclude that the representatives of ἐγὼ δὲ Χριστοῦ, while not numerous, had great influence in determining the attitude of the Church.

10. (P. 287.) The opinion of Dionysius, who was bishop of Corinth about 170 A.D., that Peter as well as Paul had part in the founding of the Churches in Corinth and at Rome (Eus. *H. E.* ii. 25. 8),—an opinion that may have been shared also by Clement of Rome (*GK*, i. 806),—probably grew up as an inference out of 1 Cor., from which source also (iii. 6 f.) Dionysius took the expres-

sions φυτεύσαντες, φυτεία. Or it is possible that a later sojourn of Peter at
Corinth may have helped to give rise to the tradition. Only at the time
when 1 Cor. was written, and even before that time, such a visit would have
been impossible, because of the division of fields of labour made between
him and Paul (Gal. ii. 7–9 ; cf. *Skizzen*, 72 f., 90 f.). Additional evidence is
found in the complete silence not only of Acts, but also of 1 and 2 Corinthians.

11. (P. 288.) The question, "Were ye baptized in the name of Paul?"
(i. 13) is directed against those who laid great stress upon the importance of
being baptized by some one particular individual. In referring to himself as
an example in this question and in the discussion that follows, Paul does not
have in view particularly the followers of Peter, nor the two or three men in
Corinth whom he had actually baptized, *e.g.* Stephanas (i. 16, xvi. 15), of
whom he has nothing but good to say : for if these men had boasted of this
fact, Paul could not have expressed his gratification that this talk had no
application to himself because of the very few instances in which he had
performed the rite of baptism in Corinth. Rather does he complain that
his carefulness about this matter has been without effect. It is another case
of the ταυτὰ μετεσχημάτισα εἰς ἐμαυτόν of iv. 6. It is possible that Apollos
baptized his own converts (above, p. 270 f., n. 11) ; but it is not likely that any
special importance would have been attached to baptism administered by
Apollos. He was a gifted teacher, but could not be considered an important
link in the spiritual succession. On the other hand, it goes without saying
that a decided impression would have been made at Corinth by a Christian
from Palestine who said, "No less a personage than Peter baptized me at
Pentecost or later" (cf. Hofmann, ii. 2. 21). The writer surmises that it was
with a thrust at Peter and the original apostles generally, whom Jesus had
actually sent to baptize (Matt. xxviii. 19 ; cf. John iv. 2), that Paul disavowed
this custom for himself (i. 17). Cf. *ZKom. Matt.* 716.

12. (P. 288.) If we make the component parts of μαραναθα (xvi. 22), מרן
and אתא, then the most natural translation is, "Our Lord has come" (not "is
coming," or "will come"). Thus : S¹ קָרָן אָתָא (according to the Nestorian
pronunciation אֲתָא, bibl. Ar. אֲתָא Ezra v. 16, or אֲתָה Dan. vii. 22), and the
interpreters more or less familiar with Syriac : Chrysostom (Montf. x. 410,
ὁ κύριος ἡμῶν ἦλθεν) ; Jerome, *Onomast.*, ed. Lagarde, 75. 24, *venit* as perfect ;
and Theodoret (Noesselt, 215), who remarks correctly that this is not Hebrew
but Syriac (cf. a scholion in Scrivener, *Cod. Augiensis*, p. 488), and who,
following the ancient Syriac usage, translates קרן, ὁ κύριος, and κύριε (*e.g.*
Matt. vii. 22, Ss), without ἡμῶν, leaving the suffix = ἡμῶν untranslated. Cf.
the three scholia in Wetstein, *ad loc.*, ὁ κύριος (with or without ἡμῶν) ἦλθε,
al. παραγέγονε, *al.* ἥκει. Linguistically this translation is entirely correct,
and was, moreover, known to a Latin interpreter of about the year 370 A.D.,
the so-called Ambrosiaster (Ambros. *Opp.*, ed. Ben. ii. App. 170). It is also
accepted by Delitzsch (*ZfLTh.* 1877, S. 215 ; see also his *Hebrew N.T.*, 11th
ed., and Neubauer, *Stud. bibl.*, Oxon. 1885, p. 57). For the incorrect translation, ὁ κ. ἔρχεται, *Onomast. sacr.*, ed. Lagarde, 195. 65, and other impossible
interpretations, cf. Klostermann, *Probleme im Aposteltext*, 224 ff. Klostermann's own interpretation קָרֶן אֲתָא "Our Lord is the token," stands or falls
with his bold exegesis of ver. 22a, "If one does not kiss the Lord Jesus,"
i.e. "If anyone refuse the fraternal kiss" (ver. 20), and more than this fails

to harmonise with the later liturgical use of this formula (see below). This is true likewise of Hofmann's interpretation מר אנתה "Lord art thou" (cf. Ps. xvi. 2). Moreover, it is doubtful whether in Palestine the original n and the final a in the pronoun were still pronounced. The most probable interpretation is that first suggested by Halévy (*REJ*, 1884, ix. p. 9), and afterwards accepted by Bickell (*ZfKTh.* 1884, S. 403) and Nöldeke (*GGA*, 1884, S. 1023 ; cf. also Siegfried, *ZfWTh.* xxviii. 128, and Dalman, *Gr.*² 152), namely, מרנא תא "(our) Lord, come." The fuller form of the suffix -*ana* מראנא to be found in Nabatean inscriptions dating from the reign of Aretas IV. (2 Cor. xi. 32), and so from the time of Paul (*C. I. Sem.* ii. Nos. 199. 8, 201. 4, 206. 7, 208. 6, 209. 8), is just as likely to have been used by the apostle as the shorter form -*an*; while תא, the common Syriac form of the imperative from אתא, was current among the Jews (cf. Dalman, *Gr.*² 357), especially in combinations of words, *e.g.* תא וחי = ἔρχου καὶ ἴδε, John i. 46, and תא שמע "come and hear" (cf. Levy, *Neuhebr. Lexicon*, i. 184 ; Buxtorf, *Lex. talmud. rabb.* 248). So interpreted, the formula is quite the equivalent of the ἔρχου κύριε 'Ἰησοῦ (S² תא מריא ישו̈); cf. Rev. xxii. 20 ; for it makes no difference in the sense whether the exclamation precedes or follows (Ps. lix. 2, lxxi. 4, 12 ; 2 Sam. xiv. 4, 9). This accounts also for the occurrence of this formula at the close of the Eucharistic prayer in *Didache*, x. 6 (*Const. Ap.* vii. 26), no matter whether this prayer which immediately precedes the Amen be regarded as an invitation to the Lord to be present with His people in the sacrament, or as a petition for His speedy return to earth (cf. *Forsch.* iii. 294 ; *Skizzen*, 315, 318, 391). The Eucharistic prayers of the *Didache* originated in a country where Greek and Aramaic were employed side by side in the Christian communities (above, p. 12 f.), and where the word " mountain " had come to be used quite in the sense of " field " ; in other words, in Palestine (cf. Schulthess, *Lex. Syropal.* 73 ; *Didache*, ix. 4, ἐπάνω τῶν ὀρέων, omitted in *Const. Ap.* vii. 25). If, as seems probable, the *Didache* itself was prepared in Egypt for the use of Gentile Christian Churches, it follows that these Palestinian prayers, and with them the words *hosanna, maranatha*, and *amen*, must have become current far beyond the borders of Jewish Christianity in Palestine. It is a question, however, whether from this fact we ought to infer that the word *maranatha* was known in the Greek Churches founded by Paul from the very first. Here there was no occasion for the introduction of Aramaic prayer words used in the very early Churches, such as that afforded by the large Jewish population in Egypt (Philo, *c. Flacc.* vi, about one million). Nor is there any evidence that *maranatha*, like such words as *amen*, had a place in the liturgy of the Churches of Asia Minor and Greece. The threat which a reader of the Church lessons on the island of Salamis in the fourth or fifth century is said to have made against one who used his grave contrary to his directions (*C. I. Gr.* No. 9303 = *C. I. Attic.* iii. 2, No. 3509), λόγον δώῃ τῷ θεῷ καὶ ἀνάθεμα ἤτω. μαραναθάν (*sic*), is very manifestly borrowed from 1 Cor. xvi. 22, but without a clear understanding of its sense. A similar use of the word is to be found in a Latin inscription discovered at Poitiers and recorded by Le Blant (*Nouveau recueil des inscr. chrét. de la Gaule*, p. 259, No. 247). In view of all this, there can be little doubt that in quoting this fragment from the liturgy of the Palestinian Church, Paul meant to make unmistakable his reference to certain Christians from Palestine. This purpose would have been obscured had he added a

Greek translation (cf. *per contra*, Gal. iv. 6 ; Rom. viii. 15). The purport of the words is quite in keeping with the Pauline spirit. When he thinks of the disturbers of peace in the Church and its destroyers, of its unskilled workers and hostile critics, his mind turns to the day of judgment (iii. 13–20, iv. 5): "Lord, come and put an end to all strife, and to all the activity of hostile forces in Thy Church."

13. (P. 291.) In the conditional sentence, 2 Cor. xi. 4, what the writer regards as really contrary to fact is put in the present (cf. Matt. xii. 26 ; Rom. iv. 14 ; 1 Cor. ix. 17, xv. 13, 14, 16, 17 ; Gal. v. 11 ; Kühner-Gerth, ii. 466 f.). Although Paul does in one instance (Gal. i. 6) call the preaching of the Judaising missionaries a ἕτερον εὐαγγέλιον, he does not do it without immediately correcting this perverted use of the name gospel (i. 7). It is certain that there was not a second Holy Spirit whom the Corinthians could or must receive through the new preachers, after they had received the real Holy Spirit through the ministry of Paul. Still less was there another Jesus who could be preached at Corinth, after the one Jesus who was the common subject of the Christian preaching had been heralded there and made the foundation of the Church (1 Cor. iii. 11 ; 2 Cor. i. 19, iv. 5). Even if it were conceivable in the light of Gal. i. 6 that Paul might contrast the Christ preached by himself with the Christ preached by his opponents, calling the latter a ἕτερος Χριστός, he could not speak of a ἕτερος, or ἄλλος Ἰησοῦς, as the subject of actual preaching, since there was no second or third Jesus, in addition to Jesus of Nazareth, who could be preached. Furthermore, if the three relative clauses here inserted were meant to characterise a false gospel differing from the gospel of Paul and actually preached in Corinth, then it would be necessary to read παρ' ὃν ἐκηρύξαμεν, παρ' ὃ ἐλάβετε . . . ἐδέξασθε (cf. Gal. i. 8 f.), and ἡμεῖς would probably be inserted in order to express contrast to ὁ ἐρχόμενος. But as the clauses actually read they simply mean that the Corinthians have already received all the essential truths that a new missionary could bring them. Moreover, the apodosis of the sentence shows that Paul is here stating a condition contrary to fact in the present tense. If with BD* we read ἀνέχεσθε, then the sentence means that in this case—but only in this case—are the Corinthians open to no censure in tolerating strange teachers among them (καλῶς ποιεῖτε ἀνεχόμενοι τοῦ ἐρχομένου κτλ.), as they are in fact doing (xi. 19 f.). On the other hand, if we accept the more common reading ἀνείχεσθε, it can hardly be regarded as a simple imperfect, merely descriptive of the attitude of the Corinthians heretofore ; because this attitude toward the strange teachers continues to the present time (xi. 19 f.). Rather is the imperfect to be taken in the sense of ἀνείχεσθε ἄν, there being a transition from the first to the fourth form of the hypothetical sentence (John viii. 39, without ἄν ; Luke xvii. 6, with ἄν after a well accredited εἰ with the present indicative ; cf. Winer, § 42 ; Kühner-Gerth, i. 215). This, however, gives practically the same sense as ἀνέχεσθε. But since the attitude of the Corinthians toward the strange teachers is in Paul's judgment highly censurable, in this instance, where it is actually represented as commendable, the case must be purely hypothetical. The frequently suggested interpretation of καλῶς in a purely ironical sense, in reality expressing strong censure (Mark vii. 9), is scarcely permissible, even from the point of view of style, following as it does a conditional clause in no sense ironical. Nor is it more

permissible from the point of view of the thought ; for, if someone in Corinth were boasting about alleged spiritual benefits which he did not yet possess, and were debating in his own mind whether he should allow them to be bestowed upon himself, it would not be occasion either for irony or censure. No difficulty to the above interpretation of 2 Cor. xi. 4 is presented by its connection with what precedes ; since it is not ver. 4 alone which is connected with what precedes by γάρ, but rather the entire passage, xi. 4–xii. 18, is introduced by γάρ, in order to explain more fully xi. 2–3. And this explanation begins very properly with the concessive statement that the Corinthians would not be blameworthy anyway, i.e. Paul would not need to be anxious about them even if the case suggested in ver. 4 were actually true to fact. To assume the possibility of such a case was just as reasonable as to ask the questions in 1 Cor. i. 13 or 1 Cor. xiv. 36 ; for the Corinthians, in listening so patiently to the strange teachers, and in permitting them to carry on their work so long without any thought of separating themselves from Paul and his gospel, were acting as if these teachers were actually imparting to them new spiritual truths. The grammatical construction of the conditional sentence forbids the assumption that the reference in this passage may be to some possible future case, in which a certain newcomer, presumably one of the original apostles, whose immediate coming the false apostles had announced, is assumed to be engaged in preaching in Corinth (cf. Hausrath, Der Vierkapitelbrief des Paulus an die Kor. 19). It is impossible also to understand how so important a matter could be referred to in a manner so incidental and enigmatical. Ὁ ἐρχόμενος does not here mean the Great Expected One (Matt. xi. 3), still less one who has already come, i.e. some influential personality who can be connected with the strange teachers who have appeared in Corinth (cf. Ewald, Sendschreiben des Paulus, 225, 295, 298). On the contrary, it is used in a quite general sense (cf. Gal. v. 10, ὁ ταράσσων ὑμᾶς ; Eph. iv. 28, ὁ κλέπτων ; also Rom. iv. 4 ; 1 Cor. xiv. 2 ff.). In order to understand the passage, it is only necessary to assume that teachers from without had appeared in Corinth (cf. Didache, xi. 1, ὃς ἂν οὖν ἐλθὼν διδάξῃ ; xi. 4, πᾶς δὲ ἀπόστολος ἐρχόμενος πρὸς ὑμᾶς ; cf. xii. 1, 2). With this interpretation is refuted also the opinion of Baur (i. 318) and Hilgenfeld (Einl. 298), that οἱ ὑπερλίαν ἀπόστολοι (2 Cor. xi. 5, xii. 11) refers to the original apostles. Even if it were possible to suppose that Paul, writing in opposition to the exaggeration of the authority of the original apostles on the part of the followers of Peter, with the corresponding denial of his own apostolic authority, might speak thus ironically of the original apostles,—to which Gal. ii. 6, 9 suggest a certain though entirely insufficient analogy,—from the connection of xi. 5 and xi. 4 it is certain that he had in mind the false apostles and servants of Satan (xi. 13-15) who were active in Corinth at this time. The same is true of xii. 11, particularly in view of the fact that heretofore Paul has not been comparing himself and engaging in discussion with the original apostles, but only with strange teachers in Corinth (xi. 7-xii. 11). Nor is there anything in this context which would indicate that these persons relied on the authority of the apostles, and were exalting it at Paul's expense.

§ 19. SURVEY OF THE SECOND EPISTLE TO THE CORINTHIANS.

Unless the close connection between 1 Cor. and 2 Cor. be broken, either by the assumption that between the two there belongs an Epistle of Paul to the same Church, which is lost, or which must be searched for (n. 1), or by the assumption of an intervening visit (n. 2), or by the combination of these two hypotheses, 2 Cor. furnishes information both regarding the immediate effect of 1 Cor. and subsequent developments.

Timothy is mentioned in 2 Cor. as a joint writer with Paul of the letter ; but the case is not parallel to that of 1 Cor. i. 1 (above, p. 267, n. 6), since Timothy was one of Paul's helpers who had had an active part in the organisation of the Churches in Achaia (i. 19 ; above, p. 264 f., n. 2 ; cf. 1 Thess. i. 1 ; 2 Thess. i. 1). This explains why, contrary to his usage in 1 Cor. i. 4, Paul employs the first person plural from the very beginning of the letter, and uses it quite uniformly up to ix. 15, never exchanging it for the singular except for some good reason, and in only one instance expressly stating who is included in the " we," namely, when he refers to the pioneer preaching of the gospel among the Christians of Achaia, in which Silvanus as well as Timothy had taken part (i. 19). Consequently, as is self-evident, throughout the letter, except where the general nature of the statements made render it clear that all Christians or all like-minded preachers of the gospel are meant, the " we " includes primarily and certainly Timothy and Paul. This is true even of the concluding section chaps. x.–xiii., where, notwithstanding the fact that the introductory αὐτὸς δὲ ἐγὼ Παῦλος indicates that what follows is an expression of Paul's own opinion, in distinction from the joint communication of Timothy and Paul that precedes, we have an occasional substitution of " we " for " I " (n. 3).

Furthermore, it is to be observed that, unlike 1 Cor., 2 Cor. is not intended exclusively for the Church in Corinth, but also for all the other Christians throughout the province of Achaia (above, p. 264 f., n. 2). But if it were intended for the Corinthians only in the same way that it is meant for the other Christians in Achaia, the designation of the readers would certainly be different : either we should have the different places where the letter was to be read enumerated (cf. Rev. i. 4, 11 ; 1 Pet. i. 1), or all the Churches would be spoken of together as those of Achaia (Gal. i. 2 ; 1 Cor. xvi. 19 ; 2 Cor. viii. 1 ; Gal. i. 22 ; 1 Thess. ii. 14). The language of the greeting shows, therefore, that while the letter was intended primarily for the Corinthians, it was applicable also, either in whole or in part, to the other Christians in Achaia, and was intended to be communicated to them. In this respect the greeting is different from 1 Cor. i. 2 (above, 297 f., n. 8). Consequently, also, the address Κορίνθιοι in vi. 11 is not to be understood after the analogy of Phil. iv. 15, Gal. iii. 1, as if directed to all the readers, but its occurrence here is due to the fact that in some degree what precedes, and in particular what is said from this point on, is applicable only to the Church in Corinth. This same circumstance explains also the mention of the city in i. 23, which, following the repeated πρὸς ὑμᾶς, δι᾽ ὑμῶν, ἐν ὑμῖν, i. 15–19, is somewhat strange, and, like Κορίνθιοι, excepting the greeting of 1 Cor., which does not need to be taken into account here, is quite without parallel. The expressions in i. 15–19 mean " to, through, and in Achaia"; what follows in i. 23 applies only to the Corinthians.

There were, on the other hand, other things which affected just as vitally the remaining Christians in Achaia, particularly the matter of the collection spoken of in chaps. viii.–ix., in which they had all had a part (ix. 2 ; Rom. xv. 26). If Titus, who, let us assume, brought the

letter from Macedonia to Corinth (see below), journeyed by
way of Athens, he is likely at once to have made known
the contents of the communication which he bore to the
Christians in Athens and in other Christian centres in
Achaia *en route*; since he could not well have passed
through these places without stopping to greet them.
And inasmuch as he was also personally to superintend
the collection in Achaia, he is not at all likely to have
left it for the Corinthian Church to see that the letter was
circulated among the Churches of Achaia, particularly
since viii. 16–24 contained recommendations and proofs
of the identity of Titus and his companions quite essential
for carrying on the collection.   But it may be questioned
whether in these transactions Titus informed the other
Churches of the contents of the entire letter, which dealt
so largely with special conditions in Corinth, or only of
such sections as i. 1–22, viii. 1–ix. 15, xiii. 11–13.

The Epistle may be divided into three clearly defined
sections, chaps. i.–vii., viii.–ix., x.–xiii.   The framework
of the *first* section consists of three fragments of an
account of the apostle's journey.   While he was still in
the province of Asia, he and Timothy, who was with him,
were threatened with what seemed certain death (i. 8–10,
n. 4).   When he reached Troas and was minded to preach
the gospel there, a favourable opportunity having offered,
he found that he was not in a state of mind sufficiently
composed to do so, because he had not been met there by
Titus, whom he had sent to Corinth, and whose return he
awaited with the utmost anxiety.   In the hope of sooner
meeting him, he and Timothy left Troas at once and went
to Macedonia (ii. 12 f.).   After their arrival in Macedonia,
where this letter was written, and manifestly not very
long before its composition, Titus met him and cheered
his heart with good news from Corinth (vii. 5 f.).

The chronological as well as geographical arrangement
of the material is retained in the two following sections.

In chaps. viii.–ix. Paul speaks of events that were taking
place at the time in the Macedonian Churches where he
was, particularly of a recent decision, a decision made
since the arrival of Titus. He tells the Corinthians what
they did not yet know, and what possibly had not been
decided upon when Titus left Corinth, namely, that of
their own accord the Macedonian Churches had decided to
help in the collection for the Christians in Jerusalem, a
collection which had been going on in Corinth now for a
year, in fact since before the sending of the communication to which Paul replied in 1 Cor. (n. 5). Moved by
the commendatory reports of Paul and Timothy about the
collections in Achaia, and without Paul's having ventured
to ask it, the poor Macedonians had at once gathered a
sum which, in view of their circumstances, was considerable (viii. 1–4, ix. 2). They had already selected one of
their own number to accompany Paul and Timothy on
their journey with the collection by way of Corinth to
Jerusalem (n. 6). The zeal of the Macedonians in this
matter, which had been dragging on in Corinth for such a
considerable time, and the news brought by Titus regarding
the condition of the offering there, led Paul to ask Titus to
return to Corinth, whence he had come only a short time
before, in company with the representative of the Macedonian Christians and another brother, perhaps the person
chosen by the Churches in Asia for this very purpose, in
order to complete the collection (viii. 6, 16–24, ix. 3–5).

All that we learn from the *second* part of the letter
(chaps. viii.–ix.) regarding Paul's anticipated visit is, that
he did not mean that it should be delayed much longer.
He does not intend to wait for the return of Titus and his
companions. The two representatives of the Churches
are to make the first part of the journey, which was
to be completed in company with Paul, somewhat earlier
than the apostle, and in company with Titus rather than
Paul himself. The three are sent ahead to Corinth to

announce his coming (ix. 5), and to deliver the letter in the middle sections of which they had been commended to the Christians of Achaia.

It is not until the *third* section (chaps. x.–xiii.) that Paul speaks particularly of his own coming. The section begins with a contrast between his anticipated presence among the Corinthians and his absence from them up to this time (x. 1–10), and concludes with the same thought (xiii. 10). Once he expresses the hope of being able to preach the gospel in the regions beyond Corinth (x. 16). But the most important purpose of his coming is to establish order in Corinth, which as yet has not been fully restored (x. 6, xii. 14 f., xiii. 1 f.). He fears that he may find many of the old disorders and be compelled to make use of harsh measures (x. 2, xii. 20 f., xiii. 7–9). As he himself indicates at the close, the purpose of the letter, which is sent from a distance in spite of the fact that he expects to come himself so soon, is to spare himself the necessity of exercising with severity the authority given him by the Lord (xiii. 10), and this is the special purpose of chaps. x.–xiii. It is with this purpose in view that he requests the whole Church to submit itself with more entire obedience than it had done heretofore (x. 6), and resents so decisively the arrogant criticisms of himself and of his letters which were still being made in the Church, particularly by the Christ party (x. 1 f., vii.–xi., xiii. 3–6, above, p. 302). For the last time he threatens those who live immoral lives, and who, in spite of all exhortations, have not repented (xii. 21–xiii. 2).

The larger portion of this section is directed against the teachers from abroad, who, as we have seen, were the followers of Peter (above, pp. 289 f., 300 f.), and the Church is requested no longer to permit these aliens to carry on their pernicious work, which more than anything else had caused the trouble and bitterness in the relations between Paul and the Corinthians (xi. 1–xii. 18).

Tradition makes the Epistle a unit; and this pre-liminary survey shows it to be such, with an order which is both natural and logical. In spirit the reader follows Paul from Ephesus through Troas to Macedonia (chaps. i.–vii.); then he lingers with him for a moment in the Churches of Macedonia (chaps. viii.–ix.); finally, he is led to the consideration of conditions in the Church at Corinth from the point of view of Paul's coming visit there. The three sections of the letter treat respectively, the immediate past with its misunderstandings and explanations, the present with its practical problems, and the near future with its anxieties.

1. (P. 307.) The theory that after Timothy's return from Corinth Paul wrote a letter to the Corinthians which he sent to them by Titus,—a letter now lost and supposedly referred to in 2 Cor. ii. 3, 9, vii. 8,—was first put forth and defended by Bleek (*ThStKr.* 1830, S. 625 ff.). This theory was adopted, with varying degrees of confidence, by Credner (*Einl.* i. 371), Neander (*Ausleg. der Kr.* 272, 293 f.), Klöpper (*Untersuch. über den 2 Kr.* 1869, S. 24 ff.), by the same author in his *Kommentar* (1874, S. 42 ff.), and by many others. According to Lisco (*Die Entstehung des 2 Kr.* 1896, S. 1), there is beginning "to be a *consensus criticus*" (it were better perhaps to say *criticorum*) on this point. Klöpper admits (38 f.) that in 1 Cor. xvi. 5–7 Paul lays before the Corinthians a new plan for his journey, the plan which he was engaged in carrying out when 2 Cor. was written, as contrasted to his original plan, which had already been put before them, and which is described in 2 Cor. i. 15–16, and he (43) finds in I. xvi. 5–7 the announcement of "an early arrival in Corinth"; though in this passage, which was written at least some weeks before Pentecost, Paul says that he may possibly remain away until the beginning of winter, and in any event will not come immediately (above, p. 268 f.). When now, on the strength of this, there is posited a lost letter sent in the interval between 1 Cor. and 2 Cor., in which Paul "put off his visit and in general made it dependent upon certain conditions" (43), thus accounting for the accusations against which he defends himself in II. i. 12 ff., it may be observed that there is nothing to suggest that at the time of 2 Cor. there was any doubt as to Paul's actually coming. There is nothing in 2 Cor. like I. iv. 18; so that the charge which he meets in II. i. 17 has no reference to what he had said in a very recent letter, nor to a recent change in the plan of his journey, but to the original plan. Of course there was no occasion for this charge until after Paul had declared that he would not follow this but another plan. This he had done, however, with emphasis in I. xvi. 5–7, and when 2 Cor. was written this other plan had been practically carried out, with no recognisable changes. The assumption that in the interval between the writing of I. xvi. 5–7 and II. i. 12–ii. 2, Paul had expressed himself again

about the plan for his journey in a letter now lost, and in a manner essentially different from I. xvi. 5–7, and that the reference in II. ii. 3–9 is to this
lost letter, cannot be harmonised with the usual translation of II. ii. 3—τοῦτο
αὐτό = "even this." Nor does it gain support from the translation, "For this
very reason" (see below, § 20, n. 5). Unless it be assumed that Paul paid a
visit to Corinth during the same interval, which changed the whole situation,
and by which also the plans that were in mind when 1 Cor. was written were
set aside, this hypothesis renders the entire defence in II. i. 15 ff. meaningless.
Paul is accordingly represented as returning, after a temporary vacillation to
which expression had been given in the intervening letter, to the definite
plan stated in detail in I. xvi. 5–7. In other words, according to II. i. 15 ff.,
this plan must have been given up temporarily, and taken up again. It
would then be necessary for him to distinguish not merely two, but at least
three, and if our interpretation of I. xvi. 5–7 (below, § 20, and above, p. 268 f.)
be correct, four different stages in the development of this affair—(1) the plan
and the promise to come immediately to Corinth from Ephesus by the direct
route (cf. I. iv. 18) ; (2) the opposite plan which is set forth in detail in I. xvi.
5–7, with reasons for the determination not to come immediately, but after an
interval by the longer route through Macedonia ; (3) the later communication to the Corinthians, of which there is no record, that plan No. 2 had been
given up, and that he had returned to plan No. 1 ; (4) the return to plan
No. 2, which, at the time when II. i.–ix. was written, had already been practically carried out. Sufficient refutation of this whole theory is the setting
forth of the actual situation (cf. § 20). More than this is unnecessary
in regard to Hausrath's theory, that the lost letter sent between 1 and 2
Cor. is to be found in 2 Cor. x.–xiii. (*Der Vierkapitelbrief des Paulus an
die Kor.* 1870). The αὐτὸς δὲ ἐγὼ Παῦλος, x. 1, it is claimed, shows that
what follows is an appendix of Paul's to an entirely unrelated letter, possibly
a letter to the Corinthians from the Church in Ephesus, or from the Church
associated with the house of Aquila in Ephesus (28). This theory rests upon
the claim that, while in chaps. i.–ix. Paul speaks in an "undisturbed, most
loving, and peaceful state of mind," addressing the Corinthians only in words
of appreciation, in chaps. x.–xiii., on the other hand, he defends himself and
his companions against the darkest suspicions in a violently polemic manner,
making against the Corinthians the most serious charges (S. 2–5). This
claim is refuted by the simple restatement of the situation (§ 20). In detail,
while it is to be admitted that as a matter of fact the praise in viii. 7 is
more strongly expressed than the thanksgiving to God in I. i. 4 f.,—since
here, as in II. i. 24 (" For as regards faith ye stand "), in addition to knowledge and speech mention is made also of faith,—yet it is to be observed that
there is the same appreciation in I. xv. 1 f. as is found in the earlier chaps.
of 2 Cor. Furthermore, in this same section (chaps. i.–ix.) boast is made
of the zeal of Paul and Timothy for the Church, and of the love in their
hearts which the Corinthians had called out, and which had been wakened
into new life by the attitude of the Corinthians toward them that had
recently come to light (II. vii. 7, 11). No mention is made, however, of the
love of the Corinthians for Paul. But this boast is made only in contrast
to their lack of zeal and of an attitude toward the collection which corresponds to the love and praise of Paul. Although the apostle assures the

readers of his love, he does it in such a way as to make clear that this love is not yet adequately requited by the readers (cf. vi. 11–13, vii. 3, xi. 11, xii. 15), and, in view of their attitude toward certain matters about which Paul was very much concerned, not deserved. Moreover, it is not to be overlooked that this appreciation of the Corinthians occurs in that portion of the letter (chaps. viii.–ix.) which is addressed especially to the whole Church of Achaia (above, p. 308). Hausrath gets his very dark picture of the condition of affairs in chaps. x.–xiii. only by mixing up all of Paul's statements, complaints, denials, and defences, irrespective of whether they were directed against the Church, individual members of the Church, or teachers from without, and then painting the whole with these dark colours. For example, from xii. 16–18, Hausrath infers that the Church had accused Paul and his messengers of dishonesty, deception, and fraud in the matter of the collection (S. 4, 10, 18); but it is difficult to see why the same inference is not drawn from vii. 2 (οὐδένα ἐπλεονεκτήσαμεν), and why this passage, which is so much more immediately connected with the frank discussion of the matter of the collection in chaps. viii.–ix. than is xii. 16–18, is not treated as a gross contradiction of the situation portrayed in chaps. i.–ix. In the second place, it is to be observed that xii. 18 does not deal with the collection at all, but with the first sending of Titus (viii. 6), which had nothing to do with the collection (see below, § 20, n. 4). Chap. xii. 16 (cf. xi. 7–12, xii. 13–15) deals with the apostle's personal conduct on the occasion of his two former visits, and xii. 17 with all the persons who since the founding of the Church had come to Corinth as Paul's messengers. The language of xii. 16 and the context from xi. 7 on, prove that the accusations which are met in xii. 16 originated with the followers of Peter, and that the latter were compelled to admit that he had not been any expense to the Church, but, on the contrary, had completely renounced the right to be supported, which as a missionary he might have claimed. The accusation (ἀλλὰ ὑπάρχων πανοῦργος δόλῳ ὑμᾶς ἔλαβον), which stands in absolute contrast to the concession made in the words οὐ κατεβάρησα ὑμᾶς in xii. 16 (cf. xi. 9; 1 Thess. ii. 6, 9; 2 Thess. ii. 8), would be pointless, if by the very same words the claim were made that Paul had imposed upon the Corinthians the burden of collecting a sum of money, but in doing so had not acted openly, but with deceit. Grammatically and logically, the accusation can only mean that the shrewd apostle, by refusing all compensation for his labours, which seemed generous, but really showed his lack of love for the Corinthians (xi. 11), had in another respect outwitted them, since by this cunningly-devised means he had succeeded in making them morally more dependent upon himself. Consequently πλεονεκτεῖν is manifestly to be taken in the same sense in xii. 17, 18 (vii. 2); for although this word may have been chosen here because of Paul's refusal to accept compensation, its meaning is by no means confined to fraud in money matters (cf. ii. 11, and any lexicon). The light which this hypothesis throws upon the obscurities of chaps. i.–ix. is as small as the foundations upon which it stands are weak. Nor is there any hint in chaps. x.–xiii. regarding the time of Paul's proposed visit to Corinth, to say nothing of the recalling of his original plan. If these chapters were written by the apostle in Ephesus before he started for Macedonia by way of Troas, this alleged four-chapter letter furnished the Corinthians no occasion whatever for the complaints which Paul answers in i. 12–ii. 2. When the latter passage was written, the plan set forth in I. xvi. 5–7 had been practically carried out, and II. x.–xiii. shows no hesitation as to this plan—certainly no promise to do otherwise, such as might have given the Corinthians cause for complaint. The only strange thing is that in II. xii. 14, xiii. 1, Paul makes not the slightest reference to the plan for his journey to Corinth, which is so emphatically set forth in I. xvi. 5–7. The explanation is that at the time when II. i.–ix. was written, which is also the time when II. x.–xiii. was written, this plan had become fact, so that only references of a retrospective character, like those in II. i. 15–ii. 2, could be made to it.   Further, Hausrath's hypothesis furnishes not the slightest help in explaining the treatment of the individual case in II. ii. 5–11, vii. 11 f., and the matter of the collection in chaps. viii.–ix. ; for in chaps. x.–xiii. the matter of the collection is not once touched upon ; and where sinners are mentioned, against whom Paul fears it will be necessary for him to take strong measures when he comes (xii. 21–xiii. 10), there is no special reference to an individual case with which II. ii. 5–11, vii. 11 f. can be connected. The reference in xii. 21–xiii. 10 is to numerous offenders, whom Paul had threatened with punishment on the occasion of his second visit (xiii. 2), which by Hausrath also is placed before 1 Cor. But if the evil-doer of I. v. 1–13 was one of these offenders, then Paul laid himself open to ridicule for speaking in I. v. 1–13 with so much passion about a case with which he had long been familiar, and with which he had dealt at the time of his last visit. How much the hypothesis is worth Hausrath himself shows when he goes on to assume that the case of incest and the matter of the collection were dealt with in a lost letter of the Church of Ephesus to the Corinthians, to which Paul attached his private communication, chaps. x.–xiii. (28) ; for that is practically to confess that there is not a single independent word in chaps. x.–xiii. on these subjects which could have occasioned what is said in ii. 5–11, vii. 11 ff., viii.–ix.   Lisco (*Entstehung des 2 Kr.* 1896, according to the preface written in 1886) undertook to improve Hausrath's hypothesis by cutting out of this four-chapter letter xii. 11–19, and inserting in its place vi. 14–vii. 1,—a passage which has often been felt to break the connection (see below, § 20, n. 7),—putting xii. 11–19 in between vi. 13 and vii. 2, and by then assuming that i. 1–vi. 13, xii. 11–19, vii. 2 f., ix. 1–15, xiii. 11–13 constitute a second letter, chaps. vii. 4–viii. 24 a third. Several other attempts at division similar in character have been made, which it seems superfluous to describe at length. Cf. the comprehensive discussion by Hilgenfeld *ZfWTh.* xli. (1899), S. 1–19. It only needs to be mentioned that Semler, who (*Paraphr. in Epist. ad Rom.* 1769, p. 305 ff.) explained the greater part of Rom. xvi. as an appendix to Rom., holding that it was meant originally for the Corinthians, in his *Paraphr. Epist. II. ad Corinth.* (1776, pref. and pp. 238, 311–314, 321), suggested that 2 Cor. be divided into the following three Epistles—(1) the Epistle which Paul sent by Titus on the occasion of the latter's second trip to Corinth, chaps. i.–viii., xiii. 11–13 ; (2) an Epistle to the Christians in Achaia, chap. ix. ; (3) an Epistle to the Corinthians which Paul wrote after he had sent Titus the second time, *i.e.* after he had despatched (1), in consequence of new reports from Corinth of an unfavourable kind, chaps. x. 1– xiii. 10. It was this evidently that led Krenkel to maintain that Paul wrote this letter, x. 1–xiii. 10 (Semler's third letter), in Macedonia, after Titus and his companions, who had delivered in Corinth the letter composed of i. 1–ix. 15, xiii. 11–13 (practically Semler's first and second letters), had returned to Paul in Macedonia with fresh and painful reports.

2. (P. 307.) Following the example of Ewald (*Sendschr. des Paulus*, 216) and of many others, Krenkel, with especially detailed proof (154–211, 377), has recently advocated the placing of Paul's second visit in Corinth in the interval between 1 and 2 Cor., making it immediately precede the alleged intervening Epistle. The main proof of this position, namely, that this visit could not have taken place before 1 Cor. was written, has already been examined (above, p. 272, n. 14); likewise (above, p. 268, n. 7) the attempt to push 1 Cor. back from the last months of Paul's stay in Ephesus to an earlier time. Moreover, it will be shown in n. 5 that the Pentecost at which Paul was about to leave Ephesus (I. xvi. 8) belongs in the same Julian year (57) prior to the end of which 2 Cor. was written. It is possible that the departure from Ephesus was delayed, because of the delay in the return of Timothy (above, p. 269, n. 7); but it is just as likely to have been hastened because of the uprising led by Demetrius. These possibilities do not need to be taken into account here, so long as it is admitted that 1 Cor. was written several weeks before Pentecost of the year (57), before the close of which 2 Cor. was written (n. 5). Then in the interval between Pentecost and the end of December it would be necessary to place the following events (Krenkel, 377):—(1) a journey by Paul through Macedonia to Corinth, and a troubled stay in the latter place; (2) a return to Ephesus instead of the projected visit to Jerusalem; (3) the sending of Titus to Corinth with a letter of Paul's now lost, wherein announcement was made of his immediate coming for a third visit; (4) Paul's journey from Ephesus by way of Troas to Macedonia, where he meets Titus, and shortly afterwards writes 2 Cor. i.– ix., xiii. 11–13. Without taking into account at all the very clear connection between 1 Cor. xvi. and 2 Cor. i., which does not permit the intervention of a letter nor of a visit (§ 20), it must be confessed that (1) and (4) in this series give rise to the suspicion of being duplicates, due to the critic's double vision; that (2) is extremely improbable; finally, that in the case of (3) the alleged contents of the supposed letter do not harmonise with 2 Cor. ii. 3.

3. (P. 307.) From the fact that the "we" is retained in i. 3–12 it is to be inferred, first of all, that Timothy shared the extreme danger which Paul encountered while he was still in Asia. Assuming that the criticism which is answered in i. 13 was occasioned by something that was said in a previous letter, from the use of "we" it is not necessary to infer that Timothy was one of the authors of the letter; for the criticism is general, and has reference to the ambiguity of Paul's utterances in his correspondence, while in replying to this criticism Paul uses a present tense which indicates nothing as to time. Since Paul was engaged in writing a letter at this very time in conjunction with Timothy, as he had frequently done before, there was no reason why at this particular point he should change to the singular. When he does so temporarily in this immediate context (ἐλπίζω δέ), it is apparent that in expressing this hope that there may never be any further misunderstanding between him and the Church in the future, he has in mind the misunderstanding and un-

favourable criticism of the changing plans for his journey, which he proposes
to discuss at greater length in i. 15 ff. Inasmuch as i. 15–ii. 11 deals with the
announcement and carrying out of plans of journeys and with communications
by letter in which Timothy had no part, Paul retains the singular in speaking
of himself, except in i. 19–22 (cf. iii. 2), which treats of the missionary preaching in Achaia. In i. 23 with ἐγὼ δέ—which stands in contrast to the preceding ἡμεῖς—Paul returns to the discussion of personal matters already begun.
This singular is retained even in ii. 12 f., although, according to i. 8, Timothy
was with Paul either before or at the time of his departure from Ephesus, and
so certainly at the time of his sojourn in Troas ; changing again to the plural
in ii. 14 f., which, in spite of the general character of the statements, is to be
connected with the sojourn in Troas. However, in a very skilful way, the
apostle indicates that the responsibility for the sudden departure from Troas
rests not upon Timothy, whose movements are dependent upon his own, but
upon himself and his disturbed state of mind. With the exception of a single
ἐλπίζω δέ in v. 11 (cf. i. 13, xiii. 6), the plural is retained up to vii. 2, i.e. up
to the point where Paul returns again to the matters already touched upon in
ii. 5–11, in which Timothy had no direct part (vii. 3–16). Since Timothy
accompanied Paul to Macedonia, and was with him when Titus met him
there, and naturally took a lively interest in the news which Titus brought,
so occasionally here also we find the "we" (vii. 5–7, 13). Once there is a
sudden change to "we" in a context where "I" predominates (vii. 14).
First of all, it was a comfort to Paul that the boasts which he had made to
Titus about the Corinthian Church had not proved false. Since, however, he
saw fit to compare the truthfulness of this praise with the truthfulness of all
that he had said to the Corinthians, i.e. of his first preaching, in which
Timothy had taken part (cf. i. 19), it was natural after this reference to the
first preaching of the gospel in Corinth (ἐλαλήσαμεν) to represent Timothy as
sharing with him the boasting before Titus (ἡ καύχησις ἡμῶν), vii. 14 (cf.
ix. 3). This, of course, was possible only if Timothy was with Paul and
agreed with what he said when he talked with Titus about going to Corinth
(cf. Hofmann, ii. 3. 196). In chaps. viii.–ix. the "we" predominates, although
occasionally the "I" occurs (viii. 8, 10). The frequent interchange of the
pronouns in ix. 3–5 affords no reason for excluding Timothy from a single
"we." In chaps. x.–xiii. also the substitution of an occasional "we" for the
predominating "I" is not without significance. By x. 11a, xi. 21a, we are
reminded that this discussion of the personal relation of Paul to the Church
and his opponents is nevertheless part of a letter of which Timothy is one of
the authors ; by x. 12–16 it is suggested that Timothy is one of Paul's missionary helpers, well known to the Corinthians, and will continue to be such.
From x. 2b–v. 7b, xi. 12, we learn that the criticisms against which he found
it necessary to defend himself were also to some extent urged against his
helpers ; x. 6, 11b, xiii. 4–9, show that Timothy was to accompany Paul to
Corinth in the near future. This is indicated also by viii. 19, where the
individual whom the Macedonian Churches had chosen to accompany Paul on
his journey to Corinth and thence to Jerusalem is called συνέκδημος ἡμῶν not
μοῦ. Moreover, in some cases it is not impossible that what Paul says of himself and Timothy by the use of this plural may be applicable also to one or
more of his other helpers. It is possible, e.g., that Aristarchus accompanied

Paul and Timothy on the journey from Ephesus to Troas and Macedonia (see n. 6).

4. (P. 309.) Since Troas is in the province of Asia, and since, moreover, Paul never uses 'Aσία except to designate the entire province (above, p. 186 f.), there is no contradiction as to locality between ii. 12 and i. 8. But it necessarily follows from ἐλθὼν δὲ εἰς τὴν Τρῳάδα that in i. 8 it is not Troas that is meant, but either Ephesus or some point between Ephesus and Troas. The reference in i. 8 is certainly not to the event hinted at in 1 Cor. xv. 32 ; for at the time when 1 Cor. was written this was so well known to the readers, that Paul was able to call it to mind by a single word which to us is obscure. It must have been something that happened earlier. In the present case, however, when 2 Cor. was written—and this was certainly some months after the event to which he refers, as is evident from the connection between i. 8–11 and i. 3–7—Paul was still actuated by feelings of grateful joy that he had been delivered out of extreme danger. Even though the Corinthians may in some way have become acquainted with the facts in the case, or might learn the same from the person who brought 2 Cor., Paul nevertheless felt constrained himself to explain to them at the very outset the terribleness of the danger to which he had been exposed. Clearly the event must have taken place sometime between 1 and 2 Cor. It is not unnatural to assume that the event in question is that described in Acts xix. 23–41. Hofmann's objection (ii. 3. 11), namely, that, according to Acts xix. 22, Timothy had left Ephesus several months before Paul, and so could not have been with Paul at the time of Acts xix. 23 ff., as is presupposed in 2 Cor. i. 8, is not decisive against this position. The account in Acts is not complete at this point ; there is no record of the return of Timothy to Paul while he was still in Asia, which we infer from 2 Cor. i. 8, and we are by no means sure whether this return took place at the time indicated by Acts xx. 1, or in the interval suggested by Acts xix. 22b. It is, however, impossible to connect 2 Cor. i. 8 with Acts xix. 23 ff., for the reason that in the latter account there is nothing to indicate that Paul's life was in serious danger. From the danger immediately threatening he escaped (xix. 30). The favour of the Asiarchs (xix. 31) would have protected him in a suit at law, such as the town-clerk (γραμματεύς, ver. 35) had in mind (xix. 38). But it did not come to this. Paul was able to depart unmolested (xx. 1). Nor would the apostle have regarded as especially terrible a death brought upon him because of his effective preaching of the gospel in Ephesus ; although, as a matter of fact, this could hardly have been the outcome of such a trial as that hinted at (cf. Phil. i. 20–23, ii. 17 ; 2 Tim. iv. 6–8 ; Acts xx. 22–24). As Hofmann suggests, it is more likely to have been the danger of drowning, possibly during a stormy voyage from Ephesus to Troas (2 Cor. xi. 25). But if Paul had left land behind, he could hardly have used the expression ἐν τῇ 'Aσίᾳ. Or he may have fallen into the hands of robbers, and have been saved from a horrible death only through unexpected aid (2 Cor. xi. 26).

5. (P. 310.) In 2 Cor. viii. 10, Paul writes that the Corinthians had begun their collection in the previous year (ἀπὸ πέρυσι), and in ix. 2 he says that recently he had boasted to the Macedonians that Achaia had been prepared in regard to this matter ever since the preceding year. Now manifestly the reference here cannot be to two entirely different facts, because the same ex-

pression is used in both instances to indicate the time (ἀπὸ πέρυσι), and there is nothing in ix. 2 which suggests that Paul had made a mistake in thus boasting about the Corinthians.   Since it was this boasting which, according to ix. 2, incited the Macedonians themselves to take part in the collection (cf. viii. 1-5), the apostle may have made it before Titus' arrival.   But this was the very time when Paul was least likely to be optimistic about conditions in Corinth (ii. 13, vii. 5).   He had not boasted that the collection in Corinth was all ready, but simply that the Churches in Greece, unlike those in Macedonia, where no preparations for a collection whatever had been made, were in a position to send a collection to Jerusalem, and that these preparations to take the collection had been begun by them in the preceding year.   This does not imply that they had not progressed in the collection since that time, nor that they had now completed it.   The question naturally arises as to the method by which the year is here reckoned.   Was it after the ecclesiastical calendar of the Jews, according to which the year begins with the first of Nisan, or the spring equinox (Hofmann, ii. 3. 211), or the Macedonian calendar (Wieseler, *Chronol.* 364), in which the year begins with the autumn equinox, and corresponds to the Jewish civil calendar, or the Athenian, which corresponds to the Olympian reckoning, and in which the year begins with the summer solstice (Credner, *Einl.* i. 371 f.) ?   It is difficult to understand why use has never been made of other calendars, *e.g.* the political year of the Romans, which began with the first of January.   This would have been especially appropriate in this letter, since Corinth, the city to which it was to be sent, was a Roman colony, founded by Julius Cæsar ; and very possibly the letter itself was written in Philippi, another Roman colony.   But just because the Churches here in question were scattered and made up of different nationalities, and therefore were without any uniform calendar, it is not likely that Paul in writing ἀπὸ πέρυσι silently took for granted one of several possible ways of reckoning the year.   Quite apart from this, however, it would have been very unnatural for Paul to say in this connection simply that the event in question took place before the beginning of the last new year.   In January or February we never speak of the last Christmas as that of the preceding year, nor of the vintage gathered in October preceding as that of last year.   We use the expressions, " in the preceding year," " last year," etc., only when the larger part of twelve months has elapsed since the event to which reference is made.   Neither, on the other hand, do we employ these expressions when considerably more than a year has elapsed.   So the only conclusion to be drawn from 2 Cor. viii. 10, ix. 2, is that about a year had elapsed between the beginning of the collection in Achaia and the composition of 2 Cor. A period of from three to six months is just as much excluded by the expression as a period of eighteen or more months.   Now, from 1 Cor. xvi. 1 (above, p. 260) we know that this matter had been touched upon in a letter from the Corinthians to which 1 Cor. is the answer.   It is probable that prior to his departure from Ephesus, Stephanas (i. 16. 15 f., cf. Hofmann, *ad loc.*) had been earnestly engaged in this work.   Since, however, the Churches in Greece, unlike those in Macedonia, had been stirred up to this service by Paul himself (II. viii. 3-5), at the very latest this earnest request of the apostle's must have been made in the letter of Paul's, now lost (I. v. 9), which preceded the letter from the Church.   Now, if 1 Cor. was written near the Easter festival (above, p. 258), then the collection in Corinth must have been begun at the very latest in February of that same year, possibly several months earlier. On the other hand, from Acts xx. 3–6 (cf. 1 Cor. xvi. 6, παραχειμάσω) we ascertain that Paul spent the three months that preceded the opening of navigation in the year 58, roughly from the 10th of December 57 to the 10th of March 58, in Greece, and naturally part of it in Corinth. Hence 2 Cor. must have been written before the end of the year 57. Not very much of this year could have remained. For, while Paul sends Titus and two other Christians on ahead, he does not expect them to return, but treats them simply as his messengers, whom he will follow shortly (II. ix. 5, x. 6, xii. 14, xiii. 1). If, then, 2 Cor. was written somewhere about November 57, the Passover near which 1 Cor. was written must have been that of 57 ; for if we assume that it was the Passover of 56, then between 1 and 2 Cor. there would be an interval of nineteen months (April 56 to November 57), and between the beginning of the collection (which in this case would be at the latest February 56) and 2 Cor. an interval of at least twenty-one months, which disagrees entirely with II. viii. 10, ix. 2.

6. (P. 310.) That the facts spoken of in viii. 1–5, the παρακαλέσαι Τίτον (viii. 6, cf. ix. 5), which grew out of the same, and the τὴν παράκλησιν ἐδέξατο (viii. 17) belong in the very recent past, is proved : (1) by the fact that Titus could not possibly have returned to Paul until after the events described in vii. 6–16 ; (2) just as certainly by the entire context, viii. 6–ix. 5, where, as is usual in epistolary style, the aorists ἐξῆλθεν (viii. 17), συνεπέμψαμεν (viii. 18, 22), ἔπεμψα (ix. 3) indicate action contemporaneous with the sending of the letter. Of Titus' companions on his second journey to Corinth, only the person first described (viii. 18–21) is expressly said to have been chosen by the Macedonian Churches to accompany Paul and Timothy on their journey to Jerusalem with the collection. The tradition which identifies this person with Luke is due to some scholar's interpretation of viii. 18. Luke was not a Macedonian. It is more likely to have been Aristarchus (Hofmann, ad loc.), who was a Thessalonian (Acts xx. 4, see above, pp. 209 f., n. 2, 212 f., n. 6), who had been with Paul for some time (Acts xix. 29, συνεκδήμους = 2 Cor. viii. 19), and who therefore had had opportunity to win commendation in a number of Churches through the part which he took in the missionary work (2 Cor. viii. 18). As a matter of fact, Aristarchus did go with Paul to Jerusalem, and accompanied him also to Rome (Acts xx. 4, xxvii. 2). Or it might have been Sopatros or Sosipatros of Berœa, who a little later was with Paul in Corinth, and accompanied him also to Jerusalem (above, p. 209). The second anonymous companion of Titus (viii. 22) is included with the first among the ἀπόστολοι ἐκκλησιῶν in viii. 23, and therefore, like him, must have been the representative of a Church or of a group of Churches. Only he was not from Macedonia, and he had no connection with the matter of the collection ; for in that case there is no reason why he should not be mentioned at once in viii. 18 along with Titus' other companion, since all that is said in viii. 18–22 would then apply equally to him. When we remember that it was Paul's plan on this journey, which as originally projected was to lead him through Macedonia to Corinth, and from Corinth to Palestine (Acts xix. 21, xx. 3), to take with him representatives also of other Churches which have no share in

this collection (above, p. 209), we find ourselves shut up to a choice between Gaius of Derbe and one of the two men from Asia, Tychicus or Trophimus (Acts xx. 4, xxi. 29, above, p. 209, n. 2). These, then, are the "brethren" with whom, together with Timothy, after the return of the latter from Corinth, Paul planned at the time when he wrote 1 Cor. xvi. 11 to start on his journey to Macedonia, Greece, and thence to Jerusalem (above, p. 269 f., n. 8).

§ 20. OCCASION, PURPOSE, AND EFFECT OF THE SECOND EPISTLE TO THE CORINTHIANS.

Answer to the much mooted question as to what took place between the two extant letters to the Corinthians and as to what in general are the historical presuppositions of 2 Cor., must be sought mainly from the first section of the letter (chaps. i.–vii.), which is retrospective, particularly from what is said between the first and second of the three historical notices (i. 12–ii. 11) that form the framework of the first division of the Epistle, together with what follows the third of these notices (vii. 5–16); since what is said between the second and third of these remarks (ii. 14–vii. 1 or vii. 4) is of a more general character, and much less closely connected with the historical notices that precede and follow (n. 1). On the other hand, what is said between the notice of the dangers that threatened Paul's life at or shortly after his departure from Ephesus (i. 8–11, above, p. 318, n. 4) and the notice of his journey through Troas (ii. 12 f.), is evidently inserted at this point because it relates mainly to this particular journey from Ephesus to Macedonia by way of Troas, and to events closely associated with the same.

Mention of the prayers of the Corinthians, of which he feels sure he shall have the benefit in all future dangers, such as those he had encountered in Asia (i. 11), gives him opportunity to call his conscience to witness that he had acted always, particularly in his relation to the Corinthians, simply and sincerely, not being governed by a spirit of worldly cunning, but acting under the guidance of the grace of God (ver. 12, n. 2). That the criticisms

which Paul here answers, both that of insincerity and
that of acting in an unsanctified and wilful manner, were
actually current in Corinth, and had been made to the
apostle himself by the Church, either through Titus or in
a communication which Titus brought, is clear from the
apologetic explanation beginning at this point. From
the sentence, " We write nothing but what ye read or
indeed understand " (ver. 13), we infer that Paul had been
criticised for having written something in his letters or in
one of them which afterwards he wanted them to understand in a sense opposed to the language, and impossible
for any ordinary reader to infer. We are reminded at
once of the misinterpretation of a passage in his first letter
(now lost) which Paul corrects in 1 Cor. v. 9–11 (above,
p. 261). That this is the case he had in mind is rendered
all the more certain, by the fact that the language in
which Paul corrects the misinterpretation in 1 Cor.
agrees exactly with the language of the criticism here
presupposed. In making this correction, he does not say,
" When I wrote the passage I meant it to be taken as
now explained, not as you understood it," but very
pointedly, " This and nothing else is what I wrote to
you " ; so that it was very natural for the Corinthians,
when they looked at the earlier communication again, and
found language which really admitted the construction
which Paul declared to be foolish and unfair, to retort,
" In his letters Paul writes what his readers cannot find
in them nor read out of them." So Paul gets back his
own criticism of their lack of εἰλικρίνεια (1 Cor. v. 8, above,
p. 276), though, as the tone of his reply indicates, in a
manner entirely polite, perhaps even deferential, designed
less to criticise Paul than to justify themselves for having
formerly misunderstood him.

One misunderstanding was now cleared up. And
with the expression of the hope that hereafter so long as
he lives the Church will understand him, and understand

him fully, he passes to the discussion of a second point with regard to which there was disagreement between himself and the Church. This disagreement concerned the journey to Corinth, which had been announced long before, and which was now being carried out in a way different from that which he had originally intended and announced. When, some time previously,—just how long is not indicated,—Paul had intended, and, as the context shows, promised the readers to come to Corinth sooner than he was now actually doing, or to come to Corinth before he went to Macedonia (n. 2), whither he had now gone without having come to Corinth at all (cf. i. 23), he made the promise in the confidence that the Corinthians would understand and appreciate his reasons. He meant then to arrange his plans so as to go directly from Ephesus to Corinth and from Corinth to Macedonia, whence he planned to return to Corinth and thence to journey to Jerusalem. His thoughtful intention was by paying them two visits to give the Corinthians not only a single, but a twofold proof of his love ; for such, in any case, his visit was to be regarded. Now, in view of the criticism that in making his original plan, which was never carried out, and informing his readers of it, Paul had acted with fickleness (i. 17a), it must be assumed that it had become quite clear to the Corinthians, either from Paul's evident intentions inferred from something he had said or done, that this plan had been given up, and, over and above this, the solemn assurance of i. 23–ii. 2 makes it clear beyond all question that in its last analysis the dissatisfaction of the Church was caused by Paul's continued absence from Corinth—in other words, by the fact that he had not carried out his original plan, but had gone first to Macedonia, and kept putting off his arrival in Corinth by the slowness of his movements. In reply, Paul assures them that this failure to come to them, which they thought showed a lack of love on his part,

was due only to his desire to spare them. With reference
to the original plan, the carrying out of which would
have met their wishes, the only criticism they make is
that it was not well considered. If Paul were con-
scientious, they thought, he ought not to have made
such a plan unless he were sure he could carry it out;
and he ought not to have aroused their expectations by
announcing it unless he were resolved to come at any
cost. Possibly, in connection with this charge of fickleness in the matter of his earlier plan, the criticism was
also made, that in changing his plans he was influenced by
purely worldly designs and by motives of self-interest.
If, as seems probable from i. 12, this was actually the
case, the apostle gives the criticism an unexpected turn,
when he asks whether generally, in making plans, he is
accustomed to act in so worldly a manner as to make his
yes and no in such matters absolute (n. 2). It is not the
making and subsequent alteration of his plans which, in
his judgment, would be a βουλεύεσθαι κατὰ σάρκα, but the
subsequent demand of the Corinthians that a promise
impossible of fulfilment be considered irrevocable, and
that a course decided upon be persisted in at all hazards.
In answer to the criticism that his promises were untrustworthy and ambiguous, he avers that what he and his
helpers had said to the Corinthians was by no means both
yes and no, but just as simple and straightforward as
their preaching of Christ in Corinth had been ; and as far
as any appearance of hesitancy on his part, dictated by
worldly or selfish motives, or any criticisms to that effect
are concerned, he calls God to witness, who makes him
steadfast and endows him with the Spirit as a pledge of
his future perfecting and as a seal of the genuineness of
his present motives. He calls upon God to witness to the
truth of his assurance that it was his considerate desire to
spare the Corinthians, which, up to this time, had kept
him away from Corinth. Even though remembering the

pain he had suffered in connection with an earlier visit (above, p. 263 f.), he felt inclined to spare himself the renewal of such sorrow ; it was, after all, the Church most of all which he would spare sorrow, because he felt it his duty to minister rather to their joy (i. 18–ii. 2).

It may be assumed that Paul is here answering complaints of the Church which had been reported to him orally by Titus, or which had been expressed in a letter from the Church to Paul brought to him by Titus. The latter is more probable, in view of the definite form these complaints must have had, if we may judge by Paul's reply. Their primary occasion, however, could not have been the journey of Paul through Troas to Macedonia. For Paul must have sent Titus to Corinth before this journey was begun, since at the time when he set out he was expecting to meet Titus in Troas, whither he was to come from Corinth through Macedonia.

If, now, we ask how the Corinthians learned about the plan for the journey which Paul was now carrying out, and which, judging from the fact that he defends it, must have been well under way, nothing is more natural than to assume that Titus, who left Paul before he began the execution of this plan, informed the Corinthians of Paul's purpose not to come to them directly by sea, but by the longer route through Macedonia.   But if, as was certainly the case, Titus was sent, and arrived later than Fortunatus, Achaicus, and Stephanas, who were the bearers of 1 Cor. (above, p. 260), he had nothing new to say to the Corinthians about Paul's plans. For example, this same plan which he was engaged in carrying out at the time when 2 Cor. was written, Paul himself had set forth in detail in 1 Cor. xvi. 5–7. Between this communication by letter and the apologetic discussion of 2 Cor. i. 15–ii. 2 nothing intervened save the partial carrying out of this plan, hence nothing had occurred in this interim that could occasion the complaints about the

carelessness with which Paul made his plans, and the
arbitrariness with which he changed the plans that had
been already made and announced. The occasion for the
complaints answered in 2 Cor. i. 15–ii. 2 must be, therefore, in part things said in 1 Cor., in part things said
before 1 Cor. was written. That this is the case is proved
by a careful consideration of the manner in which Paul
speaks of his journey in 1 Cor. xvi. 5–9. He does it with
a detail and emphasis which is intelligible only if the
readers had other expectations at the time. He does not
stop with saying that he will come to Corinth after he
has passed through Macedonia, but adds, " For I do pass
through Macedonia." This last phrase does not add any
new thought, so that its purpose must be to strengthen the
preceding statement (present διέρχομαι of a future journey,
used with ἐλεύσομαι), and, by the position of the second
Μακεδονίαν, to emphasise strongly that this was the route
that he intended to take. Change of route involved also
a change in the time of his arrival and the length of his
stay in Corinth, and this contrast is expressed even more
strongly, both in positive and negative form, than is that
between the two possible routes. He has made up his
mind not to visit them immediately (above, p. 271, n. 12),
which would necessitate his coming directly by sea instead of through Macedonia, and that would mean only a
flying visit ; whereas, according to the plan he now lays
before them, while arriving considerably later, he hopes
to be able to pay them a much longer visit. From the
detail with which he speaks in ver. 6 and again in ver. 7 of
the greater length of his visit in Corinth if the new plan
is carried out, we see that he is making an effort to justify
his present plan. It shall be only for their advantage
that he does not now come directly by sea, but arrives
considerably later, coming by the longer route through
Macedonia. Therefore, at the time when 1 Cor. xvi. 5–7
was written, Paul must have been expected to arrive in

Corinth very shortly from Ephesus, directly by sea.   For such an expectation only the apostle himself could have been responsible.   Some time before 1 Cor. was written he must have expressed this intention, the inference being that he had done so in his earlier Epistle (1 Cor. v. 9). Paul had all the more reason for fearing that the Church, or those members of it who held an immediate visit to be desirable, would be dissatisfied with the new plan which he now laid before them, involving as it did further postponement of his visit ; since there were some in Corinth who interpreted his delay heretofore as due to cowardice, and who expressed the opinion that he would never appear in Corinth again (1 Cor. iv. 18) ; therefore the detail with which he lays his newly-made plan before his readers, in 1 Cor. xvi. 5–9, aiming to forestall such complaints. It is now clear that the original plan, knowledge of which is presupposed in I. xvi. 5–7, is the same as that which he defends in II. i. 15–17 against the charge of having been made without due care ; and also that the new plan laid before the readers in I. xvi. 5–7 is identical with the plan that had been practically carried out at the time when 2 Cor. was written, and which is defended in II. i. 15–ii. 2 against the charge of changeableness, of selfish arbitrariness, and of inconsiderateness.

In spite of his careful precautions, the fears which he had when writing I. xvi. 5–7 were realised.   This communication, and his subsequent journey by way of Troas to Macedonia, had caused the dissatisfaction in Corinth which in II. i. 12–ii. 2 Paul seeks to allay.   This, taken along with the fact that in spite of its general character II. i. 13 manifestly has special reference to the misunderstanding discussed earlier in I. v. 9–11, and to the conclusion which had there been reached concerning the matter (above, p. 322), proves those to be in error who assume a lost Epistle between 1 and 2 Cor., especially those who suppose that a visit took place between the writing of these two letters (above, § 19, n. 1, 2, p. 312 f.). The principal cause for the origin of the first of these hypotheses is the observation that the news from Corinth, which is presupposed in II. i.–vii., was not brought by Timothy,—although from what is said in I. iv. 17, xvi. 10 f., we should expect Timothy to report to Paul the effect of 1 Cor.,—but by Titus, of whom no mention is made in 1 Cor. If, now, as from II. i. 8 appears to be the case, Timothy was with Paul when he started on his journey from Ephesus to Macedonia, and if, as indicated by II. vii. 14, he was also with Paul at the time when Titus was sent to Corinth (see above, p. 316 f., n. 3), it seems as if a situation had been created by the sending and the return of Titus entirely different from that produced by 1 Cor., which ended with the return of Timothy to Paul. Inasmuch, now, as mention is made in II. ii. 3, 9, vii. 8–12 of a letter of Paul's which had been received in Corinth shortly before, the effect of which is reported to Paul by Titus, it was very natural to assume that this letter was not our 1 Cor., but a later Epistle of Paul's which Titus had taken with him the first time he went to Corinth. This assumption seems all the more necessary, according as it is felt that what is said in II. ii. 3, 9, vii. 8–12, cannot be made to apply to 1 Cor. without doing considerable violence to the language. In addition to what has been said above in proof of the inseparable connection between 1 and 2 Cor., the following is to be remarked : From the fact that Timothy returned to Paul before the latter's departure from Ephesus, it does not follow that the expectations expressed in I. xvi. 10 f. were all realised. Indeed, the expectation that Timothy will arrive in Corinth after the arrival of 1 Cor. is not unconditionally expressed (n. 3) ; so that it is not unlikely, either that Timothy did not reach Corinth at all, but for some reason unknown to us had occasion to return to Paul in Ephesus directly from Macedonia ; or that, while he did go to Corinth, he arrived and departed again before

1 Cor. reached its destination.   In either case, Timothy could not have brought Paul the news about the effect of 1 Cor., which Paul hoped he would bring.   It was for this reason, then, that immediately after Timothy's return he despatched Titus, in company with another Christian, to Corinth, in order that they might bring the news concerning the effect of 1 Cor. which he awaited with so much anxiety.   That this was the purpose for which Titus was sent we are justified in assuming, since nothing is said of any other object, and since this assumption is in entire harmony with all the hints concerning the result of the journey (n. 4).

The whole question turns upon a letter of Paul's concerning the effect of which upon the Church he was so anxious before Titus' arrival, that for the time being he regretted having written it (vii. 8).   In these circumstances, it is not surprising that in Troas he was so disturbed, when Titus failed to meet him there according to expectations (ii. 13), as to be practically unable to preach.   That the letter in question is our 1 Cor. may seem doubtful if ii. 3 be interpreted to mean that Paul had actually written in that letter what is expressed in the verses just preceding, namely, his determination not to come at once to Corinth as he was expected to do, but to remain away temporarily in order not to be in Corinth a second time in sorrow (i. 23–ii. 2).   For although the plan he was now engaged in carrying out had been set forth in I. xvi. 5–7, in contrast to the earlier plan which would have brought him to Corinth by the direct route and at once, in that presentation the essential point of the statement in 2 Cor. expressly referred to by τοῦτο αὐτό is lacking, namely, the motive here indicated for the change in the plan of the journey (i. 23–ii. 2).   There is, however, nothing to prevent us from translating: " And I wrote for this very purpose, that when I come, I may not have sorrow from those who ought to give me joy; (and I wrote) with confidence in you all, that my joy is the joy of you all " (n. 5).   What has just been declared to have been his reason and purpose in remaining away from Corinth, or for changing the plan of his journey, is here assigned as the reason and purpose for his writing.   Instead of making his visit at once according to the announcement, he had sent the long letter, at the close of which he had carefully explained that he was not coming to Corinth at once, and why he had made the change.

The opinion that what Paul says in ii. 4 about his state of mind when the letter in question was written, does not harmonise with the quiet tone of 1 Cor., is not made more intelligible by being repeated.   With what tremendous wrath against the alien destroyers of the Church (I. iii. 16 ff., ix. 1, xvi. 22), against the scandalous members of the same (v. 1–5), against the Church itself which was so unruly and at the same time so self-conscious, and against the noisy brawlers (iv. 7, 18–21, v. 2, viii. 1 f., xi. 16, xiv. 37 f.), does every line of the Epistle quiver !   The tone of the eloquent description in iv. 8–13 and of the apostle's half ironical self-judgment in vii. 25, 40 is that of bitterest agony.   It required effort on the apostle's part to reply as calmly as he did to the arrogant communication which the Church had sent to him (above, pp. 277, 282). But that is the very situation which brings tears to the eyes of a man of deep feeling.   Moreover, in entire keeping with 1 Cor. is the necessity which he now feels of protesting that in the communication in question he had no deliberate intention of causing the Church pain (II. ii. 4, cf. vii. 8–11).   So far as we are able to judge from letters which are extant, there is no other Church whose open sores are so ruthlessly exposed as those of the Corinthians (I. iii. 3, iv. 6–10, v. 1 f., vi. 1–10, 18–20, viii. 10–12, x. 20–22, xi. 17–30).   When, after a deeply humiliating discussion, he says that he did not write thus in order to shame the Corinthians (iv. 14), manifestly the effect is not less painful than in another passage, where he says in so many words that his intention was to shame them (vi. 5).   The same is true also of the passage where he introduces the discussion of all sorts of disorders and of wilful violations of the custom of the Church, by the commendatory remark that they follow his instructions (xi. 2).   There is not to be found throughout this entire long letter a single real commendation of any feature of the moral or religious life of the Church, and Paul was not usually sparing of such commendations.   The only thing that he praises is what God has done for them (i. 2, 9, 26, iii. 6–10, 16, iv. 15, vi. 11, 20, xv. 1 f.) and bestowed upon them in the way of spiritual gifts (i. 4–7) (above, pp. 279, 297 f., n. 5).   In referring to a letter of this kind, he had just as much occasion to protest that he had not written it with any intention of causing the Corinthians pain, though it actually had this effect, as he had the right to assure them that they ought rather to regard it as a special token of his love (II. ii. 4, cf. vii. 8–11). Incidentally we learn that disparaging remarks had been made in Corinth to the effect that Paul praised himself (II. iii. 1, v. 12, x. 12, cf. iv. 5) and defended himself when there was no sufficient occasion for it (xii. 19). For such strictures as these ample occasion was furnished by 1 Cor.   Quite in the manner of an accused person he had questioned the competency of the tribunal before which it seemed he was charged (I. iv. 1–5).   In another passage, of which there are reflections in II. iii. 1–3 (I. ix. 1–3), he had made a very concise defence before his accusers and judges.   He had justified at length the way in which he had preached at Corinth, I. i. 18– iii. 2, and defended single points in his judgments which had been questioned, *e.g.* what he had said about the happiness of the unmarried state, I. vii. (see above, p. 276 f.).   He had pictured eloquently the self-sacrifice which his calling involved, I. iv. 9–13, xv. 32.   Again

and again he had commended his example to the Church,
I. iv. 16 f., viii. 13, ix. 26 f., x. 33, xi. 1.   Not only had
he spoken emphatically of the validity of his apostleship
(I. i. 1, ix. 1), and of his relation to the Church as its sole
founder (iii. 6, 10, iv. 15), but he also claimed to have
fulfilled his office in Corinth in a manner both skilful and
faithful (iii. 10, iv. 4).   What sort of reward and praise
he hoped one day to receive from the just Judge (iii. 8,
13, iv. 5, ix. 18) he left them to infer from his proud
assertion, that he laboured more abundantly than all the
other apostles (xv. 10).

But the serious demands which he made had also
tested severely the obedience of the Church (II. ii. 9),
especially what he had said in connection with the case of
incest (I. v. 1–13).   Assuming that practically all that
happened between the two letters was the sending of
Titus, and his return with news from Corinth, this must be
the case referred to in II. ii. 5–11, vii. 11 f.   There is no
reason why we should be surprised at the position which
Paul now takes, nor is there any justification for replacing
the data supplied by existing sources for the explanation
of these passages by conjectures which cannot be proved.
If the view of Paul's original demand set forth above
(p. 278) be correct, it is quite in keeping with the principle of Church discipline clearly stated in II. x. 6.   In
the first place, Paul must have waited for the Church to
concur in his previous judgment; for only after this
agreement had been declared could the judgment be
executed by the joint action of Paul and the Church in
the manner that Paul had proposed in 1 Cor.   But,
as a matter of fact, as appears from II. ii. 6–11, the
Church had referred the question back to Paul for his
further decision.   And, indeed, the judgments of Paul
in 2 Cor. sound so much like answers to definite
communications and questions, that the conjecture forced
upon us earlier by i. 8–ii. 4 is fully confirmed, namely,

that the Corinthians had recently communicated with Paul, not only orally through Titus, but also in a letter which Titus brought to Paul. Paul's verdict, which begins with the words, "Sufficient for this man is the punishment decreed by the majority" (ii. 6, n. 6), presupposes (1) that the offender had been definitely punished either by word or by deed, and that Paul had been informed of the fact ; (2) that this punishment had been decreed not unanimously, but only by the decision of the majority ; (3) that the Church had submitted to Paul for his decision the question whether this punishment was sufficient. This in turn presupposes (4) that the opinion had been expressed in Corinth that the punishment was by no means sufficient, or that Paul would not be satisfied with it, or both. Paul at once declares the punishment to be sufficient, not, however, in the sense that the matter is thereby settled, but with the added remark that the punishment is enough to enable the Church now to show mercy to the evil-doer and uphold him by their encouragement, lest he be entirely overcome by his great sorrow. For the Church to forgive him, Paul says, is not only permissible, but, in view of the harm which may thereby be avoided, it becomes their duty. There seems, therefore, to be sufficient reason for the apostle's request that it be formally decided to show love to the offender (ver. 8). But by the τουναντίον μᾶλλον this verdict of Paul is set in strong contrast to another judgment, which went to the opposite extreme. Instead of increasing the sentence already passed, they are to lighten the same by formal decree, or otherwise to render it less severe. Inasmuch as the judgment expressed at the outset is opposed to the opinion that the punishment already decreed is by no means sufficient, the τουναντίον μᾶλλον renders it quite certain that this other view had been submitted to the apostle by the Church for his decision. This must have been the opinion of the minority, since the punishment actually decreed represented the mind of the majority. We learn at the same time that the Church was uncertain whether Paul in turn would be satisfied with what had been done ; for he finds it necessary expressly to assure the Church that he concurs in the act of forgiveness decided upon (ver. 10).

What this punishment was which had been decided upon by the majority, naturally we are not able to determine with entire certainty. Manifestly it was not the punishment suggested by Paul in I. v. 3–5 ; since (1) the infliction of this punishment required Paul's co-operation in a manner which necessitated prearrangement, and since (2) this punishment involved the death of the offender ; so that there could have been no question about a subsequent increase of penalty, or about Paul's satisfaction with what had been done. More likely it was an ordinary case of discipline according to the rules laid down in I. v. 11 ; 2 Thess. iii. 14 f. The severer penalty demanded by the minority, and which the Church thought that Paul also might insist upon, can hardly have been any other than that which Paul proposed in I. v. 3–5. Consequently in the communication, to which Paul replies in II. ii. 6–11, the Church must have asked him whether, under the altered conditions, he still held to his original judgment. Paul reverses his decision, and earnestly requests that the punishment under which the offender is at present suffering be lessened by formal decree, lest he completely yield to despair. He was able to do this without prejudice to the seriousness of the affair, or to his own personal dignity. How strongly he felt himself under obligation to take this position, is indicated by ii. 11. He knows that nothing would please Satan more than to see him, influenced by the motive of worldly consistency which he had condemned in i. 17, stand by his original judgment and proposal. All such suggestions he rejects as cunning temptations of Satan to keep him

from permitting clemency. The primary purpose of his
original judgment had been to save the soul of the
offender (I. v. 5). That purpose was now being accomplished without resort to the extreme measures he had at
first proposed; the offender was deeply penitent. It
seems also that this person had done all in his power
to prove to the Church that he regretted his action, and,
in so far as this was possible, to atone for the wrong
which he had done to his father against whom primarily
the sin had been committed (n. 6). But if the severe
disciplinary measures adopted by the Church were enforced longer, or if they were increased, there was, Paul
now thought in the light of the news that had come to
him, extreme danger that the purpose of reforming the
offender and of saving his soul would be defeated altogether. For if this person were wholly overcome by his
sorrow, he would fall into the hands of Satan, who, by
the suggestion that Paul ought persistently to stand by
his first decision, was endeavouring to lead even the apostle
astray. Paul gives up the means which he had previously
suggested, in order to secure the end which it was altogether desirable to accomplish.

But more than this, what he had designed by his
earlier proposition to accomplish in the Church was in
large part accomplished, and promised soon to be entirely
realised. The only intention which can be directly inferred from I. v. 1–13 is the intention to move the Church
to a more modest judgment of itself and a more rigorous
disciplining of its sinful members. When, now, in II.
ii. 9, vii. 12, Paul says that he wrote as he did in order to
prove whether the Church was ready to render entire
obedience, and to give it an opportunity to show an
earnest desire to please its founder, the statement can
only be regarded as an expression of his original intention
in the light of the accomplished result. From the stirring
description of the effect of the earlier letter, vii. 7–12,

which clearly has its climax in the reference to the case
discussed earlier in ii. 5–11, we learn that now the Church
was deeply impressed with the magnitude of the offence
committed against Paul and in the sight of God, and that it
was not only exceedingly anxious to conciliate the apostle,
but had also visited its displeasure and punishment upon
the offender (vii. 11, n. 6). While as yet the majority
had not agreed to Paul's earlier proposal, they had nevertheless, in reporting the disciplinary measures proposed,
and in stating the manner in which the entire action had
been taken, practically resubmitted the whole case to him
for his opinion and decision (ii. 6–8). Finally, they had
endeavoured, not unsuccessfully, to justify themselves in
this matter. Perhaps in his joy at what had been accomplished, Paul expresses himself a little extravagantly when
he writes, "In every way ye have shown yourselves to be
pure in this matter" (vii. 11, where the εἶναι is not to be
overlooked). Although this is not equivalent to the
statement that the Church had proved itself to be quite
without fault, it does show that Paul had been convinced
by the Church's explanation (ἀπολογία)—for mere oral communication through Titus could hardly be so designated—
that the situation was not just what he supposed it was
when he wrote I. v. 1. Essentially the case seems to
have been as Paul had heard it, and possibly there were
other members of the Church who knew of it besides those
who had given the information to Paul. But the matter
was not so generally known in the Church as Paul had
supposed, and the charge that the Church as a body had
shown more than heathen indifference with regard to a
case of flagrant immorality proved to be ungrounded.
No one could rejoice that it was so more than Paul, and
he would not have been the large-hearted man and the
sincere Christian that he was, had he stood stubbornly by
his first judgment and proposal. It would be inconsistent
with his dignity and our own to defend him, otherwise

than by a statement of the facts, against the unworthy charge of endeavouring to cover up by false diplomacy an alleged defeat which he is supposed to have suffered, either by the failure of the miraculous punishment which he had predicted, or by the defiant opposition of the Church.

The greater his anxiety before the arrival of Titus lest the effect of 1 Cor. should be the entire alienation of the Church, the more easily we are able to understand the exuberant joy caused by Titus' tidings. This does not, however, prevent him, in the first division of the letter, which concludes with an extravagant expression of this joy, from taking very seriously and answering very decidedly the complaints of the Church that had reached him about the ambiguity of his letters (i. 13), the untrustworthiness of his decisions, and the lack of love which they thought was evidenced, both by the change in the plan of his journey, and by the tone of his earlier letter (i. 15–ii. 5, cf. vi. 12, vii. 3). Rejoicing that his greatest anxiety is now finally relieved, Paul looks forward to the future with confidence in the Church (vii. 16). He hopes for a complete restoration of understanding and confidence (i. 13a). This involves the admission that this hope was yet far from being realised. He must still ask the Corinthians not to close their hearts to him (vi. 13), and to restore to him the place in their midst which belonged to him (vii. 2). Between these two requests stands the exhortation suggested in vi. 1 and introduced directly in vi. 11, that they avoid altogether dangerous associations with the immoral practices of their heathen neighbours, especially with idolatry, confident that their Father will compensate them richly for all the sacrifices which they make for His sake, and that they endeavour also to live in holiness (vi. 14–vii. 1, n. 7). Just as these exhortations are made in view of the special case of heathen immorality, with regard to which Paul's mind had been set at rest by the news brought by Titus and by the communication which the Church sent by him, so it is certain that the happy turn which this matter had taken was the principal reason why Paul was so joyful. He is able now again with joyful confidence, with perfect frankness, and with a heart full of love and with sympathy for the entire Church, to exhort them and to make requests of them. And there are still many things with reference to which there is need for request and exhortation.

This was the case with regard to the matter of the collection, to which the second division of the letter is devoted (chaps. viii.–ix.). The fact that we do not find here the same mingling of strong expressions of joy and of endeavours to secure beforehand entire understanding between himself and his readers that characterises chaps. i.–vii., is explained, partly by the different subject-matter in the two sections, partly by the circumstance that in the matter of the collection he is dealing not with the Church in Corinth alone, but also with all the Christians in Achaia (above, p. 308), who had no share in the conflicts between the Corinthians and Paul. Still the underlying tone is the same in this as in other parts of the letter. His generous recognition of the willingness of the Macedonians to make sacrifice, of the zeal of Titus, of the merits of those who accompanied him, as well as of the Christian virtues of the readers (viii. 7), and his mention of the praiseworthy zeal with which the Corinthians had begun the collection more than a year before (viii. 10, ix. 2), all express indirectly his displeasure at the delay and parsimony which the Corinthians had recently shown in the matter. His various exhortations, that now this matter be brought finally to a close, are pressed upon them not so much by fault-finding, as by a statement of urgent reasons.

Quite a different tone, however, pervades the third

division of the letter (chaps. x.–xiii.). Being an expression
of Paul's own personal feelings, it is distinguished from
the preceding sections, which were written also in
Timothy's name, by the introductory phrase, αὐτὸς δὲ ἐγώ,
x. 1 (cf. xii. 13 : also ἐγώ, xii. 16, in like contrast to his
companions ; ἐγὼ μὲν Παῦλος, 1 Thess. ii. 18). He has still
upon his heart a request affecting his personal relation to
the Church, which, he intimates, must be expressed in a
spirit of gentleness and mildness, because he is compelled
continually to restrain the anger which he feels when he
thinks of the followers of Peter, who are chiefly responsible
for the disturbed relation between the Church and its
founder, and who continue to keep this relation disturbed
(xi. 1–12, 18, above, p. 289 ff.), and of the members of the
Christ party, who, assuming a superior air of neutrality,
are continually criticising him, his letters, his personal
appearance in Corinth, and his conflict with the foreign
teachers who were his rivals (x. 7–18, above, p. 292 f.).
While he everywhere distinguishes sharply between these
false apostles and members of the Church, calling the
former tempters and aliens (above, p. 287 f.), in the case
of those who boasted that they were followers of Christ
this was not possible.   Therefore he blames the Church as
a body for the currency in their midst of the disrespectful
remarks of these people (x. 1b, 2b, 9–10, 13a, 14a, xii.
19a, xiii. 3).   Particularly does he find fault with the
Church for not having silenced and ejected the followers
of Peter, thereby compelling him to defend his own case
against these servants of Satan (xii. 11, v. 12).   The
request which Paul has to make of the Church is suggested in x. 1, but its full statement is postponed by the
interjection of his prayerful wish that he may be spared
the necessity of acting with severity when he comes to
them (x. 2, cf. xiii. 7–9 ; 1 Thess. iii. 10), and of the explanations which follow (x. 3–6).   Nor is this request
stated, except in incomplete form in x. 7 (especially if

βλέπετε is an imperative), xi. 1, 16, xiii. 5. But summing up the impression as to its purpose which we get from this entire section of the letter, this request may be stated somewhat as follows : " See to it before I come that my visit be mutually peaceful, pleasant, and profitable, by repudiating the foreign teachers, by informing the haughty members of the Christ party what is their proper place, and, under threats of the severest discipline, by setting those right who are living unchaste lives." The tone of this part of the Epistle differs from that of chaps. i.–vii., in that Paul here openly attacks the opponents, with whom it was impossible to come to terms, reminding the Church in a connected statement of their duty with reference to such persons. This explains why his self-defence, which is continued through this section, takes on uniformly a tone of irony, which we do not discover in chaps. i.–vii. Naturally, also, in chaps. i.–vii., where, after days of anxious care, his unburdened heart first gives itself vent, there is an overflowing expression of joy, acknowledgment, and hope. On the contrary, in chaps. x.–xiii., where he discusses grievances not yet adjusted, naturally a prominent place is given to the expression of his displeasure and anxiety, lest things should not turn out as he wished. Taken as a whole, however, the picture of the condition of the Church and of its relation to its founder which we get from the third section of the letter, is the same as that which we get from the first section. Where there was occasion for demands such as are made in vi. 14–vii. 1, there is place also for concern such as is expressed in xii. 21, and for threats such as those in xiii. 2. The complaints which Paul found it necessary to reply to in i. 12–ii. 2 (above, p. 323 ff.) were not less serious than those in x. 1 f. The incidental denial in vii. 2b has the same value as the plain discussion of xii. 13–18. The demand at the same time that the Church sound the praises of their own apostle in opposition to the followers of Peter, thereby putting a stop to their mischievous work and sparing the apostle the necessity of commending, praising, and defending himself, which recurs so frequently in xi. 4–xii. 19, is made also in v. 12 (cf. iii. 1). Only in this latter instance it is incidental, which was appropriate in view of Paul's purpose to discuss the matter by itself later. The hope which he expresses in i. 13b is expressed in more general form in xiii. 6 (cf. also v. 11). His assurance to them of his love, which they had failed to appreciate, and his complaint because of their failure to reciprocate it (xi. 11, xii. 14), not only have a general resemblance in content to i. 15, 23, ii. 4, vi. 11–13, but are expressed in similar language (xii. 15, περισσοτέρως ὑμᾶς ἀγαπῶ, cf. ii. 4 ; ἀγαπητοί, vii. 1, xii. 19). The request of vii. 2a could stand equally well at the beginning of chap. xi. When in x. 6 expression is given to the expectation that in the near future the Church will return to a condition of entire obedience, it is practically admitted that there are yet some things lacking, of which he purposes now finally to speak. This involves no contradiction to his joyful acknowledgment that, as a result of 1 Cor., the Church had shown itself ready to submit entirely to the apostle's judgment — particularly with regard to the case of incest (ii. 9, vii. 12, above, p. 332 ff.). Nor is it inconsistent in any way with Titus' praise that the entire Church had received him, the messenger of the apostle, in a spirit of obedience, and even of fear and trembling, i.e. as a lord and master (vii. 15, cf. Eph. vi. 5). It is only an illustration of a habit of the apostle's, which may be observed variously both in his relation to men and to God, to begin by giving utterance to praise, thanksgiving, and acknowledgment for good received, and then to express the anxiety and urgency which he still felt, in request, demand, and complaint. And this was the wise way to proceed, if he wanted to put right the affairs of a Church which a

few months before had apparently been inclined to
sever its relations with him and the Gentile Church
which he had been instrumental in organising, but
which now, confessing its manifold faults, showed itself
eager to make its peace with its founder and to win
back his love, which it seemed to them they had all but
forfeited.

We have no definite information as to the reception
accorded by the Corinthians to this last message of Paul
on his way from Ephesus to Corinth. This deficiency is,
however, supplied by the facts. If in all essential respects
this letter did not accomplish its purpose (xiii. 10), particularly if the Church allowed the followers of Peter to
keep on with their work, it was impossible, after what had
taken place, for the life and death struggle between Paul
and the Corinthian Church to be kept up longer. And if
Paul had suffered defeat in this struggle, it would have led
necessarily to the separation of the Corinthian Church
from the Gentile Church. But no such separation took
place. Some forty years later the Roman Church felt
called upon, in consequence of a rebellion which, under
the leadership of a few gifted younger members, had
broken out in Corinth against the venerable head of the
Church, to interfere in the confused affairs of its sister
Church by sending it a weighty letter of exhortation.
Just as there were things in the situation which reminded
Clement, the author of this letter, of the existence of
cliques in the apostolic age, spoken of in 1 Cor. i.–iv.
(Clem. 1 *Cor.* xlvii.), so we in turn are able to discover in the
picture of the Corinthian Church, found in Clement's letter,
certain characteristics of that Church to be observed from
the Epistles of Paul. But between the troubles of the
year 57 and those of 95–97 there is no direct connection.
On the contrary, we learn that for a long time, to the joy
of the entire Church, the Corinthians had been living a
peaceful life, adorned with every Christian virtue (Clem.

i. 2–iii. 1), so that the revolution that had now broken out seemed a breach with the entire past history of the Church back to the days of Paul. Clement directs them to take up again Paul's 1 Cor. (xlvii. 1), the Romans feeling sure that they are at one with the Corinthians in paying honour to Paul.

This condition was the fruit of the "weighty and powerful letters" of the apostle (2 Cor. x. 10). Had Paul been under necessity of securing his victory, which, according to the witness of subsequent conditions, he certainly did win, by personal encounter with his opponents and with the Church which remained rebellious in spite of his letters, it is not likely that all traces of such conflict would have so completely disappeared. We learn of a three months' sojourn of Paul in Greece, ending in the spring of 58 (Acts xx. 2 f.), but nothing is said of any battles which he had to fight during that visit (n. 8). If Romans was written during this period in Corinth, its quiet tone and the careful working out of its elaborate plan prove that for Paul this period was not one of harassing struggle, but of recuperation and of preparation for new work in the far West.

1. (P. 321.) When in ii. 14–16, in contrast to the confession of the weakness which prevented him from making use of the opportunities to preach in Troas, Paul expresses his gratitude to God that in spite of such weakness his presence and preaching has proved effective in every place,— naturally therefore in Troas also,—this statement, like i. 18–22, is intended to prevent a false generalisation and interpretation of his weakness. It also furnishes a natural transition to the detailed contrast between the genuine preachers of the gospel, of whom he is one, and the wandering Jewish Christian teachers, who peddle the word of God (ii. 17–v. 21, see above, p. 290, line 15 f.). Then from vi. 1 on the discussion returns again to affairs in Corinth (see below, n. 7).

2. (Pp. 321, 323, 324.) In i. 12 the reading ἀπλότητι is to be preferred to ἁγιότητι. πρότερον, without the article in i. 15, which was not understood by numerous copyists (for this reason omitted in א*; other MSS. read τὸ πρότερον ; K has τὸ δεύτερον), is not to be taken with ἐβουλόμην, before which it would have to stand, but with ἐλθεῖν. It thus emphasises the πρὸς ὑμᾶς, if, indeed, originally the πρότερον did not precede ἵνα instead of standing in its present position Of the numerous interpretations of i. 17, that deserves the preference which

makes τὸ ναί and τὸ οὔ the subjects, and ναί, οὔ the predicates, because of what follows in i. 18 (cf. Jas. v. 12). Even if there were an actual contradiction to the latter passage, which in a general way is comparable with it, it would be no objection to this interpretation of the present passage. As a matter of fact, however, Paul is not disputing at all the truth of the general rule that a Christian's Yes and No ought to be as reliable as his oath (cf. Matt. v. 37). Indeed, in i. 18 f. he claims that he and his helpers follow this rule in the exercise of their calling. Only he goes on to explain that the application of this rule to plans for the future, the carrying out of which is dependent upon the providence of God, would be a carnal misuse of the same. In similar passages in his letters, indeed in passages more or less directly bearing upon this very question, he makes abundant use of that pious ἐάν quite in the sense of Jas. iv. 15, which excludes an unconditioned ναί and οὔ from reference to actions that are to take place in the future (cf. 1 Cor. iv. 19, xvi. 4, 7 ; 2 Cor. ix. 4, xiii. 2 ; 1 Tim. iii. 15 ; Rom. i. 10, xv. 32 [Acts xviii. 21]).

3. (P. 328.) The distinction between ἐάν I. xvi. 10 (cf. Col. iv. 10), and ὅταν I. xvi. 2, 3, 5 (cf. II. x. 6), and ὡς ἄν I. xi. 34, is not to be overlooked. Something is to be said in favour of the view of Lightfoot (*Bibl. Essays*, p. 277, 1893), who remarks that possibly the reason why Acts xix. 22 speaks of the sending of Timothy and Erastus to Macedonia only is the fact that Luke knew that Timothy went no farther than Macedonia. On the other hand, the contention that if he did actually go to Corinth, Timothy would have to be mentioned in II. xii. 17 f. is purely arbitrary ; because Timothy is one of the writers of this letter, so that if he went to Corinth, he is included in the plural of xii. 17. To mention especially the sending of Titus and the person who accompanied him from among a number of cases of this kind was natural, because it was the latest instance (see the following note).

4. (P. 329.) The reference in II. xii. 18 is not to the second sending of Titus to Corinth, on which occasion he took with him 2 Cor., although this is not precluded by the use of the aorist παρεκάλεσα (cf. viii. 6, 17, ix. 5, above, p. 320, n. 6), but to Titus' earlier trip thither. (1) Mention is made here of only one person who accompanied Titus, whereas on the second journey he was accompanied by two other Christians (above, p. 320 f.), concerning both of whom it is said, quite as much as it is said of Titus and in the same breath, that they were sent by Paul and Timothy (viii. 18 and 22, συνεπέμψαμεν ; ix. 3, ἔπεμψα τοὺς ἀδελφούς), both of whom, moreover, are called ἀπόστολοι ἐκκλησιῶν (viii. 23). To regard the person whom Paul mentions second as the principal person, in comparison with whom the first individual who is incidentally mentioned (xii. 18) can be quite ignored, is just as arbitrary as to identify τὸν ἀδελφόν, xii. 18, with τὸν ἀδελφὸν ἡμῶν, viii. 22, rather than with τὸν ἀδελφόν, viii. 18, or any other Christian (cf. 1 Cor. i. 1, xvi. 12 ; Rom. xvi. 23). Still this is done by Krenkel (351 ff.). (2) The questions in ver. 17 and ver. 18b prove that the reference is to a sending of Timothy which had taken place in the past. Krenkel, who rightly accepts this as beyond question (353 f.), tries to use it in support of his hypothesis that II. x.–xiii. is a separate letter which was sent to Corinth later than II. i.–ix. But this is possible only if it be maintained that the brother referred to in xii. 18 is

identical with the brother mentioned in viii. 22, which has been shown to be quite impossible. In no other passage does Paul have occasion to mention the fact that Titus was accompanied by another person on his first journey to Corinth, since he does not elsewhere speak of the first sending of Timothy. The utmost that can be concluded from the fact that no mention is made of Titus' companion in the passage where the return of the latter is spoken of (ii. 13, vii. 6–15), is that Titus started on the return journey from Corinth without his companion. The purpose of the first sending cannot be inferred from viii. 6, where the first and second sending are contrasted with each other. If by that which Titus had begun on his first visit, and was to finish on his second, Paul had understood the charity work of the collection (I. xvi. 3), then he must have let τὴν χάριν—either with or without ταύτην preceding or following—come immediately after προενήρξατο without καί, unless he had chosen to bring out more clearly the identity of the object in both cases by using ὁ προενήρξατο κτλ. Since, however, he describes the work begun and to be completed by Titus first in a very general way as a work directed to the Corinthians (εἰς ὑμᾶς), and then by the use of καί contrasts the work of charity in question with other things, it is clear that this is the special undertaking which at this visit Titus is to carry on and bring to a conclusion. What Titus had accomplished on his former visit, and what he is to do on this occasion, are conceived of as the beginning and the end of a comprehensive work, the general purpose of which is the restoration of normal conditions in Corinth and of normal relations between the Church and its founder. He had made a successful beginning of this on the occasion of his first visit ; now he is to fill up the measure of his service by bringing to a conclusion the troublesome matter of the collection (cf. Hofmann, ii. 3. 204 f.). Both the καί which precedes τὴν χ. τ. and the καί which precedes ἐπιτελέσῃ serve to contrast the purpose of the present coming with the results of the first. Against the interpretation of the second καί in the sense, " Among other things this also," there are the following objections : (1) It does not account for the peculiar structure of the sentence. (2) Throughout the entire context as far as ix. 5 the matter of the collection is the only reason and purpose given for sending Titus at this time. On the other hand, when Paul comes to speak of the other things which he desired to see accomplished (chaps. x.–xiii.), Titus drops out altogether ; since, as has been shown, xii. 18 is only a reference to the earlier sending. When so understood, καὶ τὴν χ. τ. does not harmonise with ἐπιτελέσῃ. (3) Neither does it harmonise with προενήρξατο, with which also it would have to be taken according to this construction ; for in the passage where Paul speaks of the results of the first sending of Titus (vii. 6–15) there is no reference to the collection. Neither does the reference in xii. 18 touch this matter (above, p. 314 f., n. 1). Paul gives no hint that Titus brought him news regarding the condition of the collection, to say nothing of a commission given to Titus regarding this matter.

5. (P. 330.) Although Heinrici still argues with great detail for the possibility of the view (ii. 23 f., 127 ff.) that ἔγραψα, ii. 3, 4, also ii. 9, refer to the words just written, or to all that precedes of the letter which Paul is now in process of writing, it may be considered certain that an earlier letter is meant. For the following reasons : (1) When referring to that which immediately

precedes, Paul is in the habit of using the present, γράφω, Gal. i. 20 ; 1 Cor. iv.
14, xiv. 37 ; 1 Tim. iii. 14 (once, 2 Cor. xiii. 10, even with reference to the
entire letter here concluding) ; so also λέγω, Rom. vi. 19 ; 1 Cor. vi. 5 (with
reference to vi. 4), vii. 6, 35 ; 2 Cor. vii. 3, viii. 8 ; Phil. iv. 11 ; 2 Tim. ii. 7 ;
Philem. 21 ; λαλῶ, 1 Cor. ix. 8, xv. 34. Only in two instances, Philem. 19
and 1 Cor. ix. 15, does he use ἔγραψα, and there because he pictures to himself
vividly the impression which the words he has just written will make upon
his readers when they come to read what had been written some time before.
With these exceptions ἔγραψα when used by Paul always refers either to a
letter which is just being concluded, Rom. xv. 15 (cf. xvi. 22 of the
amanuensis) ; Gal. vi. 11 ; Philem. 21, or to an earlier letter, 1 Cor. v. 9, 11
(cf. vii. 1 ; 2 Cor. vii. 12). (2) There would be no occasion whatever for the
assurance of ii. 4 with reference to the preceding portion of the letter. It
would not occur to anyone that what precedes was written to grieve the
Corinthians, for neither in what precedes ii. 4 nor in the chapters immediately following is there a single severe or cold word, but only a warm-
hearted and carefully considered self-defence, in which among other criticisms
he answers that of want of love. (3) Without any question the same matter
is discussed in vii. 11 ff. as in ii. 5–11 ; hence the letter referred to in ii. 9
must be the same as that which in vii. 8 is spoken of as belonging to the past.
That, however, the ἔγραψα in ii. 3, 4, 9 refers in all three cases to the same
letter, is proved by the very close sequence of thought in ii. 3–11. (4) It is
not Paul's manner to interrupt a discussion not yet finished in order to say
that in writing the letter he has shed many tears or sheds them now. It would
be more in keeping with his manner for him to write that the readers can
see how deeply he is moved, or in connection with some severe word to say
that he could not write this without tears (cf. Phil. iii. 18). If, however,
the reference in ii. 3, 4, 9 is to an earlier Epistle of Paul's, and, in particular,
the same Epistle which is spoken of in vii. 8, 12, then it is natural to infer
from the similarity of sentence structure in ii. 3 and ii. 9 that τοῦτο αὐτό, ii. 3,
means the same as διὰ τοῦτο αὐτό (I. iv. 17 א*AP), and is related in sense to
εἰς αὐτὸ τοῦτο, 2 Cor. v. 5 ; Col. iv. 8 ; Eph. vi. 22 (Rom. ix. 17) ; cf. Erasmus
(Paraphr. in ep. Pauli, 1523, p. 150) ; Rückert and Hofmann, ad loc. This
construction is good Greek (Kühner-Gerth, i. 310, A. 6 ; Winer, § 21. 3, A. 2),
occurs without question in 2 Pet. i. 5, and would certainly have to be
admitted in the present passage even if it did not occur elsewhere in Paul's
writings. But this construction does occur in Phil. i. 6, where otherwise the
αὐτό would be meaningless. In order to any other interpretation, an instance
must be shown in which a Greek writer has expressed the object of his conviction or confident expectation in the accusative after πέποιθα. Phil. i. 25
cannot be cited as a case in point ; since in this passage the τοῦτο simply
prepares the way for the following ὅτι, and belongs to οἶδα by which the clause
is governed. It is correctly translated by Peshito, " And this I know confidently." The same version translates 2 Cor. ii. 3 somewhat freely, but quite
correctly, " And (as to) my writing you, (so) is (it) this, in order that if I
come those may not cause me grief from whom I ought to have joy " ; in other
words, the reason and purpose of my coming was this. Even if τοῦτο αὐτό,
which probably belongs before ἔγραψα (DG), with a ὑμῖν inserted between it
and the verb, were the strongly emphasised object of ἔγραψα, it certainly

would not imply a mysterious reference to something which was more familiar to the readers than to ourselves (Meyer, Ewald, " The thing which is known to you"; Klöpper, "Something which causes grief"). At most it could be only a resumption of the τοῦτο of ii. 1. Then the subject of Paul's earlier communication in his letter would be the determination not to come to Corinth a second time in sorrow. But the context, i. 15–ii. 2, shows that this determination was practically identical with the determination to come to Corinth not at once by the direct route, but by the longer way through Macedonia. On this construction of the passage, then, in the letter in question Paul had expressed the same intention with regard to his coming to Corinth that he had since carried out, which, moreover, leaving quite out of account the reason for writing given in II. i. 23–ii. 2, he had set forth in detail in I. xvi. 5–7. Since, now, in the same letter the very opposite determination could not have been expressed, namely, Paul's purpose to come to Corinth at once and by the direct route, to assume, as, for example, Krenkel does (377) that this statement did actually stand in the letter written in the interval between 1 and 2 Cor. and at the same time to affirm that II. ii. 3–9 has reference to this same letter, is to involve one's self in the most glaring contradiction. But if what was said in this letter was simply a repetition of the determination expressed in I. xvi. 5–7, only in different words and with more detailed statement of the apostle's reasons, then there was no point in his appeal to the letter supposed to have been written in the interval. But now since "that very thing," which he writes in II. ii. 1 is not to be found in 1 Cor., the τοῦτο αὐτό must be taken adverbially.

6. (Pp. 333, 335, 336.) It is assumed by the present writer that οὐκ ἐμὲ λελύπηκεν, ii. 5, is a question calling naturally for an affirmative answer ; consequently that ἀλλά does not mean " but " (sondern), but is equivalent to a "nevertheless" (aber), which serves to introduce the following clauses, 5b–6. Further, it is assumed that ἀπὸ μέρους does not, as Hofmann contends, belong to the main clause of the sentence beginning with ἀλλά, but is a part of the subordinate sentence attracted out of its place on account of the strong emphasis, as is so often the case before ἵνα. " Nevertheless, in order not in a measure to burden you all, I declare the penalty imposed by the majority to be sufficient." The ἀπὸ μέρους is added, because a different judgment on Paul's part, namely, the demand for the offender's severer punishment, would be a heavy burden, especially upon the person himself, and might drive him to despair. That, in turn, would be a burden to all the members of the Church ; not only to the majority, who regarded the penalty that had been temporarily imposed as sufficient, but to the minority, who, either because they feared the effect of leniency, or because they honoured Paul's judgment, felt that a severer penalty ought to be imposed. This supposed obligation they could have fulfilled only with bleeding hearts, and the wound would not be easily healed. Instead of ἱκανή Paul writes ἱκανόν, evidently under the influence of the legal use of τὸ ἱκανόν (Acts xvii. 9 ; Mark xv. 15). There is a legal colouring also to κυροῦν (ii. 8, cf. Gal. iii. 15) and the expressions used in vii. 11 f. ἀπολογία (cf. Phil. i. 7, 16 ; 2 Tim. iv. 16 ; Acts xxv. 8, 16, xxvi. 1 f. ; Rom. ii. 15) ; ἐκδίκησις, ὁ ἀδικήσας, ὁ ἀδικηθείς (Acts vii. 24–27 ; 1 Cor. vi. 7 f. ; Philem. 18) ; πρᾶγμα (1 Cor. vi. 1 ; 1 Thess. iv. 6). If

2 Cor. followed 1 Cor. without an intervening letter or a visit of Paul's, there is no question that II. ii. 5–11, vii. 11 f. refers to the same case as I. v.   The language used points in the same direction, τίς (II. ii. 5 ; I. v. 1); ὁ τοιοῦτος (II. ii. 6, 7 ; I. v. 5).   Then ὁ ἀδικηθείς (vii. 12) cannot refer to Paul, which would imply a strangely impersonal way of speaking, but to the offender's father (above, p. 296, n. 4).   Paul might have said that the Church had done him wrong, in causing him the disgrace and the grief occasioned by the occurrence of such a scandal in a Church which he had founded ; but he could not have called it a violation of his rights, particularly since what the offender had done had no relation whatever to Paul's own person.   When, now, Paul says that he discussed this matter in his letter, not in its relation to the offender himself, nor in relation to the father whose rights had been violated, this is quite in keeping with the manner in which the affair is handled in I. v.   Nothing is said in this passage about the father, who evidently did not belong to the Church.   Neither is the offender himself the object of the discussion, but the Church in which, to its disgrace and injury, an offence of this kind remains unatoned for,—a fact, however, that does not imply that Paul was indifferent to the fate of any individual member of the Church.   But, with regard to this individual, Paul had expressed only the hope that by the judgment which destroyed his physical life his "spirit" might be saved.   What is said in vii. 12 must have been occasioned by communications from the Church concerning the offender, who had repented, and concerning the father, who possibly had been persuaded to be lenient or even to forgive the offence.   This was done in order to influence the apostle to leniency.   But Paul no longer needed such arguments (cf. ii. 10).   In their gratification at the favourable outcome of the matter, both as regards father and son, the Church is not to overlook the fact that from the beginning the apostle has been concerned about the attitude of the Church, which, therefore, has been a matter of greater importance to him than the adjustment of the legal relations between the father and son.   Consequently also his present joy does not concern these individuals, but the conduct of the Church in this matter, and the restoration of the friendly relation to himself, which had been disturbed by their earlier attitude in the affair (vii. 7–11).   Rightly recognising the fact that the matter here dealt with is one which does at least have a legal side, but falsely assuming that the matters dealt with in 1 Cor. have been pressed into the background by a long interval of time and by the intervention of new and important transactions between Paul and the Church, both by letter and in person, Krenkel (S. 306) conjectures that the occasion for ii. 5–11, vii. 11 f. was a suit at law between members of the Church (cf. I. vi. 1 ff.).   Much more common is the assumption that some member of the Church (Bleek, 1830, S. 629 ; Neander, 296, 347 ; Hilgenfeld, *Einl.* 284), or one of Paul's Judaising opponents, possibly a member of the governing body of the Church (Ewald, S. 227), had publicly offered him a grave insult, very likely on the occasion of his second visit in Corinth, putting it in legal form (Weizsäcker, S. 298), and the Church had failed to come earnestly to the insulted apostle's defence.   According to this last mentioned hypothesis, the insulted apostle was filled with wrath, and what he was unable to accomplish in person, namely, the punishment of the one who offered the insult by the very majority of the Church which had

indorsed him, he accomplished by means of the letter, now lost, which he
sent by Titus! In the exposition of this view it is not accidental, but
fundamental for the theory (perhaps we should say destructive of it) that the
words, "The insulter" and "The insulted," which are taken from Luther's
translation, recur again and again as if this were, of course, the correct translation of ὁ ἀδικήσας and ὁ ἀδικηθείς. Of course, the idea of injured reputation
comes under the general conception of ἀδικεῖν ; but in Paul's writings, where
ἀδικεῖν occurs eight times, ἀδικία twelve times, and throughout both the Old
and New Testaments, where these words (also ἄδικος, ἀδίκημα) occur very
often, there is not a single instance where the words can be shown to have the
meaning, insult, libel, still less the narrower sense of slander. On the
contrary, its universal meaning is illegal action ; or where the verb has an
object (generally personal), the illegal injury of a person, or injuring of a
thing (Rev. ix. 4), cf. Aristot. *Rhetor.* i. 10, p. 1368, ἔστω δὴ τὸ ἀδικεῖν τὸ
βλάπτειν ἑκόντα παρὰ τὸν νόμον. If it were a matter of insult or abuse by
word or deed, Paul would write the words ὁ λοιδορήσας and ὁ λοιδορηθείς ; or,
if he wanted to use a legal term in this passage, ὁ ὑβρίσας and ὁ ὑβρισθείς ; cf.
Meier-Schömann, *Attischer Prozess,* bearb. von Lipsius (1883–87), S. 394–402.
The prevailing misunderstanding of the passage is helped by the failure to
distinguish between the broader and narrower meaning of *injuria,* the latter
of which corresponds to the Greek ἀδικεῖν, ἀδικία, ἀδίκημα. Cf. Theophilus,
Paraphr. instit. Just. iv. 4 end, οὐκ ἐῶσι τοὺς ὑβριστὰς ἀτιμωρήτους οἱ νόμοι.
Γενικῶς δὲ *injuria* λέγεται πᾶν ὃ μὴ κατὰ νόμον γίνεται, *quod non jure fit ;*
ἰδικῶς δὲ λέγεται *contumelia a contemnendo,* ἣν οἱ Ἕλληνες ὕβριν καλοῦσιν. Cf.
Scholion to Leo's *Basilica,* lib. lx. tit. 21, 1, and Ulpian, *Digest.* xlvii. 10. 1 end.
The difficulty which one has in understanding how Paul, in such a deep expression of his feelings as this, which is thoroughly intense, and which is put in the
first person throughout, could in one instance designate himself by the third
person, ὁ ἀδικηθείς, as if he were a stranger, would, of course, be removed if
we could assume that possibly Timothy is "the injured person" (thus
Beyschlag, *ThStKr.* 1871, S. 670). But this interpretation gives no logically possible connection between vii. 12*b*—where Paul speaks not only of
himself, but includes at least Timothy—and vii. 12*c.* If, with a view to
lessening the contradiction, it be said that the main reason for writing the
letter was not regard for the one who had been wronged, nor for the one
who had suffered the wrong (Krenkel, 299), it is nevertheless true that,
according to vii. 12*b,* the real purpose of the letter was to give the Church
an opportunity to prove their zeal for Paul (and Timothy) ; and so, if "the
person injured" were Paul himself or Timothy, he did, as a matter of fact,
in a very real sense, write on account of the ἀδικηθείς. Moreover, this
hypothesis in all its forms stands in contradiction to ii. 5. If οὐκ ἐμὲ
λελύπηκεν be taken as a statement of fact, then it is hypocrisy unworthy of
the apostle ; if it be taken as a question, it is incomparably foolish. Nor is
it easy to see how the Church could have succeeded in making itself appear
blameless in this matter (vii. 11).

7. (P. 337.) Frequent doubt has been expressed as to whether II. vi. 14–
vii. 1 was originally a part of the letter and as to its Pauline origin. Ewald
(282 f.) held that it was taken from the writings of one who belonged to the
apostolic circle at a somewhat later date. Hilgenfeld (287, A. 1) conjectured

that it was taken from the letter mentioned in 1 Cor. v. 9,—a theory which Francke (*ThStKr.* 1884, S. 544 ff.) undertook to prove.   Krenkel rejoices (332) that the fact that this section does not belong in 2 Cor. is coming more and more to be recognised, and thinks that he discovers many similarities to the language of the *Epistle of Clement.*   The problem calls for a discussion of the context.   After the general discussion concerning the office of preaching, to which he was led through opposition to the Jewish Christian wandering teachers (ii. 17–iii. 1, v. 12), Paul, in vi. 1, returns again to the discussion of the special conditions in the Corinthian Church, which, with the exception of a few brief remarks (iii. 1–3, v. 11–13) seem to have been lost sight of from ii. 14 on.   He and his companions are not only commissioned to preach the gospel of reconciliation to the unconverted (v. 11–21), but also to help the Churches already gathered through the preaching of the gospel,—in this instance those of Achaia here addressed, and in particular those of Corinth (vi. 11),—and to warn them lest they receive grace in vain in the day of salvation (vi. 1–2, cf. i. 24).   As was recognised even by Clement (*Strom.* i. 4), and, as is clearly set forth by Hofmann (ii. 3. 166–174), vi. 3–10, which has no grammatical connection with what precedes, is the introduction to vi. 11, between which and what precedes there is undoubtedly an anacoluthon.   Conscious that his work and personal life among them have been blameless, Paul (and Timothy) now 'opens his mouth unto them,' *i.e.* he is about to tell them solemnly and frankly what he has in his heart to say to them (cf. Matt. v. 2 ; Acts viii. 34, x. 34).   And this is an exhortation like that in vi. 1, *i.e.* a warning against everything which might make their acceptance of that redemptive grace by which Christians are distinguished from the still unregenerate world seem to be an illusion.   The remark that his heart as well as his mouth is open to the Corinthians, and the request that the readers open their hearts to him, as children ought to do to their father (I. iv. 14), is a further introduction to the statement he is' about to make, occasioned by the distrust of the Church which has not altogether disappeared.   Now this statement, which has been led up to at such length and in so many different ways, and which has been held back so long, would be ridiculous if it were simply the two words χωρήσατε ἡμᾶς, vii. 2a.   That, however, would be the case if vi. 14–vii. 1 were to be set aside as an interpolation, for, in what follows vii. 2b–18 there is nothing which corresponds to the promised παράκλησις.   This is found in vi. 14–vii. 2a.   It is the demand that is found running through 1 Cor. that the Church separate itself more entirely from the heathen immorality by which it was surrounded.   With vi. 16 cf. I. iii. 16, viii. 10, x. 20–22, xiv. 25 ; with vi. 17 f. cf. I. x. 13 f., cf. above, p. 274 f., 296, n. 2.   There is nothing peculiar in the character of the words used, although ἑτεροζυγεῖν, μετοχή, συμφώνησις, Βελίαρ do not occur elsewhere in the writings of Paul nor in the N.T.   The passionate antithesis with which the section begins is quite in keeping with the mood which is reflected in vi. 3–10, vii. 1–11, while the solemn words of vi. 16b–vii. 1 harmonise with the manner of the announcement in vi. 11. These pressing exhortations have their own significance, but, in addition to that, serve appropriately as the introduction to the matter discussed in vii. 5–16, all the more so because the case of the man who had committed incest, which had caused Paul so much anxiety, had now become a source of joy to him.   Since, however, these exhortations did not touch at all Paul's personal relation to the Church, the exhortation vii. 2*a*, which is clearly different from vi. 13, forms an appropriate transition to what follows.

8. (P. 343.)   Although no representatives of the Corinthian Church are mentioned as accompanying Paul to Jerusalem along with the representatives of the Churches of Galatia, Asia, and Macedonia (Acts xx. 4, above, p. 209, n. 2), in view of Rom. xv. 25-28 we may not assume that the collection in Achaia was not completed, and that Paul's efforts in this matter (2 Cor. viii.–ix.) were fruitless.

V.

THE EPISTLE TO THE ROMANS.

§ 21. CONTENTS OF THE LETTER AND THE PROGRESS OF ITS THOUGHT.

THE Epistles of Paul, considered up to this point, have been addressed to Churches, or groups of Churches, that owed their Christianity to him. In this letter, however, he turns his attention to a Church which was undoubtedly founded without any co-operation from him or his helpers. Though individual Christians living in Rome at the time may have been personally, or even intimately, acquainted with Paul, to the Church as a whole he was a stranger, and to the large majority of the Roman Christians personally unknown. His first concern, therefore, was to establish a connection between himself and the Church. This explains why he begins with a salutation which is more elaborate than in any other of his Epistles, and why in this instance the part in which the author speaks of himself is expanded into a lengthy complex of clauses (i. 1–5), whereas, in other letters, either the characterisation of the readers (1 Cor. i. 2) or the contents of the salutation (Gal. i. 3–5) is more fully developed. Paul introduces himself to the Church, so to speak, not as if they had never heard of him before, but still in such a way that the Church can form some idea, from the very way in which he characterises himself, as to the occasion of the letter, and the grounds on which Paul based his right to address them thus in a long Epistle. He is not

merely an individual engaged in the service of Christ like
all Christians, but also an apostle ; he is not merely one
of the numerous missionaries about whose call there may
be some question (above, p. 289 f.), but he owes his position
to a definite call from God, just as the readers owe their
Christian faith to a definite call of God.   Although the
contrast with which he testifies to the genuineness of his
apostleship is not so strong here as in 1 Cor. i. 1, particularly Gal. i. 1, nevertheless the threefold repetition of
κλητός (vv. 1, 6 f.) does show the same careful premedita-
tion as 1 Cor. i. 1 f.   How anxious he is that the readers
shall realise the full import of this self-characterisation is
shown by the fulness with which he develops this particular idea, though it was familiar to every Christian of
that time.   The fact that all which follows κλητὸς ἀπόστολος in i. 1b–5 is an expansion of this idea, proves that
Paul cannot here be saying anything of himself not
equally applicable to others who have been called to be
apostles.   While in other places he speaks of his special
call to be the apostle to the Gentiles (xi. 13, xv. 16),
and so of his special gospel (ii. 16, xvi. 25), here he calls
the gospel, for the proclamation of which he has been
separated from all other avocations, a message of God.
This expression is employed here in the same sense in
which it and its synonyms are everywhere used, in distinct contrast to the conception of teaching, which is the
product of human reflection and which varies in each case
with the type of mind or the peculiar gifts of the preacher
(1 Thess. ii. 2, 8, 9, 13 ; 1 Cor. ii. 1–5 ; 2 Cor. ii. 17,
xi. 7).   When he goes on to say, further, with reference to
this same gospel, that long before God had suffered this
message of His to enter the world He had promised the
sending of the same through the prophets, and that this
promise was recorded in the Holy Scriptures (i. 2, cf.
x. 15 ; Luke iv. 17–21) ; and when, further, the central
point of this gospel is declared to be the Son of God, who

entered into a natural human life as a descendant of
David, and was appointed to become a Son of God in
power, and so to enter into a new and higher life of
which the Holy Spirit was the norm and the resurrection
the beginning, the points made are simply the close connection between the gospel and the revelations, Scriptures
and history of the O.T. on the one hand, and the exalta-
tion of the Son of David, living in the flesh, to His present
glory (cf. Jas. ii. 1 ; 2 Pet. i. 16), on the other. When,
now, at this point with the mention of Christ he passes
again by a natural transition from the description of the
gospel to a direct characterisation of his apostolic calling
(i. 5), he includes himself at once with others to whom
what he here says of himself is equally applicable. Since
this letter was not written in conjunction with anyone
else, and since from i. 8–xvi. 23 or xvi. 25 Paul uses
the singular when speaking of himself, it is self-evident
that the plural in i. 5 is to be taken literally, as always in
Paul's writings (n. 1). Since, moreover, the only thought
expressed indicating any wider or narrower circle to which
Paul belonged is that of his apostolic calling, it was perfectly clear to his readers that he included with himself
other men who, like him, were κλητοὶ ἀπόστολοι (cf. x. 15,
xvi. 7). They could say with Paul, "Through Christ we
received grace as Christians, and a call as apostles to the
end that we might arouse obedience to the faith among
all peoples, to the glory of His name." The idea that
Paul is speaking here of his special commission as the
apostle to the Gentiles, has against it not only the context of the salutation, as pointed out above, but also the
usage elsewhere of πάντα τὰ ἔθνη (n. 2). The whole human
race with its national divisions, representing as it does
the utmost diversity, is the common, originally undivided
field in which the older apostles and Paul were appointed
to labour. Nor can it be claimed that in this passage
"all peoples" must mean the Gentiles, on the ground

that otherwise in i. 6 Paul would impart the trivial information to the Romans that they are a part of the human race. Paul does not say that they are included in the πάντα τὰ ἔθνη, but that they are the called of Jesus Christ, a Church already gathered through the influence of the gospel, in that region which is the appointed field of labour for all the apostles. For this reason, neither Paul nor any of the apostles, whose call is essentially a call to preach the gospel, have any direct missionary relation to the Roman Christians. But this does not by any means render the apostles indifferent to those who are already converts. For, in the first place, existing Churches are centres of the Christian faith (cf. Phil. ii. 15 f.), the spreading of which is the distinctive function of the apostles ; and, in the second place, the word of the apostles has a right to special consideration among those who are already believers (cf. xii. 3 ; 1 Cor. xii. 28 ; Eph. ii. 20, iv. 11–16 ; 1 Pet. v. 1). Such consideration for what he is about to write Paul seeks from all the Christians in Rome at the time whose character, not only as children of God through grace, but also as those called to be saints, i.e. as a Christian Church (cf. 1 Cor. i. 2), he emphasises once more before adding his general salutation (ver. 7).

The first thought expressed after this carefully weighed greeting is that of gratitude to God for all the Roman Christians, more particularly for the fact that their conversion to the Christian faith has become known throughout the whole world (i. 8, cf. xv. 19 ; 1 Thess. i. 8 f.). How much this means to Paul is evidenced by the solemn assurance which follows, that in his private devotions, which have relation to the gospel quite as much as his outward activities, he remembers regularly also the Roman Christians, making request in all his prayers that the way may be finally opened for him, in the will of God, to come to them (ver. 10). This thought he expands by

explaining that he has a longing desire to see them in
order to impart some spiritual gift from which he expects
the Roman Christians to be strengthened, or, as he immediately adds by way of explanation and correction,
from which he expects them and himself to be mutually
encouraged by the faith that is in each (ver. 11 f., cf. xv.
24, xvi. 25).

Paul could not have spoken with greater precaution or
modesty of the result for which he hoped from this long
intended visit to Rome.   Not only does he place the
Christians in Rome on the same level with the Churches
organised by himself (cf. 1 Thess. iii. 2, 13 ; Acts xv. 32,
xvi. 5, xviii. 23), but he guards expressly against giving
the impression that they alone are to be benefited by
the visit (cf. *per contra*, 2 Cor. i. 15 ; Phil. i. 24–26).
If he had said nothing further with reference to the
purpose of his projected visit, all that could be inferred from his words would be that for Paul as a missionary the existence of a Christian Church in Rome was
a matter of great importance ; that for a long time he had
had it in mind, in further pursuance of his missionary
plans, to come also to Rome, regarding which plans,
however, nothing more definite is said ; and, finally, that
the exchange of spiritual gifts which would take place
with the Roman Christians on that occasion would be
advantageous both to them and to him.   But now he
mentions a second motive for his coming, using a phrase
which indicates the introduction of a new thought, namely,
his desire to obtain also in Rome some fruit, *i.e.* his hope
to preach the gospel with result also among the Roman
populace, the great mass of whom are unconverted.
Although he expresses himself very modestly with reference to the result for which he hopes from this contemplated missionary preaching (τινὰ καρπόν), still this seems
to have been the chief purpose of the visit to the capital
which had been planned so long and so repeatedly post-

THE EPISTLE TO THE ROMANS

poned on account of some external hindrance; for in
concluding this discussion with the words, "Such is the
willingness on my part to preach the gospel to you
(*al.* among you), *i.e.* to the people in Rome," he mentions only the missionary preaching as the object of his
coming, making no reference whatever to the hoped-for
effect of his visit upon the Roman Church (vv. 13–15,
n. 3). That he is just as willing to labour as a missionary
in Rome as he is conscious of his obligation to do so, is
proved by his declaration that he is not ashamed of the
gospel (ver. 16). The fact that until now he has remained
away from Rome is not, therefore, to be explained as due
to any lack of willingness on his part, nor this lack of
willingness as due in turn to his want of confidence in
the gospel.

In this way Paul prepares the way for statements
about the gospel which go far beyond any requirements
of the purpose manifest from the connection with the preceding context, and which are to be made the theme of more
extended discussions. Paul does not hesitate to introduce
the gospel, this weak and foolish preaching (1 Cor. i. 17–
25), into the very centre of the world's culture, because
he has learned and experienced its essence to be what he
describes in i. 16 f. It is a power of God unto salvation
for every one that believes, primarily for Jews and Greeks
(n. 4). The gospel is such a universal means of salvation,
upon the sole condition of faith, because in the same is
revealed a righteousness of God which results from faith,
and which has for its aim the creation of faith. This
is in accordance with the word of the prophet : "The
righteous shall attain to life as a result of faith" (Hab.
ii. 4 ; cf. Gal. iii. 11) ; since this prophecy contains the two
thoughts which are fundamental in the statement about
the gospel, namely, that only the righteous attain to
life, and that by no other means than through faith,
all that follows to viii. 39, or indeed to xi. 36, is in-

tended to make clear to the Romans this construction of the gospel.

In the *first section* (i. 18–iii. 20) he proceeds to show in proof of the first of the two propositions contained in the citation, that the wrath of God is directed against all unrighteousness and ungodliness of men, for which they are responsible and inexcusable, throughout the course of history (i. 18), as well as at the final judgment, when the righteousness of God, concealed from the thoughtless by the manifold proofs of God's goodness in creation, shall be revealed as retributive righteousness (ii. 3–10). Furthermore, in God's impartial determination of the destiny of the individual soul there is no distinction between Jew and Gentile (ii. 11–22). While the advantage of being an Israelite, and thus of belonging to the people of God's revelation, is not to be denied, this cannot in any way alter the fact that in the final judgment all men must appear before God as liars and sinners worthy of condemnation, for He is the only true and altogether righteous one (iii. 1–8). Finally, even Christians are not to imagine that they are exempted *a priori* from this condemnation of a sinful race under God's wrath. On the one hand, they are included in the scriptural judgment already quoted concerning the universal sinfulness of men ; and, on the other hand, they are aware that the proof furnished by the history of Israel regarding the impossibility of obtaining righteousness through the observance of the law holds for the entire race (iii. 9–20).

Although from the course of the argument condemnation seems to be the inevitable end of the entire human race, a *second section* (iii. 20–v. 11) is devoted primarily to showing how the righteousness of God necessary to life is restored in Christ, being proclaimed in the gospel which requires faith, and how by faith it becomes the possession of all Christian believers, Jews and Gentiles alike (iii. 20–30). The objection that through the doctrine of justifica-

tion as here set forth Christians are in danger of falling
into antinomianism is disposed of very briefly (iii. 31).
On the other hand, the further objection that by accepting this doctrine Christians sever themselves from the
religion of the O.T., or, in other words, render entirely
external the unquestionable relation existing between
the Christian Church and Abraham, the progenitor of
the religious community under the O.T. dispensation, is
answered in great detail. Since, according to Gen. xv. 6,
the religious attitude of Abraham was, rather, essentially
similar to that of the Christian, the opposite conclusion
follows, namely, that the theocratic community of which
Abraham was the founder has its proper continuance in
Christianity, which embraces the circumcised and the uncircumcised, but is self-consistent because it makes both
alike stand in the faith through which Abraham, being
yet uncircumcised, obtained his position of acceptance
with God, and his significance for the history of religion
(iv. 1–22, n. 5). Since, now, this exposition ends with
the reaffirmation of the original position that Christians
are justified by faith (iv. 23–25), upon it is very properly
based the assurance that Christians, being justified and
reconciled, are at peace with God, and in spite of all the
afflictions of the present may and should cherish the confident hope of their future glory or final redemption (v.
1–11, n. 6).

Here the theme stated in i. 16 f. seems to have been
developed to its logical conclusion ; since, from the preceding description of the origin and nature of the
Christian life, with the future consummation of the same
which this nature involves, it must be apparent that in
Christian experience the gospel, being a revelation of the
righteousness requisite to life, has proved itself to be a
saving power. Nevertheless, a *third section* (v. 12–viii. 39)
is added, closely connected with the one which precedes,
concluding with similar thoughts. Although the main

statement beginning with διὰ τοῦτο in v. 12 is left unfinished, and although even the comparative sentence
introduced into the main sentence immediately after the
latter is begun is not concluded, the progress of thought
can hardly be said to be obscure. As death, which was
brought into the world by Adam, more specifically by
Adam's sin, *reigned* over all Adam's descendants, so shall
the grace and the gift of God and of Christ, which had
their inception in history through Christ, more precisely
through Christ's one act of righteousness, *reign* in the
new humanity descended from Christ who is the second
Adam. Inasmuch as the Mosaic Law is described as
subordinate to the two world principles, Adam and Christ,
or sin and righteousness, or death and life (v. 20), it is
at once clear that the *reign* and supremacy of grace
under the Christian dispensation may not be limited, or,
rather, set aside, by the subordinate dominion of the law.
In proof of this last point, he calls attention to the fact
that in the very community where the law had served
only to increase sin, namely, in Israel, redemptive grace
had been revealed in its greatest fulness. This statement
is intended to guard against the possibility of grace being
looked upon as a makeshift, or as *one* means of salvation
among others, as might easily have been the case had
grace been manifested first to another people without
Israel's experiences with the law. The fact that Christ
appeared in Israel is assurance that grace may *reign*
wherever it is accepted.

The objection that if this doctrine of law and grace
be true, one needs only to continue in sin in order to
receive constantly new supplies of grace, Paul meets by
recalling the fact of the new birth connected with baptism, which makes a sinful life on the part of the Christians
seem unnatural, furnishing the strongest motive for holiness. It is just because Christians are not under law,
which in itself has no power to overcome sin, but under

grace, which in the resurrection of Christ and regeneration of the Christian proves itself to be a life-giving power, that they dare to hope for mastery over sin (vi. 1–14). But from the experience of the readers not only is this pernicious theory (vi. 1), but likewise the possibility of any practical misuse on the part of the Christian of his privileges under the gentle rule of grace, instead of under the hard discipline of the law, easily refuted as due to wrong inferences from the doctrine of justification expounded above. From being sinful and disobedient servants of God, as they were formerly, they have become servants obedient from the heart, and are, therefore, no longer slaves and mercenaries of sin, but slaves of righteousness and soldiers of God. They have only to recall their pre-Christian life, and the death which was the inevitable issue of that life, and then to observe the process of sanctification taking place in their present Christian life, and to remember that eternal life is its final goal, in order to lose all desire to sink back into their former state (vi. 15–23, n. 7).

Moreover, Paul feels that it is incumbent upon him to justify to his readers even the presupposition, namely, that the Christian is no longer under the law, but under grace (vii. 1–6), which in vi. 1–14 and vi. 15–23 is defended against false inferences. From their acquaintance with the law, the readers know that the Mosaic ordinances have authority over a man only so long as he lives, which implies that it has no power beyond death. Both these phases of the truth are illustrated by a single appropriate example, namely, the law of marriage, which unites two human lives into one. In the case of the surviving party when a marriage bond is annulled by death, we see that death frees from the law. The illustration of the marriage bond thus cited is used also as a figure in the application of the principle stated in vii. 1 to the subject under discussion. Since Christ's obligation to the law ceased with

His death, and since Christians became subsequently through baptism partakers of Christ's death, the same as though they themselves had actually died (vi. 3, cf. Gal. ii. 19, iv. 4 f.), for them also obligation under the law as a marriage bond is legally annulled, in order that they may be united to the risen Christ in a new marriage union. Not until they come into this new fellowship with Christ are they able to attain to a true moral life permeated by a new spirit; whereas, on the other hand, while they lived still under the law and served God according to the letter, sinful desires awakened by the law held sway over their bodies, and life under the law issued in death (n. 8).

Here again a conclusion seems to follow fatal to all that has been said heretofore. If exemption from the law and cessation from the life of sin go together, then we seem driven to the blasphemous conclusion that the law and sin are identical. This objection Paul answers in vii. 7–viii. 11 chiefly from his own experience with the law in his early life and now in his Christian life. This experience he describes under the presupposition that Christians who like himself have been brought up under the law have had essentially the same experience. When he became a Christian he continued to regard the law as holy, righteous, and good; and as a converted man his will gave fullest assent to it. But in individual experience, as in the life of men generally (cf. iii. 20, iv. 15, v. 20), the law has proved itself to be a power awakening and developing latent sin, thereby deepening the knowledge of sin; and even when the will gives assent to the contents of the law, it is incapable of overcoming sin. If, along with his lament due to doubt about his moral capacity, there is a place in the Christian's life for gratitude to God for His gift in Christ (vii. 24 f.), this is no effect which after all has been wrought by the law, but the outcome of the liberating work of the Spirit, begetting a new Christlike life in those who have been born again. God's very act in sending the Son was positive expression of His will that henceforth sin should no more rule in the flesh; and with Christ's coming was begun the actual fulfilment of this divine purpose (viii. 3). Through the Spirit received by the Christian from Christ the ordinances of the law are fulfilled in their unity by those who give themselves up to the control of this Spirit instead of continuing under the power of their inborn nature (viii. 4). Eventually, through the same Spirit the body also, which is still subject to death, shall be quickened (viii. 11). Finally, in language which soars higher and higher as the climax is approached, the fact is proclaimed that the sonship wrought in us by the life-giving Spirit involves not only the obligation of a present walk according to the Spirit, but warrants also the hope of future glory, and supplies the power to overcome all the sufferings of the present (viii. 12–39).

Thus the discussion of the supremacy of grace over all who have been renewed by Christ (v. 12–viii. 39) leads to the same conclusion as the discussion of the doctrine of justification (iii. 21–v. 11), and the development of the theme announced in i. 16 f. might be considered complete if in the discussion up to this point Paul had taken adequate account of Israel's special position of privilege, at which he hinted in his statement of the theme, and expressly admitted in iii. 1–3 (cf. ii. 25). When a Jewish Christian like Paul is able to describe with constantly increasing enthusiasm the glory of the redemption wrought by Christ for the whole human race, affirming that in its completion even inanimate nature is drawn into its sweep, while he passes by with a single incidental remark (iii. 3), the fact that by the vast majority of his own nation, mediators of the divine revelation though they are (iii. 2, v. 20), no benefits are enjoyed from this salvation, this omission itself requires explanation. This is given in the *fourth section* (ix. 1–xi. 35). After the song of thanksgiving in viii. 31–39, it was most fitting for Paul to aver with all solemnity that he speaks the absolute truth when he says that in his heart he suffers unceasing pain because of his unbelieving countrymen. To be sure, he does not want this to be understood as implying that God did not fulfil the promise which He made to Israel, or that the unbelieving Jews have a right by reason of their origin, and of such moral service as they may have rendered in addition, to complain of the new course taken by history with the entrance of the gospel (ix. 6 f.). From such errors he is saved by his knowledge of O.T. history and prophecy (ix. 7b–29). But nevertheless it grieves him exceedingly that while Gentiles, who are little concerned about righteousness, are saved, Israel, with all its striving after legal righteousness, obtains neither this righteousness nor the righteousness of faith, stumbling at the very point where they ought not to stumble, namely, the revelation of God in Christ (ix. 30–33). But Paul is not satisfied with merely lamenting the tragic fate of his nation. Because of their earnest, albeit blind zeal, which led them to resist the gospel, thereby giving the Gentiles their present pre-eminence, he longs for their salvation, and beseeches that it may be granted them by God (chap. x.). That there can be no question of a permanent rejection of Israel is proved by every conversion of individual Jews, like Paul, and by the existence of a body of Jewish Christians, numbering thousands (xi. 1–7a, cf. ix. 27–29). The hardening of Israel, which carries with it still other judgments of a more external kind (xi. 7b–10), is not an end in itself, but designed, primarily, to enable the Gentiles to obtain part in redemption. There is. hope that finally the conversion of the Gentiles will react upon Israel, leading to their salvation also (xi. 11 f.). Paul calls the special attention of the Gentile Christians at Rome to the fact that, in fulfilling the specific work involved by his commission as an apostle to the Gentiles, he does so always with the additional purpose in view of arousing the jealousy of his countrymen and of winning at least some of them, and thus of preparing the way for the conversion of Israel, with which event will come the end of the world (xi. 13–15, cf. ver. 12, n. 9). Similarly, applicable only to Gentile Christians is the warning against an overbearing attitude toward the Jewish people in their present hardened state (vv. 16–24), and the proclamation of the final redemption of the whole of Israel as a truth of scriptural revelation (vv. 25–32). The fourth section ends with an exclamation of wonder at God's government of the world (vv. 32–36).

To the explanation of the nature of the gospel here concluded Paul adds in a *fifth section* (xii. 1–xv. 13) a comprehensive and well-arranged statement of how one ought to walk in accordance with the same. Unlike what immediately precedes, which is directed to the Gentile Christians alone, what is here said is expressly addressed to all the Christians in Rome (xii. 3). Compared with similar parts of other letters, this section of Romans is especially noticeable for its pressing exhortation to obedience to State authority, together with the fulfilment of all the duties of citizenship (xiii. 1–7), and for the emphasis which it lays—much stronger than in Gal. v. 14—upon the principle that active brotherly love is the true fulfilment of the law (xiii. 8–10, cf. viii. 4). The exhortation to live a sober and self-controlled life in view of the constantly nearer approach of the day of Christ, and in the care of the body to avoid everything that might arouse the passions (xiii. 11–14), introduces at once the discussion of a schism among the Roman Christians regarding which Paul must have been well informed (xiv. 1–23). There were Christians in Rome who from principle avoided the use of meat, possibly also of wine (vv. 2, 20), claiming that such use was defiling (vv. 14, 30). This being their position, naturally they con-

demned severely all other Christians who used the
customary foods without distinction, and were themselves in turn despised for their superstitious scruples
(vv. 3, 10). From the opinion of the vegetarians that
those who ate meat were not steadfast, but in danger of
stumbling (ver. 4), we infer that they looked upon their
own abstinence as a means of securing religious steadfastness, and commended it as such to others (cf. Heb.
xiii. 9). Although Paul rebukes the ascetics for their
bigoted judgment of others, declaring them to be weak
in faith, and takes his own stand with those strong in
faith, as regards the actual practice in the matter he goes
no further than to state that both practices are consistent
with the Christian profession, dealing at greatest length
with the obligation of those strong in faith to avoid
offending the conscience of their weaker brethren. They
are not to influence such either by their contemptuous
treatment of them, or by their challenging example to
act against their consciences (vv. 13–23, cf. 1 Cor. viii.
7–13). The ascetic party must, therefore, have been in
the minority. That they were native Jews is probable,
as evidenced by the use of the conceptions κοινός and
καθαρός (vv. 14, 20), and made certain by the fact that
in correcting their judgment of those who eat meat Paul
argues that the use of meat is just as consistent with
Christianity, and just as much to be tolerated in the
Christian Church, as is the observance of certain days
(n. 10). This argument has weight only if the ascetics
claimed the unquestioned right to set apart on religious
grounds certain days, which could have been none other
than the Jewish Sabbaths, feasts, and fasts. From the
fact that the ascetic party were Jews it does not follow
necessarily that those who ate meat were exclusively
Gentiles. They could equally well have been Jews, like
the apostle, who, in using the phrase " we who are strong,"
identifies himself with those who used meat (xv. 1).

According to a reliable tradition, xiv. 23 was followed immediately by xvi. 25–27 (§ 22); but even if this were not its original place, it is clear that after concluding the discussion of the differences between the vegetarians and those who ate meat, Paul must have passed to a more general exhortation to preserve the unity of the Church by mutual concessions. From the fact that in the application of this exhortation to the readers united thanksgiving is declared to be the goal toward which they are to strive (xv. 6), and that in the explanation which follows (vv. 8–12) the union of Israel and of the Gentiles is proved from history and Scripture to be the final goal of the course of redemption, one sees that in these closing sentences of the fifth parenetic section Paul's aim was to remove all differences between the Jewish and Gentile Christians in Rome by which the unity of confession and of worship was imperilled.

The *sixth section* (xv. 14–xvi. 24, or –xvi. 27) begins with a retrospect of the letter itself, now nearing its close. Paul corrects the possible impression which may have been produced by the elaborateness of the letter and its strenuous tone, that he regarded the Roman Christians as in very special need of instruction. To him even it had seemed a venture to direct such a letter to them. Still this feeling was mitigated somewhat by the fact that he discussed only certain phases of Christian truth, and in doing so was always conscious of reminding them of truths with which they were already familiar. He had ventured to write them in the interest of his calling as the apostle to the Gentiles. By reason of the wide extent of the territory in which heretofore he had carried on his work, it had happened that up to the present he had found constantly new labours close at hand, and so had been prevented from realising the desire which he had often felt of coming to Rome (n. 11). And even now, when he finds no more occasion in the regions lying about the eastern part of the Mediterranean for the kind of missionary work which he recognises as his special work, namely, that of laying foundations, he cannot at once visit Rome on his way to Spain, as he had longed to do for many years, but must go first to Jerusalem to deliver the collection gathered by the Christians in Macedonia and Greece. Not until this business is finished will he go to Spain by way of Rome. So for the present he requests the prayers of the Romans for his protection against the dangers which threaten him at the hands of unbelieving Jews in Jerusalem, and for a favourable reception of the collection on the part of the Christians there, in order that by the will of God he may come to Rome in a joyful state of mind. Here the letter returns to the point at which it began (i. 1–15), and is temporarily concluded with a benediction (xv. 33). The discussion of his projected missionary journeys and his missionary plans, which is merely begun in i. 1–15, is here completed. Now for the first time we understand clearly Paul's statements at the beginning of the letter about his desire to come to Rome, and the hints about the hindrances which hitherto he had always encountered in endeavouring to carry out this purpose (i. 10, 13a). In particular is it clear why he was unable at the beginning of the letter to announce his approaching visit, but had to be satisfied with merely expressing his earnest desire, his willingness, and his hope to come. Great emphasis is laid upon the significance of the circumstance which at this time compels him to postpone his visit still longer, and which justifies the composition of this elaborate letter, namely, the journey to Jerusalem with the collection. In this collection the Gentile Christian Churches founded by him fulfil an obligation of love and of gratitude to the mother Church (xv. 25–27), and Paul hopes that this gift will be the means of producing similar kindly feeling toward the Gentile Christians among the Jewish Christians of Jerusalem (xv. 31). What he said in i. 11 about the purpose of his visit to Rome, and of the fruitful effect which he hoped to see resulting from his visit for the Roman Christians and for himself, is here repeated. He himself hopes to be quickened by his sojourn among the Roman Christians (xv. 24), and is in turn convinced that he will come to them in the fulness of Christian blessing (xv. 29). Since, however, he calls the quickening which he himself hopes to receive among the Roman Christians a " partial filling " (ver. 24), it is certain that he did not contemplate any protracted stay in Rome. This agrees with the modest way in which he spoke in i. 13 of the results which he hoped to obtain from his proposed missionary work in Rome ; but just why this was the case is made clear now for the first time, by the repeated notice (vv. 15, 24, 28) that the real objective of his more extended missionary plans is Spain, and that Rome is only a stopping-place for the missionary pressing his way to the extreme West.

The remembrances, greetings, and repeated parting wishes (chap. xvi.) require special investigation, there being more serious question as to their place in Romans than as regards any other part of the letter.

1. (P. 354.) Concerning Paul's use of the first person plural, see above, p. 209, n. 3, p. 316, n. 3. The treatise of Dick, *Der Schriftstellerische Plural bei Paulus*, 1900, betrays in the very title the lack of a distinction between the true epistolary style and the usage of the literati. As is well known, the ancient form of the introductory greeting designated by their personal names the writer of the letter in the nominative and the recipient in the dative ; in other words, with entire objectivity as third persons. Paul follows this scheme essentially in all his writings, except that he makes the greeting proper a grammatically independent sentence expressive of his wishes toward them (cf. *ZKom. Gal.* 29 f., and above, p. 177, n. 2). It appears, therefore, to be contrary to literary style, when before the greeting, which is moulded after the Semitic form into an address to the recipient, ver. 7b, an *I* and *thou*, or a *we* and *ye* appear, as ver. 4, ἡμῶν ; ver. 5, ἐλαβομεν ; ver. 6, καὶ ὑμεῖς. So Gal. i. 2, ἐμοί ; 2 John 1, 3 John 1, Tit. i. 3 ἐγώ ; Philem. 2, σοῦ, more often ἡμῶν and ἡμῖν, 1 Cor. i. 2 ; 2 Thess. i. 1 ; 1 Tim. i. 1 ; Philem. 1 ; 2 Pet. i. 1 ; 2 John 2.

This prominence of subjectivity, however, is not at all confined to the letters of the N.T. or the early Christian literature. Cf. *e.g. Berl. ägypt. Urk.* No. 405. 6, ὁμογαστρίῳ μου ἀδελφῇ, Nos. 814. 1, 892. 1, and even in Cicero, *Ep. ad famil.* xvi. 1. In inscriptions also the same thing occurs not infrequently.

2. (P. 354.) Like other Biblical writers, Paul applies the name (τὰ) ἔθνη to Gentile nations in contrast to Israel, and also, following the later Jewish usage (יוֹג mas., גּוֹיָה fem., Gentile), to individual Gentiles in contrast to Jews (Rom. ii. 14, iii. 29, ix. 24, 30, xi. 11–13, 25, xv. 9 f., 12, 16, 18, 27, xvi. 4). But since Israel also is an ἔθνος (John xi. 48–52, xviii. 35 ; Luke vii. 5, xxiii. 2 ; Acts x. 22, xxiv. 3, 10, 17, xxvi. 4, xxviii. 19 ; also יוֹג Ex. xix. 6, xxxiii. 13 ; Deut. iv. 6 ; Isa. i. 4, iv. 2), πάντα τὰ ἔθνη could not well be used to denote the Gentile world excluding Israel. In Rom. xv. 11 (Ps. cxvii. 1) the syn-onymous expression coupled with it (πάντες οἱ λαοί) shows rather that the apostle's meaning is mankind as it is divided into peoples, including Israel, and that the two parties which are distinguished in xv. 8–10 as περιτομή, or λαὸς τοῦ θεοῦ and ἔθνη, are here spoken of together. If it is perfectly plain that in Matt. xxviii. 19, Luke xxiv. 47, Israel is by no means excluded, but simply that the confining of missionary work to that nation is forbidden, *ZKom. Matt.* 714, A 9, why should the interpretation be different in Rom. i. 5, xvi. 26 ; Gal. iii. 8 ; 2 Tim. iv. 17 ; Matt. xxiv. 9, 14, xxv. 32 ; Mark xi. 17, xiii. 10 ? Moreover, in a speech to Gentiles who had heard nothing as yet of the choice of a people of God and of a special revelation to that people, it would be most inappropriate to say, *Gott alle Heiden ihre eigenen wege habe wandeln lassen* ("God suffered all *Gentiles* to walk in their *own* ways") (Acts xiv. 16). This translation of Luther's would require the reading ταῖς ἰδίαις αὐτῶν ὁδοῖς, and necessitate the placing of the words in an emphatic position. The meaning is rather that formerly, in contrast to the present preaching of the gospel to all mankind, God suffered the many nations which make up humanity to go their several ways ; cf. Acts xvii. 24–30 ; Rom. iii. 25. Even in the O.T. the term commonly includes Israel ; cf. Jer. xxv. 15, 17–25. It is also a very significant fact that the LXX repeatedly uses τὰ λοιπὰ ἔθνη, where the other modifying words do not make it quite clear that הַגּוֹיִם or כָּל־הַגּוֹיִם is restricted to nations other than Israel, Deut. viii. 20, xvii. 14 ; 1 Sam. viii. 5. But the whole of mankind is just as much the field of labour for those apostles to whom the Son of David had given grace and apostleship while He lived in the flesh (Matt. v. 13 f. [xiii. 38], xxviii. 19 ; Luke xxiv. 47 ; Acts i. 8), as for Paul, who had been called by the ascended Son of God (Acts ix. 15, xxii. 15, xxvi. 17 ; 1 Cor. i. 17–24, ix. 20 ; Col. i. 28). True, the original apostles had to begin their work with Israel and in Jerusalem (Matt. x. 5, 23 ; Luke xxiv. 47 ; Acts i. 4, 8, ii. 39), while Paul, on the other hand, was chiefly an apostle to the Gentiles. But this fact did not affect the universality of the apostleship of either, neither was it affected by the subsequent division of their field of labour (Gal. ii. 9, above, p. 266, line 23). Paul considers his mission to the Gentiles only *one* part of his calling, and indicates that even this has reference also to Israel (Rom. xi. 13 f.). But in his greeting to the Romans he does not speak as an apostle to the Gentiles, but simply as one called to be an apostle, with the same right to address them that Peter would have. He writes, not on the authority of his calling as an apostle of the Gentiles, but only in the interest of it (xv. 15 f. ;

see below, § 24, n. 1). If Paul had wished to say that by origin the Roman Christians belonged to the class indicated by πάντα τὰ ἔθνη, according to established usage he must have written ἐξ ὧν ἐστε καὶ ὑμεῖς ; cf. Gal. ii. 15 ; Rom. ix. 6, 24, xi. 1 ; Phil. iii. 5 ; Acts x. 45, xi. 2, xv. 23 ; Rev. v. 9, vii. 4–9. What he really does say is that they are a Christian community within the bounds of the apostolic field of labour. Writers as early as Ambrosiaster and Chrysostom (x. 453) give the correct interpretation of the plural ἐλάβομεν, as do also Bengel and von Hengel. There is nothing in the greeting to justify the assumption that persons like Timothy are included in this plural rather than the original apostles (Hofmann, iii. 9, who cites xvi. 21). By those who had received an ἀποστολή, the readers must have understood those who, like Paul, were κλητοὶ ἀπόστολοι, and only those (cf. i. 1). Such a full title would not be appropriate to subordinate missionary helpers.

3. (P. 357.) Since οὐ θέλω δὲ ὑμᾶς ἀγνοεῖν, i. 13 (cf. 1 Thess. iv. 13 ; 1 Cor. xii. 1 ; Phil. i. 12), introduces either a new subject or a new phase of the same subject (more certainly even than if γάρ were used ; cf. 1 Cor. x. 1 ; Rom. xi. 25 ; 2 Cor. i. 8 ; Col. ii. 1), and since ὅτι πολλάκις—δεῦρο contains nothing which has not been said before (i. 10 f.), it follows that the new point of view from which Paul here considers his journey to Rome is to be found in the new statement of his purpose in coming, namely, ἵνα τινὰ καρπὸν σχῶ καὶ ἐν ὑμῖν. By this cannot be meant the effect of his coming upon the Roman Christians, which has been already described, i. 11 f., but rather the successful missionary work he has hoped to accomplish among the Roman populace. This, too, is the only interpretation that accords with the term used (not to be confounded with καρπὸν ποιεῖν, φέρειν, καρποφορεῖν), which denotes the results of labour (cf. Rom. vi. 21 ; Phil. i. 22 ; Matt. xxi. 34 ; John iv. 36)—or, to put it more precisely, since an apostle, i.e. a missionary, is here speaking, the results of preaching, which is represented under the figure of labour in a field or garden (1 Cor. iii. 6–9). Paul's intercourse with the Roman Christians (i. 11 f.) will not require labour on his part, but will bring him quickening (xv. 24). There is no essential change in the sense, if, with D*G d g, Ambrosiaster, we read οὐκ οἴομαι (instead of θέλω) δέ, which sounds more natural, and could have been easily displaced by the other reading which occurs so frequently in Paul's writings. The ἐν ὑμῖν, i. 13, is quite synonymous with ἐν 'Ρώμῃ, just as ἐξ ὑμῶν, Col. iv. 9, means "from Colossæ" (Onesimus was not a member of the Church there, but probably had lived in Colossæ) ; πρὸς ὑμᾶς, Rom. i. 10, xv. 22, 23, 32, "to Rome" ; and δι' ὑμῶν, Rom. xv. 28 ; 2 Cor. i. 16, not directly through the midst of the assembled congregation in Rome or Corinth, but "through (via) Rome or Corinth." That in this passage the readers are addressed not as members of the Roman Church, but as representatives of the Roman populace, the vast majority of whom were as yet unconverted, appears—(1) from the fact that in i. 15, where unquestionably the reference is to the same work as in i. 13, the ὑμῖν is very clearly defined by the appositional τοῖς ἐν 'Ρώμῃ. To state that the readers are in Rome would seem superfluous, since up to this time it has always been presupposed, and according to the prevailing text of i. 7 was also formally expressed (see below, § 22, n. 3). On the contrary, it would be very much in place to remark, "When I say ὑμεῖς and ὑμῖν, I mean the people in Rome." The point is just as clear if we read ἐν ὑμῖν in

i. 15 as in i. 13 (so D* and several Latin MSS., also G with its copyist's error ἐπ' ὑμῖν, for which g substitutes *in vobis*). (2) The same conclusion follows from the meaning of εὐαγγελίζεσθαι. It is impossible longer to speak of preaching the gospel to those who are already κλητοὶ ἅγιοι (i. 6, 7). Against a perverted use of Gal. iv. 13 see above, p. 171, n. 2. (3) It is evident also from the fact that in i. 13 ἐν ὑμῖν stands in contrast not to ἐν ταῖς λοιπαῖς ἐκκλησίαις (cf. 1 Cor. iv. 17, vii. 17, xiv. 33), but to ἐν τοῖς λοιποῖς ἔθνεσιν. Thus the readers are addressed as τὸ ἔθνος τῶν 'Ρωμαίων. But that does not mean the Roman nation, even if it were possible to use such a term ; nor yet the *populus Romanus* (δῆμος 'Ρωμαίων, Just. *Apol.* i. [in the address]), the whole body of *cives Romani*, but the total population of Rome at that time, citizens and non-citizens, foreigners and natives, slaves and free men, consisting of all sorts of nationalities, Romans, Greeks, Egyptians, Celts, Syrians, and Jews,—an ἐπιτομὴ τῆς οἰκουμένης, as the rhetorician Polemo (in Galenus, ed. Kühn, xviii. 1. 347) called Rome. The sense of i. 13 would have been practically the same if Paul had written καὶ ἐν 'Ρώμῃ, καθὼς καὶ ἐν ταῖς λοιπαῖς πόλεσιν. Cf. an imperial writ of the third century (Grenfell and Hunt, *Fayûm Towns*, 120 : ἐν ταῖς πόλεσιν ἁπάσαις, ταῖς τε κατ' 'Ιταλίαν καὶ ταῖς ἐν τοῖς ἄλλοις ἔθνεσιν ; further, Galenus, *Anat. admin.* i. 1, ed. Kühn, xix. 218, ἐν 'Αλεξανδρείᾳ δὲ καί τισιν ἄλλοις ἔθνεσιν γενόμενος ; cf. Acts xxvi. 4 (above, p. 68, n. 15) ; also Acts ii. 5 (not ἐκ, but ἀπὸ παντὸς ἔθνους, above, p. 61) ; cf. further the contrast in Dio Cass. xxxvi. 41 (*al.* 24) between οἴκοι (in Rome) and ἐν τοῖς ἔθνεσιν (in the provinces, *i.e.* among the subject peoples) ; liv. 30, ἡ 'Ασία τὸ ἔθνος = the province of Asia with all its motley population. Ramsay, *Stud. Oxon.* iv. 30, compares for this use of ἔθνος *C. I. Gr.* 2802 ; Le Bas-Waddington, No. 1219 ; *Inscr. Brit. Mus.* 487. The argument remains unchanged if we make καθώς begin a sentence running through and including ver. 14, a punctuation which has much to commend it (cf. Klostermann, *Korrekturen*, 4 f.). Paul's purpose through missionary preaching to achieve some results in Rome also is in keeping with the fact that among all other peoples and in all other parts of the world he feels himself a debtor both to Greeks and Barbarians, to the cultured and uncultured alike. Although the reference here is primarily to the regions in which Paul had laboured hitherto, where he had to deal now with Barbarians who spoke Lycaonian (Acts xiv. 11), now with Athenians trained in philosophy, sometimes with Jews, sometimes with Greeks, nevertheless in the comparison of Rome with these provinces there is an indirect reference to the peculiarly varied mixture of peoples in the imperial capital. Paul is thinking, however, not so much of the different nationalities represented in Rome, as of the different degrees of culture among the individuals to whom the gospel is to be brought.

4. (P. 357.) The omission of πρῶτον, i. 16, in BG and in Marcion (Tert. *c. Marc.* v. 13 ; *GK*, ii. 515), proves merely that it was early found to be embarassing. In ii. 9, 10 there is no question as to the soundness of the text, and there is no conceivable reason why πρῶτον should have been introduced from these verses into i. 16. But, as Klostermann (*Korrekturen*, 14–24) was the first to point out, the common view, that Jews and Greeks (=Gentiles) here represent the two divisions of mankind or Christendom comprehended in the phrase παντὶ τῷ πιστεύοντι, is quite untenable. For, on this interpretation, the essential equality of Jew and Gentile and the Jew's priority over the

Gentile are asserted in the same breath. The correct interpretation is that
found in an ancient summary (*Cod. Amiat.*, ed. Tischendorf, 240, c. iii.), which
gathers up the contents of Rom. i. 13-17 in the words "de gentibus græcis
ac barbaris et primatu Judæorum atque Græcorum." The reasons for so
interpreting the passage are—(1) Paul does not use Ἕλλην, ἑλληνικός κτλ. in
the sense of "Gentile," as did other Jews who wrote in Greek subsequent to
the time of the Seleucidæ (above, p. 58, n. 2). 1 Cor. i. 22 is applicable only
to Greeks, not to all non-Jews. In Col. iii. 11 Scythians and Barbarians
are mentioned with Greeks. There are other passages (Rom. iii. 9, x. 12 ;
1 Cor. x. 32, xii. 13 ; Gal. ii. 3, iii. 28) where it is uncertain whether the
word is used in its proper national sense, or its derivative, religio-historical
sense. But here the latter meaning is impossible, for, in the immediate
context (i. 14), Ἕλλην is used to denote not Gentile in contrast to Jew, but
the Greek and the man of Greek culture, including the Hellenised Jew, the
Hellenist (above, pp. 41, n. 8, 71, n. 21) in contrast to the Barbarian, *i.e.* the
man without Greek culture ; (2) an instance has yet to be cited where πρῶτον
or a similar word inserted between τέ—καί destroys the parity of the words
connected by these particles. Even if the reading were πρῶτόν τε καί, it
would not bear this interpretation. In Acts xxvi. 20 the preaching in
Damascus and Jerusalem which afterward affected the whole country of
Judæa (cf. Acts ix. 27 f. ; Gal. i. 22 f. ; Rom. xv. 19) is treated as one
composite whole and spoken of as the apostle's first preaching, in contrast to
his later preaching to the Gentiles, which was separated from his first
ministry by an interval of several years. There is a passage in Eusebius
(*Ecl. Proph.* iii. 26, ed. Gaisford, p. 162) which may be considered parallel in
spite of the difference between πρῶτον and πρότερον, and which weighs
against the common interpretation of Rom. i. 16. Speaking of what the devil
had done to Jerusalem through the instrumentality of the Roman legions, his
agents, Eusebius says : πᾶσαν φθορὰν ἐνηργήσατο αὐτῷ τε πρότερον τῷ λαῷ
καὶ τοῖς τὴν πόλιν ἐνοικοῦσι πολίταις, ἔπειτα δὲ καὶ τῷ ναῷ καὶ τῇ πάλαι
συντελουμένῃ ἐν αὐτῷ λατρείᾳ ; (3) certainly in Rom. i.–ix. we do not find any
development of the idea that the gospel is a power of God unto salvation in
a higher degree or sooner in the case of believing Jews than of believing
Gentiles. On the contrary, up to x. 12 the whole argument is to show that,
with respect to the divine judgment and in regard to the way of salvation,
there is no distinction between Jew and Gentile. This statement is not
invalidated by the mention of the privileges of Israel in iii. 1. Not until
x. 19 (if πρῶτος be taken as a part of the preceding question—with Bentley,
Critica Sacra, ed. Ellies, 30, and Hofmann, *ad loc.*) is mention made of the
prior claims of Israel to Christ's redemption and the gospel, and their corresponding treatment at the hand of God. It is referred to again slightly in
xv. 8 f., but by this time the theme stated in i. 16 f. must have been quite
forgotten by the readers. On the other hand, the thought would be more
appropriate that, whereas the gospel exists, as it certainly does and ought,
for all men, it is intended, however, primarily, or at least in the first instance,
for the people of God's revelation and for the world of Greek culture. In
view of actual facts, this thought would not require further elucidation. As
yet, the apostolic mission had not extended to the barbarous peoples beyond
the bound of civilisation, but had been directed to Jews and Greeks, or at

least Hellenised peoples, of course without neglect of its duty toward individual Barbarians in the Græco-Roman world (Rom. i. 14), and without losing sight of its ultimate goal (Matt. xxviii. 19; Acts i. 8; Rom. xi. 11–15, 25–32; 2 Tim. iv. 17). Consequently Paul does not go to the Parthians or the Ethiopians, but, after having preached the gospel from Jerusalem to Illyricum (Rom. xv. 19), he "must see Rome also" (Acts xix. 21). Jews and Greeks are prepared beyond the rest of mankind for the reception of the gospel, and for that very reason, too, are most responsible for their religious and moral attitude. This explains πρῶτον in ii. 9 f. as in i. 16. A δεύτερον and a τρίτον are not excluded but rather implied, so there is no contradiction of the complete universality of divine providence and revelation.

5. (P. 359.) Although the different views regarding iv. 1 f. (cf. above, p. 131 f., n. 2) and iv. 16–22 cannot be discussed here, it should be observed that two aspects of Abraham's fatherhood are distinguished in iv. 11, 12 which in πατὴρ πάντων ἡμῶν, iv. 16, are combined. He is the father of uncircumcised believers (ver. 11), and more definitely by reason of circumcision he is father of those Jews who have not only been circumcised but also walk according to Abraham's faith (ver. 12). The logical and stylistic incongruity of the article before στοιχοῦσιν is perhaps relieved by Hort's conjecture (Append. 108) that we read καὶ αὐτοῖς instead of καὶ τοῖς, the only reading that has come down to us. Or perhaps the τοῖς before στοι (χοῦσιν) is due to an unconscious repetition on the part of the copyist.

6. (P. 359.) Since we are to read ἔχωμεν and not ἔχομεν in v. 1, and must accordingly construe καυχώμεθα, v. 2, 3, as subjunctive, the section v. 1–11 begins, it is true, in hortatory form. But this does not change its logical relation to what precedes, as indicated above, especially in view of the fact that from ver. 9 on the declarative form is resumed. The key to the interpretation of v. 12–21 is to be found in the word βασιλεύειν, which is five times repeated (v. 14, 17, 21, cf. also vi. 12, and κυριεύειν, vi. 14).

7. (P. 361.) The characteristics of this kingly rule are—(1) its absoluteness; (2) its independence of the will and conduct of those born under its sway. The latter applies especially to the line beginning with Adam, the former to that beginning with Christ.

8. (P. 362.) If ἁμαρτίας and ὑπακοῆς, vi. 16, cannot denote the two masters between whom choice must be made (which would require rather τῇ ἁμαρτίᾳ and τῇ ὑπακοῇ), and if both are used attributively, it follows that the readers were always servants, and servants of God. The τῆς ἁμαρτίας in vi. 17 is also to be taken attributively, which the article does not forbid (cf. Luke xvi. 8, xviii. 6; 2 Cor. i. 8); for the thing contrasted with their former state is not the choice of a *new master*, but the fact that they have become obedient *from the heart* in their conversion to the gospel. The attracted clause εἰς ὃν παρεδόθητε τύπον is to be expanded into εἰς τὸν τύπον διδαχῆς, ὃν παρεδόθητε, and the latter phrase further into ὃς παρεδόθη ὑμῖν (cf. Ewald and Hofmann, *ad loc.*; possibly also Philo, *de Josepho*, xvii, ἐν οἷς ἐπετράπησαν κατηγορηθέντες). It is plain that language like this could be addressed only to Jewish Christians who, prior to their conversion, considered themselves servants of God (cf. viii. 15), but rendered their Master only an external or seeming obedience. Really at that time they were the slaves of sin, and did not become slaves of righteousness until their conversion. The change from the

contrast between obedient and disobedient servants of God in vv. 16, 17 to the different contrast of vv. 18–23 is quite in keeping with Paul's style (cf. also John viii. 33–34), as is also the change from the figure of slavery to that of military service in ver. 23 (cf. vi. 13); observe also that while ὀψώνια (=*stipendia*) denotes regular pay (cf. 1 Cor. ix. 7; Luke iii. 14), χάρισμα means an extraordinary largess (*donativum*); cf. Tertullian's translation, *De Resurr*. xlvii, and pseud-Origenes, *Tract.*, ed. Batiffol, p. 198. 5, "stipendia salutis . . . charismatum donativa." It is perfectly clear that in vii. 1–6 Paul addresses the readers as if they, like himself, had lived under the law prior to their conversion and new birth. No rational man could possibly say this of native Gentiles. Neither could a Christian who had grown up in Judaism speak in this connection of native Gentile Christians in relation to himself as Paul does from vii. 4 (καρποφορήσωμεν) on. Consequently, for this reason if for no other the question of the nationality of the Roman Christians may be regarded as settled, for it is equally clear that Paul is not here addressing a part of his readers. Manifestly the fact that he addresses them as brethren in vii. 1 and again in vii. 4 is not an accident, since no address of this kind has been used since i. 13. He remembers that the great majority of these Christian brethren in Rome are of like origin with himself, and have stood in the same relation to the law. But there is nothing in the passage which justifies us in taking ἀδελφοί differently from the way in which it is taken in i. 13, viii. 12, xii. 1, by making it refer simply to a part of the Roman Christians, who as yet have been addressed without distinction. Had Paul wished to direct to the Jewish members of the Church in contradistinction to the Gentiles the address which begins here, it would have been necessary for him to write ὑμῖν δὲ λέγω, τοῖς ἀδελφοῖς μου κατὰ σάρκα (cf. xi. 13, ix. 3), or τοῖς ἐκ περιτομῆς; or, if after he had written the ambiguous ἀδελφοί it occurred to him that the part of the Church which he was addressing needed to be more clearly distinguished, he could have added after ἀδελφοί, ὑμῖν γὰρ λέγω, τοῖς τὸν νόμον γινώσκουσιν. As the passage reads, Paul does not make a distinction between those of his readers who know the law and those who do not; but, as he appeals to their experiential knowledge concerning the length of time the law is valid, he simply reminds himself and all his readers that he is speaking in this letter to those who know the law. It is difficult to understand how Hofmann, iii. 261, in spite of his grammatically correct rendering of the words ἀδελφοί—λαλῶ, can still hold that Paul is addressing here only the Jewish portion of his readers, and that λαλῶ refers merely to what is said in vii. 1–6. This is logically impossible. Moreover, a less important but sufficiently valid objection is the fact that if Paul had intended thus to make the word refer to the statement that follows, it would have been necessary for him to write λέγω (I say) instead of λαλῶ (talk, speak), Rom. iii. 5, vi. 19, ix. 1, xi. 13, xii. 3; 1 Cor. vi. 5, vii. 6, 8, x. 15; 2 Cor. vi. 13, vii. 3, viii. 8, xi. 21). Even where λέγω and λαλῶ occur together (Rom. iii. 19; 1 Cor. ix. 8) the distinction is not lost.

9. (P. 365.) A decision between the reading ὑμῖν δέ (אABP) and ὑμῖν γάρ (DGL) in xi. 13 is difficult, but it is not of much importance in determining the historical meaning of the passage, for evidently Paul is not thinking here of some characteristic of his readers suggested by what he is about to say (as

if, *e.g.* he had said ἔθνεσι γὰρ λαλῶ ; cf. vii. 1, n. 7). The appositive τοῖς ἔθνεσιν may be translated in one of two ways : "You who are Gentiles in distinction from other people"; or "You who are the Gentile members of this circle." Both renderings are possible grammatically (cf. the similar ambiguity in Luke xviii. 13). But the emphatic position of ὑμῖν at the beginning of the sentence shows clearly that Paul is here distinguishing a special class among the readers who hitherto have been addressed as one body (cf. Rev. ii. 24 ; Luke xi. 42-53).

10. (P. 366.) If in xiv. 5 we read ὃς μὲν γάρ (א*ACP), it is even clearer than when γάρ is omitted (BDG) that the contrast between observance and non-observance of certain days is intended only as an illustration. Moreover, according to the shorter and more correct reading in xiv. 6, only those who do observe days are mentioned and compared with those who eat meat and not those who make no distinction between days, which renders it evident that the illustration is intended to show the ascetic that the eating of meat to which he objects is just as much to be tolerated as the observance of certain days. From this it follows that the ascetics must have regarded the observance of days as right beyond all question, and made it their own practice (cf. *Skizzen*, 177, 353, n. 13). From this we are not, however, to conclude with E. Riggenbach (*ThStKr.* 1893, S. 652 f.) that the question of the observance of days was a subject of controversy between the weak and the strong parties in the Roman Church. Since the Mosaic law did not forbid to Israelites the use either of meat or of wine, these ascetics could not possibly have based their own practice and their demands upon their fellow-Christians on the doctrine that the law, particularly the Mosaic law, prohibiting the use of certain foods, was binding upon Christians. A connection with Essenism is the more unlikely, because the opinion which was first advanced by Jerome (*adv. Jovin.* ii. 14), that the Essenes abstained from the use of meat and wine, has very little to support it (cf. Lucius, *Der Essenismus*, S. 56; Schürer, ii. 569 [Eng. trans. II. ii. 200]). Philo's statement (*Quod omnis prob. lib.* xii, Mangey, ii. 457), that the Essenes do not sacrifice beasts, but purify their hearts, indicates nothing as to abstinence from the use of meat. But this statement is to be understood in the light of the more definite language of Josephus (*Ant.* xviii. 1. 5). Although in places the text of Josephus is not quite certain (Niese, ed. major on vol. iii. 143, 10), it is nevertheless clearly stated that in place of the sacrificial ritual in the Temple at Jerusalem from which they were excluded, the Essenes made the required sacrifices among themselves (ἐφ᾽ αὑτῶν τὰς θυσίας ἐπιτελοῦσιν). Farther on we learn that they considered the preparation of the bread and other food to be a priestly function (ἱερεῖς δὲ [χειροτονοῦσιν] ἐπὶ ποιήσει σίτου καὶ τῶν βρωμάτων), considered the house where they ate a temple, and looked upon their common meals as sacrificial feasts (*Bell.* ii. 8. 5). Had the food which was set before the members of the order by the cook (μάγειρος—named along with the baker—*Bell.* ii. 8. 5) consisted solely of vegetables, it would have been necessary to state the fact explicitly, since the use of θυσίας ἐπιτελεῖν to denote the preparation of food most naturally suggests the slaughter of animals. It is also to be noted that according to Philo (Eus. *Præp.* viii. 11. 4, βοσκήματα ; § 8, παντοδαπὰ θρέμματα) they engaged to a large extent in the raising of cattle in addition to agriculture. Moreover, when it is said to their credit that they were always

temperate at their meals, and that only enough food and drink to satisfy hunger and thirst was set before them, the drinking of wine is presupposed (Jos. *Bell.* ii. 8. 5). Their abhorrence of all food not prepared by themselves (*Bell.* ii. 8. 8 and 10) plainly refers not to particular kinds of food which they were forbidden to use, but to the method of its preparation (slaughter), which, in their eyes, assumed the character of worship. This feeling of the Essenes may be compared to the Jews' detestation of "Hellenic oil" (Jos. *Vita*, 13), although they made abundant use of "clean" oil. If only abstinence from the use of meat were under discussion in Rom. xiv., one might conclude that reference was intended to the School of the Sextii in Rome, under whose influence Seneca became a vegetarian in his youth (*Epist.* cviii. 17–22). But since it is implied in xiv. 17, 21 that these ascetics abstained from wine also (cf. Col. ii. 16, ἐν πόσει), and since in xiv. 5 f. it is presupposed that they and possibly other Christians in Rome observed certain days on religious grounds, the probability is that the tendency in question had a Jewish source. Upon various occasions Jews were accustomed to abstain from meat and wine—that is to say, from whatever was physically stimulating or ministered merely to pleasure. Sometimes it took the place of a complete fast as a preparation for receiving revelations (4 Esdr. ix. 24–26, xii. 51); again, it was a way with the pious of expressing sorrow for some painful misfortune. According to Baba Bathra, 60b, after the destruction of the Temple (70 A.D.), the Pharisees resolved never again to taste of wine or meat, and only earnest effort prevented this custom from becoming general (cf. Delitzsch, *Brief an d. Römer in d. Hebr. übersetzt u. aus Talmud u. Midrasch erläutert*, 1870, S. 97). The Jewish Christians in Rome, like James in Jerusalem (Eus. *H. E.* ii. 23. 5), may have practised such abstinence and urged it upon all Christians, either as a sign of sorrow for the unbelief of their people and for the approaching judgment upon Israel and Jerusalem (cf. 1 Thess. ii. 16; Rom. ix. 3), or in view of the near approach of the Parousia (cf. Rom. xiii. 11–14; 1 Thess. v. 4–8; Matt. xxiv. 37, 49, ix. 15, xi. 18 f.).

11. (P. 367.) Since διό, xv. 22, means "therefore," not "thereby," the hindrances in question could not have been formally stated in the preceding verses. Nor is the real cause which had kept Paul away to be sought in xv. 20 f.; for the reason that, if it was a matter of honour with Paul to preach only where Christ had not yet been preached, the number of places where he found it necessary to tarry would have been fewer, and rapid progress from the East to the West instead of being hindered would have been furthered. Hence διό refers to what precedes the description of the method of his missionary work (vv. 20, 21), namely, to the statements concerning its importance and wide compass (vv. 15b–19). Assuming that the rather late reading ἐλεύσομαι πρὸς ὑμᾶς, xv. 23, is spurious, and that γάρ, xv. 24, is genuine, it follows that ὡς ἂν—Σπανίαν is dependent upon the preceding participial clause, and the sentence beginning with νυνὶ δέ, ver. 23, but deprived of its proper conclusion by ἐλπίζω γὰρ—ἐμπλησθῶ, is taken up again by νυνὶ δέ in ver. 25. If this was written at the beginning of 58 A.D., the ἀπὸ πολλῶν ἐτῶν, xv. 23 (which the reading ἱκανῶν, BC, is possibly meant to weaken somewhat), would imply that Paul's mind was turning towards Rome earlier than might be inferred from 2 Cor. x. 16 and Acts xix. 21—perhaps as early as his first stay in Corinth (end of 52 until Pentecost 54)

Communications from his landlord concerning the conditions in Rome (Acts xviii. 2) may have moved him to this.   The main difficulty that prevented the fulfilment of his desire was the work in Ephesus, which occupied him for three years altogether.   After having sought in vain to reach the western coast of the province of Asia, before he crossed into Europe (Acts xvi. 6), and perhaps even on his first missionary journey (above, p. 181), Paul would not have been inclined to leave the East, nor could he have set out from Corinth for Italy and Spain without first having accomplished the preaching of the gospel in the province of Asia.   But how Paul could write xv. 23 without having been in Alexandria must find its explanation in facts about which we can only make conjectures ; cf. *Skizzen*, 343, A. 32.

§ 22. THE INTEGRITY OF THE EPISTLE TO THE ROMANS.

There are facts in the tradition of the text which are or seem calculated to arouse suspicion as to whether some parts of the received text belonged originally to the letter (n. 1).   These facts are as follows :—(1) In the West as in the East, and indeed in the East even before Origen, texts were in existence, which, though differing among themselves, agreed in that in all of them ἐν ʽΡώμῃ was wanting in i. 7 (n. 2).   There is no more probability that these words belong to the original text than that ἐν ᾽Εφέσῳ belongs to Eph. i. 1.   But because of the general conviction, which in this case also was not disputed by Marcion, that the letter was intended for the Christians of Rome, ἐν ʽΡώμῃ was inserted, only much earlier than the ἐν ᾽Εφέσῳ, in order that at once in the introductory greeting, as at the beginning of the other Church letters of Paul, this letter might have a clear designation of its recipients. This supposition would also not have any greater historical significance even were it proved by means of further documentary evidence to be beyond question. For in i. 15 the words τοῖς ἐν ʽΡώμῃ, which are lacking in only one of the witnesses for the reading of i. 7, here approved, are also for internal reasons indisputable.   It is evident besides from i. 8–13 that Romans was addressed to a locally defined group of Christians, and from xv.

22–32 that the residence of the readers lay on the road from the East to Spain. Only the one who confounds the introductory greeting with the general address can fail to feel the lack of definiteness of locality in the greeting (see above, p. 77 f.). (2) According to the testimony of Origen, when this testimony is rightly understood, Marcion not only threw out entirely the so-called doxology, xvi. 25–27, but also mutilated all that followed xiv. 23 in the text commonly used by the Church (n. 3). Now, even if the interpretation of Origen's testimony were correct, which makes Marcion throw out entirely not only xvi. 25–27 but xv. 1–xvi. 24 as well, it would not necessarily follow that Marcion's recension was based upon a copy of the text current in the Church which concluded with xiv. 23 ; for we know that Marcion threw out, either altogether or in large part, whole chapters from the text of the Epistles which he found current, partly because they did not seem to him adapted for the edification of the Church, and partly because they were contradictory to his own views. If, on the other hand, the interpretation of Origen be correct, it is proof that Marcion had a copy of Romans which contained sections beyond xiv. 23 at least similar to our text of chaps. xv.–xvi., and that these were so objectionable to him that he struck out considerable portions of them. (3) The attempt has been made to connect with the facts mentioned under (1) and (2) certain doubtful traces of the circulation of a Latin text which in chaps. xv.–xvi. is supposed to have contained only the doxology (n. 4). (4) Even as early as Origen's time there existed among the exemplars used in the Church the difference, that in some of them xvi. 25–27 stood between xiv. 23 and xv. 1, and in others at the end of the letter (n. 3). From the fact that Origen interprets the doxology as the conclusion of the letter, we may infer that this location was the one preferred in the circle to which he belonged.

When, however, he characterises this position *ut nunc est positum*, he seems to imply that the older tradition was in favour of the position after xiv. 23. Since, however, he considered it a matter of small importance, he merely expressed his opinion and refrained from all critical consideration of the question. The testimony of Origen does prove at least that the difference in the location of the doxology was not due in the first place to the systematic revision of the text (Lucian, Hesychius) which was made subsequent to Origen's time, but that it goes back to the time of the unregulated growth of text-transmission, at least back of the year 230. This fact renders our judgment regarding the original position of the doxology independent of the question as to the age of the existing sources for the text which have the doxology in one or the other of these positions, and of the very diverse opinions regarding the value of these extant sources; for all of these are later than Origen. The question as to the original location of the doxology is essentially independent of the question whether it was written by Paul or added by someone else later. For whoever wrote it could not have left it doubtful where he intended it to be placed. Assuming that the doxology is an interpolation, there is a third possibility, namely, that the writer placed the doxology after xiv. 23, but that this was at the same time the conclusion of the letter, in addition to the other two, namely, that the doxology stood originally either between xiv. 23 and xv. 1 or after xvi. 23 (24). This third possibility arises, however, only in case chaps. xv.–xvi. are also questioned.

The external evidence involved in the above problem is as follows :—I. Witnesses for the doxology between xiv. 23 and xv. 1 : (1) *Nonnulli codices* known to Origen and regarded by him as witnesses of the original tradition, or at least of the tradition most prevalent in the earlier period ; (2) the Antiochian recension of the

THE EPISTLE TO THE ROMANS

text, represented by L and most Greek cursives, by the liturgical tradition of the Greek Church, by the commentators of the Antiochian school, Chrysostom, Theodoret, and their successors, by the later Syriac (S³), and by the Gothic translation (n. 5). (3) That this position of the doxology was once widely current also in the West, is evidenced (a) by an old Latin *capitula* which divides Romans into fifty-one chapters : chap. l. begins with xiv. 15 and is followed immediately by chap. li., which began with xvi. 25–27, or consisted only of these verses (n. 4); (b) the copyist of the Greek and Latin bilingual G, who, without copying any part of the doxology itself, did, nevertheless, leave space enough for it after xiv. 23 (n. 6). To this is to be added still other evidence, that in the West also the position of the doxology at the end of the letter was not the only position (n. 5). (4) In favour of the location after xiv. 23, or partly favouring it, is the testimony of those MSS. which have the doxology twice (n. 7), after xiv. 23 and after xvi. 23 (24). II. Witnesses for the doxology after xvi. 23 or xvi. 24 : (1) the *Alii codices* of Origen, which represented the tradition preferred in his vicinity ; (2) the so-called best MSS. אBCD (regarding these see n. 6), also three or four cursives ; (3) of the versions, the Coptic, Vulgate, and Peshito (n. 8); (4) of the commentators, Origen, Ambrosiaster, Pelagius (n. 4), Augustine (n. 4), Sedulius, and possibly also John of Damascus (n. 5). To this is to be added the partial testimony of MSS. which give the doxology twice (above, under I. 4). III. So far as we know, throughout the entire ancient Church only in Marcion's N.T. was the doxology wholly omitted, which fact is referred to in a notice by Jerome, the meaning of which is not clear (n. 9). The actual omission of the doxology in G [see under I. 3 (b) above], and other facts which some have attempted to interpret in this way, cannot be taken as evidence of the existence in the ancient Church of a text without the doxology. The single case where the doxology is omitted altogether, that of a Vulgate MS. of the ninth or tenth century, which has a mixed text, is to be explained as an isolated, but very natural result in the mixing of Latin texts in which the position of the doxology varied (n. 6).

This review shows only that the difference in the tradition, which existed before Origen's time, was decided in and about Antioch and Constantinople in favour of the position of the doxology at the end of chap. xiv., by the rest of the Church in favour of the position at the end of chap. xvi. For us the question must be decided by the internal evidence, and this evidence is in favour of the opinion that originally the doxology stood after chap. xiv. For (1) while Paul not infrequently interrupts the course of a letter with a doxology ending with ἀμήν, he never concludes a letter in this manner, but always with a benediction ἡ χάρις τοῦ κυρίου κτλ. (n. 10). (2) If it is difficult to see how Paul could have written these weighty sentences, most intimately connected with the argument of the Epistle, after a long series of personal notices (xv. 14–xvi. 23), which as it grows longer shows constantly less and less connection with the theme of the letter, still less is it possible to conceive how in thus gathering up the thread of the discourse, broken so long before, he should have been suddenly so deeply moved as to be unable to conclude properly the sentence which he began. In view of this anacoluthon, the evidence for which is conclusive, it is doubtful whether originally xvi. 25–27 was a doxology at all (n. 11). (3) The subtle connection in thought between the doxology and the contents of both chap. xiv. and chap. xv. 1–13 makes it impossible to suppose that the doxology found its place so appropriately between xiv. 23 and xv. 1 by accident. Nor could it have been placed there by a reviser, who would look at the matter from a purely external point of view. However,

the position after chap. xiv. must be due to the writer of
the doxology, and this is true whether the writer is the
same as that of the letter or is to be distinguished from
the latter (n. 12). (4) That the doxology did not stand
originally at the end of chap. xvi. follows also from the
fact, that it is hardly possible naturally to explain the
confusion in the tradition of the text otherwise than by
assuming that this confusion is due either to a later
insertion of the doxology in chap. xvi. or later addition
to the same (n. 13). (5) Assuming that the doxology
stood originally at the end of the letter, there is no natural
way in which to explain its transference to the position
following xiv. 23 (n. 14). If, on the other hand, the
doxology stood originally after xiv. 23, it is easier to see
how in certain localities it came to be transferred to the
end of the letter. Since in Origen's time this transference
had been generally accepted in his neighbourhood (above,
p. 399 f.), it is probable that it was made in the second
century, i.e. at a time when as yet a general freedom
which later disappeared was allowed in the handling of
apostolic texts. Furthermore, the change was made probably in Alexandria. Because, beginning with Origen,
the oldest witnesses for the position of the doxology at
the end of the letter may be traced directly or indirectly
to Egypt. And Alexandria was the point from which a
text modified by critical reflection could spread most
easily both toward the East and the West (n. 15). The
text under discussion is of this character. The doxology
seemed to disturb the close connection between xiv. 1–23
and xv. 1–13, and, after the analogy of Jude 24 f. ; Phil.
iv. 20 ; 1 Pet. iv. 10 f. ; 2 Pet. iii. 18 ; Heb. xiii. 20 f.,
seemed to belong much more naturally at the end of the
letter, for which reason it was transferred to this position.
Or possibly criticism reached simply the negative conclusion that the doxology was not in its right place after
xiv. 23, so that it was transferred to the end, in order

that a portion of the text handed down by the tradition might not be altogether lost. There are other instances where this has happened (n. 15 regarding John vii. 53–viii. 11); and the principle involved was openly avowed in the fourth century in connection with the discussion of critical questions (Eusebius, in Mai, *Nova p. bibl.* iv. 1. 255; *GK*, ii. 913).

Presupposing the genuineness of the doxology, the attempt has been made to trace the uncertainty regarding its position back to the time when the letter was written, and to explain the uncertainty partly in a mechanical way as due to the manner in which the letter was written, partly as due to intention on Paul's part. Neither supposition has any plausibility (n. 16). More is to be said for the suspicion roused by the varying position of the doxology as to its genuineness, or even as to the genuineness of the section, xv. 1–xvi. 24, standing between the two locations of the doxology, about which there has been a question ever since before Origen's time. For, on either supposition, it is easy enough to explain the varying position of the doxology. If xv. 1–xvi. 24 is a later addition, the position of the doxology after xiv. 23 is easily explained by supposing that the new section was added, while the position of the doxology at the end of the letter only requires the supposition that in order to retain the old conclusion the new section was simply inserted between xiv. 23 and the doxology (cf. what is said regarding xvi. 24 in n. 13). On the other hand, supposing that everything else is genuine and that the doxology alone is a later addition, it is only necessary to imagine that in some cases the work of the interpolator, who, it is assumed, certainly inserted the doxology between xiv. 23 and xv. 1, was simply copied, while in other cases, where the doxology seemed out of place in this location, or where, after comparison with other MSS., its position seemed suspicious, it was omitted here and inserted rather at the close of the letter, in order that no portion of the existing text might be lost.

Suspicion as to the genuineness of the doxology was proportionally increased according as the error was accepted that in antiquity there were MSS. in the Church which did not have the doxology. Then, in addition, there were the objections, which were made to the contents of all that follows xiv. 23, so that up to the present time there are three opinions which have been maintained, supported in every case by inaccurate representation of the facts of the tradition : (1) that only the doxology is spurious (Reiche, Mangold); (2) that while xvi. 1–23 or parts of this section were written by Paul, it was intended for the Church in Ephesus (n. 20); (3) that all following xiv. 23 is a false enlargement of the original letter (Baur, n. 19). It is self-evident that the last hypothesis leaves unexplained the very ancient variations in the position of the doxology. It is equally plain also that the second view must be helped out by assuming peculiar accidents in connection with the preparation and transmission of Paul's letters. If the preceding account of the tradition be correct, taken alone it furnishes positive support to no one of these negative views. Consequently, to secure acceptance, they must have all the stronger support from the internal evidence.

Taking it for granted from what has been said above, that in the Bible used in the Church the doxology stood originally immediately after xiv. 23, the considerations which led to this conclusion are also for the most part strong arguments against the view that the doxology is spurious. The internal connections between the doxology and what precedes (xiv. 1–23) and follows (xv. 1–13), which have been already referred to (n. 12), show a subtleness of thought which one seeks for in vain in the whole body of ancient Christian literature proved to be the work of interpolators. The doxology re-echoes the

main thought of the letter ; but for all that it is not made
up of words or phrases taken from the preceding part of
the Epistle or from other letters of Paul and patched
together again, as is the case in the ancient pseudo-Pauline
Epistles to the Laodiceans and Corinthians.   On the
contrary, thoughts which had influenced the author from
the beginning of the letter are summed up again in a
manner independent and yet in entire conformity to the
context of chap. xiv. and chap. xv. (n. 17).   Furthermore, the harshness of the expression, the anacoluthon in
the construction of the sentence (n. 11), and the fulness
and intensity of the thought are strong proofs of the
genuineness of the doxology, unless it be shown that these
qualities are characteristic of the compilations made by
interpolators in the ancient Christian Church.   All clear
cases go to show only the contrary.   Finally, no reasonable motive for the forgery has yet been discovered.   If
the forger found the letter concluding abruptly with xiv.
23, he would have met the necessity for a proper conclusion to the letter by adding Paul's usual benediction,
e.g. a sentence like xvi. 24.   At most he would have
added only some blessings and greetings such as could be
found at the close of almost any of Paul's Epistles.   On
the other hand, if he found chap. xv. already a part of the
letter, the same reasons which led at a very early date to
the transference of the doxology from its position following xiv. 23, and which render it impossible to believe
that it stood originally at the end of the letter, and was
transferred later to the position after xiv. 23, would
be conclusive arguments also against the supposition
that the interpolator inserted it between chap. xiv. and
chap. xv.

Paul himself could not have concluded the letter either
with xiv. 23 or xiv. 23 + xvi. 25–27.   Nor would a simple
benediction like xvi. 20 or xvi. 24, which might have
been pushed out of its original place by the addition of

xv. 1–xvi. 20 (or –xvi. 23), have sufficed. For, leaving out of consideration the fact that elsewhere Paul is accustomed to prepare the way for the conclusion of his letters at considerable length (n. 10), in this instance there were special reasons why something needed to be added to chap. xiv. It is clear not only from the discussions of chap. xiv., but also from the entire letter, that Paul was quite thoroughly informed concerning the conditions and feeling of the Roman Church. He must have had friends there who gave him this detailed information. Is it likely, then, that he would conclude the letter without a parting greeting to these friends? Such unfriendliness would be all the more unnatural in this instance, because here he is approaching a Church the majority of whom were unknown to him and he to them. If, as any careful investigation will show, Paul's purpose in this letter was to establish a more intimate relation between himself and this Church, which up to the time had remained a total stranger to him, had he brought the letter to a close without emphasising, at least at the end, the personal relations which he undoubtedly had with individual Christians in Rome, and so making evident the connecting ties already existing between himself and the Roman Church, he would have been neglecting the most obvious means of accomplishing this end.

The surprise expressed now for more than a hundred years, that Paul should have had such an exceptionally large number of greetings to express and convey to the Church in a place that he had not yet visited, shows lack of careful observation. Not a single salutation or other communication intended for individual members is to be found at the close of letters addressed to the Churches founded by Paul at Thessalonica, Corinth, Philippi, and in Galatia. Similarly, the greetings from individuals in 1 Cor. xvi. 19 f. and Phil. iv. 21 f. are only those of persons of special importance to these Churches, and are, moreover, addressed to the whole Church in Corinth and Philippi (n. 18).   On the other hand, in the letter to the Church at Colossæ, which Paul had not organised, and which he had never visited (Col. ii. 1), he conveys the greetings of six individuals (iv. 10–14), who, with the exception of Epaphras, were quite as unknown to the Church personally as was Paul himself.   More than this, he requests the conveyance of a special greeting to an individual member of the Colossian Church; also to a member of the neighbouring Church of Laodicea, which likewise he had never visited (Col. iv. 15, 17), although at the same time he had despatched to a prominent Christian household in Colossæ a private letter dealing exclusively with personal matters.   Nor does he fail in this letter to the Church, which as yet was a total stranger to him, to make special mention of Onesimus, about whom the private letter despatched at the same time was written, and to remark expressly that Colossæ was Onesimus' home (Col. iv. 9), a fact which the readers themselves knew without being informed.   He makes exactly the same remark about Epaphras (iv. 12), who, being the founder of the Church (i. 7), was certainly well enough known to all. Who does not see that all these personal references are due to Paul's desire to make the Church feel that it is not such a stranger to him as it seems, and at the same time are indicative of an effort on his part to bring himself into closer touch with the Church where as yet he was really a stranger ?   This is exactly the case in Romans.   Furthermore, in Rom. i. 10–15 he had spoken of the desire which he had felt for a long time of coming to Rome.   But in making this statement he had not said when or under what circumstances he hoped to come, nor explained why now he sent this long letter to Rome before carrying out the plan which he had had in mind for so long. Inasmuch as he deemed the matter of sufficient importance to the Romans and to himself to be mentioned at the very beginning of his letter, it is inconceivable that he should have brought the letter to a close without answering questions which were suggested by his statements, and which must have been raised in the mind of everyone who read i. 8–15 with interest (cf. 1 Cor. iv. 18–21, xvi. 1–11). In short, he must have concluded his letter with something at least closely resembling xv. 13–xvi. 24. If this passage is a later addition, it must have been slipped in in an underhand way in place of the original conclusion of the letter, the contents of which were similar to what is found here. And this substitution must have been made before Marcion's time, since in his own recension of the Epistle he adopted portions of Rom. xv.–xvi. from the text current in the Church (n. 3). Moreover, the substitution must have been made before any copies of the letter were put into circulation ; otherwise in the widely ramified tradition there could hardly fail to be some clear trace of a copy of Romans without chaps. xv.–xvi. The substitution must have been made in the archives of the Roman Church, or just as the letter was about to be issued, before any copies were made for general circulation. Those who believe that possible must make at least an effort to render it comprehensible and clear to others. They must also advance strong arguments to prove that chaps. xv.–xvi. were not originally a part of the letter. With regard to chap. xv., these arguments are such that the number convinced by them grows constantly fewer (n. 19). Similarly, the opinion that chap. xvi. like chap. xv. was *intentionally* added to Romans has scarcely any advocates left. More popular is the view that either wholly or in large part chap. xvi. was directed to Ephesus and became attached to Romans *by accident* (n. 20). This view was first suggested by the mention of Prisca (Priscilla) and Aquila and the Church in their house, and of Epænetus, the first convert of Asia, whose name follows directly (xvi. 3–5, n. 21).

At Easter 57, Aquila and his wife were still in Ephesus
(1 Cor. xvi. 19).   If Paul wrote Romans in Corinth at the
time indicated by Acts xx. 3 (information which, presupposing that Rom. xv., xvi. are genuine, we get also
from Rom. xv. 25–xvi. 2), some ten or eleven months had
elapsed since that time.   Now, this Jewish couple, who
were natives of Pontus, who had lived for a time in Rome,
and who, after they were driven from Rome in the year
52, came to Corinth, had been closely associated with
Paul ever since, and, as the circumstances of their removal
to Ephesus show, had guided their movements altogether
in accordance with his missionary plans (above, p. 262,
265, n. 3).   It is consequently not at all impossible that
when Paul turned his attention toward Rome and prepared to give up his work in Ephesus, this couple left
Ephesus, very soon after the sending of 1 Corinthians, at
about the same time that Paul did, and returned to
Rome, where they had resided earlier, in order to prepare
quarters for the apostle there as they had done previously
in Ephesus.   That Epænetus should accompany them
thither is not strange, in view of the fact that he was the
first convert of Asia, and so probably owed his conversion
to the zeal of this couple, not becoming acquainted with
Paul until afterward.   Through these old friends and
companions, whom he mentions first among the Christians
in Rome to be greeted, he may have received news from
Rome more than once before Romans was written.   Moreover, what he says in praise of them would sound very
strange in a letter to the Ephesian Church.   For three
years the Church which gathered for worship in Ephesus
had seen them share Paul's labours, and had witnessed
their self-sacrifice on his behalf.   If Paul desired to remind
the Ephesians of this service (cf. Phil. iv. 3 ; 1 Cor. xvi.
15 f. ; 1 Thess. v. 12 ; cf., however, 2 Tim. i. 18), he must
have called their attention to the services which they had
rendered in Ephesus, instead of speaking, as he does, of

the gratitude felt toward them by all the Gentile Churches. Indeed, the use of this last expression to designate the Churches founded by Paul and his helpers and under his care, an expression not to be found in any of the letters directed to these Churches (cf., however, 1 Cor. iv. 17, vii. 17, xi. 16, xiv. 33 ; 2 Cor. viii. 18, xi. 28, xii. 13 ; 2 Thess. i. 4 ; Phil. iv. 15), can be understood only if this letter is intended for a Church outside this circle (cf. § 23). All the *Gentile* Churches are indebted to this *Jewish* couple. Like xv. 26–28, the statement in xvi. 4 is designed to make the Romans realise that in those parts of the Church which were under Paul's dominating influence Gentile and Jewish Christians were united to each other by ties of self-sacrificing love and by a pious sense of gratitude. That these remarks are not only in harmony with xv. 1–13, but have also close relation to the general purpose of Romans (§ 24), is self-evident. It is with the same purpose in mind that in three passages Paul calls particular attention to the fact that the persons to be greeted (xvi. 7, 11), or sending greetings (xvi. 21), are countrymen of his (n. 22, also § 23, n. 1). Not only does the language suggest ix. 3, but the purpose of these short notices is the same as that expressed with so much intensity in ix. 1–5, x. 1 f., xi. 1 f., xiv. He wants the Romans to know that he is anything but an apostate Jew without sympathy for his own unfortunate countrymen. The deeper his grief for the obdurate and unfortunate majority of his countrymen, the profounder his joy for every brother after the flesh who has become also a brother after the Spirit. The further remark that Andronicus and Junius were honoured among the apostles, *i.e.* in the mother Church, and that they became Christians before he did himself (n. 23), is also one of the trivial means which Paul uses to accomplish the great apologetic purpose of the letter, and is in so far evidence that these greetings were an original part of Romans. Rome is also suggested by Rom. xvi. 13. In this verse a certain Rufus and his mother are greeted, the latter of whom had at one time shown so much motherly kindness to Paul that he calls her his own mother. On the other hand, in a passage peculiar to Mark's Gospel, Simon of Cyrene is called the father of Alexander and Rufus (Mark xv. 21), which can hardly be explained otherwise than by the assumption that the sons of Simon were known to the first readers of Mark's Gospel. Since, however, Mark's Gospel was intended for Roman Christians, and since, according to the unanimous tradition, this Epistle was directed to Roman Christians, it cannot well be due to accident that in the former a Christian from Jerusalem named Rufus is mentioned as a person known to the readers, and that in the latter a Christian by the name of Rufus is greeted. The close relation existing between Paul and the family, shows that this Rufus, with his mother, must have resided earlier in the East; cf. below, § 53, especially also n. 5 of that section. Accepting these facts as conclusive evidence that the list of greetings was intended for persons in Rome, other names, which support this conclusion, deserve notice. The expressions τοὺς ἐκ τῶν ᾿Αριστοβούλου and τοὺς ἐκ τῶν Ναρκίσσου τοὺς ὄντας ἐν κυρίῳ do not refer to Christian households (1 Cor. i. 16, xvi. 15 ; 2 Tim. i. 16, iv. 19 ; cf. 1 Cor. i. 11), but to the Christian members of two larger circles not otherwise Christian (x. 11, n. 24). In all probability Aristobulus and Narcissus were two prominent men, some of whose slaves or freedmen had become Christians. Narcissus, the once all-powerful freedman of the emperor Claudius, died in Rome at the end of the year 54. Also an Aristobulus, a favourite of the emperor Claudius and brother of Herod Agrippa I., lived in Rome for a time at least during Claudius' reign. Since the slaves of such distinguished households not infrequently retained the family name, even when they passed into the possession of other masters after the death of their own, probably we have to do here with the former slaves of this Aristobulus and Narcissus. This is rendered even more probable by the mention of the Jew Herodion (ver. 11), whose name indicates that he belonged to the household of the Herodian prince just mentioned. The fact that he is mentioned co-ordinately with the group of the *Aristobuliani* does not prevent him belonging to the same, any more than the mention of Epænetus in ver. 5 prevents him from belonging to the Church in the house of Aquila. It has been shown further by Lightfoot from numerous inscriptions, that many of the names which occur in this chapter were more or less commonly used in the royal household in the first century, *e.g. Ampliatus, Urbanus, Stachys, Apelles, Tryphæna, Tryphosa, Philologus, Nereus* (n. 24). Although as yet no one of these persons has been certainly identified, nevertheless the information gathered by Lightfoot, taken together with the fact that the Christian faith made its way at an early date into the royal house-hold in Rome, winning converts among the royal servants (Phil. iv. 22), does go far to confirm the belief that these greetings were intended for persons in Rome. At the same time the tradition of the Church, even where it has local colouring, is always under the suspicion of being dependent upon what is said in the N.T., and the material which up to the present time has been gathered from inscriptions and legends with a view to clearing up the question of the names in Rom. xvi. needs to be further tested and further confirmed before it can be utilised as proof in a text-book. Without recourse to this material, however, it may be regarded as proved that Rom. xvi. 1–16 was intended for persons in Rome, and that it was, therefore, an original part of the letter. To the unity of the Epistle, which in tradition has come down to us as a single letter, other objections have been made, without reference to the facts of the tradition concerning the text,

and based on exegetical discussions and internal criticism
of the thought connection.   These can be refuted only by
a full and complete exposition of Romans, which at the
proper time the present writer hopes to be able to pub-
lish (n. 25).

1. (P. 378.) Regarding Rom. i. 7, W. B. Smith, *JBL*, 1901, pp. 1–21, and
Harnack, *ZfNTW*, 1902, S. 83 ff., have written, following the present writer.
From the literature on Rom. xv. 16, and the doxology in particular, the
present writer calls special attention to SEMLER, *Paraphrasis Ep. ad Rom.*
1769, pp. 277–311 ; GRIESBACH, *Opusc. Acad.* ii. 62–66 ; REICHE, *Comm. Crit.
in Epist. Pauli*, i. 88–120 ; BAUR, *Paulus*,[2] i. 393–409 ; LIGHTFOOT in the
Journal of Philology, ii. (1869) p. 264 f. ; iii. (1871) p. 193 f., which articles,
together with Hort's reply in the same journal, iii. 51 f., will hereafter be
cited as reprinted in Lightfoot's *Bibl. Essays* (1893), pp. 284–374 ; MANGOLD,
Der Röm. und seine geschichtl. Voraussetzungen, 1884, S. 44–166 ; LUCHT, *Über
die beiden letzten Kapitel des Röm.* 1871 ; E. RIGGENBACH, *NJbfDTh.* 1892, S.
498–605 ; 1894, S. 350–363, the latter treatise being cited here as Riggenb. ii. ;
W. B. Smith, *JBL*, 1901, p. 129 ff. ; Spitta, *Zur Gesch. u. Lit. des Urchristent.*
iii. 1, S. 6 ff.

2. (P. 378.) Rom. i. 7 reads (1) in G g πᾶσιν τοῖς οὖσιν ἐν ἀγάπῃ θεοῦ κλητοῖς
ἁγίοις. χάρις κτλ. Many clues show that this text was in early times widely
current. For (2) just the same text lay before Ambrosiaster (the Roman
commentator, *circa* 370, ed. Ben. ii. App. p. 28). According to most MSS., the
text preceding his comment is the ordinary reading of the Vulgate ("omnibus
qui sunt Romæ, dilectis dei, vocatis sanctis") ; but a "Cod. Mich." has, on the
contrary, *Romæ in caritate dei* (plainly without *dilectis dei*). This Vulgate text
(with *Romæ* and *dilectis dei*) was not that of Ambrosiaster, and even in Cod.
Mich. *Romæ* is an interpolation, as is shown by the exposition : "Quamvis
Romanis scribat, illis tamen scribere se significat, qui in caritate dei sunt."
Farther on *vocatis sanctis* is utilised, but not *dilectis dei*. Hort, in opposition to
Lightfoot in the latter's *Biblical Essays*, p. 345, cf. 288, 365, has sought vainly
to weaken this argument. Ambr. does not set over against all the Christians
in Rome those who are in the love of God, but he considers it noteworthy
that Paul, when writing to the Romans, designates his readers not as Romans,
but as persons in the love of God. (3) The Greek text of D begins with
κλητοῖς ἁγίοις, but is to be restored to τοῖς οὖσιν ἐν Ῥώμῃ ἐν ἀγάπῃ θεοῦ
κλητοῖς ἁγίοις, following the Latin text (d : "omnibus qui sunt Romæ in caritate dei, vocatis sanctis"). In d a corrector of the eleventh century (d***)
pointed, by means of a critical sign before *in*, to a correction on the margin,
which is now torn off (*Cod. Clarom.* ed. Tischendorf, pp. xxv, 537). The corrector wished either to strike out *in caritate dei*, or in place of it to read
dilectis dei. The former is the more probable, if one compares the text of E
(the former S. Germanensis, now in St. Petersburg), which, according to
a transcript furnished the present writer by C. R. Gregory, reads τοῖς
οὖσιν ἐν Ῥώμῃ κλητοῖς ἁγίοις. As is well known, E is a copy of D, a copy,
however, of D made after that MS. had gone through the hands of its correctors (Tischendorf, *op. cit.* xxv ; Gregory, *Prolegomena*, 423). Therefore ἐν

ἀγάπη θεοῦ after ἐν Ῥώμη, which was original in the lost text of D, has been
removed by a corrector, and likewise from d. (4) The diffusion in the West
of the uncorrected text of Dd is attested by old MSS. of the Vulg. like
Fuld. Amiat. ("omnibus qui sunt Romæ in caritate [Amiat. dilectione] dei
vocatis sanctis"). (5) Origen has the ordinary text, to be sure, in his Comm.
in Jo. tom. xix. 5 (ed. Preuschen, p. 304, the citation tom. ii. 10, p. 64, is not
in point), and in the Hom. in Num. (Delarue, ii. 301), preserved in Latin only.
But in such matters dependence can be placed neither on the versions nor
on such long quotations as that in John (tom. xix. 5), which Origen hardly
could have copied single-handed from the Bible. The Comm. in Rom., which
belongs to the last period of his life, gives us only his text of Rom. i. 1-7.
According to the text preceding his exposition, κλητοῖς ἁγίοις was wanting,
a lack which the exposition confirms (Delarue, iv. 467). Moreover, also,
Origen could not have read the ἐν Ῥώμῃ which the text printed above
contains. Although Origen doubted as little as Ambrosiaster that the letter
was addressed to the Romans (iv. 468, 487, etc., cf. below in § 28 his view of
Eph.), he says nothing at all of Rome in his exposition of the introductory
greeting, but writes : "dilectis dei, ad quos scribit apostolus." So his text
ran πᾶσι τοῖς οὖσιν ἀγαπητοῖς θεοῦ, χάρις κτλ. (6) A scholion of the minuscule
47 reads, τὸ "ἐν Ῥώμῃ" οὔτε ἐν τῇ ἐξηγήσει οὔτε ἐν τῷ ῥητῷ (in the text)
μνημονεύει (Griesbach, Symb. Crit. ii. 15). In the first edition the present
writer could refer this to Origen only conjecturally. Recently this conjecture
has been established by the Mt. Athos MS. mentioned below in n. 3. This
MS., it is true, in spite of the assurance that its text of Rom. is drawn from
Origen's Commentary (v. d. Goltz, S. 8), has ἐν Ῥώμῃ in the text ; yet right
here is the same scholion as in min. 47, except that τοῦ replaces τό at the
beginning (op. cit. 52 f., cf. ThLb. 1899, col. 179 f.). There existed then in
ancient times a Western (Nos. 1, 2) and an Eastern (Nos. 5, 6) text, which
agreed in leaving out ἐν Ῥώμῃ. But they differ from one another in this,
(a) that Nos. 1, 2 retained κλητοῖς ἁγίοις, while Nos. 5 (and 6?) rejected it ;
(b) that Nos. 1, 2 have ἐν ἀγάπη θεοῦ, No. 5 having ἀγαπητοῖς θεοῦ in its
place. The texts classed under Nos. 3, 4, as well as that of Ambrosiaster's
Cod. Mich. (under No. 2) and of the translator Rufinus, or his editor (under
No. 5), evidently present mixtures of the old text (without ἐν Ῥώμῃ) with
the common text. There is no satisfactory explanation of a subsequent
substitution of ἐν ἀγάπη for an original ἐν Ῥώμῃ. It was a firm belief of the
early Church (Can. Mur. lines 47-59 ; Tert. c. Marc. v. 17 ; Apolonius in Eus.
H. E. v. 18. 5 ; Ambrosiaster on Col. iv. 16, cf. GK, ii. 74 f.) that the letters
of Paul were intended for the whole Church, in spite of their being addressed
to definite localities ; but this belief has not produced the omission of the
name of the place from the introductory greeting in any of the other letters.
On the other hand, we have in Eph. i. 1 an example of how in antiquity the
name of a place, originally lacking, has subsequently been inserted, and indeed
on the basis of the still much older tradition that that letter was intended
for the Church of Ephesus (see below, § 28). The same cause occasioned
the insertion of an ἐν Ῥώμῃ in Rom. i. 7 ; for although Marcion disputed
that Ephesians was intended for Ephesus, neither he nor anyone else has
doubted that Romans was intended for Rome. Since, also, those who found
no ἐν Ῥώμῃ in i. 7, as Origen and Ambrosiaster, were convinced of this, it is

easy to understand that others wished to see this expressed in the introductory greeting after the analogy of all other Church letters, finally also of
Ephesians. To this especially led also the expression ἐν ἀγάπῃ θεοῦ κλητοῖς,
unusual in the N.T. After the analogy of καλεῖν (κληθείς) with ἐν εἰρήνῃ,
ἐν χάριτι, ἐν ἁγιασμῷ, ἐν ἐλπίδι, ἐν κυρίῳ (1 Cor. vii. 15, 22 ; Gal. i. 6 ; Eph.
iv. 4 ; 1 Thess. iv. 7), the originator of the text under consideration doubtless
desired to join ἐν ἀγάπῃ with κλητοῖς, and understand it as follows, "all, who
in (or by) God's love are called saints" (cf. Rom. viii. 28). But how natural
was the connection of τοῖς οὖσιν ἐν ἀγάπῃ θεοῦ with the inopportune recollection of τῇ οὔσῃ ἐν Κορίνθῳ, 1 Cor. i. 2, and τοῖς οὖσιν ἐν Φιλίπποις, Phil. i. 1.
At first ἐν 'Ρώμῃ may have been written alongside of ἐν ἀγάπῃ as a marginal
gloss, then have been inserted in the text before ἐν ἀγάπῃ (so D originally
and Amiat., Fuld.), and finally have fully displaced the ἐν ἀγάπῃ (so the
corrector of Dd and E). This appears to have been the history of the development of the text in the West. Also in the Greek Orient ἐν ἀγάπῃ
θεοῦ, appearing in such an unusual connection, was the stumbling-block. It
was changed into ἀγαπητοῖς θεοῦ, and κλητοῖς ἁγίοις was omitted, which appeared unnecessary alongside of κλητοὶ 'I. Χρ. of ver. 6. Only Gg and Ambrosiaster have preserved the original text entirely unchanged (see No. 1).
The question concerning τοῖς ἐν 'Ρώμῃ, i. 15, is entirely different from that
concerning ἐν 'Ρώμῃ, i. 7. Cod. G, which omits these words also, stands
entirely isolated in this respect. The witnesses, which partly or fully confirmed his text of i. 7, also Orig. and Ambrosiaster in their expositions,
failed him in i. 15. Therefore, whoever questions the genuineness of τοῖς
ἐν 'Ρώμῃ (i. 15) must hold that these words were interpolated very much
earlier than ἐν 'Ρώμῃ, i. 7. It is, however, out of the question that a place of
destination for the letter should have been missed earlier in i. 15 than in i. 7,
and that an interpolation resulting therefrom should have spread more rapidly
and universally than the ἐν 'Ρώμῃ, i. 7. In none of the passages where πρὸς
ὑμᾶς, δι' ὑμῶν, or ἐν ὑμῖν gives an undoubted designation of the residence of
the group of readers intended, so that Rome of Corinth could be substituted
(Rom. xv. 22 f., 28 f. ; 1 Cor. xv. 5-7 ; 2 Cor. i. 15 f., x. 14 f.), is such an interpolation to be found. On the other hand, the subsequent insertion of ἐν
'Ρώμῃ, i. 7 has its exactly corresponding analogy in Eph. i. 1, and in the
places of destination of the remaining introductory greetings of Pauline
Church letters its fully satisfactory explanation.

3. (P. 379.) Orig. Comm. in Rom. Interpr. Rufino ad xvi. 24-27 (Delarue,
iv. 687) : " Caput hoc Marcion, a quo scripturæ evangelicæ atque apostolicæ
interpolatæ sunt, de hac epistula penitus abstulit ; et non solum hoc, sed
et ab (al. in) eo loco, ubi scriptum est, 'omne autem, quod non est ex fide,
peccatum est' (xiv. 23), usque ad finem cuncta dissecuit. In aliis vero
exemplaribus, id est in his, quæ non sunt a Marcione temerata, hoc ipsum
caput diverse positum invenimus. In nonnullis etenim codicibus post eum
locum, quem supra diximus, hoc est, 'omne autem, quod non est ex fide,
peccatum est,' statim cohærens habetur, 'ei autem, qui potens est vos con-
firmare.' Alii vero codices in fine id, ut nunc est positum, continent. Sed
jam veniamus ad capituli hujus (al. ipsius) explorationem." A MS. of the
tenth century (Cod. 184, B 64 of the St. Laura monastery on Mt. Athos),
brought into prominent notice by E. v. d. Goltz (TU, N. F. ii. 4a, 1899),

which gives a text of Rom. drawn directly from Origen's commentary, confirms the view that this Father read and exegeted the doxology at the end of the Epistle. Unfortunately, however, two scholia drawn from Or. upon xiv. 23 and xvi. 25 are quite erased except for the abbreviated name of Or. (Goltz, S. 60). Hort (in Lightfoot, *Bibl. Ess.* 330 ; *NT. App.* 112) preferred the reading of a Parisian cod. adduced by Delarue, *in eo loco*, which, according to Riggenb. ii. 359, is found also in Cod. 88 of the library of the monastery of St. Gall ; and by the conjecture *non solum hic* (instead of *hoc*) he sought to bring out the meaning that Marcion elided the doxology not only after xiv. 23, but also after xvi. 23 (24). Among the arguments against this conjecture and the opinion built upon it (cf. *GK*, ii. 519, also Lightfoot, 353), the following ought to suffice :—Even supposing Or. had known MSS. which had the doxology twice, after chap. xiv. as well as after chap. xvi. (so Hort, 341), a thing unattested and most improbable, and even if Or. had tacitly assumed that Marcion had found the doxology in both places, a thing still more incredible, one cannot believe that a man of Origen's learning would take this remarkable way of expressing the simple thought that Marcion did away with the doxology altogether. Without changing *hoc* into *hic* (here), we can see that the clause beginning with *sed et* treats not of the doxology again, but of chaps. xv., xvi., and that after this remark Or. returns again to the doxology ("hoc ipsum caput, capitulum hoc "). The reading of *in* (instead of *ab*) *eo loco* makes no essential change in the sense, since whatever Marcion is here represented as doing to the rest, *usque ad finem* indicates the extent of his emendation. If Or. wrote ἐν ἐκείνῳ τῷ τόπῳ, he was pointing out primarily the passage where Marcion began to use his knife, and not till later did he specify how far the devastation which he wrought extended. Just as *caput hoc* and (*ab eo loco*) *usque ad finem cuncta* form a contrast, so also do the new predicates *penitus abstulit*, and *dissecuit*. The doxology he had wholly discarded ; on the other hand, all that the MSS. of the Church give from xiv. 23 on to the end of the Epistle he had cut to pieces and mutilated by omissions (cf. Reiche, *Comm. Crit.* i. 90, A. 7 ; Fr. Nitzsch, *ThStKr.* 1860, S. 285 ff., and the writer's *GK*, ii. 519 f.). An attempt has often been made to take *dissecuit* in the sense of *desecuit* (*amputavit*), this, too, in the writings of a cultured Latin like Rufinus ; moreover, the St. Gall MS. gives as its reading the otherwise unsupported *desecuit* (Riggenbach, ii. 359) ; but such a meaning is incompatible with the structure of the sentence. " Et non solum hoc, sed et" presupposes in the original that elliptical οὐ μόνον δὲ ἀλλὰ καί, to which a Latin translator (Rom. ix. 10, Vulg.), or a Latinising scribe (Cod. D, Rom. v. 3), very naturally would add a demonstrative : " not only did he do this which was just mentioned, but he also committed something other and different which is now to be mentioned." Further than this, Tertullian's words (*c. Marc.* v. 14 at the end, "bene autem quod et in clausula tribunal Christi comminatur," cf. Rom. xiv. 10) cannot prove in opposition to Or. that Marcion closed his Rom. with xiv. 23, as the present writer thinks he has shown from Tertullian's use of words (*GK*, ii. 521) more exactly than Hort (*Bibl. Ess.* 335). If it is unthinkable that Paul should have ended his letter at xiv. 23 without anything like a greeting, it is no less so that Marcion should have simply cut away all such material as he found there. He retained the personal references in Col. iv. quite fully, and accepted without change

Philem.—a letter which consists almost entirely of such references, *GK*, ii. 527, 529. On the contrary, he expunged all of Rom. iv. and 2 Cor. vii. 2–xi. 1, and all but a few sentences of Rom. ix. 1–xi. 32. But Rom. xv., xvi., including the doxology, also called for a free use of his knife. The appeal to the prophetic Scriptures, xvi. 26, xv. 2 f., 9–12 ; the recognition of Israel's prior rights, xv. 8; and the debt of the Gentile Church to Jewish Christianity, xv. 27, xvi. 4, cf. also xvi. 7, were unbearable to him ; while the names xvi. 5–15—meaningless to Churches of a later time—must have seemed to him superfluous. What he retained we have no means of finding out ; but there is nothing against the supposition that he worked up xv. 1–3*a*, 5–7, 14–24, 29–31*a*, 32, 33, and something from chap. xvi., into a tolerable whole. The present writer does not understand how Spitta, S. 18 f., without any attempt to refute the demonstration given above, can confidently repeat the old mistake that Marcion did not at all have the doxology any more than he had chaps. xv. and xvi. in his N.T. ; and then again, also on the basis of this statement, can venture the conjecture that he had found a text of the Church limited to chaps. i.–xiv. That this is due to an accidental mutilation of a copy is, to be sure, very "simply" explained by the insufficient analogy of the ending of Mark.

4. (Pp. 379, 381.) In very many Vulgate MSS. there is a list of chapters (so-called Brevis, also Capitula) belonging to Rom. which Wetstein, *NT*, ii. 91, was the first to deem worthy of notice, a notice, however, which was not exactly clear. Later, however, it was made use of for the critical question by Lightfoot, *Bibl. Ess.* 289, 355–362 ; Hort, *ibid.* 337, 351 ; also *NT., Appendix*, p. 111 ; Corssen, *Epist. Paulin. codd. græce et latine script. Spec.* i. (1887) p. 21 ; Riggenbach, 531–558, ii. 350–363. It is found, *e.g.* in the *Amiatinus*, ed. Tischendorf, 240 ; in six Roman MSS. cited by J. M. Thomasius (*Opp.*, ed. Vezzosi), i. 388 ; in many English MSS. cited by Lightfoot, 357 ; and in others cited by Riggenbach, 532. This Capitulatio Amiatina, as, for the sake of brevity, it must be called here, is in the oldest dated Vulg. MS. (*Fuldensis*, ed. Ranke, 176–179) so combined with another that its chaps. 24–51 (beginning with Rom. ix. 1) are added directly to chaps. 1–23 of the other (which embrace Rom. i.–xiv.). This naturally may be explained by saying that there was wanting in the exemplar of Fuld. a leaf which contained chaps. 1–23 of this Capit. Amiat., and that for this reason the copyist of Fuld. was induced to fill up the gap from another MS. with an altogether different Capit., taking chaps. 1–23 from this without noticing that in this mechanically combined Capit. Rom. ix.–xiv. occurred twice ; cf. Riggenbach, ii. 355. This is proved by the fact that Fuld. has the Capit. Amiat. throughout for the other Epistles, that in the very part of Rom. for which the other Capit. was used the chapter numerals of the Capit. Amiat. are inserted in the text, and that in a list of Church lections, p. 165, it follows not its own combined Capit., but the unmixed Capit. Amiat. This was present then in the exemplar of Fuld. originally, just as in the numerous MSS. mentioned. It lies also at the basis of an old concordance (*Concordia*, also *Capitulatio, Canones, Concordiæ canonum*), consisting of a hundred and one titles not numbered ; one which Vezzosi (Thom. *Opp.* i. 489) edited from a Murbach MS. and which is extant in many Vulg. MSS. in a mutilated form only, that is to say, without the first forty-three titles (*Amiat.* p. 237 ;

Fuld. p. 173 ; in three MSS. in Thomasius, i. 384, and in many others ; cf. Berger, *Hist. de la Vulg.* p. 209, n. 2. The first words "de unitate ecclesiae" = title 44 of the Murbach Concordance (Thomasius, i. 492). The high antiquity of the Capit. Amiat., which appears from the facts already adduced, is established by the Biblical text presupposed in it ; this is not the Vulg., but a text earlier than Jerome's time ; cf. Lightfoot, 362 ; Riggenbach, 531–541. But the Capit. Amiat., which the present writer quotes according to Amiat. and Fuld.,ignoring slight orthographic variations, consists of fifty-one chapters. Chap. xlvi., according to the wording of the title and the specification in the text,includes Rom. xiii. 14*b* ("et carnis curam ne feceritis") –xiv. 6; chap.xlvii., only Rom. xiv. 7–8; chap. xlviii., Rom. xiv. 9–13; chap. xlix., only Rom. xiv. 14; chap. l. has the title, "De periculo contristante fratrem suum esca sua, et quod non sit regnum dei esca et potus, sed justitia et pax et gaudium in spiritu sancto"; chap. li., "De mysterio domini ante passionem in silentio habito, post passionem vero ipsius revelato." Cf. the like sequence in the Concordance quoted in Thomasius, i. 392. From this we cannot decide definitely whether chap. l. included Rom. xiv. 15–23 or only xiv. 15–20 ; and whether chap. li. included simply the doxology, to which title 51 without doubt refers, or also something before and after. The chapter numerals in the text embarass us here, for it is not until Rom. xv. 4 that we find the numeral 51, and the doxology, to which alone reference is made in title 51, stands in the text of this Vulg. MS. not here, but at the close of the Epistle, and without chapter numeral. The only thing certain is that the Capit. Amiat. was prepared for an old Latin text of the Bible, in which xvi. 25–27 followed chap. xiv. immediately, and that whoever transferred it to Vulg. MSS. left the Capit. unchanged while allowing it to exert no influence upon his Biblical text. Since in this text the section to which title 51 refers was not to be found near at hand, the numeral 51 was put at xv. 4, apparently with the idea that xv. 4–13 contained something measurably corresponding to this title. In the lectionary of *Fuld.* p. 165, it is taken for granted that Rom. xv. 8 is contained in chap. li. Further, though the limits of the sections cannot be determined always with certainty from the wording of their titles, we cannot believe that the Capit. Amiat., which cut up Rom. xiv. into five chapters, 1 Cor. xvi. into seven, and 2 Tim. iv. into no less than eight, should have included Rom. xv., xvi. under the one title 51, which refers only to Rom. xvi. 25–27. It was consequently natural to conjecture that the Capit. Amiat. was intended for a Bible in which Rom. closed with chap. xiv + xvi. 25–27, so that of chaps. xv., xvi. only the doxology was included. Nevertheless it is exceedingly precarious to infer from what remains of the Capit. Amiat. that a Latin Rom., which contained only i. 1–xiv. 23+xvi. 25–27, existed and was more or less current. For (1) the significant diffusion of this Capit. Amiat. does not prove that it included only these fifty-one titles from the start. Even if the lists adduced by Lightfoot from English MSS., which are identical in the main with the Capit. Amiat., but include also chaps. xv., xvi., should prove to be nothing but later supplements, neither does this prove that the Capit. Amiat. is more than a fragment. The Concordance mentioned above is likewise only half preserved in the oldest and best MSS. (Fuld. Amiat. and three MSS. in Thomasius), and thus far is fully known from just a single MS. Before Heb. in Fuld. is a Capit. consisting of twelve headings, the last heading of which begins with Heb. ix. 11 (see the italic numerals in Ranke, 322. 12), so that Heb. x.–xiii., and perhaps also a part of Heb. ix., remain unnoticed. This is also the case with Cod. Reginæ Sueciæ (Thomasius, i. 428), from which the numerals xi., xii., which have fallen out of *Fuld.* p. 312. 26, 28, must be supplied. The fact that the text of Heb. in Fuld. is, besides, divided completely into one hundred and twenty-five chapters, and by a later hand again, as also in the Amiat., into thirty-nine chapters (Ranke, 492), makes the defect in the Capit., which prefaces the Epistle, and in the numerals in the text corresponding to it, all the more striking. So this Capit. also lay before the scribes of the oldest Vulg. MSS. in a mutilated form, and even yet is known in that form only. (2) Among the countless Latin Bibles, about the contents of which more or less is known, not one has been found so far which contains a Rom. consisting simply of i. 1–xiv. 23 + xvi. 25–27. Since the same is true of the Greek MSS. and of all the versions, and since even Marcion accepted fragments of Rom. xv., xvi. (above, p. 396 f., n. 2), we have not a single sure trace of this shorter form of the Epistle. Some have thought that such a trace was found in the circumstance that Irenæus, Tertullian, and Cyprian quote nothing from Rom. xv., xvi. How much this *argumentum e silentio* is worth can be seen in the case of Irenæus, who quotes nothing from the following chapters of Paul's letters :—1 Cor. xvi. ; 2 Cor. i., vi., viii.–xi. (only a doubtful reference to ix., x. in iv. 25. 3) ; Col. iv. ; 1 Thess. i.–iv. ; 2 Thess. iii. ; 1 Tim. iii.–v. ; 2 Tim. i.–ii. ; Tit. i.–ii. If this incompleteness in his quotations cannot prove that these twenty chapters and Philem. besides were wanting in the N.T. of Irenæus, neither is his silence about Rom. xv., xvi. of any weight. As for Tertullian, there should be an end of making that *in clausula*, which refers to Rom. xiv. 10, *c. Marcion*, v. 14 (above, p. 397), apply to this argument ; for even if this should mean "at the end of Rom." it would be unimportant in determining Tertullian's N.T., for everywhere in his *c. Marcion* he argues on the basis of Marcion's N.T., not his own, with only here and there a side glance at the Church Bible ; cf. *GK*, i. 601–606, ii. 453. Besides, Tertullian, *de Fuga*, 12 ("Quando Onesiphorus aut Aquila aut Stephanus hoc modo" by bribing the persecutors "eis" the apostles "in persecutione succurrerunt?"), has in mind plainly Rom. xvi. 4, the only passage from which we can gather that Aquila too, like Onesiphorus (2 Tim. i. 16–18) and Stephen (Acts vi.–vii.), had exposed himself to mortal danger. Other hints are less conclusive ; cf. Rönsch, *Das NT Tertullians*, 350 ; Mangold, 36 ff. ; it is doubtful whether Cyprian, *Epist.* lxv. 3 ("conprobantes, nec ante se religioni, sed ventri potius et quæstui profana religione servisse"), had Rom. xvi. 18 in his thought. Of other Latins who cite passages from Rom. xv., xvi., the present writer adduces pseudo-Cypr. *de Singul. Cleric.* pp. 181. 19, 212. 23 (chaps. xv. 2, xvi. 17) ; Hilary (*Trin.* iv. 8, Bened. p. 830), only the doxology ; Ambrose (Præf. *in Ps.* xxxvii., ed. Ben. i. 819) and Victorinus (*c. Arium*, iv. 17, Migne, 8, col. 1112) only Rom. xvi. 20 ; Priscillian, ed. Schepss, 92. 14 (chap. xv. 4) ; cf. the same author's *Canons and Sections*, pp. 128, 129, 131, 135, 136, 140, 141, 170 ; August. *Exposit. Præposit. Epist. ad Rom.*, ed. Bass. iv. 1222 (without touching on the doxology); *c. Maximin. Hær.* ii. 13, tom. x. 844, 845 ("in fine epistolæ sic loquitur"), then follows the doxology : *Specul.*, ed. Weihrich, pp. 204. 8–208. 21 (chaps. xii. 1–xv. 7 continuous, without doxology; then **xv.** 26, 27; further, **xv.** 30; finally, **xvi.** 17–19); Jerome often. Of the commentators, Pelagius (see the recast form of his commentary under the name of Jerome, Vall. xi. 3. 210, 216 f., and Zimmer, *Pelagius*, S. 310, 312) seems to have discussed the doxology, not after xiv. 23, but at the close of the letter, however, with xvi. 24 after xvi. 27, as his remark upon xvi. 24 ("hæc est subscriptio manus ejus in omnibus epistolis," etc.) shows, and is confirmed by the Würzburg excerpt in Zimmer, S. 64. Ambrosiaster also is important; for though elsewhere he notes differences between texts (*GK*, i. 34), he expounds Rom. xv., xvi., placing the doxology at the end, without any critical comment. Origen, too, who was once in Rome, knew only of the uncertain position of the doxology (see above, p. 396 f., n. 3). Of old quotations or allusions, aside from Jude 24 (see below, § 44, n. 13), the present writer instances the following : Ign. *Eph.* (address) (εὐλογημένη . . . πληρώματι) appears to be founded upon Rom. xv. 29, cf. *Trall.* address ; ἐκκλίνειν, often applied in later times to heretics, was used by him also (*Eph.* vii. 1, in connection with the writer's comment, *Patres apost.* ii. 11), and is drawn probably from Rom. xvi. 17. Clem. 2 *Cor.* xx. 5 ; *Mart. Polyc.* xx. 2, may have been imitations of Rom. xvi. 27. It is quite conceivable that the greeting occurring just there in *Mart. Polyc.*, Εὐάρεστος ὁ γράψας, received its form under the influence of Rom. xvi. 22. Of more weight are the *Actus Petri cum Simone*, ed. Lipsius, p. 45. 4 (Quartus from Rom. xvi. 23), pp. 48. 7, 49. 15, etc. (Narcissus from Rom. xvi. 11), also p. 52. 27 from Rom. xvi. 20 ; from which we may conclude that this writer of legends at about 160–170 considered Rom. xvi. as an integral part of Rom.; cf. *GK*, ii. 845, 855. We may add the citations in Clem. Alexandrinus (collected in Griesbach, *Symb.* ii. 493 f.), who quotes in *Strom.* v. 65, Rom. xv. 29 in loose connection with xvi. 25, and in *Strom.* iv. 9 the doxology, without stating more exactly their position in the Epistle.

5. (P. 381.) Of the uncials which give the Antioch recension in a pure state (KL), K has a gap between Rom. x. 18 and 1 Cor. vi. 13 (Gregory, *Proll.* 431). Alongside of L, Tischendorf, *NT*, ii. 442, 456, puts *al* (*i.e.* min.) *fere* 200, *item lectionaria*. Indeed Hort (in Lightfoot, 340) can find only 8–10 min. which do not have the doxology after xiv. 23, and there alone. It signifies little that a Greek, who wrote the min. 66 (Harleian MS. 5552 ; Griesbach, *Symb.* ii. 166–188 ; Gregory, p. 656) in the sixteenth century, after Erasmus had published his N.T., remarks on xvi. 24 : τέλος τῆς ἐπιστολῆς ὧδε ἐν τοῖς παλαιοῖς ἀντιγράφοις. τὰ δὲ λοιπὰ εἰς τέλος τοῦ ιδ΄ κεφαλαίου εὑρίσκεται (Griesb. ii. 180). Chrysostom (vol. ix. 718–756) and Theodoret (Noesselt, 146–162) seem to know nothing at all of another text. They see also a close connection in the sense between xvi. 25–27 and xiv. 23, and treat xvi. 24 as the end of the Epistle. Cf. the *Catenæ* (Cramer, iv. 490, 528), Œcumenius, and Theophylact (Migne, tom. 118, col. 604, 633 ; tom. 124, col. 533, 557). John of Damascus, on the contrary, who gives little more that an excerpt from Chrysostom, commented upon the doxology after xvi. 24. The scribe of our solitary MS. has on his own responsibility inserted the doxology in the section embracing xiv. 23*b*–xv. 7, for it receives no notice in the exposition there (ed. Lequien, ii. 54, 59). Influenced by the Alexandrian tradition, Joh. Dam. has here broken loose from Chrysostom. It would be an odd counterpart to this if Cyril of Alexandria had followed the Antioch text ; but this we cannot

safely infer from the order of citations in *Orat. I. de recta fide ad reginas* (Aubert, v. 2, 118 f.; Rom. x., xvi. 25–27, xv. 8), for he returns straightway to Rom. iv. In another set of citations (*op. cit.* 59) the order is Rom. xiv. 10, xv. 13 ff., xvi. 16, 20. The fragments of his commentary (Mai, *Nova. p. bibl.* iii. 1, 45) treat Rom. xiv. 6, 14, xv. 7, but not the doxology. Of the Gothic version there is preserved after Rom. xiv. 20 only xv. 3–13, xvi. 21–24, and the latter section serves as the close of the letter in a Cod. Ambrosianus which lacks xiv. 6–xvi. 20. Since this version rests in essentials upon a Greek text of Antiochian recension, it almost goes without saying that it admitted the doxology after xiv. 23, an assumption confirmed by the close of the Epistle, which has been preserved. Hort, in Lightfoot, 340, and Riggenbach, 550, by calculating the space necessary, have established the same point also in the case of the Gothic and the parallel Latin text of the Cod. Carolinus at Wolfenbüttel, which contains, among other passages, xiv. 9–20 and xv. 3–13 (Tischend. *Anecdota sacra et prof.* 155–158 ; Bernhardt, *Vulfila oder die goth. Bibel.* xlii. f., 369, 372). The Cod. Carolinus is not a strong witness for the existence of an independent Latin text which had the doxology after xiv. 23. On the other hand, Riggenbach, 553 f., through calculation and conjecture, has made it quite certain that a Latin Bible at Monza (Riggenb. 532 ; Berger, *Hist. de la Vulg.* 395), out of which all but a few leaves of Rom. x. 2–xv. 10 are torn, had the doxology after xiv. 23, the Epistle closing with xvi. 24. Moreover, there is nothing against our assuming that the exemplar of the Latin text g, as well as that of the Greek text G bound with it (see n. 6), had the doxology after xiv. 23. The Latin testimonies in n. 4 are also in point here. For the liturgic tradition of the Byzantine Church, cf. Scrivener, *Introd.*[4] i. 84 (Rom. xiv. 19–23 + xvi. 25–27, lection for Sabbath before Quinquagesima).

6. (Pp. 381, 382.) Cod. G (ed. Matthæi, 1791), written in the ninth century by an Irish monk in Switzerland, with a Latin interlinear version, leaves a third of page 18 v. blank, *i.e.* between xiv. 23 (fol. 18 r.) and xv. 1 (fol. 18 v.). Codex F, the Greek text of which is copied either from G or from the same exemplar, joins xv. 1 immediately to xiv. 23, and only in its Latin text (f) retains, in dependence on the Vulgate, xvi. 25–27 after xvi. 24, with which the whole letter closes in its Greek text just as in G. One thing is accordingly certain, that the exemplar of G did not have the doxology after xvi. 24 ; for why should a monk of the ninth century have refused to copy the verses which stand at this place in all Vulg. MSS. if he found them there also in his exemplar ? The only thing open to question is what induced him to leave a blank space large enough for the doxology after xiv. 23. The simplest explanation is that he found it at this place, but on account of his trust in the Vulg., which has no doxology here, he hesitated to copy here a passage which seemed strange to him in this connection. Leaving a space sufficient for xvi. 25–27 is in any case a half-way proceeding, and so proof of a critical reflection, serious indeed, but not carried to a conclusion. But just such reflection could be induced by the two factors mentioned, the existence of the doxology in the copyist's exemplar at this point, and the self-evident acquaintance of a Western monk with the Latin Vulg. On the other hand, it is most improbable that his exemplar contained the doxology either after xiv. 23 or after xvi. 24, and that, as Hort still assumed (Lightf. *Bibl. Ess.* 340), the mere recollection of other Greek MSS. which placed it after xiv. 23

should have aroused in him strong critical suspicions. For (1) Greek MSS. were certainly such rarities in the monasteries of Switzerland in the ninth century that it is most improbable that a scribe should reflect upon the textual peculiarities of other Greek MSS. than that lying directly before him. (2) There was surely nothing in xiv. 23 to stir a Latin monk to special reflection if the doxology was wanting here in his exemplar ; for neither in the Vulg. was he wont to read it at this point in the Epistle nor to hear it so read in public worship. The lack of the doxology could have impressed him only when he came to the end of the letter, since it appeared there in the Vulgate ; for which reason it was also attached there in the Latin text of F (f). (3) The hypothesis that, aside from the Marcionite Bibles (see above, n. 3, below, n. 9), there were Latin and Greek Bibles without the doxology, finds even less support than the assumption that there were Bibles with the doxology but without chaps. xv., xvi. (above, n. 4). Of the countless Bible MSS. of all tongues, just one has been pointed out thus far which gives Rom. xiv.–xvi. complete except for the doxology. This is a MS. at Milan hailing from Bobbio in the ninth or tenth century (Ambros. E 26 infra ; cf. Riggenbach, 556 ; Berger, Hist. de la Vulg. 138 f., 394). But what is more natural than that in mixed texts, to which class this MS. belongs, the variation of the exemplars with respect to the place of the doxology should finally result in some one instance in its complete disappearance ? In the development from G, or the exemplar of G and F, to F we can see this process going on before our eyes. The effort has been made to wring from the Græco-Latin Cod. D (Sæc. vi.), which has the doxology after xvi. 24 and no gap between xiv. 23 and xv. 1, testimony to an older text without the doxology. While the text of D is divided throughout according to the sense into short lines, the doxology is written in lines considerably longer and repeatedly breaking off in the middle of a word, ed. Tischendorf, p. 92. Corssen (Specim. ii. 27) concluded from this that the scribe of D, who with this exception copied throughout an exemplar divided into lines according to the sense, took the doxology from another MS. with lines not thus divided, the reason being that the chief exemplar did not contain the doxology at all. On the further assumption that G and F also go back to this chief exemplar of D, he holds that the absence of the doxology in G (F) can also be explained in the same way. Not to speak here of Corssen's genealogy of MSS. in other respects, we have seen already that G's attitude to the doxology definitely presupposes an exemplar in which the doxology stood after xiv. 23. But as for D, the form of the letter's close, like the same phenomenon at the end of Eph., demands another explanation. Such a one is given in GK, ii. 160 ; similarly Riggenbach, 577. The last four lines of Eph., too (from καὶ ἀγάπη, vi. 23, to ἀμήν, vi. 24), are written without reference to division according to sense. Moreover, while under all the other Epistles except the last (Philem., GK, ii. 160) the end of the preceding Epistle and the beginning of the following are marked by three lines wider apart than usual, and by the words ἐπληρώθη ἄρχεται, there stand under Romans merely πρὸς Ῥωμαίους in a single line, and under Eph. simply πρὸς Ἐφεσίους, πρὸς Κολοσσαεῖς in two lines. A glance at the requirements of space explains all. The scribe wished to begin a new Epistle always upon a new page. But there were cases where at the close of an Epistle a con-

sistent division according to the sense would have made a few words run
over to a new page, or rather two pages, since it concerned the Latin text on
the right hand page as well as the Greek on the left. So rather than leave
so much parchment blank, he determined to adopt a style of writing not so
wasteful of space, and in Eph. at least, to make the subscription shorter for
the same reason. The four long lines of Eph. vi. 23 f. would have made seven
lines divided according to sense. There are twenty-one lines on a page, and
since fifteen lines of text precede, the last of the (15+7) twenty-two lines and
the subscription would not have found room on the page. By compressing
seven lines into four, the scribe retained (15+4) nineteen lines of text and
had two left for the subscription, which for this very reason he made shorter
and more compact as before described. In the case of Rom. the ten (or
including the "Amen," eleven) lines written without reference to the sense,
would have made perhaps seventeen or eighteen ordinary lines divided
according to the sense, or including the preceding seven ordinary lines,
twenty-four to twenty-five for the page. The scribe, therefore, when he came
to a fitting break, gave up his diffuse way of writing, wrote the doxology
in longer lines, and retained this more sparing method to the end. He thus
obtained seventeen lines of text, without the Amen. By more fully utilising
the space he could have found room not only for the decoration at the end,
but also for a complete subscription as under the following Epistles, or
at least like that under Eph. But not having formed any rules as yet in
this the first Epistle of the collection, he preferred to be lavish with the
space he had saved. Contrary to the rule he afterwards followed, he put
the ἀμήν in a line by itself (18), and some distance below πρὸς Ῥωμαίους as
line 19. The present writer paid no attention to this when he saw the
MS., but is relying upon Tischendorf's copy, p. 92, cf. præf. ix. Other
isolated cases in which D's so-called stichometric writing is awkwardly
carried out, or even quite given up (p. 130. 10, where ἀδελφήν belongs
to the next line, as also καί in 130. 13, and p. 134. 2–4), need another
explanation, which Corssen, at any rate, has not found; cf. Riggenbach's
remarks in opposition to him, 575, and against Lucht, et al. 565–574.
Tischendorf, Cod. Clarom. p. 550, noticed that a corrector of the seventh
century (D**) found nothing in the doxology to correct; and that another
corrector (D***), a Greek, who in the ninth century supplied the whole
MS. with accents and made some corrections, accented only the first four
words of xvi. 25–27. Arguing from this, he was of the opinion that both
doubted the genuineness of the doxology. The first difficulty was set at
rest by the fact that the doxology in D has no mistake of grammar or
spelling. The second is explained by assuming that this Greek of the ninth
century consulted in his revision a Greek text which had the doxology after
xiv. 23, like the great majority of Greek MSS. for centuries. He had nothing
to guide him then after xvi. 24, and was unwilling to undertake the task of
accenting the rest of the text proprio Marte. Whether at the same time he
made critical conjectures as to the genuineness or relevancy of the doxology
here, is of no importance to us. A Greek text without the doxology must
be first discovered or its existence established on stronger grounds than those
found hitherto. Concerning Treschov's error, more often repeated years ago
(Tentamen descr. codd. 1773, p. 55), that the doxology is altogether wanting in

five Vienna MSS., which really have it after xiv. 23, and concerning a similar mistake of Erasmus, cf. Reiche, 89, n. 3.

7. (P. 381.) The doxology follows chap. xiv. as well as chap. xvi. in AP, some Armenian MSS., and a few Greek minusc. (Paul, 5, 17, 37, of which No. 5 is especially noteworthy in putting Phil. immediately before Thess., a proceeding very common in the West during the fourth century, GK, ii. 349). Hort's view (in Lightfoot, op. cit. 341 ff.), that the doxology was used thus twice before it came to be placed after chap. xiv. alone, has all analogies against it, and, in addition, the oldest testimony, that of Origen, who knows simply the alternatives: "either after chap. xiv. or after chap. xvi." (above, p. 396, n. 3).

8. (P. 381.) We know not how the doxology was arranged in the Syrians' N.T. before its recasting in the Syriac Vulgate, the so-called Peshito. Aphraates cites nothing from Rom. xiv. and xvi., including the doxology, but only xv. 1 (Wright, 141). Ephrem in his commentary (ed. Lat. 43, 46) passes over the doxology in both places; but this signifies nothing, for he does the same with Rom. ii. 2–16, xv. 13–16, xvi. 1–12. And it is only the inexact translation of the Mechitharists which makes it appear as if Ephrem joins xv. 1 immediately to xiv. 23a, xiv. 23b being omitted. P. Vetter kindly informs the writer that the word rendered there in line 11 by subdit is the same as that rendered by dixit in line 8. According to the Armenian original, the chapter numeral belongs after manducat, line 10. After that the translation should run: "Et ut arceat et (=etiam) credentes (without ipsos), dixit: 'Debemus inquit, nos qui potentes sumus,'" etc.

9. (P. 381.) Jerome in Eph. iii. 5 (vol. vii. 592): "Qui volunt prophetas non intellexisse, quæ dixerint, et quasi in ecstasi loquutos, cum ¦præsenti testimonio (Eph. iii. 5) illud quoque, quod ad Romanos in plerisque codicibus invenitur, ad confirmationem sui dogmatis trahunt legentes: 'Ei autem qui potest vos roborare juxta evangelium meum et prædicationem Jesu Christi secundum revelationem mysterii temporibus æternis taciti, manifestati autem nunc per scripturas propheticas et adventum domini nostri Jesu Christi et reliqua' (Rom. xvi. 25). Quibus breviter respondendum est, temporibus præteritis tacitum Christi fuisse mysterium non apud eos, qui illud futurum pollicebantur, sed apud universas gentes, quibus postea manifestatum est. Et paritur annotandum, quod sacramentum fidei nostræ nisi per scripturas propheticas et adventum Christi non valeat revelari. Sciant igitur qui prophetas non intelligunt nec scire desiderant, asserentes, se tantum evangelio esse contentos, Christi nescire mysterium, quod temporibus æternis gentibus cunctis fuerit ignoratum." That this was copied quite literally from Origen, Hort saw (Lightfoot, Bibl. Ess. 333; Appendix, 113). The present writer thinks in GK, ii. 428 f., he has pointed out and proved as well that this polemic of Origen is directed, not against Montanists, as Jerome seems to have understood it (cf. col. 589), nor yet confusedly, first against Montanists, then against Marcionites, as Hort assumed, but exclusively against the latter, and against Marcionites indeed, who when disputing with the orthodox, appealed to a text (Rom. xvi. 25 f.) which they did not receive at all themselves. Now, when Origen speaks of the doxology as contained in most MSS., the MSS. without it, which he implies, must be simply those of the Marcionites, where the doxology was indeed lacking; for among the Church MSS.

Origen had found no variation with respect to the doxology but that of position, now after xiv. 23 and now after xvi. 23 (above, p. 396 f., n. 3).

10. (Pp. 382, 387.) Doxologies in the course of Epistles, Rom. i. 25, ix. 5, xi. 36 ; Gal. i. 5 ; Eph. iii. 20 f. ; Phil. iv. 20 ; 1 Tim. i. 17, vi. 16 ; 2 Tim. iv. 18 ; cf., further, 1 Pet. iv. 11, v. 11 ; Heb. xiii. 20 f. (A solemn wish with doxological close ; 22-24 personal matters ; 25 benediction). In all these cases, and so also in Rom. xvi. 27, ἀμήν at the end of the doxology is attested by most or all sources (2 Cor. xi. 31 cannot be compared here) ; on the contrary, it is very doubtful whether Paul closed a single Epistle or benediction with ἀμήν. Also in Gal. vi. 18 it is lacking in G, Ambrosiaster, and Victorinus. A doxology as the real end of an Epistle occurs in the N.T. only in 2 Pet. iii. 18 ; Jude 25. If we compare the other Epistles of Paul, we shall find no ground at all for wondering at the endings of the letter which it is alleged are heaped up in Rom. xv. 5, 13, 33, xvi. 20, xvi. 24 (xvi. 27). Gal. vi. 11 retrospect of the completed letter, vi. 16 blessing, vi. 18 benediction. In 1 Cor. the intimation of the coming benediction (xvi. 21) is followed, after an intervening remark of warning, by a double benediction (xvi. 23 f.). 1 Thess. iii. 11–13 blessing with well attested ἀμήν, and following λοιπόν (iv. 1), so that all that follows appears supplementary to the letter already virtually ended. But it is followed by v. 23 another blessing, 26 greetings, 27 remark about the letter, 28 benediction. Similarly 2 Thess. ii. 16 f. first closing blessing (iii. 1, τὸ λοιπόν), iii. 5 another blessing, iii. 16a third blessing, 16b benediction, 17 intimation of the last greeting, 18 actual benediction. 2 Tim. iv. 18 closing doxology with Amen, 19–21 greetings with other information, 22 double benediction.

11. (Pp. 382, 386). The genuineness of ᾧ, xvi. 27, can hardly be doubted ; for, in the first place, the remarkable incompleteness of the sentence was very easy to remedy ; and, secondly, the emendations which we find are most various. Some changed ᾧ into αὐτῷ (P, Copt., min. 31, 54) ; others struck out ᾧ (B) or ᾧ ἥ (min. 33, 72), or made from ᾧ ἥ an εἴη (min. 55 and scholion of min. 43). To the latter group belong also f (the Latin text of F, the Greek text of which lacks the doxology), and Rufinus as translator of Origen (iv. 687), who here at least has not rendered fairly Origen's very peculiar text (GK, ii. 429, A. 2). S¹ treated the doxology very freely : "But to God who can stablish you in [according to] my gospel, which was preached about [περί] Jesus Christ according to the revelation of the secret, which from eternal times was hidden, but in the present was revealed through prophetic Scriptures, and by command of the eternal God was made known to all nations for the purpose of obedience of the faith : to Him, who alone is wise, glory through Jesus Christ for the age of the ages. Amen." Clement, Strom. v. 65, p. 685, and Origen, vol. i. 389, 488, iv. 104 f., 226, 257, always quote the doxology incompletely, without ver. 27.

12. (Pp. 383, 385.) The ascetics judged that their fellow-Christian of liberal views would not stand firm, but ran the risk of falling. Paul, however, assures them that he will surely be kept in his upright position, and that the Lord has the power to make him stand (xiv. 4). The liberals, on the other hand, who like Paul thought the ascetics weak, also despised them, and Paul warns them not to put in the way any stones over which these weak brethren might stumble (xiv. 13, 20 f.). The τῷ δυναμένῳ ὑμᾶς στηρίξαι, xvi. 25, refers

to both these things at once. Paul does not here utter a pious wish, but again reminds himself and the readers, as in ver. 4, with the similarly sounding words δυνατεῖ ὁ κύριος στῆσαι αὐτόν, of the power of God which is able to establish those who are in danger of unstable going, of stumbling or of falling; cf. also the expressions στήκει ἢ πίπτει, σταθήσετα, ver. 4; πρόσκομμα ἢ σκάνδαλον, ver. 13; διὰ προσκόμματος . . . προσκόπτει, vv. 20, 21. He comforts himself with this power of God, both in regard to the liberals, who in the judgment of the ascetics are in danger of falling, and also in regard to the ascetics, concerning whom he has the fear, that they might be enticed by the inconsiderate behaviour of the strong to act contrary to the dictates of conscience, and thereby to fall in the most disastrous way. As Paul, ver. 10b, unites in a *we* the two parties addressed separately in ver. 10a (cf. vv. 13a, 19), so he can unite them both in ὑμᾶς, xvi. 25, after ver. 22, which refers to the liberals, and ver. 23, which refers to the ascetics. What Spitta (S. 7 f.) has to say against the writer's proof of this connection, is at least not founded on the error that στηρίζειν means "strengthen"; it means rather "establish," either at the outset so to place something that it remains firm, or to make more secure, to support, what is already standing, but might easily become unstable or fall. The contrast between falling and destructive temptation is found, *e.g.*, 2 Pet. iii. 16 f. (ἀστήρικτοι—ἐκπεσεῖν τοῦ στηριγμοῦ); Luke xxii. 32, cf. Mark xiv. 27 ff.; 2 Thess. iii. 3; Rev. iii. 2, and the connection of στηρίξειν with the idea of standing, being stable, is unmistakable (1 Thess. iii. 2, 8, 10; 1 Pet. v. 10, 12). Also Rom. i. 11; Acts xviii. 23 (variant reading) the idea is not of *strengthening* the faith, but of *stablishing* the believers in upright bearing (cf. 2 Cor. i. 24). Here, however (xvi. 23), the question concerns a stablishing not in the πίστις τοῦ εὐαγγελίου (Phil. i. 27), but in the ethical manifestation of faith (cf. 1 Thess. iii. 13; 2 Thess. ii. 17). The connection with κατὰ τὸ εὐαγγέλιον κτλ. suits only this interpretation. The Gospel of Paul and the preaching of Jesus Christ are not named as the means of producing and strengthening faith, but as the norm of conduct, and as the standard according to which God will stablish the Romans. His personal assurance in the matter of clean and unclean things, Paul emphasises strongly in xiv. 14; at the same time, however, he expresses the thought that in this he knew that he was of the same mind as the "Lord Jesus." He desires also here to give utterance to the two thoughts, namely, (1) that the ethical principles which he has developed in chap. xiv. correspond especially with what he himself—the Apostle of the Gentiles—has preached, and (2) that, moreover, also in the preaching of Jesus Himself the outlines of these principles had been drawn (cf. Matt. xv. 1–20). In confirmation of the fact that τὸ κήρυγμα 'I. Χρ. does not mean the preaching about Christ, but the preaching and teaching of Jesus Himself, the following proofs are offered: (1) The comparison with Matt. xii. 41; 1 Cor. ii. 4, xv. 14; (2) the similarity of the genitive with εὐαγγέλιον and κήρυγμα demanded by the style; (3) the use of the personal name 'Ιησοῦ before Χριστοῦ; (4) the placing alongside of each other of the two ideas determined by the article—a position which excludes their identity (cf. below, § 48, n. 2). By means of this, however, the passage xv. 1–3 following is prepared for in more than one way. The κατὰ Χρ. 'I., xv. 5, corresponds to the κατὰ τὸ κήρ. 'I. Χρ. In xv. 3, 7, 8 there is presented as authoritative example the Jesus Christ who lived on earth, renounced self-will, cared for the needy, was calumniated by the ungodly of His own nation, and yet who all His life long served the people of the circumcision. In the διάκονον γεγενῆσθαι περιτομῆς, however, the διακονία τοῦ λόγου, the preaching, is also included as an essential element. Moreover, the further reference to the prophetic writings (xvi. 26) agrees perfectly with xv. 4, 8–12 ; and the mention of the especial gospel of the apostle to the Gentiles and the thought that the mystery of salvation formerly kept secret is intended for all nations (xvi. 26) is an excellent preparation for xv. 8–13. Moreover, xv. 1–6 also bears upon the discussion of the relations existing between the Jewish and Gentile Christians ; as is especially shown by the comparison of ver. 4 f. with ver. 13, and the close connection between ver. 6 and vv. 9–10. There is here no further discussion of the especial opposition of the vegetarians to the eaters of meat, but much more general admonitions and wishes in relation to the restoration, through mutual concessions, of unity among all the Church members—a unity which showed itself also in worship. This duty holds good for the antagonism which obtained among the Roman Christians, mentioned in chap. xiv., moreover, also, for many other existing differences, and not least for the opposition of the Jewish to the Gentile born members of the Church, to the discussion of which the general sentences, xv. 1–3, form the transition. The δυνατοί among whom the Jewish Paul classes himself, ver. 1, are naturally not the Gentile Christians ; they are also, however, not identical with the anti-vegetarians in chap. xiv., who there are just as little called δυνατοί as the vegetarians ἀδύνατοι, and with whom Paul in chap. xiv. not once identifies himself by a we. The strong are rather those whom God, who has the power to do it, has stablished, according to Paul's gospel and Jesus' preaching (xvi. 25, cf. Tit. i. 9 ; 2 Cor. xii. 10 ; Phil. iv. 13), and who, like Paul, have risen above all such oppositions (cf. 1 Cor. ix. 19–23). Hofmann, who, following Griesbach, contended for the position of xvi. 25–27 after xiv. 23 as the original one (iii. 577), tried to make it out that the sentence begun with τῷ δὲ δυναμένῳ, and resumed in μόνῳ σοφῷ θεῷ, xvi. 27, finds its regular continuation in xv. 1. No one could object to the construction of ὀφείλω with dative and following infin., cf. viii. 12, xiii. 8 ; and perhaps even the δέ, xv. 1, which is undoubtedly genuine, could be justified grammatically. But stylistically considered, the result is a monstrous form of sentence. A more probable explanation, and one much more in keeping with Paul's peculiar style, is that the sentence as he originally intended to construct it became weighted down by parenthetic remarks and, though he made an effort to carry the construction consistently through by taking up again the emphatic dative object, the doxology with its solemn "amen" forcing its way in afresh, drove the purpose from his mind.

13. (Pp. 383, 384.) After the prayer, xvi. 20a, all witnesses except DG (dg) and perhaps also Sedulius have ἡ χάρις τοῦ κυρίου ἡμῶν Ἰησοῦ μεθ' ὑμῶν (without ἀμήν). But the second benediction also, ἡ χ. τ. κ. ἡμ. Ἰ. Χρ. μετὰ πάντων ὑμῶν (with or without ἀμήν) is quite overwhelmingly attested ; only it is written sometimes after xvi. 23 (as ver. 24 ; so DG, the Antioch recension [L, the majority of min., the Antioch commentators] ; among versions the Goth. and S³, and many Vulg. MSS.), sometimes after xvi. 27 (so P, a few min., S¹, Armen., Ambrosiaster, and the true Pelagius, see above, p. 401, n. 4). It is wanting altogether in ℵABC, a few min., Copt., and important Vulg.

MSS., also probably in Origen's text. On the strength of this, Tischendorf and Westcott and Hort have stricken it out as a doublet of xvi. 20. But (1) according to the great mass of evidence it differs from ver. 20 in giving a fuller designation of Christ and in inserting πάντων ; (2) the double form of the benediction (xvi. 20, 24), is vouched for by such manifold testimony, belonging to most widely differing portions of the Church, that it must go back to high antiquity ; (3) Paul would be departing from a settled custom if he closed a letter with greetings to or from individuals without a formal benediction ; on the other hand, he never objects to a double bene-diction (see above, n. 10). These benedictions may be essentially similar and bound together like a double "farewell" (1 Cor. xvi. 23, 24 ; Eph. vi. 23, 24 ; 2 Tim. iv. 22), or they may be separated by remarks of a different char-racter, 2 Thess. iii. 16b, 18. In both 1 Cor. and Eph. he added a πάντων to the second and final benediction, exactly as in Rom. xvi. 24. Also in 2 Tim. iv. 22 the two benedictions, standing side by side, are related one to the other as the particular to the universal. Although, where Paul joins the second benediction immediately to the first, or lets it follow soon after-wards, he prefers not to repeat the same words ; yet an explanation is un-necessary when, on the other hand, in Rom. xvi. 20 and xvi. 24, where many small items intervene, he shows no hesitation in repeating the customary benediction in essentially the same words. (4) Upon the twofold presup-position that the doxology belongs to the end of the letter, and that xvi. 24 is not genuine,—a presupposition which the textual critics whose views now prevail have not proved, but have simply laid down as axiomatic in discussing this question,—the transmission of the text of xvi. 20-27 remains inexplicable. Suppose that the need arose for a benediction at the end of the letter owing to the removal of the doxology from that point to an earlier part of the letter, and that this need was met by making up xvi. 24 or by placing xvi. 20b after xvi. 23, how then are we to account for the fact that texts otherwise most various (DPS[1], Arm., Ambrost., Pelag.) agree in having the doxology in chap. xvi. and right next to it, either before or after the benediction, xvi. 24 ; and that most of them (all those named except D) retain xvi. 20b besides ? (5) On the other hand, it is easy enough to explain the fact on the presupposition that the doxology stood originally after xiv. 23. When the doxology was moved to the close of the Epistle, sometimes it was simply added at the end (after xvi. 24, so D), sometimes it was inserted between xvi. 23 and xvi. 24, so as to retain the original ending (P, min. 17, 80, S[1], Arm., Ambrost., Pelag.). A third method, followed by some apparently as early as Origen's time, was to treat the doxology as a sufficient substitute for the original ending (cf. Jude 24 f. ; 2 Pet. iii. 18), and to strike out xvi. 24, which was the easier, since essentially the same benediction was to be found in xvi. 20. In this latter opinion they agreed with those in the West who, even before the doxology was moved to the end, had stricken out xvi. 20 as superfluous alongside of xvi. 24 (G and perhaps the exemplar of D, see beginning of this note). Moreover, this misplacement had a corrupting influence upon the text of the doxology itself. The witnesses for the position after xiv. 23 (Antioch recen.) all have the simpler form εἰς τοὺς αἰῶνας, without τῶν αἰώνων, and those which have the doxology in both places (AP) prove an essential connection between the form of the text and its position by giving the shorter form of the doxology after chap. xiv. and the longer (with τῶν αἰώνων) after chap. xvi. In itself, the shorter form of the doxology is more likely to be the original one ; and this supposition is fully confirmed by such good witnesses as BC, which, in spite of the misplacement of the doxology, have retained its shorter form. The expansion of the doxology, then, which its position at the end of the letter invited, did not follow its misplacement immediately, or was not in all cases connected with this directly. But the group of witnesses which agree in giving the original *text* of the doxology deserve, as in the discussion of its *position* also, the preference over that group the great majority of which give, together with the position at the close, the corrupted text.

14. (P. 383.) Bengel, *Appar. Crit.* (ed. 2) 340 : "Videntur Graeci, ne lectio publica in severam sententiam (xiv. 23) desineret, hanc ei clausulam attexuisse, cf. var. Matt. iii. 11." He means the omission in Matt. iii. 11 of καὶ πυρί. But how can that be compared to removing a significant section from its original position ? How much more natural, with such an aim in view, to have continued the lection to xv. 4 or xv. 7, or, if transposition of the text were once allowed to enter, to have put here a prayerful wish such as that in xv. 13, which accords with xiv. 17 and with xiv. 23 also ! (through ἐν τῷ πιστεύειν). Hort (in Lightf. *Bibl. Ess.* 342) assumed that in ancient times Rom. xvi. was not read in worship, and that therefore the edifying doxology was joined to a neighbouring lection. Since this does not explain the removal of the doxology from the end of chap. xvi., but only how it came to be joined to an earlier passage, Hort arrived at the untenable hypothesis mentioned above, p. 405, n. 7. Further, the omission of xvi. 1–24 in the liturgy would not explain why the doxology was put after xiv. 23 and not rather after or before xv. 13 or before xv. 33. That the prayerful wishes there would have been no hindrance is seen from Phil. iv. 19 f. ; Heb. xiii. 20 f. ; 1 Pet. v. 10. This explanation, then, could be considered only if it could be proved that chap. xv. was also excluded from public reading in church. But the extant lectionaries give lections from chap. xv. (cf. Scrivener, *Introd.*[4] i. 82) on the seventh Sunday after Pentecost, Rom. xv. 1–7 ; on the tenth Sabbath after Pentecost, Rom. xv. 30–33 ; also Rom. xv. 7–16 and xv. 8–12 on week-days, Zacagni, *Coll. mon.* i. 587 ; *ibid.* p. 538, cf. p. 575 f., embracing the fifth lection of Euthalius, of which chaps. xviii., xix. = Rom. xv. 1–33. The lectionary in the *Fuld.*, ed. Ranke, 165, includes Rom. xv. 8 ff. There may possibly have been before Origen's time a lection system which excluded Rom. xv.–xvi. ; but even so it certainly could not have had at that early date such a powerful influence upon the shaping of the text as to make the misplacement of the doxology, which it brought about, as is claimed, appear to Orig. the older form of the text. Also Riggenbach's explanation, 603 f., that the purpose was to make Rom. close with such a blessing as the other Epistles have, is unsatisfactory. This aim could have been attained much more simply by putting xvi. 24 after the doxology, or, if this verse did not then exist, after xvi. 20, just as in Phil. iv. 23 (cf. 20) ; Heb. xiii. 25 (cf. 21) ; 2 Tim. iv. 22 (cf. 18) ; 1 Pet. v. 14 (cf. 11) the benediction follows hard upon the doxology, and some important witnesses (above, n. 13) actually do place the benediction immediately after the doxology, xvi. 25–27 in Rom.

15. (Pp. 383, 384.) As to the Peshito, back of which our search cannot

(above, n. 8), we must remember that even before its final redaction the Syriac N.T. received influences from Alexandria; cf. *GK*, i. 386, 406, ii. 560, 564. The West became acquainted with Alexandrian textual criticism at the beginning of the fourth century through Pierius, " the younger Origen " (Jerome, *Vir. Ill.* lxxvi.). The spacial separation of the two passages, xiv. 23 and xvi. 24 is much too great to be compared with transpositions like those in 1 Cor. xiv. 33–40, xv. 26, which probably arose in a merely mechanical way. More comparable is the varying position of John vii. 53–viii. 11. But, firstly, this is a pericope which did not force its way into the N.T. until the fifth century. Secondly, it is indubitable that the scribe who first connected it with the Fourth Gospel put it where the Textus Receptus and the oldest MSS. have it, and that only later critical suspicions caused it to be placed after John xxi., or also after Luke xxi. In respect of age, even such changes as the insertion of ἐν Ἐφέσῳ, Eph. i. 1, cannot be compared, but rather the changing of the original text of Rom. i. 7 mentioned above, p. 394 f. The transposing of the doxology from its original position after xiv. 23 to the close of the letter was no longer new at the time of Origen; it goes back into the second century, to the time when the effort was made in various ways to frame a fitting close to the unfinished Gospel of Mark, when Tatian compiled his *Diatessaron*, and also handled Paul's Epistles in bold fashion (Eus. *H. E.* iv. 29. 6).

16. (P. 384.) In order to explain the variant position of the doxology, and at the same time the alleged multiplicity of endings (xvi. 25–27, xv. 33, xvi. 20, xvi. 24), Griesbach, *loc. cit.*, assumed that Paul, after finishing the letter proper, chaps. i.–xiv.—since the writing material for the purpose was used up—wrote (1) on a separate sheet the sentences intended for the close, xvi. 25–27, perhaps with xvi. 24 ; (2) again, on another sheet xvi. 21–23 or xvi. 21–24 ; then (3) on a third sheet chap. xv. as a postscript to i.–xiv.+xvi. 25–27, the need for which came to him as an afterthought ; finally (4), again on a separate sheet xvi. 1–20. The sheets then, when copies were made of the Epistle, were arranged in various orders. Eichhorn, *Einl.* iii. 32, appropriated the essentials of this hypothesis ; so also Laurent, *Ntl. Stud.* S. 31, with the needful modification, however, of substituting "strips of papyrus" for "leaves of parchment" (cf. 2 John 12, χάρτης ; Birt, *Buchwesen*, S. 61 f.). But opposed to this and every such hypothesis is the following :—(1) All the texts of Rom. as we know it in literature go back to just two archetypes, one of which placed the doxology after chap. xiv., the other after chap. xvi. But on this hypothesis either all the MSS. go back to a single orderly edited exemplar, the variant position of the doxology then remaining unexplained, or the "disjecta membra epistulæ" remained in the archive of the Roman Church unarranged, and copies were made of them as the need arose. In this case we must have met in the MSS. many different arrangements of chaps. xv., xvi., instead of just two. (2) It is hardly thinkable that Paul or his amanuensis Tertius (xvi. 22) should have failed to take care, by gluing the papyrus leaves together, that the letter came to the readers in the form intended. Renan (*St. Paul*, 1869, pp. lxiii–lxxv) explained Rom. as a circular letter, which Paul himself had prepared in four copies— (1) For the Romans, chaps. i.–xi. 15 ; (2) for the Ephesians, chaps. i.–xiv.+ xvi. 1–20 (with some changes in chap. i.) ; (3) for the Thessalonians, chaps. i.–xiv.+xvi. 21–24 ; (4) for an unknown Church, chaps. i.–xiv.+xvi. 25–27. It is plain that even with some changes in chap. i. (omission of ἐν Ῥώμῃ in

i. 7, 15, perhaps), Rom. i.–xi. is still far from being suited to the Ephesians and Thessalonians. There is hardly a sentence in i. 1–16 which is not affected in form and content by the reference to Rome and to Paul's peculiar relation to the Christians there. Not to speak of the opening greeting (above, p. 352 f.), imagine i. 8–16a addressed to Macedonia, where shortly before writing Rom. Paul had spent weeks or months! But the thought of Rome suggests also the theme i. 17 f. and its whole development of this up to xi. 36. To speak of the merest externals, what would the overwhelmingly Gentile Churches of Ephesus and Thessalonica think of chap. vii. 1–6, viii. 15, or even of vi. 16 f. (above, p. 374 f., n. 8)? But if the whole letter needed a complete recasting to adapt it to other Churches than that of Rome, where do we see traces of these various recensions from which our Rom. was compiled? Lightfoot (*Bibl. Ess.* 287–320), though he sought to refute Renan's hypothesis, advanced a similar one, and maintained it in essentials (*ibid.* 352–374) against Hort's criticism (*ibid.* 321–351) ; Paul himself in later time, perhaps during his Roman imprisonment, transformed the letter originally addressed to the Roman Church, which included chaps. i.–xiv., xv. 1–xvi. 23, into an Epistle suited to a wider circle, by writing ἐν ἀγάπῃ in i. 7 for ἐν 'Ρώμῃ ἀγαπητοῖς, by striking out (τοῖς) ἐν 'Ρώμῃ in i. 15, and further by cutting off xv. 1–xvi. 23, instead of which he framed a new ending for the Epistle, xvi. 25–27. But (1) we should expect least of all from Paul himself such a partial and external procedure by which the Epistle's local reference would be merely a little obscured, not removed altogether (see above, against Renan). (2) Why should he have found xv. 1–13 less adapted to a larger circle of readers than i. 8–16 or xiv. 1–23 ? The relation of particular to universal which subsists between that section and these is just the opposite of that which Lightfoot seems to have presupposed. (3) Since Paul elsewhere seems to have had no objection to having a letter addressed to one Church read by another (Col. iv. 16), no motive can be found for this literary labour of the apostle so strange in itself. (4) The supports which Lightfoot thought he found in the text as transmitted are most decidedly weak. Marcion, even aside from the fact that he had none of the doxology, but did have parts of chaps. xv., xvi., could give absolutely no support to such a hypothesis on account of his treatment of the text (above, p. 396 f.). Just as little can Cod. G and all the witnesses for the position of the doxology after xiv. 23 ; for there is not a hint that they go back to a text without xv. 1–xvi. 23. Finally, as for the variants of Rom. i. 7 and i. 15, it has been shown to be (above, p. 394 f.) extremely probable, that in the first passage ἐν ἀγάπῃ θεοῦ was the original text, which was changed into ἐν 'Ρώμῃ ἀγαπητοῖς θεοῦ only after a considerable circulation of the Epistle in the Church, therefore certainly a long time after the death of Paul. It has also been shown that the omission of the apparently unnecessary τοῖς ἐν 'Ρώμῃ, i. 15, was only an arbitrary act, appearing only in isolated instances, and favoured by the original text of i. 7.

17. (P. 386.) A particular chain of thought suggested before, in ii. 16, the statement that in Paul's gospel the universality of God's plan of salvation was manifested more clearly than before (cf. i. 16, iii. 29); but that this gospel of Paul is not his own peculiar teaching, but the one message of salvation in a particular historical form, is maintained in i. 1 by the designation of it as the gospel of God, and here by the co-ordination of it with the preaching of

Jesus. In xvi. 26, as in iii. 21, x. 11, the reference is to the inner connection of this gospel with the O.T.; i. 2, however (cf. x. 15; Luke iv. 17 ff.)—a verse that verbally resembles xvi. 26 much more closely than do iii. 21, x. 11, which are essentially related passages—seems rather to express the thought that God had promised long before that He would send forth such a message of salvation. If the words εἰς ὑπακοὴν πίστεως εἰς πάντα τὰ ἔθνη echo i. 5 almost exactly, cf. vi. 17, x. 16, xv. 18, xvi. 19; 2 Thess. i. 8, we should also note the variation which is just what might be expected in a compiler. The στηρίζειν of the Romans, which Paul hoped to accomplish by his visit (i. 11), he must for the present leave to God, since he cannot come to Rome immediately (xv. 23-33). That a blessing certified before, indeed, but still veiled, has been made known in the gospel (iii. 21, πεφανέρωται = φανερωθέντος, xvi. 26), and repeatedly unveils itself to the believing hearer (i. 17, ἀποκαλύπτεται = κατὰ ἀποκάλυψιν, xvi. 25) was said before. But the correlate of these ideas is expressed not there, but only in xvi. 25 by μυστήριον, which only shows again that no pseudo-Paul is here copying the apostle. There the connection and the aim of the teaching involved the calling of this real blessing which is unveiled through the gospel, the righteousness of God. Here there was no occasion for it, and it sufficed to characterise the present as a time in which was revealed to all men what had been a dark secret to former generations; for in this past, which for many of the readers was not yet banished by the gospel, are rooted the wrongs and quarrels and the confused notions against which Paul had to fight in xiv. 1-23, xv. 1-13. We find μυστήριον not infrequently in the older and less disputed parts of Paul's letters (Rom. xi. 25; 1 Cor. ii. 7, iv. 1, xiii. 2, xiv. 2, xv. 51; 2 Thess. ii. 7; cf. Phil. iv. 12); but its use as a formal designation of God's plan of salvation is confined to the present passage and Eph. i. 9, iii. 4, 9, vi. 19; Col. i. 26 f., ii. 2, iv. 3—very narrow limits, it must be admitted. Indeed, Eph. iii. 3-6 and Col. i. 26 f., especially have a close resemblance to Rom. xvi. 25 f., but there is nothing in this doxology which betrays borrowing from any of these passages. Besides, it requires no proof to see that, if Paul was indeed the author of Eph. and Col., the thought expressed in these Epistles, that the sharing of the Gentile world in salvation was long hidden or remained a secret, but was revealed in the gospel, could not have occurred to him for the first time some years after he wrote Romans. The expressions ἀπὸ χρόνων αἰωνίων (cf. πρὸ χρ. αἰ., 2 Tim. i. 9; Tit. i. 2), κατ' ἐπιταγὴν ... θεοῦ (cf. 1 Tim. i. 1; similarly Tit. i. 3), τοῦ αἰωνίου θεοῦ (cf. 1 Tim. i. 17, τῷ βασιλεῖ τῶν αἰώνων), have awakened suspicions from their similarity to passages in the Pastoral Epistles. But none of them is copied, least of all the last, and the individual elements have nothing peculiar about them. Paul employs αἰώνιος outside of the doxology and the Pastoral Epistles ten times; κατ' ἐπιταγήν in 1 Cor. vii. 6; 2 Cor. viii. 8 (cf. 1 Cor. vii. 25), a common mode of speech, indeed, in such a connection (e.g. κατ' ἐπιταγὴν τῆς θεᾶς in a Phrygian inscription, JHSt. 1883, p. 388). These similarities can prove nothing alone; and even if other evidence were forthcoming, all that they could help to establish would be that Rom. xvi. 25-27 and the Pastoral Epistles were written by the same person. The case is not changed if by that person we understand Paul. On the contrary, it is absurd to claim that the same pseudo-Paul who forged the Pastoral Epistles interpolated Romans

18. (P. 388.) We find greetings from large groups of Christians to the collective body of readers in 1 Cor. xvi. 19 f. ; 2 Cor. xiii. 12 ; cf. Tit. iii. 15 ; 1 Pet. v. 13 ; Heb. xiii. 24 ; together with more particular greetings, Phil. iv. 22 ; Rom. xvi. 16. Gal., Eph., 2 Thess., and 1 Tim. have no greetings at the end ; in 1 Thess. v. 26 is simply a request to greet one another in Paul's name, cf. Rom. xvi. 16a. The only case where individuals are addressed in the course of the letter is Phil. iv. 2 f. Apart from the letters addressed to places which Paul had not yet seen, Rom. and Col. (see above, p. 388), greetings to individuals and from individuals occur besides only in the private letters, Philem. 23 f. ; 2 Tim. iv. 19–21. Even in the case of brief personal intercourse with a Church, there would be no end of greetings if the writer sought thus to express all the connections formed at that time. This is illustrated by formulas such as those in Ign. *Smyrn.* xiii ; *ad Polyc.* viii ἀσπάζομαι πάντας κατ' ὄνομα and ἐξ ὀνόματος, cf. 3 John 15 ; *Berl. ägypt. Urk.* 27. 18, 93. 28, and often. For the same reason, Paul, in his letters to the Churches founded by him at Philippi, Thessalonica, and Corinth, and in Galatia, avoids personal greetings at the close altogether. He would have done the same then probably in a letter to the Ephesians.

19. (Pp. 385, 389.) Baur (i. 394): "xv. 1–13 contains nothing which the apostle had not said better before in xii. 1 f." Answer : Paul said nothing similar in xii. 1 f. ; in xv. 1–13, for the very first time in the whole Epistle, he touches on the difference between the Jewish and the Gentile elements within the Church as an opposition which endangers unity of faith and worship, and which he exhorts both sides to put away. That there were Gentile Christians in Rome was seen before in xi. 13 ; but only the Gentile Christians were admonished in xi. 16 ff., not both parties in the Church ; and these were exhorted to a proper attitude, not toward the Jewish Christians, but toward unbelieving Jews. According to Baur 394 f., Lucht 174 ff., concessions are made to the Jewish Christians in xv. 8 f. which Paul never offers. But the historical fact that the personal activity of Christ did limit itself to Israel (γεγενῆσθαι), could not be denied by even a fanatical anti-Semite, to say nothing of Paul, who laid stress upon these very things, namely, that all revelations, including the last and greatest, were entrusted to this people and had their results in Israel (iii. 2, v. 20) ; that Jesus in the whole sphere of His life was under the law, in order that first of all He might redeem them that were under the law, *i.e.* the Israelites (Gal. iv. 4 f., iii. 13 ; Rom. vii. 4) ; and that only in consequence of His death and the unbelief of Israel did salvation turn to the Gentiles (Gal. iii. 14 ; Rom. xi. 11–xv. 30). The appearance of Christ in Israel is, indeed, made the proof of God's faithfulness in fulfilling His promises made to the patriarchs ; but so far is this from excluding the idea of grace, that promise and grace are rather correlated (Rom. iv. 13–16 ; Gal. iii. 17 f.). Yet it is emphasised no less strongly in Rom. iii. 3, ix. 4–6, xi. 1 f., 27–29, that God in fulfilling His promises toward Israel has proved His faithfulness and will still prove it. Paul never taught that the Gentiles had an historical right to salvation similar to that of the Jews. It is therefore hard to see why he could not here, as in xi. 30, emphasise as characteristic of the Gentiles' relation to salvation the fact that they owed this simply to the mercy of God. A concession to the Jewish Christians such as sets one thinking is to be found not in xv. 8 f., but in xiv. 5 ; see § 23.

Incredible as it may seem, Baur (396, 399) gathered that Paul presupposed in i. 11 a lack on the Romans' part of the "essentials of the deeper knowledge," namely, the "pneumatic," which accordingly he must needs impart to them. On this view, to be sure, the words of approbation in xv. 14, and the apologetic remark a little farther on about his writing the letter, appear like a contradiction. In reality he expressed himself much more modestly with reference to the result of his coming visit in i. 11—where, moreover, there is no mention of the letter—than in xv. 29 (above, pp. 355 f., 369). It is unquestionably true that it was a venture to write to the Romans, for Paul, who considered himself above all a missionary to the Gentiles, had no immediate connection with the Roman Church by virtue of his calling. But the attentive reader does not see this for the first time in xv. 15, it appears in the opening greeting, so diplomatically worded, and in the tone of the whole Epistle. Nowhere the tone of a teacher to his pupils, no use of νουθετεῖν (1 Cor. iv. 14 ; Col. i. 28 ; 1 Thess. v. 12, 14 ; Acts xx. 31), though this is allowable even among equal brethren (Col. iii. 16 ; 2 Thess. iii. 15 ; Rom. xv. 14), or of παραγγέλλειν (1 Cor. vii. 10, xi. 17 ; 1 Thess. iv. 11 ; 2 Thess. iii. 4, 6, 10, 12) and διατάσσεσθαι (1 Cor. vii. 17, xi. 34, xvi. 1); but everywhere the most considerate tone of one who wishes to come to an understanding with equals, and who exhorts them as a brother. The principle proclaimed in xv. 20 of preaching the gospel only where Christ has not yet been named, is held to be un-Pauline, indeed, even incompatible with the writing of a letter to the Romans. But (1) Paul says merely that he prides himself upon such pioneer work, and by no means that he regards every continuation of work begun by others as sin or folly. (2) This declaration corresponds with his actual procedure since the outset of the first missionary journey. As in Corinth (1 Cor. iii. 10), so everywhere he laid the foundations ; and he expresses himself quite similarly in 2 Cor. x. 15 f. (3) Writing Rom. is no εὐαγγελίζεσθαι, and so cannot be inconsistent with this principle. (4) Paul spoke most modestly in i. 13-15 of his missionary work in Rome (above, pp. 355 f., 369, 371). Anyone can see from Paul's actual practice why he did not wish to make Rome a centre for his missionary preaching. Wherever there was a thriving Church, whether founded by himself or by others, his tarrying was never long, and his εὐαγγελίζεσθαι not great. But it was natural surely for Paul, restless missionary as he was, to tell what was the aim of his journey to the West, since he did not intend to accomplish much in Rome. What we miss in i. 13-15 we find in xv. 22-29. Rome was his stopping-place on the way to Spain. That a pseudo-Paul regarded Rome and Italy as the province of another apostle is a thoroughly groundless insinuation of Baur's (398). It is all the more strange when we hear that this man's views agreed with those of the author of Acts (398, 408), which, as we know, closes with a terse but lively description of a two years' preaching activity of Paul in Rome, and says nothing of another apostle there. Baur (401) considered the Spanish journey "the most incredible thing told about the apostle's life." He failed to see that the possible unhistoricity of this tradition does not affect in the least the question whether the real Paul expressed such a purpose of going thither, while it is an almost insuperable obstacle to supposing that a pseudo-Paul—especially if belonging to the first century, see above, p. 388 f.—would have put such an utterance into the mouth of the apostle. This holds also against Lipsius,

HK, ii. 2, 86, 195 f., who rejected xv. 19*b*, 20*b* (including ἀλλά, ver. 21), 23, 24 as interpolations, and in ver. 28 preferred to read ἐλεύσομαι πρὸς ὑμᾶς instead of ἀπελεύσομαι—Σπανίαν, though retaining the rest of chap. 15 as genuine. That Paul should speak of preaching in Jerusalem agrees with Acts xxvi. 20, ix. 26-29, and is not inconsistent with Gal. i. 17-24. Gal. does not mention the place of his εὐαγγελίζεσθαι, about which the Churches in Judea heard at the time when he betook himself from Palestine to Syria and Cilicia (Gal. i. 21-24). But since this news, as the form of expression shows (ὁ διώκων ἡμᾶς ποτε, ver. 23), spread from Jerusalem out into Palestine, the natural assumption is that during his fifteen days' stay in the city he who before was known as a persecutor became known as a preacher of the gospel, cf. *ZKom. Gal.* 74 f. Since his aim in Rom. xv. 19 is not to tell where he had preached first and where last, but to give the most widely separated regions of his activity hitherto, he does not mention Damascus, but Jerusalem and the borders of Illyricum. He does not say that he has preached in Illyricum ; for nothing compels us to understand μέχρι as inclusive rather than as exclusive, as, *e.g.* in Rom. v. 14 ; Phil. ii. 30. The Roman province of Illyricum bordered in the south on Macedonia and was separated from Achaia, to which also Epirus belonged, by a strip of land belonging to Macedonia (Marquardt, i. 297, 318 f., 331). If Paul considered his task of preaching the gospel in Macedonia fulfilled when he had founded Churches in Philippi, Thessalonica, and Berœa, he had in so doing "fulfilled it as far as Illyricum." This way of looking at it may seem extravagant, but it was the prevailing one in apostolic times, coming to light everywhere in the N.T., and lying at the basis of Paul's missionary methods ; cf. *Skizzen*, 76-82. Moreover, it is possible that immediately after writing 2 Cor. Paul may have set forth from Thessalonica or Berœa upon a short preaching tour, which brought him still nearer to the bounds of Illyricum than he had come before. The vague expression τὰ μέρη ἐκεῖνη, Acts xx. 2, allows freest play to our imagination. Also during the three months which he spent in Greece (Acts xx. 3), he may have made in connection with his visit to all the Churches "in the whole of Achaia" (2 Cor. i. 1, above, p. 264, n. 2), a preaching tour which led him beyond the border of Achaia, and near to the confines of Illyricum, perhaps to Apollonia or Dyrrhachium. The intention of making such a tour is possibly expressed in 2 Cor. x. 16. It would be after his return from this trip that he wrote Rom. in Corinth. If his fifteen days in Jerusalem (Gal. i. 18) seemed important enough to be mentioned here, his journey to the borders of Illyricum need have lasted no longer. In short, the charge of historical improbability can be brought against Rom. xv. 19 only by those who regard the much abused Book of Acts as an exhaustive journal even when, as in xx. 1-2, it compresses the record of about ten months into four lines. And whence did the alleged interpolator get the fact ? 2 Tim. iv. 10 gives instead of Illyricum the equivalent name Dalmatia, and makes Titus go thither, not Paul.

20. (Pp. 385, 389.) Semler, *op. cit.* 293, and Eichhorn, *Einl.*[1] iii. 243, had expressed various doubts about Rome as the original destination of Rom. xvi. ; but D. Schulz (*ThStKr.* 1829, S. 609-612) developed the arguments which have given great currency to the view that this chapter or great parts of it are fragments of a letter to the Church at Ephesus. Rom. xvi. 1-20 is

claimed for Ephesus by Reuss, Lipsius, and others, following D. Schulz; xvi. 3–20 by Ewald (*Sendschr. des Pl.* 428), Mangold, and others; and xvi. 1–6, 17–20 by Lucht. The whole "list of names," which, according to Lipsius, 86, should lead to this conclusion, reduces to 3 out of the 31 (*i.e.* if we count the names Aristobulus and Narcissus and the larger groups in xvi. 5, 10, 11, 14, 15 as each a single person), namely, Aquila, Priscilla, and Epænetus. The first two, however, were at home in Pontus, Rome, and Corinth, as well as in Ephesus, see above, also p. 389 f. Concerning 2 Tim. iv. 19, to which those at least who deny the genuineness of 2 Tim. cannot appeal, see §§ 33, 37. To hold that Paul knew personally all those named or indicated in xvi. 3–15 would be a gratuitous assumption. He sends greetings to whole Churches which had never seen him and to individual members of them (Col. iv. 15, cf. ii. 1); and he directs greetings from himself or from his whole neighbourhood to the collective membership of Churches founded by him, without excepting those who had been added since his last stay, or who were personally unknown to the Christians of his neighbourhood (1 Cor. xvi. 19*a*, 20*a*; Phil. iv. 21 f. ; 1 Thess. v. 26). Consequently, also in Rom. xvi. 3–15 we can decide only from more particular statements whom of those greeted Paul knew personally. This can be claimed more or less definitely only for the persons mentioned in xvi. 3–9, 13. Those whom he knew had told him the names of these others whom he greets, and doubtless something about them also. With regard to particular ones, see below, nn. 21–24. Concerning xvi. 17–20, see § 23.

21. (P. 389.) The Antioch reading Ἀχαΐας, xvi. 5, is wholly untrustworthy, being introduced from 1 Cor. xvi. 15, which a thoughtless comparison of Rom. xvi. 3–5 with 1 Cor. xvi. 19 easily suggested. According to Acts xx. 31, cf. xix. 8–10, xx. 18, the time during which Aquila lived in Ephesus without Paul (Acts xviii. 21–xix. 1), lasted about nine months. It would be a curious assumption that he and his wife restricted their evangelistic work to the teaching of Apollos (Acts xviii. 26). It is very possible that Epænetus, like Paul, found employment as a fellow-craftsman in Aquila's trade, or even was bought as a slave by Aquila in Ephesus, and that thus his conversion was brought about. We can comprehend why it was that a congregation gathered immediately in Aquila's house in Rome as it had done in Ephesus (1 Cor. xvi. 19); for they doubtless needed a large shop in which to carry on their trade. The workmen engaged there, probably slaves of Aquila, must have formed the nucleus of the congregation. Probably all the persons mentioned as far as xvi. 10*a* belonged to Aquila's household when he was in Ephesus, and so were known to Paul. All those named as far as xvi. 13 being apparently members of the congregation in Aquila's house (§ 23, n. 1), those mentioned in xvi. 10*b*–13 would constitute the circle outside of the immediate household (xvi. 3–10*a*).

22. (P. 391.) Taken by itself, συγγενής, xvi. 7, 11, 25, may indicate blood relationship (cf. Luke i. 36, 58, ii. 44, xiv. 12 ; John xviii. 26 ; Acts x. 24). But it is exceedingly improbable that Jason of Thessalonica, Sosipater of Berœa, cf. Acts xvii. 5–9, xx. 4, above, p. 209, and a certain Lucius (ver. 21), Macedonians sojourning in the neighbourhood of Paul at Corinth, also Herodion (ver. 11), Andronicus, and Junias (ver. 7), were all relatives of Paul. Besides, the emphasising of the personal relationship would have no weight, the uniform

lack of particularity in describing the various ties of kinship (Col. iv. 10 ; Acts xxiii. 16) would be singular, and the separation of the names of these relatives living in Rome (xvi. 7, 11) would be incomprehensible. The conjecture of Semler (*Paraphr. epist. ad Rom.* 302 ; cf. Laurent, *Ntl. Stud.* 33), that συγγενεῖς means here fellow-countrymen of Paul from Cilicia or from the Synagogue of the Cilicians (Acts vi. 9) has still less to recommend it. It goes back rather, as in ix. 3, to γένος in the sense of nation (Gal. i. 14 ; 2 Cor. xi. 26 ; Phil. iii. 5 ; Acts xiii. 26).

23. (P. 391.) Rom. xvi. 7.   Since Junius, Junia was an exceedingly common nomen in all grades of society (*e.g. C. I. L.* vi. 20850-20919), it would be most natural to find here a woman, Junia.   But since Junianus is also not uncommon (*C. I. G.* 4118 ; *C. I. L.* ii. 1359, iii. 4020, v. 3489 ; Orelli, 4141, following De Vit, *Onom.*—also in a Christian inscription), there is almost nothing in the way of assuming a contracted form ʼΙουνιᾶς from this masculine name.   While the other statements, perhaps, would fit a married couple, the designation συναιχμαλώτους μου would refer more naturally to two men. Since Paul is not at present lying in prison, and, moreover, is not in the same place with these two people, this designation points even more clearly than συνεργούς μου to a community of life belonging to the past.   They must have once shared an imprisonment of Paul.   This Paul calls a captivity, just as in Col. iv. 10 ; Philem. 23, since all Christians are soldiers of Christ (2 Tim. ii. 3 f. ; 1 Tim. i. 18 ; 1 Cor. ix. 7 ; 2 Cor. x. 3), and therefore, whenever they are imprisoned, are prisoners of war.   The frequent figurative use of στρατιώτης and συστρατιώτης (Phil. ii. 25 ; Philem. 2 ; 2 Tim. ii. 3) does not commend but forbids Hofmann's view, iii. 617, iv. 2. 147, that συναιχμάλωτος, like συστρατιώτης, expresses simply the fellowship of the Christian state. Besides, on this view, Paul's language, if it is to be understood at all naturally, would imply that the persons in question were "captured from the world by Christ" at the same time as he, which was true of none of them.   Cf. the writer's article on "Paganus," *NKZ*, x. (1899) S. 38 f., and "Zur Lebensgeschichte des Paulus," *NKZ*, xv. (1904) S. 32 ff.   If Andronicus and Junius were converted before Paul, whose conversion followed hard on the death of Stephen and the first spread of Christianity beyond Jerusalem, they must have belonged to the Jerusalem Church before 35 A.D.   Consequently we are to understand by ἐπίσημοι ἐν τοῖς ἀποστόλοις : "famed, mentioned with honour in the circle of the apostles," and hardly, "eminent apostles."   The latter sense would be, in view of all that the N.T. tells us of the missionaries of that time, extravagant, to say the least.   Οἱ ἀπόστολοι alone means, in Paul's mouth, the original apostles (Gal. i. 19 ; 1 Cor. xv. 7).   Since Paul had not been imprisoned in Jerusalem before he wrote Romans, we may assume that Andronicus and Junias belonged to those fugitives who came from Jerusalem to Antioch (Acts xi. 19), that they were active in the mission there, and that sometime during the years 43-50, when we know practically nothing about Paul, they were cast into prison along with him ; cf. 2 Cor. xi. 23 ; Clem. 1 *Cor.* v. 6.   Paul may have become acquainted with them as early as his first visit to Jerusalem after his conversion (Gal. i. 18 ; Acts ix. 26), and it may have been in remembrance of experiences which he then had shared with these and others of that city now living in Rome that he mentioned Jerusalem instead of Damascus in xv. 19.

24. (Pp. 392, 393). Regarding the names in xvi. 8–15, cf. Lightfoot, *Philippians*, ed. 3, pp. 171–175 ; Riggenbach, 509 ff. (1) *Ampliatus* (ver. 8 ; D and the Antioch recension have the contracted form Ἀμπλιᾶν), a "nomen servile" De Vit, *Onomast.*), occurring also in higher circles perhaps by the third century (*Cod. Justin.* v. 56. 2). A connection with the gens Claudia is attested by *C. I. L.* vi. 14918, 15509, cf. also *Claudia*, 2 Tim. iv. 21 ; Phil. iv. 22, and below, § 33, n. 2. Under *Urbanus*, Lightfoot, p. 174, cites an inscription of the year 115 (Gruter, p. 1070, 1 = *C. I. L.* vi. 44), which, in a list of freedmen employed in the imperial mint, gives *Urbanus, Ampliatus* next to each other, as here, xvi. 8–9. In 1880 a vault was discovered in the Catacomb of Domitilla, over the entrance to which the builder and first owner is indicated by *Ampliati*, and in the interior of which an Aurel. Ampliatus, plainly a descendant of the founder, has put up a monument to his wife ; cf. de Rossi, *Bull. di archeol. crist.* 1880, p. 171 ; 1881, p. 57 (1883, p. 121 ; 1886, p. 59 other Ampliati); Hasenclever, *JbfPTh.* 1887, S. 499. If the archeologists are right in assigning the building of the vault and the inscription outside to the end of the first century, and the inscription inside to perhaps the middle of the second, it is probable that the builder of the tomb was the Ampliatus of Rom. xvi. 8 or a son of his. (2) *Aristobulus* (ver. 10). With regard to this man, mentioned in the text, p. 392, cf. Jos. *Bell.* ii. 11. 6 ; *Ant.* xviii. 5. 4, 8. 4, xx. 1. 2. A mutilated Jewish inscription at Rome (Schürer, *Gemeindeverf. der Juden in Rom.* S. 17, 40, No. 36) probably refers to a Jew, Herodion (ver. 11) rather than to an otherwise unknown Synagogue of the Rhodians. (3) The Christians ἐκ τῶν τοῦ Ναρκίσσου (ver. 11). Concerning the famous Narcissus, cf. Tac. *Ann.* xi. 29–38, xii. 1, xiii. 1 ; Suet. *Claud.* xxviii ; Dio Cass. lx. 34. Inscriptions from Rome : *C. I. L.* vi. 15640 = Muratori 1150. 4 "Claudia Veneria Ti. Claudio Sp. F. Ser. Narcissiano Filio"; Muratori 902. 5 (Narcissus and Narcissianus, freedmen of the Flavian imperial house, both names also from Pannonia, *C. I. L.* iii. 3973) ; Orelli, 4387 ; *C. I. G.* 6441b, Βαλλία Ναρκισσιανή ; *C. I. L.* vi. 22871, *Narcissias.* The name Narcissus is not uncommon outside of Rome also ; but this cannot impair the significance of the fact that from the time of the famed Narcissus there were numerous Narcissiani in Rome, or weaken the inference that it is an entire group of these which is mentioned in Rom. xvi. 11. The *Acts of Peter*, which makes Narcissus a Roman presbyter (above, p. 401, n. 4 at the end), does not draw from local tradition, but thoughtlessly selects two names, Narcissus, who is by no means presupposed as still living in Rom. xvi. 11, and Quartus (ver. 23), who was to be found really in Corinth, and places them in Rome, simply because they are mentioned in Romans (*GK*, ii. 858). (4) *Tryphœna* is naturally not the "queen" of that name in Pisidian Antioch, whom the *Acts of Thecla* connects with Paul (*GK*, ii. 906 f.). Yet the circumstance that this historical personage was related to the emperor Claudius suggests the conjecture that the Tryphœna of Rom. xvi. 12 was a servant in the court of Claudius and then of Nero, especially since Tryphœna as well as the next name here, Tryphosa, occurs among women in service at the Claudian court (*C. I. L.* vi. 15241, 15280, 15622–15626 ; cf. Lightfoot, 174). Two ancient Christian inscriptions should also be mentioned, one from the Cœmeterium of Priscilla (*Bull. arch. crist.* 1886, p. 48, No. 34, Τρυφω [ν or ωσα] . . . Τρυφα[ινη]), the other from the Cœmeterium of

Hermes (*Bull.* 1894, p. 17, ostensibly from the first half of the second century, "Tryphonillam . . . Aurelia Tryphæna parentes"). (5) Regarding *Rufus,* ver. 13, see above, p. 393, and § 53, n. 5. Of itself this very common name would suggest no special relations. It is found also among Roman Jews (Schürer, S. 36, No. 16, 17). (6) *Phlegon,* cf. *C. I. L.* vi. 15202, "Ti. Claudi Phlegontis Ti. Claudi Juliani Lib." Moreover, the writer Phlegon, a freedman of Hadrian's, lived and wrote in Rome. (7) *Patrobas* = Patrobius, cf. Tac. *Hist.* i. 49, ii. 95 ; Suet. *Galba,* xx ; *C. I. L.* vi. 15189, "Ti. Claudio Patrobio," cf. Gruter, 610. 3. (8) Concerning *Hermas* (ver. 14), Origen (iv. 683) made the modest but worthless conjecture that he was identical with the Roman Christian Hermas, who, in the time of Clement, wrote the *Shepherd* ; cf. the writer's *Hirt des Hermas,* 33. (9) *Nereus* and his sister (ver. 15). Νηρεύς and Νηρεΐς, quite common names of slaves and manumitted persons, also of some in the service of the emperor, *C. I. L.* iii. 256, vi. 8598 (Domitia Nereis, wife of a freedman and secretary of the emperor). Lightfoot, 174, cites from *Acc. di Archeol.* xi. 376, a Claudia Aug. L. Nereis, who was closely related to a mother and daughter Tryphæna (*ibid.* xi. 375). Among the earliest Roman martyrs belong Nereus and Achilleus, valets of the Christian lady Domitilla, according to the Greek legends, but prætorians rather, according to the eulogy of bishop Damasus ; cf. Achelis, *Texte u. Unters.* xi. 2. 44. These traditions cannot have sprung from Rom. xvi. 15 ; for in that case the sister of Nereus would not be wanting in the legend, nor would the names associated with Nereus be all different from those in Rom. xvi.

25. (P. 394.) It is sufficient refutation of the involved interpolation hypothesis of Völter to have stated it in the light of its results (above, p. 164). On the presupposition that xvi. 3–20 was addressed to Ephesus, H. Schultz (*JbfDTh.* 1876, S. 104–130) proposed ascribing xii. 1–xv. 7 also to this letter, which he dated in Paul's later life. This supposed " Eph." had been welded upon the older Rom. (i. 1–xi. 36, xv. 7–xvi. 2, 24) by a redactor, slight changes being made at the points of juncture. Connecting with this theory, though denying that any parts of the letter were intended for Ephesus, Spitta (*Z. Gesch. d. Urchrist.* i. 16–30), and again with more detailed proof and many not unessential changes—"Untersuchung über den Röm.," *op. cit.* iii. 1 [1901] has sought to prove that Romans, as handed down to us, and already known to Marcion, was made out of two letters of Paul addressed to the Roman Church. The longer and earlier letter has been preserved essentially unchanged in i. 1–xi. 36, xv. 8–33, xvi. 21–27 ; and the shorter and later letter appears in xii. 1–xv. 7, xvi. 1–20, likewise complete, save for a salutation which had been omitted by the editor. It is supposed that this shorter letter was not written until after Paul's release from his first Roman imprisonment and toward the end of his journey among the Eastern Churches,—a further activity attested by the Pastoral Epistles. This would date the letter probably in the beginning of 64 A.D. The longer letter, however, within the limits of which the shorter has been inserted, is a *mixtum compositum.* Paul himself is supposed to have worked over an earlier circular letter, which had been addressed soon after the apostolic council to the Jewish Christians, or to the mother Church. The original letter, which in i. 16b–xi. 10 is preserved in its essential content and word-

ing, was changed into a letter to the alleged Gentile Christian Church in Rome by prefixing i. 1–16a, by inserting iii. 1–8, vi. 12 f., 15–23, xi. 11–36, and by adding xv. 8–33, xvi. 21–27. There were still other short sentences, which Spitta has culled out with more or less certainty, as additions of the editor or later readers, as *e.g.* xi. 25 (ἵνα μή—φρόνιμοι, cf. xii. 16), xiv. 5–6a, xv. 7 (καθὼς θεοῦ); but these are inconvenient for the interpretation presupposed by him (S. 38 ff., 43, 50). Spitta also in his later and fuller treatise, which, to be sure, is not brief, has not given any adequate reason why an editor should have worked over two letters of Paul to the Romans into a single letter which must have been accomplished before the two original letters were circulated outside of Rome. By this theory the letters gain nothing in edification, and how much they lose in clearness and reasonableness would best be shown by Spitta's argument for his hypothesis if it were tenable. Still worse must be the judgment which we would have to pass upon Paul if he worked over his alleged circular letter to the Jewish Christians of Palestine into a letter to the Gentile Christians of Rome. Instead of sending the Romans a copy of the earlier letter, with a shorter note accompanying it, in which he would explain why he recommended them to read this communication, originally not intended for them, Paul sent them, without one word of explanation or excuse, a writing of motley patchwork, which in its essential content was entirely unsuited to the Roman Christians, whom, however, he is addressing (*e.g.* vii. 1–6). The other doubts concerning this, and the similar hypothesis (mentioned above, pp. 153 f., 415 f.), are indeed not lessened but rather increased by the assertion (S. 6) that not one single letter of the N.T. "is preserved in its original form."

§ 23. CONSTITUENCY AND ORIGIN OF THE ROMAN CHURCH.

In xi. 13, xv. 5–12 it is clearly stated that among the Christians in Rome, to whom, as a body, the letter is addressed, there were Gentiles as well as Jews. On the other hand, if all the Christians in Rome had been Jews, Paul would not have expressly characterised certain individuals to whom he sends greetings as countrymen of his (n. 1). At the same time, it is undeniable that in addressing the readers as a body Paul assumes that, like himself, they had lived under the law prior to their conversion (vii. 1–6, viii. 15, also vi. 16 ; see above, p. 374 f., n. 8). This does not involve contradiction any more than when Paul addresses the Churches at Corinth and Thessalonica and in Galatia uniformly as Gentile Christian Churches, though from the beginning their membership included a number of Jews and more proselytes (*e.g.* 1 Cor. xii. 2; Gal. iv. 8; 1 Thess. i. 9). The correct inference is, rather, that in Rome the Gentile Christians constituted a comparatively small minority, just as did the Jewish Christians in the other Churches mentioned. This is proved by the passage where Paul turns directly to his Gentile readers, for the first time calling attention expressly to his special commission as the apostle to the Gentiles (xi. 13). The way in which this transition is made (above, p. 375 f., n. 9) shows that Paul thought of the Church, which to this point he had addressed without distinguishing the separate elements within it, as a body of native Jewish Christians. This conclusion is confirmed by the way in which from xi. 11 on (notably in xi. 13–32) he speaks of the now unbelieving Israel. This differs altogether from the tone of ix. 1–xi. 10, in which he defends himself against the charge of heartless indifference toward his unbelieving and unfortunate countrymen (ix. 1–5, x. 1 f.). At the same time, by disavowing motives to which his solemn affirmation of sympathy for Israel might be attributed, he protests against a false grief for Israel, such as might imperil faith in the gospel and the preparatory revelation in the O.T., a grief such as only native Jews were liable to feel. The remnant of the saved, predicted by the prophets, the "seven thousand" of the present time (ix. 29, xi. 4), are not to allow themselves to be misled by the obstinacy and misfortune of the majority of their countrymen. On the other hand, from xi. 13 on the Gentile Christians in Rome are warned against an attitude of arrogant contempt toward the unbelieving Israel, and against failing to recognise this nation's importance, which will one day be made manifest. Moreover, the manner in which Paul strives to give expression to his own patriotic feeling, even in the personal notices of chap. xvi., is intelligible only on the supposition that he is speaking to Jewish Christians (above, pp. 391, 417, n. 22). The same is true

with reference to what he says about the mutual exercise
of love and gratitude between Jewish and Gentile Christians
where his influence dominates (xv. 26–32, xvi. 3 f., above,
pp. 368 f., 391 f.).   In the light of what is said in Gal.
iv. 10, Col. ii. 16, if this were a Gentile Christian Church,
Paul could not mention the observation of certain days as
he does in Rom. xiv. 5 f., as if the readers were perfectly
justified in maintaining their customs without renouncing
entirely principles tested by more than ten years of heated
controversy.   If, on the other hand, he is addressing a
Church which is predominantly Jewish, in which the Gentile Christian minority is at least under the same obligation
to submit themselves to the majority as the majority is
under obligation to defer to them (cf. xv. 1–7), what is
here said is only a statement of his view that of itself the
Jewish manner of life is just as consistent with the Christian faith as is that of the Gentiles (1 Cor. vii. 18–20, ix.
20 f. ; Gal. ii. 14, v. 6), something Paul never denied.
Had the Church been so predominantly Gentile that Paul
could have assumed that it felt itself to be one with the
Churches in the East founded by himself, he would have
referred at once to its Gentile origin, and to himself as the
apostle of the Gentiles (cf. Eph. iii. 1).   Instead of this,
however, from i. 1 on we observe he is very careful to base
his right to address the Roman Christians on the broad
foundation of the general apostleship which he shares with
the older apostles.   He also guards carefully against the
implication that his special call to the Gentiles (xi. 13 ;
xv. 15 f.) and his gospel (ii. 16, xvi. 25) prevent him
from being considered a legitimate preacher of the one
gospel of God, promised in the O.T., and first preached by
Jesus (above, p. 353).   Finally, he asks especially that his
message be received by all the Christians in Rome (n. 2).
Even the theme developed in i. 18–v. 11, the implications
of which are followed out in v. 12–viii. 39, was suggested
by his realisation of the difference between his readers'

point of view and his own construction and presentation of the gospel. Only on the theory that the letter was intended for Christians, who on account of their Jewish training still found the complete recognition of this truth difficult, was it necessary to give such a fundamental development of the thought that the gospel is a power of God unto salvation for all men under the sole condition of faith. Nothing but the fact that his readers were Jews could have made it necessary for him to answer the objections that the gospel doctrine of justification was practical antinomianism (iii. 31, compare vi. 1, 15), and broke the close connection between the Christian and the O.T. Church (iv. 1 ff., above, p. 359). Even leaving quite out of consideration the various passages where it is expressly stated that before their conversion the readers were disobedient servants (vi. 16 f.), filled with the spirit of bondage (viii. 15), not becoming free from the bondage of the law until their conversion (vii. 1–6, above, p. 360 f. 374 f.), such teaching regarding the law as is found in chaps. vi., vii. (cf. iii. 20, iv. 15, viii. 3 f., x. 4) was applicable only to native Jews who for some reason, either by their own reflection or by the influence of the slanderous assaults of their unbelieving countrymen (iii. 8), doubted whether such an entire severance of their religious and moral life from the Mosaic law, as taught by Paul, was possible. The exhortations to live at peace with their non-Christian neighbours, and to fulfil conscientiously all obligations to the State (xii. 17–xiii. 7), are fuller and more strenuous than in any other of Paul's letters, which goes to confirm our belief that Paul is here addressing the Christian part of that Jewish population, which some years before had been driven from Rome by the Emperor Claudius on account of their incessant rioting.

Many thoughts regarding law, faith, and justification similar to those in this Epistle are found also in Galatians.

But even a superficial comparison of Romans with this
or any other of Paul's Epistles addressed to Gentile
Christians, in which he antagonises the destructive influence of hostile teachers and of a false gospel, will show
that no part of Romans was occasioned by like conditions
in Rome.   Not only is the teaching under which the
Romans became Christians unconditionally approved (vi.
17, xvi. 17), but also the faith of the Church at the time
is recognised as normal (xv. 14, xvi. 19 ; cf. i. 8, 12,
xv. 24).   This is not contradicted by the occasional
reference which we find to the weakness of the flesh,
i.e. an unripe condition of moral and religious life (vi.
19, cf. 1 Cor. iii. 1 f.), to individual weakness of faith
(xiv. 1), and indirectly to the lack of close harmony
between the Jewish majority and the Gentile minority
in the Church (xv. 1–13).   Throughout the entire doctrinal discussion of the letter there is not the slightest
hint of apostasy, nor of reversion to a Jewish or Gentile
manner of life, nor of any actually threatening danger
that the readers would be deceived into accepting a
false gospel.   Nor can the injunction at the end of the
letter (xvi. 17 f.), that the Church be on its guard against
persons who stir up dissensions and create occasions of
stumbling, who do not, as they pretend, serve Christ,
but their own bellies, and who by their fine speeches,
which have a pious and friendly sound, deceive the
innocent, be taken as indicating any such condition of
things.   That in thus exhorting the Church Paul did not
have in mind persons who were actually working at the
time in Rome with success, is proved by the fact that in
this very connection he says to the readers, emphatically,
that *their* obedience has become known to all men, and
that he rejoices over *them* ; something that he could not
say of all Churches (n. 3).   Therefore the desire which he
hopes to see fulfilled by this warning, namely, that through
their experience they may become constantly wiser in

respect of the good, and remain free from the evil, has reference to the future. Accordingly, the statement that God, who desires peace in His Church, will quickly crush Satan under their feet, is made in view of the possibility that persons may come among them and disturb their peace, as had been done elsewhere (cf. 2 Cor. xi. 3). What led the apostle to insert in this peculiar place such an exhortation, designed to warn the readers against future dangers, is clear from xvi. 16. After greeting the different groups into which the Roman Church was divided without making any distinction among them, he enjoins them all to express their fellowship with one another by a holy kiss. That this fellowship, however, was wider than the bounds of the local Church, is proved by the addition of a greeting from all the Churches of Christ to the Roman Christians. Besides the Christians in Corinth and vicinity, among whom Paul was when he wrote (xvi. 1, 23), he was surrounded at the time by representatives of the Macedonian Churches, probably also of other Churches (xvi. 21, cf. xv. 26, above, p. 209). During the preceding years Paul had had a great deal of trouble in the Asiatic Churches, but especially in Corinth, with persons who disturbed the peace of the Church in one way and another. In both localities the Churches themselves had not rejected such persons with enough decision. How natural, therefore, at this point, where he conveys greetings from these Churches, to warn the Romans against such teachers! But he describes them in such general terms that it is necessary to conclude also from the passage that at the time the false teachers and disturbers of the peace had not as yet appeared in Rome. For if they had, Paul could not have failed to specify their particular character. The Church had not yet become involved in the conflict that was being waged between Paul and the Judaisers. The extremely cautious way in which Paul speaks when endeavouring to secure an understanding between himself

and the Church, proves that while the majority were not
hostile to him and his work, they did, nevertheless, feel
him to be still a stranger, and regarded him not altogether
without mistrust. This is explained, however, by the fact
that the Church was made up largely of Jews, who were
indebted for their Christianity neither to Paul nor to any
of his helpers (n. 4).

The Roman Church did not have a founder in the
same sense as did the Church in Ephesus or Corinth
(n. 5). If so, Paul could not have remained entirely
silent regarding such a person when speaking of the
teaching to which the readers owed their conversion (vi.
17, xvi. 17). The first trace which we have of the presence of Christianity in Rome is the vague statement of
Suetonius regarding the banishment of the Jews from
Rome by the emperor Claudius, which occurred probably in
or shortly before the year 52 (n. 6). Since the Jews were
banished by this decree only from Rome, not from Italy,
many may have remained in the vicinity of the city.
Others, like Aquila, left the country altogether, not, however, before they had at least heard of Christ (above, p.
265, n. 3). Soon after the death of Claudius (Oct. 54)
the Jews returned again to Rome in large numbers, and
under Nero regained their old rights. It may have been
in consequence of these disturbances under Claudius, for
which the Jews were in danger of being deprived also of
their rights of citizenship, that the Christians among the
Jews who came back, and those who now migrated to Rome
for the first time, refused probably from the very outset
to share the worship and the congregational fellowship of
the synagogues. If some such relations as existed for at
least some months between the synagogue and the
preaching of the gospel in Ephesus and Corinth had existed also in Rome, there would certainly be some trace of
it. Moreover, in spite of all the confusion and error about
the distinction between what was Christian and what was

Jewish in the year 64, the *Christiani* in Rome were known to the heathen population as a separate sect (Tac. *Ann.* xv. 44). In Romans the Jewish slanderers are spoken of as outsiders under God's condemnation (iii. 8), distinct from the "called of Jesus Christ" (i. 6). And although the majority of the latter were of Jewish birth, the Gentile minority in the Church did not feel that they were in any sense Jewish proselytes, for they needed to be warned against arrogantly despising the unbelieving Jew (xi. 13–32), and exhorted to accommodate themselves to the Jewish Christians in a self-denying spirit (xv. 1–13).

Among the Jews who during the three years prior to the composition of Romans returned to Rome or migrated thither were Christians from Palestine. Andronicus and Junias, Rufus and his mother, were not the only ones of this kind (above, pp. 392, 420, n. 24, No. 5). Paul nowhere says anything which implies that he is dealing with recent converts. Andronicus and Junias became Christians even before Paul (above, p. 418, n. 23); and in xiii. 11 it seems to be presupposed that the nucleus of the Church became believers at about the same time that Paul did, *i.e.* in the early years of the Church's growth. However this may be, the fact that a considerable number of persons who earlier had been members of the Church in Palestine now belonged to the Church in Rome, explains the warmth of tone of xv. 25–32, which would have sounded strange in a letter to a Church which had had no intimate relations either with the donors or with the receivers of the collection here mentioned. From this point of view it is also very easy to understand why, in writing this letter, Paul should have in mind and take notice of the Epistle of James, which was written some seven to ten years earlier to Christians in Palestine and adjacent regions (above, p. 128 f.). With the vigorous communication that was kept up between the Jews in Rome and in the home-land (n. 7),

it is not at all impossible that the gospel was introduced
in Rome, as it had been brought earlier to Antioch not
with the aid of regular missionaries, but by Christians
from Palestine who settled there, among whom, as among
those who settled in Antioch, there were native Cyrenians
(Acts xi. 20, xiii. 1 ; Rom. xvi. 13 ; Mark xv. 21). Their
Christian faith was proclaimed first to the Jewish population in Rome and gained here its first acceptance, without, however, involving the exclusion of proselytes and
Gentiles from the Church thus formed.   We may assume
that after the complete separation of the Roman Christians
from the synagogue, which at latest must have taken place
at the time of the return of the Jews who had been
expelled from the City, and at the time of the reconstruction of the Christian Church about 54, the non-Jewish
element began to increase in numbers and influence.
Still, up to the time when Romans was written, the
character of the Church had not yet essentially changed.
It stood in closer relation to the Churches in Palestine
than to those in Asia, Macedonia, and Greece.

1. (P. 421.) Of all the persons Paul greets he designates only three as Jews
(xvi. 7, 11) ; but certainly we cannot conclude from this that the rest were
Gentiles.   Other epithets also, like συνεργός (vv. 3, 9), ἀγαπητός (vv. 5, 12),
δόκιμος (ver. 10), and ἐκλεκτός (ver. 13), are not meant to be confined to the
persons so designated.   Of those whose names follow, we either know or infer to be Jews, though the first three are not so designated : Aquila, Priscilla
(ver. 3), Mary (ver. 6, because of her Hebrew name Μαριάμ, so אDGL, or
according to ABCP Μαρίαν), Andronicus and Junias (ver. 7, above, p. 415,
n. 23 f.), Herodion (ver. 11, above, pp. 393, 419, n. 24), Rufus and his mother
(above, p. 392).   There are thus eight in all.   But since, as these very
examples remind us, Jews at that time quite commonly bore Greek and
Latin names, the majority of those greeted may have been Jews.   Along
with six Latin names (Aquila, Prisca, Ampliatus, Urbanus, Rufus, Julia,
xvi. 3, 8, 9, 13, 15) and one Hebrew (ver. 6), we find (including Aristobulus and Narcissus, who are not themselves greeted, and Junias, in consideration of its Greek termination, see above, p. 418, n. 23) nineteen Greek
names.   Suet. Claudius, xv : "Peregrinæ conditionis homines vetuit usurpare
Romana nomina, dumtaxat gentilicia."   Exempt from this rule, as well as
from its appended restriction, were the freedmen, the many Flavii, Claudii,
Julii, who had been slaves of some member of one of these clans, or else were
descended from such, cf. Pauly, RE, v. 675.   Julia (ver. 15) must have belonged

to this class. The Church consisted for the most part of aliens, freedmen, or slaves of Greek and Oriental extraction, and especially of Jews. Twice, xvi. 14, 15, Paul strings together five names without repeating the ἀσπά-σασθε, and associates with each group the other Christians especially connected with them, though without naming individuals. Here, then, are two narrower circles within the Roman Church clearly distinguished, to which the congregation in Aquila's house (ver. 5) should be added as a third ; cf. Hofmann, iii. 615. Like the Jews (n. 6), the Christians also assembled in various places in the capital, cf. *Acta Justini*, c. iii (Otto,[3] ii. 270). Since Paul notices this grouping three times, and since we cannot think of Christians quite isolated from their fellow-believers, the only natural assumption is that the persons mentioned in xvi. 5–13 all belonged to the congregation in Aquila's house. This is probable, on independent grounds, in the case of the one first mentioned, Epænetus (above, pp. 389, 417, n. 21). The two groups in xvi. 14, 15 are indicated merely by bare names ; all those to whom Paul is more closely bound, and whom he greets accordingly, belong to the congregation in the house of that pair who had been associated with him for so many years. Mary, too (ver. 6), must have come into closer touch with Paul previously somewhere in the Orient, if the reading ἡμᾶς instead of ὑμᾶς is right. In reality the former reading is to be commended not only because of the position of Mary's name among those of persons to whom Paul stood in close relationship, but also because εἰς ὑμᾶς or ἐν ὑμῖν would be so self-evident that it would have been left unwritten, as is twice the case in ver. 12. Cf. § 53, n. 5.

2. (P. 423.) The repetitions of πάντες, i. 7, 8, xii. 3, xv. 33, xvi. 24, might perhaps of itself express the simple wish, in view of the wide diffusion and separation of the Christians in the city (see preceding note), that the letter might be made known to them all, cf. 1 Thess. v. 27. It is more natural to think of the distinction between those personally known to Paul and strangers to him. But neither motive explains why πάντες is present in xvi. 15, yet absent in xvi. 14. More probably, considering the tone in which the letter opens, Paul presupposes that the Roman Christians, the great mass of whom were personally unknown to him, might think that, in so far as they were Jews, the apostle to the Gentiles did not concern them. An address to one of these who proudly calls himself a Jew, breaks in suddenly at ii. 17 and leads up to the description of the true Jew, who is spiritually circumcised, *i.e.* who believes in Christ, ii. 29. It is not Paul's way to picture to himself a Jew taken at random from those beyond the reach of his voice, and then to address him thus. He must have assumed rather that most of his readers, being Jews by birth, needed correction upon this point. Cf. the address in the singular, viii. 2, ix. 19, xi. 17 (there the circle is narrowed by xi. 13), xiv. 4, 15 ; 1 Cor. iv. 7, viii. 10. Rom. ii. 1 cannot be compared because of its connection with what precedes.

3. (P. 425.) The forewarning, xvi. 17–20, has its counterpart in those which Paul gave the Galatians before he wrote Gal., and even before the Judaisers came to them, Gal. i. 9, v. 3, above, pp. 165, 179 f. ; Phil. iii. 1 ff. is a like case. The opinion often expressed that xvi. 17–20 could have been addressed only to a Church very long known to Paul, whether at Ephesus or at Rome after Paul's two years' stay there, has the text against it. It is

only because the readers' obedience to the faith has become known everywhere that Paul knows about it, and finds occasion to express his joy over
it (xvi. 19, just like i. 8, cf. Col. i. 9 ; Eph. i. 15). If Paul had had a
knowledge of them at first hand, we should have found some trace of it in
this or the other parts which Spitta (above, p. 420 f.) assigns to a later letter
to the Romans (cf., *per contra*, Phil. i. 27, 30, ii. 12). Besides, Paul does
not speak of obedience to himself or his teaching, but to God and the teaching which they had received from others than himself (xvi. 17, 19, essentially
like vi. 17).

4. (P. 427.) If the view of the composition and state of the Roman Church
set forth above is as firmly grounded on the text of the Epistle as it seems to
the present writer, opposing views need no detailed refutation. The so-
called Ambrosiaster (*circa* 370) developed in his commentary (Ambrosius, *Opp.*,
ed. Bened. ii. Appendix, p. 25 in the Introduction, and upon i. 5, 8, 9,
11–16, xiv. 1, 23, xvi. 17) the following view :—Certain Jews living in
Rome, who had come to believe in Christ, no one knows how, have preached
to the essentially Gentile population of Rome a Christianity altogether
fettered by Jewish legalism, and that, too, with speedy success. The founders
of the Church are just like the Judaisers in Galatia, false apostles, and the
Church gathered by them consists of Gentiles who have allowed themselves
to be brought under the law, but lack the true knowledge of Christ and the
"spiritual gift" (Rom. i. 11), which Paul wishes to impart to them by his
letter and his subsequent visit. Some few Christians, indeed, of a more
enlightened sort, have come to Rome, as may be gathered from chaps. xiv.
and xvi. ; but they have not been able to change the character of the Church
essentially. Paul does not declaim here as in Gal. against the Judaistic
Christianity of the readers ; he even commends their faith ; but the explanation of this is that the Romans, not having yet learned the true gospel,
cannot have fallen away from it, and so deserve a measure at least of praise
for receiving with faith even a Christianity so extremely defective. The
confirmatio, which Paul wishes to bring them (Rom. i. 11), is conversion to
the true gospel. A brief summary of Rom. (*Cod. Amiat.* 240; *Fuld.* 179 ;
Card. Thomassius, *Opp.* i. 391) expresses this view in the words : "Hi
præventi sunt a falsis apostolis et sub nomine d. n. Jesu Christi in legem
et prophetas erant inducti. Hos revocat apostolus ad veram evangelicam
fidem." According to a second view (Jerome *in Gal.* v. 2, Vallarsi, vii. 478 ;
Argument. solius epist. ad Rom. *Amiat.* 235 ; *Fuld.* 171 ; Thom. i. 388, the
second Prolog. ; cf. the late Catholic *Passio Petri et Pauli*, chaps. 5–10, ed.
Lipsius, 122–128, also 188–193), the Church was composed of perhaps equal
parts of Jews and Gentiles, and had been torn by fierce strife between the
two parties. The aim of the Epistle would be, according to this summary :
"His taliter altercantibus apostolus se medium interponens ita partium
dirimit quæstiones, ut neutrum eorum sua justitia salutem meruisse con-
firmet." An echo of this opinion is found in Hug, *Einl.*[3] ii. 398 ; his further
remark, however, that the letter was addressed primarily to the Jewish Christians (399), does not convey a clear idea. When Jerome in the preface of his
commentary on Galatians (Vall. vii. 371) compared Gal. with Rom., and
pointed out as a characteristic of Gal. that the readers had not come out of
Judaism into the faith, he evidently followed an old authority, which had

more definitely recognized the Jewish Christian character of the Roman Church. Until Baur's time, the commentators on Romans, whose number grew in the sixteenth century especially, considered its historical presuppositions hardly worth a thorough investigation; and if in any way they hinted at an opinion about the first readers of the Epistle, they started for the most part with the assumption that the apostle to the Gentiles was dealing with Gentiles in this letter likewise. But Baur (*TZfTh.* 1836, No. 3, S. 54; *ThJb.* xvi. 60, 184; Paulus,[2] i. 343) claimed that Rom., too, should be regarded as a letter occasioned "by special relations and needs" and arising under the "imperative stress of circumstances" (Paulus, i. 349; cf. 346), and starting from chaps. ix.–xi. as the kernel of the whole, he arrived at this conclusion: "So fundamentally and radically has the apostle aimed to refute Jewish particularism, that it lies wholly uprooted before the consciousness of his time" (380). It is therefore after all not a letter of the missionary who has regard to the "special relations and needs" of the Church addressed, but the systematic exposition of a writer who appeals to the consciousness of his time. Chaps. xv., xvi., which are peculiarly instructive as to "the special relations" under which the letter arose, are explained to be not genuine (393), and the opening greeting and the introduction, i. 8–16, where he constantly confounds the aims of the letter with those of the approaching visit to Rome, are dismissed with a few remarks, the exegetical worth of which is on a level with Ambrosiaster's endeavours; cf. *e.g.* Baur, 396, 399 on Rom. i. 11 with Ambrosiaster, p. 29. Baur expressly appeals to Ambrosiaster as an ancient authority "for the Judaistic character of the Roman Church" (391). Baur concluded from the teaching of the Epistle that the Church was of this character, and inferred further on the same grounds that it consisted predominantly of those who were Jews by birth (369–372). Even after Mangold (*Der Rm. und die Anfänge der röm. Gemeinde,* 1866, second enlarged ed. 1884) sought to prove by more careful exegetical and historical argument the overwhelming Jewish character of the Church, prominent exegetes have thought that they could still maintain that the Roman Church was for Paul "a Gentile Church like those of Thessalonica and Corinth, however many Jews might have belonged to it" (Hofmann, iii. 623). It is not to be wondered at, therefore, that those who are not exegetes, like Weizsäcker (408–424), should have returned to this view, perhaps still combined with the hypothesis that Judaistic teachers were already busy trying to win the Church to their doctrine, and to cut off Paul's approach by hatefully assailing his teaching (425). The leading proof of this, which Weizsäcker finds in iii. 8 (427), falls to the ground for the simple reason that Paul never indicates his single self by the plural (above, p. 209 f., n. 3, 316, n. 3). Cases like προῃτιασάμεθα, iii. 9, and λογιζόμεθα, iii. 28, are not comparable; for in these he classes himself with the readers whose assent to his previous discussion he presupposes. But since the connection of ideas in iii. 8 indicates a circle certainly no narrower, the "we" can be nothing less than the Christians whose theory and conduct are so slandered by the non-Christians,—plainly not by Gentiles, but by Jews (as in προεχόμεθα, iii. 9; cf. iv. 1, 16, 24, v. 1–11, viii. 4–39).

5. (P. 427.) Regarding the alleged labours of Peter in Rome before the time of Rom., see below, § 39. The Roman Jews and proselytes also, who

became believers at Pentecost (Acts ii. 10 f., 36–42), could not soon thereafter have become the first preachers of the gospel in Rome ; for they were not festival pilgrims, but persons who had settled in Jerusalem and belonged to the nucleus of the mother Church (see above, p. 61). We may more likely sift out as the kernel of fact in the romancing narrative in Clem. *Recogn.* i. 6–11, that Barnabas in very early times, perhaps shortly after his separation from Paul, had come as a preacher to Rome, where later we meet Mark his nephew, who had been his companion at that time (Col. iv. 10). To be sure, in the other recension of the same romance, Clem. *Hom.* i. 6–14, the first preacher in Rome is nameless, and Barnabas meets Clement for the first time in Alexandria. It is a question, though, whether the rather widespread tradition of Barnabas' sojourn in Rome, to which was added later the story of his preaching in Milan and other places in northern Italy, springs from the pseudo-Clementine fiction (so Lipsius, *Apokr. Apostelgesch.* ii. 2. 273), or whether the author of the *Recognitions* did not use an older tradition. The Cypriote monk Alexander, probably in the sixth century, who makes Barnabas go to Rome and then to Alexandria in the interval between Acts xi. 22 and xi. 25 (*Encomium in Barn.* chap. xx. ; *Acta SS. Jun.* ii. 442), names as his general sources Clement of Alexandria and other old writings, chap. viii. p. 438), and for particulars appeals to traditions of the ancients (chap. xiii. p. 440, γέροντες, πατέρες) ; nowhere does he appear to be dependent upon the Clement romance. Cf. *Acta Petri*, chap. iv. ; *Acta Apost. Apocr.*, ed. Lipsius, i. 49. 9.

6. (P. 427.) Suet. *Claudius*, 25 : "Judæos impulsore Chresto assidue tumultuantes Roma expulit." For the chronology see Part XI. vol. iii. Since Suetonius (*Nero*, xvi.) possessed a definite knowledge of the sect. of *Christiani* which was probably not less than that of Tacitus (*Ann.* xv. 44), it seems impossible that he should have understood by *Chrestus* the Founder of Christianity ; for in that case we must ascribe to him what is incredible enough, a belief that Christ was present in Rome in person. On the other hand, Χρηστός and Χριστός then sounded alike as pronounced by many, and confusion between them and plays upon them were not lacking (Just. *Ap.* i. 4 ; Theoph. *ad Aut.* i. 1 ; Tert. *Apol.* iii ; Lact. *Inst.* iv. 7. 5) ; nor is it easy to see why a single disturber of the peace should be allowed to keep up his disturbance ; so that we may regard it as perhaps settled that tidings of Christ's appearance in Palestine aroused fierce and long-continued quarrels among the Roman Jews, chaps. l–lii. Suetonius did not understand the report that came to his ears. It is questionable whether the scholiast on Juven. *Sat.* iv. 115 (ed. Cramer, 145), refers to this expulsion of the Jews from the city : "Inter Judæos, qui ad Ariciam transierant, ex urbe missi." According to Cicero, *pro Flacco*, xxviii, there must have been a considerable number of Jews in Italy even before his consulate (63 B.C.). At the time of this oration (59 B.C.) the Jews in Rome possessing citizenship were already a power in the popular assemblies. At all events, Philo, *Leg. ad Cai.* xxiii, speaks inexactly when he represents it as if the whole body of Jews in Rome consisted of prisoners of war who had been emancipated by the masters who had bought them, and thus had attained to citizenship. There is no stress to be laid upon the circumstance that Philo does not mention Pompey here (so A. Berliner, *Gesch. der Juden in Rom.* i. 6, n. 1) ; for of what other Jewish captives could Philo have thought than those whom

Pompey, after his conquest of Jerusalem (63 B.C.), brought with him to Rome on the occasion of his triumphal procession (61 B.C.). His statement, inexact in any case, must be reduced to this, that the body of Jews in Rome received an important addition (61 B.C.) in the shape of captives. Under Augustus they dwelt for the most part on the right bank of the Tiber (Philo, *loc. cit.*). Later, we find them settled in other parts of the city also, with various synagogues, and with cemeteries outside the gates, cf. Schürer, iii. 35, 44 (Eng. trans. II. ii. 240, 247); Berliner, i. 105. Since of the synagogues in Rome, the existence of which has been established thus far by inscriptions, one was called the synagogue of the Hebrews (above, pp. 47 f., 67, n. 14), we may assume that those who belonged to the others became Hellenised early. In 4 A.D. more than 8000 Jews in Rome attached themselves to a deputation from Jerusalem (Jos. *Ant.* xvii. 11. 1 ; *Bell.* ii. 6. 1); so that, reckoning all these as men, the Jewish population of Rome at that time amounted certainly to more than 30,000. A still larger figure can be inferred from the fact that Tiberius was able to draft 4000 men for military service from among the Jews in Rome (Jos. *Ant.* xviii. 3. 5 ; Tac. *Ann.* ii. 85; Suet. *Tiberius*, xxxvi ; cf. Philo, *Leg. ad Caium*, xxiv; Euseb. *Chron. ann. Abr.* 2050). There is something strange in the assertion of Porphyry, or of the heathen who cite him, about the *lex Judæorum* (occurring in August. *Epist.* cii. 8, ed. Goldbacher, p. 552. 2): "Postea vero prorepsit etiam in fines Italos, sed post Cæsarem Gaium aut certe ipso imperante." In spite of the express differentiation of the Christian and the Jewish religion, is there confusion here as to the time when each found entrance into Italy ?

7. (P. 428.) Cicero, *pro Flacco*, xxviii ; Philo, *Leg.* xxiii, p. 568; Jos. *Vita*, 3 ; Acts xxviii. 21 ; Berliner, i. 30 ff.).

§ 24. THE OCCASION OF THE LETTER.

Paul was on the eve of the collection journey which he made in the spring of the year 58 from Corinth, by way of Macedonia to Jerusalem (xv. 25 ; cf. Acts xx. 3–6). The elaborate plan of the letter and its quiet tone presuppose that at the time when Paul wrote he was enjoying comparative rest both of body and of mind. The excitement which, in spite of all his preparations, he had not been able to allay before his arrival in Corinth sometime in December of 57 (above, p. 338 ff.), must have been already overcome. We may assume that the letter was written in Corinth, but not until toward the close of the three winter months that he spent in Greece, mostly at Corinth, *i.e.* not before the beginning of March 58. This season of the year, when navigation was beginning to open up, and this place—Corinth—are suggested by the commendation of Phoebe, a deaconess in the Church at Cenchrea, the port of Corinth, who was about to start on a journey to Rome (xvi. 1). The hospitable Gaius, with whom Paul was lodging when he wrote Rom. (xvi. 23), we look for and find in Corinth (1 Cor. i. 14).

After the re-establishing of harmony in the Corinthian Church and the completing of the collection, Paul was in a position where, feeling that his work in the East was done, he could turn his thoughts to future undertakings, particularly to the preaching journey in the West which he had planned a number of years before (above, pp. 367 f., 377, n. 11). That this Epistle was written in connection with this plan would be manifest from the very fact that the bulk of its contents is placed between discussions of these plans (i. 8–16, xv. 15–32). But besides this proof, we have the fact that in the one passage where the composition of the letter is referred to expressly, Paul says in so many words that he wrote it because of his calling as the apostle to the Gentiles and in the interest of the same (n. 1). It is not directly the function of an apostle to the Gentiles, especially as this function is described in xv. 16–21, to write letters at all, to say nothing of letters to Churches predominantly Jewish. As a missionary in general, and in particular a missionary to the Gentiles, even if he comes to Rome, he cannot carry on his specially commissioned work in the Roman Church which is already organised. In fact, it never occurred to him to express any such intentions (above, p. 355 f.). Nevertheless, the reason for the composition of this letter was Paul's calling, which made him a debtor to all unconverted Gentiles. To him, as a missionary planning now to leave the East in order to engage in work in the West, the existence of a Church in Rome which had been organised without his help was a matter of the utmost significance (i. 9). For, in the first place, his honour as an apostle commissioned to all peoples forbade him passing by the capital of the empire without exercising his office there, at least to some extent. Not only might such action make it appear as if he had no real confidence in the cause that he represented (i. 14–16); it would lower his own sense of the scope of his calling. In the second place, the geographical situation of the Roman Church made it the natural starting-point and centre of support for all further missionary work around the western end of the Mediterranean. Rome was destined to be the metropolis of the coming Church of the West (n. 2). The person who, like Paul, intended to do missionary work in Rome itself, even though only for a time, and who purposed to accomplish the organisation of Churches in Spain, Gaul, or Africa (i. 13–15, xv. 24, 28), had necessarily to be in entire harmony with the Roman Church. The material aid obviously suggested in xv. 24 (n. 3) was of small consequence compared with the moral support of the Roman Church, which was indispensable to the apostle of the West. Accompanied by their intelligent interest and upborne by their prayers, he desires now to go to Jerusalem (xv. 30) and later to Rome, and from Rome to Spain.

Had the Roman Church been organised by Paul or by one of his helpers, and had it not subsequently become estranged from him, a brief notice of his forthcoming visit would have sufficed, particularly since Aquila and Priscilla had gone to Rome some time before (above, p. 389 f.). But, in view of the origin and character of the Roman Church, of which Paul had learned through the reports of his friends there, it seemed to him necessary to make himself perfectly understood by stating comprehensively his view of the gospel, thereby allaying the prejudices felt by most native Jewish Christians toward him and his missionary work, and guarding against future troubles. The predominantly Jewish character of the Church, its close connection with the Church in Palestine, and its location at the centre of the world's travel, made it just as easy for it to become a centre of the Judaistic propaganda, by which the apostle had been everywhere followed, as it was for it to become the centre of support for missionary work in the West, as Paul intended it should.

To what extent the apostle by his letter succeeded in warding off this danger and in accomplishing his own purpose, we learn in part from later letters of his. In more than one respect the future turned out differently from what Paul desired, hoped, and expected at the time when he wrote Romans. He was, to be sure, delivered from the hands of "unbelievers in Judea" (xv. 31 ; Acts xxi. 32). He also came to Rome, and with joy (xv. 32 ; Acts xxviii. 15), and possibly went even to Spain. But his rescue at Pentecost 58 by the Roman guard from the fanaticism of the Jews in the temple was the beginning of a five years' imprisonment. The appeal to Cæsar, which he made before the procurator Festus in the summer of 60 at Cæsarea, occasioned his transfer to Rome. Here he arrived in the spring of 61, remaining, according to Acts xxviii. 30, for two whole years, or until early summer of 63, before there was any change in his condition. Letters, in which Paul speaks of himself as a prisoner, must be considered from this point of view, whether he had written them in Cæsarea or Rome, or in an entirely different period of imprisonment.

1. (P. 435.) Hofmann, iii. 623, appealing to i. 5, xv. 15 f., remarks that Paul wrote this letter "in his capacity as Apostle to the Gentile world." But i. 5 offers no grounds for this (above, p. 370, n. 2), and the very essential distinction between διὰ τὴν χάριν, xv. 15, and διὰ τῆς χάριτος, Rom. xii. 3, or κατὰ τὴν χάριν, 1 Cor. iii. 10, Eph. iii. 7, is blurred by his ambiguous expression here, and is even quite disowned in his rendering, 613, "by virtue of which calling." No more correct is Lightfoot's translation, *Bibl. Ess.* 297, "by the grace." As so often elsewhere, διά, c. acc., denotes that in consideration of which, and with a view to which something is done, whether this end be a thing (1 Cor.

ix. 23 ; Matt. xv. 3) or a person (Rom. iv. 24 ; 1 Cor. iv. 6 ; Mark ii. 27 ; Matt. xxiv. 22). Only in the sense in which the phrase could be used of the present journey to Jerusalem with the collection (xv. 25–32), or of his earlier journey to the council of apostles (Gal. ii. 5, ἵνα κτλ.), can it be said of Rom. that Paul wrote it in his capacity as Apostle to the Gentiles.

2. (P. 436.) Th. Schott (*Der Römerbrief nach Endzweck und Gedankengang*, 1858) opposed not only the unhistorical treatment of the Epistle by most of the commentators, but also that of Baur, which is historical only in appearance, and sought energetically to explain the peculiarity of the letter as due to the state of Paul's missionary labour at the time of its composition. Not to speak of the superficial or quite mistaken explanations of individual passages bearing strongly upon the question of the composition of the Church (i. 5 f. S. 50, vi. 16 f. S. 263, vii. 1–6 S. 266–271, xv. 1–13 S. 313, nothing at all about πάλιν, viii. 15, or ὑμῖν δὲ τοῖς ἔθνεσιν, xi. 13), the success could not be great, since Schott (60, 99, 101–117), without support in the letter or the other known historical circumstances, maintained that there was an essential difference between the mission in the East and that in the West, only the latter being a purely Gentile mission.

3. (P. 436.) Regarding προπεμφθῆναι, xv. 24, cf. 1 Cor. xvi. 6, 11 ; 2 Cor. i. 16 ; but especially Tit. iii. 13 f. ; 3 John 6. As to the act itself, cf. also Ign. *Smyrn.* x. How essential it was for Paul as he pressed forward in his missionary work to leave the Churches behind him in good condition, is shown by 2 Cor. x. 15.

VI.

THE LETTERS OF THE FIRST ROMAN IMPRISONMENT.

§ 25. TIME AND PLACE OF THE COMPOSITION OF THE EPISTLES TO PHILEMON, THE COLOSSIANS, AND "THE EPHESIANS."

IF these letters were written by Paul, they were all despatched by him at the same time. Practically identical reference is made in both Eph. vi. 21, 22 and Col. iv. 7, 8 to the oral reports concerning Paul's condition which Tychicus was to deliver to the readers of both letters. In other words, the sending of Tychicus to the place where the readers were was contemporaneous with the sending of both letters. Tychicus was their bearer. In Colossæ additional reports concerning the condition of affairs where Paul was were to be made by Onesimus, whom Paul sent with Tychicus on the journey. This is all that is said in Col. iv. 9 ; it is not said that Tychicus and Onesimus would arrive in Colossæ at the same time. From the fact that Onesimus is not mentioned in Eph. vi. 21 f., it may be inferred that he was not to stop in the place, or places, to which Ephesians was directed, or that he was not to go there at all. The slave Onesimus, who had run away from his master, had fled to the place where Paul was in prison, and had been converted to the Christian faith by him. Paul sends him back to his master Philemon bearing a letter pertaining exclusively to this personal matter (Philem. 10–17). There is

no indication that Onesimus had any other commission.
The only reason why he had occasion to supplement the
oral reports of Tychicus, or to inform the Christians in
Colossæ of Paul's condition before Tychicus' arrival, was
the fact that Colossæ, whither the latter was bound with
a letter to the local Church, was Onesimus' home, and
thus the place where Philemon lived (n. 1).

So far as notices are given relative to Paul's condition
and surroundings, they are the same in all three letters.
The following persons were with him :—(1) Timothy (Col.
i. 1 ; Philem. 1), who accompanied him on his journey to
Jerusalem (Acts xx. 4), and who at the time of Philippians,
which was certainly written in Rome, was there (i. 1, ii.
19). (2) Luke (Col. iv. 14 ; Philem. 24), who, presupposing that Luke is the author of the account in Acts
xx. 5–xxi. 17, xxvii. 1–xxviii. 16, accompanied him from
Philippi to Jerusalem, and later from Cæsarea to Rome.
(3) According to Acts xx. 4, xxvii. 2, with Paul was also
Aristarchus of Thessalonica (Col. iv. 10 ; Philem. 24),
who appears to have been an earlier helper and companion
of his, and who on the occasion of the insurrection of the
silversmiths in Ephesus was deprived of his freedom, at
least temporarily (Acts xix. 29). The designation which
Paul uses in speaking of him, συναιχμάλωτος (Col. iv. 10),
may have reference to these earlier experiences (above,
p. 418, n. 23). Since Paul was never actually a prisoner
of war, this expression, like συστρατιώτης (Phil. ii. 25 ;
Philem. 2), must certainly be at least partially figurative,
and its use may be explained by supposing that at the time
when Colossians was written Aristarchus was voluntarily
sharing the dwelling in which Paul was a prisoner ; so
that, since Paul was under military surveillance, his condition, like the apostle's, might be compared to that of an
αἰχμάλωτος. The same would apply (4) to Epaphras
(Philem. 23). A Colossian by birth (Col. iv. 12), he
had laid the foundations of the local Churches (Col.

i. 6–8, iv. 12 f.) in his native city, and apparently also in the neighbouring cities of Laodicea and Hierapolis, in the valley of the Lycus (n. 2). In so doing Epaphras had taken occasion to inspire these Churches with a sense of reverence for Paul, and the main purpose of his journey to Paul in prison seems to have been to arouse the apostle's active interest in the spiritual development of these Churches (Col. i. 8 f., iv. 12 f.). It appears that originally Epaphras had undertaken to preach the gospel in his native city either by Paul's commission, or at least at his suggestion (n. 3), and it is probable that both Epaphras and his fellow-townsman Philemon became personally acquainted with Paul and Timothy during Paul's three years' residence in the province of Asia, and were converted by Paul in Ephesus. When Colossians was written, Epaphras does not appear to have contemplated an immediate return to his home. Instead of Epaphras, Paul seems to have sent back to Asia, and among other places to Colossæ (Eph. vi. 21 ; Col. iv. 7), (5) Tychicus, a native of the same province, who had accompanied Paul on his journey from Macedonia to Jerusalem (Acts xx. 4), who seems also to have acted as Paul's messenger to Ephesus on a later occasion (2 Tim. iv. 12). (6) Demas, whose greeting is sent along with that of Luke, without either praise or blame (Col. iv. 14 ; Philem. 24), was perhaps a Thessalonian (2 Tim. iv. 10 ; above, p. 213, n. 6). Greetings are also sent from (7) Mark (Col. iv. 10 ; Philem. 24) and (8) Jesus Justus (Col. iv. 11). From these greetings it is not to be inferred that those who sent them were personally known to the readers (cf. Rom. xvi. 16b, 21–23). A local Church in which Paul had a deep interest (Col. i. 8), and a household in this Church with which Paul stood in intimate relations, were also of interest to the helpers who were living more or less constantly in his companionship. To this circle Jesus Justus, who is not mentioned in Philem. 24, does not seem to

have belonged ; nor would Mark, who has not appeared
in company with Paul since the separation between him
and Barnabas (in the year 52), be mentioned in Col.
iv. 10 and Philem. 24, were it not that he planned
to go shortly to Colossæ.   News of his coming and
instructions as to his reception had reached the Colossian
Church earlier, though from whom and through whom we
do not know.   Now again, in case of his coming, Mark is
commended to the kindly reception of the Church.   For
this reason Mark, who is mentioned prominently in Col.
iv. 10 and in Philem. 24, is spoken of, on the one hand,
as the cousin of Barnabas, who was widely known, and, on
the other hand, as being at that time friendly toward Paul
and his preaching work, the purpose in both cases manifestly being to commend him to the readers (n. 4).   In
this regard Mark and Jesus Justus (and that is why he is
mentioned here) were different from the other missionaries
of the circumcision who were about Paul.   From the fact
that he praises Mark and Jesus Justus because they and
they alone of the circumcision were fellow-workers with
him on behalf of the kingdom of God, and as such were a
source of comfort to him, it is to be inferred that there
were a number of native Jewish missionaries at work
where Paul was, and that their method of work was not
a source of gratification to him.

Paul is in prison on account of the fulfiment of his
office as apostle to the Gentiles (Eph. iii. 1, 13, iv. 1,
vi. 20 ; Col. i. 24, iv. 3 ; Philem. 1, 9, 10, 13, 23).   He
feels that in suffering thus he may expect the sympathy
and the prayers of his readers (Col. iv. 18 ; Philem. 22).
Once at least he expresses the hope that through the
prayers of his friends in Colossæ he may be set at liberty
and be able to visit Colossæ at no distant day (Philem.
22, cf. Phil. i. 19).   The prayer, however, which he most
earnestly requests is not that he may be released, but that
he may be able to preach the gospel where he is with

fitting cheerfulness and with good results (Eph. vi. 19 f. ; Col. iv. 3 f. ; cf. also Philem. 10). No external hindrances seem to stand in the way of this preaching, and Paul speaks as if he intended to carry it on for a long time to come.

The question whether these letters were written in Cæsarea (Pentecost 58 to late summer 60) or in Rome (spring 61 to 63) can be decided only by a comparison of the situation at the time when they were written— which has just been described—with the meagre accounts which we have of these two periods of Paul's captivity (n. 5). At Cæsarea Paul was kept in chains in Herod's pretorium under military guard ; he was not harshly treated ; his friends were allowed to visit him, and to provide him with whatever he wanted (Acts xxiii. 35, xxiv. 23, 27, xxvi. 29, 31). Of preaching activity, how- ever, during this imprisonment there is no hint in Acts. It is also very unlikely that Paul would have felt at liberty to preach in a city of Palestine, especially if the division of their respective fields of labour, agreed upon by Paul and the older apostles a little more than six years before he was arrested, was primarily a geographical division (above, p. 265 f.). The contemporaneous missionary work of Paul and his helpers, Timothy, Luke, Aristarchus, Epaphras, Demas, possibly also Tychicus, and of numer- ous missionaries of Jewish birth, who, with the exception of Jesus Justus and Mark, were hostile to Paul, presup- poses a large city, which Cæsarea was not (n. 6). In Cæsarea dwelt the evangelist Philip, with whom Paul and his companions had lodged shortly before his arrest (Acts xxi. 8–14). How could Paul have forgotten this worthy preacher, or how could he silently imply that he was a missionary hostile to himself? Yet this is what he does if Col. iv. 11 was written in Cæsarea.

We learn more concerning this evangelistic work carried on parallel with Paul's ministry and in opposition

to himself—a work referred to in Col. iv. 11—in Philippians
(i. 14–18), which was written in Rome. The origin and
composition of the Roman Church (above, p. 421 ff.) offered
an especially inviting field to the missionaries of the circumcision. In Rome, Paul was not in prison, but lived
in his own hired dwelling. He was under military guard,
and carried a chain, but was otherwise so little restricted
that for two whole years he received numerous visitors as
he chose, and was able to carry on an important missionary
work (n. 7). Moreover, what could have induced a runaway Colossian slave to go to Cæsarea is not apparent.
Since Onesimus was not a Christian at the time, and since,
according to Philem. 11, 18, he had committed serious
offences against his master, he is not likely to have gone
for protection to Paul, a friend of his master's. To
Rome, however, streamed just such characters from all
the provinces. What brought Onesimus into contact
with Paul in Rome we do not know (n. 8). Nor are we
able from positive reports which we have from other
sources to explain on what Paul based the hope, which is
quite definitely expressed, of being set at liberty again
(Philem. 22). The longer, however, the situation
described in Acts xxviii. 30 f. continued without the
institution of a trial, the more probable it became that
eventually he would be set at liberty for lack of evidence
against him (Acts xxv. 25–27, xxvi. 31). In Cæsarea, on
the other hand, this was not to be thought of so long as
Felix was in power, since Paul could not permit himself
to offer the procurator a bribe (Acts xxiv. 16). Under
Festus the use of this means was out of the question, and
the appeal to Cæsar cut off all prospect of an early release.
But even in case of acquittal by Festus, for which possibly
he might have hoped before he made his appeal, he could
not very well have planned to make a journey to Phrygia.
For a number of years he had been anxious to go to Rome
(above, pp. 367 f., 434 f.). According to Acts xxiii. 11,

a revelation by night had confirmed anew his conviction that in spite of his arrest Rome was to be his next objective point. It was under the influence of this idea that he made his appeal to Cæsar, and the appeal proves that two years' imprisonment had not quenched the desire to go to Rome (Acts xxv. 11, 25, xxvii. 24). If, then, he had been set at liberty in Cæsarea, he would have had no motive to go to Colossæ instead of to Rome as he had planned.

To be sure, by his preaching in Rome the goal of his desire was not fully attained. But it was in part and to a degree that surpassed all expectation. Instead of doing missionary work for a few weeks on his way to Spain, he was able to preach for two entire years in the capital with zeal and good results. Judged by the standard of work during his earlier years, when these two years in Rome drew toward their close, he had completed another important period of his life history. Almost five years had passed since he had taken leave of the Church in Asia for a long period, if not for ever (Acts xx. 25). It is not, therefore, strange that Paul felt it necessary before extending his missionary work in the West to visit again his Churches in the East, also to become acquainted with the Eastern Churches that had been organised without his help (Col. ii. 1). Whether this intention was carried out this is not the place to inquire. But there is not much doubt that these three letters were written in Rome during the two years mentioned in Acts xxviii. 30. As to their more exact dating, all that can be said is that they could not have been written at the very beginning of the period. News must have reached the East that Paul was able to carry on his work in Rome before helpers journeyed from this region to Rome to support him. Nothing is said which would indicate that any one of these helpers had just come to Rome; and although we do not know all that Tychicus was instructed to report orally, we may infer from the manner in which Paul

speaks of his imprisonment, his preaching activity, and his
fellow-workers, that the readers had been for some time
acquainted in a general way with the situation in which
he was placed. Consequently, it is more probable that
the letters were written in the second than in the first of
the two years (n. 9).

1. (P. 440.) Since it was not until after his flight that Onesimus was converted through Paul (Philem. 10), and thus was not a member of the Church
at Colossæ, Col. iv. 9 must simply mean that Colossæ was his ordinary home,
past as well as future (above, p. 371, n. 3). It would have been altogether
too meaningless for Paul to refer in this fashion to the mere circumstance of
his possible birth in Colossæ had he come later into possession of a master
resident elsewhere. We must seek Philemon's house in Colossæ then, where
even in the fifth century men believed that they could still point it out
(Theodoret in the introduct. to Philem., ed. Noesselt, p. 711). The identity
of the destination of Col. and of the letter to the congregation in Philemon's
house follows from the mention of Archippus in both letters. According to
Philem. 2, he must have belonged to Philemon's household ; and if, as was
shown, Philemon's house, from which Onesimus ran away, stood in Colossæ,
that city was the home of Archippus also. It was a bold assertion of Theodore
of Mops. (ed. Swete, i. 311), that we can infer from the wording of Col. iv. 17
that Archippus dwelt in Laodicea and performed some service in the Church
there. Theodore in his exposition of Philem. does not mention the dwelling-
place of that household at all, so that he probably held it to be Laodicea, in
accordance with his remark upon Col. iv. 17 ; and Lightfoot (*Colossians*, ed.
2, pp. 244, 309), though he recognised that Philemon and Onesimus belonged
to Colossæ, felt compelled to agree with this view of Col. iv. 17. Archippus
would then be at the same time a member of the Church in Philemon's house
in Colossæ, and a servant of the neighbouring Church in Laodicea ! In reality,
after greetings are sent to the Christians in Laodicea, Col. iv. 15, and a commission is entrusted to the Colossians with reference to that neighbouring city,
iv. 16*a*, we are brought back again to Colossæ by the direction that the letter
from Laodicea be read also in Colossæ. It is there alone that we must seek
Archippus, for whom there is, in close connection with what precedes (iv. 17,
καί), a reminder to be given by the Church to which he belongs. Theodoret
was quite right in rejecting Theodore's view of Col. iv. 17. Moreover, the
more particular statement that Archippus was the first bishop of Laodicea
(*Const. Ap.* vii. 46) is worth as little as the other statements we find
there, *e.g.* that Philemon was bishop of Colossæ, and Onesimus of Berœa.
An Archippus from Hierapolis in the legend of the miracle at Chonæ
(Colossæ) can hardly have anything to do with our Archippus, as Batiffol,
Stud. patr. i. 33, conjectures ; for even according to the narrator himself this
Archippus was only ten years old ninety years after the building of a Michael
Chapel, which itself was built many years after the death of the apostles John
and Philip (*Narratio de miraculo Chonis patrato*, ed. Bonnet, 1890, pp. 3. 8,
5. 6). Nor can we infer that Philemon dwelt elsewhere than in Colossæ from

the fact that Paul had long been intimately acquainted with him and his
family (§ 26), while the rest of the Colossian Church were still unknown to
him (Col. ii. 1 ; see below, n. 3).   In that case we should have to put Philemon's home in an altogether different region ; for Paul had not yet been in
Laodicea or Hierapolis either.   Rather was the case the same with these
Churches as with the Church at Rome (above, p. 416, n. 20).   Paul does
not regard acquaintance with some of the present members of a Church as
acquaintance with the Church as a whole.   Philemon, apparently a well-to-
do householder at Colossæ (§ 26), can very easily have become acquainted with
Paul and have been converted through his labours during the apostle's residence
of almost three years in Ephesus, or if not then in some other part of the
province.   Whether or not the same is true of Apphia and Archippus we cannot tell.   From the position of these two names between that of Philemon
and the Church in his house (Philem. 2; cf., *per contra*, Rom. xvi. 5, above, p. 417,
n. 21) so much only is certain : that they were members of his family, Apphia
his wife probably, and Archippus his son.   Philemon is called the συνεργός
of Paul and Timothy, but Archippus their συστρατιώτης.   The latter expression seems to indicate an activity requiring more pains and self-denial—one
more like that of Paul and his tried helper, cf. Phil. ii. 25 ; 2 Tim. ii. 3 ;
1 Cor. ix. 7 ; 1 Tim. i. 18.   We cannot gather with certainty from the connection in Col. iv. 17 that it belonged to Archippus' office to read letters and
other writings in the meetings at Colossæ (cf. 1 Tim. iv. 13 ?), or to serve as
intermediary in the intercourse with other Churches (Herm. *Vis.* ii. 4. 3).
But that it was a service which affected the whole local Church, is plain from
the fact that the reminder about this is contained not in the letter to Philemon and the congregation in his house, but in that to the Church of Colossæ.
Ambrosiaster's imagination is a trifle too lively when he writes of Archippus:
" Post enim Epaphram, qui illos imbuit, hic accepit regendam eorum ecclesiam,"
and when in the prologue he represents the false doctrine as intruding " post
prædicationem Epaphræ sive Archippi."   But Hitzig, *Zur Kritik paul. Briefe*,
32, and Steck, *JbfPTh.* 1891, S. 564 ff., went much further astray when they
found in Col. iv. 17 an " insulting utterance," a " sharp sting," an " unworthy
insinuation," which could not be believed of the apostle, the less so as he
wrote Philem. 2 without chiding Archippus.   According to this, all Paul's
exhortations which are not confirmed by a circumstantial statement of their
occasion, would be insults.   If such a one had occurred in Philem. 2, the
critics would have seen all the more in this a proof that Col. iv. 17 was
falsely ascribed to Paul on the basis of Philem. 2.   A conjecture like that
of Hitzig, 32 (whom Steck follows), that a philosopher, Flavius Archippus,
who was condemned to work in the mines by a proconsul Paulus (Plin. *Ep.
ad Traj.* lviii–lx, lxxx, lxxxi), furnished occasion for the invention in Col.
iv. 17, must be left to its fate.

   2. (P. 441.)   For history and geography see LIGHTFOOT (*op. cit.*), 1–72 ;
HENLE, *Kolossä und der Brief des Paulus an die Kol.* 1887 ; RAMSAY, *Church
in the Roman Empire*, 2 ed. 1893, pp. 465–480, with detailed map ; *ibid. Cities
and Bishoprics of Phrygia*, i. 1 (1895), pp. 32–121 (Laodicea and Hierapolis),
208–234 (Colossæ) ; HUMANN, CICHORIUS, JUDEICH, and WINTER, *Altertümer
von Hierapolis*, 1898.   Κολοσσαί (so in the older writers, upon coins, and in the
older MSS. of the N.T. ; Κολασσαί perhaps from the fifth century A.D. onwards)

was in Persian times one of the largest and richest cities of Phrygia (Herod. vii. 30 ; Xen. *Anab.* i. 2. 6). The cities founded in the time of the Seleucidæ, Apamea (Ἀπάμεια Κιβωτός, formerly Κελαιναί) eastward and Laodicea (Λαοδί-κεια ἡ πρὸς τῷ Λύκῳ or ἐπὶ Λύκῳ) about nine miles west of Colossæ, together with Hierapolis which lay about six miles north, outstripped the ancient Colossæ (Strabo, xii. 576). Yet Laodicea did not rise to prominence until just before the time of Christ (Strabo, xii. 578, ἐφ' ἡμῶν καὶ τῶν ἡμετέρων πατέρων), and in Strabo's time (he wrote 18-19 A.D.) Colossæ still shared the prosperity of the neighbouring towns (Strabo, 578, πόλισμα does not mean necessarily "small town"), and when Pliny (*H. N.* v. 41) reckons it as one of the *oppida celeberrima* of Phrygia, we need not understand him as referring simply to historical renown. The great commercial highway which led from Ephesus through the valley of the Mæander, then through that of the Lycus to Apamea, and finally through the Cilician Gates to Tarsus and Syria, passed through both Colossæ and Laodicea (Ramsay, *Hist. Geogr.* 35 ff.). But Laodicea had the advantage of being at the junction of several roads leading in all directions (Ramsay, *Cities and Bishop.* i. 1. 12, n. 1). The chief source of its riches, to which reference is made also in Rev. iii. 17, was the trade in the jet-black wool produced in the Lycus valley, which was preferred even to that of Miletus (Strabo, 578). In addition to this was the wool-dyeing industry of Hierapolis, favoured by the nature of the water there, which rivalled the scarlet and purple dyeing of other places (Strabo, 630). Laodicea was also the chief city of the district (*conventus*) of Cibyra, which belonged to the province of Asia (Plin. *H. N.* v. 105 ; cf. Marquardt, *R. Staatsverw.*[2] i. 341). Theodoret on Col. (ed. Noesselt, 472) calls it the Metropolis of Colossæ. The Church of Laodicea, as being the most important of the three mentioned in Col. iv. 13, is the only one included under the seven Churches of the province addressed in Rev. (i. 11, iii. 14) ; and even in Col. ii. 1, cf. iv. 13, Laodicea seems to stand for Hierapolis too. A synod occasioned by the Easter disputes met in Laodicea *circa* 165-170 (Eus. *H. E.* iv. 26. 3, v. 24. 5 ; cf. *Forsch.* iv. 266, v. 26). Yet Hierapolis itself remained famous in Church annals as the long-time home of the "apostle" or rather evangelist Philip and his daughters, and as the episcopal see of Papias and of Claudius Apollinaris (Eus. *H. E.* ii. 15. 2, iii. 31. 3-5, 36. 2, 39. 9, iv. 26. 1, v. 19. 2, 24. 2). On the other hand, Colossæ falls quite into the background in the tradition. The fortress Χῶναι, built probably under Justinian, about two miles south of Colosse, afterward quite swallowed up that city (Ramsay, *Hist. Geogr.* 80, 135, 429 ; *Church in R. E.* 478). While a bishop of Colossæ still signs with that title the decrees of the Trullan Council of 692 (Harduin, *Conc.* iii. 1710), there appears at the second Nicene Council of 787 a bishop Dositheus, or Theodosius, of Colossæ or Chonæ (*op. cit.* iv. 280, 449 ; cf. 32, 120, 468). Thereafter the name Colossæ disappears. The tradition is handed down merely that Chonæ is the ancient Colossæ, *e.g.* in the historian Nicetes of Chonæ (ed. Bonn. p. 230) in the thirteenth century. One of the earthquakes frequent in this region (Strabo, xii. 578, 579) may have helped to obliterate Colossæ. Only we may not, with Lightfoot, 71, think of this as happening in the third century. Theodoret, in his hypothesis to Philem. p. 711, thinks he knows that Philemon's house is still standing in Colossæ in his day, and the continued existence of a bishopric of Colossæ without any other name affixed proves the existence of the town until 692 at least. Of the earthquakes about which we have information, only one could have any significance for the N.T. In 60 A.D., according to Tacitus (*Ann.* xiv. 27, *eodem anno*; cf. chap. xx. *Nerone IV. et Corn. Cosso coss.*, hence not, as we find it asserted more often, 61 A.D., to which the transition is not made until *Ann.* xiv. 29), Laodicea was severely damaged by an earthquake, but soon arose by its own resources and without government assistance, which probably had been rendered on a former occasion (Strabo, xii. 579). Unquestionably Eusebius has the same occurrence in mind when he states that in *anno Abr.* 2079 (63 A.D.), Laodicea, Hierapolis, and Colossæ were destroyed by an earthquake (*Chron.* ii. 154). For the Jewish Sibyllist, about 80 A.D., who knows the ground in Asia Minor, and who speaks just like Tacitus of the destruction and rebuilding of Laodicea (*Sib.* iv. 107; cf. *ZfKW*, 1886, S. 37), thus attests indirectly that no like misfortune has again befallen the city between 60 and 80 A.D. Of more importance for us is it that even from the days of Antiochus the Great (Jos. *Ant.* xii. 3. 4) many Jews had been settling in this region. From the statement of Cicero, *pro Flacco*, xxviii, that Flaccus, 62 B.C., confiscated in the district of Laodicea Jewish temple tribute to the amount of more than twenty pounds of gold, and in that of Apamea almost a hundred pounds, it has been estimated that in the former district there were over 11,000 free Jewish men, and in the latter 55,000 (Lightfoot, 20; Henle, 53, A. 2). It is unknown, to be sure, how large these two districts were; cf. Ramsay, *Cities and Bishop.* i. 2. 667. In Hierapolis there was a well-organised Jewish community, cf. *Altertümer von Hier.* 46, 96 (No. 69), 138 (No. 212), 174 (No. 342). The connection with Jerusalem was fostered, cf. also Acts ii. 10, xxi. 27. Cæsar's decrees of tolerance, issued at the instance of the high priest and prince Hyrcanus II., benefited also the Jews of Laodicea (Jos. *Ant.* xiv. 10. 20; cf. Schürer, i. 348 [Eng. trans. I. i. 382 f.], iii. 67 f. [Eng. trans. II. ii. 225 f.]. From Jews of this region the fable spread that the Ararat upon which Noah's ark (κιβωτός) grounded was near Apamea Kibotos : Orac. *Sib.* i. 261–267; Jul. Afric. *Chron.* (Routh, *Rel. S.*[2] ii. 243), and coins of the third century A.D. to be found in Eckhel, iii. 132–139; cf. Schürer, iii. 14 f. (new matter, not in Eng. trans.); Ramsay, *op. cit.* 669–672.

3. (P. 441.) If in Col. i. 7 we read ὑπὲρ ἡμῶν, which is very strongly attested (א*ABD*G, Ambrosiaster), and which has been subsequently altered in old MSS. like א and D into ὑπὲρ ὑμῶν as an easier reading, we are shut up to the conclusion that Epaphras is a servant of Christ among the Colossians for and in place of Paul and Timothy; cf. Philem. 13, ὑπὲρ σοῦ. The notion lying back of this is that properly Paul himself, as apostle of the Gentiles, and especially of the province (Acts xix. 10) to which Colossæ belonged, would have been bound to preach in that city (Col. i. 25). It was a help to him and Timothy for Epaphras to undertake this work. It is not decisive against this interpretation that we have ἐστίν instead of ἐγένετο. Epaphras' service of Christ in behalf of the Churches founded by him still continues; he prays for them constantly, actually toils for them (iv. 12 f.), and has probably been begging Paul to interest himself in them, and to write them a letter of encouragement. Hence the present in i. 7 may be non-temporal, combining past and present. But the ὑπὲρ ἡμῶν seems natural only on the supposition that Epaphras preached in Colossæ and its neighbourhood at the time when Paul and Timothy were

working in Ephesus at what they believed to be their task, namely, bringing
the gospel to the province of Asia, which included Colossæ, Laodicea, and
Hierapolis. The feeling of obligation to preach also in other cities of the
province comes out, *e.g.* in 2 Cor. ii. 12 f., and Acts xix. 10 does not exclude
the supposition that Paul himself preached in other cities too ; Acts xix. 26
may even seem to favour it. At all events, several Churches beside that of
Ephesus sprang up in the province at this time (1 Cor. xvi. 19). That
even then the gospel had penetrated as far as the Lycus valley is probable,
though it cannot be proved from Acts xix. 10, 26 ; for aside from the possibility that the expression is hyperbolic, Luke uses "Asia" in a very narrow
sense, excluding the whole of Phrygia, and hence the Phrygian cities Colossæ,
Laodicea, and Hierapolis, which belonged to the province of Asia (above, p.
186). All that we can infer with complete certainty from Col. i. 4-9, ii. 1, is
that Paul, whether on his second and third missionary journeys (above, pp.
188 ff.) or during his three years in Ephesus, had never come to Colossæ or
to that Phrygian section of the province of Asia at all. Theodoret (pp. 472,
483), differing from the older commentators (Ambrosiaster, Ephr. Syr.,
Chrys., Theod. Mops.), thought that Paul (ii. 1) has joined with the Christians
of Colossæ and Laodicea, whom he had seen, other Christians whom he had
not seen. But the lack of all hint of a contrast ("not only—but also")
and the union without distinction in ii. 2 of the Churches indicated in ii. 1,
are decisive against this view. Theodoret avoided the force of Col. i. 7 (cf.
Eph. iv. 20) by assuming that the Colossians had heard from Epaphras simply
of the progress of the gospel in the whole world (cf. i. 6a). Perhaps also
the Antiochian reading καθὼς καὶ ἐμάθετε, which Theodoret had before him,
helped to weaken the sense of the sentence.

4. (P. 442.) For particulars about Mark see Part ix. The designation
"nephew of Barnabas" hardly looks like a title for distinguishing him from
some other Mark of whom we know nothing, and it is more natural to assume
that he was then unknown in Colossæ and the neighbouring towns. On the
contrary, they had heard of Barnabas, the older and more famous missionary
(cf. also 1 Cor. ix. 6) and joint-founder of the Church in Pisidian Antioch,
which was not so very far east of Colossæ. The bare name of the next man
mentioned, Jesus, characterises him as a Jew ; his surname also, Justus, was
common among Jews ; cf. Jos. *Vita*, 9 ; Acts i. 23 (Joseph Barsabas Justus,
confused apparently in the *Acts of Paul*, ed. Lipsius, p. 108. 14, p. 116. 12, not
only with Barnabas, but also with Jesus Justus, *GK*, ii. 889), and many other
examples from literature and inscriptions adduced in Lightfoot, 238. With
Hofmann, iv. 2. 148, we may take ἐκ περιτομῆς οὗτοι μόνοι as parenthetic,
which is most natural ; or, with Bleek, we may consider that οὗτοι μόνοι
was added as an afterthought to sharpen the expression. In any event
the information here given is not simply that the men just named were Jews,
which would be quite needless in the case of the last two, nor is it that
these two or three men were Paul's only effective and agreeable fellow-
workers, for Epaphras, Luke, and Demas are also called συνεργοί, and two
of them are strongly commended (Col. i. 7, iv. 12, 14 ; Philem. 23 f.). We
are shut up to the meaning given above, which had been accepted even by
commentators who, like Lightfoot, failed to see the grammatical grounds for
their correct exegesis, because they clung to the heavy punctuation after

περιτομῆς used before Lachmann's time. But it also follows that none of the other συνεργοί then with Paul were Jews. To except Luke from this number (so Hofmann, iv. 2. 151; *Scriftbeweis*, ii. 2. 99) is impossible, for he was staying with Paul not only as physician (Col. iv. 14), but also as συνεργός (Philem. 24), and hence must have been mentioned in Col. iv. 11 if he had been a Jew. It is, if possible, still more certain that Epaphras, who is mentioned immediately after iv. 11, was a Gentile. The contrary opinion of Jerome (*in Philem.* 23, Vallarsi, vii. 762) is based on an unfortunate combination of the designation συναιχμάλωτος with the ancient tradition that Paul's family were carried away captive by the Romans at the taking of Giscala (above, p. 681 f.). All that is open to question is, whether οἱ ὄντες . . . παρηγορία refers to Aristarchus also, as most critics say, or only to Mark and Jesus, as Hofmann holds. Grammatically, we cannot decide how far back the reference of the οὗτοι extends (cf. Acts xx. 5). But since Aristarchus' relation to Paul and his work has been already sufficiently indicated by συναιχμάλωτός μου, it seems unnatural to refer ver. 11 also to him. The same principle holds in the distribution of epithets in Philem. 23 and 24. Besides, it would be strange for Paul now to assert expressly of such a tried helper that he was not a hindrance to him like others, but a furtherer of his work, and had therefore proved a comfort to him in the trouble which these others had caused. In Philem. 24, Mark, indeed, who was to come to Colossæ shortly, is mentioned, but not Jesus Justus. It is possible to suppose that an original Ἰησοῦς, as indicating him, has disappeared in the Ἰησοῦ of ver. 23, if it has not suggested, indeed, the whole phrase ἐν Χριστῷ Ἰησοῦ, which is exceedingly rare in combination with συναιχμάλωτος, συστρατιώτης, συνεργός μου.

5. (P. 443.) Among others, Reuss, Thiersch, and Weiss decide in favour of Cæsarea as the place where Eph., Col., and Philem. were written; so, too, Hilgenfeld as far as regards Philem., the only one which he considers genuine. The ancient commentators, without exception, and most of the moderns, decide in favour of Rome. At all events, the disposition not to let Paul rest altogether from letter-writing while in Cæsarea is not pertinent here. Neither have we any letter dating from the three years which may lie between 2 Thess. and 1 Cor., and we know of just a single one, which Paul wrote toward the end of this time (1 Cor. v. 9). Paul may have written twenty letters in Cæsarea. One, of which we hear in 2 Pet. iii. 15, probably falls within this period.

6. (P. 443.) According to Jos. *Bell.* ii. 18. 1, vii. 8. 7 (cf. vii. 8. 7, Niese, 362, " with women and children "), the Jewish population of Cæsarea numbered over 20,000. Though the Gentiles were in the majority there (*Bell.* iii. 9. 1), the Jewish minority was so large that, until the time of Festus, they could think of claiming the town as Jewish (*Ant.* xx. 8. 7, 9; *Bell.* ii. 13. 7). Cæsarea certainly had no more than 60,000 inhabitants.

7. (P. 444.) Acts xxviii. 16, 20, 30 f. According to the ancient *Acts of Paul*, that apostle, though, to be sure, not until his arrival in Rome the second time, hired a barn outside the city (ed. Lipsius, 104. 4; cf. *GK*, ii. 889, and below, § 36, n. 10). At any rate, Acts xxviii. 16–31 implies no little attic chamber, but a roomy abode, cf. Acts xix. 9.

8. (P. 444). Lightfoot, 312, mentions as possible occasions for the ac-

quaintance of Onesimus and Paul: a chance meeting with his fellow-countryman Epaphras, destitution and hunger, remembrance of words of Paul which he had once heard in Philemon's house, and pricks of conscience. He also cites Sallust, *Catil.* xxxvii. 5 ; Tac. *Ann.* xv. 44, to show that Rome was the great resort of the rabble.

9. (P. 446.) If the statements of Tacitus and of Eusebius (above, p. 449, line 2 ff.) refer to the same event, and if, as Tacitus says, Laodicea (with the neighbouring towns) recovered straightway from the earthquake of 60 A.D., the lack of any reference to this in letters sent from Rome to this region between the spring of 61 and 63—perhaps not till the autumn of 62, or during the winter of 62-63—is not remarkable. If Eusebius has the right date (63 A.D.), all that we need to assume is that Col. was written before the earthquake, or at least before news of it reached Rome. In no case is there any reason to deny that Tychicus and Onesimus journeyed from Rome to Asia Minor somewhere about the autumn of 62. Then Paul would have thought of the spring of 63 when he wrote Philem. 22.

§ 26. THE EPISTLE TO PHILEMON.

This is the only letter in the N.T. which gives us a glimpse into a Christian household of that time. The father, Philemon, was converted (ver. 19) through the influence of Paul, with whom he became acquainted probably in Ephesus (above, p. 447). The wife and son were also Christians. While Archippus in some regular way served the Colossian Church (Col. iv. 17, p. 446 f., n. 1), his father, Philemon, appears to have assisted more generally in spreading the gospel in his vicinity, because of which service Paul calls him the fellow-worker of Timothy and himself (ver. 1). He must have been a well-to-do citizen of Colossæ, which was at that time a flourishing commercial city. His house served as the meeting-place for a part of the local Church (n. 1). He was in a position where he could show the loyalty of his love to his fellow-believers by a rather wide-reaching beneficence (ver. 5). Only recently he had offered new proof of this practical love to "the saints" (n. 2), of which Paul is able to think only with joyful gratitude.

This liberality on the part of Philemon is emphasised so strongly because Paul is about to make a further demand upon his generosity. His request concerns Onesimus, who, in addition to being unprofitable to his master (ver. 11), had run away, apparently stealing the money necessary for the journey (ver. 18). Now, however, he has been converted through Paul's ministry in Rome, and the apostle seeks to restore him to his Master's house. This made it natural for him to direct the letter to the wife and son and the other Christians accustomed to gather there as well as to Philemon himself (ver. 2 f.), although elsewhere throughout the letter he addresses only the head of the house, with whom the decision of the matter rested (n. 3). All that Paul asks in the letter is that Philemon receive in a kindly spirit the penitent refugee who had now become a fellow-believer with him. He does not ask this in any authoritative way, although he had a right to do so, but in a brotherly spirit (vv. 8–10). No question is raised as to Philemon's right of possession in the future, recognition of which right prevented Paul from retaining Onesimus, to whom he had become attached, and who was peculiarly adapted to serve his personal needs (ver. 13 f.). This is a " fleshly " bond which, far from being annulled by the fellowship " in the Lord " established by faith, is rather sanctified by it. This " fleshly " bond serves also to render their Christian fellowship more individual and hence more intimate (ver. 16). At the most, Paul no more than hints his desire that Philemon give Onesimus his freedom, when he expresses the expectation that Philemon will do more than Paul requests (ver. 21). This expectation, however, is one with his hope that the letter may fully accomplish its purpose. For Paul by no means thinks that at once and of his own accord Philemon will receive the guilty slave with kindness, but uses every means in his power so to dispose him. At the very beginning, where he praises Philemon for his generous brotherly love, by which Paul is encouraged to prefer his request, he does not fail to

intimate that he would like to see Philemon make still
further progress in this direction (ver. 6, n. 2).   The
indignation which Philemon had felt at Onesimus' conduct
should be mitigated, among other things, by the consideration that now instead of a worthless he has a useful
servant (vv. 11, 16).   For the money which Philemon
had lost through Onesimus' unfaithfulness Paul makes
himself personally responsible, this letter in his own hand
being formal security for the debt (n. 4).   Although,
as the added remark indicates, Paul had no idea that
Philemon would hold him strictly responsible for the
payment of the sum in question, undoubtedly he did
intend a humorous thrust at the weak side of this man,
who possibly was liberal enough in large matters (vv.
5–7), but inclined to reckon closely in small affairs.   Paul
continues the same humorous vein, when he adds, "Yes,
my brother, I should like to profit at your expense" (n. 5).
Some of the salt with which he seasons his own words
(Col. iv. 6) he takes for granted in his readers.   We
observe the same humorous spirit in the request which
Paul makes of Philemon, now to make ready for him
quarters in his house, when, as a matter of fact, he was
anticipating a protracted continuance of his preaching in
Rome (Col. iv. 3 f. ; Eph. vi. 19 f.), and had said nothing
about an immediate journey to Asia in the two contemporaneous letters.   The apostle gives himself an invitation
to visit the stern householder.   It is as if he had said, "I
shall find out shortly whether Onesimus, my 'child' (ver.
10), my 'heart' (ver. 12), my beloved brother, has been
received by you in the way I requested."

The letter is a striking example of that unaffected art
by which Paul was able to touch the heart so as to win
to himself and his cause everyone not entirely devoid
of feeling (n. 6).   The humour of the letter does not
lessen its earnestness, nor does its irony affect its warmth.
It combines politeness and dignity, recognition of the

hard rights of this world with defence of the highest demands for the fuller exercise of Christian love.

The fact that this letter has been declared spurious notwithstanding its wealth of original material (n. 7), and in spite of the lack of all support from tradition and the impossibility of discovering any sufficient motive for its forgery, deserves only to be mentioned (n. 8).

1. (P. 452.) The "congregation in Philemon's house" (ver. 2) cannot be identical either with the ordinary household or with the local Church of Colossæ. In the latter case the address of this letter and of Col. would be the same. Since Colossæ at that time, though surpassed by Laodicea, was by no means decadent (above, p. 448), there is nothing improbable in the Christians' meeting for worship in various houses, as was done in other still larger cities, Ephesus (1 Cor. xvi. 19) and Rome (Rom. xvi. 5, above, p. 430, n. 1). This was the case also in the neighbouring city of Laodicea (Col. iv. 15). The reading αὐτῶν אACP, Copt. (see Lightfoot, 256) is thoughtlessly moulded after Rom. xvi. 5 ; 1 Cor. xvi. 19 ; the brethren in Laodicea must have had more than one house. The reading αὐτῆς, B, 67** presupposes that Νύμφαν, as Lachmann for this very reason wished to have it accented, indicates a woman. In the Coptic fragments of the old Acts of Paul (ed. C. Schmidt, p. 30. 19 ff., German trans. p. 54 ff.) a woman is called Nympha, who, together with her husband Hermocrates, had been baptized by Paul in Myrrha (Myra in Lycia). But Nympha is only a Doric form for νύμφη, and no more than this can it be shown elsewhere to be a personal name. Rather should we read Νυμφᾶν (=Nymphodorum, Nymphodotum, etc.), and then αὐτοῦ, with DG and the Antioch recension. The rarity of this masculine name (C. I. Att. iii. 1105, Νυνφας ; cf. C. I. G. 1290 ; C. I. Lat. ii. 557, Nyphas?) occasioned the alteration. Likewise the σοῦ, in Philem. 2, which on other grounds seems peculiar, has been altered, now into αὐτῶν, to imitate Rom. xvi. 5, 1 Cor. xvi. 19 ; now into αὐτοῦ, from stylistic considerations.

2. (Pp. 452, 454.) In itself οἱ ἅγιοι, ver. 7 (cf. 1 Cor. xvi. 1 ; 2 Cor. viii. 4, ix. 1, 12), might mean the Jerusalem Christians (Hofmann) ; but this seems unnatural here so soon after πάντες οἱ ἅγιοι (ver. 5 = all Christians). Besides, if Paul and Timothy had merely heard of a remittance of money to Jerusalem by Philemon, they would hardly have failed to say so (cf. ἀκούων, ver. 5 ; Eph. i. 15 ; Col. i. 4, 9 ; cf. per contra, Phil. iv. 10). The expression, as we have it here, gives the idea that Paul had himself recently perceived the love which Philemon had shown, and which was refreshing the saints. We might have had τῶν ἀδελφῶν here (1 Cor. xvi. 11, 12 ; 2 Cor. ix. 3 ; 3 John 3). Philemon knew whom Paul meant. He may have aided with money Christians who were travelling from Asia to Rome, or he may have sent the money by them to help needy ones of his own land and faith in Rome ; see also n. 3. According to the correct reading (ἀγάπην before πίστιν), ver. 5 treats of the love and faithfulness which Philemon shows with regard to the Lord Jesus (and) toward all saints. Consequently also the wish (ver. 6), which makes up the content of Paul's prayers for Philemon (ver. 4), can only be that "Philemon's

faithful disposition to impart may become effectual by virtue of a knowledge of all the good which it lies in the power of Christians generally (ἐν ἡμῖν) or of him and his house (ἐν ὑμῖν), to do toward Christ."

3. (P. 453.) Aside from the textually uncertain ὑμῖν, ver. 6, the plural address does not appear until ver. 22b, and then again in ver. 25, which corresponds to the opening greeting, ver. 3. The reasons for its use are in all cases clear. The joint authorship of Timothy is revealed nowhere but in vv. 1, 2 (ἡμῶν) and again probably in ver. 7 (ἔσχομεν, D* Orig. iii. 889 ; Jerome vii. 754, from which the Antiochian ἔχομεν has arisen by assimilation to the present tenses before and after it, and ἔσχον by assimilation to the singulars around it. The aorist proves that a single experience of the most recent past is meant ; cf. Phil. iv. 10 ; 2 John 4 ; 3 John 3 ; Polyc. ad Phil. i. 1, xi. 1 ; Forsch. iv. 250). In Col., too, Paul does not simply mention Timothy as one of those who send greetings, but makes him to a certain extent joint-author of the letter (Col. i. 1, 3, 9, hence ἐγὼ Παῦλος, i. 23). But he has a particular reason for so doing in Philem., namely, Timothy's personal acquaintance with Philemon—perhaps also the fact that the matter in question was of a somewhat legal nature. For signing a bond and for drawing up a recommendation for the runaway slave recourse was had to a second witness (2 Cor. xiii. 1).

4. (P. 454.) Concerning autograph writing, see above, p. 172, n. 4. It might be possible, indeed, that ver. 19a was a remark written in Paul's own hand on the margin after the letter had been all dictated. In this case ἵνα μὴ λέγω σοί would connect with ver. 18 even more easily than if with Hofmann we take ver. 19a as a parenthesis. At all events the σοί after λέγω cannot be a thoroughly superfluous enclitic dative, governed by the verb, but must emphatically express just what Paul could indeed say, but will not say directly (cf. 2 Cor. ix. 4, also 2 Cor. ii. 5). The antithesis required is not, however, to be found in ver. 19a, but simply in the ἐμοί, ver. 18. Paul says ; "Charge it (not to Onesimus, but) to me," but adds that he could properly say that Philemon should charge it to his own account, and for this reason that he owed Paul not only such trifling sums of money, but also his own self besides, i.e. every personal sacrifice. This somewhat strange thought rests perhaps on the notion that in Philemon's account-book there was no page at all on which Paul was represented as debtor, and that, therefore, it was more natural to enter a little debt of Paul to him upon the page on which his many debts to Paul were registered. He would then quickly see that the balance in favour of Paul was hardly diminished by this little sum.

5. (P. 454.) In all likelihood the words in ver. 11, ἄχρηστος, εὔχρηστος, are suggested not so much by the vulgar pronunciation of Χριστός, Χριστιανός =χρηστός (Baur, Paulus, ii. 91), as by the meaning of the name 'Ονήσιμος. Likewise it is hardly to be doubted that ὀναίμην, ver. 20, is a play upon the sound of the name. Cf. Ign. Eph. ii. 2, ὀναίμην ὑμῶν, at the end of an exhorta-tion to obey the bishop, whose name was Onesimus (ibid. i. 3, ii. 1). There are similar plays upon proper names in Theophilus, ad Autol. i. 1, Θεόφιλος—τὸ θεοφιλὲς ὄνομα τοῦτο = Χριστιανός, Eusebius, H. E. iii. 27. 6, Ebion, the poor man; v. 24. 18, Irenæus, the man of peace. Regarding Rev. iii. 1, see § 73, n. 8. There are still other examples in Lightfoot, 340. Paul does not use the polished phrase in the usual sense, "May I have joy in thee," but means it literally.

To confirm the demand hinted at in ver. 19*b*, he openly avows (*ναί*), and says to the strict householder or the carefully calculating merchant, that he on his part would like to make a profit in the transaction with Philemon, instead of letting Philemon get the better of the bargain, as was his wont.

6. (P. 454.) Among the means which Paul uses to induce Philemon to comply with his request belongs also the way in which he refers to his present situation. Four times in this short letter he alludes to his imprisonment (vv. 1, 9, 10, 13), and in the very opening greeting he designates himself, in contrast with the other letters written at the same time, simply as Paul a prisoner of Christ Jesus. In ver. 9, to be sure, it would be unexceptionable grammatically to take *τοιοῦτος—ὡς* as correlatives—the view of the ancient Greek commentators (cf. Kühner-Gerth i. 413 A. 11 ; ii. 493. 4, and Lightfoot). But in that case the present writer could see no reason for *ὡς Παῦλος* instead of *οἷός εἰμι* (cf. Acts xxvi. 29); for the name indicates no particular characteristic or situation. Moreover, *τοιοῦτος* requires no such correlative when all that is needed is to draw attention to a person's character or situation which was known before (2 Cor. ii. 6 ; Hofmann, *ad loc.*, compares appropriately, *Odyssey*, 16. 205). Philemon knows what sort of man Paul is and how circumstanced, and as such Paul makes his plea for Onesimus. This *τοιοῦτος*, which thus points by implication to the character of the pleader in all its detail, is explained in the three appositives which follow ; for since *πρεσβύτης* has no article, it cannot be construed as in apposition simply to *Παῦλος*. He pleads, as Chrysostom (xi. 780) long ago rightly distinguished—(1) as Paul, the friend whom Philemon has known so long and so well ; (2) as an old man ; (3) as one who now also wears fetters for Christ's sake. But neither the name, nor the great age, nor the imprisonment would show his right to command (ver. 8), in this matter at all events ; they are rather intended to characterise the pleader as one whose plea cannot well be refused. Thus Paul here waives altogether his official dignity and the authority growing out of his services. Bentley's conjecture (*Crit. Sacra*, ed. Ellies, p. 73), *πρεσβευτής*, which Hort, *NT*, *Appendix*, 136, adopted ; or Lightfoot's proposal, in which Westcott, in distinction from his fellow-worker, acquiesced, to take *πρεσβύτης*, after all manner of doubtful analogies, in the sense of *πρεσβευτής*, sc. Χριστοῦ (cf. 2 Cor. v. 20 ; Eph. vi. 20), introduces a foreign element which would have been in place only in ver. 8, and even there would have required much clearer expression. The *πρεσβύτης* as such, and especially when he pleads, has primarily something touching about him ; cf. Clem. *Quis Div.* xli (the plea of the gray-haired John to the erring youth) ; *Passio Perp.* v, vi (the gray hair of the father and the helplessness of the child combine to produce an effect). We do not know the year of Paul's birth. If, according to the conjecture expressed above, p. 69, his parents were carried away from Palestine in 4 B.C.,—Paul, however, not being born until after they settled at Tarsus,— still his birth may have taken place in 1–5 A.D. Considering the part which he played in 35 A.D. (Acts vii. 58–viii. 3, ix. 2), he probably was then not a "youth" of twenty, but a young man of about thirty. Consequently in 62 A.D. he must have been at all events near the sixties. His wearing life and long imprisonment may have made him old beyond his years. It was all the more natural, then, to represent himself to his friend expressly as *πρεσβύτης*.

7. (P. 455.) The circumstances and facts presupposed connect themselves in

no way with such of Paul's Epistles as are held by most critics to be genuine,
or with Acts. The names alone would arouse suspicions in every critic.
Philemon and Apphia occur nowhere else in the N.T. Onesimus and
Archippus are mentioned in Col. iv. 9, 17. But what is said about them
in the one letter touches at no point what is said in the other ; it is thus
impossible that one of these two Epistles was invented on the basis of the
other, or that both were forged by the same man. Some of the names have
a local colouring, however. The present writer is unable, indeed, to verify
for Phrygia by inscriptions from the time of the Cæsars the ancient names
Philemon and *Archippus*, or the later *Epaphras* (*e.g. C. I. G.* 2284 ; *C. I. L.* iv.
1384*a*, 1787, 1816, 1916, 1926, 1936, 2374, 2450, vi. 17174–17180, xv. 2542,
contracted form for the very common *Epaphroditus*, which Ephr. Syr. p. 169
inserts in place of it). Yet cf. Philemon and Baucis in Ovid. *Metam.* viii. 631 ;
also Aristoph. *The Birds*, 763. The name *Onesimus*, which was used especially
for slaves, is to be found as often perhaps in Rome (*C. I. L.* vi. 23459–23484)
and Pompeii (*C. I. L.* iv. 222, 1330, 1332, 2477*a*, 2777, 3163) as in Phyrgia
and the bordering regions (*C. I. G.* 2743, 2840, 2932, 2933, 3827*b*, *t. u.*, 3859 ;
Sterrett, *Wolfe Exp.*, No. 366, line 108, No. 376, lines 32, 39 ; cf. Ign. *Eph.* i ;
Melito quoted in Eus. *II. E.* iv. 26. 13). On the other hand, *Apphia* is a
Phrygian name, and has nothing to do with *Appius, Appia*. The spelling
varies between Απφια (*C. I. G.* 2775*b*, 2782, 2835, 2837*b*, 2950, 3432, 3446 ;
Ramsay, *Cities and Bishop.* i. 391, 470, Nos. 254, 309), Αφφια (*C. I. G.* 3814,
4141 ; Le Bas-Waddington, iii. Nos. 799, 911 ; Ramsay, pp. 394, 473, 559, 662,
Nos. 276, 324, 445, 624), and Αφια (*C. I. G.* 2720, 3826 ; *Wolfe Exp.* Nos. 482).
Likewise the diminutive form Απφιον (*C. I. G.* 2733, 2836 ; Ramsay, pp. 385,
391, 520, 525, Nos. 228, 254, 257, 361, 369) or Αφιον (Le Bas-Waddington,
No. 832). Derived feminine forms are Αφφιας (*C. I. G.* 3697, 3983) and
Απφιας (see below), like Αμμιας (=Αμμια, *Forsch.* v. 95, according to which
also *C. I. G.* 9916 should be read without emendation). Of especial interest
to us are *C. I. G.* vol. iii. p. 1168, No. 4380, *k* 3, 'Απφιάδι . . . γένει Κολοσ-
σηνῇ, and *Wolfe Exp.* No. 482, 'Ονήσιμος 'Αφίᾳ γυναικί. A legend of Titus
mentions an *Apphia* healed by Paul in Damascus (James, *Apocrypha Anecd.*
i. 55). Outside of Phrygia and the neighbouring regions the name seems to
be rare, cf. *C. I. L.* v. 5380 (Como), ix. 290 (Bari : *Apphiadis*). The conclusion that Onesimus became a *diaconus* Jerome drew simply from Philem.
13 (*Epist.* lxxxii. 6, Vall. i. 516, cf. vii. 755, *minister apostoli*). The real Euthalius
(Zacagni, *Coll. mon.* 528 ; cf. *Ignatii Mart.* MS. Vatic. chap. x. p. 314, 30 in
the writer's *Ignatius von Antiochien*) knew of a martyrdom of Onesimus,
according to which he suffered death under an exarch Tertullus in Rome by
having his legs broken. However, it does not pay to unravel the confused
statements of martyrologies and legends (*Acta SS. Febr.* ii. 855–859, cf. *Acta
Xanthippæ et Polyxenæ*, cap. xxxviii, in James, *Apocr. Anecd.* i. 84).

8. (P. 455.) Baur, *Paulus*, ii. 88–94, brought forward essentially nothing
against the genuineness of this Epistle except its close relation to Eph., Col.,
and Phil. (S. 89), which he rejected on other grounds. He rested satisfied
with the possibility that it was the "embryo of a Christian work of fiction,"
just as the pseudo-Clementine *Homilies* are really a Christian romance (S. 93).
Weizsäcker rejects it as a "production designed to illustrate a new doctrine of
Christian living, and betraying its allegorical character in the very name

Onesimus," as if the letter propounded a doctrine of the "usefulness" of a Christian slave, or of the "profitableness" of running away. Concerning the names see nn. 5 and 7. Moreover, cf. Deissmann, *Bibelst.* 237 (Eng. trans. 44), "to a large extent doctrinaire want of taste." Steck (*JbfPTh.* 1891, S. 571) takes offence, among other things, because this little note about a private matter has all the form of an epistle to a Church. He does not refute, or even consider the very simple explanations of the mention of Timothy, and of the household congregation (above, pp. 453, 456, n. 3). Moreover, without even reflecting that a knowledge of Latin literature was something very rare among the Greeks, Steck will have it (S. 576) that his pseudo-Paul drew in imitative fashion from Plin. *Ep.* ix. 21 (intercession for a freedman, cf. ix. 24), which Grotius, on Philem. 10 and 17, adduced as a parallel, and that he did this in the second quarter of the second century (S. 582). Marcion forbids a later date for its composition ; for he "*is believed* to have known it" (S. 575), which is Steck's incomparably delicate way of stating the fact that Marcion admitted it unchanged into his *Apostolicum.* Holtzmann (*ZflVTh.* 1873, S. 428–441) extended his view of Col. (see below, § 29) to include Philem. also. A genuine letter to Philemon was interpolated by the same man who interpolated Col. and forged Eph. The difficulty of the construction in vv. 4–6 (above, p. 455 f., nn. 2, 3), which Holtzmann exaggerates without even attempting an explanation of his own, is due, he holds, to the fact that vv. 4–6 (= Eph. i. 15–17) were inserted later. This, at least, seems to be the meaning of the discussion, S. 433–435, though according to S. 439, where it is remarked in favour of the genuineness of ver. 7, that that verse connects naturally with ver. 4, ver. 4 seems to pass for genuine. A motive for the interpolation, which certainly could not consist in making the text hard to understand, is not to be found ; nor is it explained what occasioned the remarkable position of ἀγάπη before πίστις (apparently no trace of this in Eph. i. 15), or the reference of ἐπίγνωσις to something altogether different from that in Eph. i. 17. The real parallel to this is to be found in Phil. i. 9 f. Further, if the words, "Timothy the brother," and "our fellow-worker," and "Archippus our fellow-soldier" were inserted in order to conform Philem. to Col. (S. 437 f.), this very object needs a further object as a means to which it should serve. Now, according to Holtzmann, Col. iv. 15–17 was inserted there by the same editor who enriched Philem. by these additions ; so that the whole figure of Archippus is a creation of this interpolator's. But who will admit that he is satisfied with the statement (S. 438) that Archippus was invented simply as "a sort of personal connection between the situations in the two Epistles"? And why should not the alleged interpolator have rather taken persons whom he found in the letters, Jesus Justus, Col. iv. 11, and Apphia, Philem. 2, and, by carrying them over from one letter to the other, have used them to link the two Epistles together? "Nemo tam otiosus fertur stilo, ut materias habens fingat" (Tert. *adv. Valent.* v).

§ 27. THE EPISTLE TO THE COLOSSIANS.

Simultaneously with the letter to the portion of the Colossian Church accustomed to gather at the house of

Philemon, Paul despatches a communication to the Church as a whole. It is natural to assume that both letters reached their destination at the same time. This could have happened if this letter to the Church, like the letter to Philemon, was brought by Onesimus, who did not, like Tychicus, have commissions to carry out elsewhere, but was certainly directed by Paul to return to his master by the shortest route.

Inasmuch as Paul directs the Church to see that this letter is read also in the Church at Laodicea (iv. 16), and since, moreover, in the passage where he passes from more general statements to the discussion of special conditions, Paul speaks of the Christians of Laodicea and Colossæ together (ii. 1), the inference is natural that the letter was intended originally for both these neighbouring Churches. From the absence of a similar remark with reference to the Church in Hierapolis, which was in the same neighbourhood, and just as near as Laodicea and Colossæ to the heart of Epaphras, the missionary of this region (iv. 13), it is supposable that the special conditions and dangers which led Paul to send this letter to Colossæ, and indirectly to Laodicea, were not yet present in Hierapolis.

Paul was not personally acquainted with the Churches in the vicinity of Colossæ any more than with the Colossian Church itself. In fact, with the exception of individuals like Philemon and Epaphras, he was personally unknown to them all (i. 4, 8, 9, ii. 1, 5). Nevertheless, he reckons them, as it were, in his apostolic diocese, for in organising them Epaphras had acted as his representative (i. 7, above, p. 449, n. 3). His vocation, and the sufferings which this vocation involves, are consequently on their behalf also (i. 24). They are objects of his thanksgiving and petition not merely in the sense in which all Christians are (i. 3, 9), but he is solicitous for their welfare in the same way as Epaphras, their founder (ii. 1, v. 12).

Since, now, he has been more definitely informed concerning these Churches by Epaphras, and had learned also that they feel a "spiritual" love for him though he is personally unknown to them (i. 8), it would appear that the necessity for deepening this relation were sufficient occasion for a letter. Such an occasion might explain adequately the contents of Col. i. 3, 4 ; but it does not explain why Paul did not address the letter to all the Christians in Colossæ, Laodicea, and Hierapolis, and perhaps also other cities in that region (ii. 1) ; or, if Colossæ was the centre of this group of Churches, why he did not at least address the neighbouring Churches and the principal Church together, using some such general expression in the salutation as that in 2 Cor. i. 1. And, as will be shown later, simultaneously with the letter to the local Church in Colossæ and the letter to the Church in Philemon's house, Paul despatched by Tychicus to this region still a third Epistle, which was intended for more general circulation. There must have been special conditions, therefore, existing only in Colossæ and to some extent also in Laodicea, which called for the writing of the Colossian letter. What these conditions were we learn in chap. ii., the special contents of which are led up to in various ways by chap. i. and echoed in chap. iii. In chap. i. Paul designated himself not only a διάκονος τοῦ εὐαγγελίου (i. 23), i.e. a missionary, but also a διάκονος τῆς ἐκκλησίας (i. 25), which is something quite different. When, in this connection, he speaks of the stewardship of God committed to him, he cannot mean his commission to preach the gospel, but only some calling that has reference to the existing Church. More definitely stated, it is a commission to declare *fully* the word of God which the Church had received by faith, and, more specifically still, to declare *fully* the secret of God made known to the saints, and especially revealed in all its fulness to the Gentile Church (n. 1). This πληρῶσαι τὸν λόγον, like the first λαλεῖν τὸν λόγον, *i.e.* the missionary preaching, is a making known of Christ, who in His person is this μυστήριον of God (i. 26–29, cf. ii. 2). Still this is not the preaching of an unknown person, but primarily the unfolding of the forces and norms of the moral life contained in the gospel which has been believed, and such instruction in varied knowledge as will bring the Christian personality to a well-rounded perfection. In view of the fact that Paul declares with emphasis here, and three times elsewhere, in the letter that this commission affects everyone,—naturally every Christian, and more specifically, according to ver. 27, every Gentile Christian (i. 28),—and that he makes every effort in his power to fulfil it (i. 29), it is evident that here, at the very outset, he is answering the criticism that he is satisfied to leave the Churches in his field of labour with only an imperfect declaration of the divine word; that he is not careful enough to instruct new converts in the full richness of Christian knowledge, and to guide them in the development toward Christian perfection; that, in relation to at least many of the Churches for which he is responsible, he shows a lamentable lack of concern in this matter.

What he meant by these apologetic remarks, and what his object was in making them, Paul states very clearly in ii. 1–5, which is intended to explain what precedes (n. 2). He will have the Christians in Colossæ and vicinity know that he has always recognised the obligation of Christian nurture in relation to all the Churches within his sphere of labour, and that, as is evidenced by his zealous effort in general, he is now very much concerned for them, to the end that their hearts may be strengthened through loving instruction received, and by their introduction to the full richness of Christian understanding, namely, the full knowledge of the secret of God, which is Christ. The expression used (ἀγῶνα ἔχω, ii. 1 = κοπιῶ ἀγωνιζόμενος, i. 29, cf. iv. 12, 13; 1 Tim. iv. 10) cannot properly be limited in meaning to prayer (i. 9).   There are circumstances in which the person absent in body (ii. 5) cannot do much more than pray for the loved ones at a distance.   But Paul has other means of showing that he is anxious to develop these far-distant Churches to the highest point of Christian knowledge and morality, *e.g.* by the present sending of Tychicus and the writing of the letters which Tychicus and Onesimus were to bring (iv. 8).   From his remark in ii. 4 that he makes this statement in order that none of the Colossians may be deceived by persuasive words, we learn that effort had been made to induce the Church to believe that Paul did not concern himself about their Christian nurture.   It does not require much imagination to conceive how the matter was put.   There was no need to slander the apostles. All that was necessary was to point out how in the early years of his ministry he had no sooner founded a Church than he restlessly pressed forward to some new mission station, and how now for a number of years he had been in prison, first in Cæsarea, and now in the more distant Rome.   We can see also how such remarks were well adapted to prepare the way for a doctrine which promised to lead beyond the crude beginnings of faith which had resulted from the preaching of Paul and of Paul's disciple, Epaphras, to a deeper knowledge and a fuller sanctification.   Paul opposes this teaching in ii. 8–23.

The most obvious conclusion to be drawn from this series of warnings is that the false teachers, whose dangerous influence Paul here opposes, had given the Colossian Christians regulations, more especially negative rules about food and drink, and commandments about the observation of fasts, new moons, and Sabbaths (ii. 16, 20 f.).   At the same time they criticised the Colossians for not having observed these regulations heretofore, declaring that if they persisted in their former way of living they could not attain blessedness nor indeed Christian perfection (n. 3). In opposition to this derogatory judgment of the Colossians' Christianity, Paul assures them that in Christ, as He has been preached to them and received by them through faith, they possess all essential blessings (ii. 10), and that this Christ is at once the source and the foundation of a life well pleasing to God (ii. 6 f.). Although they do need the prayers and the care of the apostle and of his helpers in order to attain the fullest Christian knowledge and the highest moral culture (i. 9–11, 28 f., ii. 1–5), there is, on the other hand, no necessity that they be brought to this state of full knowledge and true morality through doctrines entirely new to them.

The very mention of the Sabbath proves that the representatives of this doctrine belonged to Judaism. And only by assuming that he is speaking in opposition to such representatives of the circumcision, is it possible to explain why Paul reminds these Colossian Christians, who had been converted from heathenism, that in baptism they have received a circumcision which in comparison with that of the Jews is much more comprehensive and more fundamentally sanctifying (ii. 11–13, cf. i. 21). Similarly, what he says in ii. 14 about the setting aside through the death of Christ of the law as evidence of our guilt and as an accusation against us, and in ii. 17 of the ordinances of the law as being only the foreshadowing of the real blessings which have appeared in Christ, is manifestly directed against a Judaism which held firmly to the law. That the representatives of this propaganda were at the same time Christians, or pretended to be, is self-evident, otherwise they could never have come to exert a dangerous influence in a Gentile Christian Church. This is clear also from ii. 19. For only one who acknowledged Christ to be the head of the Church (i. 18) could be criticised for not retaining his connection with this head. Similarly, the criticisms of Paul, and of the defectiveness of the Christianity of the Pauline Churches (above, p. 462 f.) to be inferred from ii. 1–5, presuppose the Christian profession of the false teachers. They were Jewish Christians. But they did not teach simply the obligation of Gentile Christians to keep the Mosaic law. If, like the false teachers in Galatia, they had demanded of the Gentile Christians submission to the law, and the unconditional acceptance of circumcision, it is certain that Paul would have fought this radical demand directly and fundamentally, instead of contenting himself as he does with the statement of certain incidental consequences of their principal demand. The emphasis which Paul lays upon the spiritual circumcision of the Gentile Christians (ii. 11) is fully explained, and in its setting can only be explained on the assumption that the false teachers made the Gentile Christians feel the superiority of their Jewish training, religious and moral (Rom. ii. 17–29; 2 Cor. xi. 22). Furthermore, the regulations which they laid upon the Gentile Christians and by which they criticised the manner in which the Gentile Christians had been living, were not simply the Mosaic commandments and restrictions (n. 4). The reference is rather to regulations which, though derived from the Mosaic law in their most essential parts, were less comprehensive than the law, while in other parts they were more elaborate. This was why Paul was able to call these δόγματα (ii. 20, δογματίζεσθε), commandments and teaching of men (ii. 22 after Isa. xxix. 13, cf. Matt. xv. 9), thereby distinguishing them from the δόγματα (ii. 14) of the revealed law, and in general to treat them with the contempt that he does in ii. 20–23.

The means by which this doctrine of men works its treacherous effects is declared in ii. 8 to be philosophy. In the same passage also it is said that the traditions of men, which those who would lead them astray establish as a norm, have as their standard not Christ, but the

elements of the world (n. 5). Assuming in the light
of ii. 16–23 that by παράδοσις τῶν ἀνθρώπων in ii. 8 is
meant a summary of moral-ascetic rules (cf. Mark
vii. 3–13; Matt. xv. 2–6; 1 Cor. xi. 2; 1 Thess. ii. 15,
iii. 6), it follows that the false teachers must have
based their demands for abstinence from certain foods
and drinks upon some theory relative partly to the
materials out of which they were composed, and by which
their consistency was maintained, and partly to the effects
of these materials upon those who used them. Their
regulations regarding abstinence they derived from their
theory that even the life of the Christian was interwoven
with that of nature, and that mental and spiritual life
were dependent upon matter (ii. 20). Only by asceticism, they argued, was it possible for the Christian to
obtain the adequate freedom from matter and the forces
by which matter is ruled. If these ascetic tendencies
were like those common in antiquity, particularly if they
resembled those with which Paul has to do in Rom. xiv.,
there can be little doubt that chief among the things forbidden by the false teachers were meat and wine, the
forms of nourishment which were the heartiest and which
tended most to arouse the passions. A further element
in their teaching is disclosed by the fact that, in the midst
of his polemic against these teachers, Paul takes occasion
to emphasise the truth that Christ is exalted above all
spiritual powers (ii. 10, cf. i. 16), and by his further
statement that the God who has become manifest in
Christ has stripped off from Himself the ruling spirits
which hitherto had concealed Him from the gaze of men,
and has openly shown as a conqueror would do in a
triumphal procession that these spirits have been subdued
and are subordinate to Him (ii. 15). It is evident that
the false teachers claimed that the power of the spirit-
princes, deified in the heathen world, continued to be
exerted over Christians. Their harmful influence is not

limited to idolatrous worship (1 Cor. x. 14–22 ; 2 Cor. vi. 14 f.), but the connection between them and matter in general, or the separate elements of matter, is so close that the Christian who lives in the world, particularly the Christian who lives in the unclean heathen world, is able to escape the destructive influence of these spirit-powers that rule over matter only by stern asceticism and merciless mortifying of the body (ii. 23).   It was with this in view that Paul testified to the Colossians earlier in the letter (i. 12 f.) that through the call of the gospel, which they had accepted by faith, God had made them capable of sharing the heavenly inheritance of the Church, at the same time releasing them, as He did all Christians, from the dominion of the powers of darkness, and translating them into the kingdom of His beloved Son.   Consequently what is said further with reference to Christ (i. 14–23) is not a speculative outburst, more or less relevant, but in every particular is determined by opposition to this un-wholesome teaching about sanctification and to the dual-istic view of the world underlying it, and is designed to remind the readers of the common principles of the Christian faith.   Christians have no further need to redeem themselves, for in the forgiveness of sin bestowed upon them by Christ they have redemption (i. 14).   Nor is there any world independent of Christ and of the God who finds His image in Christ, and who dwells in Him.   The worlds of matter and of spirit alike are in Christ, the first-begotten of all creatures, and were created through Him and for Him (i. 15–17).   True, this ideal relation estab-lished at creation is not yet entirely realised.   But in the Church, which is the existing form of the kingdom of Christ, the risen Christ has now a body of which He is the sole head, and this is the hopeful beginning of the restoration of the world to harmony under His headship (i. 18).   By the same death of Jesus on the cross through which the Gentiles, who once were strangers to God and

hostile to Him, have been brought into relations of peace
with Him (i. 21), all discord in the world has been fundamentally overcome (i. 20).   Consequently, in order to be
holy in the sight of Christ, blameless and unaccused,
Christians only need to hold fast without wavering their
faith in the gospel which offers the hope of a final consummation of all things (i. 22 f.).   Thus the statements of
i. 12–23 are seen to be in harmony with the picture of the
false teachers who had come among the Colossians, which
we get from the clearer statements of chap. ii.; whereas to
admit that the old interpretation is correct, according to
which these teachers are represented in ii. 18 as worship-
ping angels, would be to introduce into the picture an in-
congruous element (n. 6).   In the first place, it is hardly
conceivable that Paul should have merely mentioned
incidentally what to him and to every orthodox Jew and
Christian of the apostolic age must have seemed a form of
idolatry as being simply a hobby of these false teachers,
instead of warning the Colossians against such idolatry.
It is hard to see, moreover, how the charge of angel-
worship could be associated with the charge of groundless
vanity and worldly arrogance, without, at least, a hint that
there was no connection between the two.   Equally difficult to explain is the fact that when he comes to speak of
this θρησκεία a second time (ii. 23) the angels are not
mentioned at all, but this supposed cult is simply charged
with arbitrariness.   Finally, in both passages θρησκεία is
very closely connected with ταπεινοφροσύνη, being dependent upon the same preposition.   Naturally the meaning
here cannot be that feeling of humility so highly praised by
Paul (Col. iii. 12 ; Eph. iv. 2 ; Phil. ii. 3 ; cf. Acts xx. 19 ;
Phil. ii. 8 ; Matt. xi. 29), but only an outward demeanour
which could be associated with the worldly haughtiness of
which these same persons are accused.   The word is not
used by Paul in this sense, and if taken by him from the
sayings of the false teachers (n. 7), we should naturally

expect it to be qualified in some way, especially where he uses it for the first time, *i.e.* we should expect τῶν ἀγγέλων to go with ταπεινοφροσύνῃ as well as with θρησκείᾳ. This is the most natural construction grammatically, for otherwise the ἐν would be repeated before θρησκείᾳ. Therefore the genitive τῶν ἀγγέλων stands in the same relation to both conceptions. But now if by ταπεινοφροσύνῃ τῶν ἀγγέλων can be meant such a demeanour as is adapted to or possible for angels, and for this reason is not adapted to men who have bodies, the same is true also of θρησκεία τῶν ἀγγέλων. The former denotes self-mortification, the latter a form of devotion, a manner of living in which men endeavour as far as possible to imitate spirits, which neither eat nor drink (n. 7). Whoever undertakes to do this certainly attempts a dangerous feat and betrays an unreasonable vanity, because he undertakes what in the nature of man and the conditions of his life is impossible. Although these ascetic practices are supposed to honour God, as a matter of fact they honour no one; they simply serve to gratify that worldly pride in which they have their source (ii. 23, cf. 18). Jewish pride, heightened by an ascetic austerity, by means of manifold judgments, verdicts, prescriptions, and instructions, had made a moral impression upon the uncircumcised Christians in Colossæ from which Paul endeavours to free them.

It has already been shown that this purpose not only dominates the discussions of chap. ii., but also determines the progress of thought in chap. i. in many ways, also the choice of language. It also dominates entirely the exhortations of iii. 1–17. In contrast with the misleading instructions regarding sanctification, against which the Church was warned in chap. ii., Paul now sets forth wherein genuine Christian sanctification consists. It is based not upon speculative investigation and arbitrary distinctions between the material elements and forces in the world, but

upon fellowship with the Christ who has been raised from
the dead and exalted to share with God dominion over the
world (iii. 1–4). In the Christian life the significant thing
is not the distinction between circumcised Jews and uncircumcised Greeks or barbarians, but a second birth or
new creation constantly appropriated anew (iii. 9–11). The
readers must not permit themselves to be disturbed by outside criticisms (ii. 16, 18), but are to let the peace which
comes from Christ have exclusive rule in their hearts, where
He dwells, and allow all questions to be decided under its
influence (iii. 15). If they give the word which comes from
Christ proper chance to unfold in all its richness, they will
not need to be instructed from outside by worldly wisdom
(ii. 8), but will be able adequately to instruct and to correct
one another (iii. 16). And the consciousness of the grace
which they have experienced will produce not only proper
feelings for the government of their intercourse among
themselves (iii. 12–14), but also a sense of gratitude to
God which will find joyful expression in inward thanksgiving and in all that they say and do (iii. 15*b*, 16*b*, 17).
That in the exhortations which follow relative to mutual
obligations within the home, by far the most space should
be given to the discussion of the relation between slaves
and their masters (iii. 22–iv. 1), is natural in view of the
contents of the letter to Philemon which was sent simultaneously with that to Colossæ. But, taking the section
(iii. 18–iv. 6) as a whole in its exhoration against all bitterness, especially against everything that might cause
bitterness (iii. 19, 21, iv. 1), its further reminder of the
necessity of thanksgiving which is to be a part of every
prayer (iv. 2), and its exhortation to the use of polite
language in their intercourse with their non-Christian
neighbours (iv. 6), there is presented the attractive picture
of a joyful Christian life lived in the midst of an evil
world, which contrasts favourably with the gloomy asceticism which Paul has been combating in the earlier sections

of the letter. Between the tendency opposed in chap. ii.,
indeed throughout this entire Epistle,—and the Judaisers
who once disturbed the Churches in the adjacent province
of Galatia, or the followers of Peter who carried on their
work in Corinth, there is no discoverable relation. There
is nothing to indicate that the teachers who caused confusion in Colossæ came from abroad. It is altogether
improbable that members of the Jewish monastic order of
the Essenes, who were settled in Palestine, would have
come to Colossæ (n. 8). False ascetic movements, such
as Paul combats in Col. ii.,—movements quite independent
of these orders,—are to be found among the Jewish Christians in Rome (above, p. 366 f., 376) and the readers of
Hebrews. Of the large Jewish population in the district
of Laodicea (above, p. 448, n. 2), there were probably some
who became members of the Christian Church in Colossæ,
and among these there may have been those who were
ascetic in their tendencies, who had some philosophic
training, and who were dissatisfied with the simple gospel
preached by Epaphras, and with the resultant type of life
among the Gentile Christians. Possibly there was an
individual of some importance (n. 9) who started the
whole movement that caused Epaphras so much trouble,
and that it was this that influenced Paul to send a special
letter to Colossæ, at the same time he despatched a circular letter of a more general character to the larger
group of Churches, of which this Church was one.

1. (P. 461.) The metaphor of οἰκονομία, οἰκονόμος is applied in 1 Cor.
ix. 17 to the calling of the missionary preacher; on the contrary, it refers
here, as in Tit. i. 7 (cf. 1 Tim. i. 4, iii. 4 f., 15 ; Luke xii. 42 ; Matt. xvi.
19, xxv. 45) to a service to the Church. The two ideas are not distinguished
in 1 Cor. iv. 1 ; Eph. iii. 2–9. The expression πληρῶσαι τὸν λόγον τοῦ θεοῦ,
i. 25, finds its analogy, so far as form is concerned, in Rom. xv. 19 ; 2 Tim.
iv. 17. But there the fulness of the gospel or of the preaching which is
attained, or is to be attained, refers to the extent of territory in which the
gospel is to be preached. Here the matter in hand is not missionary
preaching to the unconverted at all, but the word of God, as the "servant of
the Church" should offer it to the members of the Church, and as these
should constantly appropriate it (cf. iii. 16 ; Jas. i. 21 ; 1 Pet. ii. 2 ; 2 Pet. ii.

12; 1 Cor. ii. 6, xii. 8; 2 Tim. ii. 15, iv. 2). The antithesis to the incompleteness which πληρῶσαι indicates is expressed also by the διδάσκειν ἐν πάσῃ σοφίᾳ, i. 28 (cf. ii. 2, iii. 16), and the moral aim of this complete introduction to the knowledge of Christianity was expressed before, i. 9 f.

2. (P. 462.) Since Paul is not sending a treatise to the Colossian Church, but is writing them a letter, the present writer takes it as self-evident that the general statements in i. 25–29 are there for the sake of the particular statements in ii. 1–5, and not vice versa. Naturally the connection by means of γάρ does not hinder this interpretation, and the phrase θέλω ὑμᾶς εἰδέναι (1 Cor. xi. 3; Phil. i. 12)=οὐ θέλω ὑμᾶς ἀγνοεῖν (Rom. i. 13, xi. 25; 1 Cor. x. 1, xii. 1; 1 Thess. iv. 13), gives to the statement thus introduced a peculiar weight. In ver. 2 συμβιβασθέντες ἐν ἀγάπῃ cannot mean "knit together in love" (cf. ii. 19; Eph. iv. 16); for (1) it would have to be taken at best as a result of the encouragement, which, however, is not permitted by the syntax of the sentence; (2) the conception of a loving union of the members of the Church is entirely foreign to the thought in the context; (3) we should not know what to do with the following καί, the genuineness of which is undoubted. Here, then, συμβιβάζειν with a personal object has no essentially different meaning from the common one, "to teach, advise" (Ex. iv. 12–15; Lev. x. 11; Isa. xl. 13, 14; cf. 1 Cor. ii. 16), and so "to induce" to a particular act or motion (Acts xix. 33). At the same time, the basic meaning of βιβάζειν, "to cause to go," is brought out, so that συμβιβάζειν means "so to set one in motion that he shall choose and keep to a definite way, without turning to right or left" (cf. Ps. xxxii. 8). Hence also a goal may be mentioned (εἰς πᾶν πλοῦτος) to which one is directed, or a region into which he is led. καί must mean "also," cf. Hofmann, iv. 2. 51. Since the mere assurance that all the treasures of wisdom and knowledge were hidden in Christ, guards in no way against the danger of being misled by a speculation which ignored Christ, and since this misleading is not discussed at all until ver. 8, ver. 4 cannot refer to the subordinate clause in ver. 3, but to the main sentence, vv. 1, 2. In no other way can the progression in ver. 5 be explained.

3. (P. 464.) The reading in ii. 16, presupposed probably by the ancient Syrians (S¹, Ephr. Comm. in Epist. Pauli, Lat. ed. Mechith. p. 175), κιρνάτω instead of κρινέτω, which Lagarde, Proph. Chaldaïce, p. li, recommended, has against it not only the analogy of Rom. xiv. 3, 4, 10, 13, but also the construction ἐν βρώσει instead of περὶ βρώσεως κτλ. Moreover, καταβραβεύειν, ver. 18, is also a sort of κρίνειν. It indicates originally, at any rate, like βραβεύειν (Col. iii. 15) and παραβραβεύειν (Plutarch, Mor. 535 C, the unfair decision of an umpire; Polyb. xxiv. 1. 12, of any judge), an action of the βραβεύς, βραβευτής, or ἀγωνοθέτης, and that, too, of a character unfavourable to the contestant. This word, which occurs very seldom in literature (Demosth. c. Midiam, p. 544; Eusthat. Schol. in Il. i. 402 f., p. 93, ὡς οἱ παλαιοὶ λέγουσιν; ibid. De Thessal. Capta, ed. Tafel, 277), and which Jerome wrongly considered a Cilician provincialism (Epist. cxxi, Vall. i. 879), may have been used to denote various other relationships without much regard for its original meaning; but we have no cause for assuming that such was the case here; for Paul elsewhere, in using figures taken from the games, shows what a lively conception of these he had (1 Cor. ix. 24–27; Phil. iii.

14 ; 2 Tim. ii. 5, iv. 7 f.). Taking this word alone, we might conclude, quite consistently with this view, that Paul was here exhorting members of the Church not to allow themselves to be actually robbed of the blessedness set before them, for which as a prize they were wrestling or running (cf. Rev. iii. 11) ; for the umpire's judgment decides whether or not the prize shall be received. But this interpretation is here excluded by the connection and by the nature of the question. In the spiritual contest God or Christ alone in reality confers the βραβεῖον (1 Cor. ix. 24 ; Phil. iii. 14), the στέφανος (1 Cor. ix. 25 ; 2 Tim. iv. 8 ; Jas. i. 12 ; Rev. ii. 10). Men who arrogate to themselves the κρίνειν, βραβεύειν, καταβραβεύειν, and δογματίζειν, can, by presuming thus to deprive a contestant of his prize, render him in the highest degree discouraged, fearful—in general, confused. The Colossians should let no one treat them thus.

4. (P. 465.) The priests must abstain from wine and other intoxicating drinks before serving in the sanctuary (Lev. x. 9), likewise the Nazarites as long as their vow lasted (Num. vi. 2–4) ; cf. Luke i. 15, and above, p. 376 on Rom. xiv.

5. (P. 466.) Although τὰ στοιχεῖα denotes the heavenly bodies, especially the planets (cf. Valesius on Eus. *H. E.* iii. 31. 3 ; perhaps 2 Pet. iii. 10, certainly Just. *Apol.* ii. 5, τὰ οὐράνια στ. ; *Dial.* xxiii ; Theoph. *ad Autol.* i. 4, 5, 6, ii. 15 ; Clem. *Hom.* x. 25), it cannot denote these in ii. 8, 20 ; Gal. iv. 3, 9, because of the added τοῦ κόσμου. Further, it is not the observance of festivals, which, it is true, depends upon the course of the heavenly bodies, but the abstinence from certain kinds of food, a custom having nothing whatever to do with sun, moon, and stars, which is designated in ii. 20 f. as incompatible with ἀπεθάνετε ἀπὸ τῶν στοιχείων τ. κ., ii. 20 f. Paul understands by τὰ στοιχεῖα τ. κ., nothing else but the κόσμος itself, and this as composed of manifold material elements. This is shown by the exchange of the one expression for the other in ii. 20 (cf. iii. 2), and confirmed by a comparison of this passage with Gal. vi. 14. Latterly the view has been constantly gaining ground that Paul means here and in Gal. iv. 3, 9 the elemental spirits, or particularly the spirits animating the heavenly bodies (Klöpper, *Kol.* 360–389 ; Spitta, *Zw. Petr.* 260–270 ; Eveling, *Paul Angelologie*, 65–74, 92–96. Whom also Diels unfortunately followed in his otherwise so instructive writing, *Elementum*, 1899). But this meets an insuperable obstacle in the expression itself ; for while it is quite conceivable that "substances, elements," came to mean "bodies, heavenly bodies," it is incredible that it should serve to indicate its opposite, the spirits animating the substances or ruling the bodies. The confused late Christian *Testament of Solomon* (Fabric. *Cod. pseudep. vet. Test.* 1047, cf. Eveling, 70 ; Schürer, iii. 304 [Eng. trans. II. iii. 154]), in which the evil spirits call themselves τὰ λεγόμενα στοιχεῖα (Col. ii. 8), οἱ κοσμοκράτορες τοῦ κόσμου τούτου (Eph. vi. 12), and also στοιχεῖα τοῦ κοσμοκράτορος τοῦ σκότους, is palpably dependent upon misconstrued passages of the N.T., and for this reason alone cannot attest a usage which Paul may have followed. Cf. *ZKom. Gal.* 195 ff., 208 f. From Col. ii. 15 and the other passages in which Paul speaks of (good or evil) spiritual powers (i. 13, 16, 20, ii. 10), it follows simply that the false teachers ascribed to these a power to which Christians also were subject as inhabitants of the material world, in spite of their redemption through

Christ. Since these false teachers were Jews, it becomes certain that they regarded material nature as the spirits' special province, and that therefore they viewed asceticism as a means of emancipation, not only from matter, but also from the power of the spirits who ruled in it. The exegetical difficulties of ii. 10-15, which Hofmann was the first to handle, on the whole happily, can be touched upon here only lightly. The "better commentators" (Klöpper, 422), among whom none of the Greeks from Origen down are reckoned, nor Lightfoot and Hofmann—at whose head rather Ambrosiaster and Jerome are placed—are of the opinion that ἀπεκδύεσθαι, ii. 15, contrary to all usage (Col. iii. 9, ii. 11, cf. iii. 10 and ἐκδύεσθαι, ἐνδύεσθαι, δύεσθαι everywhere else), means here to strip from another his clothing or armour, to disarm him. This opinion, beyond all others, seems to the present writer an inexcusable caprice. God did not rob the spiritual powers of their clothing or their weapons, but stripped from Himself these spirits who were enveloping Him as a garment or a mist, and were hiding Him from the sight of men. It was not, however, to Israel, but to the Gentile world, that God was veiled by these spiritual powers, these λεγόμενοι θεοί (1 Cor. viii. 5). It was in the Gentile world, then, that God put these away from Himself and showed Himself in His true form to the Gentiles who had been too blind to see Him, thus at the same time setting these sham gods in their true light, while in Christ He celebrated a triumph over them, and bade them also march as captives behind Him. But this naturally did not happen at the crucifixion of Jesus ; it came about through the preaching of the gospel among the Gentiles, attended as it was by signs and wonders (cf. e.g. Acts xvi. 16-18, xix. 11-20). Since Paul is seeking to guard a Gentile Church (cf. i. 21, 27, ii. 13a, iii. 5-7) against being led astray, he begins and ends the exposition of the grace shown by God to mankind in and through Christ (ii. 11-15) with what has been experienced in the sphere of the Gentile world on the basis of the work of redemption accomplished in Israel. If in the midst of this he passes from the address to Gentile Christian readers to a statement about himself and those like him, which fits only Christians who have come out of Judaism, it is no digression. For the working of saving grace in the Gentile world depends upon what has happened in Israel. In fact, Paul says just this in ii. 14. He regards the law first as a bond or a bill of indictment testifying against the Jews, then as a wall of partition between Jews and Gentiles. The law became the former, since Israel, on the one hand, by his solemn vow to keep the law (Ex. xxiv. 3 ; Deut. xxvi. 16-28, 69) had made it, as it were, a bond written or signed by his own hand (Luke xvi. 6 ; Philem. 19) ; but, on the other hand, Israel has not met the obligation thereby assumed, has not paid the sum of money thus recognised as due, and, moreover, has no prospect of ever being able to pay off the debt. This bond God has blotted out ; He has stricken out, as we would say, the statement of debit written thereon. But He has also taken the "handwriting" itself out of the "midst" by nailing it to the cross. Paul distinguishes the bond itself from what stood written upon it and was blotted out by God, i.e. the law itself from the duties of Israel written in it, in so far as these, by being left undone, have come to indicate an equal number of debts of Israel. Quite separate from this significance of the law as a bond testifying against Israel, the law was in itself a dividing barrier, a hedge between Israel and the Gentile peoples (Eph. ii. 14). From this position which the law occupied in the midst of mankind, as was well known (hence ἐκ τοῦ μέσου with the article), and from the earth altogether, on which it formed a dividing wall of partition, God has removed the law, nailing it to the cross of Christ. Beneath the cross Jews and Gentiles who believe on the Crucified now join hands, the barrier of the law not being able to sunder them any more (Col. i. 20, iii. 11; Eph. ii. 11–22). The division of the sentences causes difficulties. Probably Paul originally intended to say all that stands between ἐν ᾧ, ii. 11, and ἐν αὐτῷ, ii. 15, in a single relative sentence. But on being developed this proved so rich that after συνηγέρθητε, ii. 12, three independent sentences arose (συνεζωοποίησεν — ἦρκεν — ἐδειγμάτισεν). The present writer translates : "For in Him dwelleth the whole fulness of the Godhead in bodily fashion, and ye are filled (fully) in Him who is the head of all principality and power ; in whom ye also were circumcised with a circumcision not performed by hand through the putting off of the fleshly body, through the circumcision of Christ, buried with Him in baptism, in which ye were also awakened with Him (shared in His resurrection). Through faith in the working of God, who awakened Him from the dead, hath He (God) made you also (Gentile Christians), who were dead by reason of your lapses and your fleshly uncircumcision, alive with Him (Christ). After He (God) in grace forgave us (Jewish Christians) all our lapses, by blotting out the bond (which testified) against us, which was opposed to us on account of the statutes, He took this itself (the bond) out of the midst, nailing it to the cross. After He (God) put away from Himself (as a garment) the lordships and authorities, He made an exhibition of them (set them before the gaze of all as that which they really are), while He led them in triumph openly in Him (in Christ)."

6. (P. 468.) The usual conception of Col. ii. 18, together with an exaggeration of the thought in Gal. iv. 8–10, first meets us in the Κήρυγμα Πέτρου, written perhaps as early as 100 (cf. *GK*, i. 823, ii. 822–832). According to Clement, *Strom.* vi. 41, Peter preached in this production as follows :—μηδὲ κατὰ Ἰουδαίους σέβεσθε· καὶ γὰρ ἐκεῖνοι, μόνοι οἰόμενοι τὸν θεὸν γινώσκειν, οὐκ ἐπίστανται, λατρεύοντες ἀγγέλοις καὶ ἀρχαγγέλοις, μηνὶ καὶ σελήνῃ. καὶ ἐὰν μὴ σελήνη φανῇ, σάββατον οὐκ ἄγουσι τὸ λεγόμενον πρῶτον οὐδὲ νεομηνίαν ἄγουσιν οὔτε ἄζυμα οὔτε ἑορτὴν οὔτε μεγάλην ἡμέραν. Aristides, who says something similar in *Apol.* xiv. 4, is plainly dependent upon the *Preaching of Peter* (*GK*, ii. 823 ; Seeberg in *Forsch.* v. 216, 393). The Gnostic Heracleon (quoted in Orig. *in Jo.* xiii. 17) cites the passage in the *Preaching of Peter.* Celsus (in Orig. *c. Celsum*, i. 26, v. 6) charges the Jews with praying to the angels and also to the heavens ; but this charge probably rests simply upon a superficial knowledge of Aristides' *Apology* (cf. Seeberg, *Forsch.* v. 233–237). Origen could reject this as a slander against Judaism that betrayed its own ignorance, not only on the basis of the O.T., but also in virtue of his wide and varied acquaintance with the Judaism of his time. He was right with respect to orthodox Judaism ; cf. Hamburger, *Realenc.* i. 507, who only should not have adduced as an exception to the rule Tob. iii. 26 (iii. 16 f.), in which he adopted a senseless reading (see Fritzsche, *Libri Apocr.* p. 116 in the Apparatus). After Jesus had unreservedly

professed adherence to the strict monotheism of His people (Mark xii. 29 ;
John xvii. 3 ; Matt. iv. 10), His true worshippers also, who had been brought
up in Judaism, could but turn away from every act of adoration of the
spirits subordinate to God (Rev. xix. 10, xxii. 8 f.), and Paul in particular
could not judge such worship otherwise than as idolatry (cf. Rom. i. 25 with
Col. i. 16 ; further, 1 Cor. viii. 4–6). Even among the Essenes, who, on
account of their alleged abstinence from flesh and wine (above, p. 376), have
been cited so often to explain the tendency opposed in Col. ii., no such
angel cultus can be proved to have existed. It may be, indeed, that their
secrecy about angels' names (Jos. Bell. ii. 8. 7) was connected with all sorts
of speculation about the angels, and that their botanical and mineralogical
investigations (Bell. ii. 8. 6) served speculative as well as medicinal ends.
But how far this was from worship of the angels is seen from the fact that
next to the name of God that of Moses was the most sacred (Bell. ii.
8. 9, 10). The Jewish Christian sects also, which seem related to Essenism,
held fast to the exclusive worship of the one God. To know the angels'
names (Clem. Hom. iii. 36) may be a valuable esoteric science (cf. even Ign.
Trall. v). But if we infer angelolatry from the statement of the Book of the
Elkesaites (Hippol. Refut. ix. 15 ; Epiph. xxx. 17), that among other things
"the angels of prayer" also should be invoked as witnesses of baptism, we
should infer from the same ritual that salt and oil were worshipped. Whoever concludes from Just. Apol. i. 6, or from the representations of angels in
the Shepherd of Hermas, that there was angelolatry in the Church, proves too
much, and therefore nothing at all. So long as we take θρησκεία τῶν
ἀγγέλων as a θρησκεία which has the angels for its object, we must understand by it simply a cult devoted to the angels, and not also a speculative
pursuit of the doctrine of angels or a superstitious veneration of them. It
was an arbitrary weakening of the conception (cf. n. 7) when Chrysostom
(Montfaucon, xi. 323, 372 ; cf. Severianus in Cramer's Catenæ, vii. 325)
thought of a mediation of our intercourse with God through the angels, or
when Theodore (ed. Swete, ii. 294) understood an indirect veneration of them
through observance of the law given by angels and the fear of the wrath of
angels who watched over the observance of the law. Ephrem came to a
view related essentially to these in that he took τῶν ἀγγέλων as subjective
genitive, but, in accordance with Syrian tradition, understood by the angels
the priests, and here the Jewish priests (Comm. in ep. Pauli, p. 175, "Ne
quis . . . seducat vos neque transmutet in legem angelorum, in doctrinam
nimirum sacerdotum"; cf. p. 57 on 1 Cor. vi. 3 ; Carm. Nisib. xlii. 10 ;
Aphraates, Hom. xxii, p. 432, under appeal to Mal. ii. 7). The Latins, plainly
at variance with the context, understood by superstitio or religio or cultura
angelorum a direct or indirect deification of nature, not by Jews, but by
Gentiles (Ambrosiaster, in Col. ii. 18 ; Augustine, Epist. cxlix. 27, ad Paul-
inum). These explanations and the silence of the ancient writers against
heresies concerning angelolatry in heretical circles (Epiphanius alone gives
any hint of it. He mentions, Hær. lx., a party of Ἀγγελικοί, but knows
nothing more of them than their name) show that circa 360–400 no angel
cult carried on by Christians which could be related to the error refuted
in Col. ii., was known in wider circles. Theodoret on Col. ii. 18, p. 290,
whom many moderns have followed (e.g. Lightfoot, 67, 71 ; Henle, 91), was

the first to seek to re-establish an historical connection between that error of apostolic times and the canons of the Council of Laodicea, *circa* 360 (*GK*, ii. 196). But certainly those decrees of this Council are not pertinent which forbid celebrating the Sabbath with Jews by resting from work (Can. 29), and receiving from Jews the presents which they were accustomed to send during their feasts, in particular the mazzoth (Can. 37, 38).   The question there was plainly not about an heretical tendency, a Judaistically coloured Christian doctrine or sect, but about real Jews.   We see that the numerous Jews of that region (above, p. 448 f., n. 2) carried on intercourse with their Christian neighbours, and induced them to make concessions to Jewish customs, in very much the same way as they do it elsewhere in the twentieth century.   The heretics, however, who are once classed with the Jews (Can. 37), but are elsewhere treated separately (Can. 6–10, 32–34), are anything but Judaists (Can. 7, 8).   The command (Can. 35) not to forsake the regular church worship for meetings in places where angels are adored, which is condemned as "secret idolatry," concerns neither Jews nor heretics.   Theodoret is probably right when he connects this command with the fact that in his time, about seventy to eighty years after the Synod of Laodicea, there existed in Phrygia and Pisidia, or particularly in Colossæ and the neighbourhood, chapels of St. Michael.   According to a legend (*Narratio de miraculo Chonis patrato*, ed. M. Bonnet, 1890 ; *Acta SS. Sept.* viii. 41–48), the apostles John and Philip, on visiting this region, foretold future miracles by the archangel, which, according to this same legend, are said to have taken place there ; and, many years after their death, a heathen priest built a small chapel to Michael as a thank-offering for the healing of his daughter, which took place there.   What was condemned as idolatry by the Council of Laodicea, and still later by Theodoret and Augustine (*De Vera Relig.* lv. 110 ; *Conf.* x. 42. 67), was soon appropriated, even by the Church.   A church built by Constantine not far from the Bosphorus was later named after St. Michael, on account of his appearances there in healing power (Sozom. *H. E.* ii. 3). In Byzantine times especially, the archangel was honoured in the interior of Asia Minor (cf. Batiffol, *Stud. patr.* i. 33 ff.; Ramsay, *Church in the Roman Empire*, 477, 480; *Cities and Bishop.* i. 541, 558, 741, Nos. 404, 441, 678). But what could this angel cult have to do with the Judaistic error of Paul's time ?   The decree of Laodicea shows clearly enough that the matter in hand was a heathen superstition in Christian garb and a merely local cult, which arose long after the time of the Apostles.   Also the legend mentioned above must be taken, in spite of the author's intention, as confirming this view.

7. (Pp. 468, 469.)   The strong Hebraism θέλων ἐν ταπεινοφροσύνῃ κτλ. (cf. Ps. cxii. 1, cxlvii. 10 ; 1 Sam. xviii. 22 ; 1 Chron. xxviii. 4 ; θέλειν, with infin., Mark xii. 38 = φιλεῖν, Matt. xxiii. 6), suggests the conjecture that Paul is here repeating expressions of the Judaists which Epaphras may have told him. This view is supported by the fact that ταπεινοφροσύνη, even if it is connected with τῶν ἀγγέλων (see above, p. 469), could not mean, according to Paul's individual usage, anything reprehensible or any external conduct corresponding to θρησκεία.   On the contrary, in Jewish phraseology ταπεινοῦν τὴν ψυχήν, Lev. xvi. 29, 31, xxiii. 27, 29, 32 ; Isa. lviii. 3 ; Ps. xxxv. 13, and ταπεινοῦσθαι, Ps. xxxv. 14 ; Ezra viii. 21 ; Sir. xviii. 20, xxxi. 26, mean "to mortify one's self" = νηστεύειν, which a scholion on Lev. xxiii.

27 substitutes for it (Field, *Hexapla*, i. 207); ταπείνωσις, Ezra ix. 5 = צנעה = νηστεία. The same meaning is attached to ταπεινοφρονεῖν, ταπεινοφοσύνη, ταπεινοφρόνησις, in the earliest speech of the Church (Herm. *Vis.* iii. 10. 6 f., *Sim.* v. 3. 7; Tert. *Jejun.* xii, xiii, xvi). To this expression so conceived is joined θρησκεία—a word used nowhere else by Paul—as a related idea; for this also indicates not a disposition, but an external religiosity, displayed especially in particular customs and a peculiar manner of life (above, p. 68, n. 3). The originally intransitive concept (Herodotus, ii. 18, 37, 64, 65) is used by later writers indeed transitively also, and then indicates the cult devoted to an object, essentially like λατρεία, λατρεύειν, with dat. (Wisd. of Sol. xi. 15, xiv. 16; Herodian, i. 11, 1, θρησκεύειν, with acc.). θρησκεία τῶν ἀγγέλων could then indicate a cult devoted to the angels, just as εἰδώλων θρησκεία, Wisd. of Sol. xiv. 27, means εἰδωλολατρεία. But this meaning is here excluded on stylistic, exegetical, and historical grounds (above, p. 469). There is therefore nothing to prevent taking τῶν ἀγγέλων as subjective genitive, and to connect it with both concepts as their necessary qualification. The subject in question is an ἄσκησις ἀγγελική, as the severe manner of life of the pious Archippus is called in the legend of the miracle at Colossæ (Bonnet, pp. 7. 11, 8. 7). The angels do not need to discipline themselves by abstaining from bodily enjoyments; but this did not hinder Paul from speaking thus any more than the circumstance that God does not grow, or that Christ did not Himself experience the baptism and circumcision of heart instituted by Him, or that we know nothing of the angels' speech, hindered him from speaking of γλῶσσαι τῶν ἀγγέλων (1 Cor. xiii. 1), or of περιτομὴ τοῦ Χριστοῦ (Col. ii. 11), or of αὔξησις τοῦ θεοῦ (Col. ii. 19). The false teachers probably taught that the Christian should become, as far as possible, an ἰσάγγελος (Luke xx. 36), a wrong striving after immateriality, which induced Paul elsewhere to call such doctrines διδασκαλίαι δαιμονίων (1 Tim. iv. 1). This interpretation finds its strongest support in ii. 23; for certainly after the analogy of similarly formed words ἐθελοθρησκεία cannot denote a cult which chooses its objects of worship arbitrarily; in this case these previously chosen objects must also have been mentioned. It may not be reprehensible in all circumstances to be a θρησκός; but he who makes it his aim to lead a peculiarly pious life beyond what God has commanded, *i.e.* of his own volition without higher commission and calling, is for this very reason to be blamed (cf. Jas. i. 26). Probably the ἐθελο- bears logically also upon ταπεινοφροσύνη, here so closely connected with θρησκεία. This pair of concepts is defined more closely by ἀφειδίᾳ σώματος, the meaning then being just this; an apparently pious manner of life, consisting essentially in an unsparing treatment of the body, that is, if with a few good authorities we strike out καί before ἀφειδίᾳ. The obscure words also which in ii. 18 are joined to the same pair of ideas seem to contain similarly a closer definition. Perhaps the only thing certain about them is that μή is a subsequent insertion (among the Syrians also, for Ephrem, p. 175, knew nothing of it) and that ἃ ἑόρακεν ἐμβατεύων gives no sense. Translations like that of von Soden (*HK*, iii. 55), "flaunting about with things that he has seen," are of course undeniably beautiful. The textual corruption which is surely here was found by so early a writer as Marcion, who read τῶν ἀγγέλων with this clause (*GK*, ii. 527). Among the

various conjectures, that of C. Taylor, ἀέρα κενεμβατεύων, is the most probable (Westcott-Hort, *Appendix*, 127 ; Lightfoot, *ad loc.*). This could mean the bold flight of an unfounded speculation (ἀεροβατεῖν, Aristoph. *The Clouds*, 225 ; Lucian, *Twice accused*, 33, or αἰθεροβατεῖν, Lucian, *Philopatris*, 25) quite as well as the vain effort by means of asceticism to break loose from earth and soar into higher regions. *Acta Andr.* chap. xiii. (Lipsius-Bonnet, ii. 43. 21) : οὐ κενεμβάτησεν (*sic cod.*), ἀλλ᾿ οἶδεν ὁ εἶπεν.

8. (P. 471.) Among the more recent commentators on Col., Lightfoot, pp. 73–113, who also added a valuable treatise on Essenism, 349–419, and Klöpper (1882), S. 58–119, have gone into special detail in trying to establish a closer connection between the errors combated here and Essenism. The chief reasons against this are :—(1) On comparing Col. ii. and Rom. xiv. we can hardly doubt that the false teachers in Colossæ forbade the use of flesh and wine ; but the Essenes set them no such example (see above, p. 376). (2) The most characteristic features of Essene customs and morality, such as the ablutions, the abstinence from marriage (cf. in brief, Schürer, ii. 568 [Eng. trans. II. ii. 200]), the absolute community of goods, the abolition of all slavery, the use of only such food as was prepared by the priests of the order, and all that is peculiar to this sect as a monastic order, could not have failed to leave a trace in Col. ii. if any of them had appeared among the false teachers there. Since they are all wanting, there is no discernible connection with Essenism to be found. (3) Moreover, the alleged angelolatry is not Essene (above, p. 476). (4) Pride in circumcision (ii. 11) and observance of feast days (ii. 16) were common to all Jews.

9. (P. 471.) In comparison with the way in which reference is made to the Judaists in Gal. i. 7, iv. 17, v. 12, vi. 12 (along with the collective singular, v. 10), and to the Cephas party in 2 Cor. ii. 17–iii. 1, v. 12, xi. 12–23 (above, pp. 167, line 17 f., 306), it is worth noting that nothing in Col. ii. 8, 16–23 points to a plurality of false teachers. Especially, the singulars μηδείς . . . θέλων, ἐμβατεύων, φυσιούμενος, κρατῶν, ii. 18 f., instead of which μηδείς . . . τῶν θελόντων κτλ. could have been written (cf. 1 Tim. vi. 5), seem more natural if Paul had in mind a single influential person.

§ 28. THE DESTINATION OF THE EPISTLE TO THE EPHESIANS.

In the same passage in which Paul charges the Colossian Church to see to it that the letter directed to them be read also to the congregation of the Church in Laodicea, he speaks of a " letter from Laodicea " which the Colossians were not to leave unread (Col. iv. 16, n. 1). Since Paul does not deem it necessary to say who wrote this letter, it is evident that, like Colossians, it was written by himself. Those who on the strength of this passage assumed that it refers to a letter directed by Paul to the

Laodiceans, and in the absence of such an Epistle composed the apocryphal *Epistle to the Laodiceans* (n. 2),
failed to give due weight to the peculiar expression τὴν
ἐκ Λαοδικείας. Marcion made the same mistake when he
identified the alleged letter to the Laodiceans with the
canonical Epistle to the Ephesians, and changed its title
to πρὸς Λαοδικέας (n. 3). If at the same time that he wrote
Colossians, Paul directed a special letter to the Laodiceans,
it is difficult to explain why he instructed the Colossians
to convey greetings to the entire Laodicean Church together with one of the household Churches in that place
(iv. 15). The reference must be, rather, to a letter which
he directed to be sent among other places to Laodicea
and "from Laodicea" to be forwarded to Colossæ, *i.e.* it
was a circular letter to the group of Churches to which
Laodicea and Colossæ belonged. That such a letter from
the apostle should be read in all the Churches whither it
was brought by Paul's messenger, and read before the
assembled congregations (iv. 16, ἐν τῇ Λαοδ. ἐκκλ. ; cf.
1 Thess. v. 27), we can readily understand. But having
received beforehand a private letter from Paul, the
Colossian Church might have thought that this letter to
the larger group of Churches of which they were one was
of no special importance to them. In iv. 16 it was taken
for granted that the Colossians would receive the letter
directed to them before they received the one from Laodicea, otherwise the Colossians naturally would not have
failed to read the circular letter directed to them with other
Churches. Furthermore, if Paul or Tychicus directed
Onesimus, who was going directly to Colossæ, to deliver
Colossians as well as Philemon (above, p. 459 f.), Colossians
would necessarily have reached Colossæ before the circular
letter which was to be read to the congregations of all
the Churches to which it was directed. Of this circular
letter Tychicus must have been the bearer, for otherwise
he would not have had occasion to go to Colossæ, and in

all probability he would not have been mentioned at all in iv. 7 f. Now, from Eph. vi. 21 f. we learn that Tychicus was actually to visit on his journey other Christians besides those at Colossæ, to inform them concerning Paul, and to deliver to them the letter at the conclusion of which this notice stands. Putting together the inference from Col. iv. 7–ix. 16 and the clear statement of Eph. vi. 21 f., the conclusion follows inevitably. Marcion's explanation of Col. iv. 16 is not exactly correct, but for having discovered in the verse the so-called Epistle to the Ephesians he deserves the title, *diligentissimus explorator*, which his opponent gives him, not without a touch of contempt. In taking this position Marcion broke with a tradition of the Church thoroughly established in his time and persistently held afterwards. Marcion's criticism of the traditional title πρὸς Ἐφεσίους, and his substitution of the title πρὸς Λαοδικέας (or Λαοδικεῖς) were not made on the ground of any tradition, but for critical reasons which may have been set forth in his *Antitheses*. Even Ignatius seems to have known the letter by its Ephesian title (*GK*, i. 819). In view of the unanimity on this point of the tradition of the Church which can be traced back to the beginning of the second century, we are justified in assuming that the Epistle had this title when it was incorporated into the collection of Pauline letters which afterwards came into general circulation in the Church. At the same time, this title is not only without support from the original text of the Epistle, but stands in irreconcilable contradiction to the entire character of the letter. Neither Tertullian nor Marcion read the words ἐν Ἐφέσῳ in i. 1, which would have disagreed with Marcion's title, since Tertullian does not criticise Marcion for changing here the text of the Epistle as he did so many other passages, but only for altering the title of the letter on the basis of alleged careful investigations and against the authority of ecclesiastical tradition, re-

garded by Tertullian as trustworthy (n. 3). Neither did
Origen, who never questioned in the least the Ephesian
destination of the letter, read ἐν Ἐφέσῳ in i. 1, as is
proved by his interpretation of this passage, and, indeed,
he seems never to have heard of such a reading (n. 4).
Jerome, whose commentary on Ephesians is little more
than a free reproduction of a commentary by Origen with
here and there a criticism (*GK*, ii. 427), thinks that Origen's
explanation of Eph. i. 1 is over-refined, and is inclined to
accept the opinion of those who "with more simplcity"
think that the salutation ought not to be read "to those
who are there," but "to those in Ephesus who are saints
and believers." The latter reading Jerome, in 387 A.D.,
cites simply as the opinion of some scholars which seemed
to clear up an exegetical difficulty. On the strength of
Jerome's statement alone, we would not be justified in
claiming that at that time the reading had found its way
into Bible MSS. The MSS. which have come down to
us from this time do not read ἐν Ἐφέσῳ (n. 4) ; and Basil,
who reproduces Origen's interpretation, gives as authority
for the text without ἐν Ἐφέσῳ, presupposed in Origen's
interpretation, not only the early theologians, but ancient
MSS. in existence in his own time (n. 4). From this
statement we infer that in 370 A.D. Greek MSS. of recent
origin read ἐν Ἐφέσῳ. By that time it had already been
incorporated in the Latin text, perhaps also in the Egyptian
and Syriac texts, and so had come to be widely circulated.
In view of all this evidence, there can be no doubt that ἐν
Ἐφέσῳ did not belong originally in the text. Furthermore, the author of the Epistle would not have placed
the words τοῖς οὖσιν ἐν Ἐφέσῳ in their present position,
but would have put them either before ἁγίοις (Rom. i. 7 ;
Col. i. 2) or after Χριστῷ (Phil. i. 1). Such an unnatural
order of the words can only be due to a corrector who
found τοῖς οὖσιν in its present place and so was compelled
to insert his addition at this point. For this same reason

it is impossible to assume that the author left a space after τοῖς οὖσιν, which, as the several copies of his letter were made, was to be filled in with the names of different places. In this case we should expect also to find in the original, in the copies of which the destination of the letter to various local Churches was to be indicated for the first time, an ἐν after οὖσιν. Only by means of such a preposition, which requires something to be supplied, as is to-day prefixed on our [German] postal cards and in similar forms, could sufficient care be taken that the necessary addition should be inserted, and indeed in the right place. It is a question whether our oldest MSS. preserve the original text intact (n. 4 end). This, however, may be regarded as certain, namely, that the late ἐν Ἐφέσῳ in Eph. i. 1 did not give rise to the very old title πρὸς Ἐφεσίους, but the reverse.

This false title has not only had an injurious effect upon the text of Eph. i. 1, but has interfered seriously with the right understanding of the letter in its historical relations. Holding that the letter was meant for the Ephesian Church, we must conclude from Eph. i. 15 f., iii. 1–4, that Paul wrote the Epistle before he went to Ephesus and became acquainted personally with the Church there. Then we must either claim, in direct contradiction to Acts, that John not Paul was the founder of the Church, or assume that Paul wrote the letter prior to the events described in Acts xviii. 18–xx. 38, which disagrees not only with Acts but with the letter itself (n. 5). When Paul first came to Ephesus (Acts xviii. 19), no Christian Church existed there. In the interval between the first arrival and the final settlement of Paul in Ephesus, Aquila taught exclusively in the synagogue, as did also the apostle himself for three months (Acts xviii. 19–26, xix. 8). A small number of persons who confessed Jesus had to be instructed and baptized before they could become members of an organised Church

(Acts xix. 1–7). The building up of an independent
Church in Ephesus was the result of his two years of
teaching in the lecture-room of Tyrannus (Acts xix. 9 f.).
Paul was thus able to claim as his own even the preliminary work of the year that preceded his coming, while
he assumed the care of the new converts made during the
two years and more of his residence in the region (Acts
xx. 18, 31).   In view of these facts, it should always have
been taken for granted as self-evident that Ephesians was
not intended for this local Church.   For Paul writes to
the readers of this letter, just as he does to the Colossians
(Col. i. 3–9), that ever since he *heard* of their faith and
their love they had been the object of his thanksgiving
and petitions (i. 15 f.).   Up to this time they had known,
not from experience, but only from hearsay, that he had
received a commission from God which authorised his
ministry to them also (iii. 2), and their first conception
of his view of Christianity they derived from this letter
(iii. 3 f.).   He speaks here of the preaching to which they
owed their Christianity (i. 13, iv. 20 f.), just as he does
in Col. i. 5 f. 23, ii. 6, as if he had no personal share in
it.   He does not, as in Col. i. 7, mention the missionary
who had brought the gospel to the readers, the inference
being that while Epaphras was with Paul and told him
of his concern for the Colossians, no such personal bond
existed between Paul and the readers of Ephesians.
All is very clear if Ephesians was not intended for a
single Church at all, but for a number of Churches, the
origin of which was due to the preaching of different
missionaries.   And this assumption is favoured by the
fact that not only in this one particular, but in every
way, Ephesians is more general in character than any
other of Paul's Epistles, especially Colossians.   There is
nothing in Ephesians corresponding to the numerous
personal notices of Col. iv. 10–18.   The only point by
which the readers seem to be distinguished from other

Christians is their Gentile origin (ii. 1 f., 11 ff., iii. 1–13,
iv. 17–24, v. 8). The greeting and concluding benediction of the letter are general enough for a communication addressed to the entire Gentile Church. This,
however, is impossible, not merely because a journey
which would have taken Tychicus to every place where
there were Gentile Christians (vi. 21 f.) would have been
out of the question, but mainly because what has been
said above in arguing against the Ephesian destination of
the letter would apply to all other Churches that were
organised by Paul and had come into personal contact
with him. Even a pseudo-Paul, who certainly would
have known that the Churches in Galatia, Ephesus, Macedonia, and Greece were founded by Paul's personal preaching, would not have been so foolish as to make the great
apostle to the Gentiles write a letter in which the entire
Gentile Church is spoken of as if he had had no part in its
organisation. The gifted disciple of Paul's, to whom the
authorship of the letter has also been attributed, assuming that such a person wrote it, makes very clear reference to the contrast between Churches to which Paul was
known and those to which he was a stranger, when he
writes (vi. 21) that Paul sends Tychicus to them in order
that he may bring them full reports about Paul and his
surroundings, so that *they also* may learn the state of
Paul's affairs and how he is, *they also*, who up to this
time have had no personal intercourse with Paul, *they
also*, as well as the Churches which he had founded, and
which since this organisation have had various communications with him, either personally or through letters,
or by messengers (n. 6). In short, the readers of this
Epistle are not simply such persons as the Christians in
Colossæ, Laodicea, and Hierapolis who have " not yet seen
Paul's face," but they are made up of the entire group of
Churches in which, according to Col. ii. 1, the two Churches
of Colossæ and Laodicea belonged. If, now, it be accepted

486 INTRODUCTION TO THE NEW TESTAMENT

as certain that Ephesians, Colossians, and Philemon, assuming their genuineness, were despatched simultaneously (above, p. 439), there can be no doubt that Ephesians is the circular letter which, according to Col. iv. 16, Paul directed to be sent from Laodicea to Colossæ. The three concentric circles to which Paul despatched simultaneously these three letters were the Church in Philemon's house, the local Church in Colossæ, and all the Churches in the province of Asia to which up to this time he had remained unknown, *i.e.* all the Churches of the province except Ephesus and Troas (Acts xx. 6–11 ; 2 Cor. ii. 12).

The very subordinate question as to the order in which the Epistles were written neither Eph. vi. 21 nor Col. iv. 16 enables us to decide. In the former passage the reference is not to a letter of Paul's (n. 6) ; in the latter, while two letters of Paul's are spoken of, there is nothing to indicate whether, at the time when this statement was written, the letter which was to go "from Laodicea" to Colossæ was already composed, or whether its composition, despatching, and final arrival in Colossæ were all to take place in the more or less remote future. All that can be inferred from Col. iv. 16 is that Paul expected Colossians to reach Colossæ before the circular letter. That this was actually the case, and how it happened, has been shown above, p. 459 f.

As soon as there came to be a collection of Paul's letters of any considerable size, the necessity arose at once of providing the several parts with brief titles indicating their destinations. In the case of the other Epistles this title was suggested at once by the geographical notice in the greeting. Thus naturally from ἐν Κορίνθῳ, 1 Cor. i. 2, came πρὸς Κορινθίους. But, like other letters of this kind (James, 2 Pet., Jude), this communication, which Tychicus was to deliver to the Churches of the province of Asia lying inland from Ephesus, has in the greeting no geographical hint whatever as to its destination. The fact that, notwithstanding this circumstance, it did receive a title like the other Pauline letters, and that the inappropriate πρὸς Ἐφεσίους was chosen, shows that those who made the collection did not have the aid of any clear and trustworthy tradition as to the letter's destination. How the error that the letter was intended for the Church at Ephesus arose, and how it could be perpetuated, is not without explanation. Ecclesiastically as well as politically, Ephesus was the metropolis of the province of Asia. Communications between the Asiatic Churches and the Churches of other countries were sent for the most part through Ephesus. So that from Ephesus this letter reached all the Churches which lay across the sea. If it was circulated as "a letter from Ephesus," it was natural for it to be regarded as a letter to the Church in Ephesus, just as Marcion thought it self-evident that a "letter from Laodicea" must be a letter "to the Laodiceans."

1. (P. 479.) Doubt cannot be cast on the reading, Col. iv. 16, ἐκ Λαοδικείας (-ίας) by a senseless ἐν Λαοδικίας (G), and by inexact translations like " eam quæ est Laodicensium" (Ambrosiaster, Priscillian, Pelagius, not corrected by Jerome). S¹ translates : "and that (letter) which was written from Laodicea (according to another vocalisation, 'from the Laodiceans') ye are to read." The same explanation was given by Theodore (Swete, ii. 310) and Theodoret (Noesselt, 501), with the qualification that it was a letter of the Laodiceans to Paul, about the contents of which, indeed, only vague conjectures were possible. Chrysostom also (xi. 413) mentions this view. Others thought that they had discovered 1 Tim. here ; see GK, ii. 567 f. It goes without saying that whoever considers Col. genuine but Eph. not, cannot recognise the latter in Col. iv. 16, especially if, like von Soden (HK, iii. 88), he holds, in spite of the mention of Tychicus (Eph. vi. 21 f.), that Eph. was addressed to all Gentile Christendom (against this see above, p. 484 f.). The same critic, S. 87, thinks it an argument against identifying the letter from Laodicea with Eph., that this designation is confusing. But confusing for whom ? Certainly not for the Colossians, who either received the circular letter at the same time as their own, or else by asking which letter was meant could find out from Tychicus or Onesimus that a circular letter was on the way, or, if it came to worst, had simply to be patient until the letter so announced arrived "from Laodicea." The further question why then Colossæ was not included in the circle of Churches to which Eph. was addressed is idle, since Col. iv. 16 itself shows that Colossæ was included from the start (above, p. 480). The question why a similar instruction as regards Col. was not given in the letter to the

Laodiceans is thus explained, that this was not a letter just to the Laodiceans, but to the Churches of Asia, and that Col. was to be read not in all these Churches, but simply in Laodicea.

2. (P. 480.) Concerning the apocryphal *Epistle to the Laodiceans*, cf. *GK*, i. 277-283, ii. 83 f., 566-585.

3. (Pp. 480, 482.) Tert. *c. Marc.* v. 17, writes under the title, *De epistula ad Laodicenos*, which he took from Marcion's *Apostolicum* : "Ecclesiæ quidem veritate epistulam istam 'ad Ephesios' habemus emissam, non 'ad Laodicenos' sed Marcion ei titulum aliquando interpolare gestiit, quasi et in isto diligentissimus explorator. Nihil autem de titulis interest, cum ad omnes apostolus scripserit, dum ad quosdam." Before this, in v. 11, he says incidentally : "Prætereo hic et de alia epistula, quam nos ad Ephesios præscriptam habemus, hæretici vero ad Laodicenos." There is no occasion to think of other heretics than Marcion's adherents. Cf. *GK*, i. 623 ff., ii. 416. By *titulus* in distinction from *ipsum corpus* of a writing (*c. Marc.* iv. 2 ; Oehler, ii. 162), Tertullian regularly understands the outside title of the book (*GK*, i. 624 A., cf. i. 83). That such is the case here is the more certain since the peculiarity of Marcion's treatment of this letter is, according to Tertullian, the falsifying of its title. The salutations he had altered elsewhere also, *e.g.* Gal. i. 1-5, *GK*, ii. 495, but the outside title in this instance only. This "title," in place of which no one but the Marcionites knew any other, is found in the literature first in Iren. v. 2. 3 ; Clem. *Strom.* iv. 65, p. 592 ; Can. Mur. l. 51, cf. Iren. v. 8. 1, 14. 3 ; Clem. *Pæd.* i. 18, p. 108.

4. (Pp. 482, 483.) *Catenæ*, ed. Cramer, vi. 102, Ὠριγένης δέ φησιν· ἐπὶ μόνων τῶν Ἐφεσίων εὕρομεν κείμενον τὸ "τοῖς οὖσιν," καὶ ζητοῦμεν, εἰ μὴ παρέλκει προσκείμενον τὸ τοῖς ἁγίοις "τοῖς οὖσιν," τί δύναται σημαίνειν, ὅρα οὖν, εἰ μὴ ὥσπερ ἐν τῇ Ἐξόδῳ ὄνομά φησιν ἑαυτοῦ ὁ χρηματίζων Μωσεῖ τὸ "ὤν" (Ex. iii. 14), οὕτως οἱ μετέχοντες τοῦ ὄντος γίνονται ὄντες, καλούμενοι οἱονεὶ ἐκ τοῦ μὴ εἶναι εἰς τὸ εἶναι. Then follows 1 Cor. i. 28 as proof text. Not only the ἐν Ἐφέσῳ but also the salutation (ver. 2) is wanting in the Mt. Athos MS. (von der Goltz, S. 75, see above, p. 396, n. 3). Origen presupposes the address to be πρὸς Ἐφεσίους, not only in the beginning of this scholion, but elsewhere also, *e.g.* as quoted in Cramer, vi. 119 ; *c. Celsum*, iii. 20. Jerome *in Eph.* i. 1 (Vallarsi, vii. 544 f.) : "'Sanctis omnibus qui sunt Ephesi.' Quidam curiosius, quam necesse est putant ex eo, quod Moysi dictum sit 'Hæc dices filiis Israel : qui est, misit me,' etiam eos qui Ephesi sunt sancti et fideles, essentiæ vocabulo nuncupatos, etc. Alii vero simpliciter, non 'ad eos qui sint (*al.* sunt)' sed 'qui Ephesi sancti et fideles sint' scriptum arbitrantur." Jerome does not say "istam epistolam scriptam esse arbitrantur," a phrase, indeed, quite inapplicable to Origen, who never doubted this ; he says rather *scriptum arbitrantur*, and hence must be speaking simply of the text with ἐν Ἐφέσῳ as contrasted with the text without it, over which Origen had puzzled ; cf. Hofmann, iv. 1, 3. It is certainly strange if this is the only hint that Jerome gives of a textual variation, for Origen's interpretation can be discussed only on the presupposition of his text (without ἐν Ἐφέσῳ) ; and we may conjecture with Vallarsi that Jerome himself prefaced his discussion by a text without *Ephesi*, and that it was only copyists who substituted the Vulgate text with *omnibus* and *Ephesi*, neither of which was known to Origen. Basil, *c. Eunom.*

ii. 19 (Garnier, i. 254), reproduces Origen's thought and text with the addition : οὕτω γὰρ οἱ πρὸ ἡμῶν παραδεδώκασι καὶ ἡμεῖς ἐν τοῖς παλαιοῖς τῶν ἀντιγράφων εὑρήκαμεν. Ambrosiaster and Victorinus are about contemporary with Basil. From the former's exposition we cannot tell whether or not he really found here "sanctis omnibus qui sunt Ephesi et fidelibus," etc., as the text in his commentary now reads. Victorinus (Mai, *Script. vet. n. Coll.* iii. 2. 88, after a previous less exact citation, p. 87) read, "sanctis qui sunt Ephesi et fidelibus in Christo Jesu" (at all events without *omnibus*). The older Syriac text, on which Ephrem wrote a commentary, expressed, as it would appear, neither οὖσιν nor ἐν Ἐφέσῳ (p. 141, "Sanctis et fidelibus, baptizatis videlicet et catechumenis "). On the contrary, S¹ literally retranslated τοῖς οὖσιν ἐν Ἐφέσῳ, ἁγίοις καὶ πιστοῖς. The essential agreement of this text with the Greek text of Antioch proves that Lucian gave it this form. Could he have been its originator ? The text of Eph. i. 1 is transmitted quite variously : (1) τοῖς ἁγίοις τοῖς οὖσιν (οὖσι ℵ) καὶ πιστοῖς ἐν Χριστῷ Ἰ. is found in ℵ*B* and the scholiast of min. 67. Whether Marcion read just this in his exemplar, and Tertullian, Origen, and Ephrem in their N.T., cannot be established. (2) τοῖς ἁγίοις (without τοῖς) οὖσιν ἐν Ἐφέσῳ καὶ πιστοῖς κτλ., D, min. 46 ; (3) τοῖς ἁγίοις πᾶσιν τοῖς οὖσιν ἐν Ἐ. κ. π., AP, corrector of ℵ, Cyrill. Al., 2 min., Copt., Ambrosiaster (?), Jerome in his commentary (?), Vulg. (sometimes *omnibus* before *sanctis*), Theod., Lat. as the text (Swete, i. 118 ?) ; (4) τοῖς ἁγίοις τοῖς οὖσιν ἐν Ἐ. καὶ π., GKL, Chrys. (probably Theodore), Theodoret, Victorinus (see above) ; (5) the same with τοῖς (instead of καὶ) πιστοῖς, pseudo-Ign. *ad Eph.* ix ; καί is thought to be lacking also in min. 37 and some MSS. of the Vulg. The reading (1) " to the saints who are also believers in Christ " is not quite satisfactory ; since, according to this, faith in Christ appears to be either a qualification of the sainthood in distinction from other saints who are such even without faith in Christ or an inference from this sainthood, neither of which meanings is very clear. The reading (2) after we expunge the ἐν Ἐφέσῳ, which is certainly not genuine, would be more likely. The origin of πᾶσιν in reading (3) is puzzling. Is it originally a variant competing with οὖσιν ? Or are both genuine (cf. 2 Cor. i. 1)? Or has a τῆς Ἀσίας been lost in the one or the other ? Or, with P. Ewald, *ZKom. Eph.* 16, is τοῖς ἀγαπητοῖς οὖσιν καὶ πιστοῖς ἐν Χρ. Ἰ. ? Cf. Rom. i. 7 above, p. 394 f.

5. (P. 483.) The older commentators, being fettered by the title "To the Ephesians," have not for the most part seriously faced the insoluble problem which thus arises. Victorinus can think of nothing to say on i. 15, iii. 1 ff. that might serve to adjust these passages to the traditional title, and asserts in the Introduction (Mai, *Script. vet. nova coll.* iii. 2. 87): " Ephesii a pseudoapostolis depravati videbantur, judaismum jungere Christianæ doctrinæ." Ambrosiaster remarks in the prologue at least : " Ephesios apostolus non fundavit in fide, sed confirmavit," without, however, grounding this more particularly on i. 15, iii. 1 ff., or reconciling it with Acts. So also writes the real Euthalius (Zacagni, i. 524), who classes the Ephesians with the Romans as Christians who were known to Paul only by hearsay. Chrysostom in his Introduction (Montfaucon, xi. 1), and on i. 15, iii. 1 ff., avoids the historical question altogether. Ephrem, p. 140, with whom Severianus also (Cramer, *Cat.* vi. 97) seems to agree, represents the apostle John as founding the Church of Ephesus, and writing his Gospel there before Paul

wrote Eph. This historically impossible view is probably traceable to some version or other of the legend about John. See especially the Syriac History of John the Son of Zebedee (Wright, *Apocr. Acts of the Apostles*, i. 1–65, also the writer's *Acta Joannis*, xxxix., lvi., cxxviii.). Theodore Mops. (Swete, i. 115 ff.) shows in opposition to this legendary view that John's stay in Ephesus does not fall earlier than the time between the outbreak of the Jewish war and Trajan's reign ; but, on the other hand, he holds fast to the conclusion drawn from exegesis, that Eph., just like Rom. and Col., is addressed to Christians whom Paul has not yet seen (pp. 112, 253). Naturally Theodore admits the truthfulness of the account in Acts xviii. 18–xx. 38, according to which Paul laboured several years in Ephesus long before his protracted imprisonment (p. 117). But the task of discovering a point in Paul's life previous to Acts xviii. 18, when he could have written as a prisoner this letter to the Church of Ephesus, and the further task of making intelligible the origin of such a Church before Acts xviii. 18, and of bringing it into harmony with Acts, are avoided by the great commentator. To amend his text by conjecture, as the present writer sought to do in *Acta Jo.* xl., is needless pains in view of the complete Latin text of his commentary, then unknown to him. Theodoret (Noesselt, p. 398) certainly must have Theodore in mind when he mentions, along with earlier commentators who considered John the first teacher of the gospel in Ephesus (*i.e.* Ephrem and Severianus), others also who claimed, indeed, that Paul had not yet seen the Church at the time when he wrote to them, but at the same time asserted that certain nameless persons were the first preachers of the gospel in Ephesus. Both views would be easy to refute from Acts. All the more inadequate, then, seems that which Theodoret remarks on i. 15, in order to make it conceivable that the letter is addressed to one of the Churches founded by Paul. In commenting on iii. 2 f. he is quite silent about this matter.

6. (Pp. 485, 486.) Hofmann, iv. 1. 266, thought that he could explain the καὶ ὑμεῖς, vi. 21, as an antithesis to the κἀγώ, i. 15. But what reader who has reached vi. 21 has still in mind a sentence from the opening of the letter ? Still more inadmissible is the common view that the contrast here is with the Colossians, to whom Paul at the same time sends news about himself by Tychicus (Col. iv. 8), or indeed with Col., which already lay before the writer (so Holtzmann, *Kritik der Eph. und Kolosserbriefe*, 1872, S. 25). The latter view is objectionable, if for no other reason, because Eph. vi. 21 f. does not treat of a letter or of several letters at all, but simply of the sending of Tychicus. Besides, Eph., if indeed it is meant at all in Col. iv. 16, was originally intended for the Church at Colossæ as well (above, p. 479). The Christians of Colossæ belong to the multitude addressed throughout Eph., and hence to those addressed in Eph. vi. 21 f. How then can they be conceived as forming a contrast to the "ye also" of Eph. vi. 21 ? Nor does Paul say that he is sending Tychicus *also* to the readers of Eph.; he says of this one mission of Tychicus, which will bring him to all the readers of Eph. (Eph. vi. 22), the Colossians among the rest (Col. iv. 7), that it should serve to inform these Churches also about his (Paul's) situation. The contrast can be formed only by such Churches as do not belong to this circle, Churches to which Tychicus is not now sent, or at least not with this aim, and which, as was well known, heard frequently from Paul ; cf. Klostermann,

JbfDTh. 1870, S. 161. Cf. also in the matter Ewald, *ZKom. Eph. Col. Philem.* 263, but on the basis of the supposition that Eph. and Philem. were written and sent somewhat earlier than Col. (*KZom. Eph.* 20 ff.).

§ 29. THE GENUINENESS OF THE EPISTLES TO THE EPHESIANS AND COLOSSIANS.

Among earlier critics many accepted the Pauline authorship of Colossians, but often questioned the genuineness of Ephesians, while only occasionally the opinion was expressed that Colossians was forged on the basis of Ephesians (n. 1). Later, Baur, followed with some divergencies by Hilgenfeld and Weizsäcker, interpreted both Epistles as products of the second century (n. 2). Hitzig made the suggestion that Ephesians was copied from a genuine Epistle to the Colossians, but that later Colossians itself was interpolated by the same author and in the same spirit. This suggestion was worked out by Holtzmann, who concluded that these changes were made either at the close of the first or the beginning of the second century (n. 3).

When the fact is taken into consideration that those inclined to this hypothesis have tended more and more to accept both the unity and genuineness of Colossians, the favour of the critics seems to have been very unequally bestowed upon these two very closely connected letters. Indeed, the Epistle most attacked is supported by the better external evidence. Whereas, with the exception of a misinterpretation of Col. ii. 18 in the *Preaching of Peter* (above, p. 475, n. 6), there are no clear traces of Colossians before the time of Marcion, even as early as the time of Clement and Hermas we begin to have traces of the circulation of Ephesians in the Church, which become clearer in Ignatius and Polycarp (*GK*, i. 817 f., 825 f.). It is hard to believe that letters which were incorporated by Marcion in 145 into his *Apostolicon* as genuine letters of Paul were not written until shortly before 140 (Hil-

genfeld, *Einl.* 680). Still less is it possible to suppose
that the writer was influenced by Montanistic ideas (Baur,
Paulus, ii. 25).

Another definite point, which cannot be overlooked
in the historical criticism of these letters, is the title πρὸς
Ἐφεσίους, which was known to Ignatius and corrected
by Marcion. In its present form this title cannot be
older than the incorporation of this Epistle into a collection of Pauline letters. On the other hand, in view of
its wide circulation and the fact that it is the only title
by which the letter was known, it cannot be later than
the formation of the collection of Pauline letters which
Marcion found circulating in the Church, and which was
in Ignatius' hands. In order to account for the historical
inaccuracy of this title, an interval must be assumed
between the letter's composition and its incorporation
in this collection sufficient for its original destination to
have been forgotten. Now this interval is allowed for,
and the perpetuation of the error in the title easily explained if Paul sent the Epistle in the year 62 by Tychicus
by way of Ephesus to the inland cities of the province
of Asia (cf. above, p. 480 f.). When, some twenty or forty
years later, the collection of Pauline letters in which this
Epistle had the title πρὸς Ἐφεσίους came into circulation
in that region, no one had longer any interest in correcting
the error. Because of its circular character, no single
Church was in a position to claim the honour of having
received the Epistle from Paul, and to contest its claim
with that of the metropolis of the province. On the other
hand, if it be assumed that the letter was forged in
Paul's name, the origin of the πρὸς Ἐφεσίους is inexplicable.
This error as to the letter's destination could not have
originated in Ephesus and the province of Asia. And
even if the letter was written in this region, the error
could not have been circulated from this centre with the
letter; while, if it be assumed that the spurious letter

was written and first circulated elsewhere, we have the still more difficult task of explaining the origin of the opinion that the letter was directed to Ephesus. For there is absolutely nothing in the letter itself which would point to a Church that had been organised by Paul, and cared for by him during the early years of its growth. If someone had been influenced in selecting a definite title by his observation of the close resemblance between this letter and Colossians,—and this was not the usual manner in which mistakes originated in the early Church,—he would have been more likely to think of Hierapolis or Laodicea (Col. ii. 1, iv. 13–16) than of Ephesus. Moreover, it is to be borne in mind that up to the present time no one has shown with any degree of plausibility that this letter was forged during Paul's lifetime, or shortly after his death. But if it had not been composed until the year 100 or shortly thereafter, there is no time for the rise and establishment of the error which had been associated with the Epistle ever since it began to have a wider circulation, indeed from the time when it was incorporated into a collection of Pauline letters.

While in the case of Ephesians it is the strong external evidence which stands in the way of the assumption of spuriousness, in the case of Colossians it is the impression necessarily made by the contents of the letter. Even the choice by a forger of Colossæ as the destination of his letter is inexplicable. In the entire literature of the ancient Church Colossæ is not once mentioned, and it is hard to see why this Church should have been chosen rather than one of the more famous Churches mentioned in Rev. i.–iii., or in Acts, or in the *Epistles of Ignatius*, or in the traditions about John and the daughters of Philip. The notices in chap. iv. would be a masterpiece without parallel in epistolary literature known to be spurious, comparable only to 2 Tim. iv. Assuming that Philemon is genuine, someone might have taken from ver.

23 f. the five names of persons sending greetings which
recur in Col. iv. But what would have influenced such a
person to add to these five the name of Jesus Justus, who
is not mentioned anywhere else in the ancient Christian
literature that has come down to us? This character
must have been invented; yet it is scarcely conceivable
that a Christian of the post-apostolic age should have
given to a character invented by himself the name
"Jesus." What is said and implied in Col. iv. 11 with
reference to the activity of Jewish Christian missionaries
in Paul's vicinity, with whom Paul was not altogether
satisfied, is confirmed by Phil. i. 15–17, but could not
have been derived from the latter passage. For it is
not said in the Philippian passage that the missionaries
hostile to Paul were of Jewish origin, which is the point
in Colossians; nor does the language in Colossians betray
the slightest dependence upon Philippians. A pseudo-
Paul might have taken the name Onesimus from Philemon,
but he could not have inferred from this Epistle that
Colossæ was the home of the slave and of his master
(Col. iv. 9). On the other hand, there is no trace in
Colossians of any of the contents of Philemon, e.g. of
Onesimus' condition of slavery, of his flight, of his conversion by Paul and restoration to his master. No
mention is made of Philemon nor of his wife. It is not
the Church in the house of Philemon at Colossæ which we
find mentioned in Col. iv. 15, but the Church in the house
of Nymphas at Laodicea. In Col. iv. 17 a ministry in
the Church is ascribed to Archippus, of which there is
no suggestion in Philem. 2. If Colossians is spurious,
chap. iv. shows that the author is very anxious, by inserting
numerous personal notices, to give his forgery the appearance of lifelikeness. How is it, then, that for this purpose
he has not made use of Philemon, assuming that the letter
is genuine? If he composed them both, how could he
have avoided repeating himself in two letters which are

represented to have been despatched simultaneously to the same destination ? The organisation of the Colossian Church is not attributed to Paul's distinguished helper Timothy, although the writer makes him share Paul's apostolic calling, as this calling is related to this particular Church (Col. i. 1, 7, above, p. 449, n. 3), and although from Philemon he must have known that Timothy as well as Paul was quite intimate with a prominent member of this Church. The place that we should expect to be occupied by Timothy is taken by Epaphras (Col. i. 7, iv. 12), who is not mentioned in the other sources, and from whose mention in Philem. 23 it could not be guessed that he had preached the gospel and organised Churches in these regions. In short, while the letters are entirely independent, their personal and historical notices are mutually supplementary, without being at any point in the slightest degree contradictory. That there is a resemblance between these two letters, as regards historical details, is not to be denied ; but it is not the resemblance that exists between two spurious letters, nor between one genuine and one spurious letter, but a resemblance such as ordinarily exists between two genuine documents, and such as in the nature of the case is possible.

The objection that there is no sufficient occasion for the letter (Hilgenfeld, 663) ought not to have been made unless the critic was in a position to show a plausible reason for its forgery, or to prove that the letter was written from pure love of writing, without any special purpose, and especially unless he was ready to show that the urgent occasion for the letter which the author himself indicates (above, p. 461 ff.) was inherently improbable. Now it cannot be denied that Paul, in addition to the responsibility which he felt for preaching the gospel to the entire Gentile world still unconverted (Rom. i. 14), bore anxiously also upon his heart the Churches already in existence (2.Cor. xi. 28). If he devoted a lengthy letter to a Church like that in Rome, which did not properly belong within the sphere of his missionary labours, but simply lay upon the route of future journeys which were to be made in connection with his work, it is evident that he must have felt himself under obligation to watch over and to promote the development of the Churches in the province of Asia which through three years of labour he had founded, and which, moreover, had received the gospel from the Ephesian Church that he himself had organised. And he would have felt this obligation all the more when it was being rumoured in Colossæ and Laodicea, as it was, that he was unable or not disposed to fulfil this obligation, when, moreover, the Christians in these two places were in danger of being led away by an unsound form of Christianity.

The claim that Colossians was not written by Paul, or that the genuine Epistle was interpolated by a later hand, cannot be upheld, save by convincing proof that historical facts or conditions are referred to in the letter which did not exist until the post-apostolic age, or by evidence of thought and language which do not harmonise with the thought and style of Pauline letters admitted to be genuine. Neither has been shown to be true. In its practical aims the movement combated in chap. ii., opposition to which, as we have seen, influenced all the didactic statements of the Epistle, was very closely allied to the movement which Paul had opposed earlier in Rom. xiv. No traces of such a movement are to be found in the post-apostolic literature. Assuming that an angel cult is really referred to in Col. ii. 18, one might search the heresy histories of the second century in vain for another reference to it (above, p. 475 f.). But when this passage is rightly interpreted, it is found to have no connection with any heretical movement of the post-apostolic age, especially those which, according to existing accounts, were influential in Asia Minor. From

the Nicolaitans of the Book of Revelation the Jewish
Christian ascetics in Colossæ are the opposite extreme.
According to trustworthy accounts, Cerinthus, the contemporary of John, was anything but a Judaiser.   He
was made such only by the ignorance of heresy writers
after the close of the fourth century, and there is no
trace in Colossians of Cerinthus' real view of the person
and history of Christ (n. 4).   On his journey through the
province of Asia, Ignatius met wandering teachers, who
insisted that the Gentile Christians there should observe
the Jewish law, e.g. the law of the Sabbath, and who at
the same time held Docetic views regarding Christ, especially regarding His sufferings.   But there is nothing said
by Ignatius about ascetic rules which were based upon
certain theories of matter and the nature of angels, nor
is there to be found in Colossians any suggestion of the
fantastic Christology which Ignatius was especially anxious
to refute.

On the surface there would seem to be points of
connection between Colossians and the so-called false
teachers of the Pastoral Epistles.   But the latter are to
be dated in Paul's lifetime (§ 37).

Baur found in both Ephesians and Colossians a Gnostic
theology and phraseology suggesting the speculation of
Valentinus, but without any "trace of even an indirect
polemic against Gnostic teachers," so that, according to
Baur, they must date from a time when Gnostic ideas were
just beginning to appear, and seemed as yet to be harmless
Christian speculations (*Paulus*, ii. 25).   On the other
hand, Hilgenfeld (*Einl.* 660, 666 ff.) makes the writer
attack Gnosticism, which is called by him philosophy
(ii. 8).   He thinks that what is said in i. 19, ii. 9 ff., is
directed against the Gnostic doctrine of the $\pi\lambda\acute{\eta}\rho\omega\mu\alpha$, that
i. 15 ff. is designed to oppose the doctrine of the creation
of the material world by spirits greatly inferior to God,
and that the presentation of Christianity as a mystery

(i. 27, ii. 2, iv. 2) and gnosis (i. 9, 10, ii. 2 f., iii. 9) is intended to offset the esoteric teaching of the Gnostics. A polemic of this sort, in which the error opposed is not so much as characterised, to say nothing of being logically refuted, would be manifestly childish. And that the error clearly designated by Paul, and really combated, has nothing to do with Gnosticism, with its doctrine of the *pleroma* and *æons,* is proved by the vain efforts which have been put forth either to prove that there are two different parties in Colossæ which are combated, or that the writer confuses the alleged Jewish Christian Gnosticism of Cerinthus with movements of an entirely different character. That the words πλήρωμα and αἰῶνες, the use of which in Colossians and Ephesians is mainly responsible for conjectures of this kind, were widely used in Gnostic circles before Valentinus, cannot be proved (n. 5). But the supposition that the teaching of Valentinus himself is either combated or appropriated in Colossians and Ephesians is ruled out, because it is chronologically impossible, in view of Marcion's acceptance and revision of the latter Epistle. Indeed, the theory is refuted by the practice of the Valentinian school, all branches of which made special use of 1 Cor., Ephesians, and Colossians in constructing their doctrine, endeavouring to show that it was derived from the esoteric teaching of the apostles. While Valentinus and his followers certainly did not derive their ideas from Paul, they did use his language for the expression of their thoughts, in order to render them less objectionable to the ordinary reader. They make the same use of the conceptions ὁ λόγος τοῦ σταυροῦ, θεοῦ σοφίαν λαλοῦμεν ἐν μυστηρίῳ, πνευματικός, ψυχικός (1 Cor. i. 18, ii. 7, 14 f.) that they do of πλήρωμα, Col. i. 19, ii. 9; Eph. i. 10, 23, iii. 19, iv. 13, and αἰῶνες, Eph. iii. 21. But since the caricatures of these Pauline conceptions constitute the basis of the Valentinian system, and are used in the technical language of all branches of the school, it is certain that Valentinus himself derived his doctrine, among other sources, from Ephesians and Colossians.

But if the genuineness of Colossians is unimpeachable, the critical question with reference to Ephesians is very much simplified; for if the latter is spurious, the numerous points of resemblance between it and Colossians prove beyond question that it is based upon this Epistle. Moreover, since mention is made in Col. iv. 16 of a contemporaneous Epistle of Paul's which was to be read, among other places, in Laodicea and Colossæ, there is no doubt that it was this passage which led to the composition of Ephesians. The relation of Ephesians to Col. iv. 16 would be the same as that of the apocryphal correspondence of Paul with the Corinthians to 1 Cor. v. 9, vii. 1. Of this possible motive for the alleged forging of Ephesians, Hitzig and Holtzmann (*op. cit.* p. 167) deprive themselves, when they explain Col. iv. 15–17 as an interpolation made by the writer of Ephesians, with the intention of making iv. 16 refer to the circular letter which he had written. But why does he do this in such unintelligible language? The reference would be intelligible only to the Colossians, who knew beforehand or learned at the time that a letter was to be sent from Laodicea to Colossæ. Only if Col. iv. 16 is genuine are there analogies from which to argue that Ephesians is a probable forgery. As a matter of fact, there was a letter forged in the second century on the strength of this passage (above, p. 488, n. 2). Although, compared with the richness of thought in Ephesians, this letter is a poor piece of patchwork, its title, *ad Laodicenos*, and its greeting, *fratribus qui sunt Laodiciæ*, are much more sensible and intelligible than the greeting of Ephesians, if the latter Epistle be likewise a forgery made on the strength of this Colossian passage. Anyone who missed the letter mentioned in this passage, and on the strength of its non-existence wrote a fictitious letter of his own, could not have left his readers to guess its destination, but, like the persons who wrote the apocryphal letters to the Corinthians and Laodiceans, he must have betrayed the origin of his invention.

In attempting to prove the spuriousness of Ephesians, a special point cannot be made of its close resemblance to Colossians, both in thought and language. For this is what we should expect if the two letters were despatched simultaneously, possibly not more than a single night intervening between their composition, and if the Church in Colossæ, to which a special letter is devoted on account of the danger threatening this Church and its nearest neighbour, was one of a larger group of Churches to which the other letter was directed. A literary man, concerned about the opinion of his critics and the judgment of posterity, in such a case might have taken special pains to secure variety of thought and language ; a great man, concerned mainly with his subject, does not take such pains (n. 6). Such a man was Paul. Moreover, it is a peculiarity of Paul's style, that having once employed a significant word he is apt soon to repeat it, or to make use of a related word (n. 7). This is true even of words that do not occur elsewhere in his writings. If, owing to the closeness of their composition, the two letters may be regarded as being in this respect a unit, the occurrence in both of expressions more or less peculiar only serves to confirm this fact. It is also to be remembered that between the composition of Romans and these letters not less than four years had elapsed, during which time Paul, torn away from his accustomed missionary work, had been receiving the greatest variety of impressions, first in Cæsarea, then for six months at sea, and finally in Rome. Under these conditions it would not be strange to find him influenced by ideas and using forms of expression with which we do not meet in the earlier Epistles.

In order to prove that Ephesians is a forgery, based either entirely or for the most part on a genuine letter to the Colossians, conclusive evidence must be adduced to show that ideas and words in Colossians were misunderstood or intentionally misinterpreted by the imitator, or clumsily copied and used in the wrong place. For these are the characteristics of all known forgeries of this sort, at least of all ancient forgeries. Consequently in handling a genuine Epistle of Paul's, whose letters were so difficult for outsiders, and so especially difficult for later generations to understand (2 Pet. iii. 16), a forger would certainly have betrayed himself in some way. Indeed, the details of Ephesians have been held to be so slavishly dependent upon Colossians as to render its composition by Paul impossible (n. 8). But this view presupposes on the part of the alleged pseudo-Paul a degree of stupidity and a lack of thought which cannot be harmonised with the unquestionable fact that the author of Ephesians was a man of profound thought, breadth of view, and no little literary power. Furthermore, the contents and plan of Ephesians cannot be said to so strikingly resemble those of Colossians as to arouse suspicion. Paul begins Colossians with the assurance that since the reception of the news of the planting of Christianity in Colossæ he and Timothy have not ceased to give thanks (cf. 1 Cor. i. 4 ; 1 Thess. i. 2) ; in Eph. i. 3 he breaks at once into praise of God, with an emotional fervour without parallel in any other of Paul's letters, not even excepting Rom. i. 8. In the Epistle intended for the group of Churches in the province of Asia the predominating tone is that of joy for the results of the gospel accomplished in his field of labour, though without his aid, which gives the Epistle throughout a solemnly exalted, soaring, even exaggerated tone that frequently passes over into praise of God (i. 3, 12, 14, 16, iii. 14 ff., 20 f., v. 20) ; the tone of Colossians, on the other hand, is influenced by the deep anxiety which both the apostle and Epaphras felt on account of the special peril to which the Christians in Colossæ and Laodicea were exposed (ii. 1, iv. 12 f.),—an anxiety that accounts for the moderate joy of its thanksgiving (i. 3), as well as for the preponderance and varied character of its petitions (i. 9, cf. i. 23 with Eph. i. 16 f.). The thanksgiving in Eph. i. 3–14 is for the redemptive grace of God, eternally shown to the Church, primarily to the Jewish Christian Church, of which grace the Gentiles have now been made partakers (i. 13). Not until i. 15 f. do we have thanksgiving for the readers themselves, with which Colossians begins. The discussions of Col. i. are entirely determined by opposition to the ethical error and confusion by which the Church was threatened, clearly characterised in Col. ii., whereas Eph. i.–iii. is concerned entirely with the contrast between the former limitation of salvation to Israel and its present extension to the Gentiles. The first main division of Ephesians concludes with a doxology ending in "amen" (iii. 20 f.), which resembles Rom. xvi. 25–27 (a resemblance all the more striking because of the similarity in thought between the latter passage and Eph. iii. 3, 5), which may also be compared to Rom. xi. 36 and the benedictions in 1 Thess. iii. 11–13 ; 2 Thess. ii. 16 f. A transition is then made with παρακαλῶ οὖν ὑμᾶς, iv. 1, to a second hortatory section of the letter (cf. Rom. xii. 1). All this is wanting in Colossians. Although there is much similarity in the language of these hortatory sections, the ethical discussion discloses a number of new points of view. There are enough independent thoughts in Ephesians to enable us to understand why Paul wanted this letter to be read by the Colossians, for whom it was intended, as well as for the other Churches (Col. iv. 16) ; on the other hand, it was so general in character that the apostle did not feel that it was sufficient to meet the needs of the Church in Colossæ.

The *lexical* proof of the spuriousness of Ephesians,

which has been thought possible, will not bear examination
(n. 9). Passing by specific defects in the argument, this
general remark is to be made concerning it. There is
error in every effort of this sort which proceeds on the
hypothesis that in and of itself the occurrence of rare
words, particularly words that are not to be found elsewhere in the N.T., or more specifically in the admittedly
genuine Pauline letters, is sufficient reason for suspecting
an Epistle. Are we to suppose that boldness in the construction of words and independence of the vocabulary of
the author whose writings he designs to multiply by his
forgery are the characteristics of the forger ? So far as
we are able to determine from the Latin version (*GK*, ii.
584), in the *Epistle to the Laodiceans*, there is not to be
found a single word, scarcely a combination of words, not
to be found in the genuine Epistles. Galatians, which is
a little shorter than Ephesians, has just as many peculiar
words (n. 10). It has been claimed that Ephesians does
not show Paul's dialectic and syllogistic style. With
double force could this objection be made to 2 Cor., in
which there occurs not a single one of those logical con-
nectives characteristic of Romans and 1 Cor. ($\mathring{\eta}$ οὐκ οἴδατε ;
$\mathring{\eta}$ ἀγνοεῖτε ; τί οὖν ἐροῦμεν ; ἄρα οὖν), whereas in Eph. (*e.g.* ii.
19) we do find an ἄρα οὖν. It has also been claimed that
the thought is not Pauline. The real Paul, it is claimed,
dealt only with individual Churches ; this alleged Paul
is dominated by the idea of *the one Church*. But it is
not to be forgotten that from the beginning to the end of
1 Cor. Paul reiterates the truth that the individual
Church cannot disregard its relation to the whole Church
and still maintain its character as a Church of God
(above, p. 281 f.). Not only does he speak of the whole
body of Christian believers as worshippers of Jesus (1 Cor.
i. 2 ; Rom. x. 12), as saints (Rom. xii. 13 ; 1 Cor. vi. 2 ;
so also Eph. iv. 12), or all the saints (1 Thess. iii. 13 ;
Philem. 5 ; Col. i. 4 ; so also Eph. i. 15, iii. 8, vi. 18), or

of all the Churches (Rom. xvi. 16 ; 1 Cor. iv. 17, vii. 17,
xi. 16, xiv. 33), but he speaks of all the Churches together
as one Church. It is not the local Roman Church which
in Rom. xii. 5 is called the body of Christ, but all the
Christians upon earth ; for he includes himself among
them. If possible, this is even clearer in 1 Cor. xii.
12 ff. In 1 Cor. xii. 28, Col. i. 18, 24, probably also in
1 Cor. x. 32 (above, p. 297, n. 7, cf. also Gal. i. 13, Phil.
iii. 6, 1 Cor. xv. 9, with Gal. i. 22 ff.), this entire organism
is called ἡ ἐκκλησία. The fact that this word, which occurs
only rarely elsewhere, is found nine times in Ephesians,
would be critically significant only if the terms which
Paul commonly uses elsewhere to designate the Church as
a whole were wanting in Ephesians. This, as we have
seen, is not the case. The idea that the conception of an
organic Church occurred to Paul only in the process of a
later development, or that the idea did not originate until
after Paul's time, is not only refuted by the use of ἐκκλησία
in 1 Cor. xii. 28, but the notion itself arises from a misunderstanding of Paul's position which is scarcely conceivable.
It is self-evident that even the possibility of speaking of
the Church in Corinth as the temple of God and of Christ,
and the only foundation of the work of God that had been
laid in Corinth (1 Cor. iii. 10–17), and the possibility of
calling this one Church the body of Christ (xii. 27), were
conditioned upon their being a microcosm of the whole
Church, and upon Christ's standing in the same relation
to their communion as He did to the whole body of
believers. Paul knew only one Christ who had died for
all men, and only one gospel which was intended for the
whole world. It is consequently self-evident that the
idea of a Church founded upon this Christ and through
this gospel could not have originated from a collective
survey of the local Churches ; on the contrary, this idea
is the presupposition of all that he says regarding the
individual Churches. The special prominence of this idea

in Ephesians is due to the fact that in this letter, and in this letter alone, he is addressing a group of Churches which, unlike those in Galatia, had not been organised by his own effort, with whose special conditions he was unacquainted save as he had learned from Epaphras and Onesimus respecting the conditions in Colossæ, and of which he thought as a group of Churches constituting a large section of the Gentile Church of which he was the head. His obligation to these Gentile Christians—an obligation which he designs to fulfil by writing this letter —arises from his commission (iii. 2, 7 f.), which puts him under obligation to all the Gentiles. Because of a lack of personal relations to the Apostle of the Gentiles, they are not to feel that they are excluded from the Gentile Church for which he labours and is in bonds (iii. 1, 13). "They also," who heretofore have had no personal intercourse with him, are to learn more concerning him (vi. 21, above, p. 490, n. 6) than they had learned from rumours (iii. 2). His design is to protect them from the danger of becoming isolated and lost—a danger to which they were exposed quite as much as the Corinthians, though for other reasons —by making them realise more strongly that they are a part of the great Gentile Church ; and since this Gentile Church with the body of Jewish Christians, built upon the same foundation, constitutes the whole Church, that they are members also of the body of Christ, and parts in the building of God.

The designation of *apostles* and *prophets* in iv. 11, as first among those who by reason of their special gifts are called to special service in this great organism, is exactly parallel to 1 Cor. xii. 28. Consequently there is nothing strange about the conjunction of these two offices in ii. 20, iii. 5. Assuming as self-evident that in all three passages by prophets Christians are meant, it is hardly likely that prophet is only a second designation of the persons who are first called apostles, for the two are clearly distinguished in iv. 11 (likewise in ii. 20, iii. 5). The use of a single article covering both the words simply indicates the closeness of their connection. And they naturally belong together, where the design is to describe the original organisation of the Church, especially the rise of the knowledge regarding the entire equality of Gentiles and Jews in the Church. In certain instances prophetic revelation and the apostolic office might blend. It was not his consciousness of apostolic duty, but a revelation, which lay outside the sphere of his apostolic office, that influenced Peter to take the first decisive steps in this direction (Acts x. 10, 34, 46, xi. 15, xv. 7). The Magna Charta of the Gentile Church was issued not by the apostles alone, but with the co-operation of the mother Church and its head (Acts xv. 22 ff.); it was proposed by James, who was not an apostle, while the author of the decree is declared to be the Holy Spirit (Acts xv. 28). The prophets Judas and Silas, acting as the ambassadors of the mother Church, strengthened the impression made by the document which they brought through their own eloquent oral exposition of it (xv. 32), and one of these, working as a missionary in conjunction with Paul, had endeavoured to actualise his prophetic knowledge that the Gentiles were fellow-heirs with the Jews of redemption. The designation of the apostles and prophets as ἅγιοι certainly cannot be interpreted as self-exaltation, which would be out of place in one who called himself an apostle (i. 1); for, as is well known, Paul very frequently designates all Christians without distinction as οἱ ἅγιοι, not because of their piety or morality, which, in certain respects, were still very deficient, and to a large extent unknown to the apostle, but simply to indicate that, by their reception into the Church, they had been separated from the world and dedicated to God. He uses the expression also in a narrower sense with reference to the body of Jewish Christians in Palestine to indicate their special distinction as belonging to God's holy people (Rom. xv. 25 f. ; 1 Cor. xvi. 1 ; 2 Cor. viii. 4), a usage which is found also in Eph. ii. 19. And why should he not use the same word, not as a special designation of the apostles and prophets,—which, in fact, is not done here, nor in Col. i. 26, nor anywhere else,—but simply to indicate through the attribute ἅγιοι that these men were endowed beyond the majority of Christians with the knowledge of the universality of redemption, and commissioned to be the representatives of this knowledge, especially in a sentence where as here he is striving for fulness of expression, as is indicated by the superfluous ἐν πνεύματι. As far as the criticism of the passage is concerned, it makes no difference whether Paul includes himself or, as in 1 Cor. xv. 7, Rom. xvi. 7, means by οἱ ἀπόστολοι the twelve apostles not including himself. The former is the more natural inference from iv. 11 (cf. i. 1) ; the latter, from ii. 20, especially in view of the historical reference of the latter passage. The same is true of iii. 5, since he has just spoken in iii. 3 of the personal revelation to him of the same mystery, since, moreover, in iii. 7 he speaks of himself as being only the chief personal agent through whom the knowledge revealed to the apostles and prophets has been practically realised, and since, finally, in iii. 8 he speaks of himself as less than the least of all Christians, not, as in 1 Cor. xv. 9, as the least of the apostles, scarcely worthy of the name. The fact that he mentions in iv. 11, besides apostles and prophets, a third class, namely, evangelists, would be ground for suspicion only if in the post-apostolic age εὐαγγελιστής was a common designation of an office in the Church, which was not, however, the case. In Paul's writings, εὐαγγέλιον always means missionary preaching (above, p. 171, n. 2). Hence by evangelists he means those preachers who, without belonging to the apostolic body proper, are engaged in spreading the gospel among those who are still un-

evangelised. When such persons happened to locate
either temporarily or permanently in communities where
Christian Churches were already in existence (Acts xxi. 8 ;
2 Tim. iv. 5), their calling brought them, quite as little as
did that of the apostles and prophets, into relation with
existing Churches, or with the local Church. This was
the particular relation sustained by pastors (Acts xx. 28 ;
1 Pet. v. 2) and teachers (1 Cor. xii. 28 ; Rom. xii. 7 ;
Acts xiii. 1 ; Jas. iii. 1), who for this reason are designated as one class. From this it is not to be inferred
that at the time when Ephesians was written the teaching
office and the office of leadership in the Church were
regularly combined, any more than it is to be inferred
from ii. 20, iii. 5 that apostles and prophets were always
the same persons. All that can be said is that the
language used is more natural if frequently the head of
the Church performed also the office of teacher (1 Tim.
iii. 2, v. 17 ; Tit. i. 9 ; Heb. xiii. 7 ; Acts xv. 22, 32).

Only on the assumption that it is a characteristic of
Paul, in season and out of season, always to say the same
thing, can it be argued that Ephesians is spurious on the
ground that there are new thoughts in this Epistle in
addition to those which are emphasised by Paul elsewhere,
such as the ideas of election and predestination (i. 4, 5,
9, 11, iii. 9, 11) of the ἀπολύτρωσις through the blood of
Christ (i. 7 ; cf. Rom. iii. 24 f.), of salvation not by works
but by faith (ii. 8 f.), of the reception of the Gentiles
among God's ancient people (ii. 11–19 ; cf. Rom. iv. 1–12,
xi. 16–24), of the old and new, and of the inner man
(ii. 15, iii. 16, iv. 22–24). The fact that Paul identifies
himself with Jewish Christians and opposes himself to
Gentile Christians certainly cannot be made an argument
against the genuineness of the Epistle ; for, in the first
place, exegetes are not agreed in their interpretations of
the interchange of " we " and " ye " in Eph. i. 12, 13,
ii. 2–10—in fact, the text is not altogether certain (ii. 8) ;

and, in the second place, quite apart from these difficulties, Paul could never have so far forgotten his Jewish origin as to identify himself with the Gentile Christians in this one point which distinguished them (cf. Gal. ii. 15 ; Rom. vii. 5 f., ix. 1 ff., xi. 1–7 ; cf. also the contrast between "we" in Gal. iii. 13, 23–25, iv. 3–5, and "the Gentiles" or "ye" in Gal. iii. 14, 26–29, iv. 6–11). In view of what is said in Gal. ii. 20, Rom. viii. 35, 37, it seems quite unlikely that the idea that Christ loved us, v. 2, 25, should be interpreted as indicating a type of thought transitional between Paul and John, or that the same interpretation should be made of the idea of love to the Lord in v. 2, 25 (cf. 1 Cor. xvi. 22 ; Philem. 5), or of the contrast of light and darkness (cf. Rom. xiii. 12 ; 2 Cor. vi. 14 ; 1 Thess. v. 4 f.), and similar conceptions (HK, iii. 99 f.). If it could be shown that the idea of the parousia has practically disappeared from Ephesians, and that its place has been taken by the idea of a long continuance of the present order of things (HK, 94), it would prove that the Epistle is not Paul's, but would at the same time take us beyond the post-apostolic age into the third or fourth century. If this is the thought expressed by τοῖς αἰῶσι τοῖς ἐπερχομένοις in ii. 7, then we have the same idea expressed in εἰς τοὺς αἰῶνας (Rom. i. 25, ix. 5), certainly in εἰς τοὺς αἰῶνας τῶν αἰώνων (Gal. i. 5 ; cf. Eph. iii. 21) ; for, without any question from the point of view of the Christian who expresses praise in this language, these æons are future. When, moreover, it is expressly said in ii. 7 that these æons are yet to come, there is implied a contrast with the αἰὼν οὗτος (Rom. xii. 2 ; 1 Cor. ii. 6 ; Eph. i. 21), to be terminated by the day of redemption and of judgment, i.e. the return of the Lord (Eph. iv. 30, v. 6).

It has frequently been argued that Ephesians is spurious, because of the enlarged significance given to Christ by which he is made to include the whole creation, even the world of spirits (i. 10, 21, iii. 10),—an argument that

certainly ought not to be advanced by those who admit
the genuineness of Colossians, which contains even bolder
statements of this kind (i. 16, 20, ii. 15).   From 1 Cor.
viii. 6 we know that Paul held the universe to have been
created and to be preserved through Christ.   Assuming
that the δι' οὗ in the Corinthian passage is only a more exact
definition of the δι' αὐτοῦ in Rom. xi. 36, which refers to
God, it is evident that Christ is not to be excluded from
the εἰς αὐτόν of Rom. xi. 36.   When Christ is described as
the second Adam (1 Cor. xv. 22, 45), the characterisation
means, not only that He is the goal of humanity, but of
the universe, which was created for humanity's sake, and
is, in principle, subordinate to humanity.   Since it was
through the sin of humanity that death became a ruling
power, and the general condition of the universe became
one of bondage to that which is perishable (Rom. v. 12,
viii. 18 ff.), it is evident that, with the removal of sin and
of its consequencies not only will humanity be restored
to its place of entire dominion in the person of the second
Adam, but the whole disordered organism will be restored,
and, finally, the dominion of death, wherever it has reigned,
will be destroyed (1 Cor. xv. 24–28 ; Rom. viii. 19, 21).
Even if it were not affirmed in so many words (1 Cor.
vi. 2 f., xv. 24), yet, from the general biblical view of the
relation sustained by angels to the natural world, it would
be self-evident that the spirit-world was to have part in
this general apocatastasis (Acts iii. 21).   In accordance
with this, the following statements contain no new thought.
The universe, including the world of invisible spirits, was
created not only in and through Christ, but also for Him
(Col. i. 16).   In Him or under Him as its head the
universe was to be gathered into one (Eph. i. 10).   The
reconciliation to God of an estranged humanity, which
had been accomplished by Christ's death on the cross,
involved the restoration of the relation between the
universe and Christ, which was a law of creation, but had

been disturbed by sin and its consequences (Col. i. 20).
It involved also the restoration of harmony within the
universe, a harmony likewise based upon Christ and disturbed by sin (Col. i. 20), just as it involved the restoration
of the ties between different branches of the human race,
which had been broken (Eph. ii. 14–16); in other words,
the bringing together of the Gentiles, who had been separated from God, and the people of His revelation to share
the benefits of this revelation (Col. i. 21 ; Eph. ii. 12 f.).
In the nature of the case, the world of spirits, which
operated in the secret background of the world's life, must
have been aware of these influences emanating from Christ
(Eph. iii. 10), and have been able to detect them before
it was possible for men to do so, who must learn of
them gradually, as they heard and accepted the gospel.
For the exaggerations of these statements by a later age
Paul is not responsible (n. 11). Similarly, the statement
that by the victorious march of the gospel through the
world God has stripped from Himself the spirit-powers
which concealed Him from the Gentile world in order to
reveal Himself in His true nature (Col. ii. 15, above,
p. 473 f.), is only an original way of expressing the thought
of 1 Cor. viii. 5 f. In view of the circumstances under which
the two letters were written, what Paul says on these
subjects in Ephesians and Colossians,—more emphatically in Colossians than in Ephesians, as was natural in
view of the false doctrine which he here opposes,—and the
echoes in Ephesians of thoughts suggested by this contest
in Colossæ, are not unnatural.

How impossible it is to accept the results of this
negative criticism of Ephesians, is shown by the inability
of this criticism to furnish a plausible motive for the
forgery of the letter. According to Baur (*Paulus*, ii.
39 f.), the purpose of the two letters is not so much the
theoretical purpose " to expound the higher conception
of the person of Christ which they both contain," as the

practical purpose to prepare the way for adjustment between the Gentile Christian and Jewish Christian parties,
and so to bring about the establishment of a single Christian Church, and again and again the primary purpose, at
least of Ephesians, is declared to be the complete union of
Gentiles and those of Jewish birth within the Church in
a firm fellowship (*HK*, iii. 84). Opposition and conflict
between the two are presupposed by Holtzmann (*Krit.* 303,
cf. S. 208, 272) when he makes this *Paulus redivivus* sound
the note of triumph and of peace in the Churches founded
by Paul. But where is the evidence that with reference
to the relation of Jews and Gentiles in the Church there
was need for an exhortation to peace? While it is true
that in ii. 11–22 mention is made of the hostility between
Gentiles and Jews which existed prior to the advent of
Christ and was removed by His death, there is no indication that where the gospel was accepted within single
Christian communities, which embraced both Jews and
Gentiles, this hostility was revived, or continued to exist
in a new form of hostility between Jewish and Gentile
Christians. Throughout the letter, like a dominant tone,
one hears naught but the note of entire restoration of
peace and of the continued equality and unity of those
who had formerly been Gentiles and Jews. Nothing is
said about events tending either to imperil or to promote
harmony between Jewish and Gentile Christians, as in
Gal. ii. 1–14 or Acts xv., nor are there exhortations to
mutual concessions on the part of Gentiles and Jews, as
in Rom. xv. 1–13. The exhortation to harmony, because
of their common interest in the benefits of redemption,
and in view of the diversity of their gifts (iv. 1–16), concerns the mutual relations of the readers (iv. 2, 25, v. 21).
But inasmuch as the readers are everywhere addressed
collectively as native Gentiles (ii. 11, iii. 1), with nothing
to indicate that there were Jewish Christians in their
circle or even in their vicinity, this exhortation can have

nothing to do with hostility between Jews and Gentiles within the Church. As regards the relation of these Churches to the Church as a whole, nothing is said of the obligation of Gentile Christians to the mother Church, as in Rom. xv. 27; 2 Cor. viii.–ix.; nor is it even mentioned that it was a matter of significance to the Churches in Asia to know that a portion of the Christians outside of Jerusalem were Jews by birth. Only two things are said: They are to love all the saints (i. 15; Col. i. 4; Philem. 5), and they are to pray for all the saints (vi. 18). Such a purpose as this cannot be rightly attributed to the forger of the letter. If so, then we must conclude that he used every means in his power to conceal his purpose and none to realise it. Neither could this pseudo-Paul have meant to express triumphant joy at the success which had crowned Paul's life-work in spite of all the opposition that he had met; for if so, how came it that he addressed the letter to Churches with the organising of which Paul had nothing to do? As a matter of fact he does not praise Paul's success in any special way; and had he wanted to do so, being without ideas of his own, he would have borrowed them from passages like 1 Thess. i. 2–10, ii. 19 f., iv. 9; 2 Thess. i. 3 f.; Phil. i. 5, iv. 1, 15, which it must be assumed he had read. That Paul had heard of these Churches (i. 15), and that they had heard of him (iii. 2), is nothing significant; and that what they had heard had been mutually favourable, is nothing to be triumphantly proclaimed. In fact, where do we hear anything about a preceding conflict without which it would be impossible to speak of victory? The list of these groundless inventions is complete only when a third alleged purpose in the composition of the letter is added, namely, reproof and punishment (Holtzmann, 304). But where in Ephesians is there any indication that the moral and religious conditions in these Churches were unsatisfactory, or where do we discover a word of reproof? Their former heathen life and the conduct of the Gentiles among whom they were living are condemned (ii. 1, iv. 17 f.); but the readers themselves are exhorted only in the most loving way to walk according to their calling, the teaching which they have received, and the love of Christ which they have experienced (iv. 1, 20 f., 32, v. 1), involving naturally as it does the avoidance of sins inherited both by birth and training. What it meant to "reprove and punish" a pseudo-Paul might have learned from Galatians or 2 Cor., or, better still, from the apocalyptic letters to which he is supposed to reply, if indeed he did not say to himself that it was unnecessary in his composition to say anything about heathen immorality in addition to what was to be found in the genuine apostolic writings expressed so trenchantly and so true to life.

1. (P. 491.) For the history of the criticism applied to both Epistles, cf. Holtzmann, *Kritik der Epheser- und Kolosserbriefe* (*sic*), 1872, S. 2 f., 18 f. In comparison with the objections raised against Eph. by Usteri, *Paul. Lehrbegriff*, 1824, S. 2 f., de Wette (from his first edition of the *Einl.* 1826 on, more and more decided against its genuineness), and Schleiermacher (*Einl.*, ed. Wolde, S. 163 ff., 166, "the whole situation of the Epistle doubtful. . . . All positive hypotheses lack foundation," hence even his own conjecture in the first draft that Tychicus or some other disciple wrote it after the pattern of Col., and with Paul's approval, cf. S. 172), Mayerhoff (*Der Br. an die Kol. mit vornehmlicher Berücksichtigung der Pastoralbriefe*, 1838) sought with considerable method to establish his hypothesis that Col. arose on the basis of Eph., which also was not written until after Paul's time.

2. (P. 491.) Baur, *Paulus*, ii. 3–49, and Weizsäcker, 541–545, without more precise dating (Hilgenfeld, *Einl.* 680), shortly before 140 A.D. Regarding the arguments for the post-Pauline origin of the Epistles, drawn mostly from their theological content, see above in the text. Hilgenfeld, 663, finds it strange that Paul should have remained personally unknown to the Churches at Colossæ and Laodicea, since he had twice travelled through Phrygia (Acts xvi. 6, xviii. 23). But Paul seems to have touched this part of Phrygia on neither his second nor his third missionary journey; above, pp. 188, 190, 449 f. Yet even had he done so, we should have to conclude from Eph. and Col. that he did not succeed either time in founding Churches in this part of Phrygia, but that these arose only after he was established in Ephesus. The placing of the Greek before the Jew, Col. iii. 11, which Mayerhoff (S. 15) had already adduced as a proof of ungenuineness, has no significance, since Paul

here is stating this contrast in a sentence addressed to Gentile Christians.
The precedence of the Greek here was just as natural as of the Jew in
1 Cor. xii. 13, a sentence in which Paul the Jew classes himself with the
Gentiles of Corinth. In the independent sentence, Gal. iii. 28, there was
nothing to prescribe which should come first.

3. (P. 491.) Hitzig, *Zur Kritik paulinischer Briefe*, 1875, S. 22-33.
Holtzmann (title in n. 1) illustrates the criticism which he applies to Col.,
S. 325 ff., by printing the whole Epistle in two kinds of type to distinguish
the genuine from the spurious. Aside from a few individual words, the
interpolations are, according to him, i. 9b-12, 14-24, 26-28, ii. 2b-iii. 7a, 9-11,
15, 17-19, 22 f., iii. 1, 2, 4-11, 14-16, 18-25, iv. 1, 9, 15-17. In the *JbfPTh.*
1885, S. 320-368, von Soden held i. 15-20, ii. 10, 15, 18 to be interpolations by another than the author of Eph.; but in the *HK*, iii. 33, these
suspected passages are reduced to i. 16b, 17. As an analogy for Hitzig's
hypothesis is adduced the procedure of that obscurantist, who about 370 or
400 interpolated the seven genuine letters of Ignatius and added six new
ones of his own devising; perhaps the same man who from the old *Didascalia*
manufactured the *Apostolic Constitutions*.

4. (P. 497.) Accounts of Cerinthus that are comparatively reliable, and
that are not in themselves contradictory, are found in Iren. i. 26. 1, iii.
3. 4 (cf. iii. 9. 3, 11. 7, 16. 5-6); Hippol. *Refut.* vii. 33, x. 21 : pseudo-
Tert. *Hær.* x. Epiphanius, *Hær.* xxviii. 1, 2, 5, and Philaster, *Hær.* xxxvi.,
who is here dependent upon him, were the first to ascribe to Cerinthus a
legalistic Judaism altogether incompatible with this representation, being
misled by the way in which Irenæus joined him to Ebion and Karpocrates
(Iren. i. 26. 2, where, according to Hippolytus, *similiter* or *consimiliter* should
be read instead of *non similiter*). This passage may have been repeated in
Hippolytus' *Syntagma*, referring, however, only to the denial of the virgin
birth of Christ. The story of the sensual chiliasm of Cerinthus (*GK*, i. 230),
started by the Alogi and spread abroad since the time of Caius of Rome, may
remain unnoticed here. We come upon difficulties only in Iren. iii. 11. 1,
which mentions as the false teachers, against whom John wrote his Gospel,
not only the Cerinthians, but along with them the older Nicolaitans, who are
designated as an ἀπόσπασμα τῆς ψευδωνύμου γνώσεως, the oldest Gnosticism.
For this very reason we could not conclude that the incidental hints here of
an æon doctrine (*Pleroma, Monogenes,* and the *Logos*, distinguished from
this as its son), refer to Cerinthus also. Further, since the æon doctrine
hinted at here presupposes the prologue of John (*GK*, i. 736 ff.), the assumption
is a likely one that Irenæus classed with the teachings of Cerinthus and the
Nicolaitans, which were being propagated in John's time and against which
he wrote, other later doctrines, the weapons for opposing which John is said
to have forged in advance (iii. 16. 5, *prævidens has blasphemas regulas*).
Moreover, the passage which follows, iii. 11. 2, confirms this assumption ;
cf. Hümpel, *De errore christol. in ep. Joannis impugnato*, Erlangen, 1897.

5. (P. 498.) We know from Iren. i. 11. 1, 30. 15, ii. 13. 8, that Valentinus
did not invent all his doctrines, but worked up the raw speculations of an
older Gnosis into an ingenious system ; the very concept πλήρωμα, however, is peculiar to the phraseology of his school, so far as we know. This
seems to be true also of the peculiar designation αἰῶνες, for the individual

beings to be distinguished in the Pleroma. It is the more certain that this arose from an allegorical interpretation of N.T. passages where measures of time, æons, years, or hours occurred (Iren. i. 1. 3, iii. 1–6); for its use cannot be explained at all from the nature of these intermediate beings as they were conceived by the Valentinians. Since Irenæus in his account of the Barbelo-Gnostics (following, to be sure, one of their own writings; cf. C. Schmidt, *Berl. Akad. Sitzungsber.* 1896, S. 842 f.), uses *æonem quendam* and *magnum æona* (i. 29. 1, 2, cf. xxx. 2), expressions which he avoids in his account of Simon, Menander, Cerinthus, Saturninus, and Basilides, we must conclude that this sect was not independent of Valentinus. Concerning Iren. iii. 11. 1, see above, n. 4.

6. (P. 500.) On April 1, 1895, in Friedrichsruh, the present writer heard two speeches by Bismarck, separated only by a breakfast, the first addressed to twenty-one professors; the second, in the presence of four or five thousand students. No one who heard the first could fail to see that the main thoughts, and many of the expressions, whole sentences indeed, were the same in both speeches; but no one on that account listened with impatience to the second, for its tone was much warmer and was artlessly adapted to the changed audience.

7. (P. 500). Examples of the characteristics of Paul's style mentioned above, p. 500, are here cited; an asterisk designates those which, outside the letter cited in any particular instance, do not occur in any of the letters pretty generally recognised as Pauline, or sometimes anywhere else in the whole N.T. outside of the letter quoted at the time : * πρὸς καθαίρεσιν, 2 Cor. x. 4 ; καθαιρεῖν, x. 5 ; εἰς καθαίρεσιν opposed to οἰκοδομήν, x. 8, xiii. 10.— * ἐν ἑτοίμῳ ἔχειν, 2 Cor. x. 6 ; ἑτοίμως ἔχειν, xii. 14 (nowhere else except Acts xxi. 13 [speech of Paul] ; 1 Pet. iv. 5).—* οἱ ὑπερλίαν ἀπόστολοι, 2 Cor. xi. 5, xii. 11.—* καταναρκεῖν, 2 Cor. xi. 9, xii. 13, 14.—βαρεῖσθαι, 2 Cor. i. 8, v. 4 ; ἐπιβαρεῖν, ii. 5 ; βάρος, iv. 17 ; ἀβαρῆ ἑαυτὸν τηρεῖν, xi. 9 ; καταβαρεῖν, xii. 16 (cf., besides, βάρος, Gal. vi. 2 ; only 1 Thess. ii. 6, ἐν βάρει εἶναι ; ii. 9 ; 2 Thess. iii. 8, ἐπιβαρῆσαι).—* ἐξαπορεῖσθαι, 2 Cor. i. 8, iv. 8.—λογίζομαι (not in the sense of "to impute," as fourteen times in Rom. and in 1 Cor. xiii. 5 ; 2 Cor. v. 19 ; 2 Tim. iv. 16, but of the estimation of a person), 2 Cor. x. 2, 7, 11, xi. 5, xii. 6 (in this sense only in 1 Cor. iv. 1 ; Phil. iii. 13 besides).—φυσιοῦν six times, 1 Cor., elsewhere only Col. ii. 18.—συνίστημι, 2 Cor. iii. 1 (here συστατικός also), iv. 2, v. 12, vi. 4, vii. 11, x. 12, x. 18 (twice), xii. 11 ; in all other Epistles together only four times.—παρακαλεῖν seventeen times, παράκλησις eleven times in 2 Cor. ; the former three or four times in Rom., six times in 1 Cor., the latter three times in Rom., once in 1 Cor.—βασιλεύειν, Rom. v. 14, v. 17 (twice), v. 21 (twice), vi. 12 ; this occurs elsewhere only in 1 Cor. iv. 8, xv. 25.—οὐκ οἴδατε, with or without ἤ preceding, 1 Cor. iii. 16, v. 6, vi. 2, 3, 9, 15, 16, 19, ix. 13, 24 ; out of all the other Epistles, only in Rom. vi. 16, xi. 2, and the substitute for it ἢ ἀγνοεῖτε, only in Rom. vi. 3, vii. 1.—* οὐδέν (μοι) διαφέρει, Gal. ii. 6, iv. 1.—* ἀνατίθεσθαι and προσανατίθεσθαι, Gal. i. 16, ii. 2, 6.—* ταράσσων, Gal. i. 7, v 10.—* πορθεῖν in conjunction with διώκειν, Gal. i. 13, 23.—* τί οὖν with a question following Rom. iii. 9, vi. 15, xi. 7, and τί οὖν ἐροῦμεν, Rom. iv. 1, vi. 1, vii. 7, viii. 31, ix. 14, 30, cf. iii. 5 ; only a distant parallel in 1 Cor. x. 19, υἱοθεσία, Rom. viii. 15, 23, ix. 4, each time in a different connection ; only other occurrences,

Gal. iv. 5 ; Eph. i. 5.—ἄρα οὖν, Rom. v. 18, vii. 3, 25, viii. 12, ix. 16, 18, xiv. 12, 19 ; only other occurrences, Gal. vi. 10 ; 1 Thess. v. 6, and in the suspected Epistles, 2 Thess. ii. 15 ; Eph. ii. 19. One observes the same thing, however, in the case of Col. and Eph. also, whether they be taken separately or conceived of together as having been written one right after the other : ἀπαλλοτριοῦσθαι, Eph. ii. 12, iv. 18 ; Col. i. 21.—εἰς ἔπαινον τῆς χάριτος or δόξης αὐτοῦ, Eph. i. 6, 12, 14.—σύνδεσμος, Eph. iv. 3 ; Col. ii. 19, iii. 14.— συνεγείρειν, Eph. ii. 6 ; Col. ii. 12, iii. 1.—* δόγμα, Eph. ii. 15 ; Col. ii. 14 ; δογματίζειν, Col. ii. 20.—* παροργισμός, Eph. iv. 26 ; παροργίζειν, vi. 4 ; perhaps also Col. iii. 21 (Rom. x. 19 from LXX).—* ἐν τοῖς ἐπουρανίοις, Eph. i. 3, 20, ii. 6, iii. 10, vi. 12 = ἐν (τοῖς) οὐρανοῖς, 2 Cor. v. 1 ; Phil. iii. 20 ; Col. i. 5, 16, 20, while ἐπουράνιος by itself occurs also 1 Cor. xv. 40, 48 f.; Phil. ii. 10 ; 2 Tim. iv. 18.—* μεθοδεία, Eph. iv. 14, vi. 11.—* συναρμολογεῖν, Eph. ii. 21, iv. 16.—σύμμετοχος, Eph. iii. 6, v. 7.—* καταβραβεύειν, Col. ii. 18 ; βραβεύειν, Col. iii. 15 (above, p. 472, n. 3), with which also ἀγών, ἀγωνίζεσθαι belong, Col. i. 29, ii. 1, iv. 12.—* σύνδουλος, Col. i. 7, iv. 7.—* ἀπεκδύεσθαι and ἀπέκδυσις, Col. ii. 11, 15, iii. 9.—ἄρχαι καὶ ἐξουσίαι, Eph. iii. 10, vi. 12 ; Col. i. 16, ii. 15, cf. Eph. i. 21 ; Col. ii. 10 (only other comparable instances Rom. viii. 38 ; 1 Cor. xv. 24).—κεφαλή of Christ, Eph. i. 22, iv. 15, v. 23 ; Col. i. 18, ii. 10 (1 Cor. xi. 3 is hardly comparable) ; hence ἀνακεφαλαιοῦσθαι, Eph. i. 10 (different in Rom. xiii. 9).—* αἰσχρότης ἢ μωρολογία, Eph. v. 4 ; αἰσχρὸς λέγειν, v. 12 ; αἰσχρολογία, Col. iii. 8.—οἰκοδομή, Eph. ii. 21, iv. 12, 16, 29.— πληροῦν, Eph. i. 23, iii. 19, iv. 10, v. 18 ; Col. i. 9, 25, ii. 10, iv. 12, 17 (in the four " main Epistles " only seven times), and πλήρωμα, Eph. i. 10, 23, iii. 19, iv. 13 ; Col. i. 19, ii. 9 (instances in all the other Epistles are, disregarding the quotation 1 Cor. x. 26, confined to Rom. xi. 12, 25, xiii. 10, xv. 29, i.e. here also within very narrow limits).—ὀφθαλμοδουλεία and ἀνθρωπάρεσκοι, Eph. vi. 6 ; Col. iii. 22.

8. (P. 501.) An instance of this dependence would be the origin of the salutation, as Holtzmann, *Krit.* 131 f., cf. 55 f., conceives it. The author who made up this letter on the basis of Col. pictured to himself the seven Churches of Rev. i. 4, 11, from Ephesus to Laodicea (S. 13 f., 245, 307), as those addressed. The error of this assumption is obvious ; the author did not have in mind Ephesus (above, p. 484 f.), which stands at the head of the list, Rev. i. 11, ii. 1, but, on the contrary, did include in his thought from the first Colossæ, which is not mentioned at all in Rev. i.–iv. (above, pp. 480 f., 486). Besides, Col. iv. 13, where the forger found Hierapolis mentioned, leaves no doubt that he intended Eph., which was composed by him, for the Church in Hierapolis also, another place not mentioned in Rev. If, however, he thought that he must address the seven Churches of Rev., though in a different sense from that of the letters there, why did he not make this plain to his readers by a salutation modelled after Rev. i. 4 ? He preferred to copy Col. i. 1, so far as it suited him. The words as far as θεοῦ suited, but then he struck out " Timothy the brother," since his "universal and ecumenical aim " required him to strip away all "individual and local limitations in the original " (Holtzm. 131) ; just as if Timothy was not mentioned as joint author in the letter addressed to all the Christians of all Achaia, a letter, therefore, which had an aim just as much and just as little ecumenical as Eph. (2 Cor. i. 1). He then copied τοῖς, and, since he could not use ἐν Κολοσσαῖς, passed at once

to ἁγίοις. Why he copied this and not καὶ πιστοῖς immediately after is not explained. While he could not yet decide upon a fitting address—as ἐν τῇ Ἀσίᾳ, perhaps—to insert at the place where he found ἐν Κολοσσαῖς, so useless to him, it was only after he had copied all of the next word ἁγίοις that he reflected "that at any rate the letter must go somewhither" (Holtzm. 132). But now his patience gave out before he could copy the καὶ πιστοῖς ἐν Χριστῷ, which belongs to ἁγίοις, and to which any number of names of places could be conveniently annexed by means of a τοῖς οὖσιν ; so he straightway decided to insert a local address in the most unsuitable place conceivable, and wrote τοῖς οὖσιν as preliminary thereto. According to Holtzm. 132, he decided, after longer meditation "over the mode of the address," to write " τοῖς οὖσιν ἐν, leaving the name in question to be filled in later." How Holtzmann thinks he knows this remains a mystery. Whether the author in his autograph originally left a space after ἐν, where his secretary was supposed to insert in the copies intended for the individual Churches the names of their respective cities, and perhaps did so insert them, or whether he himself prepared seven exemplars each with a different address after ἐν, in either case it is equally incomprehensible that the whole ancient Church until after Origen should have possessed no exemplars with ἐν, followed by a gap or by some one or other of these seven names. The ἐν Ἐφέσῳ, which has prevailed since the fourth century, is certainly, according to all extant testimony, direct and indirect (Marcion, Tertullian, Origen, Basil, Jerome, above, p. 488 f.), inserted into an older text which contained neither an ἐν nor a local address. The result of the deep reflection of this writer, who "could not at once specify [his readers] with local exactness," was therefore this : that he gave up trying to find a local designation for his letter, and then went merrily on to copy what is written in Col. i. 2. Why he omitted ἀδελφοῖς, and on the other hand inserted an Ἰησοῦ, and at the end again a καὶ κυρίου Ἰησοῦ Χριστοῦ, which is unquestionably spurious in Col. i. 2, Holtzmann has failed to explain from the "ecumenical" character of the Epistle, or more properly from its designation for the seven Churches of Rev. But without this we have gone far enough to see clearly that the author of this Epistle, which, as no one denies, is rich in great thoughts and sustained by a lofty enthusiasm, was a wretched bungler, unable even to write a salutation suited to his purpose.

9. (P. 503.) Holtzmann, *Krit.* 100 f., counts in Eph. thirty-nine words which occur elsewhere indeed in the N.T., but not in Paul's writings, and thirty-seven which occur nowhere else in the N.T., *i.e.* seventy-six un-Pauline words. The same total is given by von Soden, *HK*, iii. 88, though he assigns only thirty-five to the second class. The lists need sifting. (A) καταβραβεύειν should be stricken out, since it occurs only in Col. ii. 18, not in Eph. ; further, either ἀπελπίζειν or ἀπαλγεῖν, since we cannot read both in iv. 19 ; also ἅπας, vi. 13, which is likewise well attested in Gal. iii. 28 (quite apart from the fact that πᾶς, which Paul uses everywhere else, occurs fifty-one times in Eph.). Then all exact and inexact quotations from the O.T. should be excluded from the calculation, unless we make the absurd claim that Paul corrected on principle the text of the LXX according to his own vocabulary. Consequently without further debate fall out of consideration αἰχμαλωτεύω, αἰχμαλωσία, ὕψος, iv. 8 (Ps. lxviii. 19, Paul himself uses αἰχμαλωτίζω, Rom. vii. 23 ; 2 Cor. x. 5 ; 2 Tim. iii. 6) ; ὀργίζεσθαι, iv. 26

(Ps. iv. 5); σωτήριον, vi. 17 (Isa. lix. 17, instead of this, 1 Thess. v. 8, more freely ἐλπὶς σωτηρίας); τιμᾶν, vi. 2 (Ex. xx. 12); ἐπιφαύσκειν, v. 14 (GK, ii. 804). Further, words which occur in 1 and 2 Tim. and in Tit. should not be reckoned unqualifiedly as un-Pauline, such as ἀπατᾶν, v. 6 (1 Tim. ii. 14; aside from this, the presence of this word is without significance in view of ἀπάτη, Col. ii. 8 ; 2 Thess. ii. 10 ; Eph. iv. 22); ἄλυσις, vi. 20 (2 Tim. i. 16); διάβολος, iv. 27, vi. 11 (1 Tim. iii. 6, 7 ; 2 Tim. ii. 26); εὐαγγελιστής, iv. 11 (2 Tim. iv. 5); παιδεία, vi. 4 (2 Tim. iii. 16).   (B) Designations of things, qualities, or relations, for which there is but one ordinary expression, are of no significance in determining a man's style, unless it can be shown that elsewhere he uses an uncommon expression instead ; thus ἄνεμος, iv. 14; ὕδωρ, v. 26 ; ὀσφύς, περιζώννυμι, ὑποδέω, vi. 14 f.; μῆκος and πλάτος, iii. 18 (in conjunction with ὕψος, iv. 8, see under A, and βάθος, Rom. viii. 39, xi. 33); μέγεθος, i. 19 (neither has Paul μεγαλειότης, μεγαλωσύνη); μακράν, ii. 13, 17 (in conjunction with ἐγγύς, Phil. iv. 5); ἀμφότεροι, ii. 14, 16, 18; ἀπειλή, vi. 9; perhaps also ῥυτίς, σπῖλος, v. 27 ; κρυφῆ, v. 12 (as over against a single ἐν τῷ κρυπτῷ, Rom. ii. 29).   Also θυρεός, the large shield of the Roman soldiers, and the βέλη, against which the shield served as a protection, belong here, unless we are inclined to find fault with the apostle, who had lived for years constantly in the custody of soldiers, and who even before that had borrowed many figures from military service, because he once mentions the shield in addition to the breastplate and helmet (1 Thess. v. 8), or sums up all the weapons of defence and offence as πανοπλία, vi. 11, 13.   Since in letters very widely separated in time he is accustomed to draw figures from the games also, it can have no significance that he once, instead of the race and boxing match (1 Cor. ix. 24 ff. ; Phil. iii. 14 ; 2 Tim. iv. 7 f.), makes use of the wrestling match, and writes πάλη, vi. 12. von Soden classes among the pet words of Eph. which, he holds, never slipped from Paul's pen elsewhere (HK, 89), δέσμιος, iii. 1, iv. 1 ; but in doing so he forgets ver. 9 of Philem., a letter which he acknowledges to be genuine (cf. 2 Tim. i. 8) ; nor does he consider that it was only as a prisoner that Paul could so designate himself and talk of his δεσμοί, Phil. i. 7, 13–17 ; Philem. 10–13 ; Col. iv. 18 ; 2 Tim. ii. 9.   (C) Equally of no significance are words related in derivation to other words of Paul used outside of Eph. and Col., and in place of which he elsewhere never or very seldom uses other expressions. So a solitary ἄγνοια, iv. 18, as over against a solitary ἀγνωσία, 1 Cor. xv. 34 ; ἀγνοεῖν occurring thirteen or fifteen times ; or παιδεία, vi. 4 (2 Tim. iii. 16); related to παιδευτής, Rom. ii. 20; παιδεύεσθαι, 1 Cor. xi. 32 ; 2 Cor. vi. 9 ; παιδαγωγός, 1 Cor. iv. 15 ; Gal. iii. 24 ; or προσκαρτέρησις, vi. 18 ; along with προσκαρτερεῖν, Rom. xii. 12, xiii. 6 ; Col. iv. 2 ; or ἄνοιξις, vi. 19; from ἀνοίγειν, Col. iv. 3 ; also with στόμα as object, 2 Cor. vi. 11 ; or χειροποιητός, ii. 11 ; along with ἀχειροποίητος, 2 Cor. v. 1 ; Col. ii. 11 ; or φρόνησις, i. 8, as compared with φρόνημα, which has a somewhat different meaning (only in Rom. viii. 6, 7, 27), and the frequent φρονεῖν ; or καταρτισμός, iv. 12, as against a solitary κατάρτισις, 2 Cor. xiii. 9, καταρτίζειν being often employed similarly ; or αἰσχρότης καὶ μωρολογία, v. 4, as compared with αἰσχρὸς λέγειν, v. 12 ; αἰσχρολογία, Col. iii. 8 ; αἰσχρός (unseemly), 1 Cor. xi. 6, xiv. 35 (Tit. i. 11) ; cf. also, as regards the formation of the second word, χρηστολογία, Rom. xvi. 18 ; and πιθανολογία, Col. ii. 4, each of which occurs but once.   If in iv. 23 ἀνανεοῦν stands instead of ἀνακαινοῦν (Col. iii. 10; 2 Cor. iv. 16; cf. Rom. xii. 2; Tit. iii. 5), Paul likewise has along with καινὴ κτίσις, 2 Cor. v. 17, νέον φύραμα, 1 Cor. v. 7, which means essentially the same; and the collocation of ἀνανεοῦσθαι and καινὸν ἄνθρωπον (Eph. iv. 23 f.) has its counterpart in νέον ἀνακαινούμενον, Col. iii. 10. In 1 Cor. ix. 7, ποίμνη and ποιμαίνειν serve as a figure of labour in the Church; hence ποιμένες, iv. 11, should cause no surprise, and from this standpoint there would be no reason to object to Bentley's endeavour to read this word instead of δυνάμεις in 1 Cor. xii. 28, 29 (Ellies, *Bentleii Critica Sacra*, 37), especially since unquestionably the figure was very common in apostolic times (1 Pet. v. 2 f.; Acts xx. 28 f.; John x. 9, xxi. 15–17). If Paul represents the Church of the O.T. as well as of the N.T. under the form of a πόλις (Gal. iv. 25 f.), he must have dared to use πολιτεία also, ii. 12, and συμπολίτης, ii. 19, when occasion offered, just as elsewhere he uses πολίτευμα, πολιτεύεσθαι, Phil. i. 27, iii. 20. So also it is of no moment whatever, that the concepts opposed to these, ξένοι, πάροικοι, ii. 19, the latter is not used by Paul elsewhere, and the former only in Rom. xvi. 23, and then with a different meaning. If in 1 Cor. iii. 10–17 he regards the individual Church as a building in process of erection and as a temple, it is no mark of lexical peculiarity for him in Eph. ii. 20 ff. to apply the same figure to the whole Church, and thus in addition to οἰκοδομή, θεμέλιος, ναὸς ἅγιος, ἐποικοδομεῖν, used elsewhere by him, to use also συνοικοδομεῖν, ἀκρογωνιαῖος, κατοικητήριον, συναρμολογεῖσθαι. Since he represents Christians as forming a σῶμα (1 Cor. xii. 12–28; Rom. xii. 4 f.), σύσσωμος, iii. 6, cannot surprise us, even if Paul coined this word himself. This word shares the fault of being used by Paul only once with those of similar formation, συμφυλέτης, σύμφυτος, σύμφωνος, σύμψυχος, σύζυγος, συνηλικιώτης (σύμμορφος twice), and a hundred others in the older Epistles. It is possible that Paul, who earlier as "a Hebrew" wrote σατανᾶς regularly (Rom. xvi. 20; 1 Cor. v. 5, vii. 5; 2 Cor. ii. 11, xi. 14; 1 Thess. ii. 18; 2 Thess. ii. 9), and along with this perhaps only ὁ πειράζων (1 Thess. iii. 5), later became accustomed to say ὁ διάβολος. But all that can be adduced in support of this, outside of Eph. vi. 11, is 2 Tim. ii. 26; for Eph. iv. 27, 1 Tim. iii. 6, 7 plainly treat of human slanderers; and along with it we find ὁ πόνηρος, Eph. vi. 16; cf. 2 Thess. iii. 3; and ὁ σατανᾶς, 1 Tim. i. 20, v. 15. Similarly uncertain would be the claim that ἀγρυπνεῖν, Eph. vi. 18, which takes the place of the older γρηγορεῖν, 1 Cor. xvi. 13, 1 Thess. v. 6, 10, indicates a later usage; for the former is found nowhere else in the later Epistles, while on the other hand the latter occurs in Col. iv. 2. The remaining words in the list are ἀνιέναι, vi. 9; ἄσοφος, v. 15; ἀσωτία, v. 18 (elsewhere only in Tit. i. 6); ἐκτρέφειν, v. 29, vi. 4; ἑνότης, iv. 3, 13; εὔσπλαγχνος, iv. 32; ἐξισχύειν, iii. 18; ἐπιδύειν, iv. 26; ἑτοιμασία, vi. 15; εὐτραπελία, v. 4; κατώτερος, iv. 9; κληροῦν, i. 11; κλυδωνίζεσθαι, iv. 14; κοσμοκράτωρ, vi. 12; κυβεία, iv. 14; μεσότοιχον, ii. 14; ὁσιότης, iv. 24; πολυποίκιλος, iii. 10; προελπίζειν, i. 12; σαπρός iv. 29; συγκαθίζειν, ii. 6; φραγμός, ii. 14; χαριτοῦν, i. 6. Likewise the vocabulary of Col. has been treated statistically. In his enumeration of un-Pauline words (48=33+15) Holtzmann, 105, A. 3, 106, A. 8, has tacitly left out of account those which occur also in Eph. (see above, p. 518 f.), and which are therefore, according to him, as un-Pauline as those which occur only in the Pastoral Epistles; others, like θρησκεία, καταβραβεύειν, are wanting for no imaginable reason. In the light of the foregoing remarks on the vocabulary of Eph., the great part may be dropped out as having no significance, e.g. ἅλας, ἀνεψιός, ἀνταπόδοσις (iii. 24, cf. ἀνταποδοῦναι, aside from quotations, 1 Thess. iii. 9 ; 2 Thess. i. 6 ; ἀνταπόδομα only in the quotation, Rom. xi. 9 ; but ἀντιμισθία also occurs but twice, Rom. i. 27 ; 2 Cor. vi. 13), ἀποκρίνεσθαι, ἀπόκρυφος (ii. 3, along with ἀποκεκρυμμένος, i. 26 ; 1 Cor. ii. 7 ; Eph. iii. 9), ἀρέσκεια (ἀρέσκειν occurs thirteen times ; also ἀνθρωπάρεσκος, iii. 22 ; cf. Eph. vi. 6 ; as over against ἀνθρώποις ἀρέσκειν, Gal. i. 10 ; 1 Thess. ii. 4), ἀρτύειν, βραβεύειν, καταβραβεύειν (along with βραβεῖον, 1 Cor. ix. 24 ; Phil. iii. 14), δυναμοῦν, i. 11 (ἐνδυναμοῦν instead of this, leaving out of account Eph. vi. 10 ; Phil. iv. 13 ; 1 Tim. i. 12 ; 2 Tim. ii. 1, iv. 17 ; also only once, Rom. iv. 20), εἰρηνοποιεῖν (i. 20, as against ποιεῖν εἰρήνην, Eph. ii. 15), ἐξαλείφειν, κρύπτειν (iii. 3 ; 1 Tim. v. 25 ; but κρυπτός five times), μετακινεῖν, i. 23 (instead of this perhaps μετατιθέναι, which also occurs but once, Gal. i. 6, or in the suspected Epistle, 2 Thess. ii. 2, συλεύειν ; on the other hand, ἀμετακίνητος, 1 Cor. xv. 58), μόμφη (iii. 13, μέμφεσθαι also only once, Rom. ix. 19, more frequently ἄμεμπτος), νουμηνία (μήν, Gal. iv. 10, likewise solitary, denotes the same thing), ὁρατός (i. 16, as against ἀόρατος, cf. Rom. i. 20), παρηγορία, πλουσίως (iii. 16, from πλούσιος, Eph. ii. 4 ; 2 Cor. viii. 9), προακούειν, προσηλοῦν, σκιά, σύνδουλος, σωματικῶς (σωματικός also only in 1 Tim. iv. 8), φιλοσοφία, χειρόγραφον (ii. 14 ; cf. Philem. 19). Certain expressions are only apparently otherwise expressed outside of these letters : θεότης, ii. 9, expresses a different concept from that of θειότης, which also occurs only once, Rom. i. 20. He chooses ἀνταναπληροῦν, i. 24, instead of ἀναπληροῦν, which he uses elsewhere, since he wishes to express at the same time that he is suffering for the Church in Christ's stead, or in return for what Christ also has endured for him ; ἀπεκδύεσθαι, ἀπέκδυσις, ii. 11, 15, iii. 9, double compounds like ἐπενδύεσθαι, 2 Cor. v. 2, 4, instead of the simple ἐνδύεσθαι and ἐκδύεσθαι, 2 Cor. v. 3, 4, because the question here was not of the contrast between being naked and being clothed, but of the removal, putting away of that which has adhered hitherto. Paul puts in the mouth of the false teachers γενέσθαι, θιγγάνειν, and it is possible that not only here, but in his whole polemic against them, he has reference to their own catchwords, and that in this way we may account for certain quite remarkable expressions, such as ἐν μέρει ἑορτῆς, θέλειν ἐν ταπεινοφροσύνῃ καὶ θρησκείᾳ τῶν ἀγγέλων (above, p. 478, n. 7), from which in turn ἐθελοθρησκεία, ii. 23, is formed. Certain words are left over which Paul could have found occasion to use in the letters which are admitted to be his : ἀθυμεῖν, ἀποκαταλάσσειν, i. 20 f. (Eph. ii. 16) ; ἀποκεῖσθαι, i. 5 (2 Tim. iv. 8) ; ἀπόχρησις, ἀφειδία, δειγματίζειν, ἐμβατεύειν (? above, p. 478 f., n. 7), εὐχάριστος (ἀχάριστος, 2 Tim. iii. 2), παραλογίζεσθαι, πιθανολογία, πικραίνειν, πλησμονή, πόνος, iv. 13 (instead of κόπος, usual elsewhere, yet not with quite the same meaning) ; πρωτεύειν, στερέωμα, συλαγωγεῖν (cf. δουλαγωγεῖν, 1 Cor. ix. 27). To these should be added certain rarer words which Col. has in common with Eph.; see above, p. 516, n. 7.

10. (P. 503.) Following the method of our critics, the present writer has compiled an idioticon of Gal., which may be of use also in later investigations. In this list, however, words appearing only in O.T. quotations are omitted. Cf. Ewald, ZKom. Eph. 37. (A) Words which occur nowhere else in the

N.T.: ἀλληγορεῖν, βασκαίνειν, δάκνειν, ἐθνικῶς, εἴκειν (cedere), ἐκπτύειν, ἐπιδιπτάσσειν, εὐπροσωπεῖν, ἰουδαΐζειν, ἰουδαϊκῶς, Ἰουδαϊσμός, ἱστορεῖν, κατασκοπεῖν, κενόδοξος, μορφοῦν, μυκτηρίζειν, ὀρθοποδεῖν, πατρικός, παρείσακτος, πεισμονή, προευαγγελίζεσθαι, προθεσμία, προκαλεῖν, προκυροῦν, προσανατίθεσθαι, στίγμα, συνηλικιώτης, συνυποκρίνεσθαι, συστοιχεῖν, φθονεῖν, φρεναπατᾶν. (B) Words which occur in no other letter under Paul's name : ἀκυροῦν, ἀναλίσκειν, ἀναστατοῦν, ἀνατίθεσθαι, ἀνέρχεσθαι, ἄνωθεν, ἀποκόπτειν, διαμένειν, ἐγκράτεια, ἐκλύεσθαι, ἐνέχειν, ἐνευλογεῖν, ἐνιαυτός (elsewhere ἔτος), ἐξαιρεῖν, ἐξαποστέλλειν, ἐξορύττειν, ἐπίτροπος, εὐθέως, Ἱεροσόλυμα, καταγινώσκειν, κατάρα, κρέμασθαι, μετατιθέναι, μεταστρέφειν, μήν, ὅμοιος, παιδίσκη, παρατηρεῖν, πηλίκος, πορθεῖν, προϊδεῖν, προστιθέναι, συμπαραλαμβάνειν, ταράσσειν, ὑποστέλλειν, ὑποστρέφειν, φαρμακεία, φορτίον, ὠδίνειν. (C) Words which occur besides only in the strongly assailed Epistles (Eph., Col., 2 Thess., 1 and 2 Tim., Tit.) : ἀναστροφή (Eph.), ἐξαγοράζειν (Eph., Col.), ζυγός (1 Tim.), μεσίτης (1 Tim.), οἰκεῖος (Eph., 1 Tim.), παρέχειν (Col., 1 Tim., Tit.), στοιχεῖα τοῦ κόσμου (Col.), στῦλος (1 Tim.). To these should be added (D) peculiar phrases which occur nowhere else in the N.T., such as εὐαγγέλιον τῆς ἀκροβυστίας καὶ τῆς περιτομῆς, ii. 7 ; δεξιαὶ κοινωνίας, ii. 9 ; προγράφειν, iii. 1 (in an altogether different sense from Rom. xv. 4 ; Eph. iii. 3); οὐδέν (μοι) διαφέρει, Gal. ii. 6, iv. 1 ; κόπους παρέχειν, vi. 17 ; ἡ ἄνω (or νῦν) Ἰερουσαλήμ, iv. 25 f. ; ὁ Ἰσραὴλ τοῦ θεοῦ, vi. 16. Thus, apart from the phrases last mentioned, which are of much more significance for a truly critical inspection than the threefold list of bare vocables, there are to be found in Gal. (A 31+B 39+C 8=) seventy-eight suspicious words, and among them seventy which are decidedly " un-Pauline."

11. (P 511.) Ign. *Smyrn.* vi. 1 : "The judgment falls upon the heavenly beings also and the majesty of the angels and the rulers visible as well as invisible, if they believe not on the blood of Christ." Concerning Col. ii. 15, above, p. 473 f.

§ 30. THE HISTORICAL PRESUPPOSITIONS AND THE OCCASION OF THE EPISTLE TO THE PHILIPPIANS.

Confident that now at last, after many unsuccessful attempts, he had found the way which God wanted him to follow, and accompanied by Silvanus, Timothy, and Luke (Acts xvi. 10 ff.), for the first time Paul touched the soil of Europe in the autumn of the year 52. Without delaying at the port town of Neapolis, he went at once to Philippi, the most important city of Eastern Macedonia (n. 1). Its character was more Roman than Greek; but this was no hindrance to the apostle's work, since a knowledge of Greek was a necessity for everyone there. Here he found an organised Jewish congregation, which, though small, had among its worshippers a number of "God-fearing Gentiles," mostly women. Naturally, therefore, as was always his custom, Paul made this the centre from which to begin his preaching. To this congregation belonged a dealer in purple, a native of Thyatira, Lydia by name (possibly so called simply from the name of the place from which she came), who asked the honour of entertaining the missionaries at her house (Acts xvi. 14 f., 40). With reference to the other Christian household in Philippi, that of the unnamed jailer, there is nothing to indicate that prior to conversion its members had had anything to do with the Jews. Although it is not stated that Paul taught elsewhere than in the Jewish προσευχή, Acts xvi. 16–23, 39 gives the impression that his coming was followed at once by important results among the Gentiles, of which element the Church in Philippi seems mainly to have consisted.

The meeting with the maid possessed by the spirit of divination—a meeting which was repeated for a number of days afterward—occurred when the missionaries were on their way to the Jewish προσευχή for the first time, and the command of Paul by which she was silenced led to the interference of the authorities, which ended in the expulsion of Paul and Silvanus from the city. Consequently their entire stay in Philippi could not have occupied more than a few weeks. Apparently, however, Timothy, who rejoined Paul and Silvanus in Thessalonica,—at the latest in Berœa (above, p. 203),—and Luke, of whose whereabouts during the years immediately following we know nothing, were left behind to carry on the work which had been thus forcibly interrupted. In fact, Phil. i. 1, ii. 19–23 point to an intimate relation between this Church and Timothy. The appeal for protection which Paul made on behalf of Silvanus and himself on the ground of their Roman citizenship, after they had suffered ignominious treatment at the hands of the police (1 Thess.

ii. 2 ; Acts xvi. 22 f.), was not for their own safety, since
the command to leave the city, which Paul did not ask
the authorities to revoke, was assurance enough that at
least, so far as the authorities were concerned, they were
not to be further molested. On the other hand, the fact
that the highest officials in the city ($\sigma\tau\rho\alpha\tau\eta\gamma o\acute{\iota} = praetores$,
duumviri) visited the missionaries personally in the
prison, apologised for their unfortunate blunder, and
politely requested them to leave the city, could react
only to the advantage of the teachers and adherents of
the new doctine who remained behind. There may have
been subsequent persecutions (Phil. i. 28–30), but on the
whole the relation of the Church to those outside seems
to have been comparatively peaceful. Six years later, at
the time when 2 Cor. was written, Paul had been for
some months in Macedonia, and no inconsiderable part
of this time must have been spent with the Philippian
Christians, who were especially dear to him (i. 7 f., ii. 16,
iv. 1). Also on the last journey prior to his arrest he
seems to have enjoyed a rest of several days there (Acts
xx. 6). In the intervals there were frequent communications between Paul and the Church. A few months
after the Church was organised, Timothy was sent back
from Athens to Macedonia (above, p. 205). Whether he
reached Philippi on this journey we do not know. He
certainly did touch at Philippi when he was sent by Paul
at the beginning of the year 57 from Ephesus to Corinth
by way of Macedonia (above, p. 259 f.). Twice within a
few weeks after the Church was organised, while Paul
was still at Thessalonica, they had sent him money, and
after Paul had left Macedonia continued to contribute to
the support of the apostle and his missionary work with
greater regularity than any other Church (n. 2). The
account of these gifts, which Paul represents as containing credit and debit entries (iv. 15, 17), could in reality
hardly have been anything but a written communication

between the givers and the receiver. To this communication Paul himself refers in iii. 1. Warnings such as those introduced by the words, "To write the same things to you, to me indeed is not irksome, but for you it is safe," we do not find in any earlier passage of the extant Epistle. Consequently Paul must have written these warnings in at least one earlier letter; and if the allusion was to be understood by his readers, it must have been in a letter written not very long before the present Epistle. The fact that apart from this statement of Paul's we have no trustworthy information regarding more than one Epistle of Paul to the Philippians, is no sufficient reason for denying that there were others (n. 3).

Regarding the frequent communications between Paul and the Church which took place just before this letter was written, Paul himself gives us more definite information. For a time the contributions of the Philippian Church to Paul's support had been intermitted, which was excusable in view of a temporary stringency in their financial condition. But some time prior to the composition of this letter they had again sent to the imprisoned apostle a considerable sum of money, at least enough to meet all his needs, despatching it by one of their own members, Epaphroditus by name, who seems also earlier to have been in the service of the Church or mission (n. 4). Upon his arrival in the place where Paul was, Epaphroditus was taken dangerously ill, as implied in Phil. ii. 30, because of the efforts which he had made to discharge the commission of the Church. When this letter was written he had so far recovered as to be able to take it back to Philippi. Meanwhile, considerable time had elapsed. Not only had the news of Epaphroditus' illness reached Philippi, but the news had come back to Paul and Epaphroditus from Philippi that there was great anxiety there for Epaphroditus' life; for, when he learned how the Church felt, Epaphroditus was very de-

sirous of returning to Philippi, and Paul felt under obligation to send him as soon as possible with this letter
(ii. 25–28). With these interchanges which took place
between the arrival and departure of Epaphroditus, it is
self-evident that other news also was interchanged between Philippi and Rome and Rome and Philippi. As
the messengers came and went, they would naturally be
entrusted with letters. The news that Epaphroditus was
ill in Rome may have reached Philippi with the report of
his arrival there. But whether this announcement was
made by Epaphroditus himself, or by Timothy, or by Paul,
certainly Paul could not have failed to acknowledge the
gift of money which the Philippians had sent, and to
express his thanks, or to request the others to do so for
him. If it has been rightly inferred from iii. 1 that Paul
had written to the Philippians only a short time before,
then the most probable assumption is that this letter
contained the announcement of Epaphroditus' arrival and
of his illness, Paul's first expression of thanks for the
gift of money, warnings such as those in iii. 2 ff., and
naturally also numerous other communications. We are
able to gather from the extant Epistle to the Philippians
a fairly definite idea of the manner in which they had
replied recently to the letter of Paul's which has not come
down to us ; for throughout our Epistle is a direct reply,
not to the communications received some weeks or months
before through Epaphroditus, but to a letter which had
just arrived from Philippi. When, contrary to his usage
elsewhere, Paul emphasises strongly at the beginning of
the letter the fact that *he, for his part*, has only occasion
to thank the Lord Jesus for the substantial interest which
they had always taken in him and his work, of which
interest they had now furnished additional proof, and
that he joyfully fulfils the obligation of petition on their
behalf (i. 3–7, n. 2), there is manifestly implied a contrary view of the same facts and conditions. This con-

trary view cannot very well be that of Timothy, whom
Paul mentions in the greeting as joint-writer with him
of the letter ; for then it would be difficult to understand
how possible dissatisfaction with the Philippians on the
part of Timothy could be so silently taken for granted
and yet be made so much of.   Moreover, had this been
the case, Paul would certainly have added a Παῦλος to
the ἐγὼ μέν (1 Thess. ii. 18 ; 2 Cor. x. 1 ; Philem. 19).
Rather must this have been the view of the Church which
he addresses (1 Cor. v. 3).   The Philippians must recently
have expressed their dissatisfaction with what they had
done to support Paul and his work, and their doubt as to
whether Paul had been satisfied with the same.   The tone
in which Paul speaks of the matter throughout the letter
(ii. 17, 25, 30, iv. 10–20) is natural only on the supposition that this feeling had been very strongly expressed,
and the Church had lamented and apologised for the
smallness and tardiness of their last remittance.   Again
and again throughout the letter he assures the Philippians
not so much of his gratitude, which he had expressed
before, but of his unclouded joy and full contentment
with his condition, inward and outward.   What he desires and asks of them in the matter of charity is not
more sacrifice, in which regard the Macedonian Churches
had already distinguished themselves (2 Cor. viii. 1 f.,
xi. 9 ; 1 Thess. iv. 9), nor that simplicity in giving which
he so often commends (Rom. xii. 8 ; 2 Cor. ix. 13 ; Jas.
i. 5 ; Matt. vi. 3), but rather the opposite—a clear insight
into and a careful consideration of the circumstances and
conditions under which their charity may be exercised
consistently with uprightness and good order (i. 9–11).
Probably the unfortunate condition of their financial
affairs, hinted at in iv. 10, 19, was connected in some
way with their deficiency in these virtues (above, p.
220 f.).

A second matter with regard to which Paul found it

necessary to set the minds of the Philippians at rest was his own condition at the time. He does not leave it to Epaphroditus to give them an oral account of his state, as he did to Tychicus in his letters to the Churches in Asia (Eph. vi. 21 ; Col. iv. 7). On the other hand, he does not speak of it as if he were telling them something new ; he is simply endeavouring to set in their right light facts with which the Church was already familiar, and with regard to which they had expressed to him opinions differing from his own. The discussion begins in conversational abruptness with the words, " I will have you know, my brethren, that my affairs have fallen out rather to the furtherance of the gospel " (n. 5). As shown by this sentence, as well as by the entire discussion that follows, Paul is speaking here not of various facts and circumstances connected with his own condition and work, but specifically of his trial (ἀπολογία, i. 16). From i. 7, consequently, we must infer that the Philippians had heard of this trial some time before, and had recently expressed their sympathy with him in it. They had done so, however, with more goodwill and love than insight and discrimination (i. 9). They believed not only that the apostle's life, but also the cause of the gospel, was in extreme peril. In answer to this ungrounded fear and the expressions of deep depression resulting from it, Paul shows them that this very trial about which they were so anxious furnishes justification for entertaining the most sanguine hopes both for the cause and for him personally, and that already it has borne fruit for the cause of the gospel (§ 31). It is easy to see how anxiety about the fate of the apostle, to which was now added concern for Epaphroditus' life, together with the feeling that the sending of Epaphroditus and the gift which he carried from them had not been an adequate expression of their love for the apostle, who was now face to face with death, nor had come up to Paul's expectations — how all this had produced a feeling of utter depression in the Church. We can also understand why Paul used every means in his power to dispel this feeling and to make the Church rejoice. Hence his repeated and cordial recognition of their generosity to him (i. 3–7, ii. 17, iv. 10–20), the assurance that he is satisfied with the Church and proud of it (i. 4, ii. 16 f., iv. 1), the repeated exhortation to ˙joy (ii. 18, 28 f., iii. 1, iv. 4) and to freedom from anxiety (iv. 6, 19, iii. 15), and the most favourable representation possible of his present condition and outlook into the future (§ 31). From the noticeable circumstance that he emphasises frequently the fact that he includes all the members of the Church in his remembrances, petitions, thanksgivings, and greetings (i. 1, 4, 7, 8, 25, ii. 17, 26, iv. 21), we must infer that the opinion had been expressed that, while Paul continued to entertain friendly feelings toward individual friends of his in Philippi, he was not so satisfied with others, and consequently not so satisfied with the Church as a whole. And yet it had been the Church which, to the full extent of its ability, had shown this sympathy with him. So it is that the letter is addressed to them in their collective capacity, with special mention of their overseers and officers (i. 1). The condition within the Church was not one of complete harmony, which may have led to emphasis upon the unity of all its members. This assumption could not be made simply upon the basis of what is said in i. 17, ii. 1–5, were not certain persons expressly exhorted in iv. 2, in terms closely resembling ii. 2 f. (n. 6), to work in harmony with others. There were two women who had rendered great service to the Church at the time when it was organised, and who, when this letter was written, seem to have been engaged in some sort of work for the Church; for some unnamed person, whom Paul addresses directly as a sincere companion, probably Epaphroditus, who brought the letter to Philippi, is directed to help these two women in their work. The same is expected also of

a certain Clement in Philippi, and of others whom Paul
calls his fellow-workers, but does not mention by name.
Consequently it could not have been purely personal
differences nor differences of opinion about religious
matters that made it seem necessary to exhort these two
women to harmonious effort and labour, as is evidenced
by the peculiar repetition of the word παρακαλῶ.   Rather
must it have been a matter of Church business, such as
had taken Epaphroditus to Rome, in which Euodia and
Syntyche had had to contend with difficulties, and had
failed to agree entirely between themselves.   The sense
would be complete if iv. 2 were joined immediately to
ii. 29 f. ; what stands between in a measure interrupts the
thought.   After indicating by τὸ λοιπόν in iii. 1 that the
discussion of the principal topic of the letter is complete,
and that he is about to conclude (1 Thess. iv. 1 ; 2 Thess.
iii. 1), it occurs to Paul—there is indication that he was in
doubt for a moment whether he ought to do it or not
(n. 3)—to repeat a warning against certain persons which
he had already expressed in an earlier letter.   The same
reasons which led him to overcome his hesitation about
repeating the warning influenced him also to dwell upon
the subject somewhat at length, and to depart further
from the original plan of the letter than the τὸ λοιπόν in
iii. 1 would lead us to expect.   This had so far fallen into
the background, that when he really comes to conclude
the letter in iv. 8 he is able to repeat it.   If these persons
to whose harmful activity he directs the attention of the
Church in iii. 2 had already secured a footing in Philippi,
especially if they had secured a following in the Church
there, Paul would not have hesitated, but it would have
been his plain duty to warn the Church, and he would
not have called this warning a precautionary warning.
There is not a word of regret or complaint for any influence
which the Philippians had allowed them to gain over
them, nor any formal warning against their seductions.

"Beware of them," he says once and again. Naturally the Philippians were to do this in order not to be taken unawares. The danger is not immediate. But it is well that their work be known and recognised, as Paul had learned to know it from long experience. These persons are the old enemies, against whom he had warned the Romans in similar manner in anticipation of future troubles (xvi. 17). He calls them "those of the concision," playing upon the word circumcision, and contrasts them with himself and Timothy, likewise circumcised (i. 1 ; Acts xvi. 3, above, p. 182), who are of the true circumcision (ii. 7), thereby indicating that these persons are Jews unworthy of the name (Rom. ii. 28). This contrast and the whole exhortation would be without point if these persons were only Jews, who possibly had it in their power to persecute the Christian Church. Rather must they have been Jewish Christian teachers, like those who claimed at least the same right to preach the gospel as the true apostles who had founded the Churches in Corinth and Galatia. This is clear from their characterisation as κακοὶ ἐργάται (cf. 2 Cor. xi. 13, ψευδαπόστολοι, ἐργάται δόλιοι). Finally, Paul calls them dogs, not with the design of applying to these unworthy Jews in the name of the Gentile Christians the opprobrious title which the Jews applied to the unclean Gentiles, but having in view the troublesome obtrusiveness and roving character of ownerless dogs, such as one is accustomed to see in the streets of an Oriental city. This threefold characterisation is severe and curt, so that the persons in question could not have been Jewish Christian preachers who merely refused to carry on their missionary work in harmony with Paul and his helpers, whose lack of confidence in him grieved the apostle (Col. iv. 11 ; Phil. i. 15 ; § 31). They must have been, rather, sworn enemies of the apostle and undoers of his work, of whom he cannot say, as he does of himself, that they have broken with their Pharisaic past

(iii. 7–14), but when they became Christians they continued to be Pharisees, boasting the legal righteousness to which they had attained, and exercising genuine Pharisaic zeal for making proselytes (Matt. xxiii. 15 ; Pirke Aboth i. 1) ; engaged not in preaching the gospel among the Gentiles, but in disturbing the Gentile Christian Churches (n. 8). That there was occasion enough to warn a Church, which as yet had not been attacked by them, against their disturbing influence, Paul was well aware from earlier experience. The real occasion and purpose of the letter, however, are not to be found in this incidental warning, nor in the other exhortations which are also incidental (i. 27–ii. 18, iii. 17–iv. 9), but in the actual statements of fact and opinion in i. 3–26, ii. 19–30, iv. 10–20.

1. (P. 522.) For historical and geographical matter and inscriptions, see HEUZEY ET DAUMET, *Mission archéol. de Macedoine*, 1876, pp. 1–161 ; *C. I. L.* iii. 120, and Nos. 633–707, 6113 ; *C. I. G.* Nos. 2010*b* and 2010*c* (p. 995). The mining town Φίλιπποι, founded by Alexander's father on the site of the old Κρηνίδες, received a Roman colony after the battle of 42 B.C. (Strabo, vii. fragm. 41). This in turn was considerably augmented after the battle of Actium (31 B.C.) by settlers from Italy, who had been forced to surrender their own estates to Octavianus' veterans (Dio Cass. li. 4). Thereafter it was *Colonia Augusta Julia Philippi* with *Jus italicum* (*Dig.* li. 15. 6, and 7. 8). For that reason the inhabitants regarded themselves as Romans (Acts xvi. 21). Difficulties meet us in Acts xvi. 12, ἥτις ἐστὶν πρώτη τῆς μερίδος Μακεδονίας πόλις κολωνία ; so Tischendorf, following אAC al. On the other hand, B πρώτη μερίδος τῆς M., E πρώτη μερὶς M., D κεφαλὴ τῆς M. πόλις κολ. (cf. S¹, "which is the capital of Macedonia, and is a colony"; also several min., among them 137, Ambrosianus ; in Blass, ed. min.=M. om. μερίδος), πρώτης μερίδος τῆς M., conjecture of Blass. (ed. maj.), supported by Lat., Paris, 321 (*in prima parte*), and the Provençal Version. Hort's conjecture, put forth only tentatively, τῆς Πιερίδος M. (*Append.* p. 97, cf. Steph. Byz. on Κρηνίδες ; Herod. vii. 212 ; Thuc. ii. 99), has met with no favour. The impulse to all the changes has been given by μερίς, which must be retained. It often indicates a rather large district of a still larger province (Strabo, iv. 3, p. 191 = Cæs. *Bell. Gall.* i. 1 ; Strabo, xii. 37, p. 560 ; xvi. 2, p. 749 ; frequently in the Egyptian documents, cf. Ramsay, *Church in the Roman Empire*, 158 ; an article by the same author, in answer to the present writer, in the *Expos.*, Oct. 1897, p. 320). The Romans had divided this province into four such districts (Liv. xlv. 29 ; Marquardt, *R. Staatsverw.*² i. 317). But "the first city" of the district to which Philippi belonged was not Philippi, but Amphipolis. But it is also very improbable that Luke should have called Philippi "*a* first city of *a* district," or indeed "of *the* district of Macedonia." We should rather

read with Blass πρώτης, and paraphrase : "a city belonging to the first of those four districts of Macedonia, *i.e.* the first which Paul touched on his journey, and besides this, a colony, which is the reason for its importance." So far as place and time are concerned, the port Neapolis (now Kavala) was the first city of the province of Macedonia to which Paul came ; but without stopping there he journeyed on forthwith by the Via Egnatia, which touches the coast at Neapolis, to the much more important Philippi. To judge by the inscriptions, at least half the population were Latin in origin and speech. There among other things was a Latin theatre, maintained, it would seem, by the town (Heuzey, p. 145, No. 76 ; *C. I. L.* iii. No. 6113, *archimimus latinus et officialis,* etc.). VALENS, the name of the presbyter of Philippi who made considerable stir fifty to sixty years after the Church was founded (Polyc. *ad Phil.* xi. 1), occurs seven times in a single inscription from the neighbourhood of Philippi, which contains many names (*C. I. L.* iii. No. 633 ; cf. also Nos. 640, 671, 679, 680. In No. 633 CRESCENS also occurs twice (cf. Polyc. *ad Phil.* xiv). The names EUODIA and SYNTYCHE (Phil. iv. 2) do not occur in the inscriptions from Philippi, but are common enough elsewhere. Εὐοδία (Latin also *Euhodia,* in Victorinus on Phil. iv. 2 *Euchodia,* elsewhere even written *Heuodia*), *C. I. G.* Nos. 3002, 5711, 5923, 6390 ; *Inscr. Att.* iii. (from the time of the empire) Nos. 1795, 1888, 2079, 3160 ; *Inscr. Gr. Sic. et It.* Nos. 855, 1108, 1745 ; *Agypt. Urk. des berl. Mus.* No. 550 ; *C. I. L.* iii. Nos. 1388, 2314, 2435 ; v. No. 1173 ; vi. Nos. 17334-17339 ; viii. No. 8569. Εὐωδία also (Duchesne et Bayet, *Mission au mont Athos,* p. 40, No. 50) is different perhaps only in spelling ; it is written so even in Phil. iv. 2 in some MSS. The corresponding man's name is Εὔοδος, more rarely Εὐόδιος (Philo, *c. Flacc.* x ; Eus. *H. E.* iii. 22), also Εὐώδιος, *Ag. Urk.* No. 793. Συντύχη, *C. I. G.* Nos. 2264m, 2326, 3098, 3865k ; Le Bas-Waddington, *Asie min.* No. 722 ; *Inscr. Gr. Sic. et It.* No. 1369b ; *C. I. L.* iv. No. 2666 ; v. Nos. 1073, 2521, 8125, 8858 ; vi. Nos. 9662, 10243, 15607, 15608, 23484 ; viii. No. 7962 ; ix. Nos. 102, 116, 156, 369, 1817, 2676, 3363, 6100. It is uncertain from Phil. iv. 3 whether both these women supported Paul in the spreading of the gospel as early as his first stay in Philippi ; for at the time also when 2 Cor. was written Paul remained several months in Macedonia. He may have spent a part of this time in Philippi and utilised it among other things for an ἀθλεῖν ἐν τῷ εὐαγγελίῳ. It may appear strange that *Lydia* (Acts xvi. 14, 40) is not mentioned in this connection. But we should remember that Lydia is not a real name, but a cognomen derived from the name of her native place ; cf. Renan, *St. Paul,* 146. The Roman poets use it only of those who belong to the *demi-monde,* who hardly possess a name of their own (Hor. *Odes,* i. 8, 13, 25, iii. 9 ; Mart. *Epigr.* xi. 21). Λύδη also, which denotes the same thing, is very rare as a proper name (*C. I. G.* Nos. 653, 6975 ; *C. I. Att.* iii. Nos. 3261, 3262 ; Hor. *Odes,* iii. 28). Just as Omphale is called the Lydian (Sophocl. *Trach.* 432, cf. 70), so this dealer in purple, who had removed to Philippi from Thyatira, hence from Lydia, probably was often called the Lydian, though she had always borne a personal name besides— perhaps Euodia or Syntyche? Moreover, we are reminded of the *purpuraria* (Acts xvi. 14, Vulg.) by a mutilated inscription at Philippi (*C. I. L.* iii. No. 664), and even more definitely by a Greek inscription on a tomb at Thessalonica which the guild of purple dyers erected to the memory of a certain Menippus from *Thyatira* (Duchesne et Bayet, *Mission au mont Athos,* p. 52, No. 83). Thyatira, a Macedonian colony (Strabo, xiii. p. 625), had a guild of purple dyers (*C. I. G.* Nos. 3496-3498). The name *Clemens* (Phil. iv. 3) is also attested for Philippi, *C. I. L.* iii. No. 633, Valerius Clemens. In itself it would not be impossible to conjecture that the jailer in Acts xvi. 23 ff. was named Clemens. However, see n .6. Moreover, the indices to Tacitus, Pliny's *Epistles,* and the collections of Latin and Greek inscriptions, show that Clemens is such a common cognomen in the first three centuries A.D. that it is a hopeless venture to base any hypothesis whatever upon it alone. Merely to indicate its wide currency, some examples are adduced from the time of the Empire : *C. I. Att.* iii. Nos. 1094, 1114 (at the end), 1138 (col. 3, line 23), 3896 (all these from Athens, likewise the birthplace of Clemens Alex.) ; *C. I. G.* Nos. 3757 (Asia Minor), 4557 (near Damascus), 4801 (Egypt, cf. *Berl. Ägypt. Urk.* No. 344, four bearers of this name, *Oxyrh. Papyri* ii. 185, 313, No. 241, 376) ; 5042 (Ethiopia) ; 1829*c* (under the Additamenta from Apollonia in Illyricum) ; *C. I. L.* iii. Nos. 1739 (Epidaurus), 5211-5216 (Cilli in Styria). The river outside the town, on the bank of which the Jews and proselytes of Philippi were wont to assemble for Sabbath worship (Acts xvi. 13), is the Angites (Herod. vii. 113, now Angista, perhaps identical with the Γάγγας or Γαγγίτης, Appianus, *Bell. civ.* iv 106, 107). It flows past Philippi about half a mile west of the gates of the city, and empties into Lake Cercinitis, through which the Strymon flows, just before reaching the sea. Since προσευχή in Acts xvi. 16, at any rate, denotes the place of prayer, the present writer sees no reason to change the text in xvi. 13 (Blass, ἐνόμιζον ἐν προσευχῇ εἶναι). Though elsewhere προσευχή is used interchangeably for συναγωγή (Schürer, ii. 447 f., cf. 444 [Eng. trans. II. ii. 72 f., cf. 68 f.]), yet Luke, who uses everywhere else the latter word only, seems to express by the former an idea for which συναγωγή did not seem a suitable expression. There were seats there (Acts xvi. 13). But that it was only a makeshift for a regular synagogue is also expressed by οὗ ἐδόκει (so D, Vulg., Gigas, ἐνόμιζεν ℵ, ἐνομίζετο EHLP, ἐνομίζομεν BC) προσευχὴ (ABDEHLP, προσευχήν ℵC) εἶναι. It may have been an open hall, with or without a roof, or some other plain building. There seems to be no support in the older tradition for the statements of the *Acts of Paul* (*circa* 170) about a sojourn of Paul in Philippi (Vetter, *Der apokr. dritte Korintherbrief,* 1894, S. 54 ; *Acta Pauli,* ed. C. Schmidt, 72 ff., 77 ; *GK,* ii. 599). The names occurring in this, which have been mangled in many ways by translators and copyists, are not poorly chosen. Stratonice is an ancient Macedonian name (Thuc. ii. 101), and Apollophanes occurs in an inscription at Neapolis near Philippi (Heuzey, p. 21, No. 5).

2. (Pp. 524, 526.) Phil. iv. 15 f. The καὶ ἐν Θεσσαλονίκῃ adds force to the expression, and even when taken alone indicates that the same thing happened later also. But since the stay in Berœa, whence Paul journeyed to Athens, was short, we can hardly understand ὅτε ἐξῆλθον ἀπὸ Μακεδονίας of the moment of departure, but as the pluperfect (Hofmann) ; so that we are to think of remittances to Athens and Corinth (2 Cor. xi. 8 f.). Moreover, Phil. i. 3-7 refers to the material support of the mission on the part of the Philippians, as the present writer thinks he has shown (*ZfKW,* 1885, S. 185-202) in a somewhat more thorough way than has been done before.

Also the reading of i. 3 there defended, S. 184, ἐγὼ μὲν εὐχαριστῶ τῷ κυρίῳ ἡμῶν, must be considered established so long as no one can explain better than Klöpper, 1893, how this original reading arose from the common one, which plainly resulted from assimilation to a well-known phrase of Paul's found especially at the opening of his Epistles (Rom. i. 8 ; 1 Cor. i. 4, 14, xiv. 18 ; Col. i. 3 ; Philem. 4 ; 1 Thess. i. 2).   Klöpper (*Komm.*, *ad loc.*) conjectures that the need was felt of freeing the apostle from the connection with Timothy implied in the "address," and that in this 1 Thess. ii. 18 served as model.   Why has no one felt and satisfied this need in 1 Thess. i. 2 ; 2 Thess. i. 3 ; 1 Cor. i. 4 ; 2 Cor. i. 3 ; Col. i. 3 ? and how could 1 Thess. ii. 18, where it was necessary to distinguish between Paul and his helpers, and where, moreover, ἐγὼ μέν is followed by Παῦλος, have served as a model for the opening of a letter, where nothing is said which necessarily excludes Timothy? (see above, p. 210).   The correct text is attested not only by D*G and their Latin parallel texts, but also by Ambrosiaster, Cassiodorus, and, in a crucial point, another ancient Latin text (*Italafragm.*, ed. Ziegler, p. 74, "gratias ago domino meo "), and the imitation in the apocryphal *Epistle to the Laodiceans* (*GK*, ii. 584, "gratias ago Christo "). We should probably translate : " I for my part thank our Lord for all your substantial remembrance (of me, and indeed), always, in each of my prayers, offering up my prayer for you all with joy on the ground of your participation for the purpose of the gospel (*i.e.* your co-operation in the missionary work) from the first day until now, being confident for this very reason that he who began (such) a good work among you will (also) bring it to completion until the day of Christ Jesus ; just as, in fact, it is my duty to be mindful of this for you all (to care for you thus through joyful, continual, hopeful prayer), since I have you in my heart (must ever think of you) as those who are all comrades in my grace both (for years) in my imprisonment and also (now) in the defence and confirmation of the gospel."

3. (Pp. 525, 530.)   That τὰ αὐτά, Phil. iii. 1, refers to iii. 2 ff. and not back to χαίρετε ἐν κυρίῳ (cf. ii. 18), surely needs no further proof.   Further, since ὀκνηρός, like φοβερός or our "doubtful, fearful," and the like, is used not only of persons, but also of things which awaken in a person the mood in question, the meaning here (cf. *Oed. Rex.* 834) must be : " It seems to me unobjectionable ; I do not hesitate to write the same to you (Theod. Mops. ἐμοὶ . . . γράφειν ὄκνος οὐδείς ; cf. Plut. *Mor.* 11 D, πολὺς δ᾽ ὄκνος ἔχει με, and the frequent οὐκ ὀκνήσω, *e.g.* Papias, quoted in Eus. *H. E.* iii. 39. 3). Further, since the emphasis falls on τὰ αὐτά, not on γράφειν, we cannot complete the thought like Theod. Mops. : " I do not hesitate to say to you in writing also what I said to you orally."   We are therefore shut up to the conclusion that Paul is referring to similar warnings of earlier letters still present in his memory and in that of the readers.   In saying that it seems to him unobjectionable to repeat the same things, he acknowledges that the repetition might seem superfluous, but that he has overcome this objection or similar ones.   It is a question whether Polycarp really knew of several letters of Paul to the Philippians when he writes, *ad Phil.* iii. 2 : οὔτε γὰρ ἐγὼ οὔτε ἄλλος ὅμοιος ἐμοὶ δύναται κατακολουθῆσαι τῇ σοφίᾳ τοῦ μακαρίου καὶ ἐνδόξου Παύλου, ὃς γενόμενος ἐν ὑμῖν κατὰ πρόσωπον τῶν τότε ἀνθρώπων ἐδίδαξεν ἀκριβῶς καὶ βεβαίως τὸν περὶ ἀληθείας λόγον, ὃς καὶ ἀπὼν ὑμῖν ἔγραψεν

ἐπιστολάς, εἰς ἃς ἐὰν ἐγκύπτητε, δυνηθήσεσθε οἰκοδομεῖσθαι εἰς τὴν δοθεῖσαν ὑμῖν πίστιν ; cf. *GK*, i. 814 ff. In another place, chap. xi. (retained in Lat. only) he writes : " Ego autem nihil tale sensi in vobis vel audivi qui estis in principio epistulæ ejus ; de vobis etenim gloriatur in omnibus ecclesiis." For a discussion of more recent efforts to explain or emend the senseless *epistulæ ejus*, see *Forsch.* iv. 252. Better than all others is the suggestion of E. Nestle, communicated to the present writer in a letter, that we assume in the original ἐν ἀρχῇ τῆς ἀποστολῆς αὐτοῦ. Just as ἀποστέλλειν and ἐπιστέλλειν were not infrequently confounded (Acts xxi. 25 ; 1 [3] Kings v. 8 ; Neh. vi. 19), so here ἐπιστολῆς grew out of ἀποστολῆς. Even in Gal. ii. 8 the latter word denotes not the act of sending forth, but, quite like the modern "mission," the work committed to the one sent forth, and the performance of this commission. Polycarp renders freely and not badly the ἐν ἀρχῇ τοῦ εὐαγγελίου, Phil. iv. 15 ; but in the following sentence he refers to the Philippians the contents of 2 Thess. i. 4 also. It is the more improbable that this is a temporary oversight, since before in chap. i. 2 he seems to refer 1 Thess. i. 8 f. in like manner to the Philippians, while Tertullian *per contra* adduces in one instance (*Scorp.* xiii) several passages of Phil. as addressed to the Thessalonians. The three letters to the Macedonian Churches were classed together by many writers : Clem. *Protr.* 87 ; *GK*, i. 174 ; Vict. Petav., in the genuine conclusion of his Commentary on Rev., cf. Hausleiter in the *ThLb*, 1895, S. 196, " Paulus ad ecclesiam Macedoniam ita dixit = 1 Thess. iv. 15–17 ; Jerome, *Comm. in Gal.* lib. ii. præf. (Vallarsi, vii. 430, probably following Origen, cf. *GK*, ii. 427 ff., 1002), " Macedones in caritate laudantur et hospitalitate ac susceptione fratrum," which is confirmed by 1 Thess. iv. 9. They were also joined frequently in the MSS. (*GK*, ii. 344, 349, 353 ff.). It is in this way, then, that Polycarp also knows of several letters of Paul to the Philippians, *i.e.* the Macedonians. Following an older source, also Georgius Syncellus, *Chronogr.* ad annum 5576, ed. Bonn, i. 651, may have written in reference to Clement of Rome : τούτου καὶ ὁ ἀπόστολος ἐν τῇ πρὸς φιλιππησίους μέμνηται πρώτῃ ἐπιστολῇ. Regarding a second epistle to the Philippians in a Syrian Canon, about 400 A.D. (*Studia Sinait*, ed. Lewis, i. 11 ff.), see *NKZ*, 1900, S. 795, 799 f. ; W. Bauer, *Der Apostolos der Syrer* (1903), S. 36 ff., and the writer's *Grundriss der Gesch. d. Kanons*, 2te Aufl. 49 A. 11.

4. (P. 525.) The references in Phil. ii. 25–30, iv. 10–20, are clear in all essential features. It has been remarked already (n. 2), that in i. 3–7 the Church's very recent active fellowship with their apostle is combined with all their similar conduct before this. But the same is true of ii. 17 also ; cf. *ZfKW*, 1885, S. 290–302. The present writer translates ii. 14–18 : "Do all things without murmuring and doubting, in order that you may present yourselves free from blame and impure admixture, as spotless children of God in the midst of a crooked and perverse generation, among whom you shine as lights, holding forth the word of life [in] the world, a matter of glorying to me until (and on) the day of Christ, since (in this case, on the presupposition that you follow this exhortation) I (shall) not have striven in vain nor laboured in vain, but even in case my blood is actually poured forth as a libation (cf. 2 Tim. iv. 6), I rejoice over the offering and service of your faith (cf. ii. 25, 30, iv. 18), and delight in you all. Even so do you also rejoice and delight in me !" We might better read simply κόσμῳ instead of

ἐν κόσμῳ, which cannot possibly be dragged into the relative sentence alongside of ἐν οἷς (cf. Hofmann). Could Ephrem have read thus (*Comm.* p. 162, *apparebitis mundo*)?

5. (P. 528.) Instead of his ordinary οὐ θέλω δὲ ὑμᾶς ἀγνοεῖν, Paul writes in i. 12, γινώσκειν δὲ ὑμᾶς κτλ., with stronger emphasis upon the first word, and with reference to ἐπίγνωσις, i. 9. The reading τὰ κατ᾽ ἐμέ incurs the suspicion that it has come in from Eph. vi. 21 ; Col. iv. 7. We should read τὰ κατ᾽ ἐμέ with GS¹ (which, quite at variance with its rendering of those passages, translates as if the original had read τὴν κατ᾽ ἐμὲ πρᾶξιν) S³ on the margin, Arm. With regard to τὸ μᾶλλον = *potius*, not *magis* or *plus* (*emolumenti, quam detrimenti*), cf. the writer's Essay, *ZfKW*, 1885, S. 201.

6. (P. 529.) With τὸ αὐτὸ φρονεῖν, iv. 2, cf. ii. 2, 5, but not 1 Cor. i. 10. It does not mean the same thing as ὁμόνοια, ὁμοδοξία, but always denotes agreement for the accomplishment of practical aims ; cf. *ZfKW*, 1885, S. 193 f. Regarding the names Euodia, Syntyche, and Clemens, see n. 1. With Ambrosiaster, Lightfoot, Hofmann, *et al.*, we should take μετὰ καὶ Κλήμεντος κτλ. as the continuation not of the relative clause, but of the main clause (συλλαμβάνου), for αἵτινες introduces a motive for that request, namely, the signal rewards which these women deserve for their help in the first organisation of the Church ; but they would be only depressed if Clement and many others besides shared these rewards. Moreover, if it really should be thought that Paul's fellow-labourers in the founding of the Church are named here, we should expect to find Timothy and Silas mentioned, instead of Clement and other nameless individuals. The persons in question, then, are men who are now in Philippi, still living, of course, and so in a position to aid these women, to take hold with them of the work which they are carrying on ; for this is the meaning of συλλαμβάνεσθαί τινι (Luke v. 7 ; Artemid. *Oneirocr.* iii. 9, 37, iv. 74, as in the Attic writers, occasionally with genitive of the thing), and not to give them spiritual counsel. In the Book of Life stand the names of those who while living upon earth are enrolled as citizens in heaven (Luke x. 20 ; Rev. iii. 5, xx. 15 ; Heb. xii. 23). Paul includes among his fellow-labourers those also who, though in a different place, are carrying on the same work as he (Philem. 1, above, p. 452). Ephrem paraphrases rightly : "quorum nomina ego non hic descripsi, quia multa erant, attamen scripta sunt in libro vitæ." Paul speaks in the third person of the three whose names are mentioned, and of the nameless co-workers added at the end, and that, too, though he has a request to make of them all. This fact alone makes it exceedingly probable that the single "comrade" addressed in the second person will indeed be present in Philippi at the time of the letter's arrival and thereafter, but is now at the time of the letter's writing present with Paul. Victorinus (Mai, *Scr. vet. n. Coll.* iii. 2. 80), also Lightfoot and Hofmann, rightly conjectured that Epaphroditus is meant. If this helper sat near Paul during the writing, or served him perhaps as scribe, it must have seemed unnatural to the apostle to have his request come to Epaphroditus in the same form as to those who were absent, mediated, so to say, by the Church to whom the letter was addressed (cf. Col. iv. 17). Rom. xvi. 22 is not a parallel case. Clem. Al. *Strom.* iii. 53, p. 435, thought that Paul was speaking here of his wife, whom, according to 1 Cor. ix. 5, he did not take with him on his journeys, thus differing from the other apostles. This view is adopted

by Origen, who allegorises δοῦλος, Rom. i. 1, cf. 1 Cor. vii. 22 (Delarue, iv. 461), and appeals to a tradition which, to be sure, lacked universal acceptance (*sicut quidam tradunt*). It is also quoted by Eusebius without unfavourable criticism, *H. E.* iii. 30 ; and this must have been the cause of the further spread of the fable that Paul was married (propagated with peculiar zeal before Eusebius by Pierius, according to an excerpt in the Cod. Barocc. 142, cf. de Boor, *Texte u. Unters.* v. 2. 170 ; then by pseudo-Ign. *Philad.* chap. iv.; Epiph. *Mon.*, ed. Dressel, p. 39 ; Solomon of Bassorah, *Apis*, chap. l., tr. by Schönfelder, p. 83). Clement omitted the γνήσιε, a form incompatible, as Theodore Mops. long ago emphatically declared, with this interpretation of Phil. iv. 3, which would have required γνησία instead ; and Renan, *St. Paul*, 148, who thought that Lydia should be understood, neglected to justify the masculine. This is not one of those adjectives which vary between two and three endings for gender (Kühner-Blass, i. 1. 536). Moreover, σύζυγος γνησία could hardly denote anything else than the legitimate wife in distinction from a concubine (Xen. *Cyrop.* iv. 3. 1). The ancient Lat. translation *germane compar* (*e.g.* Ambrosiaster, Vulg.) or *germane unijuge* (Victor. p. 79) led to the mistaken idea that *Germanus* was a proper name (Pelagius = pseudo-Jerome, Vallarsi, xi. 3. 377), which in this form forced its way even into the Greek text of Cod. G. In a similar way from the Greek γνήσιε, which perhaps the Syrians had previously written on the margin, arose the remarkable proper name Chenisi or Khenesis in the Armenian Ephrem, p. 166 ; cf. Vetter, *Lit. Rundschau*, 1894, S. 111. On the other hand, Laurent, *Neutestamentliche Stud.* 134, sought to defend σύζυγε as a proper name, though such a name has not yet been pointed out either in the literature or in inscriptions. Wieseler, *Chron.* 457 f. note, thought that Christ should be understood ; Rückert, on 2 Cor. viii. 22, S. 265, an own brother of Paul's ; Völter, *ThTij.* 1892, S. 124, Timothy. With regard to modern allegorical interpretations of the passage, see § 32, n. 4.

7. (P. 531.) Inasmuch as, in spite of his mention of Timothy, i. 1, Paul has spoken of himself in the singular uniformly throughout the letter, and a great many times too, the ἡμεῖς in iii. 3, 17b is all the more striking, especially since " I " stands immediately before and after it. It cannot group the apostle with the Christians addressed, like the " We " of iii. 15 f., or with all Christians, as in iii. 20 f. In iii. 17b both are alike impossible, and Paul can mean only himself and Timothy, whom he mentions along with himself in i. 1. Why is that not true of iii. 3 also? Timothy was also circumcised (Acts xvi. 3). It is incredible that Paul should be speaking here in the name of all Christians, much less of the Gentile Christians, with reference to baptism and the new birth ; for (1) the Judaists were also baptized, and could thus appeal to the outward sign of spiritual circumcision (Col. ii. 11); (2) Paul the Jew is here speaking ; (3) he speaks in iii. 5 of his circumcision in the literal sense ; (4) he does not distinguish here between a spiritual and a carnal circumcision, in which case he must have disallowed the Judaists' claim to circumcision, *i.e.* the true one. He simply says that by reason of their evil mind their circumcision had lost its worth, has become merely a mutilation. Paul is not here giving utterance to the truth that Christians are the true Israel, a thought quite out of place in this connection ; he is rather, as in Rom. ii. 25, 28 f., contesting the worth of being a Jew outwardly, on which basis the Judaists were able to win

consideration for themselves, and is setting himself and his helpers, the founders of the Church, who sprang from Israel indeed, but who have broken with Pharisaic Judaism, as the real Jews over against these false brethren.   The Philippians then need not be imposed upon by them.   The change back to ἐγώ, iii. 4, from the ἡμεῖς, iii. 3, is fully explained by the fact that iii. 3 indeed, but not iii. 4 ff., could be said of Timothy, whose origin was only half Jewish, and who was not circumcised until adult age. Paul does not use the plural again to indicate himself until iii. 17, and even there such a transition was in itself no more necessary than in the similar passages, 1 Cor. iv. 16, xi. 1 ; Eph. v. 1.   But since Paul prefers not to set himself before the Philippians as a model without at the same time mentioning others who may likewise serve as examples, it is indubitable that he means them to understand by these others the founders of the Church, just as in 1 Thess. i. 6 ; 2 Thess. iii. 7, 9, the only difference being that in 1 Thess. i. 1 ; 2 Thess. i. 1 all three are named as writers of the letter, in Phil. i. 1 only Paul and Timothy.   We are thus to understand these two by the "we" in iii. 3, 17.   With κύνες Hofmann aptly compares Ps. lix. 7, 15, xxii. 17, 21.   Furthermore, the idea of uncleanness is more remote in this case, though elsewhere in the N.T. it is coupled with this word, Matt. vii. 6, xv. 26 ; Rev. xxii. 15 ; cf. Schoettgen, p. 1145.

8. (P. 532.)   On a superficial comparison of Phil. iii. 19 with Rom. xvi. 18 and of Phil. iii. 18 with Gal. vi. 12, we might come to the conclusion that in Phil. also the reference is to the Judaists ; moreover, the view that it was these of whom Paul had often spoken to the Philippians would agree very well with iii. 1 as rightly understood.   However, what he was reminded to say about the Judaists has already come to a close in iii. 15.   Here in a general exhortation to conduct modelled after that of the founders of the Church (cf. i. 27, ii. 12), there was need of a clear reference to iii. 2 if the thoroughly general description of the "earthy minded" was to be understood in such a special sense.   On the other hand, indeed, this is not a description of Gentile immorality outside the Church (ii. 15 ; Eph. iv. 17), but of just such immorality on the part of many Christians (2 Thess. iii. 6, 11 ; 1 Cor. v. 1) ; for it is only because the missionaries' earlier exhortations have had no effect upon them that Paul must confess that now, even weeping, he calls them the enemies of the Cross of Christ.   The words do not allow us to determine whether they have gone so far as an open renunciation of Christianity, or have simply shown by their un-Christian conduct that they will recognise none of the earnest life that the Cross demands ; cf. 1 Tim. i. 20 ; 2 Tim. iv. 10.   Polycarp, xii. 3, following Phil. iii. 18, speaks of the enemies of the Cross after he has mentioned the heathen kings, the persecutors and enemies of Christianity.

§ 31. PAUL'S SITUATION AT THE TIME WHEN PHILIPPIANS WAS WRITTEN.

The apostle was in prison (i. 7, 13, 14, 17), and must have been in Rome ; for otherwise among the greetings sent to the Philippians by the whole body of Christians in the community where he was, he could not have specified as a special group those of the Christian servants belonging to Cæsar's court (n. 1). He could not have assumed on the part of his readers the knowledge of an accidental and temporary residence of royal servants in Cæsarea, among whom were a number of Christians, but must have made special mention of the fact and have explained why they were there. On the other hand, the Philippians, who had been in recent communication with Paul (above, p. 524), might very well have known that among the Christians in Rome there were servants of the royal household (above, p. 419 f.). Moreover, Paul was in a place where there were a large number of missionaries at work, some of whom were friendly, others hostile to himself (i. 14–18), which suggests at once the situation in Col. iv. 11, and, like this passage, points to Rome (above, p. 443 f.). Finally, what is here said about Paul's trial suits Rome, but would have been impossible in Cæsarea.

Unlike the other imprisonment letters discussed, Philippians, besides mentioning the imprisonment of the apostle, speaks of his defence and confirmation of the gospel as if it were something associated with the imprisonment and yet to be distinguished from it (i. 7). The defence of the gospel was known, at least to his friends, to be the one purpose of his imprisonment (i. 16). From the repeated use of the word ἀπολογία and the usual meaning which this word has elsewhere (1 Cor. ix. 3 ; 2 Cor. vii. 11 ; 2 Tim. iv. 16 ; Acts xxii. 1, xxv. 16), it is clear beyond question that reference is had to the defence of an accused person before a tribunal, and not to that vindication of the gospel which accompanied its proclamation to non-Christians. That a trial was impending the Philippians had learned some time before, and had recently expressed their sympathy with Paul at this turn in his fortune (i. 7). Indeed, this turn of affairs had made them very solicitous about Paul and the cause of the gospel (above, p. 528). In answer to this feeling, Paul shows them in i. 12–18 that, so far as the cause of the gospel is concerned, it has suffered no harm whatever, but has only gained. One good result has been that " his bonds in Christ have become manifest throughout the whole prætorium and among all the rest." Since everyone at all interested in Paul's fate had known perfectly well, ever since the day of his arrest in Jerusalem, the fact of his imprisonment, this passage must mean (and this interpretation is favoured by the position of ἐν Χριστῷ) that it has now become clear to everyone that he had been imprisoned solely because of his relation to Christ, and not for any offences against public order (Acts xxi. 28, 38, xxiv. 5 ; 2 Tim. ii. 9). Of course, Paul's fellow-believers knew this from the first, and the pro- curator Festus had at once convinced himself of the fact (Acts xxv. 18 f., 25, xxvi. 31 f.). When, however, Paul continued year after year in prison under constant military guard, persons not intimately acquainted with him, who came in contact with him or heard of him, must have assumed that there were serious criminal charges against him. Not until the new turn in his affairs, which brought him to trial and gave him opportunity to defend himself, was this cloud removed ; and naturally the royal guard would be the first to understand the situation. To take " prætorium " (i. 13) as referring to a building, not to a group of persons, is practically out of the question, because of the co-ordination of ἐν ὅλῳ τῷ πραι- τωρίῳ and καὶ τοῖς λοιποῖς πᾶσιν. To take it as referring to the prætorian guard is justified, both by linguistic usage and the actual circumstances of this case (n. 2). If, upon his arrival in Rome, Paul was handed over to the *præfectus prætorii*, the soldier who guarded him would have been a prætorian soldier (Acts xxviii. 16, n. 2).

With the frequent daily changes of the guard, in the course of two years Paul would have come into contact with hundreds of these prætorian soldiers. How natural that they should know about the progress of his trial, and that through them it should become more widely known among the populace ! If through the trial it had become generally known that Paul had been accused by the Jews, and until now had remained in prison solely on account of his religious convictions, that was so much gained for the gospel.

A second gratifying result of the hearing which had taken place some time before is indicated in i. 14, namely, that the majority of the brethren had become confident in the Lord as to the outcome of the apostle's imprisonment (n. 3), and were venturing more than they had done heretofore to proclaim the word of the Lord fearlessly. Some there appear to have been in Rome, who, like the distant Philippians, feared the worst. From the fact, however, that the majority of the Christians about Paul who were engaged in spreading the faith were confidently expecting Paul's release, and on the strength of this confidence were preaching the gospel with increased courage and zeal, it must be inferred that on the occasion when Paul made his defence it became apparent that the Imperial Court was not inclined to suppress the gospel nor to punish men like Paul, against whom nothing could be proved except that they were engaged in spreading a new Jewish doctrine. The Roman judge must have taken the same attitude toward his case as had been taken by Gallio and Festus, and made that attitude known (Acts xviii. 15, xxv. 19). Nothing is said in Philippians about preaching activity on the part of Paul and the fellow-workers about him (Eph. vi. 19 f. ; Col. iv. 3, 10–14 ; Philem. 10, 23 f.), just as the earlier letters of the Roman captivity or Acts xviii. 16–31 are silent regarding any trial in progress. Evidently the

trial had put an end to the preaching. When his trial
began his active work ceased, being deprived as he was
of the liberty required to carry it on. Others had taken
his place in this work. Although the Philippians were
troubled when they heard that Paul was no longer able
freely to continue his preaching work, Paul himself looks
upon it rather as advantageous to the gospel, and expresses his joy at the ample substitute which exists for
his own preaching (i. 12, 18). He forces his noble heart
thus to rejoice, although he cannot conceal the fact that
this increased activity on the part of the missionaries
about him is in part influenced by motives which can
cause him no joy. A glance at Col. iv. 11 (above,
p. 442) leaves no doubt that he had in mind Jewish
Christian missionaries. From the fact, however, that he
calls all the preaching which was being carried on about
him a proclamation of Christ, expressing his own joy at
the same, taking into consideration also his purpose to
encourage the Philippians to take a hopeful view of the
situation, we must conclude that he is not referring to
false brethren, or evil workers, dogs, servants of Satan,
like those he warned them against in iii. 2, and with
whom he had had to contend in Corinth and Galatia.
The persons of whom he speaks in i. 14–18 not only
preach Jesus (2 Cor. xi. 4), but also the Saviour whom
Paul preaches ; so that their purpose, the governing
motive of their work, must have been the proclaiming of
Christ. But Paul discovers other motives and indirect
purposes in this newly increased preaching activity about
him. Now that Paul is hindered from working, there are
many who labour with increased zeal, even actuated by
ill-will toward him, καὶ διὰ φθόνον καὶ ἔριν, and governed
generally by unworthy feelings (ἐξ ἐριθείας). They avail
themselves of this opportunity to gain precedence over
him, and to lay claim to the field which he is compelled
temporarily to vacate. They have a certain malicious joy

in seeing their great rival condemned to inactivity, and do not hesitate to add to the pain of his captivity by making him envious at their success, for such, they feel, must be the effect of their work (i. 17, οἰόμενοι); but they are mistaken. There are other Christians in Rome who have been stimulated to increased activity, both by their zeal for the cause of Christ and by their love for the friend who is now before the emperor's tribunal. No matter by whom the cause of the gospel is promoted, nor with what feelings toward himself its promotion is carried on, he is able to rejoice at its progress.

But even looking at the situation from a personal point of view, he is able to contemplate both the present and the future with joyful confidence (i. 19–26). This is the third hopeful aspect of the progress of his trial, by emphasising which Paul seeks to overcome the despondency of the Philippians. He certainly cannot appreciate nor share their feeling about his trial. For him the only life worthy of the name is Christ, and of Him no one nor anything, not even death, can deprive him; in fact, if he were consulting only his own blessedness, death would be pure gain, because thereby his longing for more intimate fellowship with Christ would be satisfied. On the other hand, he has a calling upon earth to fulfil which seems to render necessary a longer continuance in the flesh. He finds himself unable definitely to decide between the two. As a Christian he comforts himself with the thought that whatever the outcome of the impending trial may be, whether it ends with his execution or his acquittal, Christ will be glorified in his body. These considerations (i. 20–24) prove that such a state of discouragement as had taken hold of the Philippians, and the surrender of their joy in the Lord (ii. 18, iii. 1, iv. 4) in contemplation of Paul's possible martyrdom, have no place whatever in the Christian life. But, leaving this out of account, this anxiety of theirs is groundless, and the danger which they

fear imaginary. Paul is firmly convinced that he is soon
to be set at liberty. " I know that this shall issue in my
salvation through your prayer, and through the supplying
of the Spirit of Jesus Christ " (i. 19). Since the petitions
of the Church for the apostle in prison, and now on trial,
could not have been offered for his death but only for his
release (Philem. 22 ; 2 Cor. i. 11 ; Acts xii. 5), the help of
the Spirit must also relate to the same. The apostle is
confident that the Spirit of Christ who has helped him
heretofore will stand by him when he makes his defence,
supplying everything that he needs in the emergency,
preserving constantly his presence of mind, and enabling
him to speak words which shall lead to his acquittal (Matt.
x. 19 f. ; Mark xiii. 11 ; Acts iv. 8). Accordingly, the
salvation which he feels sure is to be the issue of his trial
is not the blessedness nor the glorification of Christ
through him, whether by life or by death, of which he
speaks in i. 20, but his acquittal. That this is his meaning one is compelled to infer from his use of the words of
Job to express this confident expectation (n. 3). And
any possible doubt is removed by the second passage, in
which he states with even greater definiteness what he
feels sure will be the issue of his trial (i. 25). What he
says in i. 22 about the advantage of his longer continuance in the flesh is stated only hypothetically ; in i. 24
this continuance in the flesh he declares as his actual conviction, which would be impossible if his only ground of
expectation were simply a conjecture from the preceding
course of his trial that he was to escape with his life.
With even stronger emphasis he claims again to *know
certainly* that he shall continue to live, come to Philippi
again, and have fellowship not only with individual
members of the Philippian Church, like Epaphroditus, but
with the whole Church (i. 25 f. n. 3). How this conviction was formed Paul does not state explicitly. Doubtless it was due in part to the favourable opinion as to the

outcome of the trial which Paul and those about him had formed from its preceding progress, which led them confidently to expect his acquittal (i. 12–18), also to the feeling which Paul had that his life mission was not yet fulfilled (i. 22, 24). We shall not, however, be wrong—in fact, will be giving simply the impression gained from all Paul's statements about the matter—when we affirm an additional cause, namely, a longing desire on his part and a premonition which were not governed by any rational considerations (i. 19, 25). This third determining influence, which played an important rôle in Paul's life, as it does in the life of every great man and of all men having the habit of earnest prayer (n. 4), is suggested in i. 20 ; for it is not a common Christian experience confidently to hope that Christ may be glorified in one's body, whether this body continue longer to be a dwelling-place or be immediately dissolved. Paul's confidence is based upon past experiences (ὡς πάντοτε καὶ νῦν). Because in the past this frail and suffering body of his has been so often used as the instrument of Christ's miraculous power, he hopes that it will be so to the end. Therefore he cannot believe that death will come to him in the deep, or at the hands of robbers (2 Cor. xi. 25 f., i. 10 ; cf. above, p. 318 n. 4), or in feverish delirium, but he looks forward with longing and with hope to a death which itself will glorify Christ, i.e. to a martyr's death (John xxi. 19). Even more clearly does he direct attention in ii. 17 to this violent end, not as a possibility for which he and the Philippians must be prepared, but as the goal of his earthly life—not to be realised at once, to be sure, but certain to come in the end (above, p. 536 n. 4). While he speaks thus of his martyrdom only as something which he earnestly desires and hopes for (i. 20), he feels confident, for the reasons already given, that death is not now imminent, but that a period of activity lies before him. No trace of any doubt as to this outcome is to be detected in ii. 19–24.

The trial is not yet at an end. For the time being all that Paul can do for the Philippians is to pray for them (i. 4, 9), and by the sending of Epaphroditus (ii. 25–30), as well as through the letter which Epaphroditus was to bring for the quieting of their fears, to strengthen and encourage them. When he is certain how the case will go, *i.e.* when sentence has been passed, he does not plan to go at once to the East and to Philippi, but trusts that he shall then be able to send Timothy to Philippi (ii. 23). When, now, he expresses his confident expectation that he himself will shortly come (ii. 24), the ταχέως is not to be taken too strictly, since the point of comparison is the sending of Timothy immediately after his case has been decided (ii. 23, ἐξαυτῆς). Furthermore, the manner in which Paul speaks here of Timothy's relation to the Philippians and to his own apostolic work (ii. 20–22), shows that this man, who had helped to organise the Philippian Church, was not going back simply for the purpose of conveying a letter and news, but that temporarily he was to take Paul's place in Philippi while the apostle remained absent for some time longer. Finally, before he leaves Rome or goes to Philippi, Paul plans to await the return of Timothy from Philippi, hoping through him to receive good news from the Church there (ii. 19). Taking all these things into consideration, one must conclude that after the end of his trial Paul purposed to remain away from Philippi for at least some months, either intending after his acquittal to stay for some time in Rome, where he would then be able to prosecute his work with entire freedom of movement, or to carry out his long cherished plan of pressing out from Rome to the West (Rom. xv. 22–29). The former is the more natural supposition, since, if Paul had planned before returning to the East to take up a new work in the West, he could not have foreseen how soon he would be able to get release from it; so that for him to announce his early arrival in Philippi would have been

strange (ii. 24, i. 25), particularly since some time before
he had announced his intention of visiting Colossæ
(Philem. 22, above, p. 454), which involved a journey from
Rome to the East. Still these considerations are not
decisive (see below, § 36).

It is very evident that the situation depicted in
Philippians could not have preceded, but must have
followed that presupposed by Ephesians, Colossians, and
Philemon (n. 5). When the latter were written Paul
was engaged in preaching the gospel, supported by a
considerable number of helpers; nothing is said of
any external hindrances with which he had to contend.
They quite confirm what is said in Acts xxviii. 30 f. He
does not ask the Christians in Asia to pray that such
hindrances may be removed, but only that his preaching
of the gospel may be of the right kind and followed
by larger results (Eph. vi. 19 f.; Col. iv. 3 f.; indirectly,
also, iv. 5 f.). Since in Philippians there is no indication of preaching activity on Paul's part, indeed i. 14–18
can hardly be understood in any other way than as implying that other missionaries in Rome had taken advantage of the interruption in Paul's work (above, p. 592 f.),
the inference is that the letter was written, not during
the two whole years that followed his arrival in Rome
(Acts xxviii. 30), but after their close, i.e. later than the
spring of 63. This conclusion follows with even greater
certainty from the positive facts of which we learn in
Philippians. If the trial, upon the outcome of which depended Paul's fate and all his plans for the future, took
place during these two years, then the entire representation of the case in Acts xxviii. 30 f. is misleading; for
this passage gives throughout the impression that for two
whole years after Paul was delivered to the commandant
of the guard his condition remained practically unchanged,
with no judicial investigation of his case. Moreover,
assuming that the trial took place during these two years,

it is difficult to understand why this trial, which at the
time when Philippians was written was arousing the
deepest sympathy on the part of those about Paul and
of his distant friends in Philippi, and was being followed
by all with the greatest interest,—why this trial had
no apparent influence upon Ephesians, Colossians, and
Philemon. If Paul and all those about him, Christians
and non-Christians alike, were correct in their judgment
at the time when Philippians was written, he must
have been set at liberty very shortly afterward, which
excludes the possibility of Paul's having written later
during the same imprisonment letters in which his condition seems uniformly to be that of a captivity of indefinite duration, in which only once reference is made to
the prospect of liberation (Philem. 22, above, p. 454), and
that in a way purely subordinate and incidental. The
supposition of the earlier date of Philippians is just as
impossible if it be assumed that Paul and those about him
were totally deceived in their opinion, or that some un-
foreseen circumstance gave the trial an outcome different
from that which they had expected. In that case he would
have been either executed or banished to an island, or
condemned˙ to labour in the mines. Finally, another
indefinite postponement of the trial after it had been begun
in such earnest, and when it was so near decision, is extremely difficult to conceive. And even if such a delay
did take place, which at the time when Philippians was
written seemed entirely impossible, there could hardly fail
'to have been some trace of it in letters written later during
the same captivity, as well as of the bitter disappointment
of Paul and his friends caused by this delay. But the
most difficult thing of all to explain is how Paul, some
weeks or months after he and his friends had been
deceived in the expectation which they had had of his ultimate release,—an expectation based upon good and sufficient grounds,—how Paul could have expressed again,

even incidentally (Philem. 22), the hope of being set at liberty without having the strongest grounds for entertaining such a hope, and without stating to his distant friends the reasons why he felt that he and they would not be again deceived. Only one other possibility remains, namely, that the events upon which at the time when Philippians was written Paul based his definite expectation of being set at liberty, took place in the interval between the composition of Ephesians, Colossians, and Philemon and the composition of Philippians. At the close of the two years (Acts xxviii. 30), during which Paul's case remained *in statu quo*, in the spring of 63 his trial began and soon took a turn most favourable to the accused, as set forth in Philippians. The indefinite hope which he had had of being set at liberty again, and of being able to visit the Churches in Asia (Philem. 22), has become a definite expectation. Whether this expectation was fulfilled must be determined primarily by the investigation of the other letters attributed to Paul which have not yet been inquired into.

1. (P. 540.) Phil. iv. 22, μάλιστα δὲ οἱ ἐκ τῆς Καίσαρος οἰκίας. Concerning the somewhat doubtful δέ, cf. *GK*, ii. 939. Although *domus Cæsaris* (*Cæsarum*, *Augusta*, *Augustana*, *Augustiana*, later *domus divina*) is the ordinary designation of the imperial house in the sense of the ruling family with all its members, the expression which we have here (ἐκ τῆς οἰκίας, *ex domo*) never denotes relatives of the emperor. Such a meaning would be expressed by οἱ ἐκ γένους (or πρὸς γένους, Clem. *Hom.* iv. 8, xii. 8, 15), or ἀφ' αἵματος (Philo, *Leg. ad Cai.* xi ; Jos. *Bell.* i. 18. 4), or βασιλικοῦ γένους (Dio Cass. lx. 1. 3), or συγγενεῖς τοῦ Καίσαρος (*Acta Theclæ*, xxxvi). It denotes rather, according to constant usage, servants in the imperial household. In later times some of these might be of high rank, but earlier they were only slaves or freedmen (Philo, *in Flacc.* v, Mang. ii. 522 ; *Acta Petri et Pauli*, ed. Lipsius, 104. 9, 106. 15, 193. 5 ; Hippol. *Refut.* ix. 12 beginning; *Inscr. R. Neapol.* No. 6912, "ex domo Cæsarum libertorum et servorum," etc. ; *C. I. L.* vi. Nos. 8645, 8653, 8654 ; x. No. 1745). In Gregory's *Testament* (Migne, xxxvii. 389), ἐκ τῆς οἰκίας μου γενόμενος is "my former slave." We must also remember that from the earliest times οἰκέται, like *domestici* during the period of the Empire (Suet. *Otho*, 10 end ; Tert. *Apol.* vii, xxxix), denotes the "domestics" (cf., further, Lightfoot, *Phil.* 19. 165, 169–176). It was not until after Nero's time that certain court positions were filled by knights instead of freedmen, and it was later still before

this came to be the rule (cf. Friedländer, *Sittengesch.*[6] i. 83 f.); consequently Phil. iv. 22 cannot refer to persons of knightly rank. The later tradition about *equites Cæsareani* among the Roman Christians of that time (Clem. *Hypot.* on 1 Pet. v. 13, *Forsch.* iii. 83, 95) carries back into the times of Phil. iv. 22 conditions which did not arise until later.

2. (P. 541.) On τὸ πραιτώριον, Phil. i. 13, see Marquardt, *R. Staatsverw.*[2] ii. 411, 475 ff.; Mommsen, *R. Staatsr.*[3] ii. 863 ff.; Lightfoot, 97–102. As a place it denotes originally the general's tent and the part of the camp where this stands—the headquarters; then the dwelling of any prince or chief official (Matt. xxvii. 27; Mark xv. 16; Acts xxiii. 35; *Acta Thom.* 3, 17, 18, 19; Tert. *Scap.* iii); finally, any particularly aristocratic, "princely" building (Suet. *Aug.* lxxii; *Calig.* xxxvii; *Tib.* xxxix *in prætorio*=Tac. *Ann.* iv. 59 *in villa*). When the emperor dwelt in such a building *outside of Rome*, it was occasionally so designated in the dating of an edict, as, *e.g.*, *C. I. L.* No. 5050 *Bais in prætorio*; cf. Jos. *Ant.* xviii. 7. 2. The view of the Antiochian commentators (*e.g.* Theodorus, ed. Swete, i. 206), that the imperial palace in the capital which was called *palatium* in their times, went by the name of *prætorium* in Paul's time, is a worthless conjecture, unsupported by any examples. Still more untenable is the notion that ἡ Καίσαρος οἰκία (iv. 22, which, if for no other reason than the form of the phrase itself, οἱ ἐκ τῆς κτλ. cannot mean a building) is equivalent to τὸ πραιτώριον (i. 13)=τὸ πραιτώριον Ἡρώδου (Acts xxiii. 35). This is the view of O. Holtzmann, *ThLz.* 1890, col. 177, who is quoted approvingly by Spitta, *Urchristentum*, i. 34. But a palace built by Herod in Cæsarea was far from becoming ἡ Καίσαρος οἰκία simply by passing over into Roman hands or by serving presumably as the procurator's official residence; still less were the people employed in this building οἱ ἐκ τῆς Καίσαρος οἰκίας. Proof is lacking also for Wieseler's view (*Chronol.* 403), that *prætorium* denotes the guardroom or barracks in or beside the *palatium* where one of the prætorian cohorts was regularly quartered (Tac. *Hist.* i. 24, 29 ["cohortis quæ in palatio stationem egit"], 38; *Ann.* xii. 69; Suet. *Otho*, vi). Dio Cass. liii. 16. 5, like Polyb. vi. 31. 6 f., translates *prætorium* by στρατήγιον; but his meaning is simply that the emperor lived in the palace and had his headquarters there, not at all that a part of the palace was called *prætorium*. Nor can it be proved that this is used here as a name for the *castra prætoria* (Plin. *H. N.* iii. 9. 67) or *castra prætorianorum* (Tac. *Hist.* i. 31) outside of the Porta Viminalis, where since Tiberius' time the whole guard had been quartered (Tac. *Ann.* iv. 2, 7, xii. 36; Suet. *Tib.* xxxvii; Schol. on Juv. x. 95; Dio Cass. lvii. 19. 6). To begin with, we are not to think of a place at all as referred to in Phil. i. 13, since the combination "in the whole prætorium and (among) all the rest"—especially in view of the fact that the second expression has no preposition of its own—is correct and natural only if *prætorium* indicates a class of persons. Furthermore, this corresponds to an unquestionable usage; for *prætorium*, along with *cohortes prætoriæ*, is the regular name for the imperial guard. Moreover, expressions like *præfectus prætorio, militare in prætorio*, have nothing to do with a particular locality, and passages such as Tac. *Hist.* iv. 46 ("militiam et stipendia orant . . . igitur in prætorium accepti") and Suet. *Nero*, ix ("ascriptis veteranis e prætorio"), which have been adduced to support the meaning *castra prætoria*, simply establish the meaning "guard." Paul, from the time of his arrival

in Rome, was probably guarded by soldiers from this body (Acts xxviii. 16).
This passage in the other recension reads : ὅτε δὲ εἰσήλθομεν εἰς Ῥώμην, ὁ
ἑκατόνταρχος παρέδωκε τοὺς δεσμίους τῷ στρατοπεδάρχῃ· τῷ δὲ Παύλῳ
ἐπετράπη μένειν καθ᾽ ἑαυτὸν ἔξω τῆς παρεμβολῆς σὺν τῷ φυλάσσοντι αὐτὸν
στρατιώτῃ (cf. Blass, *Comm.* 287 ; ed. min. 94. 9 f.). The ancient Latin
translation of this text gives for τῷ στρατοπεδάρχῃ *principi peregrinorum*
according to one MS. (g=the so-called Gigas in Stockholm), and *præfecto*
according to another (p=Paris, lat. 321), with which a Provençal version
agrees. Even before the latter variant was known, Mommsen (*Sitzungsber. d.
Berl. Ak.* 1895, S. 495 ff.), following a suggestion of Harnack's, not only
collected all that was hitherto known about the *princeps castrorum peregrinorum*, commonly called for brevity *princeps peregrinorum*, but also sought
to show that the centurion Julius handed over Paul and the other prisoners
to this *princeps peregrinorum*, declaring, on the other hand, that the traditional
reference of στρατοπεδάρχης to the *præfectus prætorio* was "impossible historically as well as linguistically" (498). In answer to this the following must
here suffice : (1) The existence of a *princeps castrorum peregrinorum* (*C. I. L.*
vi. No. 354), and of the troops and barracks of which he was the commandant,
has yet to be established for the time preceding the reorganisation under
Septimus Severus. The occurrence of the title in a Latin text of Acts xxviii. 16
is no proof of an earlier date, for it is a hypothesis improbable and incapable
of demonstration that there was any Latin translation of Acts before the
death of Severus, 211 A.D. (cf. *GK*, i. 51–60). Besides, we do not know that
præfectus or *princeps peregrinorum* dates from the first translator. (2) Inasmuch
as this *princeps peregrinorum* occurs in a Latin text of Acts written at the very
earliest a hundred and twenty-five years after the Greek original,—therefore,
at any rate, not a translation resting on a knowledge of the events there
related, and linguistically not a translation of στρατοπεδάρχης at all, but at
best only a happily chosen *quid pro quo*, it cannot help us in our search for
the meaning of the original writer. (3) As for the alleged *linguistic* impossibility of taking στρατοπεδάρχης as equivalent to *præfectus prætorio*, it is
particularly to be emphasised that the Latin title in Luke's time and long
afterwards was rendered by the Greeks in many different ways (cf. Mommsen,
*R. Staatsr.*³ ii. 866, and the citations in Hirschfeld, *Unters. z. röm. Verwaltungs-
gesch.* i. 220–239). Josephus, Luke's contemporary, uses various renderings
(*Ant.* xviii. 6. 6, xix. 4. 6, xx. 8. 2), once having recourse to ἦν ἐπὶ τῶν
στρατοπέδων (*Ant.* xix. 1. 6), in which connection it should be remarked
that τὰ στρατόπεδα does not here mean *castra*, but is synonymous with τὸ
στρατεύματα (xviii. 6. 6, xx. 8. 2), and this in turn with οἱ σωματοφύλακες
(xix. 4. 6) ; so likewise Luke (xxi. 20) understands by στρατόπεδα troops,
while he terms their camp or barracks παρεμβολή (Acts xxi. 34, 37,
xxii. 24, xxiii. 10, 16, 32, xxviii. 16). Herodian, a Syrian, and therefore
fellow-countryman of the Antiochian Luke, uses regularly, besides the simple
ἔπαρχος (i. 9. 10), ἐπάρχων τῶν στρατοπέδων, i. 16. 5 [in this one place
ἔπαρχος τ. στ.], iii. 10. 5, xiii. 1, iv. 12. 1 [τοῦ στρατοπέδου], v. 1. 2. Philostratus renders it in various ways (*Vit. Apoll.* iv. 42, vii. 16), once (*Vit.
Sophist.* ii. 32) as οἱ τῶν στρατοπέδων ἡγεμόνες. Why should not Luke have
included in the one compound στρατοπεδάρχης what Josephus, Herodian, and
Philostratus expressed by combining its various parts—especially since the

word is used quite often to designate important commands (Dion. Hal. x. 36 ; Jos. *Bell.* vi. 4. 3 ; Luc. *Conscr. Hist.* 22 ; Eus. *H. E.* viii. 4. 3, ix. 5. 2 ; Mart. *Palæst.* ix. 2) ?   (4) The eye-witness who is speaking in Acts xxviii. 16 may have been none too well informed about military matters, or at least not specially conversant with the official titles ; but he is certainly not speaking here generally of some officer of rank or of any barracks whatever, but of the one particular στρατοπεδάρχης in Rome, and of the one particular παρεμβολή.   Consequently the former term must mean the *præfectus prætorio* and the latter *castra prætorianorum.*   From the third century onward it was a fixed rule that the emperor exercised his jurisdiction through the *præfectus prætorio* (Mommsen, *R. Staatsrecht,* ii. 972, 987, 1120) ; but even before this it was so exercised in very many cases, cf. Traj. *ad Plin.* lvii (with regard to one who had appealed from the sentence of the governor : " vinctus mitti ad præfectos prætorii mei debet ") ; Spartianus, *Severus,* iv. 3 ; Philostr. *Vit. Sophist.* ii. 32.   Whoever was so sent from the province to receive final judgment at the hands of the *præfectus prætorio* certainly had to be brought before him or his subordinates ; and who but the *præfectus prætorio* or his subordinates could have had the task of deciding where and how those under accusation and those held for examination should be lodged and guarded in Rome ?   Paul was not sent to the imperial tribunal without a report from the procurator Festus (Acts xxv. 26 f.).   To whom could the centurion Julius have delivered the prisoners and the report respecting them but to the *præfectus prætorio* as judicial deputy of the emperor ?   Previously, Mommsen (*R. Staatsr.*[3] ii. 972, n. 2) decided from Phil. i. 14 (read rather i. 13) that Paul, like other "accused persons sent from the provinces to Rome for final judgment, was given over to the *præfecti prætorio* to be guarded."   Now that is " historically impossible," since, while the *præfectus prætorio* administered criminal justice, he had nothing to do directly with the superintendence of the prisons (*Sitzungsber.* 498, A. 1 ; 498, A. 2).   But, as a matter of fact, Acts xxviii. 16 does not refer any of these things to the stratopedarch ; it says simply that after Julius had reported with his prisoners to the commander-in-chief, and, as we are justified in adding, had delivered up the writ from Festus, permission was given to Paul, in distinction from the other prisoners, who were confined in the camp in question, to dwell outside the camp guarded by a soldier, that is, to find and rent quarters for himself (cf. xxviii. 30).   The passive expression (ἐπετράπη) leaves it uncertain whether the præfect himself, or, as is more likely, one of his subordinates, decided upon the various dispositions to be made of the prisoners.   The Roman expounder of Paul's Epistles in 370 A.D. (Ambrosiaster in his prologue to Eph. p. 231), who naturally had before him the old Latin text of Acts xxviii. 16, 30 (see above, p. 552, line 5 f.), says of Paul incidentally : " quia veniens ab Hierosolymis in custodia sub fidejussore intelligitur degisse, manens extra castra in conductu suo."   To Paul, then, was granted at the outset a favour which was secured by Agrippa, later king Herod Agrippa I., only after long imprisonment of a stricter kind and as a preliminary to his final release (Jos. *Ant.* xviii. 6. 10 ; Niese, § 235, and Lightfoot's discussion of the same, 101, as against Wieseler's misinterpretations).   This case is very instructive for the study of Paul's situation.   By the emperor's order the *præfectus prætorio* Macro arrested Agrippa (Niese, § 190 ; cf. Hirschfeld, p. 219, No. 6)—the event occurring in

Tusculanum (Niese, 179). From that time on Agrippa was constantly kept in chains and guarded by soldiers, naturally of the prætorian guard (Niese, 195, 196, 203, 204, 230, 233), and that, too, in the στρατόπεδον at Rome (235), *i.e.* the *castra prætoria*, until he was allowed after the death of Tiberius to go back to his former private dwelling, though still kept under guard (235). This latter was Paul's situation during the two years. What form his imprisonment took at the end of this period so sharply defined by Luke is a question. Tradition is here silent. Yet we must conclude from Acts xxviii. 30 f. that Paul then ceased to live in his own hired house. He was not released, for at the time of Phil. he was still under arrest and in chains. On the contrary, his trial had now begun. If the *præfectus prætorio* as the emperor's deputy conducted this trial, Paul must have been lodged either in the *castra prætoria* outside the Porta Viminalis, or, since the *præfectus prætorio* had to stay in the palace as a rule (Mommsen, *R. Staatsr.*³ ii. 864 ; Dio Cass. lxix. 18, 2, cf. above, p. 551, n. 2, line 26, on Dio Cass. liii. 16, 5), in the guardroom of the prætorian cohort stationed there. The latter assumption is strongly supported by Phil. iv. 22. The special greeting from Christians who belonged among the court servants, following the greeting from the narrower circle of his friends (iv. 21) and from all the Christians in Rome (iv. 22*a*), would then be explained by the nearness of the court. Still it is possible that for the " Romans " of Philippi (Acts xvi. 21) it would be of itself peculiarly interesting and a matter of encouragement to receive a greeting from Christians in the neighbourhood of the emperor. It would thus be borne in upon the anxious hearts of the Philippians that the Christian confession and thus also Paul himself at that time were not so much in danger at Rome as they had supposed. But be that as it may, it was not for a short time merely, but ever since his arrival in Rome, that Paul had had to do with the " Prætorium," and indeed with very many soldiers of that body one after the other. Thus, and thus alone, can Phil. i. 13 be explained satisfactorily. Mommsen (*Sitzungsber.* 498, A. 1) holds it as indubitable that πραιτώριον should be understood as "the judicial board, the *præfecti prætorio* [there was only one at that time, Acts xxviii. 16] with their numerous assistants and subalterns "; but one would like very much to see examples from the usage of the first century which would confirm such a view. It does not agree well with the expression ἐν ὅλῳ τῷ πραιτωρίῳ, which suggests a large body such as the guard was (from Tiberius until Vespasian it consisted of nine cohorts of a thousand men each, Tac. *Hist.* ii. 93), and is at variance with the facts related above, which shows that Paul for more than two years had had relations with hundreds of prætorians in the ordinary sense of this word.

3. (Pp. 542, 545.) It is not merely the words τοῦτό μοι ἀποβήσεται εἰς σωτηρίαν, i. 19, which Paul borrows from Job xiii. 16, LXX ; as usual, he has in mind the whole context out of which he takes the expression ; xiii. 18 f. especially in his thought, and in his οἶδα we can even hear an echo of the words οἶδα ἐγὼ ὅτι δίκαιος ἀναφανοῦμαι ("that I shall be acquitted in the trial"). This determines the meaning of τοῦτο="the legal process in which I am involved" (essentially the same as τὸ [al. τὰ] κατ' ἐμέ, i. 12 ; cf. ii. 23), and of σωτηρία ="preservation of life" (Acts xxvii. 34), which in this case could be only acquittal by the judge. Cf., further, the writer's essay, *ZfKW*, 1885, S. 300 f., also S. 108, 201, with reference to i. 7, 12. In i. 25, τοῦτο πεποιθώς can hardly be

translated "firmly convinced of this," "sure of this," or "relying upon this." Appeal to Bernhardy's *Syntax*, 106 ; Kühner-Gerth, i. 309, A. 5 ; or to πέπεισμαί τι, Heb. vi. 9 ; or to πέποιθα, Rom. ii. 19 (acc. with inf.) ; Phil. ii. 24 (ὅτι), cannot make up for the lack of examples of πέποιθα, with acc. In Phil. i. 6, αὐτὸ τοῦτο = "for this very reason." Consequently the certainty expressed in i. 25 is not based upon the confidence in the judgment of i. 24 ; but along with this judgment, which is quite possibly only an erroneous judgment, is expressed the conviction : "And this I know assuredly, that." (Cf. ii. 24, πέποιθα, of the same thing ; Rom. xiv. 14, οἶδα καὶ πέπεισμαι.) The frequent recurrence of πεποιθέναι (in Phil. six times, in all the other letters seven times) is in keeping with his mood and situation. The construction with the dative, i. 14 (cf. Philem. 21 ; 2 Cor. x. 7), does not express the idea that these brethren put their confidence in Paul's chains, which of itself would be hard to comprehend, but that they now took a hopeful view of these chains, and awaited an outcome of his imprisonment favourable both for Paul and for the progress of the gospel. Joined to μενῶ (= ἐπιμένειν τῇ σαρκί, i. 24) in i. 25 is καὶ παραμενῶ, besides (needlessly amended in the Antioch text to read συμπαραμενῶ) added to introduce πᾶσιν ὑμῖν. It does not mean, however, "to remain with you all," for Paul was not yet in Philippi ; but παραμένειν retains its meaning "to continue in life " (Herodot. i. 30 ; Iren. iii. 3. 4), and not infrequently in this connection (Plato, *Phæd.* p. 115 ; Iren. ii. 22. 5 παρέμεινε γὰρ αὐτοῖς μέχρι τῶν Τραϊανοῦ χρόνων ; ii. 32. 4, παρέμειναν σὺν ἡμῖν ἱκανοῖς ἔτεσιν) ; therefore, "I shall continue in life, and, what is more, in fellowship and intercourse with you all."

4. (P. 546.) The supernatural agencies operating in Paul's decisions and actions are emphasised not only in Acts, especially those passages where the narrator shows that he himself was present (xvi. 6–10, 18, xx. 23, xxi. 8–14, xxiii. 11, xxvii. 23 ; cf. ix. 3–18, xiii. 2, 9, xviii. 9, xxii. 17), but also by Paul himself (Gal. ii. 2 ; 2 Cor. xii. 1–9, 12, i. 17 ; Rom. xv. 19). What he means by magnifying Christ in his body may be gathered from 2 Cor. ii. 12–16, iii. 18, iv. 11, vi. 9, x. 3–6, 11, xii. 7–10, 12, xiii. 3–10 ; 1 Cor. v. 5, xv. 30–32 ; Gal. iv. 13–15, or from the narratives of miracles in Acts.

5. (P. 548.) Since Bleek, Lightfoot in particular, pp. 29–45, has advocated the view that Phil. was written earlier than Eph., Col., and Philem. He holds (38) that the outward condition of Paul at the time of Phil. is in nowise different from that described in Acts xxviii. 30 f., and to be inferred, it may be added, in Eph., Col., and Philem. ; but this, as has been once more demonstrated (above, p. 540 ff.)., is as untenable as the assumption that Paul's prospect of release is not more strongly expressed in Phil. than in Philem. 22 (39). If Paul had had a definite prospect of release when he wrote Philem., he could not have left it wholly unexpressed in his other letters of that date, Eph. and Col. (above, p. 545) ; but aside from this, is ἐλπίζω then (Philem. 22) really equivalent to οἶδα, πεποιθὼς οἶδα, πέποιθα ἐν κυρίῳ, Phil. i. 19, 25, ii. 24 ? Further, we must regard the letters written at the same time and addressed to Christians of the same place, Col. and Philem., and in a measure also Eph., as a single reflection of a definite situation ; how then can we compare the solitary line occurring, not in the Epistle to the whole Church, but among some remarks at the close of a private letter, with the detailed description and argument in Phil. i. 12–26,

with the further assurance in Phil. ii. 24, and with the repeated reference to the contrast between absence and personal presence in Philippi, i. 27, ii. 12 ? Lightfoot's single positive argument lies in his theory of a gradual development in Paul's writings in respect of theological thought, polemic antitheses, and style, according to which he judges that Phil. has more in common with the older letters, Rom. especially, than with Eph. and Col. Here also this theory is plainly incompatible with the facts (see above, p. 200 f.). After what has been said in notes 1–3, it seems to the present writer to need no further proof that we cannot think of Phil. as having been written at a still earlier time, namely, in Cæsarea, especially as it must be accepted as proved that Eph., Col., and Philem. also were written, not in Cæsarea, but in Rome. The arguments used above, p. 443 ff., to prove this latter point, only gain force when applied to Phil. Spitta (*Urchristentum*, i. 34) finds in Phil. i. 30 a proof that Paul has only lately become a prisoner. But Paul's battle, of which the Philippians have lately heard, is not one which arises from his imprisonment, but from the change in his fortune denoted by the ἀπολογία (i. 7, 16)—those very events with regard to which he has enlightened the troubled Philippians in i. 12–26. A still stronger argument for the composition of the letter in Cæsarea is held to lie in iv. 10 ff.; but such an opinion is overthrown by the ἤδη ποτέ, which points to a long interruption of the financial aid on the part of the Philippians (above, p. 525 f.).

§ 32. THE GENUINENESS OF THE EPISTLE TO THE PHILIPPIANS.

One would suppose that the inimitable freshness of feeling betrayed in every line of this letter, the naturalness, even carelessness of its style (n. 1), the large number of facts hard to invent, regarding which the readers are not definitely informed, but which are touched upon and elucidated in a conversational way under the presupposition that they are already known, together with the strong external evidence, particularly the evidence of the Philippian letter of Polycarp, a disciple of one of the apostles—might have safeguarded Philippians more even than the other Epistles of Paul against the suspicion of being the product of a later period. Hitzig, indeed, saw (*Zur Krit. paulin. Briefe*, 24) that Baur's criticism lacked exegetical basis, and Holsten actually endeavoured by a new interpretation of the letter to secure such a basis for his own criticism, which in essentials agreed with that of Baur (n. 2). Baur directed his attention mainly to the passage so much discussed by theologians, ii. 5–11, which with all its beauty really has in the letter as a whole a very subordinate place, and contains scarcely more dogmatic material than is to be found in a sentence like 2 Cor. viii. 9. According to Baur, the author of Philippians here denies of Christ what Valentinus had taught concerning his σοφία (*Paulus*, ii. 51–59), although, as a matter of fact, Valentinus' σοφία did not grasp after likeness to God, but sought to unite itself with the divine First Cause; while, between the sinking of the baser part of this σοφία into matter and the self-emptying of Christ, there is nothing in common except the fact that both the Pauline κενοῦν ἑαυτόν and the Valentinian name for matter (κένωμα) are derived from the word κένος. According to Baur's representation, the author of Philippians, like the pseudo-Paul of Ephesians and Colossians, was influenced and governed by the very Gnostic ideas which he here seems in some measure to oppose; and this view is maintained notwithstanding the fact that Philippians was adopted with some changes by Marcion into his N.T. (S. 51, 59, cf. above, p. 497 f.). Instead of admitting the natural agreement between Phil. iv. 15 and 2 Cor. xi. 8 f., Baur finds (S. 62–65) the repeated relief of Paul by the Philippians, which he thinks had been arranged beforehand, to be in contradiction to the principles laid down in 1 Cor. ix. 6–18, apparently forgetting that the same contradiction exists between 1 Cor. ix. and 2 Cor. xi., and that to allow one's self to be supported and paid by those who hear one's preaching is, in fact, a very different thing from accepting the freewill offerings of a grateful Church towards the carrying on of new missionary work, that is, towards defraying the expenses of travel and making the preaching of the gospel without cost in other places. The indifference to false teachers shown in Phil. i. 15–18 is also found to be un-Pauline (Baur, ii. 72; Hitzig, S. 15). As a matter of fact, this expression of unselfish joy on the apostle's part for the spread of the Christian faith in Rome shows that the preaching of all the missionaries who were working there, even those who were hostile to Paul, was in his judgment really a proclamation of Christ. The thing which he shows himself magnanimous enough to overlook is not the corruption of the gospel, but the unfriendly, to him painful, rivalry of certain preachers (above, p. 543).

If, now, it be asked, what purpose there was in the forgery of the letter, a twofold answer is given. Baur—and at this point Hitzig agrees with him—finds this purpose to be—(1) the glorification of the extraordinary success of Paul's preaching in Rome, and (2)—and at this point it is Holsten especially who follows in Baur's footsteps—to lessen the opposition between the Jewish Christian and Gentile Christian parties. The former purpose is inconceivable, since throughout the entire letter nothing is said about Paul's preaching in Rome. Neither the imperial guard nor the larger group to whom reference is made in i. 13 owed their conversion to the knowledge, secured through Paul's trial and from contact with him, to the effect that he was not a violator of the laws of the State, but the representative of a religious doctrine relating to a certain Christ (above, p. 541). Furthermore, reference is made in i. 14–18 not to the spiritual success of the preaching, but to the favourable impression made by Paul's defence before the court, and to its effect, not so much upon those who had heard Paul's preaching before his trial began, as upon the missionary activity of other teachers, some of whom were ill-disposed toward Paul. There is nothing to indicate that the royal servants (iv. 44, above, p. 550, n. 1), whom Baur makes relatives of the imperial house (ii. 65 f.), were converted through Paul's influence, and a pseudo-Paul of the second century would not have regarded the privilege of conveying greetings from some servants of the court as any special honour to the apostle. This supposition, namely, that the author of Philippians meant to glorify Paul at the expense of historical accuracy, was further supported by Baur and others, by assuming as self-evident that the Clement mentioned in iv. 3 was identical with the distinguished head of the Roman Church at the close of the first century, or was so represented, and by assuming that the latter was, or is here, represented to be the same as T. Flavius Clemens, related to the Flavian royal family, and consul in the year 95 A.D., who was likewise a man of some note (n. 3). The latter identification is a fiction of the pseudo-Clementine *Romances*, which were written certainly not earlier than the year two hundred, and has no basis whatever in fact. Even if the identification were possible, it would have no significance with reference to Philippians, since the person referred to in Phil. iv. 3 was an influential member not of the Roman, but of the Philippian Church, and so cannot be identified with Clemens Romanus.

That the purpose of the author was to lessen the opposition between Gentile and Jewish Christians is likewise inconceivable ; because in the one passage, where Jewish Christians are clearly referred to (iii. 2), they are spoken of in the severest tone of disapproval, and declared to be base enemies of Christianity. And those who are opposed to them as being real Jews both in feeling and by circumcision are not the Gentile Christian party, but Paul and his helpers (above, pp. 531, 538 f., n. 7). There is not a single passage in the letter containing exhortations to harmony or to co-operation among the members in which there is indication that there were differences of faith and doctrine in the Church which needed to be overcome (above, p. 529 f.). In order to discover such opposition and an attempt to overcome it in iv. 2 f., one must have recourse to an allegory of the most fantastic sort, and to an interpretation of words contrary to their natural sense (n. 4).

Not more successful in discovering a plausible motive for the composition of the letter have been the efforts of those who think that Philippians is made up of a number of letters or fragments of letters, some of them genuine, others spurious (n. 5). Before the original unity of the letter can be called in question, essential contradictions must be shown to exist with reference to the facts referred to in the letter; and before the genuineness of the whole or of single parts of the letter can be regarded as in doubt, it must be shown that there are ideas in the letter out of harmony with the Epistles generally conceded to be Paul's. Like Corinthians and Thessalonians, this Epistle is not an essay, but a real letter, in which the succession of ideas is not always strictly logical. We should certainly be able to understand its details better if our knowledge of the correspondence between Paul and the Philippians which preceded it were derived from existing documents and historical reports, not simply from inferences drawn from the Epistle itself. However, what we do have is enough to show that Philippians is the product of actual conditions, which could not have been invented, and which are only partially reflected by the letter itself.

1. (P. 556.) Genuine epistolary style is to be seen in the passages where reference is made to remarks of the Philippians without any quotation of them, or even a statement to the effect that they are the occasion of the discussion which follows, as in 1 Cor. vii. 1. The most striking of these are i. 3, ἐγὼ μέν (above, p. 535, n. 2; i. 12, μᾶλλον, above, p. 528), also iv. 10. Observe the carelessness in sentence construction in i. 22, 27, 29, iii. 8, 14. It is also genuinely Pauline (cf. above, p. 516, n. 7) that certain expressions should recur very frequently in this short letter: πέποιθα (above, p. 555, n. 3); φρονεῖν ten or eleven times, in all the other letters twelve times; πλήν three times, elsewhere only twice; κοινωνία, κοινωνεῖν, συγκοινωνός, συγκοινωνεῖν six times altogether; χαίρειν, συγχαίρειν, χαρά sixteen times in all; δέησις four times, in Rom., 1 and 2 Cor., Gal., Col., 1 and 2 Thess., and Philem. altogether only three times, in Eph. twice, in 1 and 2 Tim. three times.

2. (P. 556.) Holsten in JbfPTh. 1875, i. S. 425 ff.; 1876, ii. S. 58 ff., 282 ff. The arguments of the Tübingen school are judged (i. 425, ii. 329 f.) to be in part incomplete, in part unfortunate, and on the whole deserving

oblivion. The demand for a new interpretation (i. 426) is met by the conclusion (ii. 372), "I have brought criticism back again to the basis of exegesis." How it fares with this reconstructed criticism the present writer has shown by the citation of characteristic examples (cf. his *Abhandlungen, ZfKIV*, 1885, S. 183, 186, 188, 189, 194, 201, 291).

3. (P. 559.) Baur (*Paulus*, ii. 66–72, 85 f.), Hitzig (11 ff.). In the groundless identification of this Clement of Philippi with Clement of Rome the moderns have been anticipated by Origen (tom. vi. 36, *in Jo.* ed. Preuschen, p. 163), who also recognised Hermas, author of the *Shepherd*, in Rom. xvi. 14 (Delarue, iv. 683), and Luke the Evangelist in 2 Cor. viii. 18 (see below, Div. ix.). But Origen certainly did not base his conjectures on such a monstrous assertion as that of Baur (S. 66), that "neither history nor legend knows of any other Clement at this time" (cf. above, p. 534). With regard to the relation between Clement of Rome and the consul T. Flavius Clemens, the present writer can no longer appeal unconditionally to what he wrote thirty years ago in his *Hirt des Hermas* (S. 44–69). Lightfoot has the best discussion of the whole question, *St. Clement* (1890), i. 14–103. When it was brought to Baur's attention that there is no hint that the Clement of Phil. iv. 3 had any connection with Rome, but that we should rather seek him in Philippi, he made a point out of this very thing against the genuineness of the letter (S. 86), holding that we cannot tell where the persons whom it mentions belong; as if the letter were to blame for this, and not rather its inattentive readers. There is not the slightest unclearness as to the whereabouts of Paul, Timothy, Epaphroditus, Euodia, Syntyche, Clement, the bishops and deacons (i. 1), the imperial guard (i. 13), or the brethren who were preaching Christ (i. 14–17). The Judaists alone, against whom the Philippians are warned in iii. 2, are mentioned without a hint of their local habitation ; and for the simple reason that reference is made not to individual persons, but to a whole class, which had its representatives throughout Asia and Europe.

4. (P. 559.) Schwegler (*Nachapost. Zeitalter*, ii. 135), whom Baur (ii. 72, 86) followed, found in the women Euodia and Syntyche the Jewish Christian and Gentile Christian parties respectively, and in the "true comrade," Peter. Volkmar (*ThJb.* 1856, S. 310 ff.) on this theory explained Εὐοδία (from ὁδός = doctrine) = ὀρθοδοξία, ὀρθοδία, the Jewish Christian party, which considered itself as alone orthodox, Συντύχη = *consors*, the Gentile Christians, who had become partakers of salvation. Unsatisfied with this distribution of the characters, Holsten (ii. 71), without mentioning Hitzig, who (S. 10) considered that he had refuted Schwegler's view by showing that the rôles could be reversed, declared Euodia to be the Gentile Christian party, which has always been on the right way, Syntyche the Jewish Christian party, which has met the former upon the right way, and the Synzygos, as his name implies, the one who yokes together (!), *i.e.* who has the task of uniting the Churches. Finally, Völter (*ThTij.* 1892, p. 123) left the question open again as to how the two women's names shall be divided between the two parties in question, and tacitly made the copyist's error Εὐωδία (instead of Εὐοδία, above, p. 533, line 17) the basis for his interpretation of these names. But Hitzig (S. 5–10) had proved long before that the names in question came rather from Gen. xxx. 11, 13, namely, Συντύχη from Leah's exclamation at the birth of Gad, Εὐοδία from the name Asher. Since the LXX gives only an

562 INTRODUCTION TO THE NEW TESTAMENT

uncertain support (ἐν τύχῃ) for the formation of the first name and none at
all for Euodia, the author must have drawn from the Hebrew text. According
to Hitzig (S. 9), he drew even the name of the mother of these sons of Jacob,
Zilpah, into his etymological investigations, which included derivations from
Armenian, Aramaic, and Arabic. Her name signifies "the foreskin." Her
daughters (sons they were in the history) Euodia and Syntyche are, then, two
classes of Gentiles into which the Church was divided, the Roman or Latin
and the Greek. The author, according to Hitzig, xiii.–xxi., belonged to the
former class ; for, in addition to his acquaintance with Oriental languages
and his easy handling of Greek, he was very familiar with the latest produc-
tions of Latin literature. Though writing no later than Trajan's time, he
had read, in particular, the *Agricola* of Tacitus, perhaps also the letters of
Seneca and of Pliny. The only passages that can be compared are i. 16 with
Agric. xli, "optimus quisque amore et fide, pessimi malignitate et livore"; or
ii. 3 with *Agric.* vi, "vixerunt mira concordia per mutuam caritatem et invicem
se anteponendo." The presupposition of all these fantastic conceits is the
claim that Euodia and Syntyche are unheard of proper names (made with
especial emphasis by Hitzig, 6); but cf. the twenty-three or twenty-four
instances of Euodia and the twenty-five of Syntyche above, p. 533. A longer
search might perhaps yield double that number. Moreover, it was shown
above, p. 537, n. 6, that the nameless comrade was not to reconcile these
women who were at variance, but to help them in their work. Even if Phil.
were not a letter addressed by its founder to the Church in Philippi and
received by it, but a literary fiction, and if there had never been in Philippi
a Euodia and a Syntyche, a Clement and another comrade of Paul's, who
would have understood immediately what he wished to say to them, no
reader could have found in the simple words of iv. 2 f. the secrets which the
critics have sought to find beneath their surface with such various results.
This supposed pseudo-Paul must have intended at least to make himself
understood. Holsten (i. 431) had no trouble in finding even in Phil. i. 5
the author's endeavour to bring about the unity of faith which the Philippians
lacked. The fellowship among the Philippians in the matter of the gospel,
which, if we are to believe this passage, had existed since the founding of the
Church, Holsten makes the subject of Paul's prayers for them. To contend
continually against such exegesis seems to the present writer as superfluous
as it is vain (cf. the writer's *Abhandlungen*, S. 189 ff.). To characterise
Holsten's treatment of the Epistle as over-critical (P. W. Schmidt, *Neutesta-
mentl. Hyperkritik*, 1880), seems uncalled for.

5. (P. 560). After many suggestions had been offered which met with
little response, D. Völter (*ThTij.* 1892, S. 10–44, 117–146), sought to establish in detail the hypothesis that Phil. consists of a genuine and a spurious
letter of Paul to the Philippians, combined by a redactor with the aid of
a few additions of his own. The genuine letter embraces, i. 1 (without
σὺν ἐπισκόποις καὶ διακόνοις), vii. 12–14, 18b–26, ii. 17–20, 22–30, iv. 10–21,
perhaps also iv. 23. The spurious letter, likewise addressed to the Philippians, and perhaps furnished with similar opening and closing greetings,
embraces i. 8–11, i. 27–ii. 16, iii. 1b–iv. 9, 22. To this should be added,
perhaps, a sentence to which Polycarp refers, ad *Phil.* xi. 3 (p. 29 ; see above,
p. 535, n. 3). The redactor interpolated the Church officers in i. 1, also

i. 15-18a, ii. 21, iii. 1a. The spurious letter was written at the very earliest under Trajan, more probably not until Hadrian's reign (S. 146), let us say about 125. Völter does not think it worth while even to mention when the redactor made the combination which Marcion regarded as a genuine letter of Paul's about twenty-five years after the writing of one of its component parts. Nor does he point out any more clearly an idea which could have suggested to the redactor his remarkable work, or an aim which he might have thus sought to attain. For the desire to commend a certain form of Church polity, which, it is held (S. 24), gave rise to the insertion of the bishops and deacons in i. 1, is discernible again neither in the other alleged interpolations of the redactor, nor in the whole altogether aimless undertaking of making one letter out of two. The redactor, it is claimed, inserted iii. 1a as a transition to the section iii. 1b–iv. 9, introduced from the second letter. At the very moment, then, when he was preparing to insert into the exemplar, which he had been using, an exceedingly significant section, whereby the conclusion must be deferred, he is made to declare expressly by the use of τὸ λοιπόν that he really had nothing more of importance to say, but was hastening to the conclusion ; and he is made further to use as a transition to the insertion from the second letter an exhortation to joy in the Lord, which certainly is not adapted to introduce the warning against Judaists. And it is this stupid compiler we have to thank for our Phil. ! The postponement of the conclusion is explained naturally enough when we regard Paul as the sole author, and follow the hints which he himself has thrown out (see above, p. 529 f.). There is no trace of two conclusions to the letter, which, of course, if they existed, would have to be assigned to two different letters. At any rate, the second alleged conclusion cannot be made to begin with iv. 10, where sentences follow which in themselves could stand just as well at the beginning of a letter (Polyc. ad Phil. i. 1, imitates this very passage). It should rather begin with iv. 4, or with iv. 8, where the χαίρετε and λοιπόν respectively of iii. 1 are taken up again after the matters have been discussed which for a time delayed the apostle when he was already hastening to a close. Likewise the assertion, that in i. 3–7 and i. 8–11 there are two introductions of similar content, can be made only by one whose linguistic knowledge is such that it can allow him to characterise the translation of i. 4 f. (S. 33) ("while I . . . remember in prayer your fellowship with regard to the gospel"), as adequate (cf. in refutation, above, p. 534, n. 2, and the writer's *Abhandlungen, KfKW*, 1885, S. 188). While in iii. 1 there is in reality an interruption of the thought which is indicated by Paul himself, Völter (S. 16) laboured vainly to point out a wide gap before i. 27. As in Gal. ii. 10, v. 13, μόνον introduces the mention of a duty upon the performance of which the applicability of what has been said before is conditioned. It is only on condition that the Philippians walk in a manner worthy of the gospel, and that, too, whether Paul is there to see it or is absent and only hears of it (cf. ii. 12), that their pride and joy will be increased by his intended visit to Philippi (i. 26). In the opposite case his visit would only bring shame to them and pain to himself (cf. 2 Cor. xii. 20–xiii. 10). In this way, as in Gal. v. 13, Paul makes a transition to an extended exhortation of independent significance (i. 27–ii. 18). But this comes in very fittingly between the description of his *present* situation and mood (i. 3–26) and the statements about what he intends to do *in the future* in order to make his relation to the Philippians again a more personal one (ii: 19–30, sending back of Epaphroditus, sending of Timothy, his own coming) ; for the exhortations are plainly intended for this interval primarily. At first sight we might call iv. 10–20 a doublet of i. 3–8 ; but even if this were the proper designation of the relation of these two sections, analogies to it are not lacking even down to the trivial formula, "Thanking you again," at the end of modern letters which have begun with an expression of gratitude. As a matter of fact, we see that the money which the Church had sent by Epaphroditus was kept in mind by the apostle throughout the letter ; again and again he refers to it (ii. 17, 25, 30). But in i. 3–8 this is combined in such a way with other similar actions of the Philippians, that no one could tell that this was specially implied here unless he were acquainted with the facts, or at least had read iv. 10–20, thus coming to understand also ii. 17, 25, 30 ; indeed, only a purpose on Paul's part to express elsewhere in the letter due appreciation of this last gift of the Philippians, can explain why in i. 3–8 he merely refers to this along with other similar acts of the Philippians, and then only to say that on his part the prevailing mood was not depression, least of all dissatisfaction, which might lessen his confiding love for them, but rather thankful joy.

END OF VOL. I.

Printed by MORRISON & GIBB LIMITED, *Edinburgh*

The International Theological Library.

EDITED BY

PRINCIPAL S. D. F. SALMOND, D.D., AND PROFESSOR C. A. BRIGGS, D.D.

'A valuable and much-needed addition to the theological literature of the English-speaking nations.'—*Academy*.

The First Seventeen Volumes are now ready, in Post 8vo, viz. :—

An Introduction to the Literature of the Old Testament. By Professor S. R. DRIVER, D.D., Oxford. Seventh Edition. Price 12s.

The *Guardian* says: 'By far the best account of the great critical problems connected with the Old Testament that has yet been written. . . . It is a perfect marvel of compression and lucidity combined.'

Christian Ethics. By NEWMAN SMYTH, D.D. Third Edition. Price 10s. 6d.

The *Bookman* says: 'It is the work of a wise, well-informed, independent and thoroughly competent writer. It is sure to become *the* text-book in Christian Ethics.'

Apologetics; or, Christianity Defensively Stated. By the late Professor A. B. BRUCE, D.D., Glasgow. Third Edition. Price 10s. 6d.

The *Expository Times* says: 'The force and the freshness of all the writings that Dr. Bruce has hitherto published have doubtless led many to look forward with eager hope to this work; and there need not be any fear of disappointment.'

History of Christian Doctrine. By Professor G. P. FISHER, D.D., LL.D., Yale. Second Edition. Price 12s.

The *Critical Review* says: 'A clear, readable, well-proportioned, and, regarding it as a whole, remarkably just and accurate account of what the course and development of doctrine throughout the ages, and in different countries, has been.'

A History of Christianity in the Apostolic Age. By Professor A. C. McGIFFERT, Ph.D., D.D., New York. Price 12s.

The *Literary World* says: 'A reverent and eminently candid treatment of the Apostolic Age in the light of research.'

Christian Institutions. By Professor A. V. G. ALLEN, D.D., Cambridge, U.S.A. Price 12s.

The *Christian World* says: 'Unquestionably Professor Allen's most solid performance; and that, in view of what he has already accomplished, is saying a great deal.'

Volumes now ready (continued)—

The Christian Pastor and the Working Church. By WASHINGTON GLADDEN, D.D., LL.D. Price 10s. 6d.

The *Baptist Magazine* says: 'There is scarcely a phase of pastoral duty which is not touched upon luminously and to good purpose.'

Canon and Text of the New Testament. By Professor CASPAR RENÉ GREGORY, D.D., LL.D., Leipzig. Price 12s.

The *Scotsman* says: 'A brilliant contribution to New Testament scholarship.'

The Theology of the New Testament. By Professor G. B. STEVENS, D.D., Yale. Price 12s.

The Ancient Catholic Church. From the Accession of Trajan to the Fourth General Council [A.D. 98–451]. By the late Principal RAINY, D.D., Edinburgh. Price 12s.

The Greek and Eastern Churches. By Principal W. F. ADENEY, D.D., Manchester. Price 12s.

Old Testament History. By Professor HENRY P. SMITH, D.D., Amherst. Price 12s.

The *Academy* says: 'The history of the little nation out of which was to arise the Sun of Righteousness, is clothed with an added charm of actuality, as it is presented in these sane and balanced pages.'

The Theology of the Old Testament. By the late Professor A. B. DAVIDSON, D.D., LL.D., Edinburgh. Second Edition. Price 12s.

The *Bookman* says: 'Contains the essence and strength of the whole work of one whom the best judges have pronounced to be a leader in Old Testament learning.'

The Christian Doctrine of Salvation. By Professor G. B. STEVENS, D.D., Yale. Price 12s.

The *Expository Times* says: 'It is a great book upon a great subject. If preachers want to fit themselves for a winter's work of strong, healthy, persuasive preaching, this book will fit them.'

The Christian Doctrine of God. By Professor W. N. CLARKE, D.D., Author of 'An Outline of Christian Theology.' Price 10s. 6d.

The *Baptist Times* says: 'It is as masterly, as inspiring and helpful a treatise as can be found in the famous series to which it belongs.'

History of the Reformation. By Principal T. M. LINDSAY, D.D., Glasgow. In Two Volumes.

VOL. I.—**The Reformation in Germany, from its beginning to the Religious Peace of Augsburg.** Second Edition. Price 10s. 6d.

VOL. II. —**The Reformation in Lands beyond Germany.** With Map. Price 10s. 6d.

The *Times* says: 'At last the English public possesses an adequate History of the Reformation.'

*** *A Prospectus giving full details of the Series, with list of Contributors, post free on application.*

A Grammar of New Testament Greek. By James Hope
Moulton, D.D., Didsbury College.   Part I., The Prolegomena.
Third Edition now ready.   Demy 8vo, 8s. net.

Note.—Dr. Moulton has spent much labour upon this New Edition. It has been
thoroughly revised and contains a large amount of important additional matter.

*No other grammar takes adequate account of those wonderful discoveries of Greek papyri,
which within the last few years have altered the entire basis of the study of New Testament
Greek.*

'This book is indispensable, really a first requisite to the understanding of the New
Testament Greek.   We do not see how it could have been better done, and it will
unquestionably take its place as the standard grammar of New Testament Greek.'—
Principal Marcus Dods, D.D.

CONCORDANCE TO THE GREEK TESTAMENT. MOULTON-GEDEN.

A Concordance to the Greek Testament : According to the
Texts of Westcott and Hort, Tischendorf, and the English Revisers.
Edited by W. F. Moulton, D.D., and A. S. Geden, M.A.   In crown
4to (pp. 1040).   Second Edition, *Revised throughout.*   Price 26s.
net; or in half-morocco, price 31s. 6d. net.

*⁎⁎⁎ It will be generally allowed that a new Concordance to the Greek Testament is much needed
in the interests of sacred scholarship.   This work adopts a new principle, and aims at providing
a full and complete Concordance to the text of the Greek Testament as it is set forth in the
editions of Westcott and Hort, Tischendorf (8th), and the English Revisers.   The first-named
has throughout been taken as the standard, and the marginal readings have been included.   Thus
the student with any one of these three editions in his hands will find himself in possession of a
complete Concordance to the actual text on which he is engaged.   While the method employed, it
may fairly be claimed, precludes the omission of any word or phrase which, by even a remote
probability, might be regarded as forming part of the true text of the New Testament, on the
other hand, passages disappear as to the spuriousness of which there is practical unanimity
among scholars.*

*Professor W. SANDAY, D.D., LL.D., Oxford, writes : 'There can be no question as to the
value of the new "Concordance." It is the only scientific Concordance to the Greek Testament,
and the only one that can be safely used for scientific purposes.'*

Prospectus, with Specimen Page, free on application.

The Fourth Gospel.   Its Purpose and Theology.   By Prof.
Ernest F. Scott, D.D., Kingston.   Second Edition.   Demy 8vo,
6s. net.

'One of the most instructive and suggestive studies of the Fourth Gospel that has
appeared in later New Testament criticism. . . . Written from a thorough knowledge
both of the sources and of the later authorities on the subject.'—*Christian World.*

'The most elaborate and thorough-going treatment of the whole theology of the Fourth
Gospel that has yet appeared in English.   He has put the theological world under a
debt of gratitude to him for supplying the best solution of the problems of the Fourth
Gospel.'—*Glasgow Herald.*

The Bible : Its Origin and Nature.   By Principal Marcus Dods,
D.D., Edinburgh.   Crown 8vo, price 4s. 6d. net.

Contents :—The Bible and other Sacred Books — The Canon — Revelation —
Inspiration — Infallibility of Scripture — Trustworthiness of the Gospels —
Miraculous Element in the Gospels.

'The very book on the Bible that multitudes of thinking people are asking for
in order to meet the questions that are now pressing upon them.   The subject is
here treated with the lucidity and frankness, the firmness of handling and force of
expression, which characterise all its author's writings.'—*Review of Theology and
Philosophy.*

A New Topographical, Physical, and Biblical Map of Palestine.
(Scale—4 miles to an inch.) Compiled from the Latest Surveys and Researches, including the Work of the English and German Palestine Exploration Funds. Showing all identified Biblical Sites, together with the Modern Place Names. Prepared under the Direction of J. G. BARTHOLOMEW, F.R.S.E., F.R.G.S., and Edited by Prof. GEORGE ADAM SMITH, LL.D. With complete Index.

Prices : Mounted on cloth and in cloth case, with Index, 10s. 6d. ; mounted on rollers and varnished, with Index separate, 15s. May also be had in two sheets, enclosed in leather-wallet, for tourists, 15s.

This new Map has been designed to present in a clear and readily accessible form the results of recent Surveys and Research in Palestine. It represents a complete survey of the country as it exists at the present day, while superimposed upon this are all the scriptural names of the past. The Map is drawn to the scale of four miles to an inch, and includes the country from Beirut in the north to the Arabah in the south, extending as far east as Damascus and Jebel Haurân. All the modern place names are given, while the accepted identified Biblical sites have been added in bolder lettering.

The Physical Relief of the country is effectively shown by colouring in contours, and there are diagrammatic cross-sections illustrating the configuration of the plateaux and the Jordan valley depression. Inset maps show the Environs of Jerusalem and the Vegetation of Palestine. All the names on the Map, numbering about 3180, are contained in the accompanying Index. Each place is indexed under its modern as well as ancient name, and cross-references are given.

Besides meeting the special requirements of the student and the teacher, the Map will be found invaluable as a Touring Map for Travellers in Palestine. It shows all modern roads, railways, and places of interest.

'The most welcome gift of the season. We are greatly struck with its beauty of workmanship. That it will supersede all maps in existence there can be no doubt. We expect to see it soon in all our church halls, and it will find its way into the knapsack of the traveller. It will also take its place as a very suitable companion to the "Dictionary of the Bible," edited by Dr. Hastings, the ordinary case-form being folded in the same size as the Dictionary and bound to match.'—*Expository Times.*

BY THE LATE *PROFESSOR W. HASTIE, D.D.*

The Theology of the Reformed Church in its Fundamental Principles.
By the late Professor W. HASTIE, D.D., Glasgow. Crown 8vo, 4s. 6d. net.

'*The work so long looked for is now published, and it is to be hoped that it will be widely and kindly received. No intelligent reader of it can fail to find in its pages much information, eloquently stated, regarding both the history and the characteristics of the Reformed theology.*'—From Prefatory Note by Prof. R. FLINT, D.D.

'A strong and able performance, giving a rigorous defence of the Reformed theology and a closely reasoned appreciation of it as superior to the other great typical forms of theology. Dr. Hastie has no doubt whatsoever as to the justice of his plea, and he puts it forward here with all the strength of profound conviction.'—Principal SALMOND in the *Critical Review.*

Outlines of Pastoral Theology for Young Ministers and Students.
Crown 8vo, 1s. 6d. net.

'How Professor Hastie discovered this book, and how he was drawn to it, how it had to be laid aside, and how it would not lie,—all this is told with thrilling simplicity in the Introduction. We do greatly need a small competent sympathetic guide to the work of the ministry. This is the book we need.'—*Expository Times.*

ImTheStory.com

CPSIA information can be obtained at www.ICGtesting.com
Printed in the USA
LVOW101755230113

316973LV00035B/1751/P